The Economics
of Health
and Health Care

Second Edition

The Economics
of Health
and Health Care

Sherman Folland

Associate Professor of Economics
Oakland University

Allen C. Goodman

Professor of Economics
Wayne State University

Miron Stano

Professor of Economics and Management
Oakland University

 Prentice Hall, Upper Saddle River, NJ 07458

Executive Editor: Leah Jewell
Associate Editor: Gladys Soto
Editorial Assistant: Kristen Kaiser
Editor-in-Chief: James Boyd
Marketing Manager: Sandra Steiner
Production Editor: Maureen Wilson
Production Coordinator: David Cotugno
Managing Editor: Carol Burgett
Manufacturing Buyer: Kenneth J. Clinton
Manufacturing Supervisor: Arnold Vila
Manufacturing Manager: Vincent Scelta
Composition: Omegatype
Cover Art/Photo: Comstock

Library of Congress Cataloging-In-Publication Data

Folland, Sherman.
    The economics of health and health care / Sherman Folland, Allen
C. Goodman, Miron Stano. – 2nd ed.
        p.   cm.
    Includes bibliographical references and index.
    ISBN 0–13–565987–6
    1. Medical economics.   I. Goodman, Allen C.   II. Stano, Miron.
III. Title.
RA41O.F65   1997
338.4′33621—dc20   96-23953
                                                        CIP

Prentice-Hall International (UK) Limited, London
Prentice-Hall of Australia Pty. Limited, Sydney
Prentice-Hall Canada Inc., Toronto
Prentice-Hall Hispanoamericana, S.A., Mexico
Prentice-Hall of India Private Limited, New Delhi
Prentice-Hall of Japan, Inc., Tokyo
Simon & Schuster Asia Pte. Ltd., Singapore
Editora Prentice-Hall do Brasil, Ltda., Rio de Janeiro

Printed in the United States of America

10   9   8   7   6

Contents

Preface

The economics of health care has burgeoned as a field of study over the last two decades. Emerging beyond institutional and descriptive commentaries on hospital costs, health professions and health professionals, labor shortages, and public health concerns, the field has evolved to one in which a set of distinctive principles are systematically applied to a surprisingly wide range of health-related issues.

We first wrote this book to synthesize contemporary developments around these principles and to make them accessible to undergraduate as well as to graduate students. Rather than organizing the book around the institutions specific to the health care economy, we have used core economic themes as basic as supply and demand, as venerable as technology or labor issues, and as modern as the economics of information. Moreover we have sought to improve accessibility to the wide range of health services to students and practitioners whose knowledge of economics may be more limited.

We have used the philosophy that one must have a working knowledge of the analytical tools of economics and econometrics to appreciate the field of health economics. Students may be ready to plunge directly into the Production of Health (Chapter 4) upon completion of the introductory chapter. However, Chapters 2 (Microeconomics Tools) and 3 (Statistical Tools) allow the students and their teachers to develop or to review the needed analytical concepts before tackling the core subject matter of the course. In these chapters, students with as little as one semester of microeconomics may review and study how economists analyze problems, using examples that are relevant to health economics. No calculus is needed.

Consistent with our emphasis on clarity of exposition, we make extensive use of graphs, tables, and charts. We provide discussion questions and exercises to help students master the basics and to prompt them to think about the issues. We also provide features on up-to-date applications of theory and policy developments, as well as the occasional tidbit containing purely background information.

Finally, we caution that some of the chapters, though devoid of advanced mathematics, may still require considerable effort from the student. There is no painless way to appreciate the scope of the contributions that scholars have made in recent years. Sections or subsections that are more demanding and/or peripheral to the core material have been marked with asterisks. These sections can be omitted without detracting from the flow of the book. Finally, for more advanced students of the health care economy who wish to be challenged yet further, we provide a comprehensive references section so that our (and their) work can be enriched through referral to original sources.

ALTERNATIVE COURSE DESIGNS

As an evolving field, the economics of health care has an evolving literature, and there is no single "correct" order for the course design. *The Economics of Health and Health Care* offers instructors considerable flexibility. We have divided the 25 chapters into nine sections:

1. Basic Economic Tools (Ch. 1–3)
2. Supply and Demand (Ch. 4–6)
3. Information (Ch. 7–10)
4. Insurance and Organization of Health Providers (Ch. 11, 12)
5. Technology (Ch. 13, 14)
6. Labor (Ch. 15, 16)
7. Hospitals and Nursing Homes (Ch. 17, 18)
8. Social Insurance and Health System Reform (Ch. 19–23)
9. Policy Issues and Analyses (Ch. 24, 25)

The organization follows an "economics" model in which consumers and firms are analyzed in a world without government and governmental policies. As a result, explicit discussions of government policies do not come until Chapter 19, although regulation, licensing, mandates, and the like, are discussed in reference to other topics much earlier. Some instructors may wish to follow the chapters in this order.

Other instructors, particularly those who are interested in governmental policies, may wish to "tool up" on some of the early analyses, and then skip directly to Part 8, in which we look at social insurance, health care regulation, and health care reform. After that, they may wish to browse selected topics. Although some analyses build on each other within chapters, we have sought to avoid cross-referencing among chapters.

ACKNOWLEDGMENTS

Since this book emerges from years of classroom and professional interaction, we thank those students and colleagues who have discussed the economics of health and health care with us, and who have challenged our ideas. Perhaps our most significant debts go to Annie Todd, who suggested the endeavor and first got us together, to Jill Leckta, editor of our first edition, to Leah Jewell, our current editor, and to Tom McGuire, whose intellectual and collegial support convinced us that we could succeed. We certainly thank our colleagues at over 100 universities in the United States, Canada, and abroad, who have provided the market test for our work by adopting the book.

We have been helped all along by capable research assistants, including Kimberley Klett, Kalyani Velagapudi, and Daniel Armijo. Donna Hill and Stuart May provided secretarial assistance.

Numerous professional colleagues were generous in their time and energy in reading and critiquing various chapters. We thank:

- Carson Bays, East Carolina University
- Frank Chaloupka, University of Illinois—Chicago
- Hope Corman, Rider College
- Merton Finkler, Lawrence University
- H. E. Frech, III, University of California—Santa Barbara
- John Goddeeris, Michigan State University
- Warren Greenberg, George Washington University
- Michael Grossman, City University of New York
- Jack Hadley, Center for Health Policy Studies
- James Hamilton, Wayne State University
- Janet Hankin, Wayne State University
- Ronald Horwitz, Oakland University
- Harold Hotelling, Lawrence Technological University
- Tom McCarthy, National Economic Research Associates
- Catherine McLaughlin, University of Michigan
- Eleanor Nishiura, Wayne State University
- Martin Pernick, University of Michigan
- Joann Richards, Oakland University
- John Rizzo, Yale University
- John M. Tilford, University of Arkansas
- Scott Vander Linde, Calvin College
- Rob Verner, Kent State University
- Kenneth Warner, University of Michigan
- Gerard Wedig, University of Pennsylvania
- Burton Weisbrod, Northwestern University
- William White, University of Illinois—Chicago
- Barbara Wolfe, University of Wisconsin—Madison
- Michael Woolley, University of Southern California

We also thank the following colleagues who, with their classes, test-taught and test-learned parts of the text:

- Randall Ellis, Boston University
- Gail Jensen, Wayne State University
- Thomas McGuire, Boston University
- Lee Mobley, Oakland University

- Kathleen Possai, Wayne State University
- Richard Scheffler, University of California—Berkeley
- Nancy Wolff, Rutgers University

The staff at Prentice Hall has been outstanding in their support. Kristen Kaiser and Teresa Cohan have provided important advice and Maureen Wilson has managed production.

Once again, we thank our wives and daughters who spent several more New Year's Eves watching their husbands and fathers learn about health economics.

S. F.
Rochester, Michigan

A.C.G.
Detroit, Michigan

M.S.
Rochester, Michigan

The Economics
of Health
and Health Care

CHAPTER

Introduction 1

- ■ The Relevance of Health Economics
- ■ Economic Methods and Examples of Analysis
- ■ Does Economics Apply to Health and Health Care?
- ■ Is Health Care Different?
- ■ Conclusions

ealth and health care are dominant economic and political issues in the United States and many other countries. Because most nations have experienced rapid rises in health care spending over the past 30 years, it is not surprising that health economics has emerged as a distinct specialty within economics. In a formal sense, health economics is the study of how resources are allocated to and within the health economy. The production of health care and its distribution across populations fall within this definition. Several examples will be introduced in this chapter to illustrate economic analysis of health care issues.

A second objective here is to demonstrate the magnitude and importance of the health sector. Various measures of size and growth will be used to establish the relevance of the health economy to both individual and national policy concerns.

Our final goal of this chapter is to promote the theme that economics will have much to say about how health care markets function. However, we will also stress the importance of recognizing features distinctive to health care markets so that appropriate modifications can be made to the economist's conventional analytical tools. Despite continuing controversy on many major issues, health economists have been able to provide answers to many questions of academic and policy interest.

THE RELEVANCE OF HEALTH ECONOMICS

We have selected three interrelated ways in which the study of health economics proves important and interesting. These three factors are (1) the size of the contribution of the health sector to the overall economy, (2) the national policy concerns resulting from the importance many people attach to the economic problems they face in pursuing and maintaining their health, and (3) the fact that many other health issues have a substantial economic element.

The Size and Scope of the Health Economy

The health economy merits attention alone for its sheer size. It contributes a large and growing share of gross national product (GNP) in the United States as well as other countries. It also represents a substantial capital investment and a large and growing share of the labor force.

HEALTH CARE'S SHARE OF GNP IN THE UNITED STATES

One of every seven dollars spent on final goods and services in the U.S. economy goes to the health sector. To put this figure in perspective, as recently as 1976, the share of GNP devoted to health care was one dollar in twelve, and in 1950 it was less than one in twenty.[1] Figure 1.1 tracks the health economy's share of GNP from early in the century with projections to the year 2000. The conclusion? The health care sector is a large and growing portion of our economy.

In calculating the share of GNP spent on health care, both spending and GNP are measured in current dollars; thus, the effects of general inflation are netted out. Therefore, only three major possibilities exist to explain the substantially increased ratios shown in Figure 1.1:

1. People, for various reasons, may be buying more health services. Patients may be consulting with health providers more frequently; more tests are being ordered, or more drugs are being prescribed.

2. People, for various reasons, may be buying higher-quality health services, including products and services that previously were not available. Laser surgery, measles vaccines, and new treatments for burn victims have raised the quality of care since 1960. Economic theory suggests that people are willing to pay more for better quality.

3. There may have been health care inflation over and above what occurred in the general economy. Higher incomes and the increased prevalence of insurance, including large government programs such as Medicare and Medicaid, each may have led to increased health care prices over time.

A major challenge is to understand these phenomena and their contributions to total spending. The study of demand, insurance, production, technology, and labor supply, among other topics, will help meet this challenge.

---

[1]GNP is the current value of all final goods and services produced in a given period. In 1991, the United States began a practice already followed by many other countries of reporting national income data in terms of gross domestic product (GDP). GDP, which measures only domestic output, is equal to GNP minus net factor income from abroad. The two measures are often very similar in value. We will usually present historical series for the United States using GNP, but we will make comparisons with other countries in terms of GDP.

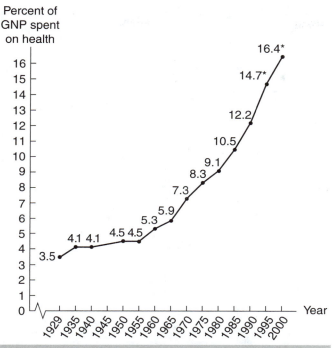

FIGURE 1.1   Percent of GNP spent on health, 1929–2000.

Sources: Sonnenfeld et al. (1991) for 1975 to projected figures (*);
Office of National Cost Estimates (1990) for 1960–1975; Gibson and
Mueller (1977) for 1929–1955.

HEALTH CARE SPENDING IN OTHER COUNTRIES

Our understanding of the U.S. health economy may be enhanced if we examine other countries. In particular, we will show that the issues of concern in the United States are also major issues elsewhere. The size of the health care sector is large not only in the United States but also elsewhere. Table 1.1 shows that in most countries the share of health care in the gross domestic product (GDP) grew rapidly between 1960 and 1980. However, unlike most other nations, the rate of increase in the United States has continued to grow. The data also indicate the relative size of the U.S. health economy compared to those of other countries. For example, its share of GDP in the United States is approximately twice as big as its share in the United Kingdom—a country with national health insurance. Is care costlier in the United States? Is the care of higher quality or is more simply being consumed? We will address such questions in Chapter 22.

IMPORTANCE OF THE HEALTH ECONOMY IN PERSONAL SPENDING

Because it accounts for such a large share of the national product, the size of the health economy is also reflected through other key indicators. Two of these are especially easy to relate to at the personal level: (1) share of income spent on medical care, and (2) number of jobs in the health economy.

TABLE 1.1   Share of Gross Domestic Product in Health Care in Selected OECD Countries: Selected Years

Country	1960	1970	1980	1990	1993
Australia	4.9	5.7	7.3	8.2	8.5
Austria	4.4	5.4	7.9	8.4	9.3
Belgium	3.4	4.1	6.6	7.6	8.3
Canada	5.5	7.1	7.4	9.4	10.2
Denmark	3.6	6.1	6.8	6.5	6.7
Finland	3.9	5.7	6.5	8.0	8.8
France	4.2	5.8	7.6	8.9	9.8
Germany	4.8	5.9	8.4	8.3	8.6
Greece	2.9	4.0	4.3	5.3	5.7
Iceland	3.3	5.0	6.2	7.9	8.3
Ireland	3.8	5.3	8.7	6.7	6.7
Italy	3.6	5.2	6.9	8.1	8.5
Japan	3.0	4.6	6.6	6.8	7.3
Luxembourg	n/a	3.8	6.3	6.5	6.9
Netherlands	3.8	5.9	7.9	8.0	8.7
Norway	3.3	5.0	6.6	7.5	8.2
New Zealand	4.3	5.2	7.2	7.4	7.7
Portugal	n/a	2.8	5.8	6.6	7.3
Spain	1.5	3.7	5.7	6.9	7.3
Sweden	4.7	7.1	9.4	8.6	7.5
Switzerland	3.3	5.2	7.3	8.4	9.9
Turkey	n/a	2.5	3.4	2.9	2.7
United Kingdom	3.9	4.5	5.6	6.0	7.1
United States	5.3	7.3	9.3	12.7	14.1

Source: Organization for Economic Cooperation and Development Health Data, 1995.

Table 1.2 provides data on the ways in which U.S. consumers spend their disposable incomes. By 1992 medical care had supplanted food and tobacco as the largest category of expenditures. Consumers spent 17.4 percent of their budgets on medical care, as opposed to 16.0 percent on food and tobacco, and 14.4 percent on housing. This represents a major shift in spending patterns. As recently as 1960, food represented about 25 percent of spending, housing about 15 percent, and medical care only 5 percent.

IMPORTANCE OF THE HEALTH ECONOMY TO THE LABOR FORCE

The flip side of spending is reflected through the jobs that have been created in the health economy. Table 1.3a shows that over 10 million people, almost 9 percent of the labor force, worked at various health service sites in 1993; almost half of them worked in hospitals.

Table 1.3b indicates the considerable growth in health care personnel since 1970 for selected professions. In 1970 there were 290,862 physicians, or 143 per 100,000

TABLE 1.2   Total Personal Consumption Expenditures (in $ billions), by Type, 1993

	Total $	Percent	
Total	4,378	100.0	
Food and Tobacco	700	16.0	
Housing	629	14.4	
Medical Care	761	17.4	
Drugs/Sundries	69		1.6
Physicians	166		3.8
Dentists	39		0.9
Private Hospitals	347		7.9
Health Insurance	46		1.1
Other	94		2.2
Transportation	504	11.5	
Household Operation	508	11.6	
Recreation	340	7.8	
Clothing	294	6.7	
All Other	642	14.7	

Columns are subject to rounding errors.

Source: Health Insurance Association of America (1994, Table 4.5).

population. By 1992 the number of physicians more than doubled, as had the number of registered nurses. The number of registered nurses per 100,000 population had also more than doubled from 369 to 742.

Reflecting the increases in spending, the health care sector is increasingly a source of employment. Thus, cutbacks in spending on health care will typically mean cutbacks in employment opportunities.

TABLE 1.3a   Employed Civilians at Health Services Sites: 1993

Category	Total Employment (in thousands)
All Employed Civilians	119,306
All Health Services Sites	10,553
Hospitals	5,032
Nursing and Personal Care Facilities	1,752
Offices and Clinics of Physicians	1,450
Offices and Clinics of Dentists	567
Offices and Clinics of Chiropractors	116
Other Health Services Sites	1,635

Source: U.S. Department of Health and Human Services, *Health United States 1994,* Table 97.

TABLE 1.3b Active Health Personnel and Number per 100,000 Population: Selected Years			
Profession	*1970*	*1980*	*1992*
Physicians	290,862 (143)	427,122 (190)	614,050 (242)
Dentists	95,700 (47)	121,240 (54)	153,800 (61)
Optometrists	18,400 (9)	22,300 (10)	27,000 (11)
Pharmacists	112,570 (55)	142,780 (63)	165,300 (65)
Podiatrists	7,110 (4)	8,880 (4)	12,500 (5)
Registered Nurses	750,000 (369)	1,272,900 (560)	1,893,400 (742)

Note: The numbers per 100,000 population are shown in parentheses.

Source: U.S. Department of Health and Human Services, *Health United States 1994,* Table 102.

CAPITAL INVESTMENT IN THE HEALTH ECONOMY

In addition to labor, a substantial amount of capital has been drawn to the U.S. health care system. The number of nursing home beds increased from about 1.3 million in 1976 to 1.6 million in 1991 (beds per person, however, decreased slightly). The number of beds in over 5,000 short-stay hospitals peaked in the early 1980s but the total number remains on the order of 1 million. There are also considerable and growing amounts of other capital—such as diagnostic equipment—per bed.

OTHER RESOURCES

Data on expenses for health care and data on health care labor and capital inputs reflect only some of the inputs used by people to produce health. Inputs that are not bought and sold in the marketplace are also important, including a person's own contribution of time and effort. These inputs entail real costs to society. For example, when one's time is given over to producing better health, the cost to the individual and society is the value of the leisure that is foregone. Thus, the value of the inputs we use to produce and maintain our health is much greater than the measured costs of the health care that we buy.

Although we have stressed inputs, the contribution of health resources to the economy is ultimately a measure of the value of the output—health itself. The value of improvements to our health is measured both in consumption and production. This means that we value being healthy both for its own sake and for its contribution to the production of other goods.[2] The intrinsic value of being healthy is ultimately the value we attach to life and limb, which people commonly describe as infinite in certain circumstances and at least substantial in most circumstances. The value of health in the production of other goods is exemplified not just in reduced absenteeism rates but also in output per worker on the job. In both its consumption and production aspects, the output of the health sector makes a substantial contribution to the economy.

---

[2]This idea was developed further in an essay by Fuchs (1972).

THE IMPORTANCE ATTACHED TO ECONOMIC PROBLEMS OF HEALTH CARE DELIVERY

The health sector receives attention from policymakers because of its widely perceived problems. The data we have shown reflecting the substantial resources devoted to health care are reflected in a more meaningful way through the average level of this nation's spending for health care. Table 1.4 provides various measures of health care spending and its growth since 1950.

Table 1.4 shows how national health expenditures have grown from $27 billion in 1960 to $884 billion in 1993, a thirty-three fold increase. During that period, the U.S. population grew by 48 percent, from 181 million to 267 million. Thus, national health expenditures per capita rose by a multiple of 23, from $143 in 1960 to $3,299 in 1993.

However, the real increase is what matters most. Prices, as measured by the broad-based consumer price index (CPI), grew by a factor of about 4.9. After deflating by this factor, we find that real expenditures per capita in 1993 were approximately five times the 1960 level—still a hefty increase.[3]

INFLATION

Although we have deflated the spending values using the consumer price index, medical care prices have grown faster historically than the general level of prices. Table 1.4 also shows the pattern of health care inflation in the United States in recent years. Note that hospital and physician care prices have risen much faster than prices overall. Their increases between 1960 and 1993 were about double the increase in prices for the overall economy. Even since 1982, while consumer prices rose by 44.5 percent, hospital bed prices increased by 126.4 percent and physicians' services prices increased by 91.3 percent.

Growing costs are a common problem for maintaining health programs, and they have spurred numerous cost-containment efforts by government in the past two decades.

TABLE 1.4   National Health Expenditures (NHE) and Other Data for Selected Years, 1950–1993 ($ billions)

							Price Indexes	
Year	NHE	% Growth	GNP	NHE per Capita	NHE (% of GNP)	CPI	Hospital Rooms	Physician Services
1950	$ 12.7	12.2	$ 288	$ 84	4.4	24.1	4.9	15.7
1960	27.1	8.7	515	143	5.3	29.6	9.3	21.9
1970	74.4	13.1	1,016	346	7.3	38.8	23.6	34.5
1980	250.1	15.5	2,732	1,063	9.1	82.4	68.0	76.5
1982	323.8	12.2	3,166	1,348	10.2	100.0	100.0	100.0
1990	666.2	10.5	5,463	2,566	12.2	138.7	175.4	160.8
1993	884.2	7.8	6,260	3,299	14.1	144.5	226.4	191.3

Source: Levitt et al. (1994, Table 13).

---

[3]This is determined by dividing $3,299 (spending in 1990) by 4.9 and dividing the result by $143 (spending in 1960).

Understanding and evaluating the effects of such regulatory measures are important tasks for the health economist.

ACCESS

For many, the rising costs significantly reduce accessibility to health care. Financial affordability influences demand for most goods and services, and there are many reasons why some people do not have health insurance. What is clear is that the number of uninsured has risen in the United States; about 40 million people now lack insurance. Many more are considered to have inadequate insurance. The problems of cost, inflation, and uninsured people have led to numerous proposals for some form of national health insurance. Later in this book, we will examine several broad groups of plans as well as the national health insurance programs that exist in several other countries.

QUALITY

Increases in the quality of care contribute to increases in spending. Often the focus is on ensuring quality through professional licensure and certification and, especially for hospitals, through quality assurance programs. At the same time, there are concerns about access to high-quality care for those without insurance or with minimal insurance. Interestingly, also there are concerns that the quality of care in the United States is often excessive, especially for some forms of "high-tech" treatment. For such treatments, the costs of resources may exceed the benefits to patients. The interplay among insurance, technology, and consumption is of growing interest to economists.

The Economic Side to Other Health Issues

Production, costs, and insurance are naturally issues that involve economics, but many other health issues have economic components, even though they may seem to be purely medical concerns. A few examples illustrate the point.

The choice of a health care treatment seems purely medical to many people, but physicians and other providers are increasingly aware that alternative treatments can be evaluated and compared on economic grounds. It is necessary to examine the costs of alternative techniques. Physicians are also increasingly sensitive to the economic side of the patient–physician relationship. The patient's preferences are considered to be a valid factor in determining the appropriateness of a given treatment.

We must also explore the economic reasons behind people's choices about their health. People take care of themselves well at some times and poorly at other times. The desired health status of an individual can be usefully understood as an economic choice. Even addiction to a harmful substance can be understood better when analyzed as a possibly rational economic choice.

Other health issues clearly have an economic aspect: What role should government play in health? What health care investments should a developing country make? Should cigarette advertising be banned? Questions like these do not solely concern economics, but they obviously have an economic side.

ECONOMIC METHODS AND EXAMPLES OF ANALYSIS

We have already provided a formal definition of health economics as the study of the allocation of resources to and within the health economy. From another perspective, however, economics is what economists actually do and how they apply economics to health. What economists do in practice is to use certain characteristic approaches to their analysis of the world.

Features of Economic Analysis

Many distinctive features of economics might be exhaustively identified, but we emphasize only four:

- the assumption of rationality
- the use of abstraction
- the use of marginal analysis
- the use of models as metaphors.

RATIONAL DECISION MAKING

Economists typically approach problems of human economic behavior by assuming that the decision maker is a rational being. Rationality is effectively defined as making choices that best further one's own ends given one's resource constraints. Some behaviors may appear irrational. However, when disputes over rationality arise, economists often attempt to point out, perhaps with some delight, that so-called irrational behavior often actually makes sense when the incentives facing the decision maker are properly understood.

USE OF ABSTRACTION

Most contemporary economic analyses choose to draw the world abstractly. Whether models are too abstract is a matter of legitimate dispute. However, abstraction itself is not the culprit, since the details of economic phenomena are inherently too complex to permit direct comprehension. As an example, it would be difficult for a first-time visitor to the New York Stock Exchange to understand the economics of financial markets from direct observation of the confusing flurry of activity on the floor of the exchange.

Similarly, a map serves as a model for abstractions. If you wanted to find the Library of Congress in Washington, D.C., a completely realistic aerial photo would not be of much use, since you would have neither the street names nor the appearances of the buildings on the map. You would prefer an abstract drawing with the names clearly marked, and the Library of Congress plainly indicated, perhaps in a different color. Abstraction in economics is the art of eliminating the nonessential detail in order to make the remaining model more useful to the purpose at hand. Abstraction is always necessary, but eliminating essential features (such as the location of the White House in a map of Washington) is an error in anybody's book.

MARGINAL ANALYSIS

Mainstream economic analyses feature reasoning at the margin. The marginal unit means the next unit. To make an appropriate choice, a decision maker must understand the cost as well as the benefit of the next, or marginal, unit. One could contemplate the appropriate total number of pounds of beef to buy, for example, by considering iteratively whether the next pound is worth the cost. Similarly, marginal analysis often entails the mental experiment of trading off the costs of something against its benefits at the margin. Trade-offs of this sort are ubiquitous in both economics and in the real world, so that Nobelist Milton Friedman once proposed that one could sum up economics with the following phrase: "There's no such thing as a free lunch."

USE OF MODELS

Finally, economics characteristically develops models to depict its subject matter. The models may be described in words, graphs, or mathematics. We feature word and graph in this text. These models may be usefully understood as metaphors for reality. We say, "This is the market for physician care," but what we mean is that "this is like the market for physician care." We understand that any metaphor can be pushed too far and must be tested against one's intuitive sense of reality and ultimately against the facts. Nonetheless, metaphors can be apt, and we can learn from them.

In economic analysis, the models are often abstract. Abstract models help to make sense of the world, in economics as in everyday life. A young child asking what the solar system is like will undoubtedly be shown the familiar drawing of sun and planets in their orbits, an abstract model. The drawing is quickly grasped, yet no one supposes that the sky looks like this, either during the day or at night.

Examples of Health Economics Analysis

What do economists do? Here are some examples of economic analysis. On the one hand, physicians, clinics, and hospitals use labor and machines just like other segments of the economy. They charge prices for their services, and they hope to earn at least enough to keep themselves from wanting to switch to other types of work. In this sense, the theories that tell us what firms do, and how they combine resources to maximize profits, may provide some insights into how the health care sector works.

On the other hand, the health sector is complicated. Consumers must often depend on health providers to tell them whether they are ill, and, if so, what they should do. Treatments are often prescribed seemingly irrespective of their costs. Physicians may not only be entrepreneurs themselves, but they may also manage their own laboratories, control hospitals, or influence insurance companies that also affect the health care sector.

Some of the earliest work in health economics addressed several of these issues. Milton Friedman and Simon Kuznets, both of whom became Nobel laureates, studied the so-called physician shortage of the 1930s. They discovered that although physicians earned 32 percent per year more than dentists, their training costs were 17 percent higher. The remaining difference was still large, however, and Friedman and Kuznets

Who Are Health Economists and What Do They Do?

A survey of 518 health economists from the United States and Canada provides information on what they do, where they work, and how they view important policy issues. About 85 percent of the respondents hold Ph.D.s in economics, but only half of those wrote Ph.D. dissertations specifically on a health-related subject. The remainder were principally trained in various other disciplines within economics. Also, about 60 percent of health economists work in universities, though most work outside of economics departments in settings such as schools of public health and medicine. Those without Ph.D. degrees tend to work in government or in industry.

Table 1.5 provides response rates to questions about some major policy issues. The table reveals not only the concerns of many health economists, but also indicates the depth of disagreements on many issues. For example, the applicability of the competitive model splits the health economists right down the middle (49 percent each way). In contrast, 81 percent of the economists believe that physicians can generate some demand for their own services; only 17 percent feel that this does not occur.

As for some other issues, there is also considerable disagreement as to whether technology is primarily responsible for increasing costs, the superiority of the Canadian health care system, and whether requiring employers to provide health insurance for their employees is desirable. Though it is premature to focus on these issues at this time, we will introduce the necessary conceptual and institutional material to enable students to evaluate the arguments on both sides of the questions.

TABLE 1.5   Health Economists' Opinions About Health Policy Issues[a]

Issue	Opinion				
	1	*2*	*3*	*4*	*5*
Physicians generate demand	27%	54%	2%	14%	3%
Competition model cannot apply	23	26	2	33	16
Canadian system is superior	23	29	10	28	10
Hospitals shift costs	11	52	11	23	2
Employer-mandated insurance is good	9	29	6	44	11
Insurance causes welfare loss	18	45	5	26	6
Technology is the culprit	8	38	6	42	8

[a] 1 = strongly agree, 2 = agree, 3 = don't know/no opinion, 4 = disagree, 5 = strongly disagree.
Source: Feldman and Morrisey (1990, Table 7).

(1945) attributed part of the higher returns on investment enjoyed by physicians to barriers to entry into the medical profession. Barriers to entry tend to lower the supply of physicians, hence raising physicians' incomes and raising the rate of return on their investment in their own education. The situation also meant that the value to society of producing one more physician exceeded the costs of producing one more physician.

Reuben Kessel addressed the practice common some years ago for physicians to charge different fees to different patients. The practice was often interpreted as an act of charity, for it was thought that physicians were charging lower fees to poorer patients. Kessel (1956) showed, however, that the practice of charging different fees could also be understood as a form of price discrimination that allowed physicians to increase their profits by charging more to those with greater ability to pay.

Kessel presented historical analysis supporting his case. He argued that physicians used the system of hospital privileges as a means of perpetuating price discrimination. Physicians, in order to practice, must be affiliated with hospitals. Historically, those who adopted competitive economic practices were often branded as "unethical" and could be denied membership in county medical societies, access to specialty certification, or hospital privileges.

These examples also illustrate two features of health economics. The first is the interdisciplinary nature of health research. Economists must know how health care is delivered. This information comes from health care providers, as well as from members of other disciplines such as public health, sociology, and psychology, who study how organizations operate.

The second feature is that one needs to understand the institutions in the health care system, including hospitals, insurers, or regulators. Examples of these include the following:

- relations of doctors to hospitals
- the organization and practices of the health insurance industry
- licensing and certification of health care providers.

Such institutional concerns do not necessarily distinguish health economics from other forms of economic analysis, but the particular history and present form of health care institutions do set health economics apart from other fields. We must take care to describe the institutional characteristics of the health sector in order to devise appropriate models.

DOES ECONOMICS APPLY TO HEALTH AND HEALTH CARE?

A frequent complaint by many who are exposed to applications of economics to health is that economics is irrelevant. This issue is raised often enough in serious contexts to require serious consideration. The complaint suggests a model of health care in which health is considered to be primarily a technical issue of medical science, better left to experts. One gets sick, and one sees a doctor who provides the medically appropriate treatment.

On a most general level, the claim that economics does not apply to health care is untenable. If economics, as we have stated, studies how scarce resources are used to produce goods and services and then observes how these goods and services are distributed, then clearly economics applies. Certainly health care resources are scarce; in fact, it is their cost that concerns most people. Certainly health care is produced and distributed.

Nevertheless, one can question whether the characteristic approaches of economics apply to health care. Are health care consumers rational? Do they calculate optimally at the margin? Imagine a loved one suffering a cardiac arrest. Is there time or reasoning power left to calculate? Would anyone question the price of emergency services under such circumstances?

Much of health care simply does not fit this emergency image. A considerable amount of health care is elective, meaning that the patient has and will perceive some choice over whether and when to have the diagnostics or treatment involved. Much health care is even routine, involving problems such as upper respiratory infections, back pain, and diagnostic checkups. The patient often has prior experience with these concerns. Furthermore, even in cases of real emergency the consumer has an agent, the physician, to make or help make decisions on his or her behalf. There is thus the capability for rational choice.

The primary objective of this text is to show that economics can help us understand how decision makers throughout the health economy make choices. It is in fact the special characteristics of health care markets and products that make the study of health economics both challenging and rewarding.

An Example: Does Price Matter?

To illustrate, does price matter? This question would not even be raised in the study of any other commodity. In the case of health care, however, many have argued that health care is so different from other goods that consumers do not respond to financial incentives. These views have been justified by arguments that demand is based on need or arguments that patients leave decisions entirely to their providers who are concerned with their own interests, not with how much patients have to pay.

Data from the Rand Health Insurance Experiment give an unequivocal answer to this question: Yes, economic incentives do matter to a considerable extent. Figure 1.2 describes results from the Rand study; amounts of health care consumed are measured along the horizontal axis. These amounts are scaled in percentage terms from zero to 100 percent, where 100 percent reflects the average level of care consumed by the group that used the most care on average. This group, not surprisingly, is the group with "free" care. The vertical axis measures the economic incentives as indicated by the coinsurance rate—the percentage of the bill paid out directly by the consumer. Thus, a higher coinsurance rate reflects a higher price to the consumer.

The curve shown in Figure 1.2 is similar to a demand curve in that it shows people consuming more and more care as the care becomes less and less costly to themselves directly. What is more to the point is that the curve demonstrates that economic incentives matter.

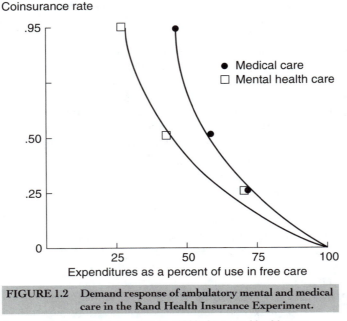

FIGURE 1.2 **Demand response of ambulatory mental and medical care in the Rand Health Insurance Experiment.**

Sources: Keeler, Manning and Wells (1988) for mental health care; Keeler and Rolph (1988) for medical care.

IS HEALTH CARE DIFFERENT?

While economics certainly applies to health care, it is more challenging to answer the question of how directly and simply it applies. Is available economic theory so easily applicable that a special field of health economics is not even necessary? Is health care to the contrary so special as to be unique? Or is the truth somewhere in between?[4]

A reasonably satisfactory answer to these questions suggests that health care has many distinctive features, but that it is not unique in any of them. What is unique, perhaps, is the combination of features and even the sheer number of them. A review of these distinctive features serves the purpose of alerting the student to those salient features of health care that require special attention. In each case where health is distinctive in economic terms, there is nevertheless a body of economic theory and empirical work that illuminates the issue.

Presence and Extent of Uncertainty

When Nobelist Kenneth Arrow (1963) directed his attention to the economics of health, he helped to establish health economics as a field. His theme stressed the prevalence of uncertainty in health care, both on the demand side and on the supply side. Consumers

---

[4]For further development of the following issues and for a variety of views, see Arrow (1963), Pauly (1978), and Fuchs (1972).

are uncertain of their health status and need for health care in any coming period. This means that the demand for health care is irregular in nature from the individual's perspective; likewise, the demand facing a health care firm is irregular.

Uncertainty is also prevalent on the supply side. Standard economic analysis often assumes that products, and the pleasures that they bring, are well-understood by the purchasers. The purchase of steak, milk, new clothes, or a ticket to a baseball game all provide expected well-being that is easily known and easily understood. In contrast, several cases of product uncertainty exist in the health field. Consumers often do not know the expected outcomes of various treatments without their physicians' advice, and in many cases physicians themselves cannot predict the outcomes of treatments with certainty.

Arrow argued that uncertainty on both the supply and demand sides was such that markets for insurance for various risks would often fail to arise. These factors suggested a role for government. While others disputed the conclusion, the point stands that uncertainty is a prominent feature in the field of health and the tools of economic analysis of uncertainty and risk will need to be used to analyze health issues fully.

Prominence of Insurance

The fact of uncertainty and risk in health implies a role for insurance. Consumers purchase insurance to guard against this uncertainty. Because of health insurance, neither most Americans, nor indeed citizens of other countries, pay directly for the full costs of their health care. Rather, the costs are paid indirectly through coinsurance and through insurance premiums that are often, although not always, purchased through participation in the labor force.[5]

Table 1.6 provides data on the sources of payment for personal health care services for selected years since 1960. In the 1960s approximately 56 percent of all personal

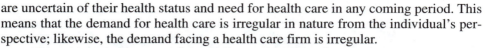

TABLE 1.6   Personal Health Care Expenditures ($ billion) by Source of Payment for Selected Years: 1960–1993

Year	Total	Out of Pocket	Private Health Insurance	Other Private	Government State/Local	Total Federal	Total Third Party	Pct. Third Party
1960	$ 23.9	$ 13.4	$ 5.0	$ 0.4	$ 3.0	$ 2.1	$ 10.6	44.4
1965	35.6	19.0	8.7	0.8	4.3	2.9	16.7	46.9
1970	64.8	25.4	15.3	1.6	7.8	14.7	39.5	61.0
1975	116.2	39.0	29.1	2.8	14.4	30.9	77.2	66.4
1980	220.1	61.3	64.1	7.7	23.6	63.4	158.8	72.1
1985	380.5	98.8	119.8	13.9	36.7	111.3	281.7	74.0
1990	612.4	138.3	206.7	24.0	65.3	178.1	474.1	77.4
1993	782.5	157.5	258.0	30.0	78.1	259.0	625.0	79.9

Source: U.S. Department of Health and Human Services, *Health United States 1994,* Table 124.

---

[5]Analysts are becoming more concerned about the insurance coverage of those who are not in the work force, or those who are not covered through their jobs.

health care expenditures were paid out-of-pocket, meaning that 44 percent was paid by third-party payers (either private or government). By 1993, almost 80 percent was paid by third parties, with the increase due to the growth of both private insurance and public programs. Certainly such separation from the direct payment must weaken some of the price effects that might be expected in standard economic analysis. Insurance changes the demand for care, and it potentially also changes the incentives of providers.

The possibility of changed provider incentives becomes more of a concern as the insurance portion of the bill increases. How the insurers pay the health care firm thus becomes a critical fact of economic life. Whether a procedure or a professional's services are accepted for coverage by insurers may determine whether providers use the procedure. Furthermore, changes in insurance payment procedures can substantially change provider behavior and provider concerns, as evidenced by Medicare's decision to change their hospital payment system during the 1980s in order to control costs more effectively.

Problems of Information

The problem of uncertainty can be understood in part as involving lack of information. Actual and potential information problems in health care markets raise many economic questions. Sometimes information is unavailable to all parties concerned. For example, neither the gynecologist nor her female patient may recognize the early stages of cervical cancer without a Pap smear. At other times, the information in question is known to some parties but not to all, and then it is the asymmetry of information that is problematical.

The problems of information mean that the careful economic analyst must modify standard methods of analysis. Standard analyses often assume that consumers know what is necessary to know about the quality of the food or the clothing that they purchase. People purchase beef as opposed to fish, or cotton as opposed to nylon fabrics. They base their decisions on the characteristics of the goods, their prices, and their abilities to bring pleasure to the buyers.

The purchase of health goods and services departs substantively from this model. Consumers do not necessarily know who is a good physician, or which is a good hospital. They may not know whether they are ill or what should be done if they are. This lack of information often makes the consumer, sometimes referred to as the principal, dependent on the provider, as an agent, in a particular way. The provider provides both the information and the service, leading to possibilities of conflicting interests. Health economics must address the provision of health services in this context.

Large Role of Nonprofit Firms

A durable assumption of economic analysis is that firms maximize profits. Economic theory provides models that explain how businesses allocate resources so as to maximize profits. Yet many health providers, including many hospitals, insurance companies, and nursing homes, have nonprofit status.

What, then, motivates these nonprofit institutions, if they cannot enjoy the profits of their endeavors? It is necessary that the economist analyze the establishment and perpetuation of nonprofit institutions, and understand the differences in their behaviors from for-profit firms.

Restrictions on Competition

Economists and policymakers generally laud the competitive market, since the entry of firms or providers in the face of high prices and/or profits will cause the other firms or providers to lower their prices. This entry and the resulting price reduction improve the well-being of consumers.

Nevertheless, the health sector has developed many practices that effectively restrict competition. These practices include licensure requirements for providers, restrictions on provider advertising, and standards of ethical behavior that enjoin providers from competing with each other. We must explain the forces that generated such practices and understand their potential benefits, but we must also understand their anticompetitive impacts and measure the magnitudes of the higher costs they may impose on society.

Regulation to promote quality or to curb costs also reduces the freedom of choice of providers and may have an impact on or restrict competition. There is often substantial interest in regulating the health care sector. The causes as well as the impacts of the regulations require considerable attention. There are industries, such as the pharmaceutical industry, that contend that patent protection is crucial for their financial stability. Economists must consider how regulations are developed, as well as who gains and who loses from them.

Other types of government intervention, particularly antitrust action, can serve to promote competition. Economic theory suggests that in the case of monopoly power, production may be restricted with a corresponding increase in price. Control of the monopolies or antitrust action to curb monopolistic practices may thus benefit the consumer.

Role of Need

Poor health of another human being often evokes a feeling of concern that distinguishes health care from many other goods and services. Many advocates express this feeling by saying that people ought to get the health care they need regardless of whether they can afford it. In practice, need is difficult to define, and distributing care under certain definitions of need may cause more economic harm than good. Yet the word signals a set of legitimate concerns for analysis.

Government Subsidies and Public Provision

In most countries there is a major governmental presence in the provision of health services. Programs such as Medicare and Medicaid inject the government into the financing of and payment for services. In addition, under many circumstances governments provide health care services through clinics and hospitals. All told, government spending in the United States of $388 billion in 1993 accounted for about 44 percent of total national health care spending of $884 billion.

CONCLUSIONS

The features we have discussed are distinctive, but is the health sector unique in these respects? No! Accounting for the features of the health sector falls well within the scope of economic inquiry. Uncertain events affect much of life and they are a prominent concern for the cases of automobile transportation, household security, and the fortunes of most businesses. Insurance programs cover many of these instances and every financial decision entails an element of risk.

Much of health care, arguably, finds the consumer relatively well-informed. In instances where the physician is asymmetrically better informed, the case is often not unlike the information deficit faced by the typical purchaser of auto repair services or a complex camera.[6]

We commonly speak of needs for food and housing, and we have government programs to provide or subsidize the poor in these markets. Other professions are licensed in many states, and various industries are regulated. Nonprofit firms provide symphony music as well as college education. Special tools of analysis are needed in all these cases, not just for health care.

Nevertheless, health and health care are unique in having this combination of distinctive features and perhaps in possessing the sheer number of them. It is not surprising that a distinctive field of economic inquiry with a distinctive set of questions has arisen regarding health.

The relevance of health economics hinges on its ability to inform, and possibly influence, the decisions of those who make health care policy. In his January 1996 presidential address to the American Economic Association, distinguished health economist Victor Fuchs concluded:

> In the past three decades economics has made a positive contribution to health and medical care, and I believe that future contributions will be even greater. Now that the basic ideas of economics are gaining acceptance, it will be more important than ever for economists to master many of the intricacies of health care institutions and technologies. We will also have to consider the problems of dissemination in order to ensure that when we agree on research results, these results are understood and accepted by all relevant audiences including the media, politicians, and health professionals. (Fuchs, 1996, p. 20).

We believe that Professor Fuchs's optimistic statement represents both a useful conclusion to this introductory chapter, and an important point of departure for the chapters that follow.

---

[6]See Pauly (1978) for a well-reasoned analysis of the differences between health care and other goods and services. He argues in particular that in many cases information problems are no more severe for health care than for many other commodities.

Summary

1. Health care spending has grown rapidly in absolute and relative terms. It accounts for about one-seventh of the GNP in the United States and its share of GNP is projected to continue to grow.
2. The growth in health care spending is attributable to more services, higher-quality services, and relative increases in the prices of health care services. A major goal of health economics is to determine the underlying causes of these phenomena.
3. The size of the health economy is also reflected through other measures such as the number of jobs in health care professions and amount of capital.
4. The health economy is considerably larger in the United States than in other countries.
5. There are significant policy concerns not only with the growth of spending but also with access and quality.
6. Economists use models to explain economic behavior. The models are abstract simplifications of reality.
7. Health economics is a relatively young and evolving field of study. As a result, health economists still disagree on some fundamental issues such as the extent to which the competitive model applies to the health economy.
8. Health care services and the health economy are associated with a unique set of distinguishing features. The uniqueness of health care lies in the entire set rather than with individual distinctive features such as the prevalence of uncertainty or insurance coverage.
9. Despite these features and unresolved issues, health economics has much to say about how health care markets function.

Discussion Questions

1. Suggest several reasons why health care spending is higher in the United States than in other countries. Is the fact that the U.S. population spends more per capita on health care than people in any other developed country evidence of a failure of the U.S. system? What issues do you think are involved in answering the question?
2. Describe several key issues facing policymakers with regard to health care spending.
3. If greater health care spending leads to more jobs, why are we so concerned about the rapid growth rates of spending?
4. Do consumers take the net price (including insurance and time) they face into consideration when choosing health care? What evidence suggests that "price matters?" Suggest real-life scenarios in which price may affect choices regarding health care.
5. What is meant by marginal analysis? Provide an example in which marginal analysis is useful in looking at policy questions.

6. Give three examples of quality of care in the provision of health services. Why might consumers be willing to pay more money to have each of them?

7. Describe the size of the health economy when measured by the quantities of capital and labor used to produce health care. What important inputs to the production of health are not being counted among these?

Exercises

1. Identify at least three reasons why health care spending has grown rapidly.

2. Identify five distinctive features of the health economy. Taking each one separately, describe other commodities or sectors that share those features. Are there any other commodities or sectors that have all the features you listed?

3. In Table 1.6, we see increases in health expenditures by consumers and by the government. From year to year, in the table, which grew by a larger percentage? Over the entire period, which grew by larger percentages?

4. In Table 1.1, calculate which country had the largest and smallest percentage increase in GDP share from 1960 to 1980. Compare these to similar calculations for the period 1980 to 1993. Discuss your results.

CHAPTER

2

Microeconomic Tools for Health Economics

This chapter provides an explanation of the microeconomic tools that are used in the text, by reviewing material that may be encountered at the introductory and intermediate levels of learning. These tools are useful for a deeper understanding of ideas in health economics. This review does not substitute for an introductory course in the principles of economics. Although we present the material in a way consistent with more detailed and thus rigorous developments in a standard microeconomics course, we have eliminated mathematical detail.

While health economics sometimes involves macroeconomic concepts such as gross national product (GNP) or the consumer price index (CPI), it deals primarily with microeconomic concerns involving individual decision makers such as households and providers, and specific industries such as the health insurance and hospital industries. The behavior of individual decision makers is the focus and subject of microeconomics. Health economics also addresses the problem of the efficient use of scarce resources, which too is a microeconomic issue.

The chapter starts with the concept of scarcity and reviews supply and demand analysis. After these introductory treatments of supply and demand, the chapter returns separately to demand first and then to supply, developing the underlying ideas behind these tools. We then combine them into models of market structures, emphasizing those featured in health economics.

SCARCITY AND THE PRODUCTION POSSIBILITIES FRONTIER

A fundamental idea in economics is that there is no such thing as a free lunch. The fact that little if anything is free implies that to get something one must usually give up something else, such as time or other resources. A helpful theoretical tool that illustrates this idea is the *production possibilities frontier* (PPF).

The production possibilities frontier is a curve drawn in a graph to illustrate the trade-offs between two categories of goods. The curve shows how our choices are constrained by the fact that we cannot have all of everything we want. The idea that we face resource constraints and must make trade-offs is central to the PPF, but similar ideas also apply to the individual firm or the individual consumer.

We begin the production possibilities problem with a table illustrating a classic dilemma. A classic PPF problem concerns society's trade-off between guns and butter. Table 2.1 shows data on the amounts of guns or butter that a hypothetical society could produce with its resources. Guns and butter are meant metaphorically to refer to all goods and services with a military use versus those that have a domestic consumption use. The PPF could in principle also be drawn in many dimensions. What is essential is that the goods represented exhaustively account for all the goods in the economy.

TABLE 2.1 Society's Trade-off Between Guns and Butter

Point	Butter	Guns	Opportunity Cost: Butter Given Up to Produce 100 Units of Guns
A	936	0	
B	891	100	45
C	828	200	63
D	732	300	96
E	609	400	123
F	444	500	165
G	244	600	200
H	0	700	244

Table 2.1 contains many numbers but illustrates two central ideas. Note first that as the numbers of guns increase, the numbers for butter fall, indicating that to produce more of one good we must give up some of the other. The amount of butter given up in order to produce an extra 100 units of guns is called the opportunity cost of 100 units of guns. Opportunity cost can be measured per 100 units of guns as here, but more commonly we are interested in the opportunity cost of the single next unit of guns, called the marginal unit. In either case, the opportunity cost represents what is given up.

The opportunity cost column reporting the costs of each 100 units of guns in terms of butter foregone illustrates a second idea, that of increasing opportunity costs. As guns increase, the opportunity cost gets larger. If society is to increase its production of guns, say from 200 to 300 units, it must transfer the resources, labor, and capital previously used in butter production to gun production. The idea that this is a frontier means that we are hypothetically representing society's best possible production. Thus, when we first shift butter resources toward gun production, we can arbitrarily choose to shift those resources relatively best suited to gun production first. By choosing laborers who are more handy at gun making than at butter making, we will gain the most guns per unit of butter we give up. But, as we shift more and more resources toward guns, we will necessarily have to dig deeper into our relatively good butter-producing resources, and hence give up greater quantities of butter. Increasing opportunity costs thus also illustrate the specialization of society's resources of labor and capital.

Graphing and its usefulness are illustrated by transferring the data in Table 2.1 into the graph in Figure 2.1. Note that if this society devotes all its labor and capital to butter production, the most butter it can produce is 936 units. The two numbers—936 units of butter and 0 units of guns—can be represented by point A in Figure 2.1. The other points are transferred in the same manner. We assume that the missing points between these data points will fit the same pattern, resulting in the curve labeled PPF.

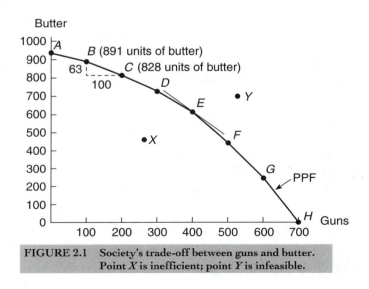

FIGURE 2.1   Society's trade-off between guns and butter.
Point *X* is inefficient; point *Y* is infeasible.

In the graph, the idea of no free lunch is illustrated by the downward slope of the PPF curve. In this example, increased gun production means we have to give up some butter production—hence, we get no free lunch. Second, the opportunity cost itself is illustrated in the slope of the curve. For example, the line between points *B* and *C* has a slope of 63 (the rise) over 100 (the run), and 63 units of butter per 100 units of guns is the opportunity cost we had observed in the table.

The opportunity cost of one single unit of guns is virtually the slope of the PPF at a single point, which equals the slope of a line tangent at that point. Therefore, at point *E* the opportunity cost is identical with the slope of the tangent line to the PPF at *E*.

Finally, the idea of increasing opportunity cost is illustrated by the bowed-out shape of the PPF, showing its concavity to the origin. Recall that the slope is the opportunity cost. Thus, the slope becoming steeper means that the opportunity cost is increasing.

Society could choose any point on the PPF, but society can only be at one point at a time. How society makes and achieves its choice are other matters to discuss, but at present we have merely illustrated the best possible practices of some hypothetical society. An interior point such as *X* means that the particular society is not doing the best it can; it is inefficient. Second, a point such as *Y* is unattainable because of insufficient resources to produce the indicated amounts of both guns and butter.

PRACTICE WITH SUPPLY AND DEMAND

The most familiar ideas in economics are probably supply and demand curves. We will illustrate supply and demand analysis for a hypothetical market for apples.

The Demand Curve and Demand Shifters

In Figure 2.2A, a demand curve illustrates the demand for apples in a hypothetical market for a given period of time, say one week. The demand curve drawn shows a quantity demanded in this market for this time period for each possible price. For example, at a price of $5.25 per bushel, the consumers would wish to buy a total of 345 bushels that week. The theory of demand suggests that quantity demanded would be less at higher prices—for example, 215 bushels at a price of $7.50. Some consumers may find that the price rise represents "the last straw" so that they buy none, while others may buy fewer apples than before, and yet others would not change their purchases. It is doubtful that anyone would use the occasion of a price rise as a reason to buy more.

This analysis is done ceteris paribus, meaning that we are assuming that all other things are held constant. The price of apples rises while people's tastes, perceptions, incomes, and so on stay the same. In life it is common for two or more things to change at the same time. If, for example, the price of apples rises at the same time as tastes change, the result would be theoretically ambiguous, meaning that we cannot predict the direction of the change. In contrast, the demand curve depicts the behavior of consumers as price only changes.

As long as people buy less at higher prices, then the demand curve will be downward sloping. In statistical analysis, estimated demand curves are almost always downward

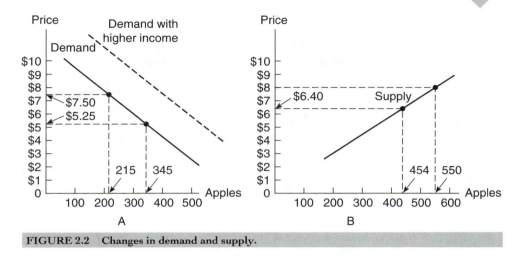

FIGURE 2.2   **Changes in demand and supply.**

sloping. The responsiveness of demand to price is measured by the elasticity. We will discuss elasticity in a later section.

Other variables will also affect the demand for apples. For example, the amount of various foods that people buy may depend on their incomes; richer people tend to buy more. Demand may be affected by the price of other substitutable goods. When any other variable affects demand, its effect will be shown as a shift in the curve. For convenience, we call such variables demand shifters. A list of demand shifters includes the following:

Income: Generally the quantity of a good that people wish to buy depends in part on their incomes. People with higher incomes tend to demand more of most goods. Such goods are called *normal* goods. But some goods, such as used clothing or generic brand goods, are purchased less often when people become richer. Such goods are called *inferior* goods. Let us assume that apples are normal goods. In Figure 2.2A, increased income in the community would tend to shift the demand curve outward.

Other Prices: Prices of related goods will also affect demand. Related goods may be either substitutes or complements. If oranges are regarded as substitutes for apples, an increase in the price of oranges would cause the demand for apples to increase, shifting the demand curve to the right. In contrast, a complement is something that is used with apples, such as caramel. If the price of a complement rises, the demand for apples decreases or shifts left.

Insurance: A variable that makes no sense for apples, but that is essential on a list of demand shifters in health contexts, is insurance. Insurance has the effect of decreasing the costs of purchase at the point of service; this will increase demand for health care.

Tastes: There are many other shifters of demand that may be grouped under the heading of tastes. Tastes can be literally what the word means, as when a new recipe increases interest in apples. The term can be less literal as well, as when we say that an older population has a greater demand for health care because it has a greater taste for health care.

The Supply Curve and Supply Shifters

Supply can be approached in a similar way. Figure 2.2B shows an upward sloping supply curve for apples. It illustrates, for example, that apple growers would be willing to offer 454 bushels of apples for sale if the price were $6.40. At a higher price, say $8.00, more would be offered. Apple growers might be more willing to divert apples from cider production, to make greater efforts in harvest, or even to bring formerly unprofitable trees into production if the price were higher. Such reasons would suggest an upward sloping supply curve such as the one shown.

We may likewise generate a list of supply shifters:

Technological Change: As technology improves for producing a given product, the good becomes cheaper to produce. Certainly technological changes that make products more costly without improving quality would be ignored. As the product becomes cheaper to produce, suppliers will be willing to offer more for sale at a given price. This will increase supply, thus shifting the supply curve to the right.

Input Prices: If the wage of apple pickers were to rise, this increase in an input cost would reduce suppliers' willingness to offer as much for sale at the original price. The supply would decrease, shifting the curve to the left.

Prices of Production-Related Goods: The price of a good related in production, such as cider, would also be relevant. Since farmers can use raw apples for eating or for cider, generally a rise in cider prices will cause apple supply to decrease, thus shifting the supply curve to the left.

Size of the Industry: As more firms (in this case apple growers) enter a market, the supply of the product will be greater. Thus, entry of firms will cause supply to shift to the right.

Weather: For a number of products, acts of God like the weather will tend to affect production. The direction of the effect is obvious: Good weather increases supply.

Equilibrium

Under conditions of competition, the equilibrium in a market will be at the point where the demand and supply curves intersect. This is the point at which demanders' and suppliers' plans agree. In Figure 2.3, the equilibrium occurs at the price of $5.00 and at the quantity of 350 bushels. At higher prices there will tend to be excess supply, and suppliers who were unable to sell all their goods will be willing to bid prices down. At lower prices there will be excess demand, and demanders who went undersupplied would have been willing to pay more and will tend to bid prices up.

Comparative Statics

An equilibrium as depicted in Figure 2.3 is called a static equilibrium. It shows a picture of an unchanging equilibrium at a point in time. It is more interesting to assess how the equilibrium will change when the market is affected by some economic event. Figures 2.4A and B give two examples. Consider in Figure 2.4A what would happen to the market for coffee if there were a freeze in Brazil. This worsening of the weather

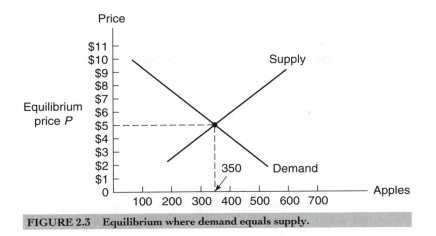

FIGURE 2.3   Equilibrium where demand equals supply.

would tend to shift supply to the left as shown. At the new equilibrium, the price of cof-fee is higher and the quantity consumed is lower.

Similarly, in Figure 2.4B, consider what happens to the market for tea when the price of sugar rises. Since sugar is a complement, this event causes a shift to the left in the demand for tea as shown. The new equilibrium will have a lower price and a lower quantity.

A few exercises help to generate experience with comparative statics and to demonstrate the applicability of this analysis:

1. A national health insurance proposal is passed that provides comprehensive health insur-ance to everyone. How would this affect the markets for health care in the short run?

    Answer: The competitive model is robust enough to give some guidance. Insurance cov-erage will probably increase on average, causing the demand for health care to increase, shifting the curve to the right. This will increase the equilibrium price of care as well as

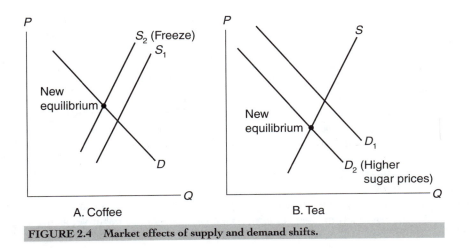

FIGURE 2.4   Market effects of supply and demand shifts.

the quantity consumed. The two results combined will increase the total money spent on health care. The analysis here is conducted ceteris paribus. If a successful cost control program were put into effect at the same time, the net result might be different.

2. A law is passed requiring that hospitals only hire nurses with baccalaureate degrees. How would this affect the market for hospital care?

   Answer: Hospital markets are not perfectly competitive, but the predictions of the competitive model would tend to hold. Such a law would increase an input price, thus shifting the supply of hospital care to the left. The equilibrium price of hospital care would tend to rise and quantity would fall.

3. Suppose the government lowers the rates paid to physicians for Medicare patients. How would this affect the market for non-Medicare patients?

   Answer: The government action probably serves as a supply shifter because Medicare patients are a production-related good. Physicians would shift more time and other inputs into non-Medicare patient production, shifting the supply to the right, lowering equilibrium price, and raising quantity.

FUNCTIONS AND CURVES

Most economic discussions consider how two or more economic variables are related to each other. For example, consider what we have theorized about the relationship of the price to the quantity demanded. We say that the quantity demanded is a function of the price. Mathematically, a function is an arrangement whereby we plug in the value of the independent variable, here the price, and the function generates the value of the dependent variable, here the quantity demanded. Alternatively, we can say that quantity demanded depends on price.

Linear Functions

Before considering the writing of supply and demand in functional notation, consider the linear function. A linear function is that of a straight line and can be written as follows:

$$y = a + bx \qquad\qquad (2.1)$$

where y is the dependent variable and x is the independent variable.

A linear function, no matter what idea it represents, has characteristic features: an intercept and a slope, both of which are constants. The y-intercept is the value of the function evaluated when x equals zero. Here the intercept is a.

The slope of a function is the rise over the run. To determine the slope of this particular function, examine this function drawn as a curve in Figure 2.5. We use the word *curve* for all functions, including the straight line. As noted, the y-intercept is a. Similarly, the function crosses the x-axis at a value of zero for y. Setting y to zero and solving for x yields a value of $x = -a/b$. Now to find the slope divide the change in y, $-a$, by the change in x, $-a/b$, thus generating a value for the slope of b, the slope of this linear function. The value of b in this case must be negative, as the slope is downward.

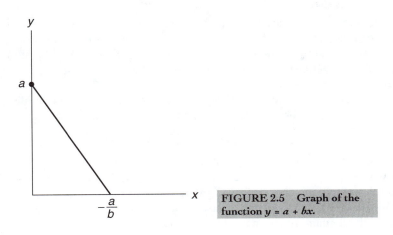

FIGURE 2.5 **Graph of the function $y = a + bx$.**

Demand Functions

The demand functions up to this point have been linear. In general, though, linear demand is only one special case. Even when demand is linear, however, there is a minor complication. Consider the following linear demand function:

$$Q_d = a - bP \qquad (2.2)$$

where Q_d is quantity demanded and P is price.

A complication arises because economists customarily draw demand and supply curves with the independent variable, price, on the y-axis and the dependent variable, quantity demanded, on the x-axis. In standard mathematics the dependent variable is usually drawn on the x-axis.

Most commonly, we will be considering cases where the dependent variable, such as quantity demanded, is a function of not one but several variables. For example, the quantity of spaghetti demanded, Q_d, may depend not only on the price of spaghetti, P_s, but also on the price of substitutes for spaghetti (such as other pastas), P_o, the individual's income, Y, and a taste factor, Z. Mathematically, using the general notation, we would write the demand function for spaghetti as follows:

$$Q_d = f (P_s, P_o, Y, Z) \qquad (2.3)$$

Here the notation $Q_d = f (\dots)$ is read, "Quantity demanded is a function of P_s, P_o, Y, and Z."

If the function in (2.3) also happens to be linear, its more specific form would have a characteristic linear look to it. Statisticians frequently use this case and it is useful to look at an example. A linear spaghetti demand function, for example, might look like this:

$$Q_d = 500 - 10P_s + 5P_o + 20Y + 40Z \qquad (2.4)$$

Linear equations with several independent variables have some things in common with the simple linear equation in (2.1). There is an intercept constant calculated by setting all the independent variables equal to zero; here the intercept is 500. The slope values in such linear cases will be the coefficients of the independent variables in question. For example, the slope value for the income variable Y is 20. The slope gives information regarding the contributions of changes in the independent variables to the value of the dependent variable.

Again, it is worthwhile emphasizing that functions in economics need not be linear. For example, the true spaghetti demand function might instead look like this:

$$Q_d = AP_s^{-.05}P_o^{.002}Y^{0.8}Z^{.01} \tag{2.5}$$

which is not linear. Our theory says only a few things about a demand function: It is downward sloping in own price, shifting rightward (leftward) with higher prices of substitutes (complements), shifting rightward (leftward) with income increases for normal (inferior) goods, and shifting rightward with a positive shift in tastes. Beyond these features, the demand function mathematically could take on many different forms.

CONSUMER BEHAVIOR THEORY: IDEAS BEHIND THE DEMAND CURVE

Consumer theory examines how rational individuals make consumption choices when faced with limited resources. The limited resources determine what options a consumer can afford. From among these options, the consumer attempts to pick the best one. The theory has two parts. One is a description of what the consumer prefers, what he or she thinks is best; for this description we use both the ideas of utility and of indifference curves. The second part is a description of what the consumer can afford; for this part we use the idea of budget constraints. The use of indifference curves and budget constraints together constitutes indifference curve analysis.

Utility

Consider a consumer, Kathy Richards. Let us suppose she is an experienced consumer who knows what her tastes are for kinds of houses to live in, cars to drive, food to eat, and books to read. She can't afford everything she would like to have, but she knows what she would prefer if she could afford everything.

In summarizing this information about Kathy's preferences, we suppose that she has a utility function. Utility is a measure of her level of satisfaction with various combinations of consumer goods. It includes a market basket filled with a combination of housing, food, transportation, and so on, with perhaps many different types of each. Bundles preferred over other bundles are given a greater value of utility. Since more utility, thus defined, is always better, Kathy will logically seek to maximize her utility subject to the constraint of what is affordable to her.

Using functions, we say that Kathy's utility is a function of the goods and services she consumes. In practice, the level of detail we use will vary. On some occasions we must specify most of the detailed consumption of Kathy's life. Then we would describe her utility as a function of each good or service she buys, perhaps compiling hundreds of them. But in many cases it is useful to abstract from this detail and describe

Kathy's utility as a function of one or two goods of special interest plus another ge. good representing all other goods she considers. At still other times we will find it useful to describe Kathy's utility as a function of wealth. We will develop two examples in the following discussion.

Theories using the idea of utility may propose that utility is either cardinal or ordinal. Cardinal utility would mean a metric measure, like a measure of weight or volume. It is characteristic of cardinal measures that the difference as well as the ratio between two measurements has meaning. One can meaningfully say, for example, that 5 quarts is 3 more than 2 quarts and for that matter it is two and one half times 2 quarts. Under ordinal utility, to the contrary, only the ranking has meaning. Examples of ordinal numbers are first, second, third, and so on.

It is preferable to theorize that consumers' utility is ordinal. It is safer to assume that consumers can rank their preferences than to assume that they can both rank and scale them. It seems safer to suppose someone can say that he is happier to have gotten a raise, but it seems questionable to suppose that he is 1.07 times as happy. Most theories of demand assume only ordinality. In a few cases, such as the theory of behavior under risk and insurance, some degree of cardinality is assumed.

To illustrate ideas about utility, we should begin with the simplest case to draw. Figure 2.6 depicts Kathy's utility as a function of her wealth. The curve illustrates two ideas. First, the upward slope indicates that utility increases with wealth. Second, the bowed shape, concave from below, indicates that her utility increases with wealth at a decreasing rate.

Marginal utility is defined as the extra utility achieved by consuming one more unit of a good. Here the only good is wealth, so marginal utility is the extra utility Kathy gets from one more dollar of wealth. An extra convenience of drawing the function graphically is that the marginal utility is the slope of the curve at a given point. Starting at any point on the curve and adding a single dollar to Kathy's wealth leads to extra utility for that dollar, which we have just defined as marginal utility (MU).

If we understand marginal utility as the slope, for Kathy the marginal utility of wealth gets smaller as she gets wealthier. That is, the slope gets flatter. An extra dollar means more to Kathy when she is poorer than when she is richer. Does this notion apply to most people? That it might apply seems plausible to most students, but the notion also introduces an element of cardinal utility.

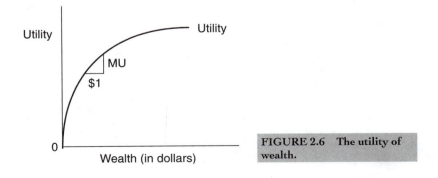

FIGURE 2.6   The utility of wealth.

Indifference Curves

Often we wish to depict the consumer's preferences over two or more goods. The most convenient case to draw is when there are only two goods. To capture the sense of the real world in a two-good drawing, let one of the two goods represent all other goods generally, as if they were a conglomerate. Call this conglomerate OG, meaning Other Goods. Suppose that the good of special interest is Food. Figure 2.7 depicts a graph with these two goods, OG and Food on the axes. Any point in the space, such as A, represents a consumer bundle. The bundle A includes the combination of 8 units of Food and 4 units of Other Goods. Other bundles that are labeled include B, C, D, E, F, and G, but any other point in the space is also a bundle.

Suppose we focus on bundle A and that we hypothetically ask Kathy to identify all other bundles as well that for her are indifferent to A (that is, points that give her the same utility as A). The entire set of such points is labeled U_1; as noted in the graph, any point along U_1 affords Kathy 112 utils (we will call the units of utility *utils*).

This curve is downward sloping as well as bowed toward the origin. Notice, for example, that Kathy did not choose point C as being indifferent to A. This seems plausible because C represents more of both goods, and as long as she is not satiated with these two goods then she would prefer C to A. Likewise, she has not picked point D as indifferent to A because D has less of both goods. Instead, she has picked points such as E, which has more Food but less OG. Presumably at E she has just balanced the loss of OG against the gain in Food. These considerations suggest that it is understandable that the indifference curve through A is downward sloping.

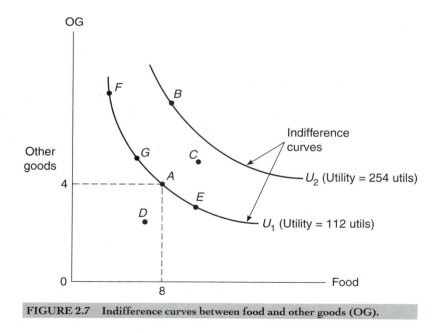

FIGURE 2.7   Indifference curves between food and other goods (OG).

The curve is also convex to the origin. Consider that at point *F* Kathy has relatively a lot of OG and little of Food. As Food is relatively scarce for her, she is willing to give up a lot of OG to get more Food. The rate at which she is willing to trade off the two goods is represented by the slope of the indifference curve, which is very steep at point *F*. In contrast, as we move down the indifference curve, Kathy gains relatively more Food, and the more she gets the less ready she is to give up still further OG to gain yet more Food. Thus, the curve becomes flatter.

Indifference curves for Kathy summarize and represent her preferences. Every possible combination of goods will lie on some indifference curve so that in principle there would be an infinite number of indifference curves in Figure 2.7, with higher curves representing greater satisfaction.

Budget Constraints

Indifference curve analysis uses preference maps and budget constraints. The budget constraint indicates the set of bundles the consumer can afford with a given income. Suppose that Kathy Richards must allocate $30 of her family food budget per week between beef *B* and chicken *C*. If the price of beef is $2.00 per pound, and the price of chicken is $1.00 per pound, then she can afford any combination of *B* and *C* that costs less than or equal to $30, and her budget constraint is:

$$30.00 = 2.00B + 1.00C \tag{2.6}$$

If we draw this constraint in Figure 2.8 with beef *B* on the vertical axis, then the budget constraint will start at 15 pounds of beef and proceed downward sloping to 30 pounds of chicken as the horizontal intercept.

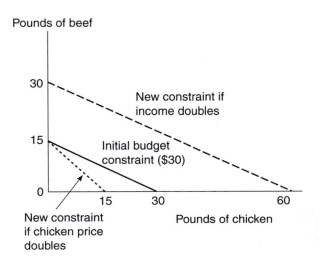

FIGURE 2.8 Changes in budget constraints due to changes in price or income.

It is convenient to demonstrate this pattern by examining the mathematical function. Equation (2.6) can be transformed using algebra so that *B* appears on the left-hand side, and all other terms on the right. Thus, the budget constraint equivalently is:

$$B = \frac{30}{2} - \frac{1}{2}C = 15 - 0.5C \qquad (2.7)$$

a linear function with an intercept of 15 and a slope of −0.5.

If, in Figure 2.8, the price of chicken were to rise, the amount that Kathy could buy, if she spent all $30 on chicken, would be less than before. If the price doubled, the chicken axis intercept would shift inward, permitting her to buy only 15 pounds of chicken rather than 30. The beef intercept is not affected when the price of chicken rises.

Consider instead an increase in the portion of her budget allocated to beef and chicken. A doubling to $60 would allow Kathy to increase the amount of beef from 15 to 30 pounds, or the amount of chicken from 30 to 60 pounds. As shown, the new budget constraint is parallel to the original budget constraint. When the income doubles, this in itself does not cause the prices to change. Since the slope of each budget constraint is the ratio of prices, then the new constraint will be parallel. The intercepts will double.

Consumer Equilibrium

To maximize satisfaction, given a budget constraint, the consumer will want to be on the highest attainable indifference curve. In Figure 2.9, the indifference curve U_1 is not the best possible, while the indifference curve U_3 is unattainable. Rejecting such alternatives, the consumer will find that she maximizes utility at a point of tangency, shown as

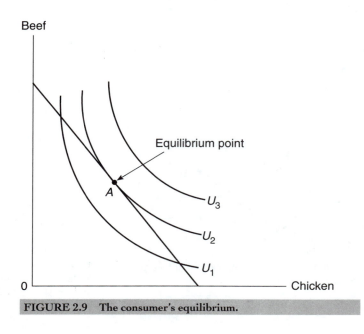

FIGURE 2.9   **The consumer's equilibrium.**

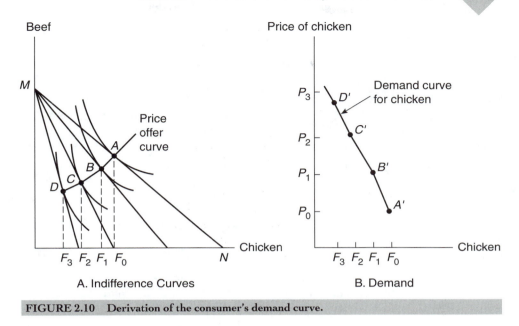

FIGURE 2.10 Derivation of the consumer's demand curve.

point *A* in the figure. At this point, the rate at which the consumer is willing to trade beef for chicken, the slope of the indifference curve is equal to the rate at which the consumer is able to trade the two goods at market prices, the slope of the budget constraint.

One can derive the equilibrium for different prices and/or for different values of income. For example, in Figure 2.10A, as the price of chicken rises consecutively, Kathy consecutively chooses points *A, B, C,* and *D*. The collection of such points is called the price offer curve. The information from these data points along the price offer curve can be used to generate her demand curve. For example, point *A* at the left represents her best choice for a given budget and set of prices. Suppose the price of chicken for budget constraint *MN* is P_0. Then plotting P_0 together with the quantity demanded at *A*, namely F_0, in the graph at right generates point *A'*. In the same manner, data on price P_1 and the quantity demanded F_1, at point *B*, generate point *B'* in the graph at right. Repeating this process generates the demand curve.

INDIVIDUAL AND MARKET DEMANDS

The theory of consumer behavior focuses on the demand relationships of individual consumers. Many applications of demand theory, however, consider market demand. The extension from individual to market demand is straightforward. In Figure 2.11, health care demand is shown for two people who constitute a market for health care. For example, Mary demands 3 units at the price $p_H = 30$, and John demands 2 units. Market demand here at $p_H = 30$ is (3 + 2) or 5 units. The market demand in panel C is derived by adding the quantities demanded at every price. The process can be extended

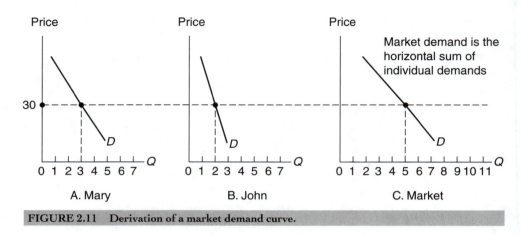

FIGURE 2.11 **Derivation of a market demand curve.**

to all of the consumers in the market, and it yields a market demand curve. If everyone's demand curve conforms to the Law of Demand, the market demand curve must also be downward sloping.

Finally, note that as with individual demand functions, there also are other variables such as income and the prices of other related goods (the shift variable we discussed earlier) that affect market demand. Thus, the market demand for some commodity X might be expressed in functional notation. Consider, for example

$$QD_x = f\ (P_x,\ Y,\ P_o,\ E) \tag{2.8}$$

where Y represents income, P_o are the prices of other goods, and E represents a socioeconomic variable such as average educational attainment (in years of schooling).

ELASTICITIES

We are often particularly interested in the responsiveness of the quantity demanded to other variables. For example, if the price of health care rises, will the quantity demanded fall by a large amount or a small amount? Economists use the term *elasticity* to describe the responsiveness of *any* term y (in this case, quantity demanded of health care) to changes in some other variable x (here, price of health care).

Elasticity is defined as the percent change in the dependent variable resulting from a 1 percent change in the independent variable under study.[1] In the case of the price elasticity of demand it is as follows:

---

[1] Percentages allow us to "standardize" our measure. In particular, the use of percentages eliminates problems comparing various goods that may be measured in pounds, gallons, or feet. Here they are all measured in percent. For example, it becomes possible to compare demand elasticities for beef with automobiles, even though the price levels and quantities are different.

E_p = (% change in quantity demanded)/(% change in the price), or

$$E_p = \frac{\Delta Q/Q}{\Delta P/P} = \frac{\Delta Q}{\Delta P}\frac{P}{Q} \qquad (2.9)$$

where Δ refers to change in the variable. The price elasticity is always algebraically negative because an increase in price leads to a decrease in quantity demanded. Other elasticities, such as the income elasticity of demand, are derived similarly.

E_y = (% change in quantity demanded)/(% change in income), or

$$E_y = \frac{\Delta Q/Q}{\Delta Y/Y} = \frac{\Delta Q}{\Delta Y}\frac{Y}{Q} \qquad (2.10)$$

Income elasticity may be positive (if a normal good) or negative (if an inferior good). If there is no response to a variable at all, then elasticity is 0.

Numerical values for price elasticities are often reported in absolute values, eliminating the minus sign. Absolute values for price elasticities indicate the responsiveness of demand to price in that the greater the elasticity the greater the responsiveness. Absolute values greater than 1 are considered relatively responsive and are called elastic. Elasticities less than 1 in absolute value are called inelastic. In the limiting cases, zero price elasticity means that the demand curve is perfectly vertical, while infinite price elasticity means that the demand curve is perfectly flat.

The importance of price elasticity to policy questions can be illustrated with an example regarding cigarettes, clearly a health concern. In 1994 the State of Michigan instituted a 50-cent tax per pack of cigarettes sold in Michigan. How much will this tax cause the purchase of cigarettes and the level of smoking to fall, if at all? The answer depends critically on the price elasticity of cigarette demand. In Figure 2.12 three alternative demand curves for cigarettes are illustrated, each with a different pattern of

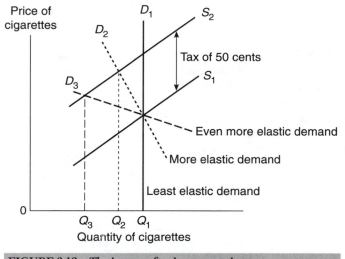

FIGURE 2.12　The impact of a cigarette excise tax.

response. The vertical demand curve D_1 illustrates the least elastic curve (closest to 0), indicating the possibility that smokers do not respond to price at all because they are completely hooked. The demand curve D_2 illustrates a more responsive set of consumers (more elastic demand), while curve D_3 illustrates the hypothetical demand curve that is most responsive.

Now assess the effect of the 50-cent tax increase. An excise tax shifts the supply curve upward by 50 cents. Assuming that the original equilibrium quantity of cigarettes was Q_1, after the supply shifts, the new equilibrium quantity either stays at Q_1 (perfectly inelastic demand), or adjusts downward to Q_2 or Q_3 for the alternative demand curves. Thus, the more elastic the response, the greater the effectiveness of an excise tax in inducing people to reduce their levels of smoking. Lewit and Coate (1982) indicate that teenagers, for example, are more responsive to cigarette prices than adults. In such cases, taxes on cigarettes will be relatively more effective with teenagers.

PRODUCTION AND MARKET SUPPLY

If market demand is one "blade of the scissors" in determining the price of a good, market supply by individual firms is the other. A typical firm will be faced with decisions on production levels, prices, production methods to be used, levels of advertising, and amounts of inputs to be purchased. The theory of the firm, much like the theory of consumer behavior for buyers, develops a framework for understanding how these choices are made.

The key assumption for most models of firm behavior is that the decision makers wish to maximize profits. It follows that the firm will try to minimize the costs of producing any given output and will undertake activities such as advertising only so long as they add to profits. Before examining such decisions, we will review production and cost relationships.

The Production Function

The production function shows the maximum sustainable output that can be obtained from all of the various possible combinations of inputs such as labor, materials, and machinery, with existing technology and know-how. It is useful to begin our discussion of production functions with a simple case, one in which there is just one input and one output. Suppose that food, perhaps in a hunter–gatherer society, were produced solely with labor. Let the production function be as shown in the top panel of Figure 2.13. The fact that the production function is rising indicates the idea that labor is productive; more labor means that more food is produced. The bowed shape of the curve illustrates a second idea, the law of diminishing returns.

It is understood in Figure 2.13 that the production takes place during a specified period of time. Thus, the output axis represents a flow of output per unit of time. Likewise, the labor input represents labor services applied during a specified period of time.

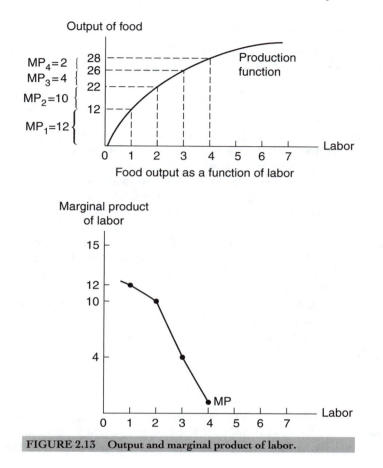

FIGURE 2.13   Output and marginal product of labor.

The law of diminishing returns represents the idea that the marginal product (MP) of an input will eventually tend to fall as more is added. The marginal product, here of labor, is defined as the extra output that can be generated when one adds an additional hour of labor, holding all other inputs constant. In the figure, the food output increases from zero to 12 units when the first hour of labor is added. Thus, 12 units of food is the marginal product of the first unit of labor. When a second hour of labor is added, the output of food increases from 12 units to 22 units. The extra amount is thus 10 units, meaning that the marginal product of the second hour of labor is 10 units of food. The bottom panel of the graph illustrates the marginal product of consecutive hours of labor. The pattern of the marginal products in this illustration is clear: They tend to get smaller as more labor is applied. This illustrates the law of diminishing returns. Notice that total output need never fall during diminishing returns. That is, the production curve itself never turns downward in this illustration, although it may in some applications.

Production Functions

In practice, production processes may involve several different inputs, not just labor. It is convenient to express the production relationship for a firm, or a unit of the firm, as follows:

$$Q = f(X_1, X_2, \ldots, X_n) \tag{2.11}$$

Here Q represents output, and X_1, X_2, and so on are quantities of the various inputs.

Consider, for example, the output of hospital X-ray services, which require the use of labor by technicians, nurses, and radiologists, and machinery, such as X-ray machines, computers, film, and typewriters. As with demand functions, production functions may take on many different mathematical forms. The theory of production functions only specifies certain patterns for these functions.

One commonly applied functional form that fits the theoretical patterns for such functions is called the Cobb-Douglas form. Historically, it was one of the earliest production functional forms to be studied and applied to firms. It derives its name from the two authors who developed it, mathematician Charles Cobb, and economist and later U.S. Senator, Paul Douglas. Many other functional forms of production have since been investigated, but this form is still commonly used in the classroom to illustrate the mathematics of the production process.

If the production of X-ray services just discussed fits the Cobb-Douglas form, and if inputs of all kinds are grouped into the categories of capital, K, and labor, L, the production function actually estimated might look like this:

$$Q = L^{0.8}K^{0.2} \tag{2.12}$$

Here, as with any production function, there will be a unique level of maximum output for any combination of inputs.[2] For example, Table 2.2 shows values of output corresponding to changes in L, holding K constant at 5 units. The change in output

TABLE 2.2 Production Schedule for X-ray Services				
K	L	Q	MP	AP
5	0	0.00		
5	1	1.38	1.38	1.38
5	2	2.40	1.02	1.20
5	3	3.32	0.92	1.11
5	4	4.18	0.86	1.05
5	5	5.00	0.82	1.00
5	6	5.79	0.79	0.97
5	7	6.54	0.75	0.93

---

[2]There can always be less output if workers are shirking or if machines break down. As with the production possibilities frontier, there cannot be more than the maximum.

associated with a one-unit change in L is the marginal product of labor. More L (e.g., technicians) with the same amount of K will typically produce more Q (hence, a positive marginal product of labor), but as the machines become crowded or break down, the marginal product may fall as L increases. Hence, the marginal product in Table 2.2 is shown as diminishing. This decreasing marginal product again illustrates the Law of Diminishing Returns. The average output or average product (AP) for each worker is Q/L, as shown in the last column.

Alternatively, we can derive various input combinations needed to produce a given output level. Table 2.3 illustrates several combinations that produce 10 units of output for the production function represented by equation (2.12). This method closely parallels the indifference curve analyses introduced in an earlier section, except that we actually observe and measure the quantities produced (in contrast to the levels of utility that could only be ranked). Combinations of inputs producing equal output levels lie on an *isoquant* (literally, "the same quantity"). The isoquant in Table 2.3 is illustrated graphically in Figure 2.14. The isoquant map, representing all possible values of Q, would be the geometric representation of a production function.

The negative slope to an isoquant indicates the possibility of substituting inputs in the production process and of the positive marginal product of the inputs. Consider, again, the example of X-ray services. The numerical value of the isoquant slope, indicating how much capital (X-ray machines, typewriters, computers) must be given up per unit increase in labor (nurses, technicians, radiologists), is called the *marginal rate of technical substitution* of labor for capital ($MRTS_{LK}$).[3]

Isocost Curves

In order for the X-ray unit to maximize profits, suppose that the unit wishes to minimize the costs of providing any given quantity of X-rays. Suppose for the moment that it decides to produce a given level of X-rays. Under the assumptions, it will want to minimize the cost of producing this output. Letting TC represent total costs, w the price

TABLE 2.3 An Isoquant Schedule

Q	L	K
10	1	100,000.00
10	5	160.00
10	7	41.60
10	8	24.40
10	10	10.00
10	11	6.80
10	13	3.50
10	20	0.63

---

[3]Isoquants are typically convex to the origin, i.e., the numerical value of the slope diminishes as one moves to the right. This is consistent with a diminishing marginal rate of technical substitution.

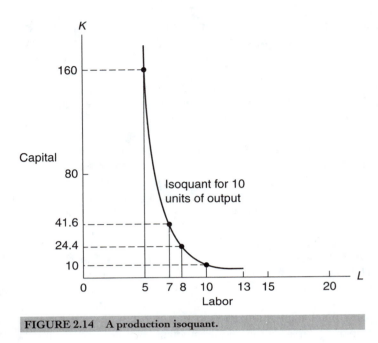

FIGURE 2.14 A production isoquant.

(wages, salaries, fringe benefits) of labor, and r the cost of buying or renting machines for the production period, the total cost is as follows:

$$TC = wL + rK \tag{2.13}$$

where L and K are the amounts of inputs used, labor and capital. For example, if $w = 50$, and $r = 20$, when the unit uses 30 hours of labor, and 10 machines, $TC = 1,700 = 50 \times 30 + 20 \times 10$. As with the consumer's budget problem, it is helpful to determine all of the combinations of L and K that cost a given amount, such as \$1,000. The equation for this isocost curve is

$$1,000 = 50L + 20K \tag{2.14}$$

Again, as with the consumer example, we can rearrange the equation by placing capital (or labor) on the left-hand side, to yield

$$K = 50 - 2.5L \tag{2.15}$$

which is a linear equation as shown in Figure 2.15. The isocost curves for $TC = 686$ is also shown.

More generally, equation (2.13) can be written as

$$K = TC/r - (w/r)L \tag{2.16}$$

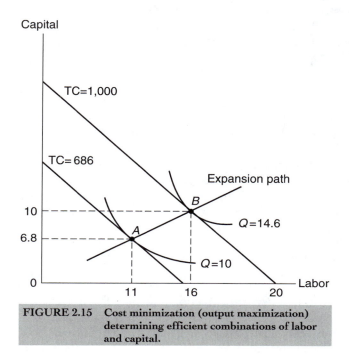

FIGURE 2.15 Cost minimization (output maximization) determining efficient combinations of labor and capital.

Equation (2.16) shows the impacts of changes in wages and/or rental rates on the costs of purchasing various amounts of labor and/or machinery.

Cost Minimization or Output Maximization

In the example just given, the assumption that firms maximize profits requires that the X-ray unit select the least-cost method of producing its output. To produce Q^* units of output, the firm will wish to minimize the costs of that Q^* output, and hence be on the lowest possible isocost curve. The case where Q^* equals 10 units is illustrated in Figure 2.15. This will occur at point A, where the isocost curve is tangent to the isoquant representing 10 units of output. Higher isocost curves are unnecessarily wasteful; lower ones will not attain 10 units of output.

Suppose, on the other hand, that the firm has a budget of exactly $686 and wishes to maximize its output. It is easy to see from Figure 2.15 that the same equilibrium condition will hold, and that the most the firm can produce is 10 units. Cost minimization and output maximization in the manner described lead to the same results.

Marginal and Average Cost Curves

By varying the production levels and finding the respective isocost curves, we can find the minimum cost of producing each output level. This is shown by the set of tangencies in Figure 2.15. The curve connecting these tangency points, A and B, is called the expansion path. Thus, the expansion path contains the information on the total cost and the average cost (cost/unit) of producing any output level.

If all inputs can be varied, then the long-run total cost and long-run average cost (LRAC) functions are generated. The LRAC curve is illustrated first in Figure 2.16. Total and average costs are related to the scale of the activity. If higher levels of production lead to improved ability to take advantage of specialization providing a better division of labor, it may be possible to reduce average costs; the case of decreasing long-run average costs is referred to as the case of economies of scale. If, on the other hand, the increased level of output leads to difficulties in managing and coordinating production activities, then long-run average costs may rise; this is referred to as the case of diseconomies of scale. Such issues are relevant for determining the optimal size for firms. For example, the socially optimal size and distribution of hospitals will depend on estimates of scale economies. As another example, it is clear that enough patient volume is needed to cover costs of such high-priced items as CAT scanners, a case of economies of scale. Too many patients may lead to crowding of patients or to increased labor costs that could again increase costs, producing a case of diseconomies of scale.

In our specific Cobb-Douglas production function example, the LRAC will be a horizontal line reflecting constant average costs (about $68.60 per unit). This occurs simply because of the specific production function chosen as an example. Figure 2.16 shows the classical U-shaped relationship, which starts with economies of scale, and then yields to diseconomies of scale. The long-run marginal cost (LRMC) curve shows the cost of producing an incremental unit when all inputs (both machinery and labor) can be varied. It will go through the minimum point of the LRAC.

The short run corresponds to a period where at least one input (typically machinery or plant) cannot be changed. This form is particularly applicable to big-ticket machinery items in hospitals, for example. In such cases, there are some fixed costs (the machine costs or plant costs that cannot be changed in the short run). The other costs are called variable costs (here, for example, the labor costs).

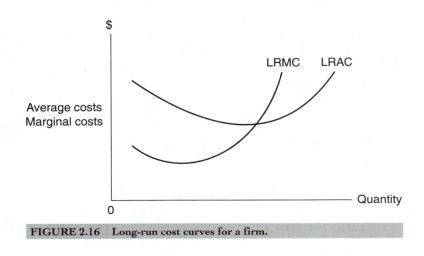

FIGURE 2.16   Long-run cost curves for a firm.

THE FIRM SUPPLY CURVE UNDER PERFECT COMPETITION

The cost curves we have reviewed can be used to develop a theory of the supply curve for a firm, but to do so we must know something about the demand curve for the firm's product. In our earlier practice with supply and demand, the demand curve represented the market demand for the product. The demand for a single firm's product may be different. To gain an idea of what a typical firm's demand curve will look like, we must know what type of market structure we are talking about.

There are several market structures that are of interest, either for the insights they provide to an idealized world or for their applicability to the real world. One defining principle that distinguishes the various market structures is the degree of control that individual firms have over the price that they get paid. Two cases define the extreme forms of market structure: the competitive and the monopoly cases. We will look first at the competitive model, then discuss market structure more generally, and finally follow that discussion with the monopoly case.

The competitive model is rarely seen in the world in its idealized form. It requires several assumptions that ensure perfect competition. The assumptions are as follows:

- There are sufficient numbers of buyers and sellers of the good so that no single actor has any power over the price.
- The good is homogeneous; that is, all producers produce the exact same good so that the market cannot be segmented on the basis of difference of goods.
- There is perfect information. All buyers and sellers have information on all relevant variables such as prices and qualities.
- There are no barriers to entry or exit. A producer starts producing, buying necessary machinery, patents, or anything else, on terms that are equivalent to those already in the industry.

These assumptions ensure that a short-run market equilibrium can be represented by the price and the quantity at which demand and supply curves intersect. Figure 2.17 illustrates the model. Under the assumptions of competition, the demand curve facing the firm will be flat, as shown by the curve $D = MR = P$. To understand this point, consider a mental experiment. Suppose that the market for wheat was competitive and that it had determined, by the actions of market demand and supply, some equilibrium price for wheat, say \$3.50 per unit, as shown. Suppose now that a single firm determined to raise its price above \$3.50. Would anyone buy its product? They would not because they know (perfect information) that they can buy its identical product (homogeneous product) elsewhere for \$3.50. In theory, at even a slightly higher price, the quantity demanded would slide horizontally to zero. On the other hand, suppose that the farmer wished to double the output. Would the farmer have to lower the price in order to sell it all? This would not be necessary because the farmer's output is small relative to the whole market (numerous buyers and sellers); hence, the farmer could sell as much as he or she wanted at the going price of \$3.50.

The demand curve for this firm is labeled $D = MR = P$, indicating that it represents demand, as well as the marginal revenue for the firm and the going market price.

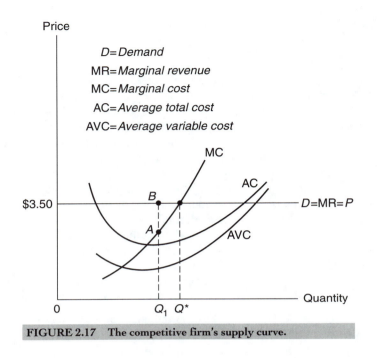

Price

D=*Demand*
MR=*Marginal revenue*
MC=*Marginal cost*
AC=*Average total cost*
AVC=*Average variable cost*

MC

AC

$3.50 — B — D=MR=*P*

A

AVC

Quantity

0   Q_1 Q^*

FIGURE 2.17   The competitive firm's supply curve.

It is worth noting that the market price is identical to the firm's marginal revenue. Marginal revenue is defined as the extra revenue obtained by selling one more unit of product. Since this firm can sell all it wants at the going market price, it can sell the marginal unit at that price as well. Thus, marginal revenue equals price in the competitive model. It is only in cases where a firm has some monopoly power that marginal revenue will differ from price.

The profit-maximizing output for this competitive firm can now be deduced. The firm will maximize its profits at that output where marginal revenue (the price) equals marginal cost; this occurs in the figure at output Q^*. This output is called the firm's profit-maximizing output. The common sense of this seemingly technical proposition can be understood by examining a "wrong" output level, one that is not profit maximizing, for example, Q_1. Suppose a firm that is currently producing Q_1 units were to produce one more unit. The cost of this one extra unit would be A, by definition the point on the marginal cost curve at $Q = Q_1$. The revenue from this one extra unit would be B (which equals the price), the point on the marginal revenue curve at $Q = Q_1$.

The firm would increase its profits by producing that extra unit and would continue to increase its profits as long as the marginal revenue curve were above the marginal cost curve. Hence, maximum profits would only occur where MR = MC.

The supply curve for a firm shows the firm's profit maximizing output at each possible price. The competitive firm is producing at the output where price equals marginal cost. If the market price thus were to rise in steps, the firm's adjustment steps would just be to follow the marginal cost curve on up. The competitive firm's supply curve will be its marginal cost curve, as long as the price is sufficiently high to make it worthwhile to produce at all. Price must at least cover the firm's average variable cost (AVC).

The competitive market supply will be determined by the horizontal sum of the individual firm supply curves. This horizontal summing is done much in the manner in which we found market demand curves. The market supply curve in the competitive case, the sum of firm marginal cost curves, will also represent the industry marginal costs of production. In general, under competition the supply curve is the industry marginal cost curve.

What then determines the market price of a good? The answer is that combination of output and price at which market quantity demanded equals market quantity supplied, or the intersection of market demand and supply.

The assumption of free entry and exit, however, offers further insight into the workings of the competitive market. Suppose, for example, that the equilibrium price in the wheat market in the short run is high enough so that producers in the sector may earn attractive economic profits.[4] Any positive economic profit will be attractive to potential entrants. With perfect information and no barriers to entry, other suppliers will enter the market. This will increase market supply and drive down market prices. The entry process logically would continue in the long run until the prices have fallen enough to eliminate economic profits. In the long run, equilibrium profits will be zero, and price will be at the lowest point on each firm's long-run average cost curve.

However, if barriers to entry in the form of licensure or other restrictions exist, this adjustment process will be impeded. Sellers will be able to earn economic profits over long periods of time, perhaps indefinitely. Such a situation is not perfectly competitive even though the forces of demand and supply determine price at any moment. It is thus important to evaluate the extent to which *all* of the four conditions for competition stated at the beginning of this section are satisfied.

MONOPOLY

The preceding section describes the case of perfect competition, where no seller or buyer can affect prices. The exact opposite is the case of monopoly where there is only one buyer or seller. In perfect competition, everyone else's good is a perfect substitute for the seller (and the buyer). In monopoly, by contrast, there are no competitors and no close substitutes. Although, as with perfect competition, few situations approach this limiting case, it is possible to apply the ideas of the pure monopoly model to many other situations in which firms also have some power over price. In the health sectors, pharmaceutical firms that control patents for certain drugs may be considered to be monopolists. Although individual physicians are not monopolists, they may have some

---

[4]Economic profits represent profits after considering all costs including opportunity costs. A "normal" level of profits is necessary to keep firms in the market, and is a factor payment to the entrepreneur, just like a factor payment to workers or to owners of machines or materials.

power to influence their own prices. Many other firms of various kinds in the health sector probably have some degree of monopoly power; that is, they face some portion of a downward sloping demand curve.[5]

Equilibrium for the monopolist is illustrated in Figure 2.18. The demand curve facing the monopolist firm is downward sloping because the monopolist faces the whole downward sloping market demand curve. With a downward sloping demand curve, the incremental, or marginal revenue, MR, is less than the demand price. Why is this the case? Suppose the monopolist were selling Q_0 units at price P_0. Total revenue, TR_0, would be P_0Q_0. The monopolist would be selling to everyone who is at least willing to pay the price P_0. In order to sell one more unit of the good, the monopolist would have to induce more consumers to buy by lowering the price. It may be impossible to lower the price to extra consumers without also lowering to all previous consumers. In this case, since the monopolist must lower the price to everyone else, the marginal revenue will be the price of the extra unit of the good sold minus the loss of revenue from everyone else who now pays less.

To maximize profit, the monopolist produces where MC = MR, at Q_0 in Figure 2.18. The corresponding price is P_0 and total profit is the rectangle P_0ACB. If barriers to entry are persistent, the economic profits can be maintained and even increased through advertising, promotion, new product development, or other means.

The fact that the monopolist is earning excess profits suggests that the monopolist has reduced the amount produced from the competitive amount. The monopolist in the graph chooses point A on the demand curve. If the monopolist had acted like a competitor by setting price equal to marginal cost, MC, it would have chosen point E, providing more output and charging a lower price. The induced scarcity caused by the monopolist necessarily raises the price to the consumer.

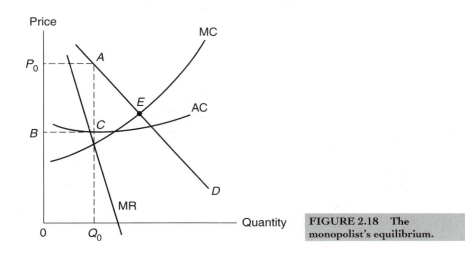

FIGURE 2.18 The monopolist's equilibrium.

---

[5]Degree of monopoly power is a recurring theme in the discussion of market power and the need for regulation. We will return to this subject repeatedly.

WELFARE LOSSES

A major objective of economists is to compare different economic situations, or to examine the effects of different policies. In doing so, economists often use the concept of allocative efficiency. One of the most widely used examples to illustrate the problem of inefficient resource allocation is found in the comparison of monopoly and competitive equilibria.

Consider once again the case of monopoly. Figure 2.19 shows the long-run marginal cost curve in an industry with constant marginal costs. With demand curve D, the competitive market equilibrium is at P_c and Q_c. Suppose, somehow, that the providers are able to form a monopoly. If so, it will be in their interest to raise prices by withholding services from the market. The resulting monopoly will produce at quantity Q_m, consistent with price P_m, where price is higher than marginal cost. The result reflects a loss to the consumer due to the monopoly. The total loss is indicated by the triangle *ABC,* called the welfare loss.

Welfare loss can be better understood if we think in terms of marginals. Consider first that the demand curve measures the highest price that people are willing to pay for an extra unit of the good. The price they are willing to pay measures their marginal benefit.

Now consider what the consumer and society as a whole have to give up when they face a monopoly. The monopolist will choose output level Q_m. If we somehow could have produced one more unit of the good, the $(Q_m + 1)$th unit, we would have made a net gain for society. The benefit of that extra unit is Q_mA in the graph because by marginal benefit (here equal to the height of the demand curve) we mean the benefit of the extra unit. Similarly, the cost to the monopolist, and thus to society as well, of the extra unit is Q_mB. Since the marginal benefit is greater than the marginal cost, the extra unit yields society a net gain of the rectangular shaded area.

Reasoning iteratively, another unit again yields another net gain to society, this time somewhat smaller than the first net gain. Net gains will continue to occur until we

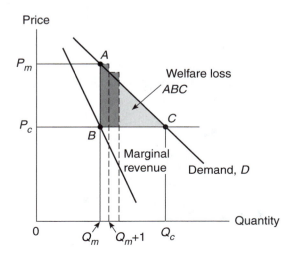

FIGURE 2.19   **Welfare loss of monopoly.**

reach the output at which society's marginal benefit (demand) intersects its marginal costs, which occurs at *C*. The total net gain to society from increasing output up to the point at *C* equals the triangular area labeled *ABC*.

THE EDGEWORTH BOX

The monopoly example applied methods of partial equilibrium analysis where one firm or industry is isolated from the rest of the economy. The example has clear implications and can be useful in many cases.

In many other applications, however, individual firms and markets exist with other firms and markets in a complex interrelated economy. In an earlier example, we considered an excise tax on cigarettes, and showed what would happen to cigarette consumption. We did not discuss the impact of the tax on the consumption of other goods, nor did we consider its impacts on the producers of cigarettes, or the producers of other goods, or the decrease in the need for health services because people are now healthier. For some policy questions, these may be very important considerations.

The Edgeworth box is a useful tool to describe interrelated markets without complex mathematics. The box is also convenient for describing the mutual gains from trade and for defining the Pareto concept of efficiency.

Suppose that persons A and B, say Abner and Belinda, inhabit a desert island, forming a two-person economy. Further suppose that there are only two goods available on the island: Food is gathered and is available in a fixed total amount, and medicine is likewise available in a fixed amount. Medicine consists of natural growing herbs and other medicinal plants.

To form the Edgeworth box, consider Figure 2.20. Abner's preference map is illustrated in the "southwest" corner. The only difference between this map and any others is that there is no reason to draw the axes out further than M_0 and F_0, which

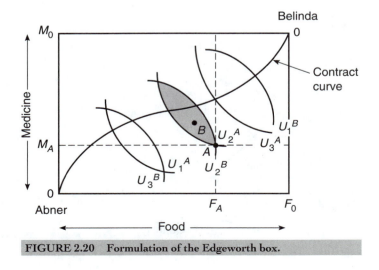

FIGURE 2.20 Formulation of the Edgeworth box.

represent the total amounts of medicine and food available on the island. Belinda's preference map is similar to Abner's except that it starts at the "northeast" corner. It is also constrained by amounts M_0 and F_0.

Any point in the box represents a complete and exhaustive distribution of the island's endowment of food and medicine. For example, point *A* represents a distribution in which Abner has OM_A units of medicine and Belinda has M_0M_A units of medicine. Similarly at *A*, Abner has OF_A units of food while Belinda has F_0F_A units of food.

The economist Pareto defined an efficient (optimal) situation as one in which it is impossible to improve the lot of any one person without harming the lot of someone else. It would be inefficient to do anything less than apply and exhaust all possibilities for mutual gain.

Only when a society has exhausted all avenues for mutual gains among people will it be efficient. It follows that in a Pareto efficient situation there are no further opportunities for mutual gain left to exploit.

Under this definition, is point *A* a Pareto efficient distribution? It is *not*. This can be shown by example. Point *B,* within the "eye" formed by the two people's intersecting indifference curves, is at once a superior bundle for Abner and a superior bundle for Belinda. Thus, the two people would mutually gain by moving to *B*.

Point *B* also may not be Pareto efficient. Only when a distribution point is such that the two indifference curves are tangent with one another will the distribution be Pareto efficient.

There will be many alternative Pareto efficient points in the Edgeworth box. Every indifference curve of Abner's will have a point on it where an indifference curve of Belinda's is just tangent to it. The collection of all Pareto efficient points will tend to lie along a curve extending from one origin to the other. The resulting curve, the collection of all Pareto efficient points, is called the contract curve.

CONCLUSIONS

The microeconomic tools developed in this chapter consist of the production possibility frontier, demand and supply analysis, utility and indifference curve analysis, production and cost curves of a typical firm, firm behavior under competition and monopoly, the measure of welfare loss, and the Edgeworth box. The economic tools used later in the text are direct applications or extensions of the tools developed here. By learning these ideas, you will gain an understanding of the terminology used in health economics as well as an understanding of the type of reasoning used.

Summary

1. The concept of scarcity underlies much economic thinking. Scarcity necessitates that decision makers make trade-off decisions at the margin. The production possibilities frontier represents these trade-offs, and its slope represents the opportunity cost of one good in terms of the other.

2. Supply and demand analysis of competitive markets is a basic tool of economics and provides insights that extend beyond the theoretical perfectly competitive markets. Supply reflects sellers' offers as a function of price, and demand reflects buyers' offers as a function of price. The intersection of demand and supply describes the market equilibrium.

3. Comparative static analysis of demand and supply finds the new equilibrium after economic events shift either curve. Demand increasing (decreasing) events tend to raise (lower) equilibrium price while supply increasing (decreasing) events tend to lower (raise) equilibrium price.

4. A relationship between one or more independent variables yielding a unique value for the dependent variable is called a function. The linear demand function, showing demand as a straight line, is only one special case of the many possibilities.

5. The utility function summarizes a consumer's preferences. Higher utility numbers are assigned to consumer bundles that provide higher levels of satisfaction, meaning that the consumer prefers these bundles.

6. Indifference curves are collections of points describing bundles that yield the same utility and hence the same level of satisfaction. Well-behaved indifference curves are downward sloping, continuous, and convex to the origin.

7. The budget constraint represents the combinations of goods that the consumer can afford given his or her budget. The budget constraint is downward sloping, and its slope is the negative of the ratio of prices.

8. In consumer theory, the consumer maximizes utility subject to a budget constraint. This means that the consumer picks the most preferred consumer bundle from among those he or she can afford. The equilibrium occurs at the tangency between the budget constraint and the highest attainable indifference curve.

9. Price elasticity depicts the responsiveness of demand to changes in price. It is defined as the ratio of the percentage change in quantity demanded to the percentage change in price. Each other elasticity also represents the ratio of a percentage change in a dependent variable to a percentage change in a given independent variable.

10. The production function describes the relationship of inputs to output. The marginal product of an input is the increase in output due to a one-unit increase in the input holding all others constant. That marginal product tends to decline as more input is added describes the law of diminishing marginal returns.

11. The average total cost curve of a firm shows the total cost per unit of output. The marginal cost curve shows the extra cost required to produce an additional unit of output.

12. The competitive firm in the short run produces that output where price equals marginal cost. The marginal cost curve is therefore the supply curve of the competitive firm.

13. In long-run equilibrium, entry by competing firms forces the typical competitive firm to produce an output level such that its price equals its minimum average cost. At this output, the competitive firm is producing the economically efficient output and it is earning zero economic profits.

14. The pure monopolist faces the entire downward sloping market demand curve, and this implies that its marginal revenue lies below the demand curve. The monopolist restricts output, by comparison to the competitive case, and it charges a higher market price.

15. The pure monopoly case is one instance of a market in which there is a welfare loss. A welfare loss, represented by an area under the demand curve and above the marginal cost curve, is an opportunity for mutual gains that is being foregone by the market.

16. The Edgeworth box for exchange represents compactly the indifference curves of the consumers in a two-person society. Pareto efficient points are those where all opportunities for mutual gain have (efficiently) been exhausted. The collection of Pareto efficient points in the box is called the contract curve.

Discussion Questions

1. Explain the difference between cardinal and ordinal utility.

2. If a consumer always prefers more to less, can the indifference curves between the two goods be upward sloping? Explain.

3. The law of diminishing marginal returns states that eventually the marginal product of an input will tend to fall as more input is added. Describe real-life scenarios, explaining why this is likely to happen.

4. Describe the long-run equilibrium of the competitive firm. Which of the assumptions of perfect competition are important in generating this result? Which are most important? Why do economists argue that in competitive markets, long-run profits should be normal, or "zero" profits? Is this necessarily the case in the short run?

5. What are the welfare losses due to monopoly? Do they mean that the monopoly does not earn profits?

6. What is a demand shifter? Use the concept to resolve the following: "The price of ice cream increased in the summer, yet quantity also increased. Therefore, the Law of Demand does not apply to ice cream."

Exercises

1. Draw the production possibilities frontier between guns and butter and show how it would change if there were an improvement in the technology of producing butter. Show the change if there were an increase in the available productive resources, capital and labor, in society.

2. Draw a production possibilities curve between health and all other goods. Insert a point in the drawing that illustrates an economy with an inefficient health system. Insert two additional points that illustrate two efficient economies but two which contrast in their relative emphasis on health care versus all other goods. Is there a cost to society of policies that lead to increases in health care? Explain.

3. Using a supply and demand graph assuming competitive markets, show and explain the effect on equilibrium price and quantity of the following:
   A. A technological change that reduces the cost of producing X-rays on the market for physician clinic services.
   B. Increased graduations of new doctors on the market for physician services.
   C. The virtual elimination of smoking in the population on the market for hospital services.
   D. A price ceiling placed on physician fees in the market for physician services.
4. Graph the following demand functions:
   A. $Q_d = 110 - 3.3P$
   B. $Q_d = 100P^{-1.3}$
5. What is the Other Goods (OG) axis intercept of a budget constraint? What is the *x*-axis intercept? How does the budget constraint shift if the consumer's income level and the two prices all double?
6. Calculate the price elasticity for a $1 change in price at initial price level $300 for the demand function $Q_d = 1,500 - 1.5P$.
7. What is the slope of the isoquant described by the data in Table 2.3 when evaluated from a labor input of 7 to 8?
8. Assume that a monopoly firm has a linear demand curve and a constant marginal cost curve. Graph this firm's optimal output choice before and after a per-unit excise tax is placed on the output. Does the equilibrium price rise by as much as the tax?
9. In prisoner of war camps during World War II, it was common for each prisoner to receive identical Red Cross packages containing amounts of cigarettes and other goods. Using an Edgeworth box for two prisoners, illustrate the Red Cross "endowment" of cigarettes and other goods. Are prisoners likely to trade? Using indifference curves, illustrate a trade from the initial endowment that makes both prisoners better off.
10. Using equation (2.4), what is the demand equation as a function of P_s if the price of other pastas (P_o) is $2, the individual's income (Y), in thousands, is $25, and tastes ($Z$) are represented by 20? What happens if the individual's income increases to $30?

A P P E N D I X

Discounting

Discounting is used in many applications involving comparisons of different streams of returns and/or costs over a number of periods. For example, an analyst might be asked to compare Investment A, which provides $20 at the end of Year 1, and $20 at the end of Year 2, with Investment B, which provides $12 at the end of Year 1, and $29 at the end of Year 2. Although Investment B returns $41 over the two years, compared to $40 for Investment A, most of the return on Investment B comes later, at the end of Year 2. It is often necessary to compare the investments with a criterion that considers the timing of the returns. The analytical tool used for such comparisons is usually referred to as *discounting.*

Suppose George is offered the opportunity to buy a bond that will return $1, one year from now. How much will he be willing to pay now? George always has the option to keep his money and earn interest rate *r.* He will buy the bond if he can pay a price far enough below the $1 return next year, such that that price, multiplied by one plus the interest rate, equals $1. Algebraically, if the rate of interest is *r,* and the unknown amount is x_1, then:

$$x_1 (1 + r) = 1$$

The value for x_1, then, can be solved as:

$$x_1 = \frac{1}{(1 + r)}$$

If the rate of interest is 5 percent (or 0.05), then x_1, the discounted value of $1, one year hence, equals $1/1.05$, or 95.24 cents.

Similarly, the discounted value of $1 *two* years hence, is:

$$x_2 (1 + r)^2 = 1$$

leading to:

$$x_2 = \frac{1}{(1 + r)^2}$$

If, again, the interest rate is 5 percent, then x_2 equals $1/1.05^2$, or 90.70 cents.

Returning to the preceding example, we can calculate that the present discounted value (the sum of x_1 and x_2), or PDV, for Investment A, will equal $37.19, or $20/1.05 + 20/(1.05)^2$. The PDV of Investment B is $37.73. Thus, George will prefer Investment B.

In summation notation, the present discounted value of a stream of returns, *R,* and costs, *C,* over time is given by

$$PDV = \sum_{t=1}^{n} \frac{(R_t - C_t)}{(1 + r)^t}$$

It is easy to demonstrate that the relative amounts of the PDVs of Investments A and B may depend on the interest rate chosen for the analysis. If an interest rate of 15 percent were used instead in the preceding example, the PDV for Investment A would be $32.51, compared to $32.36, for Investment B. Intuitively, the higher interest rate gives the larger, but later, return in Investment B less weight.

CHAPTER

3

Statistical Tools
for Health Economics

- ■ Hypothesis Testing

- ■ Difference of Means

- ■ Regression Analysis

- ■ Multiple Regression Analysis

- ■ The Identification Problem

- ■ Discrete Choice Analysis

- ■ Statistical Inference in the Sciences and Social Sciences

- ■ Conclusions

The ideas from economic theory need to be tested and measured according to the standards of real-world data. Statistical techniques applied to economics are collectively called econometrics. In Chapter 2, we discussed supply and demand, as well as the importance of price and income elasticities. Economic theory predicts that demand curves will slope downward, but it does not predict the degree of responsiveness of demand to price and other variables; it is the task of statistical analysis to estimate these magnitudes. When close substitutes are available for a good, theory predicts that demand will be more sensitive to price than if no close substitutes were available. Yet it is hard to know whether a 1 percent increase in price will decrease the demand for the good by 10 percent, 1 percent, or 1/10 of a percent, yielding elasticities of -10.0, -1.0, or -0.1, respectively. Measurements of the economic behaviors of both people and firms may be crucial in analyzing whether drug companies raise drug prices, whether income subsidies will cause people to buy more medicines, or whether mandated levels of health care are economically efficient.

This chapter considers statistical methods that econometricians use to draw inferences from data that are collected. Many students with natural science backgrounds are familiar with laboratory experiments, where the environment is held as constant as possible and treatments are administered to experimental groups. The results are then compared to those of untreated control groups. One form of this design is called the *dose-response* model in that the results or responses are generally related to the experimental treatment, or the dose.

Social science analysis of human behavior is rarely so fortunate as to find an experimental group that can be matched with a convenient control group. Social scientists, and economists among them, must usually collect information from people doing day-to-day activities. Using statistical methods, they try to control for the confounding differences among the people that they are analyzing. The more successful they are in controlling for such differences, the more reliable the analysis will be.

This chapter begins with discussions on how we form hypotheses. It then considers difference of means analysis as a way of introducing statistical inference. Most of the rest of the chapter concentrates on simple regression and multiple regression analyses that are most often used in economic and econometric analysis.

HYPOTHESIS TESTING

Economists have been confronted on occasion by statements that, while plausible, demand some validation:

"Twenty-year-old men have different cholesterol levels than twenty-year-old women."

"Rich people spend more on health care than do poor people."

"Monopolists make more money than competitive firms."

These are all statements that either logic or casual observation would suggest to be true.

It would be useful, however, to have a rigorous method of determining whether the assertions were correct. Statistical methods suggest formulating these statements as hypotheses, and collecting data to determine whether we are correct.

Take, for example, the first assertion, about cholesterol levels for twenty-year-olds. It is useful to state clearly both the hypothesis we wish to disprove (the null hypothesis), as well as the hypothesis the theory suggests to be the case (the alternative hypothesis). The null hypothesis, H_0, presently is:

The men's levels (c_m) equal the women's levels (c_w), or

$$H_0: c_m = c_w \qquad (3.1)$$

against the alternative hypothesis H_1, that c_m does not equal c_w:

$$H_1: c_m \quad c_w \qquad (3.2)$$

To indicate that 20-year-old men's levels are, in fact, different from their counterpart women's levels, it is necessary to show convincing evidence that c_m is different from c_w. Hypotheses that are designed to test for equality among two or more items are sometimes called simple hypotheses.

Consider the second hypothesis, which asserts that rich people spend more on health care than do poor people. If we define health care expenditures of the rich (poor) as E_r (E_p), then the null hypothesis is:

$$H_0: E_r = E_p \qquad\qquad (3.3)$$

Here the alternative is

$$H_1: E_r > E_p \qquad\qquad (3.4)$$

In this analysis, it may not be enough just to show that E_r is different from E_p. Certainly, evidence that E_p was greater than E_r would not validate the hypothesis. Having seen, then, how one might address the hypotheses in question, it is now necessary to discuss how to test them. Hypotheses that are used to test whether two or more items are greater (or less) than each other are sometimes called composite hypotheses.

DIFFERENCE OF MEANS

Let us return to the hypothesis about men's and women's cholesterol levels.[1] Some cholesterol is necessary to life; too much can be threatening, leading to coronary heart disease (CHD). Levels are measured in milligrams per deciliter (one-tenth of a liter). Levels typically range from 100 (extremely low) to 400 (extremely high). For individuals with levels between 240 and 300, the likelihood of CHD is increased up to fourfold above that for those with levels below 200 mg.

Cholesterol levels may depend on many factors. For example, those raised in more affluent families may have been better fed than those in poor families. Alternatively, poor children may have had diets higher in certain fats or starches. We would want to avoid bias in our results by making sure that our sample of women was not drawn primarily from one income level while the men were drawn from another.

We could attempt to avoid this sort of distortion by drawing our samples randomly from among all possible 20-year-olds, called the universe of data. Alternatively, we may try to choose samples of 20-year-old men and women from the same general income group. A sample of college sophomores, for example, from the same location, with similar socioeconomic status, may be a good group for holding many factors constant.

Even this example shows how difficult things may be to control. People at the same age (at the same college) may have had different prenatal care, birthweight, genetic composition, nutrition, vitamins, or exercise. The level exhibited at a given test may depend on what the subject ate that morning (physicians often ask for a "fasting" cholesterol test, to avoid this problem).

To compare men's and women's cholesterol levels, we need a test that can determine the differences between two distributions of continuous data. Continuous data are

---

[1] Sources for this discussion are U.S. Department of Health and Human Services (November 1990), and Rifkind et al. (1979).

natural measures that in principle could take on different values for each observation. Examples include height, weight, income, or price. Categorical data refer to arbitrary categories such as gender (male or female), race (black, white, or other), or location (urban or rural). In this chapter, unless we specify categorical data, our methods will refer exclusively to the analysis of continuous data.

Suppose at this point that the econometrician tests one woman and finds her cholesterol level to be 180 ($c_w = 180$). The first man tested has a level of 150 ($c_m = 150$). This provides evidence that women have higher levels than men, since $c_w > c_m$, or $180 > 150$. It is not very convincing evidence, however. The man, or woman, or either, may not be typical of the entire group. What if a different man and/or woman had been selected? Would the answer have been different?

It seems logical to test several men, and to compute the mean or average level, by summing the levels and dividing them by the total number of men tested. Suppose, for example, that there were 30 men, and that the mean, or average, level $\bar{c}_m$ was 163.3. Suppose, also, that there were 30 women, and that the average level $\bar{c}_w$ was 173.5. The difference, $d = \bar{c}_w - \bar{c}_m$, then, is 10.2.

The Variance of a Distribution

Although a difference of the two means is improved evidence, the econometrician desires a more rigorous criterion. It could be that the true level for both men and women is 170, but our sample randomly drew a higher average level for women (173.5) than for men (163.3). Figure 3.1 plots each observation. Although the mean levels differ (women have higher levels than men), some men have higher levels than some women. Statisticians have found the variance of a distribution to be a useful way to summarize its dispersion. To calculate the variance of women's levels, we subtract each observation from the mean (173.5), square that term, sum the total, and divide that total by the number of observations N. Hence, variance V equals:

$$V_w = \frac{(110 - 173.5)^2 + (125 - 173.5)^2 + \ldots + (215 - 173.5)^2}{30} \tag{3.5}$$

This term reflects the variance of any individual term in the distribution. If V is large, then the dispersion around the mean is wide, and another woman tested might be far from our mean. If V is small, then the dispersion around the mean is narrow, and another observation might be pretty close to the mean.

Standard Error of the Mean

The variance is often deflated by taking the square root to get the standard deviation s, yielding:

$$s = \sqrt{V} \tag{3.6}$$

As with V, a large (small) value of s indicates a large (small) dispersion around the mean. Statisticians have shown that we can calculate the standard error of the mean itself, by dividing s by the square root of the number of observations. Suppose, then, that the women's variance V_w equaled 587, so the standard deviation would equal the

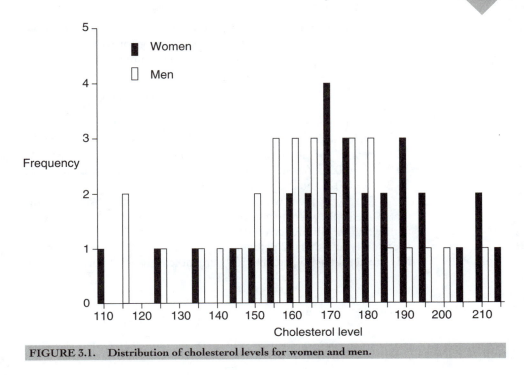

FIGURE 3.1. **Distribution of cholesterol levels for women and men.**

square root of 587, or 24.2. The standard error of the mean would then equal s_w divided by the square root of 30, or (24.2/5.5), which equals 4.4.[2]

A powerful theorem in statistics, the Central Limit Theorem, states that no matter what the underlying distribution, the means of that distribution are distributed like a normal, or bell-shaped curve. Hence, we can plot the normal distribution of means of women's levels with a mean of 173.5, and a standard error of 4.4.

Statisticians have also shown that a little over 68 percent of the area under the curve would be within one standard error, or between levels of 169.1 (173.5 − 4.4) and 177.9 (173.5 + 4.4), and that 95.4 percent would be within two standard errors. This means that we could be about 95 percent sure that the true mean cholesterol level for 20-year-old women was between 164.7 [173.5 − (2 · 4.4)] and 182.3 [173.5 + (2 · 4.4)].

A similar calculation can be done for men, yielding a similar measurement. Intuitively, the further apart the means, and the smaller the dispersions (standard errors), the more likely we are to determine that the average level for men is smaller than that for women. To test the hypothesis formally, we then construct a "difference of means" test. We wish to compare the measurement $d = (\bar{c}_w - \bar{c}_m)$ to 0, which was the original hypothesis.

---

[2]Formally, in a sample, we calculate the standard error by dividing by $n - 1$.

Here $d = 10.2$. The variance of the difference is defined as the sum of the variances of the standard errors. If the standard error for women was 4.4, as we calculated it, and the standard error for men, given the sample in Figure 3.2A, was 4.1, then the standard error of the difference would be:

$$s_d = (4.4^2 + 4.1^2)^{.5} = (19.36 + 16.81)^{.5} = (36.17)^{.5} = 6.02 \qquad (3.7)$$

The difference and its distribution can also be plotted.

The most probable value of the difference, as noted in Figure 3.2B, is 10.2. About 68 percent of the distribution lies between 4.18 (i.e., $10.2 - 1 \cdot 6.02$) and 16.22 (i.e., $10.2 + 1 \cdot 6.02$). About 95.4 percent of the distribution lies between -1.84 (i.e., $10.2 - 2 \cdot 6.02$) and 22.24 (i.e., $10.2 + 2 \cdot 6.02$).

This experiment would find good, although not absolutely conclusive, evidence that 20-year-old women have higher cholesterol levels than 20-year-old men. The probability that the difference of 10.2 would have been found, when the true difference is 0, is certainly less than 32 percent (100 percent less than the 68 percent figure); however, it is greater than 4.6 percent (100 percent less the 95.4 percent figure).

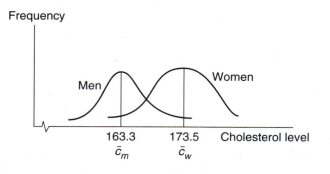

A. Means of Cholesterol Level

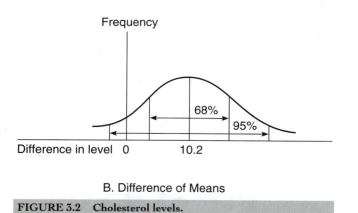

B. Difference of Means

FIGURE 3.2 **Cholesterol levels.**

Alternatively, the *t*-statistic, comparing the numbers 10.2 and 0.0, equals 10.2/6.02, or approximately 1.70. Statisticians calculate tables of *t*-statistics, whose critical values are related to the size of the sample. With a sample of 30, a *t*-statistic of approximately 1.70 is statistically significant at approximately the 90 percent level. Still another way of phrasing this is to say that there is not more than a 10 percent chance that this difference of 10.2 between women and men was the result of a random draw from two distributions that have the same means.[3]

Hypotheses and Inferences

This process illustrates the steps that are necessary to test hypotheses appropriately. The econometrician must do the following:

1. State the hypotheses clearly: $c_m = c_w$.
2. Choose a sample that is suitable to the task of testing: a matched sample of men and women of the same age, in the same location.
3. Calculate the appropriate measures of central tendency and dispersion: the mean and the standard error of the mean for both men and women, leading to the difference of the two means.
4. Draw the appropriate inferences: 20-year-old men have different cholesterol levels than 20-year-old women.[4]

No matter how sophisticated the method used, good statistical analysis depends on the ability to address these four criteria, and stands (or falls) on the success in fulfilling them.

There are, of course, measures of central tendency other than the mean. For example, analysts may worry that someone with a particularly high cholesterol count may influence the mean. A different measure, the median, calculates a statistic such that half of the observations are greater than the median and half are less. Thus, a median cholesterol level of 173.5 would imply that half of the sample was higher than 173.5, and half lower. The median is less sensitive to extreme values in the data (e.g., someone with a count of 400 would have no more effect on a median of 173.5 than does another with a count of 300). However, the use of the median presents some serious mathematical problems in hypothesis testing. Simple formulae for standard errors of medians are not available; hence, hypothesis testing is difficult.

REGRESSION ANALYSIS

The difference of means analyses are extremely useful in treating continuous data that can be broken up by categories, such as gender, race, or location.[5] Yet many interesting economic variables occur naturally as continuous variables. Health care expenses,

---

[3]The difference in this example is approximately the difference found in Rifkind et al. (1979). Their standard errors are smaller because they have larger samples.

[4]Econometricians often use more rigorous standards for hypothesis testing, requiring significance at the 5 percent or even the 1 percent levels.

[5]Although difference of means considers only two categories, analysis of variance methods allows the consideration of three or more categories. Newbold (1995) presents good discussions on this and other statistical topics.

physician visits, firm profits, as well as prices and/or incomes could take large numbers of values naturally, and are grouped into categories only with serious loss of information. If we have information on income, in terms of dollars per year, we can distinguish among households with $10,000, $20,000, $30,000, and so on. If we were to define high income as greater than $40,000, for example, thus separating all of the different incomes into two categories, we would then have no way of distinguishing between households with $10,000 and $20,000 (or for that matter, between households with $50,000 and $100,000).

Regression analysis allows the econometrician to fit a straight line through a set of data points. Consider, for example, an economist who seeks to estimate consumer demand for aspirin (e.g., Bayer brand). Although one might argue that aspirin is not "chosen," it is clear that the amount of aspirin purchased is likely to be related to prices of substitutes, incomes of consumers, worries about side-effects, and other factors. Using a carefully tested survey instrument, or observing consumer purchases at supermarkets and drugstores, the economist collects information about various determinants of demand. These include the amount of aspirin that is purchased each year, the price that is paid per box of aspirin, the prices of other types of medicines, whether there are any children in the household, and (usually last) the household's income.

Assume that we have collected data where the unit of observation is the individual person. We have noted the amount of aspirin consumed for the year, and we have noted the price paid. By basing our estimates on such individual data, we can assume that our resulting estimates reflect the demand function.

FEATURE

The Treatment of Income in Survey Research

Americans are notoriously reticent about revealing incomes to survey researchers. Yet, in many surveys, it is desirable to have measures of the income and/or wealth of the respondents. Most survey researchers have come to realize that they should ask questions about income at the end of the questionnaire. This means that if the respondent refuses to answer the question, and, in fact terminates the interview, at least the rest of the interview is valid. Moreover, people are often more willing to provide information about income if the questions do not ask for exact levels. Goodman and Hankin (1981), in a needs assessment for the Baltimore community, found that a card coded with income categories such as the following elicited good subject responses:

    1 = 0–$4,000

    2 = $4,001–$8,000, through

  10 = $36,001–$40,000

  11 = $40,000 or more.

While not exact, the responses provided useful information and were far better than refusals by the interview subjects.

Suppose that the economist wishes to relate the amount of aspirin purchased to the price of the aspirin. Even though other factors are likely to influence the quantity of aspirin purchased, it is useful to plot the quantity purchased against the price per box, as noted in Figure 3.3. Upon examination, the plot of points in Figure 3.3 looks like a higher price per box is related to lower purchases, and vice versa. We would like to know, however, how much they are related, or as we noted before, how responsive quantity demanded is to the price (the demand price elasticity). Recall that the price elasticity relates the percent change in quantity to the percent change in price. It would be useful to draw a straight line that would summarize the relationship.

Ordinary Least Squares (OLS) Regressions

Two rules are commonly used to determine this line. The first rule is that the deviations (unless the line fits perfectly) from the line must sum to 0. Positive deviations must be offset by negative deviations. We can show, however (see Figure 3.3), that many lines have this characteristic. For example, dashed lines R_1 and R_2 both have 0 net deviations. It is necessary to have a second criterion by which to distinguish among the large number of lines where the sum of the deviations equals 0.

The second criterion is to minimize the sum of the squared deviations of the actual data points from the line that is fitted. Even though the sum of the deviations equals 0, the sum of the squared deviations must be positive (any number multiplied by

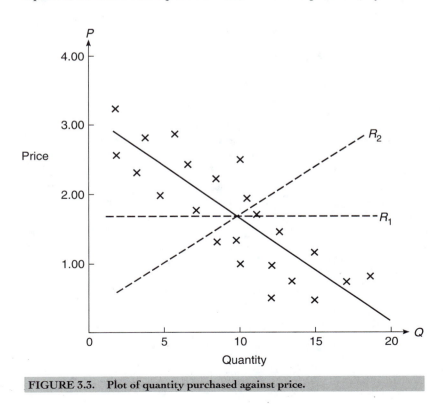

FIGURE 3.3. Plot of quantity purchased against price.

itself is either 0 or positive). Hence, one can choose among the many lines that have sums of 0 deviations, by picking the one line with the minimum or least sum of the squared deviations. Such analyses are called ordinary least squares, or OLS analyses.

The resulting equation would have the following form:

$$q = a + bp + \epsilon \qquad (3.8)$$

where p and q refer to price and quantity, and a and b are the parameters to be estimated. Parameter a is sometimes referred to as the constant, or the intercept. It might refer to the demand for q in the unlikely event that the price of aspirin were zero. Parameter b refers to the slope of the line and shows the direction and magnitude of the impact of a change in p on the quantity demanded. Since we expect a higher level of p to decrease the amount of aspirin purchased, we expect b to be negative.

The last parameter is the *error term* ϵ. No regression analysis will fit the data exactly. There are likely to be errors that may reflect several causes. We may have omitted a variable, such as age (children should not take aspirin), the possibility of drug interaction (if one is taking one type of drug, it may not be advisable to take aspirin), or health status (pregnant women should not take aspirin). We may have measured one or more of the explanatory variables, or the dependent variable (the amount of aspirin) inaccurately. All of these may stand in the way of our predicting the amount demanded exactly. In advanced econometric work, the characterization of the term ϵ is crucial for assuring that the estimated parameters are accurate. In our exposition here, however, we will assume that ϵ obeys the appropriate rules to allow us to make appropriate inferences with OLS analyses. We will examine some exceptions later in the chapter.

A Demand Regression

Suppose we estimate the following regression from a survey of 100 consumers:

$$Q = 20 - 6.1P \qquad R^2 = 0.10$$
$$(2.5) \qquad (3.9)$$

This equation indicates that a one-dollar increase in the price of a bottle of 100 aspirins leads to the purchase of 6.1 fewer bottles in a given year. The standard error of estimate for the coefficient of price P is 2.5. This term is similar to the standard error of the estimated mean in the example of men's and women's cholesterol levels, earlier in the chapter. As before, the smaller the standard error, relative to the estimated value of b, the better the estimate.

In this regression, the standard error is relatively small compared to the absolute value of the coefficient, 6.1; hence the coefficient is significantly different from zero. The expression R^2 is used to measure the fraction of the variation of the quantity of aspirin explained by the price alone. An R^2 of 0.10 implies that 10 percent of the variation was explained.

It is useful to examine this simple regression in detail, since it has many features that occur in more complex analyses. Consider the following hypothesis:

H_0: Price doesn't matter; that is, $b = 0$

against the alternative hypothesis, which is:

H_1: Price is significantly related to quantity demanded; that is, $b < 0$.

The test of the hypothesis is similar to a difference of means test. In particular, we are testing the difference between -6.1 (estimated with standard error 2.5) and 0. Remember that since demand is downward sloping, the coefficient will be negative. The *t*-statistic here is 2.44; that is, the value of the coefficient, 6.1, divided by the standard error of 2.5. The value of 2.44 suggests that we can be more than 95 percent sure that the price has an effect on quantity of aspirin demanded. This term is statistically significant in its difference from 0.

If 10 percent of the variation of the quantity of aspirin demand is explained, then 90 percent is unexplained. In part, this occurs because the regression does not include some variables that are likely to be important. These include the consumers' incomes, the prices of other pain-relieving drugs, as well as some taste variables. For example, given the well-documented concerns about the use of aspirin for young children, families with young children may purchase less aspirin than others. When variables indicating the numbers or ages of children are included in the regression, the equation may explain things better.

This example illustrates *cross-sectional* analysis, which provides "snapshots" of a "slice" of the population at one period in time. Since we do not follow the people in the sample over time, we may not be aware of continuing health problems, changes in wealth or income, or systematic differences in ability that cannot be measured, and which in the cross-sectional model will be treated as "random noise." As a result, cross-sectional regressions often explain less variance than either panel data, which follow households over time, or time-series data, which calculate aggregates over time.

Estimating Elasticities

Regressions are also used to estimate elasticities. Recall that the definition of the price elasticity of demand (E_p) is the percentage change in quantity demanded, elicited by a 1 percent change in price. This is written as

$$E_p = \frac{\Delta Q/Q}{\Delta P/P}, \text{ or } E_p = \frac{\Delta Q}{\Delta P}\frac{P}{Q}$$

The term ΔP stands for a one-unit change in the price, while the term ΔQ represents the resulting change in the quantity demanded. It follows that $\Delta Q/Q$ is a measure of the percentage change in quantity whereas $\Delta P/P$ is a measure of the percentage change in price. In rearranging terms at the right, the portion $\Delta Q/\Delta P$ represents the ratio of changes and thus is the reciprocal of the slope of the demand curve. With a linear function as in this case, this is the coefficient of price, that is, -6.1.

In calculating an elasticity from the coefficients estimated in a regression, there may be a different elasticity calculated for each different starting price that is assumed. So it is also necessary to have reference values for P and Q, and the mean (or average) values are often used. Suppose that the mean price for a box of 100 aspirins was $2.50. Then the predicted quantity demanded would be

$$Q = 20 - 6.1 \cdot 2.5 = 4.75 \text{ boxes} \qquad \textbf{(3.10)}$$

Hence, calculated at the mean,

$$E_p = -6.1 \cdot (2.5/4.75), \text{ or } -3.21$$

This says that a 1 percent increase in the price of aspirin would lead to a 3.21 percent decrease in quantity demanded. Does this make sense? A demand elasticity of this size suggests the availability of numerous alternatives, or that there is considerable competition in an industry, with many substitutes. Such a characterization might serve the market for cold remedies very well.

MULTIPLE REGRESSION ANALYSIS

Students of economics are aware that real-world relationships are seldom two-dimensional, as useful as this situation would be in drawing graphs. As noted, demand for aspirin is probably related to income Y, the prices of other pain relievers, P_o, such as acetaminophen (e.g., Tylenol), ibuprofen (e.g., Advil), or generic substitutes, and maybe some family characteristics, G. For example, given the well-documented concerns about the use of aspirin for young children, families with young children may purchase less aspirin than other families would buy. Indeed, the omission of important variables may lead to particular behavior in the error term ϵ.

One could graph quantity of aspirin independently against any of these other variables, just as was done with price. Graphing quantity against income, for example, would likely yield, as noted in Figure 3.4, an upward sloping curve.[6] Graphing quantity of aspirin demanded against the price of acetaminophen would probably also produce an upward sloping curve. Since acetaminophen is presumably a substitute for aspirin, an increased price of acetaminophen is likely to increase the demand for aspirin.

If each of these relationships could be graphed, assuming that nothing else were changing (i.e., if the only thing varying was the price of acetaminophen, and the amount of aspirin purchased), then simple regression would work fine. Fortunately, the mathematics necessary to estimate the appropriate relationship can accommodate more than two dimensions. It is easy to write the following multiple regression:

$$Q = a + bP + cP_o + dY + eG + \epsilon \qquad (3.11)$$

Although the econometrician is fitting a surface through five dimensions now, rather than the two dimensions, he or she is using exactly the same least squares criteria as before. The interpretation of the coefficients is similar to before, but is done with more confidence. With the simple regression, relating Q only to P, the econometrician would not know whether income Y or the price of alternative medications P_o were varying. Including them in this regression allows the econometrician to "hold constant" these other variables and reduce the error. As a result, he or she can now calculate elasticities, under the condition that "all else is equal."

---

[6]If, however, aspirin is a "poor-man's substitute" for a trip to the physician, an increase in income may lead to more visits to the physician and to less aspirin purchased.

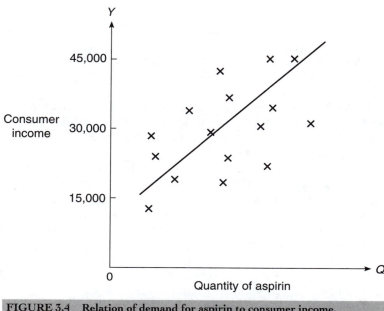

FIGURE 3.4   Relation of demand for aspirin to consumer income.

The R^2 measure of variation explained earlier is also available here. R^2 will always rise with more variables (if you add variables you can't explain less of the variation!). Several methods can be used to interpret R^2, and some statisticians wish to maximize R^2, that is, to explain as much variation as possible.[7] While this may be desirable, most econometricians are at least as interested in the values of the parameters that are estimated.

Interpreting Regression Coefficients

Consider, now, a regression estimated in the following form:

$$Q = -5.0 - 4.1P + 3.2P_o + 0.25Y - 2.6G, \quad R^2 = 0.25$$
$$(2.0)\quad(2.5)\qquad(0.20)\quad(1.1)$$

$$(3.12)$$

---

[7]Often R^2 is adjusted for the number of explanatory variables and the number of observations, and is termed as the adjusted R^2 or $\bar{R}^2$. Its relation to R^2 is:

$$1 - \bar{R}^2 = [(n - 1)/(n - k - 1)](1 - R^2)$$

where n is the number of observations, and k is the number of explanatory variables. Adding additional variables k will raise R^2, but will not necessarily raise $\bar{R}^2$.

where the standard errors of the coefficients are in parentheses below the regression. This regression says that, holding P_o, Y, and G constant, a one-dollar increase in the price of aspirin P, implies a decrease in quantity of aspirin demanded of 4.1 boxes. Similarly, a one-dollar increase in the price of acetaminophen, P_o, implies an increase in the quantity of aspirin demanded of 3.2 boxes. It may be convenient to measure income in thousands of dollars; hence, an increase in income from \$20,000 (20) to \$21,000 (21) is a one-unit increase, implying an increase in aspirin demanded of 0.25 boxes per year. If G represents the number of children below the age of 5, then it indicates that households with more young children purchase less aspirin.

In this regression, the values of the coefficients of P and G are at least twice as large as their standard errors. This is usually fairly good evidence that the relationships are statistically significant. The coefficients of the price of acetaminophen, P_o, and income, Y, while in the expected directions, are not statistically significant at the 95 percent confidence level. That is, although these coefficients differ from zero, there is less than a 95 percent probability that the true values are different from zero. Also, as was done with the simple regression, predicted values of the dependent variable as well as values of the elasticities can be computed. As before, hypotheses can be tested. Most often, again, econometricians are interested in whether coefficients are positive or negative, and whether they differ significantly from zero.

Dummy Variables

Often in health care research, econometricians are interested in whether particular groups of patients or subjects differ from others. These groups can be indicated by using binary, or *dummy* variables. For example, an econometrician may wish to indicate whether a household is white (WHITE = 1), or not (WHITE = 0), or whether it is headed by a woman (FEMALE = 1) or not (FEMALE = 0).

Figure 3.5 shows how the estimated coefficients of these two variables can be treated. The "northwest" box indicates an observation for which both FEMALE and

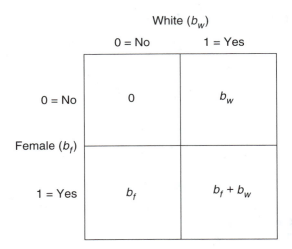

FIGURE 3.5 Interpreting the effects of dummy variables.

WHITE equal 0. If FEMALE $= 1$, then the coefficient b_f for both lower boxes indicates whether the household purchases more or less aspirin (and whether this is significant). This is a *row effect.* If WHITE $= 1$, then the coefficient b_w indicates whether white households purchase more or less aspirin (and whether that is significant). This is a *column effect.* If the household is both white and female-headed, then the combined effect is $(b_f + b_w)$.[8]

THE IDENTIFICATION PROBLEM

Up to this point, all of the exposition has concerned the estimation of a single equation. The examples have concerned an econometrician looking at the individual-demand equation for aspirin. Suppose, now, that the econometrician is concerned with measuring the demand for aspirin from data that represent market outcomes. The market outcome—that is, the amount of aspirin actually consumed—will depend on the interaction of both supply and demand. Thus, the econometrician would like simultaneously to measure market demand and market supply for aspirin.

Suppose, assuming that each state represents a market, he gets data on the reported price of aspirin as well as on the quantity sold, in the 50 states. He then sets up the demand regression such that

$$Q = A + BP + \epsilon \tag{3.13}$$

Previously, when dealing with data on individual consumers, the econometrician knew that he was dealing with a demand function, because, at least with respect to aspirin, individuals take the price as fixed, and do not produce aspirin. Hence, the econometrician was estimating demand.

Yet in a market setting, the quantity consumed in equilibrium represents simultaneously both the quantity supplied and the quantity demanded. If the econometrician graphs the data, as in Figure 3.6, from the market for aspirin in the 50 states, he sees a set of points that reflect the intersection of 50 pairs of demand and supply curves. Will the pattern found and estimated by the computer reflect the supply curve or the demand or a messy mixture of both?

This problem is known in econometrics as the *identification problem,* for the reason that the data at hand are not sufficient to identify whether the price and quantity data indicate a demand function, a supply function, or some combination of the two. If the econometrician does not realize that this problem exists, and estimates the regression above, it is likely that the parameter B will not reflect either the underlying demand or supply curves exactly.

This leads to the econometrician's task, which is to identify the true equations. If, somehow, the econometrician can find a variable that affects only the supply curve, then by shifting the supply curve, he will trace (or identify) the equilibria on a demand

---

[8]In fact, if one felt that white females may have particular attitudes or preferences for aspirin, one could estimate a coefficient that addresses the interaction of the two effects (1 if white and female, 0 otherwise). This would be coefficient b_{fw}. Here, then, the impact of being white and female would be $(b_f + b_w + b_{fw})$.

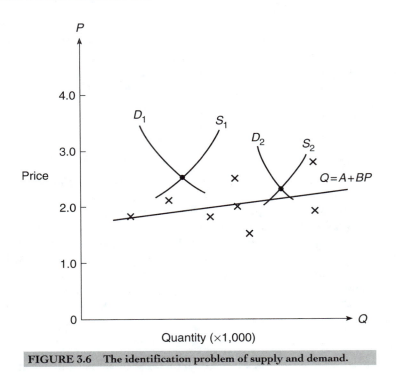

FIGURE 3.6 **The identification problem of supply and demand.**

curve. Conversely, if somehow he can find a variable that affects only the demand curve, then similarly he will trace (or identify) the equilibria on a supply curve. The complete correct procedure is beyond the scope of the present book. The discussion, however, shows that particular care is necessary, especially when dealing with cross-sectional economic aggregates. We will see examples of the identification problem in later parts of the book.

DISCRETE CHOICE ANALYSIS

The exposition in this chapter has moved from variables that are characterized in categories to those that are continuous. It was argued that many economic outcomes are measured with continuous variables; hence, ordinary least squares (OLS) regression methods are appropriate.

There are, however, classes of economic problems that do not meet these criteria. For example, someone needing treatment may choose to go to one doctor over another. Or a patient, together with a physician, chooses treatment A rather than treatment B. One chooses among a small number of insurance plans. These analyses are known as discrete choice analyses, referring to the fact that there are small numbers of possibilities, or discrete choices, rather than a continuous set of possibilities.

Suppose we wish to predict the factors that make people in a certain small town choose Dr. Lewis as their physician rather than Dr. Arnold. Let variable Y equal 0 if patients choose Dr. Arnold, and 1 if they choose Dr. Lewis. The underlying relationship between the independent variables and the dependent zero–one variable is often understood as probabilistic. We say that given certain prices, consumer incomes, and the like that "the probability that this patient will choose Dr. Lewis is _____." The probability in such choice problems often follows a pattern that can be graphed as an S-shaped curve, as noted for example in Figure 3.7.

Although the econometrician only sees values of 0 or 1 for Y, it is convenient to assume that there is an underlying response variable Y^*:

$$Y^* = bX + \epsilon \qquad (3.14)$$

where variable ϵ reflects random or unknown terms. Each person may have some threshold value of Y^*, related to common parameters b, and to the person's error term. If Y^* is greater (less) than the threshold, then he or she chooses to go to Dr. Lewis (Arnold).

Some of the independent variables that might push the individual over the threshold between Dr. Lewis and Dr. Arnold would be the prices charged by each doctor, the distance from each doctor's office, the length of time that the person has lived in the town (old-timers may prefer Dr. Lewis), and so on. The interpretation of positive and negative coefficients in the resulting estimated equation and the testing of hypotheses are very similar to that under ordinary least squares regression.

Two popular discrete choice analyses are the *probit* and the *logit models*. They differ by the mathematical form of the distribution that the error term is assumed to take, but they both provide the S-shaped curve. Maddala (1983) is a standard reference for these analyses.

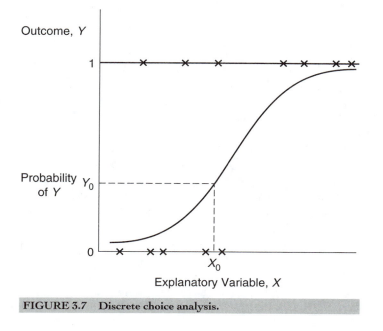

FIGURE 3.7   Discrete choice analysis.

STATISTICAL INFERENCE IN THE SCIENCES AND SOCIAL SCIENCES

The natural sciences attempt, if not always successfully, to control experimentally for all of the other possible sorts of variation. By contrast, econometricians are seldom so fortunate. Occasionally experimental economic studies are done, but such projects are very expensive. One attempt to formulate such a study was the multimillion dollar Health Insurance Experiment of the late 1970s and early 1980s, funded by the Department of Health, Education and Welfare, and analyzed by health experts at the Rand Corporation. We discuss parts of that study in several later sections of the book.[9] Even with the careful planning that went into the experimental design, this experimental study was not immune to major analytical concerns.

Other fields have similar problems. A 1988 report from the Panel of the Institute of Mathematical Statistics referred to analytical problems in chemistry:

> The data are frequently complex with a large number of dimensions, may sometimes have a time element, and can be further complicated because of missing values. In some instances, standard multivariate or time series methods may suffice for analysis, but, more commonly, novel developments are required, for example, to handle the problem of multivariate calibration. . . . (p. II-1)

Econometricians must most often use natural experiments, and must seek ways of accounting for the other variation. Since many policies, such as the provision of public health services, or the regulation of the prescription drug industry, depend on accurate measurement of economic phenomena, it is essential that the measurements be carefully and scientifically accomplished.

CONCLUSIONS

This chapter has attempted to give a "taste" of the statistical methods necessary to address questions that occur in health economics, and to make more understandable the occasions where statistical material is presented later in the text. The needed ideas for understanding the text include formulating questions in terms of hypotheses, reading statistical test results to determine if the result is significant, understanding statistical significance, and interpreting reported regression results.

The emphasis on problems to watch for in statistical analysis is not meant to generate undue skepticism over the statistical data to be reported. We do not wish to promote thinking that states, "Lies, damn lies, and statistics." On the contrary, the discussion is meant to help one to distinguish the better studies where confidence can best be placed. Statistics applied to health economics provide a useful tool even though

---

[9]There are excellent reviews by Manning and his collaborators (1987), and Newhouse et al. (1993).

individual statistical analyses may be flawed by the use of improper techniques. A lab dish may be dirty, but one does not conclude that it is impossible to prove anything through laboratory experiment.

Summary

1. Economists must usually collect information from people doing day-to-day activities and use statistical methods to control for the confounding differences among the people that they are analyzing. The more successful they are in controlling for such differences, the more reliable the analysis will be.

2. Statistical methods suggest formulating economic assertions as hypotheses, and collecting data to determine whether the hypotheses are correct.

3. Hypotheses that are designed to test for equality among two or more items are called simple hypotheses. Hypotheses that are used to test whether two or more items are greater (or less) than each other are called composite hypotheses.

4. There are several steps necessary to test hypotheses appropriately. The econometrician must:
   - state the hypotheses clearly
   - choose a sample that is suitable to the task of testing
   - calculate the appropriate measures of central tendency and dispersion
   - draw the appropriate inferences.

5. Regression analysis allows the econometrician to fit a straight line through a set of data points. In ordinary least squares regression, the sum of the squared deviations of the actual data points from the line is minimized.

6. R^2 measures the proportion of the total variation explained by the regression model. While it may be desirable to maximize R^2, most econometricians are at least as interested in the values of the parameters that are estimated.

7. Identification is the problem of estimating the underlying functions (structural relations) within the context of a joint (simultaneous) relationship, such as demand and supply.

8. Important skills in statistical analysis include:
   - understanding statistical significance
   - interpreting reported statistical results
   - detecting problems in reported statistical findings.

Discussion Questions

1. List at least three ways in which natural experiments differ from laboratory experiments.

2. What is the difference between a simple hypothesis and a composite hypothesis? Why might economists choose to use one over another?

3. In considering the difference in cholesterol levels between men and women, what is the null hypothesis? What is the alternative hypothesis? Is the alternative hypothesis simple or composite?

4. Suppose that we wish to compare the health status of two groups of people. What variable might we use to measure the status? What variables might we wish to control, in order to draw the appropriate inferences?

5. If someone reports that the mean weight for fourth grade boys is 50 pounds and for fourth grade girls is 48 pounds, what must you know to test hypotheses using the difference of means?

6. If one is trying to relate output to labor inputs and capital inputs, using regression analysis, would we expect the coefficients of the regressions to be positive or negative? Why?

7. What are *dummy variables?* How are they useful in identifying differences among groups?

8. Suppose that you used regression methods to estimate the demand curve for physician visits and found a positive relationship. That is, you found that the higher the price, the more visits are demanded. What problem has likely arisen? Explain the problem in words. Why might it make statistical inference difficult?

9. What is *discrete choice analysis?* How does the variable to be explained differ, in this case, from ordinary least squares analysis?

10. Rich people consume more health care services than poor people. Explain two ways one might test this hypothesis.

Exercises

(For students with access to spreadsheet computer programs such as Excel, Lotus 123, Quattro, or others) Consider the following data for a cross section of individuals in the population, in which

Q = Quantity (in 100s) purchased in a year
P = Average price of aspirin in that year
Y = Annual income
A = Age of buyer

Obs	Q	P	Y	A
1	1	1.5	20	25
2	2	1.5	40	20
3	4	1	12	25
4	2	1	10	30
5	2	1	8	30
6	3	2	30	35
7	3.5	1.5	30	40
8	4	2	20	40
9	7	1	20	45

Obs	Q	P	Y	A
10	1	3	15	40
11	2	2	18	30
12	3	2	20	32
13	3.5	2	15	36
14	4	2	10	30
15	2	3	25	20
16	1	4	15	25
17	8	2	15	55
18	9	1	40	50
19	1	4	10	45
20	10	1.5	30	55
21	6	1.5	35	60
22	2	1	30	40
23	3	1	25	40
24	3	2	20	35
25	3	2	15	35
26	4	3	20	35
27	1	4	20	25
28	1	4	25	30
29	2	5	28	30
30	3	1	30	32

Now consider questions 1–4:

1. If we divide the population into two groups, up to age 35, and over age 35, which group purchases more aspirin?

2. If we divide the population into three groups, up to age 30, over 30 and up to 45, and over 45, do the purchases vary by age?

3. What is the relationship in a regression analysis between Q and P? Between Q and Y? Between Q and A?

4. Calculate the multiple regression that relates Q with P, Y, and A. Which variables are statistically significant? What is the elasticity of Q with respect to P, to Y, and/or A?

5. In Equation (3.12), suppose income Y is 20, the price of aspirin P is $2, the price of acetaminophen P_o is $3, and there are no children. Calculate the elasticities of demand for aspirin with respect to Y, P, and P_o.

6. Consider demand curves for aspirin, estimated for two different sets of consumers:
   (a) $Q = 20 - 5P + 0.2Y$
   (b) $Q = 30 - 5P + 0.2Y$

   If $Y = $20 and $P = $1, calculate the price and income elasticities for group (a) and group (b). Whose elasticities will be higher? Why?

7. Given the regression estimate of the demand equation of

$$Q_x = 1{,}000 - 3.3P_x + .001Y$$

where Y is income, what is the change in demand if price rises by $1 holding income constant? What is the percentage change in demand if price rises by $1 from an initial price of $P = \$200$ given $Y = \$10,000$? What is the effect on demand of a $1 increase in income holding price constant?

8. Given the estimate demand equation of

$$Q_x = 1,000 - 3.3P_x + .2P_z + .001Y$$

$$(3.5) \quad (2.1) \quad (0.5)$$

with t values in parentheses, where P_z is the price of another good Z, and Y is income. Is good Z a substitute or a complement? Can we say confidently whether good X is a normal good or an inferior good?

Part Two: Supply and Demand

C H A P T E R

4

The Production of Health

■ The Production Function of Health

■ On the Historical Role of Medicine and Health Care

■ The Production of Health in the Modern Day

■ On the Role of Schooling

■ Conclusions

The production of health is a central concern to the health economist and to public policy. Consider that the role of health care in society, including medical care provided by physicians, is ultimately a production question. What is the contribution of health care to the health status of the population? Secondarily, what is the best way to produce and distribute health care?

THE PRODUCTION FUNCTION OF HEALTH

A production function summarizes the relationship between inputs and outputs. The study of the production of health function thus requires that we inquire about the relationship between health care inputs and health. The answers that economists and medical historians offer to this question are surprising to many people. First, the contribution of practitioner-provided health care to the historical downward trends in population mortality rates was probably negligible at least until well into the twentieth century. Second, while the total contribution of health care is probably substantial in the modern day, its marginal contribution is small.

This distinction between total and marginal contributions is crucial to understanding these issues. To illustrate this distinction, consider Figure 4.1A, which exhibits a theoretical health status production function for the population. Set aside the difficulties of measuring health status in populations, and assume that an adequate health

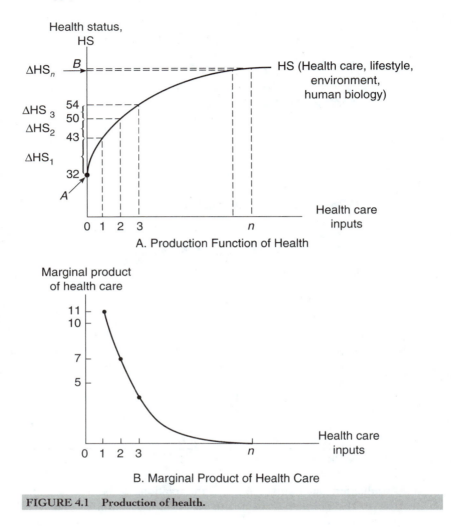

FIGURE 4.1 Production of health.

status (HS) measure has been agreed on. Health status is shown here to be an increasing function of health care. To avoid a perspective that is too narrowly focused on health care, we specify further that health status depends at least also upon the population's biological endowment, environment, and lifestyle.[1] Thus, HS = f(Health Care, Lifestyle, Environment, Human Biology). Improvements in any of these latter three factors will shift the curve upward.

A production function specifies the relationship of flows of inputs and flows of outputs over a specified time period, so the inputs and output in Figure 4.1A are measured over an implied period of time, such as a year. In practice, we might use the

---

[1]The categorization of groups of inputs follows, for example, Lalonde (1974).

number of healthy days experienced by the population per capita or the reciprocal of a reverse indicator such as mortality rates or disability days to indicate health status.

To simplify the depiction of the production of health process, we have reduced all health care inputs into one scale called Health Care. In reality, health care consists of many different health care inputs. Many of them include types of medical care provided by doctors of medicine or osteopathy, but many also are provided by other professionals in the health care field. Conceptually, the health care measure, HC, may be thought of as an aggregate of all these types of health care, the aggregation being based on dollar values.

The marginal contribution of health care is its marginal product, meaning the increment to health caused by one extra unit of Health Care, holding all other inputs constant. Increasing Health Care from zero to 1 unit in Figure 4.1A improves health status by ΔHS_1, the first unit's marginal product. Numerically, this first unit of Health Care has increased the health status index from 32 to 43; thus, $\Delta HS_1 = 11$ Health Status units. The next unit of medical care delivers a marginal product of $\Delta HS_2 = 7$, and so on. That these marginal products are diminishing in size illustrates the law of diminishing marginal returns. If society is employing a total of n units of Health Care, then the total contribution of Health Care is the sum of the marginal products of each of the n units. This total contribution as shown, *AB,* may be substantial. However, the marginal product of the nth unit of medical care is ΔHS_n, and it is very small. In fact, we are very nearly on the "flat of the curve." Marginal product is graphed on Figure 4.1B.

We have drawn the health production function as a rising curve that flattens out at higher levels of health care but never bends downward. Would the health production function eventually bend downward? Is it possible to get too much health care so that the health of the population is actually harmed? This is a logical possibility under at least two scenarios. Iatrogenic (meaning provider-caused) disease is an inevitable by-product of many medical interventions; for example, each surgery has its risks. If the rate of iatrogenic disease does not fall while diminishing returns sets in, it is possible for the balance of help and harm from health care to be a net harm.

Secondarily, a provocative writer in the 1970s, Ivan Illich, has argued that medicalization could effectively lead to less personal effort to produce health on the part of the consumer and perhaps less personal determination to face the problems in living that have incorrectly come to be treated as medical problems. In this event, the net effect could be a harm to the health of the population.[2]

Return to the distinction between total product and marginal product. Often it is the marginals that are relevant to policy propositions, not the totals. For example, no one seriously recommends that society eliminate all health care spending. However, it is reasonable to ask whether society would be better off if it could reduce health care expenditures by $1 billion and invest those funds in another productive use, such as housing, education, transportation, defense, or other consumption. We could even reasonably ask if health itself could be improved by transferring the marginal billion dollars to environmental or lifestyle improvements.

---

[2]For those interested in pursuing study of these ideas, see Illich (1976) and Carlson (1975).

Many of our government programs are designed to encourage health care use in certain population groups, such as the poor and the elderly. Many programs, such as tax preferences for health insurance, benefit people who are neither poor nor elderly and encourage their consumption of health care. The theoretical issues raised here necessitate that we question the wisdom of each of our programs.

The theoretical questions can be investigated with data of several kinds either directly or indirectly relevant to the production-of-health issue. It is useful to begin with the historical role of medicine, which indirectly bears on the issue of health production. After providing an overview of these efforts, largely the work of medical historians, we then turn to econometric studies of the modern-day production function.

ON THE HISTORICAL ROLE OF MEDICINE
AND HEALTH CARE

Among many medical historians, it is agreed that practitioner-provided medical interventions played only a very small, perhaps negligible, role in the historical decline in population mortality rates in countries where data are available. Effective medicine is a fairly recent phenomenon, and the delivery of effective medical interventions on a scale sufficient to affect population health indicators most likely appeared only well into the twentieth century. Though the magnitudes of other causes of mortality declines are still disputed, it is clear that a larger role, perhaps the most significant one, might be attributed to public health measures and the spread of knowledge of the sources of disease. However, at least one provocative scholar in this field attributes the lion's share of the credit to improvements in environment, particularly to the greatly increased supply of foodstuffs that became available due to the agricultural and industrial revolutions.

The Rising Population and the Role of Medicine

The notion that medicine played a relatively minor historical role is certainly not new, and it has been asserted by researchers of various ideologies. Most recently, this point of view is associated with the work of Thomas McKeown (1976) who focused on the dramatic rise in population in England and Wales from 1750 to modern day.

The pattern over time of world population growth, including population growth in England and Wales, is one that has posed a significant research question to many scholars including McKeown. Our best estimates suggest that the world population rose and fell for hundreds, perhaps thousands, of years without any significant long-term upward trend. It is clear that an extraordinary change took place after 1750. From roughly this point in time, population began a distinctively strong upward trend that by the present day has tremendously expanded world population. Why did this extraordinary historical change occur?

The large rise in the English and Welsh population in the period roughly following 1750 is largely a story of the population's health. Population increase comes from three sources: increased births, reduced mortality, or increased net in-migration. Migration was probably not an important source of population increase in England and Wales; when accurate birth and death data become available from about 1841, these data alone proved able to account for the population change. Likewise, fertility probably did not account for the change because recorded birth rates actually declined during the period since data became available. Declines in birth rates are a common finding in countries undergoing industrialization or modernization. In contrast, recorded mortality rates did decline substantially.

To assess the role of medicine, McKeown began by investigating which diseases contributed to the decline in death rates. Mortality data are often limited prior to the mid-1800s, but from available records he produced an emerging picture. Table 4.1 shows death rates by disease category for three different time periods. The table shows that airborne infectious diseases account for the largest single portion of mortality reduction, and waterborne infectious diseases also make up a substantial portion of known causes. Regarding the airborne diseases, other data suggest that the main airborne diseases showing a decline in mortality included tuberculosis, bronchitis, pneumonia, and influenza.

What Caused the Mortality Rate Declines?

Many presume that the declines in the mortality rates were due to improvements in medical science provided to the public through medical practice. Nevertheless, counterarguments to this proposition bring this presumption into question. In most cases, an effective specific medical intervention was not available until late in the period, well after the greater part of the mortality decline had occurred.

For example, the argument can be illustrated for the cases of respiratory tuberculosis and a group of three upper respiratory diseases—bronchitis, pneumonia, and influenza. Mortality rates for these diseases fell to relatively low levels prior to the availability of effective medical interventions, whose availability occurred respectively

TABLE 4.1   Death Rates[*] (per million) in 1848–1854, 1901, and 1971

	1848–1854	1901	1971	*Percentage of reduction (1848–1854 to 1971) attributable to each category*	*For each category, percentage of reduction (1848–1854 to 1971) which occurred before 1901*
I. Conditions attributable to microorganisms:					
1. Airborne diseases	7,259	5,122	619	39	32
2. Water- and foodborne					
diseases	3,562	1,931	35	21	46
3. Other conditions	2,144	1,415	60	12	35
Total	12,965	8,468	714	72	37
II. Conditions not attributable					
to microorganisms	8,891	8,490	4,070	28	8
All diseases	21,856	16,958	5,384	100	29

[*]Standardized to the age/sex distribution of the 1901 population.

Source: McKeown (1976, p. 54). We have corrected misprints in the original.

after 1930, and for some cases well into the 1950s and 1960s. The picture is shared by waterborne diseases. About 95 percent of the mortality declines in cholera, diarrhea, and dysentery occurred prior to the 1930s when intravenous therapies became available. Likewise, typhoid and typhus mortality already had fallen to low levels by the beginning of the twentieth century.

The pattern McKeown found for England and Wales can also be illustrated for the United States. McKinlay and McKinlay (1977) provided data for the United States from 1900 to 1973. Figure 4.2 shows these patterns for several infectious diseases. In most cases, as is shown, the availability of the effective medical intervention occurs well after the larger part of the mortality declines.

One of the most important changes in mortality in the twentieth century was the decline in infant mortality. Does this type of mortality follow the same pattern? A highly readable account of the modern historical pattern of infant mortality is offered in Victor Fuchs's *Who Shall Live?* (1974). Fuchs noted that infant mortality rates in New York City improved markedly from 1900 to 1930 and that this decline was significantly due to declines in deaths from "pneumonia–diarrhea" complex. Fuchs concluded as follows:

> It is important to realize that medical care played almost no role in this decline. While we do not know the precise causes, it is believed that rising living standards, the spread of literacy and education, and a substantial fall in the birth rate all played a part . . . (p. 32).

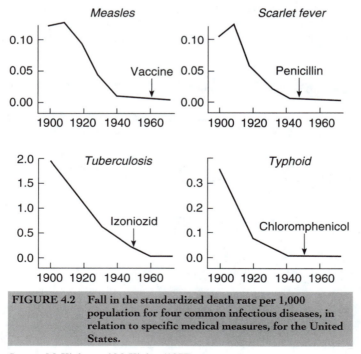

FIGURE 4.2   **Fall in the standardized death rate per 1,000 population for four common infectious diseases, in relation to specific medical measures, for the United States.**

Source: McKinlay and McKinlay (1977).

Tuberculosis and the Magic Mountain

Thanks to the efforts of writers such as Nobelist Thomas Mann, the tuberculosis (TB) sanitarium of 100 years ago has found a permanent place in literature. Mann's novel, *The Magic Mountain,* describes with a mastery of medical detail, often admired by physicians, a sanitarium retreat in the Alps, its colorful clients and their experiences with the deadly disease. Mann's incomparable development of characters and dialog bring a reality to the society unique to this sanitarium, representing one he had himself visited. Hans Castorp, a young German engineer, is smitten with Clavdia Chauchat, a young woman at the "good" Russian table. The Italian Settembrini's intellectual arguments with Naptha can only result in a duel. We grieve when Hans's cousin Joachim, a good, simple military man, succumbs to TB and his body is sledded down the mountain. Hans survives to return to the lands below.

Though effective chemical interventions were not available until after 1940, doctors did treat TB prior to 1940, notably with the widespread use of sanatoria, such as the one in *The Magic Mountain.* Declines in TB mortality during the period studied by McKeown represented perhaps the single most important example of declines in the mortality rate. Can we credit the sanitoria for this progress? This is unlikely because it is unlikely that sanatoria capacity or the capacity of sanatoria dispensaries were ever large enough to affect the pattern of mortality in populations. For an account of the retreat of tuberculosis, see Smith (1988).

In the 1930s, antimicrobial drugs were introduced. During the period 1935–1950, the fall in infant death rates accelerated. Fuchs proposed that during this period "both medical advances and rising living standards contributed to the reduction in infant deaths" (p. 32). Declines in infant deaths flattened somewhat beginning about 1950 but resumed a stronger decline about 1965.

Returning to McKeown's work, if specific effective curative medicines were largely not responsible for mortality declines, is it nevertheless possible that other tools in the physician's black bag were effective? The problem is that there probably were not many effective tools in the physician's metaphorical black bag until well into the twentieth century.

On the Role of Public Health and Nutrition

If medicine cannot be credited with the large declines in population mortality rates after 1750, what then can be credited? Other alternative candidate causes seem together sufficient to explain the decline: reduction in exposure to infection, and improvement in the human host's ability to resist infection. Of these two, reduction in exposure was the primary method through which public health measures could be effective. The role of public health measures is of interest in itself.

The magnitudes of the effects of these alternative causes, including importantly the role of public health, are open to dispute, a dispute whose settlement lies largely outside of an account of health economics. For the present purpose, however, an overview of the issues may suffice.

Available evidence is sufficient to establish that public health contributed significantly to mortality declines, though some historians dispute the proposition that public health was the major contributor. McKeown disputed the preeminence of public health. His argument is that while surely public health was effective for many diseases, its effects were noted primarily through the limitation of exposure to waterborne and foodborne disease organisms, and it cannot account for the large decline in airborne infectious disease mortality.

Public health measures include, among other things, immunization of populations, quarantines, standards for sanitary water supplies and sewage systems, and standards for the sanitary handling and treatment of foodstuffs. During the historical period of study, the most important public health influences appear to be on the waterborne and the foodborne diseases. Here public health measures appear to have notably helped to improve the quality of water supplies.

However, public health measures came into widespread use late in the period of population mortality declines. For example, among foods carrying pathogens, milk was perhaps most important because it became more widely available in the eighteenth century and it was a carrier of microorganisms for such diseases as dysentery, typhoid, streptococcal sore throat, and infantile gastroenteritis. It was not until the late nineteenth century that commercial pasteurization was developed, and it was widely used only in the twentieth century.

Control of water purity and sewage systems came into play in the latter part of the nineteenth century, and these changes surely had a positive effect. McKeown argued

> From the evidence it is clear that the death rate from water- and food-borne diseases declined continuously from the second half of the nineteenth century. . . . There is no doubt that [this decline] was due to reduced exposure brought about by improvements in hygiene . . . and their decline coincided with advances in hygiene, particularly, in the nineteenth century, purification of water and sewage disposal (p. 121).

In acknowledging a significant role for public health, the remaining dispute is over its relative importance in comparison to other health-enhancing improvements. McKeown argued that the public health contribution was less important than improvement in population nutrition. He emphasized the lateness of the arrival of widespread public health practices and the limitations of public health measures in improving mortality experience from airborne diseases.

Nevertheless, more recent studies emphasize the importance of public health. Notably, Woods and Hinde (1987) demonstrated that improvements in mortality in England and Wales during the study period showed a narrowing of the gap between urban and rural areas. They argued that dietary differences between urban and rural populations were probably less important than adverse environmental conditions for which public health efforts probably were effective. They corroborate the conclusions regarding medical care by finding that the local availability of physician care had no significant bearing on mortality.

McKeown's argument in favor of the role of nutrition also has some credibility to many scholars. The introduction of two American foods—corn and potatoes—may alone have made a significant contribution. Agriculture experienced large advances, including new crops, crop rotation, seed production, winter feeding, and improvements in farm implements.

The connection between improved nutrition and infectious diseases is fairly clear.[3] Infectious disease creates a relationship between host and agent of disease. While control of the agent is directly helpful in reducing disease incidence, the condition of the host helps to determine its resistance to disease. A person who is better housed, better rested, and, with emphasis here, better fed, will be more resistant and less likely to die subsequent to exposure.

What Lessons Are Learned from the Medical Historian?

This examination of the history of declines in the population mortality rate may be summarized as one of some controversy over the relative importance of public health measures and other environmental factors such as nutrition. There is a fairly clear consensus over the relatively minor role of medical practice. What conclusions for modern health policy can be drawn?

First of all, we cannot infer from this historical record that medical research is unimportant or overrated either historically or in our modern day. Medical research is significant not only today for its contribution to medical practice but also for its influence on other health-enhancing practices.

The instance of typhoid provides a good example. As we have seen, mortality from typhoid declined primarily before the availability in about 1950 of chloramphenicol. Medical research, however, was instrumental in understanding the cause and transmission of the disease and led to public health measures in filtering public water supplies, chlorination of water supplies, and establishment of drinking water standards. All of these factors occurred historically in time to have a major effect on mortality.[4] Selma Mushkin's (1979) estimates on the contribution of medical research to mortality experience tend to confirm this idea. She estimates that medical research accounts for almost one-third of the cost savings to society from reduction in sickness or death rates in the United States from 1900 to 1975. The period 1900–1930 accounts for half the value of medical research effects, even though it came largely before the specific effective medical practice interventions.

Second, the question of whether a given medical intervention works with afflicted patients requires both a different numerator and a different denominator. For example, if we wish to assess the effectiveness of a given treatment for a particular form of cancer, the numerator more plausibly should be the mortality, not in the general

---

[3]And, we may presume, a similar argument holds for improvements in housing conditions.

[4]The ideas in this paragraph owe to discussion in Schneyer, Landefeld, and Sandifer (1981).

population, but that due to the cancer. Likewise, the denominator would more plausibly be the number of afflicted patients, not the general population.[5]

Finally, the argument regarding the role of medicine is after all an historical one. Successful medical intervention came very late in the period, but it did come. In the present day, the arguments must be different. For example, we might be called on to advise a developing country on the best strategy for investment in health care relative to investment in industry or education.

If the inferences suggested earlier are, as we have argued, overdrawn, or even invalid, what then can we conclude from the historical record regarding modern health care policy? Perhaps the best result of this overview is a healthy skepticism toward the effectiveness of any given medical practice, and more importantly, to its significance and benefits to the population. It is in this spirit that the U.S. government has increasingly come to fund outcome studies. Outcome studies are intended to address the effectiveness and appropriateness of specific medical practices on patient outcomes. The studies attempt to reduce the prevalent uncertainties in medical practice, and they offer important inquiries into the wisdom of using the marginal billion dollars on medical care delivery, particularly in terms of costs and benefits to the population as a whole.

THE PRODUCTION OF HEALTH IN THE MODERN DAY

The investigation of the modern production function of health entails the application of econometric techniques. An understanding of the strengths and limitations of these contributions requires attention to the underlying conceptual issues.

Preliminary Issues

There are two conceptual issues that bear on our interpretation of the results. These two issues can be posed as questions faced by every researcher: (1) how to measure health, the dependent variable in these studies, and (2) how to eliminate biases in the estimates.

HOW TO MEASURE HEALTH

Consider first the measurement of health. We desire a measure of population health status that has at least two characteristics: It must capture the aspects of health status that are meaningful to us, and it must be measurable with adequate precision. It is difficult to attain both of these goals. We are most confident of the accuracy of mortality rate data; however, mortality rates do not adequately capture several very meaningful aspects of health status, such as reduction in pain and suffering, and other improvements in the quality of life. The approach of researchers in this field is understandable. Mortality data have necessarily been emphasized both because of their accuracy as well as because of their importance in the public mind. But other indicators of health status, such as morbidity (illness) rates and disability days have also been used.

---

[5]The ideas in this paragraph owe to work by Pernick (1991).

In discussing the empirical literature, we begin with the mortality studies and then go on to consider studies of morbidity.

HOW TO ELIMINATE BIASES?

Second, consider the difficulties of eliminating biases in the estimation process. Conceptually, the statistical estimates should be based on combinations of all health care inputs actually used and the resulting outputs. Such data, along with appropriate econometric techniques, would permit the estimation of the production function directly, the goal of much of this research. Unfortunately, available data have often permitted only a more indirect approach. Researchers have often used data on the availability of some health care inputs in the population, not on the amounts of all inputs actually used.

It is safe to say that empirical work in this area has been developing and improving over time, and this progress includes a more recent emphasis on more direct and unbiased estimation of the production function. The problems that can introduce bias into other estimates can be illustrated with an example. Suppose we have measures for the availability of one health care input, say physicians per capita, but lack data on some other input measure such as the amount of exercise that local people generally do. Unfortunately for the econometrician, these two input variables may themselves be related. More physicians may be demanded in areas where people do fewer health-promoting activities on their own. Unaware of this correlation, or simply lacking the needed data, the econometrician might underestimate the productivity of physicians. One way in which this literature has been progressing is in having greater success in eliminating such biases. This is noteworthy, for example, in the studies of neonate mortality, which we will report shortly.[6]

The Production of Population Mortality Rates

An early contribution by Auster, Leveson, and Sarachek (1969) helps to illustrate several central issues of research on mortality rates. These authors econometrically studied death rates across states using 1960 data. They estimated the contribution to these death rates for several variables, including among them medical services, education, income, and cigarette consumption. The estimated elasticities for these variables alone suggest several policy ideas.

The elasticity of medical services expenditures in their equations was approximately 0.10 and was statistically insignificant. This suggests that a one percent increase in medical services expenditures would reduce mortality rates by 0.1 percent, and because the coefficient is statistically insignificant we cannot confidently rule out the possibility that the marginal product is zero. We would appear to be at or near the flat of the curve of the mortality rate production function. This has understandable implications from a cost–benefit perspective. Estimates of the cost of mortality developed by

---

[6]The issue of bias discussed here involves the distinction between reduced-form equation studies, which suggest incorrect inferences about input productivity, and structural equation studies, which more directly estimate the productivity of inputs. For a fuller discussion of the importance of the distinction between reduced-form studies and the structural function approach, see Grossman and Joyce (1990).

Dorothy Rice (1966) at that time suggested a total cost in terms of future earnings loss of from $40 to $50 billion in then-current dollars. A one percent increase in medical expenditures would have reduced the cost of mortality by about $40 to $50 million, but the increase in expenditures would have cost almost $320 million. Rice thought it was likely that nonmortality costs of illness would be less substantial than the mortality costs, but she reasoned that even if the nonmortality costs of illness were as substantial as the mortality costs, it would be cost-beneficial to reduce gross expenditures on medical services.

A second feature of the study is of equal interest. Auster, Leveson, and Sarachek found that while the elasticity of medical services was small, the elasticity of education was a somewhat larger and significant 0.2. Even though the cost of increasing education levels by 1 percent was substantial, calculations suggested that a marginal transfer of expenditures from medical services to education would improve population mortality rates.

Finally, these authors also found that cigarette consumption per capita is significantly associated with higher mortality rates. In this case, the direction of causation is probably not in doubt; we know that cigarette smoking causes diseases that are often fatal. It is noteworthy that this lifestyle variable is easily significant in a context where medical services expenditures are insignificant.

On the Importance of Lifestyle

The importance of accounting for lifestyle factors in affecting a population's health is illustrated by an international study by Barbara Wolfe (1986). She investigated the trends in health status in several industrialized countries, and looked at trends in medical expenditures and lifestyle factors such as cigarette and alcohol consumption. Previous international studies had suggested little or no significant effect of medical expenditures, but by controlling for lifestyle factors she could demonstrate a positive relationship between expenditures and health trends in several countries. This was corroborated recently in findings of a cross-national study showing that health expenditure is effective in reducing mortality rates (Hitiris and Posnett, 1992).

The role of lifestyle is also illustrated very effectively by Fuchs (*Who Shall Live?*). He compared death rates in Nevada and Utah with averages for 1959–1961 and 1966–1968. These two states are contiguous, and they share "about the same levels of income and medical care and are alike in many other respects" (p. 52). Nevertheless, average death rates in Nevada are much in excess of those in Utah. Table 4.2, from Fuchs's work, tells this story. Fuchs argued that the explanation for these substantial differences surely lies in lifestyle differences:

> Utah is inhabited primarily by Mormons, whose influence is strong throughout the state. Devout Mormons do not use tobacco or alcohol and in general lead stable, quiet lives. Nevada, on the other hand, is a state with high rates of cigarette and alcohol consumption and very high indexes of marital and geographical instability (p. 53).

The role of lifestyle is strong and tragic in a recent study of the consequences of maternal substance abuse in New York City (Joyce, Racine, and Mocan, 1992). The

TABLE 4.2 Excess of Death Rates in Nevada Compared with Utah, Average for 1959–1961 and 1966–1968

Age Group	Males	Females
< 1	42%	35%
1–19	16%	26%
20–39	44%	42%
40–49	54%	69%
50–59	38%	28%
60–69	26%	17%
70–79	20%	6%

Source: Fuchs (1974, p. 52).

alarming increase in low birth weight births, particularly among blacks, in the 1980s was to an important extent the result of an epidemic of illicit substance abuse by pregnant women. The explosion of cocaine use had horrendous consequences for these babies.

Production of Mortality Among the Medicare Population

Let us return to the production function literature in the line of Auster, Leveson, and Sarachek's work. Their contribution is historically important and entails issues still current, but it leaves several issues unaddressed. First, it is a highly aggregative study dealing with state averages. A natural complementary investigation is to examine smaller geographic areas or even individuals. Second, it is now quite old, even pre-Medicare, and many changes have occurred in the health system since then.

Hadley (1982) investigated a cross section of county groups in the United States (the groups consist of one or more whole counties with a combined population of at least 250,000). The study, which uses data for 1970, also disaggregates mortality by age, sex, and race. Hadley's measure of medical expenditure is a variable describing Medicare expenditures per enrollee within the county group. He demonstrated from other data that these Medicare expenditures were approximately proportional to total medical expenditures per capita, so he used the Medicare variable for all age groups (other expenditure data were not available by county group). However, we shall emphasize his results for the elderly cohorts.

An examination of the first row of Table 4.3 indicates that the Medicare expenses elasticities are somewhat larger in absolute value than those previously examined. These results suggest, for example, that a 1 percent increase in medical expenditures will reduce mortality rates among elderly black males by about 0.16 percent.

Notice, as well, that education again is often found to be significantly related to lower mortality rates and that cigarette sales per capita are a significant contributor to higher mortality rates. Finally, income in the reported equations is not a significant factor. This is not too surprising because the existence of Medicare means that income is no longer as serious a barrier to health care for the elderly.

TABLE 4.3 **The Elasticities of Age-Sex-Race Mortality Rates with Respect to Medicare Expenditures, Education, Income, and Cigarette Consumption, 1970 County Group Data**

Independent Variable	White Males 65+	Black Males 65+	White Females 65+	Black Females 65+
Medicare Expenses	−.123**	−.163**	−.141**	−.173**
Education	−.128**	−.060	−.025**	−.106
Income	−.020	−.012	NS	−.011
Cigarette Sales	.053**	.134*	.110*	−.045*

Medicare Expenses = Medicare expenditures per Medicare enrollee; Education = average number of highest education year attained; Income = total family income and other unearned income; Cigarette Sales = cigarette sales per capita.

NS = coefficient is not significant and rounds to zero.

 * Significant at the 5 percent level.

** Significant at the 1 percent level.

Source: Jack Hadley (1982). Medicare expense elasticities from tables, pp. 61, 62. Cigarette sales elasticities from table, p. 69. Income elasticities from row one of table, p. 112. Education elasticities are based on regression coefficients reported in tables on pp. 61, 62 with elasticities evaluated at sample means of the relevant variables.

A picture emerges in which health care appears to have a small marginal contribution. On the margin, it competes with education and lifestyle factors such as cigarette consumption in importance. However, in contrast to the previous results, medical services expenditure does appear to be a statistically significant contributor to health status.

But how small is small? The relevant test of the importance of the contribution of medical expenditure to health is whether it is an efficient investment in comparison to other health-enhancing policies such as improvements in lifestyle, education, or environment. Hadley's own estimates on this comparison issue suggest that medical expenditure is effective in comparison to estimates that have been made for various environmental and other risk reduction programs.[7]

CONTRIBUTION OF MEDICAL CARE

Consider again the question of the total contribution of medical care to health status today. As we pointed out, even when the marginal contribution is small, the total contribution may be substantial. Consider a crude extrapolation of elasticity estimates by Hadley, say between 0.1 and 0.3; in extrapolating a 100 percent reduction in medical care, we would estimate a consequent worsening of mortality rates by 10 to 30 percent. Most Americans would consider this range to be very substantial. But this extrapolation is at best very crude. The econometric cross-sectional estimates from U.S. data invariably entail few to no observations of states or county groups with

---

[7]For further development on Hadley's estimates and views on these issues, see Hadley (1982).

extremely low levels of health care. To extrapolate to zero health care moves us far out of the sample, a risky proposition statistically. A measure of total contribution is thus not realistic with cross-sectional data from a highly developed country.

The results reported in Table 4.3 are reinforced by a more recent study again by Hadley (1988). Using data from a 5 percent sample of the 1980 Census of Population, Hadley aggregated the necessary variables to the county group level. Focusing on the elderly, he found that Medicare spending per enrollee is significantly related to mortality rates; the relationship is stronger than previously observed. For whites, a 1 percent increase in Medicare expenditures tends to reduce mortality rates by 0.2 to 0.4 percent. For blacks, the increase is much higher, from 0.5 to 1.0 percent. Cigarette consumption has a "positive and statistically significant association with mortality rates for the four younger cohorts. . . . [while] Higher education is associated with lower mortality rates, although it is statistically significant for only three of the cohorts" (p. 490).

Hadley's findings suggest the importance of examining not only population aggregates but also disaggregates; that is, population subgroups by age, sex, and race. Or more generally, the point is that we must pay attention to the details. If medical expenditure on the margin has a small effect on average, it may nevertheless have significant and important effects for specific population groups. Furthermore, while aggregate spending on medical services has small marginal effects for many population groups, it may nevertheless be true that many specific types of medical expenditures and programs have significant and important effects.

The importance of these disaggregated results should be emphasized. Consider again the value of spending the marginal billion dollars on medical expenditure. Average estimates over the entire population will substantially understate the impact of the additional dollar of expenditure compared to the impact achieved by targeting these expenditures at those groups in society where the money is most effective.

Neonate Mortality

The point of focusing on the experience of population subgroups is reinforced by the neonate health production function studies. In the latter part of the 1980s, Corman and Grossman (1985) and Corman, Joyce, and Grossman (1987) reported studies of the determinants of neonatal mortality rates in cross-sections of counties in the United States. A neonatal mortality rate is the ratio of deaths of infants aged one month or less per thousand live births. Between 1964 and 1982, the U.S. average neonate mortality rate dropped from 17.9 to 7.7, a very substantial decline. An investigation into the causes of this decline illustrates another useful purpose of production of health studies. Corman, Joyce, and Grossman's production function estimates enabled them to estimate the contributions of specific types of medical care and specific types of neonate-related programs.

Table 4.4 presents their estimates of the contribution of each measured factor to the reported mortality rate decline. Use of medical services—both for neonatal intensive care and for prenatal care—are included. The WIC program is a shortened name for the governmental program designed to provide improved nutrition for Women, Infants, and Children; it is a means-tested program, meaning that it is directed to the poor. The BCHS project use measure is the authors' measure combining various Bureau

TABLE 4.4   Contribution of Selected Factors to Reductions in Neonatal Mortality Rates, 1964–1977

Factor	Whites Total Effect	Blacks Total Effect
Organized family planning	0.084	0.526
WIC	0.425	1.330
BCHS project use	0.002	0.030
Neonatal intensive care	0.140	0.534
Abortion	0.824	2.109
Prenatal care	0.434	1.949
Total explained reduction	1.9	6.5
Total reduction	7.5	11.5
Percentage explained	25.3	56.5

Note: Figures record estimates of the reduction in deaths per 1,000 live births predicted to have been caused by various factors.

Source: Corman, Joyce, and Grossman (1987, p. 356).

of Community Health Services (BCHS) projects, including maternal and infant care as well as community health centers.

The data recorded in Table 4.4 indicate that of the total reduction in neonate mortality for whites during the period, 1.9 deaths per 1,000 live births or 25.3 percent can be explained by the observed factors, whereas for blacks a greater amount, 6.5 or 56.5 percent, can be explained. The table is read, for example, as follows: During the period studied, the WIC program resulted in a reduction of white neonate mortality rates of 0.425 deaths per thousand live births, while for blacks WIC reduced neonate mortality by 1.330 deaths per thousand live births.

The contribution of neonatal intensive care was important but more modest in effect than the role of prenatal care, which had a particularly large effect for blacks. WIC was also important, again particularly for blacks. Notably, the availability of abortion services in the county, which increased during this period after legalization of abortion, was significant in terms of its contribution to mortality declines.

Morbidity Studies

Up to this point, the production of health might be better termed a production of mortality rates. Research has focused on mortality for good reasons: These data are more widely available, they are measured quite accurately, and they are meaningful in themselves. But they do not tell the whole story. Anderson and Morrison (1989) put it perhaps more forcefully than many:

> The authors of the 1970s raised the question: Do personal health services reduce mortality rates? And they answered with a resounding "No!" . . . The health policy analysts of this decade have revealed an increased sophistication by asking: Is it appropriate to measure the effectiveness of personal health services by gross measures of mortality? And they have answered that question with an equally resounding "No!" (p. 148).

We would argue somewhat to the contrary, that personal health services *do* reduce mortality in populations significantly, and while the marginal contribution is small on average, it nevertheless is probably cost-beneficial on the margin for some population subgroups. Second, data on mortality rates such as we have examined *are* meaningful; that is, they tell an important part of the story. However, the point is well taken that mortality rates tell *only* part of the story, and for many people who use health care, it may not be the most important part. Other measures of health should also be examined. These include morbidity data, self-reported health status, and other indicators of health. Work is also being done on developing a measure of the quality of life, and quality of life may also become the subject of production studies.

OTHER MEASURES OF HEALTH STATUS

Newhouse and Friedlander (1980) recognized the need for production of health studies to examine nonmortality measures of population health status:

> If, as many believe, most diseases that are currently treated are either selflimiting or irreversible, the possibilities for additional medical services to reduce mortality are small. In this case, . . . the observed effect of medical care will be both small and hard to detect. By contrast, there may be some diseases, such as hypertension or periodontal disease, where additional medical-care resources can make a difference (p. 201).

These researchers examined six physiological measures taken on individuals evaluated in the Health Examination Survey between October 1959 and December 1962. The measures included blood pressure, cholesterol, electrocardiogram abnormalities, abnormal chest X-rays, varicose veins, and periodontal disease. Using econometric techniques, the authors found that the availability each of five types of health care resources was rarely significantly related to these physiological measures. In the few exceptions, the effect of health care was very small; the estimated elasticity was very small. In contrast, better educated individuals often had better health indicators, but the effect of income was small where significant. Better-educated people tended to have much better gums, that is, better periodontal indicators, whereas the availability of dentists per capita did not seem to matter. The authors concluded that "the results are consistent with the view that what the individual does (or does not) do for himself affects health more than do additional medical resources" (p. 200).

The Rand Health Insurance Experiments offered confirmation of this research, and they are unique in providing experimental data for analysis. The Rand study experimentally investigated the role of health insurance on people's demand for health care and their health status. Reductions in insurance resulted in reductions in health care use, and provided the opportunity to investigate the effects of this reduced use on subsequent health status.

Brook and colleagues (1983) asked whether free care improves adults' health. Their study is appropriate to our present inquiry as well because they used nonmortality measures of health status. Their measures included health status evaluation scores, self-reported health status scores, and several physiological indicators. They compared mean values on these measures between people in the free-care plan versus those under a cost-sharing plan. Of approximately one dozen measures of health status, only "corrected far vision" was statistically significantly improved under free care. The better financial access to care thus influenced very few health effects for the average person. However, for the subgroup of poor people who had elevated health risks, the free plan did reduce the risk of dying.

The effects on children showed a somewhat similar pattern. Valdez et al. (1985) examined data for 1,844 children in the Rand study, children who differed primarily by the type of insurance plan their families obtained. Children under the cost-sharing plans consumed up to one-third less care. However, the reduction in care was not significantly related to health status measures. It appears clear that while free provision of health care to children might be justified on equity grounds, it may not be justified on the basis of benefits to health.

ON THE ROLE OF SCHOOLING

In this exploration of the evolving literature on the production of health, we have frequently encountered the finding that ceteris paribus, people with higher levels of education tend to be healthier. This again raises the policy question discussed by Auster, Leveson, and Sarachek—that is, should we transfer resources on the margin to education in order to achieve an improvement in population health status? The apparently simple economic question involves an interesting and thorny issue. The crux of the issue is whether increased education *causes* better health status or whether health status and education are correlated for other reasons.

Two Different Theories about the Role of Schooling

The ideas and work of two health economists serve to develop and contrast the two theories. First, Michael Grossman's (1972a,b) theory of demand entails a central role for education. Under Grossman, better-educated persons tend to be economically more efficient producers of health status. Better-educated people understand the technology or "know-how" needed to stay healthy, and they know better how to use medical and other market inputs and their own time to produce health. Under this view, the marginal transfer of resources makes fairly good sense.

Other health economists have put forward hypotheses under which schooling and health status are correlated only because they are both related to one or more other factors. The problem can be seen as the familiar self-selection problem. Do people who self-select to choose higher levels of education have an unobserved characteristic that also makes them likely to be more healthy?

Victor Fuchs (1982) has suggested a theory that serves as a prime example and involves certain microeconomic aspects of time discounting. Chapter 24 on cost-benefit analysis will explain why decision makers must discount future benefits and costs of a social investment to make them comparable in terms of present values. It will also show that a decision maker with a high rate of discount will tend to prefer projects with immediate payoffs versus long-term projects. Now consider individuals facing a possible investment in education. Since education requires current costs to gain distant payoffs, individuals with relatively low discount rates will be the more likely to invest in education. Similarly, health investments require substantial current outlays to gain distant payoffs; for example, the payoffs may be extended years toward the end of life. It follows that individuals with low time discount rates, or long *time horizons*, will tend to invest both in education and health. This will cause health status to be correlated with education, but further increments to education will *not* cause improvements in health status.[8]

Empirical Studies on the Role of Schooling in Health

Health economists have investigated the reasons why education is associated with better health. In these studies, we are concerned with formal education, also called *schooling*. Berger and Leigh (1989) examined data on thousands of individuals in two separate samples. One, the Health and Nutrition Examination Survey, used blood pressure as a measure of health status. The other, the National Longitudinal Survey of Young Men, used measures of functional limitations and disability.

The authors' statistical methods permitted a useful test. They first observed the individual's choice of schooling, using standard techniques. They found that years of schooling for an individual are related to several demographic characteristics such as age, race, ethnic background, family characteristics, and IQ. But they also developed a measure of the effect of unobserved factors, which would include factors such as personal time preference. They then posed the question: Do such unobserved self-selection factors affect health status or does schooling directly improve health status? Their results are consistent for both samples and for all measures of health status. Schooling directly improves health status measures, but there is no significant effect of unobservables such as time preference. This result is consistent with the view that schooling improves one's ability to produce health.

The issue of schooling and health is also of crucial importance to health in developing countries, and studies of families in Nicaragua by Jere Behrman and Barbara Wolfe are relevant. Behrman and Wolfe (1989) posed the question, "Does more schooling make women better nourished and healthier?" They took steps to control for the influence of other factors that affect both schooling and health. In particular, they controlled for the women's childhood background factors. They concluded that "the estimated positive health impact of the woman's schooling is largely representing schooling per se rather than unobserved fixed endowments so that . . . the woman's schooling does seem to make the woman healthier" (p. 660).

If a woman's schooling makes her a more efficient producer of health, then we should also expect that it will improve her children's health. Standard estimates of the effect of a woman's schooling on her children's health indeed show this effect. However, other work by Wolfe and Behrman (1987) casts serious doubt. The two authors collected data for sisters in Nicaragua. This allowed them to compare the health status of the children of the more educated of the sisters, using econometric techniques. Since the sisters had essentially the same childhood background, these data and

---

[8]Fuchs (1982) proposed as well the alternative related hypothesis that schooling tends to effect a change in people's time preferences. Both of the Fuchs hypotheses and the Grossman hypothesis would imply the observed positive correlation between schooling and health.

methods allowed them to control for unobserved elements in childhood background. Their results were very clear: Once childhood background is controlled for, a mother's education has no significant effect on her children's health status.

Thus, not all pieces of evidence fit the same pattern, and this will be a continued area of health economics research in this decade. We must recognize as well, that the major evidence we have examined addresses schooling per se, not necessarily schooling in health production. Introspection will serve quickly to show that most of one's schooling from elementary school through college or graduate school deals with knowledge and intellectual skills most often not related to personal hygiene. Even a negative result on the effect of schooling is consistent with a policy of increased investment in specific education devoted to health information—that is, to health production technology.

CONCLUSIONS

In this chapter, we have investigated several topics, each related directly or indirectly to the production of health. The concept of the health production function exhibiting diminishing marginal returns emphasizes the distinction between total product contributed by health care, which is surely substantial, and by marginal product, which is fairly small.

Historically, much of the declines in population mortality rates occurred prior to the introduction of specific effective medical interventions. Thus, historically both the marginal and the total contributions of health care provided by the health practitioner were probably small until well into the twentieth century.

However, modern production function studies show a statistically significant marginal contribution of Medicare expenditures to the health of elderly populations. Though in controlled experiments the better insured appear to experience few improved morbidity indicators, it is probably better to say that health care is productive on the margin at least for selected population subgroups and for selected mortality categories.

Whether education or schooling is a better investment toward improving health is still subject to alternative theories and somewhat mixed empirical work. Each of the health production topics we have investigated will probably prove fruitful as continued areas of research in the future.

Summary

1. The production function for health exhibits diminishing marginal returns. In developed countries, the total product of health care is probably substantial at the same time that the marginal product is relatively small.
2. The historical declines in mortality rates in representative industrial countries were substantially responsible for the large growth of populations.
3. The historical declines in population mortality rates were not due to medical interventions because effective medical interventions became available to populations

largely well after the mortality had already declined. Instead, public health, improved environment, and improved nutrition probably played substantial roles.

4. Studies show that the marginal product of health care in the United States is small. Early studies suggested that this marginal product in mortality production was not significantly different from zero. However, more recent studies of the Medicare population find significant elasticities in the range of 0.10 to 0.30, but as high as 0.50 to 1.00 for some population subgroups.

5. Experimental insurance coverage studies suggest that reduced use of health care on the margin has very little effect on the illness rates of the study population.

6. Lifestyle factors are major and statistically significant determinants of population health status.

7. Health care is an important and statistically significant contributor to health status for subgroups of the population, including infants and also including certain minority ethnic groups.

8. Education, as measured by years of schooling, is significantly related to population health status; however, the reason for this relationship is subject to mixed evidence. One theory proposes that schooling improves the efficiency by which one produces one's own health. Other theories suggest that both schooling and health are linked to other unobserved variables.

Discussion Questions

1. Assume that health production is subject to diminishing returns and that each unit of health care employed entails a constant rate of iatrogenic (medically caused) disease. Would the production of health function eventually bend downward? Explain.

2. What evidence is there to suggest that the United States is on the "flat of the curve" in health production? Is a typical developing country likely to be on the flat of its health production function? Discuss the differences.

3. Of birth rates, death rates, and net migration rates, which are important in explaining the modern rise in population in England and Wales? Describe the evidence.

4. "Medical interventions were not important in the historical declines in mortality rates, but that does not imply that medical research was unimportant." Explain this viewpoint.

5. What role did public health play in the historical decline in mortality rates?

6. Suppose you were hired as an adviser to a developing country and you were versed in the theory of production, the historical role of medicine, and the modern-day health production function studies. Their government seeks advice on the wisdom of a relative emphasis on health and health investment versus other forms of developmental investment. Given what you know, what would be your advice?

7. What are the main differences in the results of the Auster-Leveson-Sarachek mortality rate production study and the studies by Hadley? What might account for these differences?

8. Someone says the following: "Lifestyle may be the most important determinant of health status, but changing lifestyles may not be the least costly way to improve population health status." Explain the circumstances under which this opinion could be true. Is it likely to be true in reality? What does the evidence on lifestyle suggest about government policies to improve the public's overall health?

9. Summarize the two theories on how schooling is correlated with health status. Wolfe and Behrman investigated the health status of the children of pairs of sisters in Nicaragua. The sisters, who shared a common environment as children, often had different levels of schooling. Which of the two theories does the Wolfe and Behrman evidence support?

10. Research has shown that the returns to prenatal (before birth) and infant health care are very high, whereas it may cost hundreds of thousands of dollars to keep some elderly alive. What does this suggest about the appropriate allocation of resources among members of society?

Exercises

1. Graph the production of health function $HS = 10HC^{.5}E^{.3}LS^{.4}HB^{.2}$ in a graph with axes HS and HC assuming $E = 10$, $LS = 5$, and $HB = 7$. Graph the marginal product of health inputs. Is it increasing or decreasing? Show how the curve changes when E is increased to 15.

2. Which factors in Table 4.4 were important in explaining improvements in black neonate mortality rates? White neonate mortality rates? Speculate on why some of these factors may have been more important for blacks.

3. What are the differences between mortality and morbidity? Would you expect the two variables to be related to each other? If so, how?

CHAPTER 5

Demand for Health Capital

T he previous chapter considered the production of health in the aggregate. That is, it looked at the impacts of various factors on health for society as a whole. In this chapter, we show how individuals allocate their resources to produce health.

Economists' understanding of this decision has been deepened by the important work of Michael Grossman and subsequent extensions of his model. His model has enabled us to understand thoroughly the role of several variables such as age, education, health status, and income in the production of health through the demand for health capital.

THE DEMAND FOR HEALTH

The Consumer as Health Producer

Grossman (1972a, 1972b) used the theory of human capital to explain the demand for health and health care. His work has become a standard beginning point for much subsequent work. According to human capital theory, individuals invest in themselves through education, training, and health to increase their earnings. Grossman shows the way in which many important aspects of health demand differ from the traditional approach to demand:

1. It is not medical care per se that the consumer wants, but rather health itself. Medical-care demand is a derived demand for an input to produce health. People want health; they demand inputs to produce it.

2. The consumer does not merely purchase health passively from the market, but instead *produces* it, spending time on health-improving efforts in addition to purchasing medical inputs.

3. Health lasts for more than one period. It does not depreciate instantly, and thus can be treated like the capital good that it is.

4. Perhaps most importantly health can be treated both as a consumption good and an investment good. As a consumption good, health is desired because it makes people feel better. As an investment good, health is also desired because it increases the number of healthy days available to work, and thus to earn income.

Consider the consumer as a producer, as a firm that buys market inputs (e.g., medical care, food, clothing), and combines them with his or her own time to produce the services that increase the individual's level of utility. The consumer not only increments his or her stock of health, but using market inputs and personal time produces the other satisfactions and enjoyments of life.

These satisfactions and enjoyments are meant to include virtually all other things that the consumer does. Included are time watching television, time spent reading, time spent playing with and teaching one's children, time spent preparing meals, baking bread, or watching the sun set. While we call these activities satisfactions and enjoyments, we do not mean that they are all simply pleasures. Instead, they are intended to represent a composite of other things we do with our "leisure" time, both for pleasure as well as out of a sense of duty to family and community. We shall call this composite *home good B*.

Time Spent Producing Health

An increment to capital stock such as health is called an investment. Each period the consumer produces an investment in health, *I*. Health investment *I* is produced by time spent improving health T_H, and market health inputs (providers' services, drugs, exercise) *M*. Likewise, home good *B* is produced with time T_B, and market-purchased goods *X*.[1]

---

[1] If, for example, we considered good *B* as baking bread, the market goods might include flour, yeast, kitchen appliances, and gas, water, and/or electricity.

Thus, the consumer is using money to buy health care inputs *M,* or home good inputs *X.* He or she is using leisure time either for health care (T_H) or for producing the home good (T_B).

Using functional notation:

$$I = I \ (M, T_H; E) \tag{5.1}$$

$$B = B \ (X, T_B; E) \tag{5.2}$$

These functions indicate that increased amounts of *M* and T_H increase *I,* and that increased amounts of *X* and T_B increase *B.* The variable *E* in these functions is included to suggest that productivity in producing *I* or *B* may vary from person to person. Grossman proposed that this technical efficiency level would be related to the individual's education level, *E.* That is, educated people may produce one good or the other more efficiently.

In this model, Ed Kramer's ultimate resource is his own time. Treat each period of analysis as being a year in length, and assume that Ed has 365 days available in the year. To buy market goods such as medical care, *M,* or other goods, *X,* he must trade some of this time for income; that is, he must work at a job. Call his time devoted to work T_W. Since our focus is on the health aspects of living, we realize that some of his time during each year will be taken over by ill health, or T_L. Thus, we have accounted for his total time in the following manner:

$$\text{Total time} = T = 365 \text{ days} = T_H \text{ (time spent improving health)}$$
$$+ T_B \text{ (time spent in producing home goods)}$$
$$+ T_L \text{ (time lost due to illness)} \tag{5.3}$$
$$+ T_W \text{ (time devoted to work)}$$

Recall that his leisure time is spent either improving his health or producing home goods.

DISCOUNTING AND THE EVALUATION OF HEALTH CARE INVESTMENTS[*]

Since the investment aspect to health expenditure is critical to the model of demand for health capital, it is appropriate to discuss the evaluation of investments. Economists are often asked to compare investments that provide different streams of income over a number of periods. Why, for example, should Ed pay for a physical checkup (Investment *H*), when instead he can have his car serviced (Investment *S*) for the same cost?

Compare Investment *H,* which provides $20 at the end of Year 1, and $20 at the end of Year 2, with Investment *S,* which provides $28 at the end of Year 1, and $11 at the end of Year 2. Although Investment *S* (car service) returns $39 over the two years,

---

[*]Here we review the discussion of discounting found in the appendix to Chapter 2. More advanced readers may wish to skip this section.

TABLE 5.1 Relative Present Discounted Values of Investment			
a. Interest rate = 5%			
Health, H	**Return**	**Car, S**	**Return**
Period 1	20	Period 1	28
Period 2	20	Period 2	11
PDV	37.19	PDV	36.64
Health has a higher PDV!			
b. Interest rate = 15%			
Health, H	**Return**	**Car, S**	**Return**
Period 1	20	Period 1	28
Period 2	20	Period 2	11
PDV	32.51	PDV	32.67
Car has a higher PDV!			

compared to $40 for Investment *H,* most of the return on Investment *S* comes earlier, at the end of Year 1. Since we address the allocation of resources among numerous uses that may have long-term impacts, it is useful to compare investments with respect to their present discounted values.

Using the methods presented in Chapter 2's appendix, we can calculate the present discounted value (PDV), using a 5 percent discount rate, for the two investments as noted in Table 5.1. The PDV for Investment *H,* his physical checkup, will equal $37.19, or $20/1.05 + 20/(1.05)^2$. The PDV for Investment *S,* car servicing, is $36.64. Thus, Ed will prefer Investment *H,* or health care.

The relative PDVs of Investments *H* and *S* may depend on the interest rate chosen for the analysis. If an interest rate of 15 percent were used instead in the preceding example, the PDV for health care would be $32.51, compared to $32.67, for car care. Intuitively, the higher interest rate gives the larger and earlier return in Investment *S* more weight. This may be appropriate for an asset such as a car, that is shorter lived, with more uncertainty in its return.

LABOR–LEISURE TRADE-OFFS

The potential uses of Ed's time are illustrated by the labor–leisure trade-off. Our variation on this analysis also helps to illustrate the investment aspects to health demand.

Trading Leisure for Wages

In Figure 5.1, the *x*-axis represents the amount of time Ed spends in other activities—that is, with other enjoyments, T_B. Suppose that he considers his time spent creating health investment to be "health-improvement time" and that he calls T_B his leisure. In reality, he may do some health-improving activities at work, may obtain some enjoyment

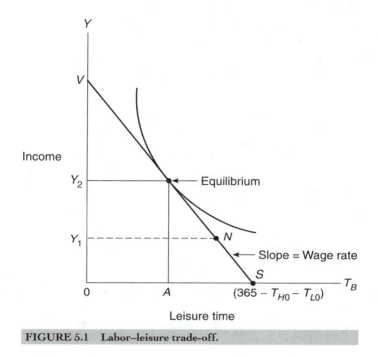

FIGURE 5.1   Labor–leisure trade-off.

or satisfaction from healthful time, and so on, but assume, here, that these categories are exclusive. Assume further that the number of days lost to ill health and the number of days spent on health-enhancing activity are fixed (we relax this assumption later). Variables T_{L0} and T_{H0}, refer to time lost and time spent on healthy activities respectively. The maximum amount of time that he has available to use for either work, T_W, or leisure, T_B, is thus $365 - T_{H0} - T_{L0}$, so:

$$\text{Time Available for Work or Leisure} = 365 - T_{H0} - T_{L0} = T_W + T_B \qquad (5.4)$$

Thus, leisure time T_B is measured toward the right while time spent at work T_W is measured toward the left. For example, if Ed chooses an amount of leisure time indicated by *OA*, then he has simultaneously chosen the amount of time at work indicated by *AS*. These are indicated in Figure 5.1.

Recall that Ed's total amount of time available for either work or leisure is given by point *S*. If he were to choose point *S* for the period, he would be choosing to spend all this available time in leisure, that is, in the pursuit of the enjoyments and satisfactions of life (albeit without the wage income to produce them). The *y*-axis represents income, which can be obtained through work. This income can be used to purchase either market health goods, *M*, or other market goods, *X*. Thus, if he chooses point *S*, he will be able to purchase no market goods because he has no earned income.[2]

---

[2]Income may also be earned through nonwork efforts—for example, through returns to financial investments. We ignore such income here.

If, beginning at *S*, Ed gives up one day of leisure by spending that day at work, to point *N*, he will generate income equal to OY_1. OY_1 thus represents his daily wage. In economic terms, this quantity represents income divided by days worked—that is, the daily wage. Thus, the slope of the line *VS* depicting the labor–leisure trade-off is the wage rate.

Preferences Between Leisure and Income

The consumer has preferences regarding income and leisure, just as he or she had among other goods in Chapter 2. As before, the consumer would like more income and more leisure, so the indifference curve map is normally shaped. In Figure 5.1, in equilibrium, Ed's trade-off of leisure and income is the same as the market trade-off, which is the wage rate. Here, he takes amount *OA* of leisure, and trades amount *AS* of leisure for income OY_2.

In Figure 5.2, Ed has made a different choice with respect to time spent investing in health status. To illustrate, suppose that time spent on health-producing activities, T_H, is increased from T_{H0} to T_{H1}. Correspondingly, suppose that the number of days lost to ill health has been reduced from T_{L0} to T_{L1}. What effect will this have on the horizontal intercept, the total time remaining for work or leisure? On the one hand, time spent producing health reduces time available for other activities. On the other hand, time spent on health investment increases health stock and in turn reduces time lost to illness.

If the net effect is a gain in available time, then this illustrates the pure investment aspect of health demand. The health investments "pay off" in terms that not only add to potential leisure but that also increase the potential income, shifting the income–leisure

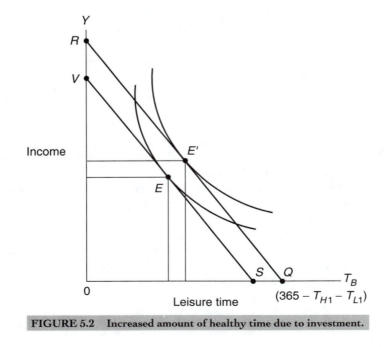

FIGURE 5.2 Increased amount of healthy time due to investment.

curve outward from *VS* to *RQ*. The expenditure of time (and medical care too) for health-producing activities may *later on* improve Ed's available hours (because he is sick less) of productive activity.

As a result of his investment, Ed can increase his utility, moving from point *E* to point *E'*. Not only does investment in health lead to his feeling better, but it also leads to more future income and may lead to more leisure as well!

The improvement in health status might also increase Ed's productivity at work, perhaps resulting in a higher wage and thus a steeper income–leisure curve. In any case, it is clear that Ed might wish to engage in activities to improve his health, even if the only value of health is its effect on his ability to earn future income.

THE INVESTMENT/CONSUMPTION ASPECTS OF HEALTH

The Grossman model describes how the consumer simultaneously makes choices over many periods or years. It is also instructive, on occasion, to represent a whole life span as a single period. This can show the dual nature of health as both an investment good *and* a consumption good.

Production of Healthy Days

Health is a productive good that produces healthy days. This production function relationship is illustrated in Figure 5.3. The horizontal axis measures health stock in a given period. The greater one's stock of health, the greater the number of healthy days, up to a natural maximum of 365 days. The bowed shape of the curve illustrates the law of diminishing marginal returns (additional resources have decreasing marginal impacts on the output). Note also the concept of a health stock minimum shown as H_{min}. At this point, production of healthy days drops to zero, indicating death.

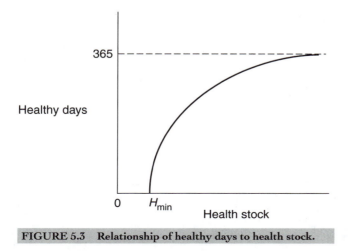

FIGURE 5.3   Relationship of healthy days to health stock.

Production of Health and Home Goods

Consider the possibilities for producing health H and home good B, given the total amount of time available. Figure 5.4 shows this production possibilities trade-off. Note that the curve differs from the usual production possibilities curve in several respects. First, from point A to point C, increments to health increase the amounts of both home good B and health H attainable. It is necessary to increase health beyond H_{min} in order to obtain income and leisure time from which to produce B.

Moving along the production possibilities curve, Ed Kramer is shifting his uses of available time and is distributing his purchases of market goods. Thus, the move from E to C indicates that he has made more time available for health and that this move has reaped the side benefit (increased leisure time) of increasing the availability of market goods and time used to increase production of bread.

Suppose that Ed gets no psychic benefit at all from health; that is, health is desired solely for its effect on the ability to produce B. This would imply that his indifference curves between H and B would be vertical lines (Ed places no intrinsic value on H, so he would not trade any B to get additional health). In such a case, he would maximize his utility by producing as much B as possible. The utility-maximizing choice would be at point C, a point of tangency between indifference curve U_1 and the production possibilities curve. He produces amount B_O of the home good, and H_O of health.

Now assume instead that Ed achieves utility not only from producing B, but also directly from health itself (he likes feeling better). In this case, his indifference curves U_2 have the more familiar shape in Figure 5.4, sloping downward from left to right. It is more realistic to say that he values health both as a consumption good, as is shown in Figure 5.4, *and* as an investment in productive capacity. The former suggests that he enjoys feeling healthy; the latter, that feeling healthy makes him more productive, thus allowing him to earn more. In general, by including Ed's "feeling healthy" in this consumption feature of the model, he will choose a higher health stock than under the pure investment model. Health stock H_1 exceeds H_0 in Figure 5.4. This is achieved by Ed's taking less home good, or $B_1 < B_0$.

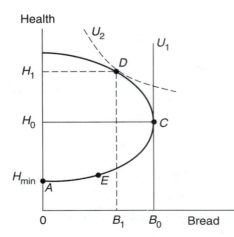

FIGURE 5.4   **Allocation of resources between health and bread.**

INVESTMENT OVER TIME

Choices are made for the many periods over one's life cycle, rather than just for one representative period. As a beginning point for each analysis, we feature the pure investment version of the model (point *C* in Figure 5.4). We then discuss the analytical changes when consumers, in addition, value health intrinsically (point *D* in Figure 5.4).

Since health is a capital good, it is necessary to understand the cost of capital as well as the capital good demand process. A health clinic, for example, purchases thousands of dollars of X-ray equipment. The return to the X-ray equipment is in the future earnings that ownership of the equipment can provide.

Suppose that an X-ray machine costs $50,000, and that its price does not change over time. Suppose that the annual income attributable to the use of the X-ray machine is $10,000. Is purchasing the machine a good investment? Consider the alternative: Instead of purchasing the X-ray machine, the clinic could have put the $50,000 in a savings account, at 5 percent interest, yielding the following:

$$50,000 \cdot 1.05 = 52,500, \text{ at the end of Year 1.}$$

$$52,500 \cdot 1.05 = 55,125, \text{ at the end of Year 2.}$$

$$55,125 \cdot 1.05 = 57,881, \text{ at the end of Year 3.}$$

$$57,881 \cdot 1.05 = 60,775, \text{ at the end of Year 4.}$$

$$60,775 \cdot 1.05 = 63,814, \text{ at the end of Year 5.}$$

For the investment in an X-ray machine to be desirable by these criteria, it should provide at least $13,814 in incremental revenue over the five years.

The problem is more complicated, however, because most capital goods depreciate over time. Suppose that the clinic knows that the X-ray machine will wear out (or depreciate), so that after five years, the equipment will be worth only half its original value. The clinic must earn enough not only to cover the opportunity cost from the bank, but also to maintain the value of the machine. For the investment to be worthwhile, then, it must not only earn the competitive 5 percent return each year, but it must also provide enough return to cover depreciation of the machine. This suggests that the cost of holding this capital good for any one year, as well as over time, will equal the opportunity cost of the capital (interest foregone) plus the depreciation (deterioration of value).[3]

THE DEMAND FOR HEALTH CAPITAL

Conventional economic analysis provides a powerful conceptual apparatus by which to analyze the demand for a capital good. The cost of capital, in terms of foregone resources (for health capital, both time and money), is a *supply* concept. The other needed tool is the concept of the marginal efficiency of investment, the MEI, a *demand* concept that relates the return to investment to the amount of resources invested.

---

[3]Had the price of the asset changed, leading to capital losses or gains, this feature too would have to be considered.

Marginal Efficiency of Investment (MEI) and Rate of Return

The MEI can be described in terms of the X-ray machine example. A busy clinic may wish to own more than one X-ray machine. But how many? The clinic management may logically consider them in sequence. The first machine purchased (if they were to buy only one) would yield a return as we have discussed. Suppose that return each year were $10,000.

We can also calculate the rate of return, which would be $10,000/$50,000 or 20 percent per year. The management would buy this machine if the incremental revenue brought in covered its opportunity cost of capital and the depreciation. In terms of rates, management would choose to own the first X-ray machine as long as the rate of return, 20 percent, were greater than the interest rate (the opportunity cost of capital) plus the depreciation rate.

If management considered owning two machines, it would discover that the rate of return to the second X-ray machine would probably be less than the first. To understand this, consider that a clinic buying only one X-ray machine would assign it to the *highest*-priority uses, those with the highest rate of return. If the clinic were to add a second X-ray machine, then logically it could only be assigned to lesser-priority uses (and might be idle on occasion). Thus, the second machine would have a lower rate of return than the first. The clinic would then purchase the second machine as well, only if its rate of return was still higher than interest plus depreciation.

The Decreasing MEI

Other machines could probably be added at successively lower rates of return. In Figure 5.5 the marginal efficiency of investment curve, MEI, describes the pattern of rates of return, declining as the amount of investment (measured on the horizontal

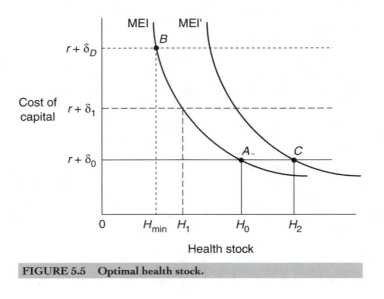

FIGURE 5.5   Optimal health stock.

axis) increases. In Figure 5.5, the cost of capital (that is, the interest rate r plus the depreciation rate δ_0) is shown as the horizontal line labeled $(r + \delta_0)$. The optimum amount of capital demanded is thus H_0, which represents the amount of capital at which the marginal efficiency of investment just equals the cost of capital. This equilibrium occurs at point A.

Like the marginal efficiency of investment curve in this example, the MEI curve for investments in health would also be downward sloping. This occurs because the production function for healthy days (see Figure 5.3) exhibits diminishing marginal returns. The cost of capital for health would similarly reflect the interest rate plus the rate of depreciation in health. Understand that a person's health, like any capital good, will also depreciate over time. Thus, the optimal demand for health is likewise given at the intersection of the MEI curve and the cost of capital curve $(r + \delta_0)$.

CHANGES IN EQUILIBRIUM:
AGE, WAGE, AND EDUCATION

The model depicted in Figure 5.5 provides a useful way to investigate several important model implications. Return to Ed Kramer. How does his investment in health change in response to changes in age, wage, and education? Consider age first.

Age

One may ask in this context how the consumer's optimal stock of health varies over a lifetime. In this model, the person's death itself is endogenous! Endogenous means that this variable is determined within the model, not external to it. Ed chooses his optimal life span, a life span that is not infinite. By this model, all of us, at some time, will optimally allow our health stock to dissipate to $H_{min.}$ This feature depends in a critical way on how the depreciation rate varies with age.

The rate at which Ed's health stock depreciates may increase during some periods of life and decline during others. Eventually, as he ages, the depreciation rate is likely to increase. In other words, the health of older people is likely to deteriorate faster than the health of younger people.

Consider then the effect of aging on Ed's optimal health stock. Return to Figure 5.5. We assume that the wage and other features determining the MEI are not substantially altered by this aging. But, by hypothesis, the depreciation rate, δ, increases with age from δ_0 to δ_1 and ultimately to δ_D. These assumptions imply that the optimal health stock decreases with age.

This situation is shown in Figure 5.5 by the fact that the optimal health at the younger age, H_0, is greater than H_1, the optimal stock at the older age. Higher depreciation rates increase the cost of holding health capital stock. We adjust to this by holding greater amount of health in periods when health is less costly. In very old age, health depreciation rates are extremely high, δ_D, and optimal health stock falls to H_{min} at point B.

This conclusion is consistent with the observation that elderly people purchase a greater amount of medical care, even as their health deteriorates. Grossman explains the phenomenon:

> Gross investment's life cycle profile would not, in general, simply mirror that of health capital. . . . This follows because a rise in the rate of depreciation not only reduces the amount of health capital demanded by consumers but also reduces the amount of capital supplied to them by a given amount of gross investment (p. 238).

Other features of the model suggest that people will generally increase their gross investment (the amount of dollars spent) in health as they age. This suggests in turn that the elderly would demand more medical care than the young, as we frequently note to be the case.

Thus, the pure investment model generates the prediction that optimal health will decline as the person ages. Will this prediction change when we more realistically assume that an individual will also value health for consumption reasons (good health makes one feel better)? The issue turns on whether older persons get more or less direct utility from the enjoyment of healthy days. If people increased their valuation of healthy days as they age, this would offset the predicted health stock decline somewhat. But we have no theoretical reasons, intuition, or empirical evidence to suppose that this would be true.

Wage Rate

Figure 5.5 illustrates the effect of a change in wage rate on Ed's optimal level of investment. The wage change will not affect the cost of capital, so the $(r + \delta)$ line remains constant. Increased wage rates do increase the returns obtained from healthy days (8 hours' work will bring in $80 rather than $72, if the wage rate rises to $10 from $9). Thus, higher wages imply a higher MEI curve, or MEI′.

Assume now that the original MEI curve describes the lower-wage case and yields optimal health stock H_0. MEI′, above MEI, shows the marginal efficiency of investment for someone with higher wages. At new equilibrium point C, the higher wage will imply a higher optimal level of health stock H_2 in this pure investment model. The rewards of being healthy are greater for higher-wage workers, so increased wages will tend to increase their optimal capital stock.

The model illustrates an additional rich implication of the wage factor. Consider that when Ed retires, his wage effectively drops to zero. The pure investment version implies that he would change his optimal health stock to H_{min} upon retirement! Once he retires, he would make no further investment in health, but instead would allow health to depreciate until death.

How would our analysis be amended by considering the consumption aspects of health—that is, that good health makes one feel good? First, the retired person would presumably continue to obtain utility directly from healthy days. Thus, optimal health stock would not necessarily drop to H_{min} directly upon the person's retirement, but it would only do so when depreciation rates became sufficiently severe.

Second, if retirees, and those who are still working, obtain utility directly from healthy days, then the only significant change upon retirement would be the pure investment aspects. Therefore, even when we include the consumption aspects of health, we would expect people to reduce their health stock upon retirement. This prediction suggests an interesting field for future research.

Education

Finally, the role of education is of special interest in the demand for health. Recall that education is seen as a factor that improves the efficiency with which one can produce both investments to health and the home good. The effect of education is illustrated in Figure 5.5. Here the MEI curve illustrates the marginal efficiency of investment for the consumer with a low level of education (measured, for example, by years of schooling), while the MEI$'$ curve illustrates the same person with a higher level of education. This model indicates that since education raises the marginal product of the direct inputs, it reduces the quantity of these inputs required to produce a given amount of gross investment.

It follows that a given investment in health can be generated at less cost for an educated person, and thus he or she experiences a higher rate of return to a given stock of health. The result, as shown, is that the more educated person will choose a higher optimal health stock H_2 than the less educated person who will choose H_0.

This explains the widely observed correlation between health status and education. Educated people, ceteris paribus, tend to be significantly healthier. However, this explanation only explains the correlation of health status and education from the supply side, in that it considers only the increased efficiency with which we produce health. One might also wish to explain education from the demand side.

Educated people are likely to recognize the benefits of improved health. They may enjoy eating nutritious food or doing physical exercise. They may recognize the dangers in smoking, and the long-term problems of overexposure to the sun. They may enjoy feeling and looking good. As such, all else equal, they would have a greater taste for health relative to other goods.

The demand for health due to education is difficult to separate from the supply effect of education, which implies more productivity in producing health. Clearly, however, both exist and are important.

EMPIRICAL ANALYSES USING GROSSMAN'S MODEL

In the last several years a wide range of literature has emerged using Grossman's model. This literature examines the separable impacts of age and education. It also looks at the various time components of health investment within families. Finally, the analytical methods permit researchers to examine the impacts of health status (and those factors which affect health status) on the demand for health and health care.

Strauss et al. (1993) examine the depreciation of health capital by using indicators of adult health for men and women in Malaysia, Jamaica, Bangladesh, and the United States. They find that "activity limitation" increases with age; in Grossman's terms, this would imply that health decreases. Furthermore, this activity limitation tends to occur more frequently for women than for men. They also find that increased education leads to improved health, but that the impact of education decreases for older people.

Mwabu, Ainsworth, and Nyamete (1993) examine the impacts of both market goods and time prices on the production of health care in Kenya. Higher relative prices

Rational Addiction—An Adaptation of the Demand for Health

The economists Gary Becker and Kevin Murphy (1988) have provided an interesting perspective on addictive behavior, and are able to describe conditions under which a rational person would choose to consume an addictive good or service. Their work is challenging both because of its economic content and because it challenges our common moral concepts and attitudes toward addiction. It also provides interesting similarities and contrasts with Grossman's model of the demand for health.

Becker and Murphy argue that addictive behavior (as any current or former smoker would agree) must provide some pleasure, or else people would not pursue it. One necessary condition for a good to be addictive, in their model, is that past consumption of the good increases the marginal utility of current consumption of the good. Becker and Murphy conceive of past consumption as contributing to "consumption capital" regarding the good in question. For example, smoking cigarettes presently may entail a "learning" experience, in the sense that future consumption of an additional cigarette becomes more enjoyable. This important feature of their model is also very general in the sense that it applies to many goods and services and does not necessarily separate out those goods that society has made taboo or bad. For example, listening to Mozart presently may also entail a learning experience. It is quite plausible that Mozart symphonies will become more enjoyable in the future as this learning experience continues.

A characteristic of many addictions, however, is that they *are* harmful. Harmful, in the Becker and Murphy context, means that the capital good in the model, that is, the consumption capital, may also have harmful effects similar to a reduction in health status in the Grossman model. Smoking cigarettes, for example, may reduce health and healthy days, and this may reduce the amount of income the person can earn. Such harmful effects are part of what Becker and Murphy call the "full price" of the addictive good.

In the model, a good is potentially addictive to the consumer if a certain pattern obtains over time for the consumer. It occurs when the effects of present consumption of the good tend to increase future marginal utility more than they increase future full price. This pattern is called "adjacent complementarity."

For example, the potential cigarette smoker would choose to start smoking, even knowing that it is "addictive," if smoking tends to increase future enjoyment from smoking more than it increases future harmful effects from smoking. The interesting aspect is that this dynamic model explains why a rational person may choose to ingest a harmful substance, fully knowing its future effects.

In this model, a permanent increase in the tax on cigarettes may reduce consumption by a considerable extent, even though we would describe smokers as being addicted. Estimates of the price elasticity of cigarettes are usually thought to be between 0.2 and 0.7 in absolute value, with some estimates higher (toward 1.0). This evidence suggests that addictive consumption patterns for cigarettes do respond rationally to economic stimuli. How the individual values the present relative to the future determines how reactive he or she will be to the imposition of such a tax. Current researchers are making use of such models to consider the implications of many public health policies regarding addictive behavior. Chaloupka (1991) provides provocative results in applying the model to the impacts of cigarette taxes.

lead consumers to shift among (from more expensive to less expensive) health care providers, and the higher relative prices also move some consumers either to treat themselves, or to use traditional healers. The authors also find that women are more responsive to time and monetary costs of medical care than are men, but that they use medical care more frequently.[4]

Kenkel (1994) investigates health investment through demands for preventive care. He estimates the determinants of women's purchases of medical screening services, designed for the early detection of breast and cervical cancer. Annual use of these screening tests decreases with age, a result consistent with women rationally reducing care as the payoff period shortens over the life cycle, and as the depreciation rate rises. Furthermore, increased schooling tends to increase the use of the screening services, implying more efficiency in producing health.

Grossman's model also suggests ways in which health status can impact demand for health. Wedig (1988) finds that those who are less healthy have reduced demand elasticities to seek care. However, health care declines have no measurable impact on the elasticity of demand at mean levels of health care consumption.

Mullahy and Sindelar (1993) examine the relationships among alcoholism, income, and working. Poor health may reduce income either by reducing productivity, which results in lower wages, or by reducing labor market participation (whether and/or how much one is working). Alcoholism is an illness which reduces people's health capital. Mullahy and Sindelar find the labor market participation effects are more powerful than the wage (productivity) effects in reducing earnings, and hence reducing the return to health. By these criteria, successful alcoholism treatment would appear to have significantly positive economic returns.

Grossman's model has guided cross-disciplinary work to examine other health and family issues. Mauldon (1990) looks at the impact of marital disruption on children's health. She proposes three models based on factors in which marital disruption could impact children's health.

1. In the *health investment* model, marital disruption might reduce resources including family income, parental time, and health care.

2. In the *stress* model, events and environmental factors may lower the child's resistance to injury or illness.

3. In the *selection* model, a child with a decreased initial stock of good health may be "selected" into families with marital disruption.

Mauldron finds more support for the health investment model than for the stress model. Her data reject the selection model.

In short, Grossman's model has yielded considerable insight into the determinants of health and into the allocation of resources (both time and money) into health-creating activities. It has crossed fields of economics, including labor and development economics, and has provided fruitful results in cross-disciplinary demographic and sociological research as well.

---

[4]These papers come from a conference on families, with considerable emphasis on Third World countries. Many of the papers were published in the *Journal of Human Resources*. For more discussion, see Schultz (1993).

AN INTEGRATED FRAMEWORK FOR THE GROSSMAN MODEL[*]

In the text we saw four separate analyses for the Grossman model. In maximizing utility subject both to time and money constraints in a given period, the consumer must do the following:

1. Allocate time between work and leisure.
2. Spend remaining leisure time on health and nonhealth activities.
3. Spend earned income on health (medical) and nonhealth (e.g., baking) resources.
4. Produce health capital that may help in future years.

Although Grossman's fundamental model is complicated, it can be presented, with some modest changes, in an integrated geometric framework. The first three decisions are treated explicitly in this analysis. The investment in health capital is considered indirectly by adjusting the model from year to year.

The Labor–Leisure Trade-off

Consider, then, Figure 5.6. As is customary, the quadrants are labeled counterclockwise, starting from the "northeast" corner. Quadrant I indicates the labor–leisure trade-off with respect to the allocation of time to wage-earning activities. The x-axis going "east" from the origin reflects Ed's entire time constraint; the y-axis going "north" indicates the amount of income possible from the labor–leisure choice. The budget constraint indicates the trade-off (a steeper line indicates higher wages) between labor and leisure in the market, and the slope of the indifference curve U_1 indicates the consumer's subjective trade-off between leisure and earnings.

Ed's optimal division of time between market work T_W and leisure is indicated where the two curves are tangent. Assuming that no days are lost to illness T_L, at equilibrium point A, he has chosen how many days to work $(365 - T^*)$, and how much income G^* to earn for spending on the medical (for health production) and home good inputs that he will purchase. Although the market work–leisure decision may be made simultaneously with the others, it is useful to treat the process in a two-stage sequence. First, he decides how much income and leisure to take in a given year; then, he decides how to divide each of them.

Optimal Levels of Health and the Home Good

It still remains to be seen how Ed will allocate his income and his leisure time to produce the optimal levels of health investment I and home good B. Quadrant II shows a trade-off that looks like a standard production-possibilities curve between I and B, given Ed's time and money resources. As before, the y-axis going "north" indicates money to be spent on market inputs to the home good, or on medical inputs; some of

---

[*]May be omitted without detracting from the flow of the book.

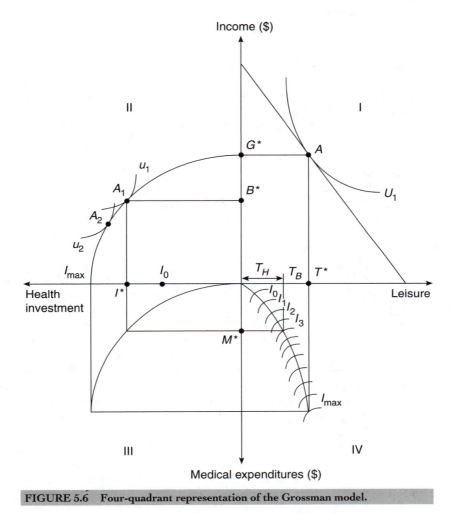

FIGURE 5.6 Four-quadrant representation of the Grossman model.

the money will be used to produce health and the remainder will be used to produce the home good. The *x*-axis going "west" indicates the amount invested in health. It illustrates the premise that Ed divides his time and his money in producing health investment *I* and home good *B*, based on his preferences, and on his productivity in producing both. This production-possibilities curve is derived next in analyzing Quadrants III and IV.

One other aspect of Quadrant II is important for Ed. Consistent with the analysis of health as both a consumption and an investment good, Ed knows the amount of health investment that is necessary to keep his long-term capital stock constant, and thus indirectly to augment it or decrease it. We can indicate I_0 as the level of health production in any given period to maintain Ed's health capital at the same level from year to year, thus replacing health capital that depreciates. If Ed produces more (less) health capital than I_0, his health capital stock will increase (decrease) for future years. The effects of this decision will be made clear in the discussion that follows.

Production of Health and the Home Good

Quadrant IV indicates how health is produced. Ed spends his leisure time in the production either of health or the home good. Although all of these decisions are made jointly, it is again helpful to consider them in a sequential fashion.

His resource constraints can be thought of as an Edgeworth box (as discussed in Chapter 2) with two dimensions. The "width" of the box indicates the amount of time remaining after the allocation of time between work and leisure, and the "height" of the box, the number of dollars G^* of income that was earned. Amount G^* is divided between medical expenditures, M, and home good materials ($G^* - M$). Hence, level G^* is the same distance "south" as the intercept G^* is "north." The amount of money spent on medical expenditures is measured downward from the origin; the remainder is spent on expenditures for home good inputs.

Ed can use his money and time to produce either health investment I, or home good B. The health investment isoquants go from northwest to southeast; the more resources (medical goods M and time T_H) spent on health, the more health investment is produced. If he spends no money or time on health, he is spending all of both on B, and is at the origin. This can be thought of as the highest B isoquant going "northwest" from the southeast corner of the box. Similarly, if he spends all of his money ($M = G^*$) and time (T_H = nonwork time) on health, he is spending none on B, and he is at the southeast corner of the box. The points in between are related to the relative productivity of his time and goods on I and B. An illustrative graph, or contract curve, is plotted, and one can read the amounts of I and B from the appropriate isoquants. All points on the contract curve are more efficient for Ed than are points off the curve.[5]

The contract curve describes, however, only the combinations that are efficient for Ed in producing I or B. It does not indicate how much I or B he would like, that is, his preferences between the two, which are part of the same preference process that determined the trade-off between leisure and work. We must relate these preferences to his possibilities for production in Quadrant II. This involves translating the efficient points from Quadrant IV through Quadrant III.

Quadrant III relates the level of market medical expenditures M, reading down, to the level of health investment, which is plotted moving left from the origin on the x-axis, a production function for I. This is done by reading the level of health investment off the contract curve, and then calibrating the x-axis to the left of the origin with the appropriate level of health investment. This gives the amount of health investment consistent with any amount of M.

---

[5]Technically, Ed maximizes his utility with respect to health H, and home good, B, allocating M and T_H such that:

$$\max U [B (G^* - M, T^* - T_H), I (M, T_H)].$$

The optimum condition with respect to the marginal products of the production function is the tangency of I and B isoquants. As drawn here, the production of I is relatively labor intensive compared to the production of B (isoquants not shown).

Thus, the trade-off between all income G^* and health investment I, to be plotted in Quadrant II, is related to the curve in Quadrant III. Begin at point G^*. An increase in health investment is related to a decrease in market inputs to the home good (or an increase in medical care M). The production function from Quadrant III can be lifted up to Quadrant II to give the trade-off between I and B, and it becomes a production-possibility curve.[6]

The Four-Quadrant Equilibrium

We can now tell the whole story. Ed picks point A in Quadrant I to determine the amount of income G^* and leisure T^*. Quadrant II shows point A_1 as Ed's optimal level of health investment I^*, and home good $B^* = (G^* - M^*)$. Since, in this example, I^* exceeds I_0, he will increase his future health capital. Translating through Quadrant III, amount M^* determines the amounts of time T_H spent on health care, and $(T^* - T_H)$ spent on B.

This framework addresses several analyses in the text. Improved education may improve the productivity in health care, thus affecting Quadrant IV. This would shift out the curve in Quadrant III, and the production-possibilities curve in Quadrant II. This would lead to increased health investment *and* increased B. Improved education may also change his tastes for health relative to home good, as noted in Quadrant II. It may move his preference function toward more health, as noted by point A_2.

We have thus far treated health services and health capital as being the same. Although Ed's health brings him pleasure in the year in which he spends, increases in his health capital may *also* improve his life in future years by improving the amount of leisure available. Since, in this example, I^* exceeds I_0, then he has made a positive net investment $(I^* - I_0)$ in health capital. This increases the stock of time available for both earning and leisure, affecting Quadrant I.

Quadrant I shows how much leisure time is available to Ed. Earlier in this section we ignored sick time. Assume, instead, that he has typically been unable to work, because of illness, 10 days per year T_L, and that this is termed "sick time." On the assumption that Ed does not enjoy leisure when he is sick, the budget trade-off between leisure and goods would cross the x-axis at 355 days (that is 365 days, less 10 sick days). The slope of the trade-off reflects Ed's wage, conditional on his productivity, which, of course, is related to his health.

The health production in Year 1 of $I^* > I_0$ increases Ed's stock of health capital in Year 2. Improved health allows more days for more productive activity. The optimal amount of health capital for Ed is not modeled here (although it was modeled earlier in the chapter), but we can consider succeeding years as succeeding snapshots of the four-quadrant diagram. Hence, the increased health capital from health production in Year 1, if I^* exceeds I_I, shifts out the labor–leisure trade-off in Year 2, and possibly increases its slope (indicating higher wages because Ed is more productive).

The improved health may also influence Quadrant II in Year 2 by changing Ed's preferences between health and the home good, and possibly Quadrant IV by improving

---

[6]It can be shown that if the units of B are defined appropriately, i.e., such that one unit of the home good costs one dollar, then B^*, the maximum amount of B, will equal G^*, and the y-axis can be labeled as dollars spent on B.

his productivity in producing either *I* or *B* or both. Although a complete discussion is outside the scope of the analysis, the Grossman model provides a rich means of analyzing the allocation of resources to health-producing activities, in any given year, and over time.[7]

CONCLUSIONS

This chapter has addressed the demand for health and medical services from an individual perspective. It has treated health as a good that is produced like all others, using market inputs, as well as an individual's time. People benefit from health in four important ways:

1. They feel better when well.
2. They lose less time to illness, and hence can work more.
3. They are more productive when they work, and can earn more for each hour they work.
4. They may live longer.

By analyzing the demand for health in this way, we recognize that the demands for health care inputs, from physicians' services, to drugs, to therapy, are demands that are derived from the demand for health itself. Consumers, jointly with providers, allocate resources among health care inputs, based on the demand for health. We address the specific demand for health inputs in Chapter 6.

Summary

1. It is not medical care per se that consumers want, but rather health itself. Medical care demand is a derived demand for an input that is used to produce health.
2. Consumers do not merely purchase health passively from the market, but instead produce it, spending time on health-improving efforts in addition to purchasing medical inputs.
3. Health lasts for more than one period. It does not depreciate instantly, and thus can be treated as a capital good.
4. Demand for health has pure consumption aspects; health is desired because it makes people feel better.
5. Demand for health also has pure investment aspects; health is also desired because it increases the number of healthy days available to work and thus earn income.
6. Consumers prefer more income and more leisure, so indifference curves between income and leisure are negatively sloped. The slope of the line depicting the labor–leisure trade-off is the wage rate.
7. Since health is a capital good, the cost of holding health for any one year, as well as over time, will equal the opportunity cost of the capital (interest foregone) plus the depreciation (deterioration of value).

---

[7]Goodman, Stano, and Tilford (1995) perform further analyses using this framework.

8. The MEI curve for investments in health are downward sloping. This occurs because the production function for healthy days exhibits diminishing marginal returns. Thus, the optimal demand for health is likewise given at the intersection of the MEI curve and the cost of capital curve $(r + \delta)$.

9. The pure investment model generates the prediction that optimal health will decline as the person ages if the depreciation rate of health increases as a person ages.

10. The rewards of being healthy are greater for higher-wage workers, so those with increasing wages will tend to increase their optimal health stock.

11. Health can be generated at less cost for more highly educated people, resulting in a higher optimal health stock than for less educated people.

Discussion Questions

1. Why do we treat leisure and earnings as ordinary utility-increasing goods?

2. Describe the aspects of health that make it a consumption good. Describe those that make it an investment good.

3. Give examples of how health is produced from market and nonmarket goods.

4. Why is the depreciation of a capital good a cost to society? In what ways does a person's health depreciate?

5. Why might older people's health care expenditures increase, in the Grossman model, even though their desired health stock may be lower?

6. List at least three factors that might increase an individual's marginal efficiency of investment in health capital.

7. Suppose that Amanda Robertson goes on to medical school and becomes a physician. Would you expect Amanda's expenditures on medical goods for her own health to be higher or lower than a nonphysician? Why?

8. From your experience, do you think that the typical person becomes less healthy upon or shortly after retirement? What does the Grossman model predict?

9. People who earn a higher salary can afford more of all goods, including health care. However, according to Grossman, they will choose a higher desired health stock. Why is this so under the model?

Exercises

1. Draw an isoquant between medical inputs and other inputs in the production of a given amount of health investment. What does the isoquant mean? How would the isoquant look if substitution were very limited? If a high degree of substitution were possible?

2. Suppose that no amount of other goods can compensate for a loss in health. How would the individual's indifference curves look? Is this a reasonable assumption in terms of what we actually see taking place?

3. Suppose that a person gets promoted to a job that causes two changes to occur simultaneously: he earns a higher wage, and a safer environment causes his health

to depreciate less rapidly. How would these two changes together affect his desired health capital?

4. Suppose that John Smith could work 365 days per year, and could earn $200 per day for each day he worked. Draw his budget line, with respect to his labor–leisure choice.

5. Suppose that John Smith chooses to work 200 days per year. Draw the appropriate indifference curve, and note his equilibrium wage income and labor–leisure choices.

6. Suppose, in exercise 5, that John's wage rises from $200 to $210 per day. Show how his equilibrium level of income and labor–leisure will change.

7. Suppose that John is ill 10 days per year. Draw the impact of this illness on the equilibrium defined in exercise 5. How will it change his equilibrium allocation of earnings and labor–leisure?

8. a. Depict Sara's optimal stock of health capital at age 18, with a high school diploma, and a wage of $5 per hour.
   b. Suppose that she invests in a college education, expecting to get a better and higher-wage job. Show how her optimal stock of health capital changes by the age of 30 due to the increased wage. Then show how her education would affect her optimal health stock if education also made her a more efficient producer of health.
   c. Suppose after age 30, her wage stays the same. As she ages, show what happens to her optimal stock of health capital, assuming that the depreciation rate of health increases with age.

CHAPTER

Consumer Choice and Demand

6

In the previous chapter we showed how the demand for health care services is derived from the demand for health, and how the consumer produces health. In this chapter, we examine the rational consumer as one who chooses the best alternative from among those that are affordable.

Many might object to this approach at the start, believing that there is little choice for us when we need health care; sometimes little rationality seems possible, at least for the urgently ill. If you are lying on the pavement and the ambulance arrives, do you ask for a list of prices and providers?

Nevertheless, a theory of rational choice over health care and other goods is defensible on several grounds. First, many health care options leave room for some thoughtful consideration or at least some planning. Second, the physician serves as an agent for patient-consumers and can make rational choices on their behalf even in urgent situations.[1] Finally, the ultimate test of any theory is whether it predicts well, and we will show empirically that people, as consumers of health care, do respond to economic incentives.

---

[1]Problems may occur in describing a relationship where the provider, acting as an agent for the patient, helps to determine the amount of care. This is known as *supplier-induced demand,* and is explained in Chapter 8.

The traditional approach to consumer choice in health economics views the consumer as choosing a best combination or bundle of health care and other goods from among the set of bundles that is affordable. We then study how these choices change in response to changes in economic incentives.

APPLYING THE TRADITIONAL MODEL

Because the traditional approach is especially useful in showing how changes in income and prices affect consumer equilibrium, this chapter begins with extensions of indifference curve analysis for health care. This analysis can address features such as health insurance and differences in health status and can formulate demand functions that can be estimated. We then provide some examples of research that consider these features.

In economic theory, the logic of consumer choice is straightforward. The logic is that the consumer can choose any affordable combination or bundle of goods, and from among these affordable bundles, he or she will choose the one preferred. The depiction of this choice thus requires two elements:

- The consumer's preferences—described by a set of indifference curves.
- The consumer's budget constraint—described by the straight budget line.

To make the graphical depiction possible, it is essential to abstract from the multiplicity of goods available in the real world and assume instead that there are only two goods available. Fortunately, the results we get for this two-good world tend to continue to hold when the model is extended to many goods. Let one of these two goods represent a composite of other goods, and call this good Other Goods, or OG. Assume that the health care good is physician office visits consumed during a year, or VISITS. The consumer's name is Ellen Anderson.

The Consumer's Equilibrium

Figure 6.1 depicts these elements of the choice problem. The indifference curves labeled U_1, U_2, and U_3 represent some of Ellen's indifference curves (not all are presently depicted) and together the indifference curves describe her preferences. The indifference curve U_1, for example, represents all points—that is, bundles of OG and VISITS—that provide this consumer with the utility level U_1. Utility is an index of preferences that can most easily be understood as a measure of satisfaction.[2] Since OG and VISITS are both "goods" to the consumer, it follows that indifference curve U_2 is preferred to U_1 and so on; that is, "higher" indifference curves are preferred.

Let Ellen's budget be Y dollars for the period. If the price of other goods OG is P_{OG}, and the price of VISITS is P_V, then the sum of her expenditures, $P_{OG} \times OG$, plus

---

[2]Utility, as discussed in Chapter 2, is an index of preferences in which higher numbers are assigned to "higher" or preferred indifference curves. Utility need not correspond to a physically measurable level of satisfaction, although it may be easier to imagine it as such a measure. In this chapter, calling utility *satisfaction* will not lead to errors in the logic of choice.

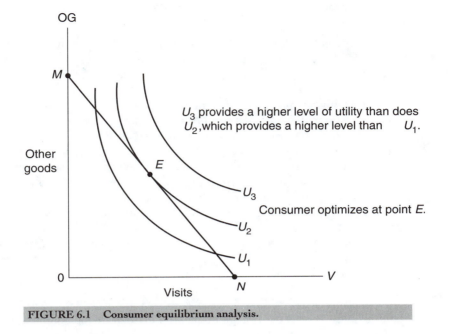

FIGURE 6.1   Consumer equilibrium analysis.

$P_V \times$ VISITS cannot exceed her income Y. To spend all her income means to be on the budget line, which is given by the equation:

$$Y = P_{OG} \times OG + P_V \times VISITS$$

Point M represents the amount of other goods consumed if no visits occur. Point N represents the amount of visits if no other goods are purchased. The budget line is shown as line MN in Figure 6.1, and its slope will be given by $-P_V/P_{OG}$, the negative of the ratio of prices.

The consumer equilibrium is shown as point E in Figure 6.1, a point of tangency between the highest indifference curve attainable, U_2, and the budget line. In contrast, all points on indifference curve U_3 are unattainable, and points on U_1 are not chosen because the consumer can afford points she prefers to these. The equilibrium point E is a point of tangency, meaning that the slope of the indifference curve equals the slope of the budget line at this point.

The slope of the indifference curve is called the marginal rate of substitution or MRS. It tells the rate at which Ellen is *willing* to trade other goods for physician visits. Recall that the slope of the budget line is the negative of the ratio of prices. This is the rate at which she is *able* to trade other goods for physician visits at current market prices. An equilibrium is thus reached only if the rate at which she is willing to trade the two goods, the MRS, is equal to the rate at which she is able to trade the two goods, $-P_V/P_{OG}$. This will have the result that in equilibrium, a dollar's worth of OG will yield the same extra utility as a dollar's worth of VISITS.

Demand Shifters

Ellen's response to price changes can be determined by examining the new equilibria that would obtain as the price of V varies. Figure 6.2 shows the effects of changes in prices at constant income y, dropping from the highest price P_V^1, to a lower price P_V^2, to the lowest price P_V^3.

At the highest price P_V^1, income y buys V_1 visits at equilibrium point E_1. At the lower price P_V^2, Ellen chooses equilibrium point E_2 (with V_2 visits), and at the lowest price P_V^3, Ellen chooses equilibrium point E_3 (with V_3 visits). The amount of visits V increases because visits have become less expensive relative to other goods.

Figure 6.3 plots a demand curve, relating the price of visits to equilibrium quantity demanded. The data come from Figure 6.2. Point E_1 from Figure 6.2 corresponds to point A in Figure 6.3, and similarly points E_2 and E_3 correspond to points B and C. The demand curve summarizes Ellen's response to price changes, holding income and preferences constant.

The responsiveness of the consumer's demand to price is measured by the *price elasticity*. Price elasticity, E_p, is the ratio of the percentage change in quantity demanded to the percentage change in price. Algebraically it is

$$\text{Elasticity} = E_p = (\Delta Q/Q)/(\Delta P/P) \tag{6.1}$$

Here the numerator is the change in quantity divided by the quantity level; that is, the numerator is the percentage change in quantity. Since the demand curve is downward

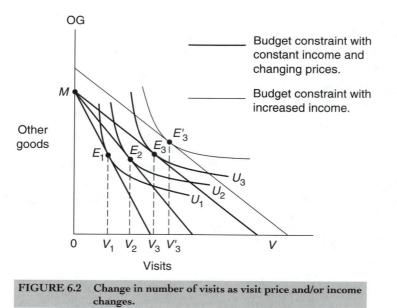

FIGURE 6.2 Change in number of visits as visit price and/or income changes.

Number of visits increases from V_1 to V_2 to V_3 as the price of visits decreases from P_V^1 to P_V^2 to P_V^3.

Number of visits increases from V_3 to V'_3 as income rises.

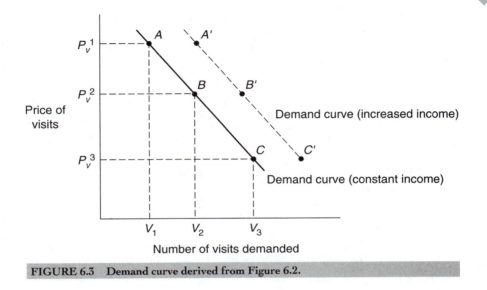

FIGURE 6.3 Demand curve derived from Figure 6.2.

sloping, the percentage change in quantity (the numerator) will always be negative in response to a rise in price. Likewise, the denominator is the percentage change in price. The higher the elasticity in absolute value (the farther away from 0), the more responsive is the consumer to price. Note that (6.1) can also be written as

$$E_p = \frac{\Delta Q}{\Delta P} \frac{P}{Q}$$

A similar analysis develops the consumer's response to changes in income. Returning to Figure 6.2, recall that point E_3 is determined by income, preferences, and price $P_V{}^3$. Suppose that Ellen's income now increases. Since the relative prices are not changed by the income increase, the slope of the budget line is not changed, but Ellen can now buy more of both visits and other goods. Her new equilibrium point is E_3'. This is translated in Figure 6.3 to point C'. We can similarly draw points A' and B' on Figure 6.3 to indicate the impacts of an income change and prices $P_V{}^1$ (new point A') and $P_V{}^2$ (new point B').

The responsiveness of demand to changes in income is measured by the *income elasticity*. Income elasticity, E_Y, is the percentage change in quantity demanded divided by the percentage change in income:

Income elasticity $= E_Y = (\Delta Q/Q)/(\Delta Y/Y)$, or

$$E_Y = \frac{\Delta Q}{\Delta Y} \frac{Y}{Q}$$

(6.2)

Finally, although two-dimensional indifference curves are not well suited to the handling of larger numbers of substitute and complement goods, the effects of changes in the prices of other goods can be analyzed. One would expect that increases in the prices of substitutes to physician visits (hospital outpatient services, visits to other providers) would increase the demand for office visits; that is, an increase in the price of a substitute will shift the demand curve to the right in Figure 6.3. Increases in the prices of complements (diagnostic services) would reduce demand for office visits.

Health Status and Demand

Figure 6.4 illustrates how differences in patient health status can be handled. Suppose that Ellen is viewed in two different time periods in which her situation is the same in all economic respects except her health status. In Period 1 (equilibrium point *E*) she is fairly healthy. In Period 2 her overall health status is lower because she is ill. The change in health status will affect Ellen's preferences (often referred to as tastes) over VISITS and OG as reflected by *different* sets of indifference curves and changed levels of physician care, here point *E'*.

Note that although Ellen consumes more visits in Figure 6.4 when she is ill, in both cases she has the same marginal rate of substitution, or MRS, of visits for other goods at the equilibrium. Indeed, as long as the prices of the two goods do not change, all consumers in equilibrium will adjust to the prices until all consumers have the same MRS.

The analysis thus far suggests that price, income level, tastes, health status, and other circumstances influence the consumption of physician services. There are other considerations, however, that cannot be overlooked. Two such considerations are the roles of insurance and of time.

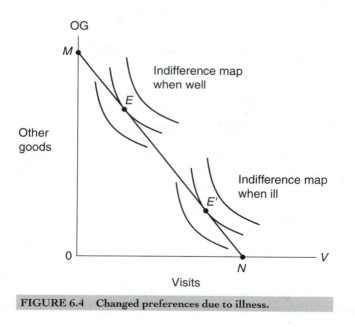

FIGURE 6.4   Changed preferences due to illness.

TWO ADDITIONAL DEMAND SHIFTERS—
TIME AND COINSURANCE

Two other factors distinguish the literature on health care demand. First, the consumer's time represents a significant portion of the full cost to the consumer. Second, health insurance may serve to distance the consumer from direct contact with the stated prices of physician services, hospital services, or prescription drugs.

The Role of Time

Recall from Chapter 5 that time is an important element in the demand for health. The consumption of health care services requires time—considerable time for some services and procedures. Economic analysis suggests that people value their time. Many have had the experience of turning down additional work, even at increased wages. Still others have declined driving across town to save five or ten dollars on an item, even though the cost of driving was far less than the five or ten dollars. Both of these refusals to spend time in return for retaining money occurred because the additional time spent "wasn't worth it."

With an opportunity cost to time, a focus on the money costs of health care ignores a substantial portion of the economic costs. The discrepancy between the total economic costs and the money costs will be especially large for low-priced services, for other services where patient copayments are small, and for a patient with a high opportunity cost of time.

An example of the effect of time costs is instructive. Suppose that Ellen must go to the doctor for a 10-minute visit. It will take her 15 minutes to travel each way (30 minutes in all), 20 minutes to wait in the office, and 10 minutes with the doctor. Suppose further that the money cost of the visit is $25, and that she values her time at $10 per hour. Traveling and parking costs total $5. The full price of each visit is then $40:

- 1 hour of time valued at $10.
- 1 visit priced at $25.
- Travel and parking costs at $5.

Since the money price of care is only a portion of the full price, the elasticity of demand with respect to the full price (including time) will be higher than the elasticity with respect to money price. Leaving insurance aside, a money price increase to $30 represents a 20 percent increase in money price ($25 to $30), but only a 12.5 percent increase in the full price (i.e., $40 to $45). Figure 6.5 gives an example of Ellen's demand as a function of money price.

At money price $25, she demands 6 visits. If the money price is raised by 20 percent to $30, she reduces quantity demanded by 16.6 percent to 5 visits. The measured money price elasticity is (-16.6 percent change in quantity) / (20 percent change in price), or -0.83.

Note, however, that the full price, as graphed using the axis on the right of Figure 6.5, represents a vertical shift of $15 at each quantity demanded. Return to Ellen's

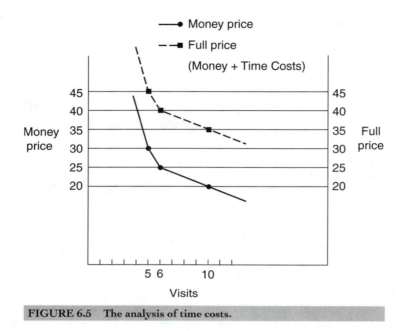

FIGURE 6.5   The analysis of time costs.

demand at a money price of $25, but a full price of $40. A $5 increase here represents only a 12.5 percent increase in full price; this implies a higher elasticity of −1.33. The greater the difference between full price and money price, the more elastic the full price demand will be relative to the money price demand.

The Role of Coinsurance

Insurance also plays a major role in health services demand. Many health care purchases are at least partially covered by health insurance, so that some part is paid for by someone other than the consumer. Although the topic of insurance is covered in Chapter 11, we introduce it here by showing the effect of copayments on demand. Here, as elsewhere, *coinsurance* refers to the percentage paid by the patient; *copayment* refers to the amount paid by the patient. With a patient coinsurance rate of 50 percent, the patient pays for 50 percent of the money price, as does the insurer. Thus, a change in the coinsurance rate from 100 percent to 50 percent represents a change from having no insurance to a case of having an insurance policy that pays 50 percent of the bill.

INDIVIDUAL EFFECTS

Figure 6.6 shows Ellen's demand for physician services without insurance as D_1. The vertical axis measures the price of the service in money terms. At an out-of-pocket price of $30, Ellen consumes 5 visits, as noted at point *A*. However, a 50 percent coinsurance rate, which is applied to the out-of-pocket price, reduces the out-of-pocket price to $15, as noted on the righ-hand axis. At $15, Ellen will consume 10 visits, as

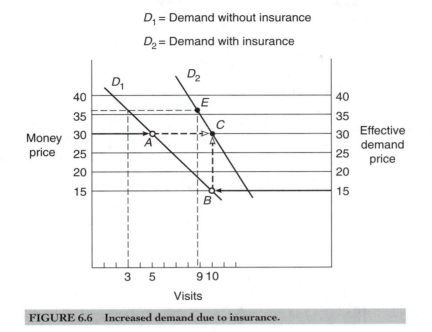

FIGURE 6.6 **Increased demand due to insurance.**

noted at point *B*. Ellen's effective demand will be determined by the price indicated at point *A,* and the quantity indicated at point *B*. The dashed arrows show that the point indicated is at *C*, with 10 visits demanded, at a price of $30.

By following this procedure for other prices, Ellen's new demand curve D_2 is determined. It rotates clockwise from original demand curve D_1 from the point at which D_1 would intercept the *x*-axis. Furthermore, the lower the coinsurance rate (the less Ellen paid), the greater the clockwise rotation until the demand becomes vertical in the case of zero coinsurance (i.e., she pays nothing).

This example illustrates several points about coinsurance and the demand for health care. First, the impact of coinsurance depends critically on the price elasticity. If consumers do not respond to changes in price in the absence of insurance, changes in the coinsurance rate will have no impact on quantity of services demanded.

Second, instituting any coinsurance regime makes the demand curve less responsive (less elastic) with respect to the price. The demand curve becomes more vertical (less price elastic) in Figure 6.6. In effect, the consumer is cushioned from the entire impact of a price change. As a result, the quantity response is smaller for any given price change (thus, the demand is less elastic).[3]

Without insurance, an increase in price from $30 to $36 reduces quantity from 5 visits to 3 visits. With insurance, her copayment increases from $15 to $18. This is the

---

[3]The change in elasticity is related to the level of the coinsurance. A change from full pay to 20 percent coinsurance will have a greater effect on the elasticity than a change from full pay to 50 percent coinsurance.

same percentage increase, but her new quantity, read from D_2, is only a little less than 9 visits (point E). Thus, insurance tends to do the following:

- It increases demand, shifting the demand curve to the right.
- It reduces the elasticity of demand; that is, it makes the demand curve steeper (other things held constant).

Insurance coverage and time costs interact in important ways in the description of health care demand. It is clear that changes in money prices do not address all of the parameters of health care demand. It would seem that if the coinsurance rate went to zero, people would demand very large (or even infinite) amounts of care. However, the analysis of time cost in Figure 6.6 suggests that even with zero copayment, the full price of treatment to Ellen would be substantially more than zero. There have been economic analyses that have argued that improved accessibility (cutting the time costs) is at least as important to health care demand as is lowered prices (or improved insurance). We will present one of these analyses later in the chapter.

MARKET EFFECTS

The effect of a coinsurance change alone, for Ellen, is seen to be an increase in the quantity demanded. Ellen does not demand enough care to influence market prices. Individual consumers are price takers; their individual actions have no effect on the price, so they face essentially a horizontal supply curve.

Suppose, however, that the coinsurance rate is changed for many consumers in the market. For the market as a whole, the relevant supply curve may be upward sloping, indicating that higher prices might be required to motivate producers to offer greater market quantities supplied.

Figure 6.7 shows an equilibrium of price and quantity with an upward sloping supply curve. The original market equilibrium price is P_o and the equilibrium utilization is V_o. In this case, if coinsurance rates are generally reduced, the increased market demand will raise market quantity demanded to V_1 and the market price to P_1. Total health care expenditures will rise from $P_o V_o$ to $P_1 V_1$. Many economists feel that such effects are major reasons for the increases in health care costs in the United States. We address this issue in considerably more detail in Chapter 11 on insurance, and again in Chapter 14 on technology.

ISSUES IN MEASURING HEALTH CARE DEMAND

With the current concern about health care expenditures, it is crucial to have reliable estimates of health care demand elasticities. Recall that an elasticity measures the responsiveness of demand to a change in the value of a related variable. A price elasticity is important in determining the effects of changes in health insurance practices or policies. The effectiveness of public policies that improve the accessibility of health care will depend on the time-price elasticity.

We will find that prices, incomes, time prices, and coinsurance rates do matter. Increased prices, time prices, and coinsurance rates do decrease demand for services.

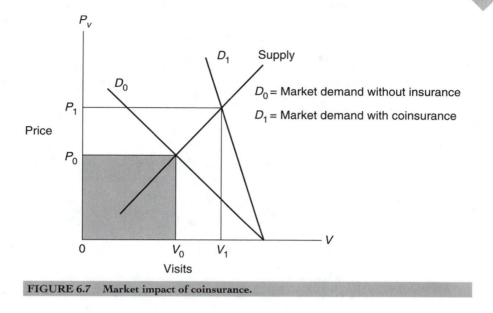

FIGURE 6.7   Market impact of coinsurance.

Increased incomes increase the demand for services. Economic considerations are important in the demand for health care resources.

In this section, we review some of the better studies of health care demand elasticities. We focus on those variables most often of interest to scientific and public policy issues. We examine, in particular, how health care demand responds to changes in money price, insurance coverage, and time price. In addition, we examine the effects on market demand of changes in income and other variables. Each study has attempted to estimate a demand function statistically; all variables thought to be relevant to demand are considered simultaneously in the actual statistical work. For ease in exposition, we consider the important variables separately.

It will first be helpful to review some of the difficulties faced by researchers and some of the differences between the many studies. In effect, we must ask the following question: Why do these reported elasticities often vary so much from one study to another? In almost all cases, the differences can be accounted for by spotting the particular choices the researcher made in the face of problems faced by all researchers in this field. We have identified five such issues.

Individual and Market Demand Functions

Our modified demand analysis has focused on the individual. It has suggested the following type of demand function for physician visits, referred to as V

$$V = f(P, r, t, P_O, Y, HS, AGE, ED...)$$

where P is price per visit, r is the patient's coinsurance rate, P_O is the price of other goods, Y is a measure of income, t is a time price, HS is the patient's health status, and

AGE and ED represent variables such as age and education to reflect other need and taste factors. This functional notation shows that certain variables are likely to affect V, without specifying the relation exactly.[4]

Often, however, economists are interested in *market* demand functions. Care is needed in order to move from individual to market demand. Even the measure of utilization poses a challenge. For example, most studies will use the number of visits per person (rather than the total quantity of visits) as the dependent variable. They then attempt to control for the size of the market by considering total population. This has been shown to lead to serious problems in the interpretation of results.

Measurement and Definitions

Unlike the carpenter's simpler problem of measuring the length of a wall, there are alternative definitions of health care quantities to be measured, as well as many alternative measuring tools. Investigators often measure the *quantity* of services in terms of dollar expenditures. One major problem is that the expenditures reflect a complex combination of price of care, quantity of care, and quality of care.

An alternative way of measuring quantity may be to look at units of care such as number of visits, or patient days, or cases treated. Yet these measures do not necessarily measure the intensity of care. One person may spend five days in the hospital for observation; another may spend five days for brain surgery. Consequently, the literature contains a variety of measures and thus a variety of reported elasticities.

A second problem is in the definition of prices of services. Because of the prevalence of health insurance, most patients do not pay the full price for their treatments. Moreover, the price they pay may be related to the size of the bill because of deductibles, coinsurance, or limits. A $50 treatment, for example, may cost $50 if it occurs before the deductible limit is reached, or $10 (assuming 20 percent coinsurance) if it occurs after the deductible limit has been reached. The statistical problems in this case are fairly complicated, but it should suffice here to note that the resulting price elasticities may vary.

Differences in the Study Populations

Different researchers, quite naturally, often use different samples or populations. Elasticities will differ between populations and even within populations at different points in time. For example, many health economists believe that income elasticities for health care have become smaller over the years in the United States, presumably because of the effects of programs like Medicare and Medicaid.

Furthermore, it is quite possible, in theory, for people in California to have a different price elasticity for physician services that people have in Minnesota. People in one state may be older (for example, Florida) than in another, or have better access to

---

[4]Econometricians often use the OLS method discussed in Chapter 3. In this case, the regression is:

$$V = b_0 + b_1 P + b_2 r + b_3 t + b_4 P_O + b_5 Y + b_7 \text{AGE} + b_8 \text{ED} + \epsilon$$

with the variables defined as before, and ϵ is the error term.

larger varieties of health providers. Similarly, it is possible theoretically that people will exhibit a different price elasticity for dental care than for pediatric care. Thus, some variation in reported elasticities is inevitable even when one uses the same measures, definitions, and techniques.

Data Sources

Even when the population studied is the same between studies, the sources of data may differ in ways that result in different elasticity estimates. For example, one common source of health care demand data is the insurance claim. Such claims data, however, are limited to services covered by insurance and used by the insured. Furthermore, they often lack detail on individuals' demographic characteristics, such as education level, as well as on economic characteristics such as income. In contrast, health interview survey data often incorporate considerable personal data, but their accuracy depends on the recall ability of the person being interviewed.

Experimental and Nonexperimental Data

Much of the health care demand research has used nonexperimental data, cases where the researcher cannot control the environment to assure that other extraneous things are indeed held constant. These data typically represent samples across individuals or markets—that is, a slice of experience. If the necessary assumptions hold for such data, then available statistical techniques can provide valuable analytical insights.

An alternative is sometimes preferred, involving the natural experiment. A natural experiment, for example, may occur when a given Canadian province changes its health insurance plan. The change enables one to observe differences in health care utilization before and after. In a natural experiment, we presume that only the policy changes and all other things are held constant. Unfortunately, often other demand-related factors may also change.

In a *controlled* experiment, subjects can be randomly assigned to treatment and control groups to measure responses directly to changes in the levels of demand-related variables. Such experiments, however, are costly to perform and are not without their own difficulties. Fortunately, we have the benefit of a controlled experiment on health insurance conducted by the Rand Corporation. Where the relevant Rand results are available, we will close each section with a report on them.

EMPIRICAL MEASUREMENTS OF DEMAND ELASTICITIES

Price Elasticities

The central focus of health care demand studies in the United States has been on the price elasticity. Table 6.1 reports a selection of price elasticity estimates for various types of care as well as for aggregate expenditures.

The dependent variable in each of these equations is a measure of quantity demanded. In some cases, the measure used is a market aggregate, such as admissions

TABLE 6.1 Price Elasticity Estimates from Selected Studies

Study	Dependent Variable	Price Elasticity
All Expenditures:		
Rosett and Huang (1973)	Expenditures for hospital and physician services	-0.35 to -1.5[a]
Manning et al. (1987)	All expenditures	-0.17 to -0.22
Physician Services:		
Fuchs and Kramer (1972)	Physician visits per capita	-0.15 to -0.20
Newhouse and Phelps (1976)	Physician office visits	-0.08
Cromwell and Mitchell (1986)	Surgical services	-0.14 to -0.18
Hospital Services:		
Feldstein (1971)	Hospital admissions per capita	-0.63
Newhouse and Phelps (1976)	Hospital length of stay	-0.06
Manning et al. (1987)	Hospital admissions	-0.14 to -0.17
Nursing Homes:		
Chiswick (1976)	Nursing home residents per elderly population	-0.69 to -2.40
Lamberton et al. (1986)	Nursing home patient days per capita elderly	-0.69 to -0.76

[a]Rosett and Huang report that price elasticity varies by level of coinsurance. Elasticities reported range from -0.35 for 20 percent coinsurance to -1.5 for 80 percent coinsurance.

per capita; in other cases, the unit of observation is the individual consumer. Most reported elasticities are in the inelastic range (between 0.0 and -1.0), indicating that consumers tend to be responsive to price changes but that the degree of price sensitivity is not very large compared to that of many other goods and services. Suppose that the price elasticity for physician services were between -0.08 to -0.20 and that physician services prices were to rise by 10 percent. This would reduce consumption by 0.8 to 2.0 percent.

A further distinction among studies should be made at this point. The price elasticities reported in Table 6.1 are each measures of the individual consumer's or the market response to price changes. That is, they are not firm specific, but represent the demand for the health care good or service in general.

The demand for a good or service would tend to be less elastic than the demand for the services of a particular firm. For example, suppose a medical symptom is worrisome and the patient chooses to see a physician. The more worrisome the symptom, the less responsive he or she is likely to be to market price. Which physician to see is a completely different question. Knowing with some certainty the quality level of each physician and the price, one would likely choose the lower-priced physician among those of equal quality. The point is that there are few substitutes for physician care as such, although there are many substitutes *between* individual physicians. Thus, firm (physician)-specific demand will be more price responsive than overall demand.

This point is illustrated in Table 6.2, which reports a few studies of firm-specific demand elasticities. As we observe, these firm-specific elasticities do tend to be considerably higher in absolute value than are most of the overall elasticities reported previously in Table 6.1.

TABLE 6.2   Firm-Specific Price Elasticities

Study	Dependent Variable	Price Elasticity
Physician Services:		
Lee and Hadley (1981)	Physician price	-2.80 to -5.07
McCarthy (1985)	Physician visits	-3.07 to -3.26
Hospital Services:		
Feldman and Dowd (1986)	Hospital patient days	-0.74 to -0.80
	Hospital admissions	-1.1

The firm-specific elasticities have further significance. They indicate the degree of competition in the market. Under perfect competition, firm-specific elasticities will tend to approach negative infinity. At some lower level, the reported elasticities may be large enough so that competition is a reasonable approximation. Even the elasticities reported in Table 6.2 for physician visits would be large enough for some analysts to argue that competition is a good approximation. In contrast, the estimates reported for hospitals suggest considerable market power.

While firm-specific elasticities are useful in terms of the degree of competition in a market, the more policy-relevant aspect is the demand elasticity for services. Two findings are salient. Price elasticities are significant; that is, prices matter. Second, the elasticities are usually between 0 and -1.0, or inelastic. This means that price increases (decreases) will usually tend to increase (decrease) expenditures.

Time-Price Elasticities

We turn now to the demand elasticities with respect to time. Acton (1975, 1976) provides one of the first examinations of the treatment of leisure time. He chooses to model the numbers of visits for various types of care, as determined by travel times and waiting times, as well as by income, and other sociodemographic variables (including race, education, and household size).

Table 6.3 shows Acton's elasticity estimates for outpatient visit demand in column 1, and physician services in column 2. For outpatient care, T_{out} is the *own-time price,* and T_{phys} refers to the other good (*cross-time price*).

Table 6.3 shows that the own-price elasticity (-0.958) of a public outpatient department is about four times as large as for a private physician (-0.252), presumably because there are numerous substitutes. The cross-elasticities are positive, indicating

TABLE 6.3   Acton's Time Valuation Equations

Dependent Variable	Outpatient Visits	Physician Visits
Elasticities:		
Elasticity with respect to T_{out}	-0.958	0.640
Elasticity with respect to T_{phys}	0.332	-0.252

that the two types of care are substitutes rather than complements. Waiting own-time elasticities (not shown) are considerably smaller in absolute value regarding a private physician's office, implying that there are fewer close substitutes.

Subsequent work has built on these results. Coffey (1983) seeks to explain: (1) whether or not an individual seeks health care; (2) the individual's choice of provider; and (3) how much health care is chosen, given the decision to seek care. She finds that a 10 percent increase in time price leads to a 1 percent reduction in the probability of seeking care, while quantity of care is similarly unresponsive, also with an elasticity of –0.1. However, a 10 percent increase in the time price of a public provider relative to a private provider leads to a 4.8 percent decrease in the probability of seeing the public provider, a considerably more elastic response.

Mueller and Monheit (1988) estimate the time-price elasticities of dental care demand. Their results contrast with Coffey's findings in that they find relatively elastic responses to time prices for quantity of care, but only modest responses to time prices in determining whether or not care was used.

Individual Income Elasticities

Conventional theory suggests that for most goods, increased income will lead to increased purchases. Goods with positive income elasticities are referred to as *normal* goods; those with negative elasticities are referred to as *inferior* goods. Table 6.4 reports estimated income elasticities for a selection of studies covering several types of health care. In most cases the magnitudes are quite small. This indicates that while health care is generally a normal good, since its demand increases with income, the response is relatively small.

TABLE 6.4   Income Elasticities from Selected Studies

Study	Dependent Variable	Income Elasticity
All Expenditures:		
Silver (1970)	Expenditures	1.2
Rosett and Huang (1973)	Expenditures	0.25 to 0.45
Hospital Services:		
Newhouse and Phelps (1976)	Admissions	0.02 to 0.04
Dental Services:		
Silver (1970)	Expenditures	2.40 to 3.20
Andersen and Benham (1970)	Expenditures	0.61 to 0.83
Physician Services:		
Silver (1970)	Expenditures	0.85
Andersen and Benham (1970)	Expenditures	0.22 to 0.41
Fuchs and Kramer (1972)	Visits per capita	0.20 to 0.57
Newhouse and Phelps (1976)	Visits	0.01 to 0.04
Nursing Homes:		
Chiswick (1976)	Residents per elderly population	0.60 to 0.90

Income elasticities also help define when goods are necessities or luxuries. We note that when income elasticities are between 0 and +1, goods are defined as necessities (demand is not terribly responsive to income, although it does increase). When income elasticities exceed +1, goods are defined as luxuries. From the properties of elasticities, a 1 percent increase in income increases the budget share devoted to a luxury, and decreases the budget share devoted to a necessity. From Table 6.4, the results are not really surprising; people commonly perceive health care to be a necessity.[5]

Income Elasticities Across Countries

Given these findings, it may be quite surprising that studies that examine aggregate expenditures across countries report substantially higher income elasticities. Often the magnitudes are above unity. A good example of such cross-national studies is one published by Newhouse in 1977. Newhouse regressed per capita medical expenditures for 13 developed countries on a variable representing per capita income. From the estimated coefficient of this equation, he then calculated the implied income elasticity for various levels of income. The elasticity estimates ranged from 1.15 to 1.31. He concluded that despite within-country results showing health care to be a necessity, health care in fact is a luxury good!

Parkin and colleagues (1987) point out several potential weaknesses in most existing cross-national studies.[6] Despite their objections, their improved results tend to support our belief that cross-national income elasticities for health care tend to be substantially higher than within-country results. More recent work by Gerdtham et al (1992) supports the conclusion that cross-national income elasticities are greater than 1.0.

It may at first seem inconsistent that within-country estimates of health care income elasticities tend to be small while cross-national estimates tend to be greater than 1.0. Health care appears to be a necessity at the individual and market levels, but a luxury at the country level. However, these various estimates are not necessarily inconsistent, and none need be incorrect.

How does one reconcile these disparate findings? Individual demand is usually measured for specific types of care, with quality of service and substitutions among types of care strictly controlled by statistical methods. Many individuals use no care, or use care infrequently. As a result, their demand will generally be unresponsive to income changes. What is important to a policy analyst is that if these people are given additional money, their demand response will be small.

A hypothetical example illustrates that income elasticity results at the aggregate level do not necessarily apply to individual behavior. Suppose that two countries, one rich and one poor, each provided free health care to their citizens irrespective of

---

[5]There are also issues of the appropriate definition of income, particularly with respect to short-term versus long-term (or permanent) income. Those interested should examine Goodman (1989).

[6]Three of these arguments are especially noteworthy. First, highly aggregated data such as national income or national health care expenditures do not necessarily imply individual behavior. Second, most studies use exchange rates to convert foreign country values to U.S. dollars, but exchange rates may not accurately reflect the purchasing power of the currency. Finally, the results are sensitive to the functional form (econometric method) used.

income. Then within-country income elasticities might be small if not zero. Yet the richer country might provide greater quantities, higher technology, and better qualities of health care to each of its citizens. Thus, the cross-country income elasticities could be high.

Country expenditures include price and quantity, as well as quality of care, which would certainly increase the expenditures. The measures are aggregates, and the cessation of one type of care might be offset by the beginning of another. This would imply considerably more responsiveness of expenditures in the aggregate than individually. It might also help explain the disparity between aggregate and individual income elasticities as well.

Insurance Elasticities

Consumer responses to changes in insurance are important because insurance coverage has grown dramatically in the past 30 to 40 years and because we frequently must consider possible changes in social insurance. Among such changes is a possible national health insurance plan. While the issue of insurance effects must be treated separately from price effects, it is closely intertwined with the issue of price elasticities.

Consider a health insurance policy where the consumer pays a fixed percentage of the bill—that is, a fixed coinsurance rate, *r*, regardless of other circumstances. In such a case, the net price that the consumer pays, NP, would be a simple multiple of the market price, *P*:

$$\text{Net price} = rP$$

When the market price rises by 1 percent, so does the net price; that is, $(1.01)\,\text{NP} = r\,(1.01P)$. Under such an insurance plan, the coinsurance elasticity would be the same as the price elasticity.

However, most health insurance plans are not so simple. In practice they have many features, often including deductibles and maximum dollar expenditure (MDE) limits in addition to the coinsurance rate. The result is that the effective coinsurance rate—that is, the proportion of the bill paid by the patient—may depend in part on the size of the bill. In consequence, price elasticities and coinsurance elasticities will differ somewhat in practice.

A further difficulty stems from the fact that most studies have been performed on nonexperimental data. One of the major concerns with nonexperimental data is that the groups compared are not always randomly selected. For example, suppose that a company allows its employees to enroll in a *high*-coverage plan or a *low*-coverage plan. Some people may choose to work for the company because it offers the high insurance plan. Others, who expect to use large (low) amounts of services, will naturally enroll in the high (low) coverage plan. Still others, if sufficient insurance is not available from the company, will purchase more generous insurance privately. If the demand analysis proceeds by comparing these groups, the results may misstate the true effect of coinsurance. This is because the major decision was made in deciding *which* group to join. The behavior is known in economics as *adverse selection*.

The Rand Corporation, funded by the United States Public Health Service, mounted an experiment beginning in 1974. Households at six sites across the nation were randomly assigned to groups that had different levels of cost sharing, ranging from free care, to care with 95 percent coinsurance, and including a maximum dollar expenditure limit. The families were paid a lump-sum payment to be sure that no family was made worse off by the experiment. Since the assignment was random, adverse selection could be minimized, and the random assignment of coinsurance also allowed researchers to investigate the effects of coinsurance on expenditures.

They observed family health care use and expense experience over a period that varied from three to five years for various experimental groups. This intensive and expensive experiment was immensely important to our understanding of the response of health care consumers to economic incentives. Table 6.5 summarizes some of the key results of the Rand Health Insurance Experiment.

We note that coinsurance has a considerable effect on the level of average medical expenditures. Going from an extreme of a 95 percent coinsurance to the opposite extreme of free care, or zero coinsurance, the average family's medical expenses increase by nearly 50 percent, from $534 to $777. Even hospitalization rates are responsive, increasing from 7.75 percent of those in the 95 percent coinsurance group to 10.37 percent in the free care group, representing an increase of about 33 percent. We must conclude from the Rand experimental data and analysis that both price and insurance do matter considerably![7]

TABLE 6.5 A Summary of the Effects of Coinsurance on Mean Annual Use of Medical Services in the Rand Health Insurance Experiment

Plan	Likelihood of Any Use (%)	One or More Admissions (%)	Medical Expenses (1984 $)
Free	86.7	10.37	777
	(0.67)	(0.420)	(32.8)
Family Pay			
25 Percent	78.8	8.83	630
	(0.99)	(0.379)	(29.0)
50 Percent	74.3	8.31	583
	(1.86)	(0.400)	(32.6)
95 Percent	68.0	7.75	534
	(1.48)	(0.354)	(27.4)
Individual Deductible	72.6	9.52	623
	(1.14)	(0.529)	(34.6)

Notes: Standard errors shown in parentheses. Medical services exclude dental and outpatient psychotherapy.
Source: Manning et al. (1987).

---

[7]The Rand researchers ignored those households with zero expenditures. Inclusion of such households may move the estimated price elasticity closer to zero.

Other Variables Affecting Demand

The studies we have reviewed often incorporate many other variables of interest in the demand function estimates, and considerable information relevant to policy issues has been obtained. Many studies examine race, and it is frequently found that blacks tend to consume less medical care when other factors are held constant. Similarly, several studies have determined that females consume somewhat more health care.[8]

Studies occasionally find differences due to rural status, though the variable is not always significant. If rural residents tend to consume somewhat less care, the reasons are not necessarily clear. Rural status may be linked to tastes, health status, and other variables. However, rural residents will also tend to face greater travel distances and hence greater time costs. Thus, researchers must control for these related variables.

Education is often found to be relevant. In at least one study that employs a single average education level variable, higher education is associated with lower health care demand. This would suggest, as noted in Chapter 5, that better-educated people use health care more efficiently. However, others have used several categories of education levels and have found the relation to be more complex than can be captured by a single variable.[9]

The correlation of demand with age is clear. Older people tend to consume larger amounts of health care. This result is not surprising to most people, and it is linked to the health status levels of older people, or perhaps more precisely to the positive correlation of health status depreciation rates and age. This again verifies some of the predictions from Grossman's model regarding the demand for health capital.

The link between health status and age is not unique among these variables, however, as there may also be a link between health status and race, sex, and education. A number of studies have attempted to learn more about these relationships by incorporating health status measures into the study. The relationship of health status to demand is clear: Healthier people tend to demand less health care, other factors held constant.[10]

Perhaps more interesting is the relationship of health status to the price elasticity of health care demand. Theory is not clear on this point, but it is plausible that sicker people will tend to be less sensitive to price.

Wedig (1988) finds that the price elasticity of the decision to seek health care tends to be lower in absolute value for those with poorer health status, regardless of which measure is used to record health status. However, no clear pattern over health status can be determined with respect to level of care—that is, the amount of health care consumed given that the consumer has chosen to seek health care.

---

[8]For blacks, see Andersen and Benham (1970) and Newhouse and Phelps (1976). For females, see Newhouse and Phelps (1976), Silver (1970), and Scheffler (1984). Scheffler actually found that while females have an increased probability of entering a hospital, mean hospital expenditures thereafter tend to be somewhat lower for females.

[9]See, for example, Stano (1985) and Wedig (1988).

[10]See, for example, Andersen and Benham (1970), Cromwell and Mitchell (1986), and Goodman and Tilford (1991).

IMPACTS OF INSURANCE ON AGGREGATE EXPENDITURES

Using their estimated coinsurance and income elasticities (each approximately 0.2), Rand researchers attempted to estimate what portion of the sevenfold post-World War II increase (adjusted for inflation) in U.S. health expenditures could be attributed to the spread of health insurance.[11] The answer was "not much"—approximately 10 percent of the increase. All else equal, the spread of health insurance should have increased aggregated health care expenditures by 70 percentage points, rather than the 700 percent measured.

Income increased by a factor of 3 in the period considered. If the income elasticity was 1.0, this would have indicated an increase in expenditures, also by a factor of 3. The income elasticity was, in fact, 0.2, according to Rand estimates, indicating that only $0.6 = 3 \times (0.2)$, or 60 percentage points of the 700 percent increase could be explained by increased income. Adding 60 percent to the 70 percent attributed to insurance, yields a 130 percentage point increase, or less than one-fifth of the entire increase of 700 percent.

The Rand researchers attribute the remainder to increased costs brought on by technological change. Certainly products such as kidney dialysis or organ transplant procedures have improved technology dramatically, at increased costs. The extent to which every technological development is desired, or efficient, however, is still open to question.

CONCLUSIONS

This incursion into the traditional theory of demand for health care, and into the empirical work on health care demand, reveals that a considerable amount has been learned about health care demand. This is true particularly when we include the period of work through the completion of the Rand experiment.

It is important to reemphasize the general findings of the demand results. Price, coinsurance rate, time price, and income all do matter. Lowering the price or lowering the waiting time increases demand for the services. Providing income subsidies to users also increases the demand and hence the utilization. Economic incentives have substantive, although not always large, impacts.

Summary

1. The theory of rational choice over health care and other goods is useful since many health care options are not urgent, leaving room for thoughtful consideration or at least some planning.
2. In addition, physicians serve as the patient-consumer's agents and can make rational choices even in urgent situations.

---

[11]Rand researchers also attempted to measure the impacts of possibly excess insurance, or "welfare loss." We address this analysis in some detail in Chapter 11.

3. Depiction of the consumer's choice requires knowing preferences, as described by a set of indifference curves, and resource constraints, described by the budget line indicating income and market prices.

4. Consumer equilibrium occurs only if the rate at which they are willing to trade, or MRS, equals the price ratio at which they are able to trade the two goods. In equilibrium, a dollar buys the same utility from all goods.

5. Price elasticity, E_P, is the ratio of the percent change in quantity demanded to the percent change in price. Income elasticity, E_Y, is the percent change in quantity demanded divided by the percent change in income.

6. The time spent acquiring services constitutes a substantial portion of the economic costs. The discrepancy between the total economic prices (including time) and the money prices will be especially large for low-priced services, services where patient copayments are small, and for patients with high opportunity time costs.

7. Insurance plays a major role in health services demand. Many health care purchases are at least partially covered by health insurance, so that a portion is paid for by someone other than the consumer.

8. The impact of coinsurance depends critically on the price elasticity of demand for health care. If consumers do not respond to price changes in the absence of insurance, changes in coinsurance will have no impact on quantity of services demanded.

9. Coinsurance makes the demand curve for health services less responsive (less elastic) with respect to the price.

10. Quantity of services is often measured by dollar expenditures. One problem is that expenditures reflect a combination of price of care, quantity of care, and quality of care. Alternatively, quantity may be measured in numbers of visits, patient days, or cases treated.

11. It is often difficult to define prices of services since insured patients usually do not pay the full price. Moreover, the net price paid by consumers is influenced by deductibles, coinsurance, or other limits.

12. Most reported price elasticities indicate that consumers respond to price changes. However, these elasticities (between 0.0 and -1.0) are not large compared to many other goods and services.

13. In most cases, income elasticities are low. While health care is a normal good, since its demand increases with income, the response is relatively small.

14. Coinsurance has a considerable effect on the level of average medical expenditures. Both price and insurance matter.

15. Income and insurance changes since World War II may explain approximately 130 percentage points of the 700 percent increase in U.S. health expenditures, through increased demand for services. Researchers attribute the remainder to increased costs brought on by technological change.

Discussion Questions

1. Discuss the various types of waiting time whose costs may affect demand for health care.
2. Define price elasticity of demand. How does an increase in the coinsurance rate affect the consumer's price elasticity?
3. Why are firm-specific demand price elasticities higher than elasticities for demand in general? Why does a high elasticity indicate a very competitive market?
4. For the following pairs of services, which of the two services would you expect to be more income elastic? More price elastic?
   A. Surgical services versus allergist services.
   B. Heart surgery versus cosmetic surgery.
5. It has been discovered that countries with higher per capita incomes spend more than proportionally as much on health care. What does this imply about the cross-national income elasticities? Why might this occur, even though individual income elasticities seem to be quite low?
6. The frequencies of health care visits are often used to measure service demand. Many, however, criticize the use of this variable. What are some pros and cons of the use of visits?
7. We often speak of how price rations goods. What are other rationing measures in clinics in which free care is provided?
8. Explain or show why the impact of changes in coinsurance rates on demand depends on the elasticity of demand. What sorts of health care goods or services will be responsive to changes in coinsurance rates? What sorts will tend to be relatively less responsive?
9. A profit-maximizing firm finding that its demand is inelastic will necessarily find it profitable to increase its price; therefore, its equilibrium price elasticity will necessarily be greater than 1.0 in absolute value. Are the market- and firm-specific elasticity data reported here consistent with this theory?
10. The consumer's indifference curves in Figure 6.1 indicate substitutability between visits and other goods. What will the indifference curves look like if the consumer perceives no substitutability? What will happen to the elasticity of demand in this case?

Exercises

1. Suppose that Martha's income is $20,000 per year. She can spend it on health care visits, which cost $40 per visit, or on groceries (standing for all other goods), which cost $50 per bag of groceries. Draw Martha's budget constraint. Using indifference curves, show Martha's optimum, if she buys 300 bags of groceries per year.
2. Suppose that Martha's income rises to $21,000 per year, and that she increases her consumption of health care visits by five visits. Using the graphs for Exercise 1,

draw the new equilibrium. What is her income elasticity of demand for health care visits?

3. Consider the following information on Alfred's demand for visits per year to his health clinic, if his health insurance does not cover (100 percent coinsurance) clinic visits.

P	Q
5	9
10	9
15	9
20	8
25	7
30	6
35	5
40	4

Alfred has been paying $30 per visit. How many visits does he make per year? Draw his demand curve.

What happens to his demand curve if the insurance company institutes a 40 percent coinsurance feature (Alfred pays 40 percent of the price of each visit). What is his new equilibrium demand?

4. Suppose that a consumer makes V_o physician visits each year at a price of P_o. If the price elasticity is -0.4, what will happen to the number of visits, if the price rises by 10 percent? What will happen to total physician expenditures? Why?

5. If the price elasticity of demand is -0.5 and the income elasticity is +0.3, then what will be the effect of a simultaneous 10 percent increase in price, and 10 percent increase in income on health expenditures?

6. Draw a diagram for hospital care that reflects the income-elasticity estimates found empirically. As income increases, what happens to the proportion of income spent on hospital care?

7. Would the opportunity cost of waiting time be higher for higher-income people or lower-income people? Given your answer, for which income group would money price tend to be a smaller portion of the full price?

Part Three: Information

CHAPTER 7

Asymmetric Information and Agency

- ■ Overview of Information Issues
- ■ Asymmetric Information
- ■ Application of the Lemons Principle: Health Insurance
- ■ The Agency Relationship
- ■ Consumer Information, Prices, and Quality
- ■ Conclusions

T he traditional theory of demand, as we have seen, begins with the assumption that individuals are fully informed about prices, quantities, and the relationships of medical care and other inputs to their levels of health. We examined decision making within a model that assumed perfect information. Depending upon the purpose of the model, such an assumption may be justified even if it is not realistic. However, a more complete understanding of the health economy requires particular insight into the effects of various informational problems in health care markets.[1]

Though imperfect information has long been regarded as prevalent throughout the health economy, until recently, insight into its specific effects has been lacking. The economics of information has emerged as a distinct specialty, and needed tools to study informational problems have developed. Health economics has been greatly enhanced by the study of asymmetric information and agency relationships. The former encompasses situations where buyers and sellers have different levels of information; the latter concerns situations where, for lack of information, buyers or sellers rely on other parties to help make decisions.

---

[1]The emergence of health economics as a distinct field is often traced to Kenneth J. Arrow's (1963) seminal article, "Uncertainty and the Welfare Economics of Medical Care." Arrow emphasized the role of imperfect information and uncertainty, especially the features of health care markets due to the "imperfect marketability of information."

OVERVIEW OF INFORMATION ISSUES

The markets for many health care services and for insurance, especially but not exclusively in the health economy, are marked by significant degrees of asymmetric information and agency. Our study of these markets would be deficient if we did not account for these features. Many characteristics of the health care sector can be understood as problems of asymmetric information and agency. These characteristics include both institutional features as well as behaviors of buyers and sellers.

Apart from its relevance to demand, other important market features can be attributed to information problems. These include the possible preference for health care delivery by nonprofit hospitals and nursing homes (Chapter 18) and the phenomenon of adverse selection. The former has been attributed to patients' lack of information and inability to discern quality. For some patients, a nonprofit status might be taken as reassurance of higher quality, with caring and decisions made independent of a profit motive.[2]

Adverse selection, a second kind of information problem, arises because the beneficiary has better information than the insurer about his own health status and expected demand for health care. As a result, premiums for higher-risk patients will be underpriced so that these patients tend to overinsure while the opposite holds for lower-risk patients. Consequently, adverse selection reduces the efficiency of health insurance markets.

The present chapter is the first of four chapters that develop themes in health economics with the information problem. This chapter introduces the nature of information asymmetry, its relative prevalence and consequences in the health sector, and the rise of the agency relationship and related health economic issues including adverse selection in health insurance. It quickly becomes clear that adverse selection is only one special case of the more general phenomenon of asymmetric information so common in health care markets.

A second important case is taken up in Chapter 8 where the controversial issue of the supplier-induced demand (SID) is treated as an information and agency issue. A third chapter with ties to information theory is Chapter 9 on advertising. Finally, the last chapter in this book section (Chapter 10) treats as an information problem the issue of *small area variations,* a phenomenon relating to the wide interarea variations observed in the per capita utilization rates of many medical and surgical procedures.

This chapter will provide an introduction to the basics of asymmetric information and agency and will discuss related issues. A major goal of our work is to focus on a careful study of how imperfect information may affect the functioning of markets. An equally important goal is to identify and discuss the institutional arrangements that commonly evolve to reduce the disadvantages for the less informed parties.

---

[2]Lack of quality information is thought also to be an important motive for licensure and various quality assurance schemes.

ASYMMETRIC INFORMATION

Basic microeconomic theory usually includes an assumption that the market being analyzed exhibits perfect information. Under conditions of perfect information, all decision makers, meaning all consumers and producers, have complete information on all prices as well as the quality of any good or service available in the market. Consumers will also be as well informed about the product as the seller.

Obviously, information is never perfect in the real world. However, theories in many disciplines are necessarily developed with concepts that are rarely or never actually obtained in practice. Examples from other sciences include the idea of a perfect vacuum, frictionless motion, or the idea of a geometric point that has no dimensions. In economics, perfect information is often a useful starting point because the properties and predictions of the standard models relying on this assumption are so well understood.[3] The researcher's task is then to assess whether the actual functioning of a given market is close enough to the predicted behavior so that the application of the model is useful, even though all of the assumptions of the models are not fully satisfied.

On the other hand, there are cases where imperfect information does seem to matter. During the past two decades, economists have developed new insights into the effects of imperfect and asymmetric information. This section examines some of that work, including contributions by health economists to the specific problems of the health sector.

On the Extent of Information Problems in the Health Sector

Before investigating several contributions to the economic theory of information, we begin by asking how prevalent information problems are in the health sector. It is obvious not only that imperfect information is prevalent in health care markets, but also that there is asymmetry of information. Levels of information will differ among participants in many transactions, such as between physicians and patients. Often the patient is poorly informed, as compared to the provider, about his or her condition, the treatment available, expected outcomes, and prices charged by other providers. Furthermore, it is our presumption that information problems exist in the health sector that are prominent enough to require the special analysis of the economics of information.

However, while we can agree that information problems arise in health care markets, we must avoid the temptation to overgeneralize or to draw the point too far. To say that information problems exist in the health sector does not mean that these problems are necessarily worse than in any other market. For example, markets for insurance, other professional services, automobile and appliance repairs, and many other market goods and services also exhibit asymmetries. Also we should not necessarily conclude that information asymmetries in health care markets make it impossible for corrective

---

[3]These include not only the perfectly competitive model but also standard theories of monopoly and monopolistic competition that include the assumption of perfect information.

The Extent of Consumer Knowledge

The extent of consumer knowledge about health issues as well as their responsiveness to information should not be judged a priori, but, as shown earlier, are matters that need to be determined through empirical study. Newhouse and colleagues (1981) administered a questionnaire to a large sample of nonelderly individuals in order to evaluate the American public's knowledge of its health care system. They determined that the public is knowledgeable about some issues (e.g., "Two doctors who are equally good at their jobs may still suggest different ways of treating the same illness"), but not at others (e.g., "Doctors are checked every few years before their licenses are renewed"). The response pattern suggested that consumers are relatively knowledgeable about particular health care problems but much less so with regard to general information about health care delivery and about choosing a physician.

---

institutions, practices, or products to evolve; nor does it necessarily preclude the possibility of competition.

Pauly (1978) notes that half or more of physician visits are customarily made for services like general checkups or chronic care for which the patient has some if not considerable experience. From data on the portion of medical expenditures attributable to ambulatory physician care, we can estimate that if half of this care is reasonably well informed, that implies that about 8 percent of total medical care is informed. Reasoning in this manner about all sorts of medical care and products, Pauly concluded that plausibly "one-fourth or more of total personal health-care expenditures might be regarded as 'reasonably informed' " (p. 16). By adding nursing home services and chronic conditions, Pauly (1988a) subsequently argued that this ratio is about one-third.

The second branch of this argument notes that the information gap in several medical care issues is shared by the provider. As we will emphasize when describing the "small area variations" literature, the physician is often uncertain if not uninformed about the outcomes of many medical procedures. In such cases, information asymmetry does not necessarily arise even though it may well be correct that the patient is ill informed.

Finally, economic analysts of information asymmetry problems have been able to show that markets may perform well in the face of some degree of information asymmetry provided that a sufficient portion of the consumers are reasonably well informed.[4] For example, perhaps a majority of consumers who use VCRs are relatively poorly informed about their technical aspects and relative qualities and prices. However, a significant minority of consumers tends to be highly informed. In markets like this, it is possible that the informed minority is sufficient to provide the economic discipline it

---

[4]See Salop (1976) and Grossman and Stiglitz (1976).

takes to make the market perform well so that the rest of us will tend to find reliably that the higher priced VCRs also tend to be higher quality VCRs.

We conclude this section by summarizing its main point. Certainly information gaps and asymmetries exist in the health sector. They are perhaps more serious for health care than for other goods that are also important in household budgets. This makes it useful for the student of health economics to investigate the theory of information asymmetries and its application to health care. However, it may be unwise either to overgeneralize or to extend the claim to the point of asserting that information gaps preclude the possibility of having a high degree of competition. In particular, mechanisms to deal with information gaps should not be overlooked. These mechanisms include licensure, certification, accreditation, threat of malpractice suits, the physician–patient relationship, ethical constraints, and having some informed consumers.

Will a state of relative consumer ignorance preclude high levels of competition? Will health care markets be characterized by a high degree of price dispersion and the provision of unnecessary care or care which is not in the patient's best interests? Can some of the characteristics of health care markets and the evolution of their institutional arrangements be related to asymmetric information? The following sections attempt to address these and other questions by beginning with the pioneering work on asymmetric information.

Asymmetric Information in the Used Car Market: The Lemons Principle

Akerlof (1970) is often credited with introducing the idea of asymmetric information through an analysis of the used car market. Though seemingly unrelated to health care, his classic article is well worth studying for two reasons. First, it tells us much about adverse selection and the potential unraveling of health insurance markets. Adverse selection is one of the keys in our understanding of some major contemporary issues such as the uninsured and the performance of HMOs or other delivery systems. Second, Akerlof's example leads right into the issue of agency.

In Akerlof's example, used cars available for sale vary in quality all the way from cars that are still in mint condition to some that are complete "lemons." Information asymmetry arises, if, as is often plausible, the sellers know better the true quality of their cars, than do the potential buyers. Akerlof devised an example that showed that cases may arise where such information asymmetry causes the market for used cars to perform poorly or even to disappear entirely.

To illustrate the nature of the used car example, consider a somewhat simpler example, but one that retains the essential features. In particular, suppose there are nine used cars to be sold (potentially) that vary in quality from 0, meaning a lemon, to a high of 2, meaning a mint condition used car. In fact, suppose that the nine cars have respectively quality levels (Q) given by the cardinally measured index values of 0, 1/4, 1/2, 3/4, 1, 1 1/4, 1 1/2, 1 3/4, and 2. Under a cardinal index, a car with a value of 1 has twice the quality of a car with an index of 1/2. The distribution of these cars is shown in Figure 7.1, where the horizontal axis shows the quality level and the vertical axis shows the uniform probability, 1/9 in this case, of randomly picking a car of each given quality.

Probability

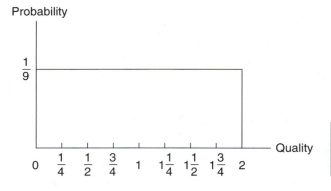

Quality

FIGURE 7.1   The availability of products of different quality (uniform probability of picking each car).

Suppose further that the owner of a car knows its quality level exactly but that the nonowners (potential buyers) know only the distribution of quality. It is known that the owners have a reserve value on their cars, so that Reserve Value to the seller = $1,000 × Q. That is, the owners would sell their car only if they could get at least $1,000 for every unit of quality that the car has. On the other hand, the nonowners are more eager for used cars and value them so that the Value to Nonowners = $1,500 × Q. To make this experiment a complete market, suppose that an auctioneer is hired to call out market prices; sales take place when the auctioneer finds a price that successfully equates quantity demanded with quantity supplied.

DOES A MARKET EXIST?

Consider what would happen here under asymmetric information. Suppose the auctioneer calls out an initial trial price of $2,000 per car. At this price, all owners know it is worthwhile to sell their cars, so all nine cars will be supplied. However, nonowners, knowing only the distribution of quality but not the quality of each individual car, will make a best guess that a given car is of average quality, that is $Q = 1$. They would not buy any cars at a price of $2,000, since they are only willing to pay $1,500 per unit of quality; and they guess that all cars have quality of 1, for a product of $1,500 × 1 = $1,500, which is less than the $2,000 asked. They would only be willing to buy cars if the price were less than or equal to $1,500.

So the auctioneer, perhaps trying to accommodate the potential buyers, tries a lower price, say $1,500. Unfortunately, at this price, the owners of the two best cars will withdraw from the market. Why? The owner of the car with 2 units of quality is receiving only $1,500/2, or $750 per unit of quality; the owner of the car with 1 3/4 units will act the same way. The withdrawal of the two best cars causes the average quality of the seven remaining cars to fall. With nine cars, the average of the distribution was $Q = 1$. But now at a price of $1,500 per car, the best car offered will have a quality level of 3/2, and the average quality will now be 3/4. Potential buyers would now only be willing to pay $1,500 per unit quality × (3/4 unit of quality per average car) or $1,250 for any car. Just as the previous price of $2,000 per car was too high before, again the new price of $1,500 is too high for buyers.

Will an equilibrium price ever be found? Surprisingly, in this example, an equilibrium, one that satisfies both buyers and sellers, will not be found. The reader can discern this by trying several successively lower prices. In the end, the cars will not be sold even though nonowners value the cars considerably more than their current owners. Akerlof saw the problem this way: When potential buyers know only the average quality of used cars, then market prices will tend to be lower than the true value of the top-quality cars. Owners of the top-quality cars will tend to withhold their cars from sale. In a sense, they are driven out of the market by the lemons. Under what has become known as the Lemons Principle, the bad drives out the good until, in some cases such as this one, no market is left.

IMPERFECT VERSUS ASYMMETRIC INFORMATION

To see that the problem is asymmetric rather than imperfect information for both buyers and sellers, consider what would have occurred if information had been symmetric. Suppose, in particular, that both owners and nonowners were uncertain of the quality, that they knew only the average quality of used cars on the market. Again, let the auctioneer start with a trial price of $2,000 per car. All owners, at their best guess, may presume that their car is of average quality, and that the average will again be $Q = 1$. Thus, at a price of $2,000 per car, all the nine cars would be offered for sale. But the nonowners would be willing to pay, at most, $1,500 based on their guess that a given car is of average quality (that is $1,500 per unit of quality, multiplied by expected quality of $Q = 1$). Again, suppose the auctioneer tries to accommodate the potential buyers by offering a lower trial price, say $1,500. If the owners have imperfect information, rather than better information, they will guess that their cars are of average quality, and thus worth (to them) $1,000 per unit of quality, multiplied by average quality of 1. So the owners are willing to supply nine cars at a market price of $1,500, and the buyers are willing to purchase them at that price. The market thus exists, and clears (supply equals demand) if the information is symmetric, in this case equally bad on both sides.

This example is extreme in several respects. The assumption of an auctioneer, the assumption that there is only one price for the used cars, the implicit assumption that the parties are not influenced by risk, and even the assumption that the quality of the cars is exogenously given could each be modified to add more realism. Since the lemons example was published, several analysts have worked on models that modify these assumptions. In some cases this changes the result significantly. However, Akerlof's main point remains illuminating. Phlips (1988) notes:

> Obviously, the example is extreme. It is meant to make the point that the presence of unidentifiable lemons makes it difficult to sell cars of better quality at a good price. . . . The more general phenomenon of asymmetric information coupled with a reduction of average quality of the goods and services traded in the market has received the name "adverse selection" (p. 70).

APPLICATION OF THE LEMONS PRINCIPLE: HEALTH INSURANCE

Adverse selection is a problem for markets involving health insurance, as well as for analysts studying the relative merits of alternative health care provider arrangements. The application of the Lemons Principle to the problem of health insurance can be seen directly with the help of the previous example, which is a mirror image of the insurance problem. In Figure 7.2, let the horizontal axis measure the expected health expenditure levels of a population of n potentially insured people, instead of measuring the quality of used cars. Assume that they have the same demographic characteristics and that their expected health expenditure levels for the insured period range from a low of $0 up to an expenditure level of $M. The vertical axis represents the probability with a uniform distribution (so that the probability of any level of spending is $1/n$). The insurer must at least break even, which means that the premium (or price) received from each insured must cover the insured population's average expenditure and other expenses (including marketing and overhead).

Information asymmetry is likely to occur here because the potential insured person knows more about her expected health expenditures in the coming period than does the insurance company. To illustrate, assume the potential insured knows her future expenditure exactly but that the insurance company knows only the distribution of expenditures for all insured persons.

Again, use the device of the auctioneer to illustrate the point. Suppose this time that the auctioneer attempts a first trial price of $0! All potential beneficiaries would certainly demand coverage at this price. Just as certainly, the insurance company, expecting an average expenditure of $ $(1/2)M$ would require a premium of at least $ $(1/2)M$.

Following Akerlof's analysis, suppose the auctioneer tries a higher price, say $ $(1/2)M$, hoping that this will clear the market. In this case, all potential beneficiaries who expect an expenditure level below $ $(1/2)M$ will choose to self-insure, that is, leave the insurance market altogether, because this premium is higher than their privately known levels of health expenditure. When these healthier people leave the market, the average expected expenditure level of the remaining insured persons, those with expected expenditures from $ $(1/2)M$ to $M, rises to $ $(3/4)M$. Thus, the higher health risks tend to drive out the lower health risk people and a functioning market may even fail to appear at all for some otherwise insurable health care risks.

Observe again that it is the asymmetry of information rather than the problem of incomplete information that leads to this result. If patients were no better at predicting

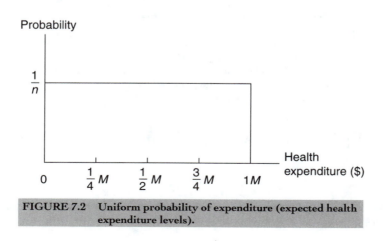

FIGURE 7.2 **Uniform probability of expenditure (expected health expenditure levels).**

their health expenditures in our example than the insurer, adverse selection would not take place. That is, all potential beneficiaries would have expected expenditures of $ (1/2)M$ and would be willing to purchase insurance at the premium of $ (1/2)M$.

Inefficiencies of Adverse Selection

This example illustrates the effects of adverse selection. Analysts of the health insurance industry recognize that even in its less extreme forms, adverse selection will appear. Even if functioning health insurance markets do evolve in the presence of information asymmetry of this kind, the resulting adverse selection tends to result in economic inefficiencies.

What are the inefficiencies? Unlike the example, few people can exactly know their future level of expenditures. Risk is the main reason for insurance. However, if the lower risks are grouped with higher risks and all pay the same premium, the lower risks face an unfavorable rate and will tend to underinsure. They sustain a welfare loss by not being able to purchase insurance at rates appropriate to their risk. Conversely, the higher risks will face a favorable premium and therefore overinsure; that is, they will insure against risks that they would not otherwise insure against. This too is inefficient.[5]

If information asymmetry threatens to lead to inefficiency and even to the elimination of functioning markets in some cases, we would expect consumers and providers to resort to other economic devices and institutions to help to overcome the problem. To illustrate, reconsider the used car example. While the lemons problem in used car markets is real, many economic devices have evolved to help counter it. For example, a buyer may hire a mechanic to examine the car of interest, the seller may offer a warranty, agencies or consumer unions may arise to provide quality information. Similar features have evolved in health care markets. In health insurance markets, beneficiaries are often not covered for preexisting conditions. Premiums for individual policies may be based on other information that insurers use to predict expenditures. They may consider factors such as age, employment status, and occupation.[6]

Relevance to Health Care Services Markets

Aside from insurance markets, asymmetric information is prevalent in the markets for health care services. In most cases, the provider will be much better informed than the patient. That there exist large and extensive markets for many health care services indicates that various arrangements have evolved or have been introduced to deal with asymmetric information. Consider licensure and certification. These and other regulatory arrangements are often promoted as quality assurance schemes.

Another solution to the problem of adverse selection in health insurance markets is to get health insurance companies to use information (and generate information)

---

[5]Of course, in addition to efficiency, there is also a redistribution of income toward higher risks. Equity issues are taken up separately in Chapter 20.

[6]The emphasis placed by many large insurers on employment-based group rather than individual policies is itself a partial manifestation of the problem of asymmetric information. Under group policies, employees usually have more limited choices and insurers have relatively good information about group experience.

The Benefits of Asymmetric Information

Lest our examples suggest that asymmetric markets are always undesirable, Tibor Scitovsky (1990) alerts us to the benefits of such markets. First, by noting that asymmetric information is the inevitable byproduct of specialization, where individuals know more about their specialty than they do about others' specialties, he points out that asymmetric markets are the norm rather than the exception. Second, he emphasizes that the nonprice forms of competition that emerge in many asymmetric markets, such as guarantees and selling through franchises, are highly desired by the public. Perhaps, more important, he argues that intense nonprice competition in asymmetric markets is the major factor in innovation and technical progress.

about their customers and then risk rate their customers: charge groups of customers different premiums depending on their riskiness of becoming ill. Data analysis shows that the welfare loss due to adverse selection can be reduced substantially by using just a few risk factors.[7] If risk rating can pass ethical muster in a health system, then this problem, the authors suggest, is soluble.

Similarly, the health maintenance organization (HMO), a form of health care delivery to be introduced in Chapter 12, is widely seen as a mechanism that limits unnecessary or marginally beneficial care that a fully informed patient might otherwise not choose to consume. In addition to the asymmetry of information, an agency relationship is established under which the patient relies on the insurer to hire or contract with providers who will make appropriate recommendations.

Before we further pursue these arrangements, it is necessary to focus on the overriding feature in the health care transaction. This is the agency relationship between patient and provider, often a physician. The agency relationship is a direct consequence of the provider's informational advantage. Thus, as these selections of insurers and reliance on provider situations illustrate, the role of asymmetric information in health care cannot be studied without an understanding of agency.

THE AGENCY RELATIONSHIP

An agency relationship is formed whenever a *principal* (for example, a patient) delegates decision-making authority to another party, the *agent*. In the physician–patient relationship, the patient (principal) delegates authority to the physician (agent), who in many cases will also be the provider of the recommended services. The motive behind this delegation of authority is that the principal recognizes that he is relatively uninformed about the most appropriate decisions to be made and that the deficiency is

---

[7]Van de Ven and van Vliet (1995).

best resolved by having an informed agent. Thus, asymmetric information and agency are closely related phenomena.

The Perfect Agent

What would the perfect agent do? Following Culyer (1989), the perfect agent physician chooses as the patient himself would choose if only the patient possessed the information that the physician does.[8] This is in line with the medical code of ethics to the extent that the patient's own interest focuses on his health. When any conflict arises, the perfect agent focuses on the patient's preferences, not his own.

The problem for the principal is to determine and ensure that the agent is acting in the principal's best interests. Unfortunately, a divergence of interests may commonly arise.

FEATURE

Agency Problems in Other Fields

Health care is not the only field with agency problems. Long ago, Berle and Means (1932) described the problem of the corporation that is "management controlled." The manager is the agent of the owners, but he may have considerable autonomy in a firm where ownership shares are widely dispersed. Baumol (1967) described a theory of this situation in which he showed the outcomes if the manager operated with a different utility function from the owners. Owners will wish to maximize profits, but the manager may prefer nonpecuniary benefits such as extra staff or amenities or sales. The problem is notorious. It can be solved only if the owners can devise a contract with the manager that assures his functioning as a perfect agent.

This issue of finding the right contract is illustrated in the case of the Department of Defense (DOD) contracting. The problem for the DOD is to establish a contract that induces defense contractors (agents) to accept the contract and to meet its specifications at the lowest costs. This outcome is unlikely to arise unless the DOD can effectively monitor the agent's performance and enforce the contract.

Consider two possible contracts for a new weapons system: one is a fixed-fee arrangement, and the other is a cost-plus arrangement where the contractor is paid on the basis of cost plus a "fair" rate of return. The fixed-fee system forces the contractor to bear all the risks, and it may be difficult to get low bids. With the cost-plus system, the agent has no strong motive to avoid compliance with the specifications, but it also has no strong incentive to be efficient.

Hospital reimbursement has experienced both kinds of contract. The cost-plus system of reimbursement has been the traditional one in hospital care used by Medicare and other third-party payers. Since 1983, Medicare has reimbursed hospitals on a fixed-fee basis.

---

[8]See also Clark and Olsen (1994) for a model and analysis that makes use of the assumption of perfect agency.

Agency and Health Care

Thus far, we have identified the problems posed by asymmetric information as well as the difficulties inherent in the principal–agent relationship. In the process, we have encountered devices or schemes that have arisen to help to counteract such problems. Examples of such schemes are warranties and guarantees, licensure, consumer unions, special manager–owner contracts, and so on. Such devices seem to arise naturally because they fill a void and make participants in the market better off. It seems natural to expect them to arise in markets with information asymmetries. Like Sherlock Holmes's dog that didn't bark in the night, we may be puzzled when the devices don't arise.

As an example, Dranove and White (1987) ask why physicians are not reimbursed on the basis of improvements in patient health. More simply, why are they not reimbursed only if the patient is cured? It would appear that such a contract would be a naturally arising device that would merge the interests of both principal and patient. The authors suggest that the unavailability of such contracts in health care lies in the problem of asymmetric information, although in this case it is the physician who may lack information about the patient's well-being.

To illustrate, take a patient with low back pain. Regardless of her improvement, the patient has a financial incentive to understate the extent of her improvement. The provider also has an incentive to overstate the difficulty in treating the patient and in improving her health in order to increase the payment (which, let us assume, is based on the difficulty of the case). Further, it is these information problems and not other special characteristics of health care delivery that preclude payment based on the degree of improvement of the patient's condition.

Dranove and White further apply agency theory to explain other features in the organization of health care delivery. A feature we commonly find is that patients often establish a long-term relationship with a physician and pay that physician on a fee-for-service basis. As discussed earlier, such an arrangement would appear prone to lead to conflict between patient and provider. It is thus natural to ask the following questions: Why does this particular physician–patient arrangement arise and why is it so common?

Dranove and White explain this phenomenon with an argument based on information theory. They argue that a continuous relationship between patient and physician provides the patient with increasing information with which to monitor the physician. This information places constraints on the extent to which the provider is able to deviate from an agency responsibility. Monitoring also encourages the physician to make appropriate referrals to other providers when he or she is unable to provide the services alone.

We can also add to their argument by further pointing out that a continuous relationship reduces the information cost of transferring information about medical history, circumstances, and preferences from patient to provider. These advantages of the usual physician–patient relationship would be eroded if patients and providers were to switch to limited period contracts under which providers are reimbursed on a different basis.

Other Applications of Asymmetric Information and Agency

Though we reserve discussion of supplier-induced demand until Chapter 8, other applications are found throughout the health economy. Dranove and White further apply information and agency theory to explain other institutional features of the U.S. health care system. They seek to explain the historic prevalence of autonomous physicians, their decline in recent years, and the growth and organization of HMOs. At this point, we investigate two other applications.

CONTINGENCY FEES AND MEDICAL MALPRACTICE

Guarantees of satisfaction are common in the market for many consumers' goods. Most large retailers will accept returns, without question, if the customer is not satisfied. However, guarantees have also found their way into some services such as for car tune-ups and even hair styling. One of the most interesting and controversial examples of a service guarantee is the contingency fee system in tort cases, particularly for malpractice suits. Under the contingency fee system, the plaintiff (party that sues) pays only if he or she wins damages (at a rate that is usually at the legal maximum, about one-third of the award in many states). Contingency fees are possible because, unlike with many medical services, the outcome is clear.

Opponents of this system charge that it leads to unnecessary litigation and frivolous suits. Supporters, by contrast, claim that it provides access to the courts to those with more limited financial means. They also suggest that the client and attorney share the common goal of maximizing the award. Although at first glance this appears to be an obvious proposition, there remain significant problems of agency and asymmetric information under the contingency fee system.

An inherent conflict arises because the rational client would want an attorney to spend more and more time on the case, so long as each additional hour would yield some positive benefit. In Figure 7.3, the marginal benefit curve $(2/3)$ MB, represents the benefit of each additional hour (in terms of additional monetary gain) to a client who keeps $2/3$ of the court-awarded damages or settlement and pays an attorney the remaining $1/3$ as a contingency fee. Thus, the fully informed client wants an attorney

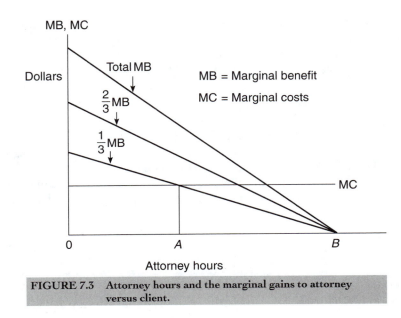

FIGURE 7.3 **Attorney hours and the marginal gains to attorney versus client.**

to spend a total time of *OB* hours on the case, the point at which $(2/3)$MB becomes zero. The attorney, on the other hand, wants to maximize his or her own income net of costs. The attorney's marginal benefit curve is given as $(1/3)$MB and the marginal cost is represented by MC. The attorney maximizes net income at *OA* hours where $(1/3)$MB equals MC. He or she has a different utility function and will recognize that there is an opportunity cost to the time spent. Thus, the attorney will prefer to spend less time on the case than would be desired by a fully informed client. The extent to which attorneys deviate from client responsibilities is not known. Nevertheless, some critics of contingency fees have recognized this conflict and have thus charged that the system promotes early settlement of cases that would be further pursued if attorneys acted solely in the best interests of their clients.

HOSPITAL REVENUE REGULATION

Blanchard and colleagues (1986) applied asymmetric information and agency theory to explain the case of hospital revenue regulation by state hospital commissions. They studied the case in which the Washington State Hospital Commission (principal) regulates the revenues of Washington hospitals (agents). Under the regulatory mechanism that was in place, each of the regulated hospitals submits a budget to the commission. The commission then constrains allowable revenues that are determined by the budget and adjusted for differences between the actual and budgeted volume (measured by patient days). If the adjusted budget exceeds revenues, the hospital is in conformance. If revenues exceed the adjusted budget, there may be a deduction in the following year's authorized budget.

The principal's inability to monitor agents perfectly enabled hospitals to increase revenues by providing biased budget data to the commission. More specifically, the authors assume that a hospital knows its fixed costs, variable costs per unit, and volume at the beginning of a period. The commission determines only the total costs and volume at the end of the period. Thus, when a hospital's volume is increasing, it is in the hospital's interests to overstate the impact on budgeted costs by inflating estimates of its variable costs (and deflating estimates when volume is decreasing). The authors found evidence of such biased reporting and concluded that "at least some agents appear to be acting in their own (and not the principal's) interests and with guile" (p. 14).[9]

CONSUMER INFORMATION, PRICES, AND QUALITY

A further objective of this chapter is to examine the effect of imperfect information on the price and quality of medical services. Would relatively poor consumer information reduce the competitiveness of markets? Does increasing physician availability increase

---

[9]The evidence is also consistent with the *industry capture* theory of regulation. Under the industry capture theory, government regulation benefits special interests (hospitals) that have gained control over the regulatory process rather than benefitting the public interest. Industry capture theory is also relevant to our discussion of licensure and other regulatory controls found in Chapter 19.

competition and lower prices as traditional economics suggests? What happens to quality? How do consumers obtain and use information? Although research on these issues is still limited, several studies provide helpful insight.

Consumer Information and Prices

One of the most novel approaches to issues of consumer information and competition was introduced by Satterthwaite (1979) and Pauly and Satterthwaite (1981). The authors identify primary medical care as a reputation good—that is, a good for which consumers rely on the information provided by friends, neighbors, and others to select from the various services available in the market. Each firm offering physician services provides a service that is differentiated from others. That is, the firms do not offer identical services. As such, the market can be characterized as monopolistically competitive.

REPUTATION GOODS

Under these conditions, the authors show that an increase in the number of providers can increase prices. The reasoning behind this surprising prediction is actually quite logical. Recall that a typical consumer relies on other consumers for information regarding their experiences with physicians. Thus, when physicians become very numerous, the average number of friends who see any provider diminishes; this, in turn, diminishes the average level of information available. The consumer's responsiveness to prices and other practice characteristics depends on his or her knowledge of—that is, his or her information on—the available alternatives. Thus, this reduced information reduces the price responsiveness (i.e., the elasticity) of the firm demand curves, causing the equilibrium prices to rise. The economic idea is that reduced information tends to give each firm some additional monopoly power.

That reduced information enhances monopoly power and reduces the elasticity of the firm demand curves is consistent with standard theory. That such a situation may arise as the number of sellers increases is an unconventional idea. It is understandable if the results run counter to one's intuition. The authors have, however, provided empirical support for their theory, and the interested reader is referred to their work for further study of the issue.

THE ROLE OF INFORMED BUYERS

The degree to which imperfect price information contributes to monopoly power should not be overemphasized. Recall that it is not necessary for every buyer of a commodity to have perfect price information to elicit relatively competitive pricing conditions. Realistically, most consumers lack complete price information about many of the goods and services that they buy (that is, they don't know what alternative sellers are charging). Yet, despite variations in the prices of individual items among, for example, grocery stores, the average charges for a set of items across similar types of stores are likely to be quite similar and close to competitive pricing. There is a growing literature showing that it is sufficient to have enough buyers who are sensitive to price differentials to exert discipline over the marketplace. This is likely to hold especially also where there is the damaging threat of having any systematic differentials publicized by consumer organizations or the low-priced merchants themselves.

Consumer Behavior and Price Information

Several other studies shed information on consumer responsiveness to price and quality information. In an experimental design, Hibbard and Weeks (1989) examined whether patient access to physician-fee information will reduce their expenditures. The authors found that while those who received information had an increased awareness of fees, they did not reduce expenditures for care. One of the reasons suggested by the authors is that patients receive relatively small financial gains from choosing lower-priced services.

The thrust of these arguments is to suggest that while imperfect price information is likely to produce higher prices, there may be substantial limits to this phenomenon. In health care markets, where many services are fully or partially covered by insurance, there are added considerations. Thus, while a patient may become less sensitive to both price levels and price differentials in the choice of providers, third-party payers, such as insurers, have assumed a monitoring function. Through selective contracting and other fee agreements, the actual reimbursement is often lower than the provider's usual charges.

Price Dispersion The distinction between the effective transaction price and a provider's usual charge also obscures evidence of dispersion of fees as distinct from the average level of fees. Under conditions of imperfect consumer information, Nobel Laureate George Stigler (1961) argued that variation in prices will increase.

Building on Stigler's insight, Gaynor and Polachek (1994) have developed measures of the degree of both buyer and provider ignorance by using frontier regression methods. These authors separated price dispersion into measures of incomplete buyer information, incomplete seller information, and random noise. They found that both patients and physicians exhibited incomplete information with the measure of ignorance being one and a half times larger for patients than that for physicians.

In addition, Juba (1979) found that the variations in physician fees appear to be larger than those found in other relatively competitive markets. It is not clear, though, that variations in effective transactions pricing resulting from insurance agreements lie outside of competitive norms.

Consumer Information and Quality

Because quality is not easily monitored, the search for information regarding it can be costly to the consumer. At the same time, the consequences of poor quality care can likewise be very severe. Thus, as previous discussion suggested, despite asymmetric information patients rely on a variety of countervailing arrangements that are intended to reduce their search costs. These include licensure and certification, the threat of malpractice suits, codes of ethics, and quality assurance schemes that are either mandated or voluntary. The public's demand for regulation and licensure, the role accreditation such as that offered by the Joint Commission on Accreditation of Healthcare Organizations (JCAHO), and other arrangements are taken up in Chapter 19.

At this point, we pursue the consumer's direct role through the Dranove and White argument that the physician–patient relationship enables patients to monitor providers and to encourage physicians to make appropriate referrals. To the extent that many specialists rely on referred patients, it would seem that these specialists have incentives to maintain quality. Are they also rewarded with higher prices when they provide higher-quality services? Theory would suggest that if consumers have the ability to distinguish between quality, then the demand for higher-quality providers and thus price should be greater than for lower-quality providers. Haas-Wilson (1990) examined this proposition using data from the psychotherapy services market. She investigated whether the prevalence of referrals from informed sources affects the price of social workers' psychotherapy services. Informed sources include other health providers and other professionals such as school counselors and clergy.

Regression analysis of a sample of social workers' fees indicated that fees are positively and significantly affected by the percentage of clients who were obtained through informed referrals. The evidence thus shows that patients rely on informed sources (agents) for information and that higher quality, as measured by informed referrals, is rewarded by higher fees. Although more research is needed on other services, this work indicates that asymmetric information does not necessarily lead to market failure.

Other Quality Indicators

Luft and colleagues (1990) examined the influence of quality indicators and other variables on the choice of hospitals for patients with seven surgical and five medical conditions. Various quality indicators—such as teaching status, transfer and referral patterns, medical school affiliation, and various indexes of outcomes—were examined. The authors found that medical school affiliation increased the probability of selection for seven of the twelve conditions studied and that poorer-than-expected outcomes index measures were associated with a lower probability of selection.

Studies such as the previous one raise interesting questions about quality indicators and patients' perceptions of quality. The medical literature has been strongly influenced by the structure, process, and outcome distinctions established by Donabedian (1966) to represent quality. Owing to its relative ease of measurement, the focus is often on structural indicators, which refer to the availability of resources such as personnel per bed.

There is, however, an extensive marketing literature that focuses on expressive quality as manifested through caring and communication skills. The marketing discipline has also stressed the credence properties of health care services.[10] These are dimensions of quality that cannot be evaluated, even after experience, and that are

---

[10]See Bopp (1990) and Lynch and Schuler (1990).

thought to be especially relevant to high-skill services. There is considerable interest in the extent to which price, advertising, and other sources of information serve as signals for credence properties.

Finally, despite licensure requirements and other schemes to promote quality, the media has disseminated claims by those within the profession that approximately 10 percent of physicians are incompetent or seriously impaired by drug and alcohol addiction. Consider also reports that some medical doctors are not actually medical doctors but have falsified credentials, work under the assumed names of deceased physicians, or practice without licenses. Though the extent of these problems of incompetence, impairment, and fraud are not known with any accuracy, their acknowledged existence raises troubling questions about patients' perceptions of quality and their ability to monitor quality. The role of licensing boards and other organizations is similarly called into question.

CONCLUSIONS

There is little doubt that information gaps, asymmetric information, and agency problems are prevalent in provider–patient transactions. However, for some health care services, the problems are not necessarily great or larger than those for other goods. Patients are likely to be relatively poorly informed about treatment for conditions that they have not previously experienced and about care involving newer technologies. The informational asymmetries and reliance on provider-agents are likely to be most pronounced in these situations.

However, while there is a potential lack of competition, even wide information gaps do not necessarily lead to market failure. Leaving aside the role of licensure and regulation, arrangements have evolved to enable patients or their insurers to monitor the quality and prices of providers. Furthermore, higher-quality producers are rewarded by greater demand and higher prices. There is evidence that the variation in physician fees is greater than what is found in more competitive markets. Price dispersion data indicate some ignorance on both parts, physician and patient, with the patient being the lesser informed. Nevertheless, because of the use of referrals, accreditation, and other arrangements, the provider's ability to raise prices profitably above those charged by others and to sell low-quality services at high-quality prices is significantly constrained.

Summary

1. Health care markets tend to be characterized by both imperfect information and asymmetric information. Asymmetric information describes a situation in which those on one side of a transaction have better information than those on the other side.

2. Often providers are relatively well-informed (e.g., about the patient's illness and possible treatments). In other cases buyers are relatively well-informed (e.g., the

purchaser of insurance knows more about his health status and pertinent habits than the insurer).

3. The extent of consumer information problems should not be exaggerated. Consumers are reasonably well-informed on about one-fourth to one-third of their health care spending.

4. One possible consequence of asymmetric information is that a market will not exist. Even if it exists, there may be a general reduction in the quality of goods available (the "Lemons Principle").

5. The Lemons Principle appears as the problem of adverse selection in health insurance and other health care markets.

6. Adverse selection results from asymmetric information, not equally imperfect information. Adverse selection in insurance results in inefficiencies through higher-risk consumers overinsuring, relative to the amounts they would purchase at actuarially fair rates, and lower risks correspondingly underinsuring.

7. An agency relationship tends to be formed when a party (principal) delegates decision making to another party (agent). The problem for the agent is to develop a contract or relationship to ensure that the agent is acting in his or her best interests.

8. Various agency relationships have evolved to mitigate the problems associated with asymmetric information between patient and provider. These include the continuous physician–patient relationship and the health maintenance organization.

9. Other constraints, such as licensure and accreditation, codes of ethics and the threat of litigation, limit the ability of providers to deviate from their agency responsibilities.

10. Many health care services are reputation goods. In markets for reputation goods, an increase in the number of providers can lead to an increase in monopoly power and higher prices.

11. The existence of informed buyers helps exert discipline over the market by limiting price increases and price differentials among sellers.

12. Higher quality tends to be rewarded with higher prices. Patients also respond to quality indicators in selecting a hospital.

Discussion Questions

1. The market for higher education may be another example where there is likely to be a high degree of information asymmetry. What mechanisms have evolved to help students in their choice of schools and classes within schools? Do you have confidence that higher-priced institutions provide higher-quality education?

2. The situation where an individual is interviewing for a job also exhibits information asymmetry. Explain why. How does the relatively poorly informed party deal with this?

3. The use of professional and independent buyer-agents to help individuals purchase automobiles or houses is becoming a more common phenomenon. Given the conflict

of interest facing the physician-agent, why do we not see greater use of a buyer-agent who is retained by the patient?

4. In the used-car market there are publications that provide information on the quality and prices of used cars. Are there similar avenues of information available to health consumers? What kind of information do they provide? Is it more or less effective than the information available on used cars? How would you, as a patient, find information about a provider's quality or prices? How would you assess the confidence you have in that information?

5. What is a reputation good? What are examples of reputation goods outside the health care sector? Show what Pauly and Satterthwaite predict will happen to the demand curve for health services as a result of an increase in the number of providers.

6. Stigler argued that the variation in fees increases as buyer information decreases. Suppose that you observe that each seller in a market is charging the identical price. What potentially conflicting inferences can you draw?

7. Why don't physicians guarantee their work as do many auto repair shops?

Exercises

1. Suppose that in the Akerlof example, there are only eight cars ranging in quality from 1/4 to 2 (i.e., there is no complete lemon). Hence, the mean quality level is 1.125. Determine whether the market disappears completely and, if not, how many cars will be sold.

2. Using Figure 7.3, explain how the two MB curves shift if the attorney receives 1/5 of the expected gain. What will happen to the number of hours she would prefer to spend on the case? What will the client prefer?

3. Give three examples of asymmetric information in which the health consumer has information that is unavailable to the health provider. Give three concrete examples in which the health provider has information that is unavailable to the health consumer.

4. In the Akerlof example, the individuals are treated as indifferent to risk. What would you expect to see in these markets if individuals wanted to avoid risk? What if there were some "risk lovers?"

CHAPTER

8

Imperfect Agency and Supplier-Induced Demand

- The Need to Consider SID

- A History of SID

- A Common Representation of SID

- Other Models of SID

- The Identification Problem and the Evidence on SID

- Evaluation of SID

Chapter 6 followed conventional microeconomic principles in developing theoretical relationships between the quantities of health care services demanded and prices, incomes, health status, and other determinants of demand. Put simply, health care was treated like any other economic commodity. But can the demand for health care be studied solely like the demand for food, clothing, and other goods? In particular, can we safely neglect the potential problems created by a consumer's relative lack of information, hence the appearance of markets characterized by varying levels of asymmetric information and agency?

THE NEED TO CONSIDER SID

The literature provides clear answers to these questions. No single issue in the relatively brief history of health economics has generated more interest and controversy than supplier-induced demand (SID). The thesis of SID is that health care providers have and use their superior knowledge to influence demand for self-interests. For many, the SID idea has intuitive appeal and seems consistent with anecdotal evidence. Others support this idea, using more formal arguments involving information gaps between patient and provider and the latter's dual roles as provider-agent.

167

Were this influence not present so that providers typically acted as well-meaning agents who recommend care solely in their patients' interests, SID would be largely of intellectual interest. However, it is commonly argued that providers have actually used their influence to generate substantial demand and subvert the ways markets normally function. In other words, there is great concern that SID can lead to market failure.

As a result, there is also a strong policy motive to study the issue. On this point, Uwe Reinhardt (1989) went so far as to declare:

> The issue of physician-induced demand obviously goes straight to the heart of probably *the* major controversy in contemporary health policy, namely, the question whether adequate control over resource allocation to and within health care is best achieved through the demand side . . . or through regulatory controls on the supply side (p. 339).

Here Reinhardt is questioning whether health care markets function according to the standard demand–supply paradigm. In the standard model, consumers are sovereign and the volume and kinds of goods and services produced respond to independent consumer demands. If, however, consumers' demands are strongly influenced by providers, market forces are much less likely to restrain prices, limit the consumption of care, and allocate resources to their best uses. Thus, if SID is a major problem, Reinhardt argues that regulation should be seriously considered as a policy option.

In the following two sections of this chapter, we provide a brief history of SID as well as a simple and common representation of the phenomenon. We then examine the other more elaborate attempts to represent SID. We close with discussions of econometric problems and empirical evidence.

A HISTORY OF SID

The origins of SID can be traced to contributions by Shain and Roemer (1959), and Roemer (1961). Shain and Roemer found very close correlations between the availability of short-term general hospital beds per 1,000 population and rates of utilization as measured by hospital days per 1,000 population.[1] The relationships held across states as well as across upstate New York counties. The apparent phenomenon was interpreted as a "bed built is a bed filled," and this observation became known as Roemer's Law or the Roemer Effect.[2]

Roemer's Law and the Post Hoc Fallacy

Many economics textbooks alert students to the post hoc (false cause) fallacy. Can Roemer's Law be such an example where analysts have mistakenly ascribed the availability of beds as the cause and utilization as the effect? Consider Figure 8.1 in which

---

[1] Roemer (1961) also reported on a natural experiment where a sudden increase in hospital beds in one county, with no changes in other factors, led to a sharp increase in utilization rates.

[2] The terms *Say's Law* or *Parkinson's Law* for hospital beds as well as the availability effect have also been used to describe this phenomenon.

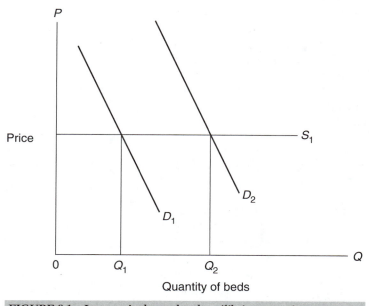

FIGURE 8.1 **Increase in demand and equilibrium quantity.**

D_1 and D_2 represent original and new demand curves, respectively, and in which hospital care including the availability of beds is provided at constant costs as shown by S_1. What happens to quantity as demand increases? It is clear from Figure 8.1, where the hospital market is described within a competitive demand–supply framework, that utilization will be highly correlated with availability not because supply creates demand, but because changes in demand lead to changes in equilibrium quantities. That is, the equilibrium and observed quantity will increase from Q_1 to Q_2. Utilization and beds will be perfectly correlated even though the increase in demand led to the increase in beds.[3]

The principle of Roemer's Law was thought by some to apply as well to physician services, and the general term identified as *supplier-induced demand (SID)* seemed a natural extension of the same basic idea. The underlying notion can be understood as an agency problem in that the reliance of the patient on a physician gives the physician a degree of discretionary influence. SID is not only intuitively appealing but appears to be supported by three well-documented phenomena. First, attempts to impose physician fee controls have often led to increases in utilization. This idea will be further discussed later in this chapter. Second, there are those who claim that the wide geographic variations in utilization rates that have been observed across geographic areas are, in part, due to inducement. Third, suggestions of the potential for

---

[3]Shain and Roemer were aware of this possibility but argued that the close correlations between availability and utilization also held before the large increases in insurance coverage and incomes in the period following World War II.

inducement come from evidence that physicians' clinical decisions can be influenced by financial incentives. For example, Hemenway et al. (1990) examined a chain of for-profit ambulatory care centers that paid physicians a flat hourly wage. After the centers experimented with bonuses that were determined by the revenues generated by physicians, the number of visits and laboratory tests per patient rose substantially. Similarly, Hillman and colleagues (1989) found that HMOs that use capitation or salaries to compensate physicians have significantly lower rates of hospitalization and outpatient visits than HMOs that use fee-for-service.

Not all health economists, however, accept the SID proposition; they are divided into two camps. Those who believe that SID is an important phenomenon are labeled as the "broads" (Bs); those who challenge the phenomenon are called the "narrows" (Ns).

A COMMON REPRESENTATION OF SID

Figure 8.2 illustrates a commonly used model to explain SID as well as to distinguish between the Ns and the Bs. Here, D_1 and S_1 represent the initial demand and short-run supply of physician services with an equilibrium at Q_1. Suppose there is an increase in physician supply to S_2, ceteris paribus. The Ns would use standard analysis to predict that the price would fall from P_1 to P_3 and that the quantity demanded would increase from Q_1 to Q_3. Total spending would increase or decrease depending on the elasticity of demand. For services with an inelastic demand, such as physician care, total spending would decrease. Also, because there are more physicians dividing up a smaller pie, the typical physician's share of patients and earnings will also diminish.

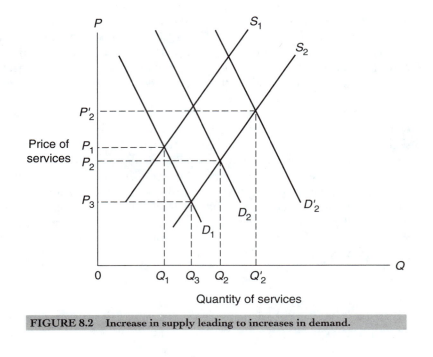

FIGURE 8.2 Increase in supply leading to increases in demand.

According to the Bs, however, an increase in supply leads directly to an increase in demand through the SID effect. Physicians are motivated by what otherwise would be a loss of patients and earnings to use their discretionary influence to shift demand. That is, demand will not remain independent and stable at D_1 but will be shifted out. Where it increases to a level such as D_2, the equilibrium price declines to P_2 with equilibrium quantity Q_2. However, if the increased demand is sufficiently large, such as shown by the shift to D_2', the equilibrium price may even rise above the initial level to P_2' with equilibrium quantity Q_2'.

Thus, as shown through Figure 8.2, the new equilibrium fee may be lower or higher under this view of SID. The case where the fee becomes higher came to be called the Reinhardt fee test of inducement. Under this test, evidence that fee increases follow increases in supply is interpreted as unequivocal support of the SID proposition.[4]

Correlations Between Physician Availability and Utilization

Much of the early empirical support for SID, however, came not from evidence regarding fees but from studies showing correlations (either simple or through multiple regression analysis) between physician availability and utilization rates. Although this evidence is consistent with SID, it is also consistent with standard analysis, as can be seen in Figure 8.2. Note that the equilibrium quantity of health care is larger after the supply curve shifts outward—regardless of whether or not the demand curve also shifts outward. Unless the study carefully distinguishes between shifts in demand versus a movement along a demand curve, the evidence of positive correlations does not support one theory over another.

Furthermore, even evidence that determines that demand has shifted somewhat following increases in supply is consistent with traditional economic arguments. An explanation of a demand shift is plausible under standard theory when the opportunity cost of patient travel times is a significant component of total cost. When increases in physician availability reduce travel times or waiting times, one would predict that the demand will increase. Furthermore, if increases in availability also lead to improvements in the quality of care, this too will shift the demand curve.

Theoretical Problems with the Commonly Used SID Model

There is another difficulty with the model of SID as described graphically through Figure 8.2. Using demand and supply implies that SID occurs in a competitive market in the sense that prices adjust to their equilibrium levels so that the market clears. However, it is difficult to construct an economically meaningful competitive model with SID. To illustrate the conceptual challenge, return to Figure 8.2. Following a shift in supply to S_2, suppose that the price immediately drops to P_3. At this price, by providing the quantity of services on the original demand curve D_1, suppliers will be on their supply curves. To be on one's supply curve means to produce and offer the

---

[4]Recall though from Chapter 7 that the Pauly/Satterthwaite consumer information model offers an alternative explanation of higher fees.

quantities one wishes to provide. In other words, there is no motive to induce demand when prices rapidly adjust to market clearing levels. The motive and mechanism for inducement have not been made clear within the context of the demand–supply paradigm in Figure 8.2.

OTHER MODELS OF SID

Thus, the attempt to describe a simple intuitive notion of SID in the familiar context of a competitive market raises important questions that must be answered by a better working model. What is the motive to induce demand? Why would providers induce demand to a certain degree at one time and to a lesser degree at another? Why do not providers simply induce fully all the time? What is the mechanism through which they induce demand? How does inducement change in the face of increased supply? To answer questions like these, economists have developed several models of SID.

Price Rigidities and SID

One approach that can provide a logical explanation of demand inducement within the context of a competitive market model is to argue that prices tend to be rigid; that is, price does not adjust quickly to changes in demand or supply. To elaborate, suppose that prices in Figure 8.2 do not drop from their initial equilibrium at P_1 as supply increases. With the new supply curve S_2, there is now an excess supply at P_1 if physicians continue to provide the original quantity of services. An excess supply means that at least some physicians are not on their supply curves providing the quantities they would like to sell at the existing price, and thus they would clearly have a motive for inducing additional quantities if that is possible.

The ability to induce demand depends on the agency responsibility that gives physicians opportunities for inducement. But the motive to use this power and the extent to which it is used depend on the relative gains from the additional earnings versus the costs of the additional inducement activities. Aside from direct costs, time costs are incurred because it may take time to persuade patients to consume more care. There is also a potential loss of patients who detect that the physician is not acting in their best interests.

Thus, while the demand may ultimately be shifted to the right, there is no way of theoretically determining just how far to the right. It depends upon the relationship between the incremental earnings and incremental inducement costs. If the incremental costs of inducement are relatively large, because of serious damage to a physician's reputation, then we would expect very little or no inducement. If it is easy to persuade patients to consume more services and there are minimal professional and ethical constraints, then the demand shift can be substantial. We suggest though that demand will never be shifted to a level such as D_2' where there would be an excess demand at the price P_1. Given the costs of inducement activity, there is simply no reason for providers to shift demand to the point where the quantity demanded exceeds the quantity providers are willing to supply at P_1.

Some previous work on price rigidities in the physician services market found evidence of SID.[5] Despite these contributions, however, price rigidities and disequilibrium models have not received wide attention in the literature so that the corresponding picture remains incomplete. Further, the support has been weakened by empirical evidence for the hospital services markets which is consistent with a standard demand–supply model rather than with various disequilibrium models which incorporate inducement.[6]

The Target-Income Model of SID

The target-income model is often used to explain the rapid increases in physician fees experienced in the 1960s and 1970s. These increases occurred despite rapid increases in physician availability. Under the target income hypothesis, instead of leading to lower fees and incomes, increases in physician availability lead to higher fees in order for earnings to be maintained. Consumer ignorance provides physicians with discretionary influence to manipulate demand when, for example, fees are controlled. Physicians also have an untapped degree of monopoly price power that could be used to raise fees and incomes to some target level.

Evidence of physician behavior under fee controls, especially under the Economic Stabilization Program introduced in the early 1970s, has been cited to support the target-income hypothesis. The imposition of fee controls which limited the annual increases to 2.5 percent is often offered as a natural test of inducement.

Under conditions of price controls, several investigators found that utilization tended to increase—evidence consistent with the target-income model. Similar support comes from studies of Medicare utilization in Colorado.[7] In 1977, Colorado restructured its Medicare reimbursement rates by virtually freezing rates for urban physicians while providing large increases for nonurban physicians. Rice (1983) found that the relative decrease in fees for urban physicians led to increased surgical and ancillary services as well as to more intensive medical and surgical care (measured by the number of standardized units per service).

Despite strong initial interest in target-income pricing, this approach has been largely discredited within the academic community. Significant problems arise in explaining how the target income is established and why physicians do not consistently exploit their monopoly power by always pricing at profit-maximizing levels. Note also that the target-income concept is similar to often heard claims that large corporate firms have unexploited monopoly power to be able always to pass on tax increases or increases in other costs in order to maintain profit margins. Such claims, which would otherwise require these firms to price below profit-maximizing levels, are largely unsupported by empirical evidence. Furthermore, if physicians had the ability to target price, it would be reasonable to predict that physicians would have little concern about

---

[5]See Stano et al. (1985) and Cromwell and Mitchell (1986).
[6]See Hay and Anderson (1988).
[7]See Rice and Labelle (1989) for a review of this work.

increases in costs, such as increases in malpractice insurance premiums, since they could always pass the increased costs on to customers in the form of higher prices. Such, however, is not the case.

The Disutility of Discretion Model of SID

To understand the SID literature as a progression of ideas, we should reconsider one of the problems identified with the target-income approach. In particular, we will direct our attention to the problem of accounting for the chosen target. Why are physicians satisfied with a given target income? How can we explain the equilibrium inducement level and income level within the model itself?

A major innovation in this regard was introduced by Evans (1974). Evans represented the physician as a utility-maximizing provider whose utility function is expressed as follows:

$$U = U(Y, W, D)$$

where Y is net income, W is hours of work, and D represents the discretionary influence used to augment demand. The physician has monopoly power so that he or she faces a negatively sloped demand curve that shifts inward as the number of physicians increases. A key feature of the model is the assumed increasing marginal disutility of augmenting demand. That is, physicians, according to Evans, prefer not to induce demand, and find greater incremental displeasure with greater inducement. This displeasure must be counterbalanced by the gains to income that inducement provides. When competition tends to reduce income, the physician may increase inducement to help offset this.

By placing limits on the extent to which demand will be increased, this feature addresses a weakness of earlier SID models that had no apparent brakes on physicians' abilities and willingness to increase demand. In the Evans framework, a physician will augment demand to the point where the marginal utility of the additional income equals the marginal disutility of the added work plus the marginal disutility of the discretionary influence.

GRAPHICAL REPRESENTATION OF THE EVANS MODEL

Several essential ideas of the Evans model can be made clearer with the aid of a graph. To do this, let us suppress the variable W, the work effort of the physician. Work effort was important to Evans's empirical tests, and thus we refer the interested reader to the original article. In this simplified model, let the physician's utility depend solely on income, Y, and discretionary demand, D.

In Figure 8.3, the indifference curves represent the physician's preferences. The indifference curves slope upward because one of the two "goods," that is D, is really a "bad." Can you see why they must slope upward? In order to remain on the same indifference curve, the physician must be compensated for engaging in a higher level of D. As is the usual case, however, higher curves are preferred.

To make the example straightforward and the measure of discretion concrete, let discretionary demand, D, be measured in units representing the number of induced units of service. If these induced units are sold at a constant profit rate of π, and if the

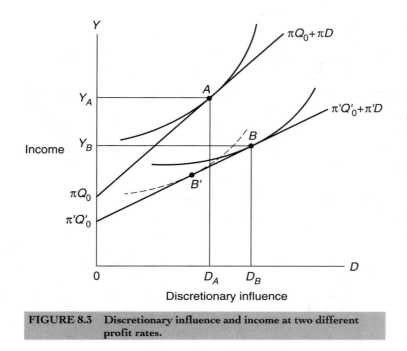

FIGURE 8.3   Discretionary influence and income at two different
profit rates.

maximum profit level with zero inducement is πQ_0, then the physician's total profit (income) can be described by $Y = \pi Q_0 + \pi D$. This equation is seen to be a linear equation with an intercept of πQ_0, and a slope of π. This linear equation represents the attainable combinations of Y and D available to the physician, and thus it represents the physician's income possibilities.

Figure 8.3 can now be used to describe a disutility of discretion equilibrium. In the figure, the physician seeks to reach the highest indifference curve attainable, and this outcome occurs at the point of tangency shown as point A. Furthermore, the figure illustrates the physician's response to increased competition. Let increased competition be represented as a reduction in the average profit rate the physician receives from providing units of service. A lower profit rate, π', results in a budget constraint with a flatter slope and a lower intercept. The new equilibrium occurs at point B. In this example, increased competition has led the physician to choose a higher degree of inducement (i.e., $D_B > D_A$).

LIMITATIONS OF THE MODEL

This simplified version accounts for inducement and income endogenously, one of the benefits of Evans's original model. The figure also illustrates a drawback of the original model, the fact that the model is ambiguous in its predictions of the effects of increased physician availability on the level of D. To see this, experiment with Figure 8.3 by drawing other indifference curves representing physicians with different preferences. You will find that a physician might alternatively reduce the inducement level, D, when the budget constraint rotates downward. That is, tangency can be achieved at point B' with a lower level of D on the indifference curve represented by the dotted curve. Economists summarize this ambiguity by saying that the comparative static properties of the model are not determinate. Using a different utility function, Ellis and McGuire (1986) note that imperfect agency may, in some circumstances, lead to an undersupply of care.

Another concern with the approach stems from the fact that physician producers are firms. In conventional economic theory of the firm, economists have found that the profit-maximization model often yields strong results. An alternative SID approach would determine whether a profit-maximization model yields stronger predictions in the context of SID.

A Profit-Maximizing Model of SID

Before describing such a framework, begin with the standard profit-maximizing conditions for a firm with a negatively sloped demand curve. This is shown in Figure 8.4 (at the intersection of the marginal revenue curve with the marginal cost curve) to produce the equilibrium price–quantity combination P_1, Q_1. One of the key distinctions between monopoly and competition is that, at the monopoly equilibrium, price exceeds marginal cost: In competition, to the contrary, price equals marginal cost.

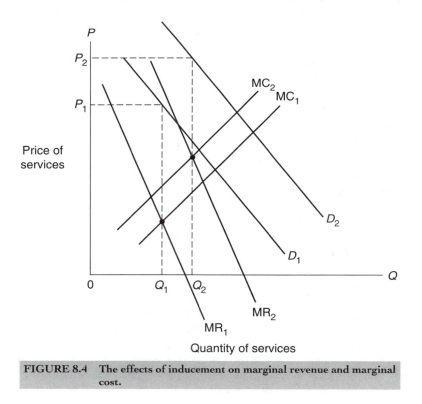

FIGURE 8.4   The effects of inducement on marginal revenue and marginal cost.

The gap between price and marginal cost in imperfect competition, much like the price rigidities case for price takers, creates an incentive to enhance demand. Why? If the seller can sell more at a price that is higher than marginal cost, profitability increases. Of course, alternatively, if there had been perfect information and perfect agency, the seller could not thus improve its position.

THE PARALLEL BETWEEN INDUCEMENT AND ADVERTISING

On the other hand, with imperfect information and the ability to induce increases in demand, sellers can often improve their profits by inducing customers to buy more output. This idea is similar to theories of more typical commodities where sellers have an incentive to introduce advertising and product promotion in order to raise demand.[8] But these activities also raise costs so they should be undertaken only to the point where their marginal revenues equal marginal costs. The new equilibrium is illustrated in Figure 8.4 by the price–quantity combination P_2, Q_2.

As we have noted, the decision to induce, under this theory, has elements that are similar to standard advertising/product promotion decisions. The physician expects revenues to increase, but costs in the form of reputation loss and time costs also have to be recognized. Following Stano's (1987) representation of SID within this context, several observations follow from the advertising analogy.[9] First, the incentive to advertise will be linked to the gap between marginal revenue and marginal cost. A small gap, which arises under a relatively elastic demand, reduces incentives. If the typical physician has a high degree of monopoly power, the gap will be large. Empirical evidence indicates that while the overall elasticity of demand for physician care is quite low, the elasticity of demand facing individual providers is considerably higher.[10] That is, the market for physician services is monopolistically competitive. Further, with suggestions that the market has become more competitive,[11] the foregoing approach predicts that the incentive to induce demand is likely to be diminishing.

A second important consideration follows in that the optimal level will depend on the relative costs and gains of manipulating consumer demand. Previous discussion of agency suggested that consumers are not as ignorant as is often assumed. Ethical and professional considerations restrict physician activities, and, notably, various contracts between principal and agent have evolved to limit physicians' informational advantages. These include the monitoring feature of the traditional physician–patient relationship as well as other arrangements introduced by third-party payers. The effects of the various constraints on physician behavior are to raise costs of imperfect agency and thereby reduce the extent of SID.

---

[8]We do not consider here the distinction between advertising that enhances information and that which is directed at manipulating the preferences of buyers. A firm will not normally provide the former unless it expects that information to increase its demand.

[9]Although it appears that the utility approach introduced earlier has been abandoned, in order to simplify the analysis, the various costs associated with foregone leisure and imperfect agency can be incorporated into the cost function.

[10]See Langwell and Nelson (1986) for a review of the evidence.

[11]See Feldstein (1986) and Newhouse (1988).

Finally, if we draw the advertising analogy closely, we can also somewhat expand our concept of physician inducement. That is, we can recognize some forms of inducement by physicians that are no more or less harmful to the patient than are some forms of advertising to the general consumer. Certainly, if inducement takes the form of a physician providing misinformation, recommending procedures or risks not suitable for the patient, or recommending excessive levels of care, then inducement is correctly characterized as a problem of imperfect agency. This is understandably the form of SID that is worrisome to policy analysts. But, just as advertising may sometimes work its demand-enhancing effects through its informational function, so sometimes may physician inducement take the form of providing enhanced information to the patient.

THE IDENTIFICATION PROBLEM
AND THE EVIDENCE ON SID

Despite an extensive literature on the subject, the difficulties of developing and testing theoretically consistent models of SID have limited the applicability of much of the empirical work. The problem is that in much of the empirical work, the SID effect cannot be econometrically identified. The identification problem in econometrics was explained in Chapter 3, and reference to that chapter may be helpful.

The Identification Problem: An Algebraic Example*

The problem will be illustrated next with the help of an algebraic example. For those readers who wish to forego the algebraic derivations, we summarize as follows. Begin with demand and supply curves such as those illustrated in Figure 8.2. The identification problem is exemplified by the following fact: If we construct an algebraic model *with no SID,* the resulting equation that is commonly estimated by researchers will look much the same as the equation derived from an algebraic model *with SID.* This fact is suggestive of the problem faced by the econometrician in that SID often cannot be distinguished from no SID by the statistical evidence.

To confirm this point, following Folland and Stano (1990), we begin with an algebraic demand–supply model without SID as represented by the following linear equations:

$$QD = a_0 + a_1P + a_2Y + u_1 \tag{8.1}$$

and

$$QS = b_0 + b_1P + b_2X + b_3\text{MD} + u_2 \tag{8.2}$$

where QD and QS represent quantities demanded and supplied and P represents price. Exogenous demand variables such as income and education are represented in the demand equation by Y; while exogenous variables in the supply equation, such as the price of inputs, are represented by X. The variable MD represents the availability of

---

*May be omitted without detracting from the flow of the book.

physicians. From these two equations plus the condition that the quantity supplied, *QS,* equals the quantity demanded, *QD,* we can solve for the equilibrium quantity:

$$Q = c_0 + c_1 X + c_2 Y + c_3 \text{MD} + v \tag{8.3}$$

The coefficients in equation (8.3) are complicated combinations of those in equations (8.1) and (8.2), as will be discovered when one performs the algebra (see Exercise 5). When the econometrician estimates the parameter c_3 and discovers it to be greater than zero, he or she can conclude correctly that increased physician availability (that is, increased MD), has a positive effect on equilibrium utilization. But this cannot be taken as evidence of SID; recall that by assumption we started with a model with *no SID.*

For SID to exist would mean that physician availability affects demand directly; that is, it would mean that MD appears directly in the demand equation. To illustrate, suppose that SID does exist. In that case, a model of demand with SID would be as follows:

$$QD = a_0 + a_1 P + a_2 Y + a_3 \text{MD} + u_1 \tag{8.4}$$

Here the availability of physicians (that is, the variable MD), appears directly in the demand equation as a demand shift variable. Upon solving algebraically equations (8.4) and (8.2), the resulting equation with SID looks just like equation (8.3) without SID.

Furthermore, the econometrican will usually not be able to use the resulting estimates to determine whether or not SID exists. As Auster and Oaxaca (1981) have shown, this identification problem is not easily resolved, even when more sophisticated estimation methods are used. This finding has been reinforced through an innovative approach involving the demand for childbirths. Dranove and Wehner (1994) show that a statistical method (two-stage least squares) often used to estimate the inducement effect produces "evidence" of inducement for childbirths even though one would not expect to find inducement here. The apparent anomaly arises because that method does not properly deal with identification issues.

As a result, we conclude that much of the reported evidence of SID is unreliable. An account of the evidence must appeal to studies that have in some way successfully avoided the identification problem.

The Evidence on SID

One way of overcoming the identification problem is through the study of the effects of fee rigidities or price controls. These studies, some of which were reviewed earlier, generally indicate that the volume of services increases after controls are imposed— that is, some SID effect is found. The magnitude of the effect, however, tends to be modest.

Another way of overcoming the identification problem is to circumvent it. In this regard, Hay and Leahy (1982) formulated a simple proposition. If imperfect agency leads to a higher volume of services provided, we ought to see those with more complete information consuming fewer services. The authors, in fact, found that, after controlling for other socioeconomic factors including health status, medical professionals and their families are at least as likely to visit physicians as others who are presumably less well informed.

The contributions by Rossiter and Wilensky (1983, 1984) are also noteworthy. These authors distinguished between patient-initiated visits, presumably not subject to physician control, and what may be subsequent physician-initiated visits. The authors attempt to identify the extent of SID by focusing on the relationship between the physician-initiated component and variables representing physician self-interests. In particular, if SID exists, increases in physician availability would be expected to increase physician-initiated services, ceteris paribus, but would not affect patient-initiated visits. The authors found exactly this pattern; however, the estimated SID effect elasticity, although it was statistically significant, was very small, less than 0.1. This means that a 10 percent increase in physician availability produces an inducement effect of less than 1 percent.

In a similar study of Medicare beneficiaries, Escarce (1992) found that greater availability of surgeons increased initial contacts with surgeons but had little effect on the intensity of subsequent services. The higher utilization resulting from an increased supply of surgeons is thus associated with patients' preferences for access to care or referrals rather than to SID.

Finally, Grytten and colleagues (1995) also distinguished between patient and primary physician-initiated visits under the fixed-fee schedules of Norway's public health care system. The investigators did not find any evidence of either SID or rationing of physician-initiated visits, though there was some indication of inducement for laboratory tests.

Other Limitations on SID

Two other contributions provide theoretical grounds to suppose that there are inherent limits on the physician's ability to influence demand. Rochaix (1989) recognized that a patient is not fully dependent on any physician and in fact forms prior expectations about his or her own condition. If the physician's suggestions deviate sufficiently from those expectations, the patient may not consent to the proposed care, but rather seek another opinion. This ex ante monitoring constrains physicians' behavior. The author demonstrates that it takes only a small number of informed patients to constrain physicians to act as "better agents."

Similarly, Dranove (1988) proposed that patients form expectations about the severity of their conditions. In the inducement decision, a physician is concerned about the loss of business were he or she to develop a reputation as overly aggressive. Among various factors, Dranove showed that improvements in patients' diagnostic skills reduce the gains from inducement.

EVALUATION OF SID

Our partial review of the SID literature has selected from a wide range of contributions and ideas. The whole of the SID literature shows that the intuitively simple idea of physicians inducing demand actually has many, often interesting complexities.[12]

---

[12]Pauly (1988b) has even suggested that the complexities inherent in the SID–imperfect information controversy mean that the issue may never be completely settled.

We argue that elements of competition, agency relationships, and consumer search place substantial limits on the ability and willingness of physicians to generate increases in demand. Even those more recent contributions that lend support to SID indicate that inducement activity is less extensive than supporters had previously believed. For example, while Fuchs (1978) estimated an inducement elasticity of about 0.3 for surgeons' services, Cromwell and Mitchell's (1986) improvements of that work generated estimates in the 0.1 range. Given these theoretical and empirical advances, one could reasonably conclude that some deviations from perfect agency and demand inducement exist. However, SID is certainly not the problem it once was thought to be.[13]

Therefore, it seems safe to suggest that health care markets can often be studied using models that postulate stable demand functions even though there may be some degree of SID. In other words, consumers are not nearly as helpless as many might imagine in that they take steps to protect their self-interests when those interests are threatened. It follows that it would be reckless to argue market failure, at least on the basis of SID, and to dismiss readily as ineffective policy analysis based on standard models.

Summary

1. Supplier-induced demand (SID) refers to the phenomenon of physicians deviating from their agency responsibilities to provide care for their self-interests rather than their patients' interests.

2. SID represents one of the major intellectual and policy controversies in health economics. Its origins can be traced to Roemer's Law, which predicts that a "bed built is a bed filled."

3. SID is typically represented graphically by increases in demand following increases in supply, though there are theoretical flaws with this representation.

4. The target-income hypothesis is a related idea that suggests that physicians use their discretionary advantage to achieve a target level of income.

5. Evans theorized that the utility of the gain in income has to be balanced by the disutility of inducement and the disutility of the work in providing care. This idea establishes theoretical limits on the level of inducement.

6. The disequilibrium approach to SID resulting from price rigidities establishes a gap between demand and supply and a motive to induce increases in demand.

7. Another approach develops the analogy between inducement and advertising. It predicts that inducement will diminish as competition reduces the gap between a physician's marginal revenue and marginal cost.

8. The identification problem, which refers to the difficulty of determining the extent of SID, has plagued much of the empirical literature on the subject.

---

[13]Labelle, Stoddard, and Rice (1994) argue that the inducement controversy should consider the effectiveness of services as well as the effectiveness of the agency relationship. This expanded framework could help distinguish among different categories of utilization (e.g., as between induced care that helps or harms the patient). The authors claim that these categories have very different policy implications. See also Pauly's (1994a) criticism of this proposal.

9. The empirical work that has overcome or sidestepped the identification problem has found evidence of SID. However, the magnitudes tend to be much smaller than was originally believed by supporters of the hypothesis.

10. Though conventional economic analysis oversimplifies the physician services market, the standard competitive and monopoly models provide useful insight into the effects of changes in demand and physician availability on prices and quantities.

Discussion Questions

1. Suppose that insurers monitored all health care payments to determine whether the services were appropriate. Would you expect to see more or less tendency toward SID?

2. Figure 8.3 shows how increased competition can lead to a higher degree of inducement at point *B*. This suggests that providers try to induce more usage to compensate for lower profit margins. Suppose, however, that the physician ends up at point *B′*, where there is less inducement. What types of preferences would lead to reduced inducement in response to less profits?

3. How is the possibility of SID related to the price elasticity of demand for services? Does increased demand elasticity increase or decrease the possibility of SID?

4. If prices are relatively rigid so that they do not adjust rapidly to changes in supply, explain how SID can be manifested.

5. What are some criticisms of the target-income approach to SID? In the target-income model, what determines the physician's target income? Would target incomes differ between physicians in practice? Would some physicians choose instead to be income maximizers?

6. What forces limit a provider's ability and willingness to engage in SID? In the profit-maximizing model of SID, what are the costs to the physician of inducement? Give examples of inducement costs.

7. Assume that SID is prevalent and that there are few forces to limit or check this phenomenon. What are some of the implications for policy?

8. In what ways is inducement similar to advertising? In what ways is it different?

9. How do the medical care consumption patterns of physicians and their families differ from those of nonphysicians? If physicians may be considered well-informed, what does this suggest about the SID hypothesis? Does it matter for this point that physicians tend to have larger than average incomes? Discuss.

Exercises

1. Using Figure 8.1, explain why a strong positive relationship between the availability of health care resources (e.g., beds) and the use of those resources does not prove that increases in supply lead to increases in demand.

2. Explain why the standard demand–supply framework in which prices adjust immediately to a new equilibrium is inconsistent with SID.

3. Explain why the indifference curves in Figure 8.3 are positively sloped.

4. If the use of discretionary influence were not a "bad," what would the indifference curves in Figure 8.3 look like? Where would the equilibrium solution along the physician's income locus be found?

5. Set QD in equation (8.1) equal to QS in equation (8.2) and solve for P, showing that it is a linear function of the remaining variables.

   Substitute your solution for P back into either (8.1) or (8.2) and solve for $Q = QD$ (or QS) to find equation (8.3). Alternatively, solve for P in each of the equations by putting P on the left-hand side. These are known as the inverse demand-and-supply equations. Then eliminate P by setting the two equations equal to another and solve for Q.

6. Consider the evidence that fee controls or price ceilings tend to be followed by utilization increases. Why doesn't this evidence necessarily support either the target income pricing or SID hypotheses? *Hint:* Consider a physician with some degree of monopoly power and, for simplicity, constant marginal cost. Examine the profit-maximizing price and quantity combinations before and after a price ceiling is introduced to determine what will happen to utilization and spending.

CHAPTER 9

Health, Health Care, and Advertising

- A Background on Advertising by Health Care Firms

- The Firm's Optimal Level of Advertising

- The Effects of Advertising on the Health Care Sector

- Advertising and Health: The Case of Cigarettes

- The Effect of Price on Cigarette Consumption

- Conclusions

The health economics of advertising addresses not only the advertising by health care firms, but also the advertising of products and services that potentially affect people's health status. We examine both issues in this chapter. We begin with the study of advertising practices of health care firms, and close with a section surveying the controversial subject of the advertising of cigarettes.

The growth in advertising by health care firms raises questions about why this has occurred; economic theory can provide some of the answers. First, economic theory describes the optimal level of advertising by a firm. Inasmuch as many health care firms are adopting advertising for the first time, analysis of the optimal advertising level helps to explain the adoption of advertising by such firms.

Second, economic theory addresses the effects of advertising on society's well-being, in particular, its possible effects on consumers. Does advertising by health care firms help or hurt the consumer, the health care professional, and society as a whole? Advertising could affect society's well-being through changes in prices, degree of competition, ability of new firms to enter the market, or quality of care. The first sections of this chapter develop the themes just described: the optimal level of advertising, and the effects of advertising.

The final section of this chapter addresses a question just as important to health economics, the issue of health status and advertising. We have chosen the controversial field of cigarette advertising. The issues of health and advertising are different from the issues of health care and advertising, even though they are related. The salient feature is that here the product advertised is viewed by many as a "bad" or at the very least as a "good" that imposes harmful effects on others. A central economic question in this regard is whether and to what degree cigarette advertising increases the total consumption of cigarettes. A closely related policy question is whether proposed bans on cigarette advertising in the United States would be effective in reducing consumption. We begin the chapter by addressing advertising by health care firms.

A BACKGROUND ON ADVERTISING BY HEALTH CARE FIRMS

Advertising in the health care sector is in some ways a very old phenomenon and in some ways very new. Advertising, meaning "a paid communication from an identified sponsor using mass media to persuade or influence an audience," has a long history in health care.[1] For example, it is associated in the public mind with ads for medicines and healers that were common in the nineteenth century.

Advertising practices by health care firms, however, have different histories among the diverse health professionals and health care institutions. Some industries within the health care sector (for example, the pharmaceutical industry) and some professionals (for example, chiropractors) have advertised historically. In other cases, advertising has been unpopular, and frequently professional groups have placed prohibitions or severe restrictions on advertising in their professional codes of ethics. The American Medical Association from its beginning incorporated a ban on advertising in its code of ethics published in 1847.[2]

Throughout much of the twentieth century, advertising by health care professionals and hospitals was common only in a few exceptional cases, and professional prohibitions on advertising were generally followed and accepted. This situation changed recently due to at least two factors. First, remaining professional prohibitions were removed, beginning in the 1970s, partly due to legal actions and court decisions that demanded their removal. Second, even where prohibitions apparently had been less of a factor, there was growing interest in advertising and marketing practices in an increasingly competitive environment. For example, a survey of 437 hospitals, reported in 1984, showed that the number of hospitals with established marketing departments grew by over 75 percent in the prior three years.[3]

Of these two factors, one can identify more clearly the role played by the courts. During the twentieth century in the United States, and especially culminating in the 1970s, the Supreme Court has in steps come to assert the applicability of antitrust law

[1]Wells, Burnett, and Moriarty (1989, p. 585).
[2]Pollard and Leibenluft (1981).
[3]Fontana (1984).

to the "learned professions." Applications of this law to advertising came directly. In the landmark case, *Bates and O'Steen* v. *State of Arizona* (1977), the Supreme Court ruled that it is unconstitutional for bar associations to prohibit their lawyer-members from advertising.

A decisive application to the health professions followed. By the mid-1970s, the American Medical Association (AMA) guidelines on professional advertising practice had been revised. The Federal Trade Commission (FTC), however, determined that the remaining AMA guidelines on advertising were in restraint of trade. The case involving the medical profession reached the Supreme Court when in 1982 the Court effectively ruled in favor of the FTC. The applicability of these various rulings to other health professional groups is not in doubt.

The removal of professional restrictions and also probably the growing interest in advertising as a response to competition led to an era of greater advertising in the health care sector. The response of health care institutions and of health care professionals was evident. For example, reported advertising expenditures in the category "medical and dental" increased over tenfold during approximately the first half of the 1980s.[4] By the mid-1980s, over half of hospitals did some form of advertising. It has been reported that "while less than 5 percent of self-employed physicians advertised in 1982, by 1987 this figure had risen to 20 percent."[5]

THE FIRM'S OPTIMAL LEVEL OF ADVERTISING

We begin by viewing the advertising question from the point of view of the health care firm. The firm must determine whether to advertise, and if so, at what level. Economic theory invokes a basic principle: the profit-maximizing firm will advertise when it is profitable to do so and to the extent that it is profitable. It is necessary first to examine clearly what this principle entails. We then consider its applicability to the health care sector. The inquiry also clarifies what distinguishes health care professionals who advertise from those who do not.

Optimal Advertising Conditions

Consider a profit-maximizing firm that sells a single product and faces a downward sloping demand curve for its product. Suppose further that advertising by this firm tends to increase its demand to some degree and that the marginal effect of advertising on demand varies with the level of advertising. In particular, we expect that there are diminishing returns to the advertising dollar. We can understand this firm's choice problem as that of simultaneously choosing the levels of two variables, its output level and its level of advertising, to maximize its profits.

[4]Montgomery-Karp (1983).
[5]Rizzo and Zeckhauser (1990).

The two-variable maximization problem can be understood step by step. The firm will increase its output level up to the point that the cost of one more unit of output (that is, the marginal production cost) equals the revenue gained from one more unit of output (that is, the marginal revenue of the output). At the same time, the level of advertising will be increased up to the point where the marginal costs attributable to advertising are just offset by the marginal revenue attributable to that extra advertising.

EQUATING AT THE MARGIN

In Figure 9.1, panels A and B help to describe this process. In panel A, let the firm's demand curve $D(A_1)$ represent the level of demand that would obtain if the firm spent A_1 dollars on advertising. With this level of demand, the optimal output level for the firm, Q_1, would occur at the output at which the marginal revenue curve, MR (A_1), crosses the marginal cost curve, MC. This output level may not maximize profit overall, however. We must further consider whether an alternative advertising level would be better.

In panel B, we see that at advertising level A_1 the marginal cost of advertising (MCA) is less than the marginal revenue attributable to advertising (MRA). In this panel, let us define each unit of advertising as a dollar's worth; thus, the marginal cost of advertising is always $1. At point *F,* the fact that the marginal revenue from advertising curve, MRA, lies above the marginal cost of advertising means that an increase in advertising by this firm will lead to higher profits.

Finally, at output Q_E in panel A and at point *E* in panel B, the firm has satisfied both marginal conditions simultaneously. Profits at output level Q_E and advertising level A_E are at a maximum. Further output would add to revenue, but the addition to revenue would not cover the addition to costs. Similarly, further advertising would increase demand still further, but this demand increase will be too small to cover the extra advertising cost. Thus, the optimal level of advertising for this firm is A_E.

Dorfman and Steiner (1954) have shown that these conditions imply also that the firm will advertise to the degree that the marginal revenue product of advertising is equal to the price elasticity of demand. The Dorfman-Steiner result and the marginal conditions we have examined both make clear that optimal advertising depends on the costliness of advertising, its effectiveness, and the conditions of demand.[6] It is useful to inquire into the applicability of these conditions and of advertising in general to the health care sector.

On the Appropriateness of Advertising by Health Care Firms

The question of whether advertising is appropriate to health care firms can be asked in at least two very different ways. On the one hand, health care professionals, and the

---

[6]Note also the similarities of the advertising model to the profit-maximizing inducement model of SID described in Chapter 8.

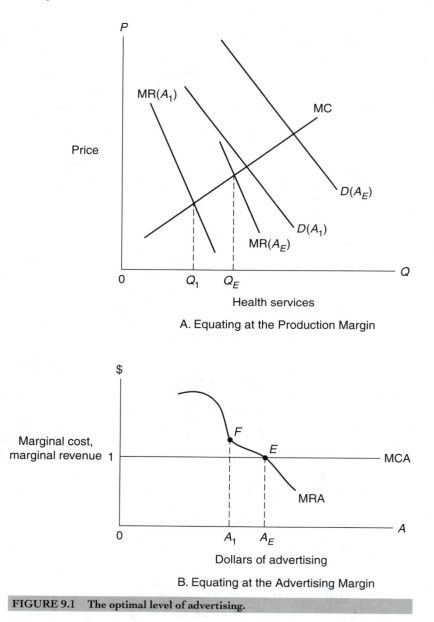

FIGURE 9.1   The optimal level of advertising.

public as well, often question whether advertising is really ethical for health care firms, whether it violates a provider–patient trust, and whether it is appropriate to the professional image. But the economist will ask the question differently. Are the economic conditions for successful advertising met in this sector? Will advertising increase the demand for the health care product or service? Will it provide economically valuable information?

On the first issue, it is clear that health care professionals often show a distaste for advertising, question its ethics, and question whether it fits a professional image.[7] The public also often questions health care advertising but seems more accepting of advertising than the professionals themselves. A survey of consumers published in 1984 by the AMA, for example, reported that 62 percent felt that advertising would be useful in helping them choose a physician.[8]

Nevertheless, because of the historical role of advertising in health care and the attitudes of health professionals and some consumers, advertising by health professionals may convey an unwanted signal. It has been observed in other settings that when information about quality is incomplete, consumers may regard advertisements of lower prices as a signal of lower quality. This may serve to help explain why even physicians who advertise rarely advertise their prices.[9] A recent study reported little effect on the use of care from giving consumers information about prices.[10] That study suggests that in the case of physician services consumers do not use price information to find the lowest-cost providers, and that price advertising in physician services markets may have little effect on consumption.

Furthermore, personal distaste for advertising among many health professionals may influence their behavior even if advertising were to increase profitably demand for service. If health professionals were pure profit maximizers, such feelings would not affect their economic behavior. It seems plausible, however, that some form of utility maximization better describes the economic behavior of many health professionals and that reluctance to advertise at least partly reflects a professional distaste for the practice.

On the pure grounds of profit and loss, however, is advertising economically appropriate to the health care sector? To answer this different question requires an inquiry into the market structure of health care industries as well as into the nature of the product or service.

Advertising is quite common in what we may call the intermediate market structures between the extremes of perfect competition and pure monopoly. These market structures include monopolistic competition and oligopoly, and most health care firms can probably be classified into one of these two market structures. In these market structures, the firm demand is downward sloping, and yet each firm has competitors, thus representing imperfect competition. Advertising is common in such markets.

SEARCH GOODS AND EXPERIENCE GOODS

Given that the market structure seems appropriate, what about the nature of the product or service? Nelson (1970, 1974) distinguishes between *search goods* and *experience goods,* and these terms are useful in one's advertising vocabulary. Nelson argues that advertising tends to be more effective and more important for experience goods than for search goods. He explains that search goods are goods that can be evaluated

---

[7]Folland (1987).

[8]Freshnock (1984).

[9]Monroe (1973), Petroshius and Monroe (1987), and Folland (1987).

[10]Hibbard and Weeks (1989).

upon inspection, such as nails, clothing, and furniture. Advertising such goods is useful, but the repetition of this advertising gives a smaller payoff than for experience goods. The reason is that such ads merely repeat information that the customer can observe alone.

In contrast, experience goods or services are difficult to evaluate prior to purchase. Such is the case with food and automobiles, by Nelson's account. We may add that the quality of medical care is difficult to assess prior to experience. According to Nelson, for experience goods, direct observation of the important characteristics of the good is impossible or difficult prior to purchase, and thus advertising becomes an important device. Thus, at least by a superficial application of Nelson's theory we would expect health care firms to advertise more heavily than many others.

THE SIGNPOSTING PHENOMENON

Going beyond Nelson, however, we should add that the quality of several health care services, such as physician care, may be very difficult for the consumer to judge even after experience. As such, physician care provides an example of what others have called the "sign-posting" phenomenon.[11] The point is that advertisers inevitably advertise only certain characteristics of the product that consumers will interpret. Sellers will typically have the incentive to suppress some negative information they possess. It is critical that consumers can decode the signposts. In the case of health care services, where the consumer cannot judge quality independently, he or she may interpret price information negatively. For example, a physician advertising a low price may be interpreted as doing so because other knowledgeable consumers have judged the provider's quality as being low. Under this theory, physicians, for example, might advertise but they probably would not advertise such items as their prices.

HEALTH CARE AS A REPUTATION GOOD

Along similar lines, there are several characteristics of the health care industry that suggest a limited role for advertising for some health care firms. In any industry, advertising must compete in both the buyer's and the seller's mind with other forms of information and persuasion. In health care, word of mouth is often very important. Pauly and Satterthwaite (1981) have argued that physician care, for example, is a *reputation good*. Demand for a physician's services depends on his or her reputation for both technical ability and ability to relate well to patients. Reputation often depends on word of mouth, the recommendations of friends and relatives. Furthermore, many physicians obtain patients through referral, and referrals may depend on the physician's reputation—in this case, his or her reputation among other doctors.

These theoretical ideas on the role of advertising in the health care sector provide several insights, but some suggest substantial advertising while others suggest a smaller role for advertising. What will the future hold? Probably advertising practices will differ among the diverse elements of the health care sector. We do not yet have studies of each health care industry, but a case study of the advertising behavior of physicians sheds some light.

---

[11]Zeckhauser and Marks (1989).

Physician Advertisers: A Case Study

The ideas we have studied regarding the optimal level of advertising for a firm can be summarized as suggesting that the decision to advertise and the degree of advertising chosen will depend on two factors: the profitability of advertising to the firm, and, in the case of utility maximizers, on the degree of distaste or acceptance of advertising by the firm's decision makers.

Rizzo (1988) used a sample of over 2,500 self-employed physicians that contained information on whether the physicians were advertisers. Advertisers, for the purposes of this study, were defined as those who had advertised their practice in newspapers, magazines, radio, or television at any time over the previous five years. To focus on new forms of advertising, he omitted Yellow Pages advertising, which had long been common. His statistical techniques estimated how several physician characteristics affected the probability of advertising in the past five years.

Table 9.1 presents a selection of results based on Rizzo's estimates. In almost all cases, the numbers can be directly interpreted as representing a change in probability. Consider row (2), identified as "Member of group practice of size SIX TO TEN MDs." Physicians in a group practice of size 6–10 will be more likely to advertise (the increase in probability is 0.13) than the reference group, in this case solo practitioners.

In Table 9.1, physicians in succeedingly larger group practices are more likely to advertise. Second, board certified physicians (row 4) are less likely to advertise than the reference group, non-board certified physicians. Third, foreign medical graduates *and* female physicians (rows 5 and 6) are each more likely to advertise than their

TABLE 9.1 Change in the Probability That a Physician Will Advertise Given Selected Characteristics

Physician Characteristic	Estimated Change in Probability*
(1) Member of group practice of size TWO TO FIVE MDs	0.01
(2) Member of group practice of size SIX TO TEN MDs	0.13[a]
(3) Member of group practice of size ELEVEN OR MORE MDs	0.28[a]
(4) The physician is BOARD CERTIFIED	-0.04[b]
(5) The physician is a FOREIGN MEDICAL SCHOOL GRADUATE	0.07[a]
(6) The physician is FEMALE	0.06[b]
(7) The physician is a specialist in SURGERY	-0.08[a]
(8) The physician is in one of SELECTED SPECIALTIES	-0.10[a]
(9) The effect of additional EXPERIENCE**	-0.07[a]

Notes: *Probability change estimates reported here are based on probit function estimated coefficients. Probability data were calculated at the sample means.

**EXPERIENCE is measured in years of experience normalized to the zero-one interval. Change in EXPERIENCE for this table is evaluated as one additional standard deviation of the EXPERIENCE variable. The reported standard deviation is 0.11.

[a]Coefficient on which the probability calculation is based is significant at the 1 percent level.

[b]Coefficient on which the probability calculation is based is significant at the 5 percent level.

Source: Rizzo (1988).

counterparts. Fourth, in the two examples of Rizzo's specialty categories that we have selected to show, Surgery and Selected Specialties (rows 7 and 8), physicians in each of these specialty categories are less likely to advertise than the omitted reference group, General/Family Practice. Finally, more experienced, older physicians are less likely to advertise than are the younger physicians.

IMPLICATIONS OF THE FINDINGS

The data in this table are specific to the case of physicians, and it requires some speculation to see relationships between these data and the theoretical discussion. However, in several instances, the results seem to accord with the idea that the physicians who chose to advertise are more likely to be those who expect that advertising will be more profitable for them.

Reconsider the result that physicians in larger group practices are more likely to advertise. It is plausible that certain economies of scale exist in advertising that may apply to medical group practice advertising.[12] The physicians, for example, may be able to divide up the advertising costs into smaller shares. Economies of scale in advertising would tend to make advertising more profitable to the physician in larger groups.

In addition, the results showing that board certified physicians are less likely to advertise and the results implying that General/Family Practice physicians are more likely to advertise than many specialties are also both understandable. "Board certified physicians are likely to have stronger referral networks than are uncertified physicians . . . [thus] they may have less need to promote themselves through advertising."[13] Using similar reasoning, General/Family practice physicians rely less heavily on referrals than many other specialists.[14]

Other results are also of interest. Why are female physicians in this sample more likely to advertise? Similarly, why are foreign medical graduates more likely to advertise? In both cases, the answer may be that they are more likely to be building their practices or simply that they are less averse to advertising.

Finally, the result that more experienced physicians are less likely to advertise confirms a frequent result in the literature on advertising by professionals. This fact allows alternative explanations. On the one hand, younger physicians may find advertising more profitable because they do not yet have extensive referral networks and advertising may help them to establish a practice. Alternatively, older physicians may have a stronger distaste for advertising.

Summary

This section has examined the optimal advertising level of the firm, the appropriateness of advertising to the health care industry, and a case study of the determinants of the physician's decision to advertise. The discussion serves to introduce the health professional or student to the theory of advertising from the firm's perspective, the appropriateness of

---

[12]Comanor and Wilson (1979); Albion and Farris (1981).
[13]Rizzo (1988, p. 1241).
[14]Shortell (1973).

advertising given the nature of the health care industry, and the factors important to the physician's decision about whether to advertise.

These discussions, however, do not help to explain or predict the effects that health care advertising will have on the consumer. Nor do they address the historical opposition to advertising by many health care professional groups, or the reason why public policy has been decided in favor of freedom to advertise. These issues are addressed in the next section.

THE EFFECTS OF ADVERTISING ON THE HEALTH CARE SECTOR

Many health professionals have made the decision to advertise, and undoubtedly more will do so. What effects will this have on the consumer? Many health professionals when surveyed are skeptical that advertising does the consumer much good. Historically, health professional groups have opposed advertising by their member professionals. Policy analysts have increasingly questioned the motives behind these professional groups, or perhaps more accurately, public officials have gained the authority to do something about this opposition. The present public policy in the United States is decidedly in favor of freedom for professionals to advertise their services. Nevertheless, some analysts voice skepticism over whether the consumer benefits of advertising exhibited within some health services markets will extend to all or even to many parts of the health care sector. An examination of the relevant economic theory and evidence will help one to understand these contrasting views. It will also reveal a corresponding scholarly controversy over some of these issues.

A Contrast of Theories About the Effects of Advertising

There are two theories in this literature about how advertising works. In one, advertising is a form of information, and generally positive effects on markets come through improved information. In the other, advertising is persuasive rather than informative so that it is possible for consumer tastes to be changed by advertising. In this view, advertising at profit-maximizing levels may be harmful to markets inasmuch as it may create barriers for new firms to enter the market.

It is useful to consider examples of each theory in more detail. Here we present the advertising-as-information approach developed by Nelson (1970, 1974) and contrast this theory with the view of advertising as a barrier to entry as developed by Comanor and Wilson (1974).

ADVERTISING AS INFORMATION

Nelson studied the implications of the information contained in advertising. Viewed as information, advertising is capable of generating lower average equilibrium prices, better access to the market for new entrants, and better matches of consumer preferences with available qualities. To understand the connection, begin by considering the role of available alternatives in the consumer's choice problem.

Imagine a consumer who is perfectly informed about all available brands of a product in the market. His interest in brand A will depend on its price, quality, distance and so on. But his interest will also depend on his alternatives. If he can comfortably forego the product entirely, or if he can easily opt for another brand, then he has flexibility. A flexible consumer is more likely to resist undesirable changes in brand A (such as a drop in quality or a rise in price). This greater responsiveness to price implies a more elastic demand.

Now consider, more realistically, a consumer who is imperfectly informed about available brands. He will desire information about available products because it makes him more flexible. Information comes at a price. He must expend effort to obtain information through recommendations from friends and relatives, the advice of agents he hires, or he may use available advertising. More information about available substitutes will make his demand curve for the relevant product relatively more elastic.

Understood this way, the consumer desires the information contained in advertising, and the product seller is willing to provide the advertising. This source of information, while costly to the consumer in time and energy, is also beneficial in alerting the consumer to better buys. If advertising is prohibited by law, this prohibition effectively makes information more costly to obtain. Anything that encourages advertising or lowers its price to the consumer tends to make demand more elastic.

The effect of advertising under the information theory is illustrated in Figure 9.2. In this figure, the demand curve D_1 represents the demand for a particular brand under conditions where advertising is prohibited. By changing the rules to permit or encourage advertising, the consumer demand for a given brand becomes more elastic,

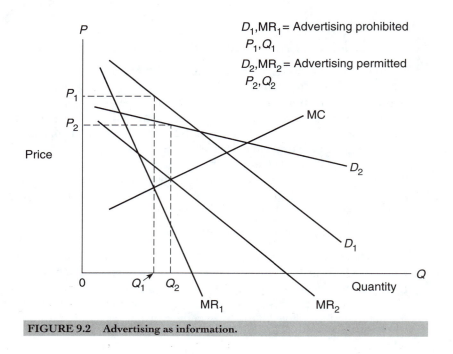

FIGURE 9.2   Advertising as information.

as represented by demand curve D_2. Now contrast the equilibrium outputs and prices in the two cases. Prior to advertising, the marginal cost curve and the relevant marginal revenue curve, MR_1, intersect at output level Q_1, implying a price of P_1.

When advertising is permitted, the equilibrium changes. First we note that the marginal cost curve does not change (as shown) or at most would change very little. This reflects the assumption that for most firms advertising will not vary much with the output level; thus, the advertising increases fixed costs but not variable (and thus marginal) costs. The intersection of the marginal cost curve with the new marginal revenue curve, MR_2, occurs at output level Q_2 and corresponds to the price level Q_2. The result is that the equilibrium price has fallen because of the advertising.[15]

Nelson went on to consider the relationship of product quality and advertising. Under this view, if firms differ in quality of product, then advertising, because it informs the consumer, will be most beneficial to the firms with the higher quality. More exactly, advertising will be most beneficial to firms whose combination of price and quality represent the better buy. If advertising is more beneficial to such firms, it follows that they will also advertise more. Theoretically then, the level of advertising by a firm can be taken as an indicator of its quality level per dollar.

ADVERTISING AS A BARRIER TO ENTRY

In contrast to Nelson's view in which advertising is generally beneficial to the consumer, other theories suggest that advertising may have anticompetitive effects. Bain (1956) argued that advertising is often used in practice to differentiate one brand from others—that is, to create a sense that the brand is different in a way that is more valued. This differentiation may result in loyalty to the brand so that consumers will become more resistant to price rises.

This effect of advertising on tastes can lead to higher prices. The primary mechanism is that consumer loyalty leads to lower cross-elasticities of demand between the products of established firms and new entrants. For example, in Figure 9.3, the demand curve under the no-advertising case is represented by demand curve D_1. Following the principles of profit maximization, the firm depicted would produce where the relevant marginal revenue curve, MR_1, intersects the marginal cost curve, MC. The equilibrium price and output are respectively P_1 and Q_1. If advertising makes consumers more loyal to this brand, then the demand curve under advertising will become less elastic, such as the demand curve D_2. Thus, price will rise to P_2, higher than under no advertising.

OTHER CONSIDERATIONS

Although this graphical analysis may seem sufficiently straightforward, the required theory underpinning this view is necessarily more complex. Consider first that the other firms in this industry will also have incentives to advertise, and advertising by competitors will tend to offset the brand loyalty to the firm depicted. Second, new

---

[15]An alternative theory in the advertising literature also explains how price could fall under advertising as the result of economies of scale. In particular, if the firm's average cost curve is declining in the relevant range, and if advertising causes the firm to sell a greater quantity in net, then average costs of production would tend to fall. This could lead to lower prices.

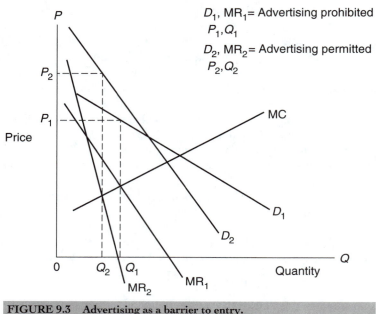

FIGURE 9.3   Advertising as a barrier to entry.

entrants will also be able to use advertising to enter the market and thus add to the level of competition.

The theoretical work supplied by Comanor and Wilson (1974) shows that the result of lessened demand elasticity is nevertheless plausible because of the asymmetric effectiveness of advertising for incumbent firms versus potential entrants. Under Comanor and Wilson, a dollar spent on advertising has a higher marginal product for incumbents than for entrants. Consumers have greater experience with established firms and greater recognition of them, and thus it is easier for them to maintain an incumbent position with advertising than it is to break into the market with advertising. The result of this theory would be as depicted in Figure 9.3, and it would suggest that average prices under advertising will tend to be higher than under no advertising.

Furthermore, work by others reconsiders the issue of quality. Schmalensee (1978) argues that the consumers envisioned under Nelson's advertising-as-information theory are somewhat implausible. Instead, consumers who are very responsive to advertising are often also likely to be misled. Schmalensee showed with an example that when consumers' perceptions of quality are influenced by advertising, and when these perceptions are somewhat slow to change in the face of other evidence, then low-quality firms may find it beneficial to be among the heavy advertisers.

Thus we have at least these two quite different theories about the effects of advertising. Under the advertising-as-information theory, advertising tends to make consumers more responsive to price and quality differences, and this may lead to lower average prices and a better matching of products to consumer tastes. Under the theory that regards advertising as a barrier to entry, advertising may favor incumbent firms and thus lead to less competition and higher prices than otherwise.

The Effects of Advertising: Empirical Studies

Theoretical disputes are often best settled by empirical work, that is, by looking at the evidence. Evidence from the health care sector is most relevant to the present purpose, but it will be useful first to provide a sample of results from other sectors to establish a benchmark with which to contrast findings from the health sector.

STUDIES FROM OTHER INDUSTRIES

Inasmuch as the opposing theories differ in their predictions about the effect of advertising on the elasticity of demand, we begin with evidence on elasticities. The evidence is mixed. Some studies found lower elasticities (in absolute value) associated with greater advertising in the given industry; several others found higher elasticities.[16]

Although the two theories are not as sharply distinguished regarding the effects of advertising on average prices, effects on price are what ultimately count. Some studies have shown that while individual nationally advertised product brands tend to be higher priced, the average prices for the product group as a whole tend to be lower with advertising.[17] Coincidentally, some of the most widely cited studies regarding advertising and prices come from studies within the health care sector. We treat these separately.

Other studies have addressed the relationship between advertising and product quality. Some studies have reported that advertised brands tend to be of higher quality than nonadvertised brands—for example, for such products as canned foods, running shoes, and other consumer products.[18]

In assessing the kind of evidence presented so far, we must naturally ask questions. Do studies from other sectors apply to the health care sector? For example, how relevant is a result for running shoes to the personal and complex service provided by a health care professional? Clearly, the questions of interest to us can only be settled by studies of each health industry, and only a select few studies are yet available. We turn to a summary of these.

STUDIES OF THE PHARMACEUTICAL INDUSTRY

The effects of advertising have been studied for pharmaceutical products. These studies address both the role of advertising by retail pharmacies and the advertising of drugs by drug companies.

Cady (1975) assembled evidence on the average prices of drugs sold by retail pharmacies and investigated the effects of advertising on the average prices. He compared pharmacy price-index levels in states that had regulatory restrictions on advertising with states that permitted freer advertising, using multiple independent variables to control for other factors. He found that states that restricted pharmacy advertising tended to have higher average pharmacy prices. The difference in prices was about 4 percent.

---

[16]Among the former, see Comanor and Wilson (1974), and Lambin (1976); among the latter, see Wittink (1977), Eskin (1975), and Eskin and Barron (1977).

[17]Albion and Farris (1981).

[18]Telser (1964), Archibald et al. (1983), Rotfeld and Rotzoll (1976).

A 4 percent rise in prices may appear trivial, but consider its significance. Inasmuch as advertising costs money, laypeople often believe that the cost of advertising by firms is inevitably passed on to the consumer in the form of higher prices. This evidence regarding retail pharmacies shows empirically what we have explained theoretically, that it is possible for advertising to lead to lower average prices. Furthermore, this kind of evidence supports public policies that permit or encourage the practice of advertising by pharmacies.

The role of advertising by drug companies, however, is distinctive in many respects and needs to be assessed on its own merits. Here the advertising and promotion that drug companies undertake are directed at the physician.

Hurwitz and Caves (1988) found that promotional expenditures[19] by an established brand-name drug tend to have a stronger effect on its market share than the offsetting effect of promotion by new competing generics. That is, their evidence suggests a net advantage of advertising to the incumbent in this case.

These studies probably will not decide the issues raised regarding the pharmaceutical industry and advertising. However, the studies are clearly related to the theories we have discussed, and they suggest that the effects of advertising may differ even between different elements of the same industry.

STUDIES OF OPTOMETRY

Optometry provides the strongest and most consistent instance of support for the advertising-as-information view. The initial work on the effects of advertising in optometry was done by Benham (1972), who compared average price levels for eyeglasses between areas in the United States where advertising was permitted and where it was not. Benham found that areas that restricted advertising tended to have higher average prices of eyeglasses. Supporting Benham's results, another study found for a large national sample that advertising restrictions raised prices for eye examinations by 5 to 10 percent.[20]

Studies of advertising and optometry have also addressed the issue of quality. Kwoka (1984) reported on an analysis of a large sample regarding optometry collected by the Federal Trade Commission. This study included data on individual practitioners' prices, advertising behavior, and quality of care characteristics. Data on optometrists from seven cities were able to represent the different possible advertising environments.

The results indicated that the prices among optometrists in cities where advertising was permitted were lower than the prices of optometrists in nonadvertising cities. The quality of care was measured by the amount of time taken by the optometrist per examination. The results indicated that there was no significant difference in quality between the advertisers and the nonadvertisers.

This evidence on quality is indirect, and the quality of optometric care might not be truly measured by the time spent with each patient. However, in other studies conducted

---

[19]Promotional expenditures include both advertising in medical journals and direct contact with physicians by what are called pharmaceutical detail men. According to Leffler (1981), somewhat more than 20 percent of promotional expenditures is journal advertising.

[20]Feldman and Begun (1978).

with FTC data, similar results have been obtained for other measures of quality.[21] Furthermore, an "index of thoroughness" was found to be highly correlated with the amount of time spent per patient. All these results tend to suggest that the optometrist advertisers were not of lower quality.

The evidence from optometry supports the view that advertising benefits the consumer by reducing prices. This evidence supports the advertising-as-information theory proposed by Nelson.

TWO STUDIES FROM THE PHYSICIAN CARE INDUSTRY

A recent study of physicians and advertising supports the conclusion that advertising effects will differ among elements of the health sector. Rizzo and Zeckhauser (1992) analyze a large sample of individual physicians using a data set on physician advertising practices, prices, and quality indicators. They find that, controlling for the factors which cause a physician to self-select as an advertiser, physicians who advertise tend to have higher prices and higher quality levels than those who do not. The authors conclude that physicians may tend to advertise to obtain a more desirable clientele, perhaps including a wealthier one. This study contrasts with the results for optometry, and so also does a companion study of the effects of advertising on entry into physician markets.

While in other industries the bulk of evidence supports the view that advertising facilitates entry,[22] the first results regarding advertising and entry in the physician industry suggest otherwise. Rizzo and Zeckhauser (1990) study the determinants of earnings levels for physicians who advertise and those who do not. One can infer ideas about advertising and ease of entry into physician care markets from their data. Using regression analysis, these authors estimated the contribution to earnings of each of many factors. They suggest that experience is more valuable among advertisers than among nonadvertisers. More experienced physicians earn higher incomes in both groups; however, experience is more important among physicians who advertise.

It appears that the advantage of experience is accentuated among the advertisers. This suggests that older, more established physicians have more to gain from the spread of advertising than do entering physicians. These results tend to support the advertising-as-barrier-to-entry theory for the case of physician markets.

Conclusions About the Effects of Health Care Advertising

The effects of health care advertising differ across health professional groups and institutions. Health care advertising has elements of both persuasion and information. In several instances, the balance is strongly in favor of benefits to the consumer. However, the available evidence also shows that the benefits found in one part of the health care sector do not automatically extend to the other parts. In particular, the early results from the physician care industry suggest that advertising tends to raise prices and to inhibit entry.

To emphasize this point, consider that the strongest case for the benefits to the consumer of advertising in the health sector have been found for the case of optometry.

---

[21]Bond et al. (1980).
[22]See Kessides (1986).

Optometric products and services, however, are somewhat more standardized than the more technically complex and personal services of a physician to a patient. More to the point, consumers are better able to assess the quality of optometric care. Furthermore, optometric advertising heavily features price, whereas physician advertising does not. For advertising to lower price, it may be the case that products must be fairly standardized and that the seller must advertise price. While both of these practices are common in optometry, neither commonly applies in the market for physician services.

Finally, what does both theory and evidence suggest for public policy? Should we return to advertising restrictions, at least in the case of physician care? Advertising can have important beneficial effects for the consumer in that it may encourage competition and may lead to better information and lower prices. There is substantive evidence of such benefits for instances within parts of the health care sector already.

Furthermore, it has not been clearly demonstrated that advertising harms the consumer in selected health care industries. In the physician studies, we find that price *and* quality rise with advertising, leaving uncertain the net effect of physician advertising on society's well-being.

There is little justification at this point in either available theory or evidence for a return to the historical restrictions on advertising. Most advertising in this field contains some information, and in some of the known cases the balance is toward information. To restrict advertising in any health care industry may mean to curtail information and to curtail the freedoms of people to provide information.

ADVERTISING AND HEALTH: THE CASE OF CIGARETTES

Up to this point, we have discussed the role of advertising in the health care sector. The role of health care firm advertising is an advertising issue of interest within the field of health economics, but it is not the only one. We are also concerned with advertising that takes place outside of the health care sector but that potentially affects peoples' health. Of a few such cases, one of the most prominent as well as controversial instances involves the advertising of cigarettes.

In a market-oriented economy, the consumer's decision to buy is usually regarded as a private matter: The consumer is free to choose. However, one can identify several exceptions in any otherwise free society, cases where the private decision to buy is either encouraged or discouraged by society as a whole. We encourage the purchase or provision of motorcycle helmets, automobile emissions control devices, old age pensions, and prenatal maternal nutrition. Conversely, we often seek to discourage the purchase of alcohol, other recreational drugs, and cigarettes.

The rationale for intervention in such private decisions may be paternalistic in some cases, but in other cases the intervention may arguably improve economic efficiency. Cigarette smoking affects not merely the cigarette buyer and seller—effects that are internal to the cigarette market—but it also affects the health of nonsmokers nearby, an external cost. Similarly, since health insurance markets often do not distinguish between smokers and nonsmokers, perhaps because of high monitoring costs, nonsmokers may pay higher premiums than warranted by their actual health risks. It is known that smokers have higher lifetime health expenditures than nonsmokers even though their lives are shorter.[23] When an activity has such external costs, the market output may exceed the efficient output; in this case, too much smoking occurs. This is an economic efficiency rationale for the antismoking movement. When smokers tend to underestimate the probabilities of ill health due to smoking, this too suggests an efficiency rationale for some measures such as taxes that tend to curb smoking.[24]

We may expect, however, that many antismoking advocates would oppose smoking even if it could be shown that the smokers themselves bear most of the health costs. It is true that smoking has extremely substantial health consequences. We showed in Chapter 4 that cigarette consumption is more important for population mortality rates than marginal variations in health care expenditure. Knowing this, many Americans would choose to do something about it, even if the treatment intruded on the smoker's private decisions.

The economist as citizen may choose one side or the other of this cigarette controversy depending on his or her own values. The economist as scientist, however, can help to illuminate the policy issues of current interest. For many, the question is not whether to curb smoking in the population but how to do it most effectively and unobtrusively. This hinges on two economic questions. First, what is the relationship of price to cigarette demand? And second, what is the relationship of cigarette advertising to smoking behavior? We begin with the advertising issue, the focus of this chapter.

A word of caution is in order. This is an issue over which people differ and hold their views strongly. A report of the U.S. Surgeon General (1989) concludes at one point that:

> There is no scientifically rigorous study available to the public that provides a definitive answer to the basic question of whether advertising and promotion increase the level of tobacco consumption. Given the complexity of the issue, none is likely to be forthcoming in the foreseeable future (pp. 516–517).

Even this conclusion is disputed by parties on both sides of the issue.

The Effect of Cigarette Advertising on Aggregate Consumption

When an imperfectly competitive firm advertises, it may improve its own demand in part by inducing consumers to switch brands and in part by inducing consumers to consume more of the product. Upon reflection, however, it is clear that other firms will tend to advertise for these purposes, and the advertising among the various firms may tend to be partially or even totally offsetting. The practice of advertising in the industry may have little effect on total industry demand. It may also have a positive effect on total industry demand.

---

[23]See Hodgson (1992).
[24]See Viscusi (1994).

Whether or not advertising tends to increase total industry demand for the product was a question raised by Galbraith in a popular book called *The Affluent Society* (1958). Galbraith's view was that powerful and large firms had the power to create or substantially influence demand for products. In his belief, such manipulated demands are somewhat artificial and socially less valuable than goods that are needed in the public sector. Galbraith's argument, regardless of whether one is either pro or con, is not itself a health policy issue, but the effect of cigarette advertising on total cigarette consumption is the crux of the key health policy issues regarding cigarette advertising.

Laypeople often conclude that the answer is obvious. Surely cigarette advertising must lead to more smoking, or else cigarette companies would not spend so much money on it. Cigarettes are among the most heavily advertised categories of products. A similar argument is also made among some economists who argue that the many available brands are really owned by a few companies and that the degree of brand switching (around 10 percent of smokers switched brands in a recent representative year) is not sufficient to justify the billions spent on advertising.[25] Table 9.2 shows the average market shares of the leading firms in U.S. sales during the period 1971–1982 and confirms that the industry is oligopolistic and concentrated.

Others argue that brand switching is a sufficient motivation for heavy advertising in principle. Two points help to explain this view: (1) the firm's decision to advertise is

TABLE 9.2	Average Market Share of Cigarette Firms 1971–1982 Categorized by Tar Content
High Tar	*Market Share (%)*
Philip Morris	25.7
R.J. Reynolds	31.8
American Brands	13.9
Brown and Williamson	16.5
Lorillard	7.2
Liggett and Meyers	4.8
Low Tar	
Philip Morris	27.4
R.J. Reynolds	31.9
American Brands	10.4
Brown and Williamson	15.5
Lorillard	14.3
Liggett and Meyers (1977-82)	1.0

Source: Roberts and Samuelson (1988).

---

[25]Tye, Warner, and Glantz (1987).

made ex ante with available information, and (2) the firm's decision criterion is what would have happened if it did not advertise. On the one hand, the firm commits money to advertising based on the effect it expects advertising to have. It may not have the econometric data published later, may not believe what is published, or admittedly it may have better information. On the other hand, the number of smokers who actually switch on average is less relevant than the unknown number who would switch if the firm did not advertise.

INCREASE IN DEMAND OR BRAND SWITCHING?

To evaluate this argument, we must examine what statistical evidence is known regarding the effects of advertising on aggregate consumption in the case of cigarettes. If advertising of cigarettes increases aggregate consumption, could we not reduce smoking in the population by either increasing the price of advertising, or, more directly, by outright banning of cigarette advertising? Health professionals are increasingly interested in such bans, but the evidence to date suggests caution.

As has been noted, the introduction of advertising in an industry has several effects on firm demand. The firm's own advertising can be expected to increase demand for its product. However, advertising by the firm's competitors will tend to decrease the firm's demand. The effect on aggregate consumption is thus not self-evident from theory.

Several studies of cigarettes have estimated the effect of advertising on aggregate cigarette consumption. The results of these studies tend to show that advertising effects on aggregate cigarette consumption are very small. In several of the most prominent studies, the estimated effects are insignificantly different from zero. A study by Baltagi and Levin (1986) illustrates this point. Their methods allowed for the possibility that cigarette advertising effects depend on both past and current advertising. They examined data for U.S. states over the years 1964–1980. In all equations estimated, aggregate cigarette advertising effects were insignificantly different from zero. Their results are effectively the same as those obtained earlier by others.[26]

Several notable studies have reported a statistically significant effect of cigarette advertising on aggregate demand; however, such studies tend to report a very small effect. McGuiness and Cowling (1975), for example, report a significant but small effect for data on the United Kingdom.[27] The highest reported significant estimate is apparently Seldon and Doroodian (1989) who found an elasticity of 0.2. A more recent estimate is by Tremblay and Tremblay (1995) who report 0.11. Most commonly, the estimated response of aggregate demand to advertising is an elasticity of around 0.1. The Toxic Substance Board of New Zealand (1989), a strong advocate of advertising bans, conservatively uses an elasticity of 0.07 in estimating the benefits of a ban.

The issue of whether cigarette advertising primarily affects brand switching or aggregate demand has nevertheless been renewed as an issue. A study by Roberts and

---

[26]Schmalensee (1972), Hamilton (1972), and Schneider, Klein, and Murphy (1981).

[27]McGuiness and Cowling reported a long-run elasticity of approximately 0.20 for the post-1962 period. Johnston (1980), however, argues that properly interpreted the McGuiness and Cowling estimates imply that an increase in advertising expenditures of 10 percent would in the long run increase cigarette consumption by less than 1 percent.

Samuelson (1988) is unique in that it simultaneously estimates both the degree of brand-switching effects and aggregate demand effects. They find no statistically significant effects on brand switching but statistically significant effects on aggregate demand. They do not report the size of the effect, however.

Suppose we agree that cigarette advertising affects aggregate demand but that the size of the effect is very small. Should we then conclude that a total advertising ban would be ineffective in curbing smoking? There are at least two reasons to consider carefully. First, even a small effect may be worthwhile. Suppose the correct elasticity for cigarette advertising is 0.10. If we could safely extrapolate this result to a total ban, a 100 percent reduction in cigarette advertising, we would reduce smoking in the population by 10 percent. Ban advocates and ban opponents both may claim such estimates support their case.

Second, most of the econometric studies of cigarette advertising were necessarily estimated over samples in which advertising levels were fairly high. For example, in a study of U.S. cigarette demand from 1964 to 1980, cigarette advertising levels were far above zero in every year; tobacco products were among the most heavily advertised of all products in the United States. The estimates might be quite different if the range of advertising expenditures were larger. It is statistically unsafe to extrapolate this far out of sample, so we should also study the effects of actual advertising bans.

The Effect of Cigarette Advertising Bans

World experience with cigarette advertising bans is informative. Several countries have banned cigarette advertising outright, and the United States installed a partial ban (a ban of cigarette advertising on broadcast media) in 1971.[28] Studies of the effects of these changes supply some relevant information, though only a few studies are available. The picture is fairly clear regarding the U.S. experience and we begin at this point.

THE PARTIAL BAN IN THE UNITED STATES

What of the U.S. experience with a partial ban, the banning of cigarette advertising on television and radio in 1971? It has been argued, somewhat paradoxically, that this U.S. ban actually increased cigarette consumption.[29] Hamilton's argument illustrates the historically relevant issues. Prior to the 1971 ban, a 1968 FTC ruling required television and radio stations, under the Fairness Doctrine, to give equal time to anti-smoking messages.

The result was a flurry of often memorable commercials showing the harm of smoking. In one, a father is shown walking in the forest with his young son. They stop to rest, lean back against a tree trunk and the father reaches for a cigarette. The boy watches in admiration as his dad lights up. But the father sees this, thinks, and stops. He gets the message, and so does the viewer.

Hamilton argued that such antismoking messages were effective in reducing smoking in the population. Hamilton's own evidence (as we have noted) showed cigarette

---

[28]Warner and colleagues (1986) survey this literature.
[29]Hamilton (1972); Schneider, Klein, and Murphy (1981).

advertising expenditures to have a small and insignificant effect on consumption. Thus, when the advertisement ban of 1971 eliminated *both* procigarette messages and mandatory anticigarette messages at once, the combined effect may actually have increased smoking.

Hamilton's argument was acknowledged by both sides of the cigarette advertising controversy and was widely accepted for many years. Subsequent estimates provided by Baltagi and Levin (1986) suggest that the net effect of the U.S. ban was probably closer to zero—that is, it had no net effect.

EFFECTS ON YOUTHS

Perhaps what is more important, however, is the effect of the antismoking messages we described on young potential smokers. Lewit, Coate, and Grossman (1981) studied data on over 6,000 individual youths. They found that television watching significantly increased the probability that a youth would start smoking. And they found that the Fairness Doctrine ads reduced the probability that a youth would start smoking. This suggests that the antismoking message was getting through to the very group we might most wish to reach. If youths can be encouraged not to begin smoking, we may have the most effective means to reduce smoking in the population.

ADVERTISING BANS INTERNATIONALLY

But what of the effects of the numerous, often recent restrictions on tobacco advertising across countries? For many years the basic statistical cross-national study of the effect of advertising bans was by Hamilton (1975). He showed that bans to that date had no significant effect on the level of cigarette consumption in the country. More recently, incorporating many new years of data and experience with bans, Laugesen and Meads (1991) have reported that these bans do have an effect.

These two authors developed data on tobacco consumption, price, advertising restrictions, and other variables for 1960–1986, and they defined an index measuring the degree of advertising restriction in the country. Estimates of the advertising restrictions effects over time show that restrictions did not reduce consumption in the early years (suggesting an explanation for Hamilton's results) but that they increased in effectiveness over time. The estimates also show that if countries without a total ban in 1986 had imposed such a ban, the effect would be a reduction in tobacco consumption of 6.8 percent. Thus, this estimate of the effect of a total ban is close to our estimate from extrapolating the econometric results of the previous section. Nevertheless, it will require confirmation and updating.

A possible additional effect of a total ban is worth noting. Several researchers have investigated the relationship between magazine editorial policy and the degree to which the magazine depends on cigarette advertising.[30] These studies show that magazines with higher cigarette advertising income tend to have significantly fewer articles on the harms of smoking. Though causality is difficult to identify in these studies, they do present a possible benefit of total bans.

---

[30]See Warner and Goldenhar (1989).

THE EFFECT OF PRICE ON CIGARETTE CONSUMPTION

The present chapter addresses advertising, but it is wise to consider price elasticity if we are to complete the assessment of cigarette advertising issues. The two fit together in some minds because excise tax increases on cigarettes appear as a policy alternative. Their effectiveness in reducing consumption depends, however, on the price elasticity of demand for cigarettes. Advertising bans and excise tax hikes are two pills proposed to cure the patient of smoking. To some analysts, however, such bans are of doubtful effectiveness and have a serious side effect—the possible restrictions on individual rights and the raising of constitutional issues. To such analysts, tax hikes seem the treatment of preference. To other analysts, however, both treatments are effective and both should be used.

Consider the potential for using excise tax increases to reduce smoking in the population. An excise tax on cigarettes is a per-unit tax collected and paid to the government by the cigarette seller. One effect of such a tax is to increase the equilibrium price of cigarettes. If smokers are responsive to rises in price, then the effect of the tax will be to curb consumption. The question is, how much? The greater the elasticity of demand, the greater will be the effectiveness of the tax in reducing the level of smoking. Thus, the question becomes, "What is the price elasticity of cigarette demand?"

Price Elasticity of Demand

The importance of price elasticity has not been lost on economists, and most econometric studies of cigarette consumption report price elasticity estimates. Reported price elasticities in absolute value range rather widely, from as low as 0.20 to occasional estimates greater than 1.0. The high estimates are the exceptions, however, and a consensus range of estimates is probably somewhere between 0.20 to 0.70. If the true elasticity at present were to be exactly 0.40, it would mean that a 10 percent rise in the

---

[31]DiFranza et al. (1991).

Antismoking Sentiment

The U.S. Food and Drug Administration, in declaring cigarettes a drug in 1995, has taken on the cigarette industry in its most serious challenge to date. The challenge comes at a high point in the influence of the antismoking movement in the United States. The same sentiments are growing in Europe. Europe boasts some of the highest smoking rates, but even this is changing. European smoking rates are coming down. "Today, 34% of the European Union population smokes, compared with 37% in 1987. (By comparison, 25% of the U.S. population smokes, compared with 30.4% in 1985.)" (Parker-Pope, 1995, p. B1). The goal of the European Region of the World Health Organization is a reduction of the adult population smoking rate to 20 percent in the near term (Trigg and Bosanquet, 1992).

---

price of cigarettes would cause consumption to decrease by 4 percent. Elasticities of this size suggest that price hikes are a fairly powerful tool in the effort to curb smoking. Consider that by simple extrapolation of these elasticity estimates, a doubling of the price of cigarettes in the United States would reduce cigarette consumption by 20 to 70 percent! Again, such out-of-sample extrapolation is risky statistically, but the illustration serves to show the potency of the tax tool.

Direct measures of the effect of cigarette taxes on mortality also show the potency of tax policy. Michael Moore (1995) tests tax variables in equations to predict mortality from several smoking-related diseases. Higher taxes significantly reduce mortality from lung cancer, cardiovascular disease, and asthma. For example, he reports that a 10 percent cigarette tax hike would save 3,700 lives per year in the United States.

While some other countries have vigorously applied tax hikes in order to reduce population smoking, tax rates in the United States had declined substantially as a percentage of the average price of cigarettes up to the late 1980s. Furthermore,

> The Federal excise tax has declined in real terms since 1964, despite the rising concern about the adverse effects of smoking on health that followed the release of the 1964 Surgeon General's Report and the adoption of specific Federal tobacco control policies (Surgeon General of the United States 1989, p. 529).

Figure 9.4 shows the average price of cigarettes and the average tax in cents for both federal and state/local average taxes. The federal cigarette excise tax has recently been increased, but even this increased level is a small portion of the price.

LONG-RUN EFFECTS

Studies of cigarette price elasticities in recent years may alter our understanding of the price responsiveness of cigarette demand. Studies focusing on long-term effects rather than short-term effects suggest a greater price responsiveness. This is illustrated

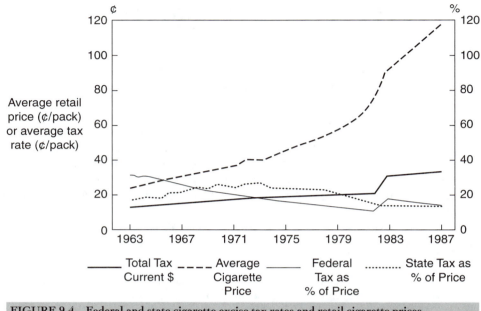

FIGURE 9.4   Federal and state cigarette excise tax rates and retail cigarette prices.

by data from Seldon and Doroodian (1989). They estimate not only the short-run effect of price on consumption but also the degree of habit persistence. Their short-run elasticity estimate is 0.40. With their habit persistence estimates, we can infer that the long-run price elasticity would be close to twice as large.

Similarly, long-run effects are theoretically greater in the "rational addiction" models of cigarette demand as discussed in Chapter 5. Chaloupka (1991) applies the rational addiction approach and estimates the long-run effects to be twice as great as the short run; however, in this instance, the long-run elasticity estimate is less than the value presented by Seldon and Doroodian (1989).

In contrast, Wasserman et al. (1991) suggest that state and local regulations that control smoking in public places (and sometimes private workplaces) may be the true source of some of the statistical power of price. When state-level smoking regulations are included in the analysis, price elasticity estimates drop to the neighborhood of 0.20 to 0.25. A lower level of price elasticity was also found by Chaloupka and Saffer in 1992. Their estimate is 0.24 in absolute value, which they report is an estimate "consistent with other recent studies" (p. 79).

PRICE ELASTICITY AND YOUTH

A focus of several cigarette studies has been the responsiveness of youths to cigarette prices. If youth are responsive to price (hopefully even more than adults), then tax strategies may be very effective. As noted by Lewit and Coate (1982), ". . . an excise tax increase . . . might continue to discourage smoking participation by successive generations of teenagers and young adults and gradually impact the smoking levels of older age groups as the smoking-discouraged cohorts move through the age spectrum" (p. 143).

It was originally thought that youth price elasticity was indeed very high as based on a finding by Lewit, Coate, and Grossman (1981). These authors studied the effect of price on both the decision to smoke (participation elasticity) and on the decision of how much to smoke. The participation price elasticity for this group was approximately 1.20 to 1.40. This means that for teenagers, many of whom may not have a lot of ready cash, the decision to smoke or not to smoke appeared to depend importantly on cigarette prices.

However, more recent estimates have raised questions about the early results. Two studies have now reported that price has little or no impact on teenage smoking decisions.[32] One concludes that it "finds no evidence that higher cigarette prices would have a significant impact on teenage decisions to pick up the smoking habit" (p. 213).[33]

CONCLUSIONS

This chapter examines two aspects of advertising of concern to the health economist: advertising by health care firms, and advertising that has potential health effects. Beginning with health care firm advertising, we describe the profit-maximizing level of advertising, suggesting that optimal advertising will equate the marginal revenues of advertising with its marginal costs. We find that health professionals are increasingly choosing to advertise in patterns that suggest both an attention to the profit impacts of advertising and the importance of personal feelings about the appropriateness of advertising to the profession.

Advertising in theory may be beneficial to the consumer to the extent that it provides economically valuable information; or it may be detrimental to the prices that consumers face to the extent that it tends to be of the persuasive kind. Evidence from the health sector indicates that advertising effects will differ from industry to industry within the sector. Optometric advertising appears to offer an unqualified benefit to the consumer, lowering price with no harm to quality. In contrast, studies of physician services indicate that here advertising works to raise entry barriers and price. The lesson is one of diverse effects for a diverse sector.

The other major advertising concern of health economics is the potentially detrimental effect of advertising products that are harmful to one's health. The cigarette advertising literature shows that the responsiveness of total industry demand to advertising levels is small at the margin. Excise tax increases appear to be potentially effective tools in public efforts to curb smoking, given the range of elasticity estimates available. For advertising bans, the greatest potential effect appears to be on the young, those in the age group who are more often forming habits that will tend to persist over time.

---

[32]See Wasserman et al. (1991) and Douglas and Hariharan (1994).

[33]See Douglas and Hariharan (1994).

Summary

1. Advertising by health care firms has increased substantially in the past two decades. This trend has been influenced by court actions that increasingly supported the health care firm's freedom to advertise and by an increasingly competitive environment in health care markets.

2. Optimizing by the firm requires the simultaneous optimal choice of firm output level and advertising level. This requires production so that marginal cost equals marginal revenue, and it requires advertising so that the marginal cost of advertising equals the marginal revenue induced by advertising.

3. The advertising adoption choice by the health care firm is probably affected by the health professional's personal distaste or acceptance of advertising as well as profitability criteria.

4. There are two contrasting theories regarding the effects of advertising. One describes advertising primarily as information, and holds that better information leads to greater competition and possibly lower prices. The other describes advertising as a potential barrier to entry, which increases monopoly power and prices.

5. Evidence from the health sector indicates that advertising effects differ by industry within the sector. Studies from the optometry and retail pharmacy industries support the advertising-as-information theory. Studies from the wholesale drugs and physician services industries support the advertising-as-barrier-to-entry theory.

6. The theory of advertising suggests that cigarette advertising can affect brand switching and/or aggregate cigarette demand. Empirical studies tend to conclude that the elasticity of aggregate cigarette demand with respect to advertising is small where significant and sometimes is statistically insignificant.

7. The effect of an advertising ban cannot be predicted from studies of aggregated demand advertising elasticities. The partial ban in the United States, which eliminated both prosmoking and mandatory antismoking messages on television, had little effect on smoking levels and may have increased them. A recent study of bans internationally reports that these and related restrictions on advertising have a significant effect on smoking, though the effect is less than 10 percent.

8. The price elasticity of cigarette demand is large enough to be an important potential public policy tool in any effort to curb smoking in the population.

Discussion Questions

1. Would you be more likely or less likely to choose a physician who advertised in the newspapers or broadcast media? Are there any theoretical or empirical grounds to support your view? Discuss.

2. "Advertising by health care firms is more likely to promote competition where the product is relatively standardized and where advertisers advertise prices." How well does this view accord with the evidence from various parts of the health sector?

3. Advertising may have informative content or persuasive content roughly corresponding to the advertising-as-information theory and the advertising-as-barrier-to-entry theory. Which is most representative of the health care advertising you have seen? Discuss.

4. Advertising in optometry appears to promote lower prices, while advertising in physician care does not appear to have this effect. How can you account for this difference?

5. Someone says: "The advertising elasticity of cigarette demand may be small, but it is big enough to warrant policy curtailing advertising." Under what circumstances could this view be correct? What is your view?

6. What does the evidence regarding the effects of the partial U.S. ban on cigarette advertising suggest about the relative effectiveness of cigarette advertising versus antismoking advertising?

7. How does the responsiveness to both cigarette advertising and cigarette price differ between youths and adults? Why is this important?

8. Suppose that wheat farming were a perfectly competitive industry. Would the typical wheat farmer be likely to advertise? Why or why not? Would an organization representing all wheat farmers be likely to advertise? Compare and contrast the individual farmer with the farmers' organization with respect to advertising.

9. Explain how it is possible to advertise too little or too much.

10. Advertising is normally associated with a rightward shift in demand. Under what circumstances can advertising lead to a decrease in demand? In those situations, what is the optimal level of advertising?

11. Under what circumstances will advertising lead to an increase in a seller's elasticity of demand? A decrease?

12. Advertising has been variously described as a provider of information or as a barrier to entry. Compare the two hypotheses with respect to the ultimate effect on price of the good to be sold.

Exercises

1. How would each of the following likely affect the firm's optimal level of advertising? (A) an increase in the marginal product of advertising at every level of advertising; (B) a law disallowing advertising expenditures as an expense for tax purposes; (C) a firm is just starting out and has not yet developed a clientele.

2. Distinguish between search goods and experience goods. Which of the following are more likely to be experience goods: (A) a meal at Sam's diner; (B) an automobile; (C) a diet cola; (D) 1.5-inch hexagon bolts.

3. How are the following characteristics related to a physician's likelihood of being an advertiser? (A) firm size; (B) specialty category; (C) physician age. Why?

4. If the elasticity of aggregate cigarette demand to advertising were estimated at 0.15, by extrapolation what effect on cigarette consumption would be caused by a 10 percent reduction in advertising? A 50 percent reduction? A 100 percent

reduction? How and why does one's confidence in prediction change over this range of reductions?

5. Draw a demand curve and a marginal revenue curve for a profit-maximizing firm in a market where advertising is prohibited. Draw a marginal cost curve for the same firm and identify the optimal output. Show the appropriate shifts in demand and marginal revenue that would be caused by a removal of the advertising restrictions under the advertising-as-information theory.

6. Suppose the price elasticity of cigarette demand is –0.4. If we increased the prices of cigarettes by 50 percent, what would we expect to happen to the quantity purchased? To total expenditures on cigarettes?

CHAPTER 10

Physician Uncertainty and Small Area Variations

- The Small Area Variations Phenomenon

- The Physician Practice Style Hypothesis

- SAV and Inappropriate Care

- The Cost of Inefficient Variations

- Conclusions

Chapters 7 and 8 focused on the problems that can be created in health care markets by asymmetric information and flawed agency relationships. We emphasized the consequences of a patient's informational gap as well as the limits imposed on the ability of a physician to deviate from his or her agency responsibility in order to induce increases in demand.

There is, however, a different set of information problems relating to technology that has become equally if not more important to health care delivery and policy. These problems relate to information gaps or physician uncertainty regarding the appropriateness of care and the outcomes and relative effectiveness of alternative treatments. The process of disseminating information to providers and the diffusion of know-how and technology are also relevant. Although these subjects have only recently attracted the attention of economists, they have been extensively examined by scholars in other health-related disciplines.

That a physician does not have complete knowledge on all factors that bear on a patient's condition is not a startling proposition. For each of many existing medical procedures, medical scientists have often not yet fully evaluated either the probability of the various outcomes or the cost-effectiveness of the procedure. Those within the medical community have on occasion acknowledged this state of affairs. Perhaps to draw attention to the problem, Dr. David Eddy, a scholar of medical practice, has expressed the problem in strong but simple language: "We don't know what we're

213

doing in medicine."[1] Dr. Eddy and others have recognized the importance of such information gaps both to medical decision making and to the efficient use of health care resources. However, much of the present interest in the problem has come to the attention of analysts through the empirical work of Dr. John Wennberg and various colleagues whose characteristic approach has been the study of *small area variations.*

THE SMALL AREA VARIATIONS PHENOMENON

The small area variations (SAV) phenomenon refers to the wide variations in the per capita utilization rates for many medical and surgical procedures that are commonly found in comparing small, contiguous hospital service markets. Figure 10.1 illustrates the findings for seven common surgical procedures in regions of New England, the United Kingdom, and Norway. The rates, which have been age and sex adjusted to correct for differences in age and sex distributions across populations, have two distinct features. First, the rates vary widely for some procedures, as shown by the ranges in

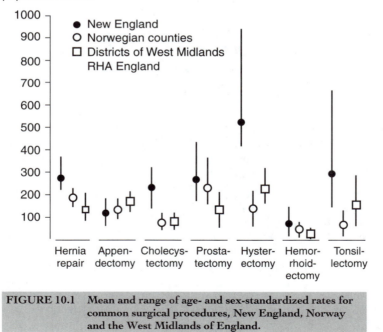

FIGURE 10.1 Mean and range of age- and sex-standardized rates for common surgical procedures, New England, Norway and the West Midlands of England.

Source: McPherson et al. (1982, Figure 1).

[1]*Detroit Free Press,* February 4, 1990, p. 7H.

Figure 10.1. Second, there are wide intercountry differences in the mean rates, such as hysterectomy with a rate (per 100,000 at risk) of 540 in New England, 118 in Norway, and 220 in England. This finding is consistent with many other studies that have shown similar wide variations across small market areas. Even larger areas including states, provinces, and census regions of the United States exhibit the variations. To illustrate, we consider the age- and sex-adjusted surgical rates of low back pain hospitalization, one of the most common sources of hospital admission. In 1987, the rate ranged from 77 per 100,000 adults in the northeastern U.S. census region to 138 in the western region.[2]

In addition to documenting the extent of the variations, Wennberg and others have argued that much of the observed variation is closely related to the degree of physician uncertainty with respect to diagnosis and treatment. Where physicians are uncertain about the effects of and value of a medical procedure, and where a wide range of physician practices are considered to be within the bounds of appropriate care, then there is little consensus and a wide range of practice styles can develop. After he examined the variations in a large number of medical and surgical causes of hospital admission, Wennberg (1984) argued that there is a close association between the variations and the degree of physician discretion in whether or not to hospitalize.

Although evidence supporting the variations is well established, controversy arises from conflicting explanations of the causes of the phenomenon. Some have asked whether or not SAV in part reflects subtle measurement problems. Diehr and colleagues (1990) have demonstrated that due to random variation the observed variation across small areas can be high even when the underlying rates across the areas are the same. By examining variations in hospitalization rates using more than one year of data, Schwartz et al. (1994) found that the variations are substantially reduced. Most of the controversy, however, has focused on the role of practice style and on the related question of whether the observed variations are evidence of unnecessary or inappropriate care. The resolution of this controversy is understandably important for policy. If the variations can be reduced by providing more scientific information, then perhaps welfare gains can be achieved from substantial expenditures in medical science research. Further, some may even suggest the imposition of practice norms, a possibility that illustrates the dangers of misinterpreting the SAV evidence. A careful examination of economic issues involved in the SAV theory and evidence and especially regarding the role of practice style is warranted.

THE PHYSICIAN PRACTICE STYLE HYPOTHESIS

As noted previously, the focus of SAV analysis is often on small, contiguous hospital markets. The purpose of this approach is to evaluate utilization patterns in populations that are relatively homogeneous. In this case, the investigator will be more confident in ruling out differences in population characteristics, such as in health status, education,

---

[2]Volinn, Turczyn, and Loeser (1994).

income, and insurance coverage, as the sources for the observed variations in utilization rates.

SAV researchers have suggested that standard socioeconomic variables cannot fully account for the observed variations in utilization rates. In light of this difficulty, the concept of *practice style* was introduced. According to Wennberg and others, there is substantial uncertainty in diagnosing many conditions, and there is uncertainty associated with outcomes of alternative interventions. This uncertainty has resulted in a lack of agreement about appropriate standards of care so that a physician's set of beliefs will in part determine his or her actions.

Modeling Practice Style

It is useful to provide an operational definition of practice style. The care actually provided and observed ex post (that is, after the fact) is the result of the confluence of many factors of which practice style is only one. Instead, practice style, more in keeping both with the SAV literature and with the economist's understanding of markets, is a before-the-fact, or ex ante, concept describing the physician's set of beliefs about the efficacy of particular forms of care.

One approach to describing practice style in economic terms was introduced by Folland and Stano (1989) and is illustrated in Figure 10.2. The figure shows two production functions for a patient with uterine leiomyoma (fibroids). This condition often leads to hysterectomy, itself a high-variation procedure. The vertical axis in Figure 10.2 represents health status (HS) after treatment, and the horizontal axis represents increasing units of care. One may imagine that the horizontal axis measures a composite of

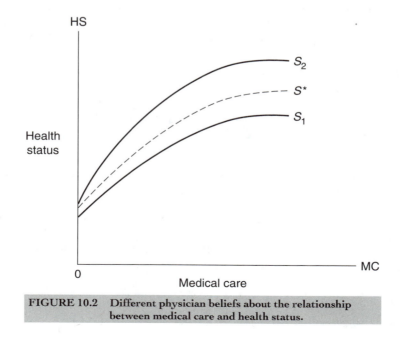

FIGURE 10.2 Different physician beliefs about the relationship between medical care and health status.

various kinds and degrees of medical care (MC). As we move along the units-of-care axis to the right, these increasing units might represent a progression from a simple initial office visit on up to complex surgical interventions.

Differences in practice style are shown by S_1 and S_2, which are representations of two different physicians' beliefs about the true production function. These reflect differences in beliefs by the two physicians about the marginal productivity of higher values of medical care. Here Physician 2 is shown as believing at each step that additional units of medical care are more effective (that is, more productive) than Physician 1 believes them to be. For example, Physician 2 might be a physician who believes that surgery is quite effective, whereas Physician 1 has doubts about the effectiveness of the surgery.

Differences in practice style, therefore, provide a possible accounting for interarea differences in utilization rates. If physicians of type 1 and 2 are not similarly distributed across markets, then the hysterectomy rates will vary between those markets.[3] However, it is also possible to have wide differences in practice style across physicians within markets, but yet little interarea variations if the distribution of practice styles is similar across markets. That is, the average practice style, as represented by the dashed curve S^* in Figure 10.2, could be similar across markets. In these instances, the mean per capita rates of utilization across markets will be relatively uniform even while practice styles vary widely within markets. This possibility marks one of the deficiencies of studying the practice style phenomenon through population-based utilization data.

Testing the Practice Style Hypothesis

A problem with the concept of practice style, including the account we have described, is that the empirical researcher has no apparent objective measure of practice style. In the absence of a directly observable measure, evidence for the thesis will necessarily be indirect. However, relevant indirect evidence is available and it comes from several sources.

EDUCATION, FEEDBACK, AND SURVEILLANCE

First, some studies show that educational, feedback, and surveillance programs directed at physicians can alter their behavior and thus presumably their practice style.[4] For example, one study found that an informational program significantly affected the tonsillectomy rates in 13 New England areas. Similarly, another study found that the rate of unjustified hysterectomies dropped by two-thirds subsequent to a review program introduced in the Canadian province of Saskatchewan. Such evidence supports one's intuitive reasoning that monitoring should change behavior. Nevertheless, there are also studies that suggest that the effects may not be large. In 1985–1986, a system of mandatory review was implemented for inappropriate claims under the Medicare

---

[3]As a corollary to the practice style hypothesis, it is claimed that the interarea variations in utilization will be higher for those procedures for which there is greater uncertainty in diagnosis and treatment.

[4]The ones discussed here are Wennberg et al. (1977), Dyck et al. (1977), and Nyman et al. (1990).

Program (Part B) for 13 procedures. An investigation of the effects of this feedback mechanism on practice behaviors found only a marginal reduction in the rates at which inappropriate claims were submitted.

COMPARING UTILIZATION RATES IN HOMOGENEOUS AREAS

A second empirical approach in investigating the practice style hypothesis is illustrated through an early but influential study by Wennberg and Fowler (1977). The authors extensively studied use rates and population characteristics for six areas in Vermont. They applied the *chi-square* test[5] and found that population differences on many socioeconomic variables, such as "percent with health insurance" and "percent with any restricted days in last 2 weeks for chronic condition," were generally not statistically significant at the 5 percent level. Thus, by ruling out differences in morbidity and other factors (covariates) as accounting for the large differences in the utilization rates which they observed, they concluded that the differences are probably due largely to practice style differences across areas.

Though practice style differences can contribute to differences in utilization across areas, the inference that interarea differences in utilization rates, even in apparently similar areas, are due largely to differences in practice style is incorrect. Green and Becker (1994) performed a SAV analysis for acute cardiac ischemia (ACI) in which they compared two demographically similar towns in Michigan whose ACI discharge rates differed by a factor of three. An examination of medical records suggested that the large differences in admission were due more to differences in the proportions of patients with ACI who went to their hospital emergency department rather than to differences in physician decision making. In other words, area variation does not necessarily mean variation in practice style.

MULTIPLE REGRESSION APPROACHES

The Wennberg and Fowler study also has certain limitations in comparison to approaches that investigate the influence on utilization of many variables simultaneously. That study does not directly control for differences in the covariates. It is generally useful to examine interarea utilization through multiple regression and other multivariate methods that control for the other factors.

The inclusion of many or conceivably all relevant measurable variables in the analysis suggests another indirect approach to the practice style issue. As more variables are added to the analysis, one learns better how much of the observed variations can be explained by standard socioeconomic variables without resorting to the hypothesis of practice style. In cases where the variations are largely explained by the usual set of socioeconomic variables, then the potential role of practice style is small and much of the mystery of the variations phenomenon is eliminated. On the other hand, an inability to explain the variations in terms of the usual variables leaves open the possibility that practice style and possibly other unknown factors are responsible for much

---

[5]This is a simple test that is often used to compare whether proportions in paired or independent samples are significantly different.

of the variations. Practice style is then essentially the residual when other impacts have been explained.

A review of the available multiple regression studies shows that moderate to substantial amounts of the interarea variations are typically explained.[6] Often when a study explains a large portion of the variation by standard socioeconomic variables, we find that it has focused on aggregates of procedures. An aggregate of procedures is typically a weighted average of many procedures. One common example of an aggregate of procedures is medical expenditures per capita. Several studies have found that socioeconomic variables are important in explaining variations in aggregate measures of utilization for small area hospital service markets.[7]

Regression analysis at the small area level[8] for individual procedures, as opposed to aggregates over large numbers of procedures, has generally been less successful in explaining the variations. Nevertheless, Phelps and Parente (1990) found that standard demand and supply variables typically account for between 40 and 75 percent of the variation in their study of 134 separate diagnostic categories. Elsewhere Escarce (1993) found that 43 percent of the variation in cataract surgery rates for the Medicare population is explained by economic and sociodemographic variables. This still leaves a potential 57 percent that may be due to practice style. But, after "purging" the surgery rates of any possible practice style influence, Escarce found that the variation in cataract surgery rates was reduced by only a small amount.

FEATURE

Small Area Variations and the Diffusion of Medical Technological Information

Both demand and supply will be influenced by information available to providers and patients as well as by the availability of a service in a market. Many existing studies of variations have not accounted for the uneven diffusion of information and technology. Legnini et al. (1990) observed large changes in the discharge rates of anal procedures and cardiac catheterization between 1981 and 1986 in Connecticut hospitals. For the former, the increasing availability of outpatient treatment greatly reduced the rate and greatly increased the variations. For cardiac catheterization, increasing information about its use as well as increasing use of new technologies, such as coronary angioplasty, accounted for a large increase in the use rate and a sharp decrease in the variability.

---

[6]See Folland and Stano (1990). Also Folland and Stano (1989) show the conditions under which the residual variation from multiple regression can be taken as an upper bound for the contribution of practice style. They show that practice style is relatively unimportant for large aggregated sets of commodities.

[7]McLaughlin et al. (1989) and Clark (1990).

[8]The size of the geographical area representing a hospital service market is commonly represented by combinations of zip codes. There are various algorithms to determine these areas, but basically the population in a zip code is assigned to the hospital service area determined by where the plurality of its residents received their care.

These contributions indicate that practice style could be important for some procedures, but the contribution of other variables should not be overlooked. As Escarce demonstrates, it would also be wrong to attribute all or most of the unexplained variation in utilization rates to practice style. For many procedures, conventional economic and demographic influences may well dominate the as yet undetermined effects of practice style.

SAV AND INAPPROPRIATE CARE

Perhaps the most controversial issue in the SAV literature is the proposition that substantial variation in utilization rates across market areas is an indication of inappropriate care. Can we say that high-use areas are likely to be using unnecessary care, and that low-use areas experience underutilization? It is tempting to reach these conclusions and to extrapolate savings under the assumption that high-use areas experience the rates found in lower-use areas. This is just what Wennberg and colleagues did after comparing utilization rates in Boston and New Haven.[9] The authors argued that the cities are demographically similar but Boston has much higher utilization rates so that substantial cost savings are possible.

The potential savings from reducing excessive utilization has led to a national focus on this issue. Indicative of this new priority, Congress in late 1989 created the Agency for Health Care Policy and Research. The agency's primary mission is "to determine what works and to develop practice guidelines and standards to assess and assure quality of care." A large number of multidisciplinary Patient Outcomes Research Teams (PORTS) have been funded to fulfill this mission.

Defining Inappropriate Care and Patient Preferences

Although the assessment of medical practice and the development of guidelines would appear to be largely noneconomic problems, the economist's contribution could be important. First, economists are typically skeptical of the notion that a correct rate of use can be determined on the basis of medical science alone. The economically correct rate is one at which the marginal benefits to the informed consumer equal the marginal costs. In consequence, it may be difficult to identify "unnecessary" utilization without having extensive knowledge of the consumer's preferences and local cost conditions. A graphical illustration helps to identify the issues.

Assume two populations identical in size. In Figure 10.3, panel A shows two demand curves, D_1 and D_2, representing different demands for a particular service. Differences in demand can arise because both economic and noneconomic characteristics of the two populations differ. These different demand curves represent different marginal valuations being placed on health care utilization. People may differ in their

---

[9]Wennberg, Freeman, and Culp (1987); Wennberg et al. (1989); Fisher et al. (1994).

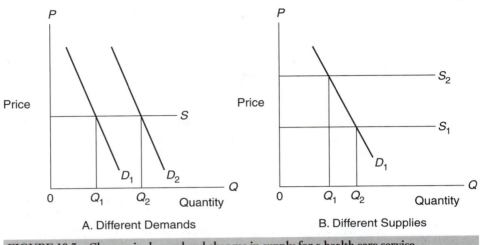

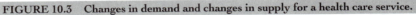

A. Different Demands   B. Different Supplies

FIGURE 10.3   Changes in demand and changes in supply for a health care service.

Clinical Decision Making—Patient Preferences and Prostatectomy

The role of information, medical science, and preferences in clinical decision making was studied by Eddy (1990). Eddy breaks the decision into two main components—evaluating the outcome of alternatives and then comparing and choosing from among the options.[10] The first component is largely a scientific one determined primarily through clinical studies of patient outcomes. However, for many patient conditions, even a fully informed physician will face the problem of inadequate scientific information.

The second component, comparing the alternatives, involves judgment and patient preferences. Eddy emphasizes that "it is the patient's preferences that should determine the decision" (p. 442).

A failure to make appropriate decisions can arise from failures in both stages. Clearly, a physician's inadequacies in education and training as well as deliberate attempts to misrepresent outcomes will distort information needed at the second step. Similarly, if patients misrepresent, or physicians misinterpret, their preferences, or if inadequate information is communicated to patients, the second step will be flawed.

The realization within the medical community of the role of the patient has encouraged the development of new information technology that can improve the decision-making process. For example, Wennberg and colleagues have developed an interactive videodisc that is designed to help patients make a choice regarding prostatectomy. To help with the decision, a patient answers questions designed to measure his attitude toward risk and his ability to tolerate discomfort.

[10]Eisenberg's (1986) work on physician decision making and practice patterns is also highly recommended.

preferences with regard to health care, their attitudes toward risk, their ability to pay, and so on. These demands would tend to differ even if scientific knowledge were complete and identical in both markets.

To illustrate the implications of this theory, suppose further that the supply curves are identical in both markets as represented by curve S in panel A. The correct rate in each market occurs at the intersection of the supply and demand curves. Here the correct rate is defined as the one under which the marginal benefit to users will equal the marginal cost of providing the service. The correct rates will thus differ if the fully informed demand curves differ. Furthermore, where supply conditions differ between two markets, as in Figure 10.3 panel B, the correct utilization rate will be different even if demand were identical in both markets at D_1.

The importance of patient preferences in utilization decisions is being increasingly emphasized in the medical community. Included in patient preferences are attitudes toward risk or the tolerance of pain and discomfort. As a result of this interest in preferences, Wennberg, Eddy, and others have urged physicians to involve patients in medical decisions.

Economically Inefficient Levels of Care

A second important role for the economist is to identify inefficient levels of care and to assess the costs of these inefficiencies. As we have noted, economists argue that resources should be used to the point where marginal benefits are equal to marginal costs to society. Under certain circumstances, the marginal benefit to society will be given by the consumer's demand curve. In Figure 10.4, the efficient utilization from society's perspective is thus Q^*, derived from the intersection of the marginal benefit curve with the marginal cost curve. With this understanding, inefficient care would be

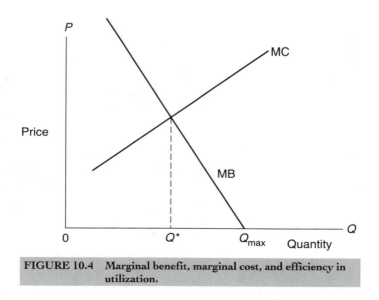

FIGURE 10.4 Marginal benefit, marginal cost, and efficiency in utilization.

indicated by any level of care different from Q^*. Excessive care is utilization beyond Q^* even though the additional care still provides positive benefits to the patient. Shortly, we will apply this approach to the assessment of the cost of inefficient levels of care. Before taking that step, however, consider a dilemma for the physician that arises from this analysis.

If the patient pays for the care out-of-pocket, then he or she will also elect the level of care indicated by Q^*. That is, this patient will arrive at the social optimum. If, instead, the patient is fully insured, then he or she will maximize well-being by consuming the quantity Q_{max} in Figure 10.4. We have previously identified this increased consumption as the moral hazard problem. A physician acting as perfect agent would also recommend or agree to provide the fully insured patient the quantity Q_{max}. It is clear, though, that the physician may be placed in a difficult position, particularly if society demands in addition that he or she act as an agent for the broader interests of society as a whole. Society's broader interest requires that the physician recommend and provide the quantity Q^*.

What should the physician do? Should he or she act in society's best interests to ration resources efficiently, regardless of the financial circumstances of the patient? Or should the physician provide all the medical care that provides a positive benefit even if the marginal benefit is much smaller than the marginal cost of the required resources? This is, after all, what physicians have been trained to do and also what is consistent with the Hippocratic oath.

THE COST OF INEFFICIENT VARIATIONS

Given the economic understanding of what constitutes the correct—that is, the efficient—level of health care, Phelps and Parente (1990) developed a model to measure the cost to society of inefficient or incorrect rates of use. Their approach is still evolving[11] but the basics are illustrated with the help of Figure 10.5. In this figure, the true marginal benefit curve for medical care involving procedure X is given by the curve MB*. This curve reflects the true benefits in the sense that it reflects what patients' valuations of the care would be, given full and complete medical scientific information. The efficient fully informed quantity (expressed as a rate of utilization) is thus R_2, where MB* crosses the marginal cost curve, MC.

With underutilization, such as at R_1, a gain in consumer surplus could be achieved by increasing utilization up to R_2. The gain in consumer surplus is measured by the area under the true marginal benefit curve and above the marginal cost curve. This potential gain is indicated by the area labeled A. Thus, triangle A represents the net forgone benefit to society from underutilization. The forgone benefit is a welfare loss, and it represents the cost to society of the inefficiency. In a similar fashion, one can measure the welfare loss of inefficiently excessive utilization. The utilization rate R_3 exceeds the efficient rate R_2 and causes a welfare loss equal to the triangle B.

---

[11]Dranove (1995) and Phelps (1995).

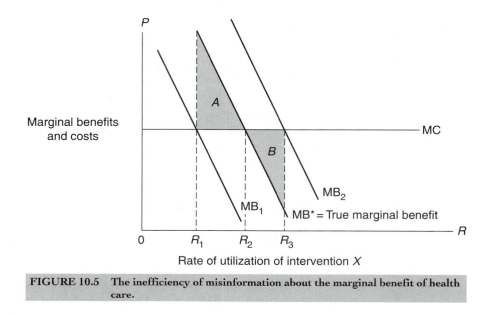

FIGURE 10.5   The inefficiency of misinformation about the marginal benefit of health care.

Measuring the Welfare Loss

Phelps and Parente show that the total welfare loss (W) to society resulting from inter-area deviations from the correct rate is approximated by:

$$W = \frac{0.5 \times (\text{Total Spending on } X) \times \text{CV}^2}{E_p}$$

where the abbreviated terms have the following meanings: CV is the coefficient of variation of inappropriate use, and E_p is the absolute value of the price elasticity of demand. While the elasticity has been defined in Chapters 2 and 6, the CV as used in the present context will require additional clarification.

A coefficient of variation is a measure of dispersion commonly used in statistics and defined as the ratio of the standard deviation to the mean. However, as discussed earlier, variation due to differences in preferences and many other socioeconomic factors are legitimate determinants of the correct rates. In the present context, the total variation in utilization rates must be adjusted to remove that portion of the variation that is due to legitimate differences in the correct rates across market areas. The only variation that causes a welfare loss is the residual variation, that due to inefficient use. In the preceding formula, CV represents the coefficient of variation purged of the legitimate differences. The CV in the present equation thus means only the amount of variation due to medical disagreement and lack of medical technology information. Thus, if total spending or the variations as noted with the CV rise, so does welfare loss W. The more elastic the demand (higher E_p), the smaller the welfare loss.

TABLE 10.1   Annual Welfare Loss Nationally from Variations in Medical Practice When Average Rate Is Correct

Procedure	Per Capita Loss	Aggregate Loss, U.S. Annually ($ billion)
Coronary bypass procedures	$3.10	$0.74
Psychosis	2.97	0.71
Circulatory diagnoses except AMI, with cardiac catheterization	1.86	0.45
Chronic obstructive pulmonary disease	1.71	0.41
Angina pectoris	1.33	0.32
Adult gastroenteritis	1.15	0.28
Adult pneumonia	1.14	0.27
Alcohol and drug use	1.08	0.26
Major joint replacement and limb reattachment	1.03	0.25
Back and neck procedures	0.93	0.22
Chemotherapy	0.83	0.20
Depressive neurosis	0.81	0.19
Extracranial vascular procedures	0.76	0.18
Medical back problems	0.70	0.17
Pediatric pneumonia	0.70	0.17
Cardiac valve procedures	0.68	0.16
Adult bronchitis and asthma	0.65	0.16
Heart failure and shock	0.64	0.15
Acute myocardial infarction	0.59	0.14
Pacemaker procedures	0.57	0.14
Respiratory infections/inflammations	0.57	0.14
Infectious disease diagnosis	0.56	0.13
Pediatric bronchitis and asthma	0.54	0.13
Cardiac arrhythmias	0.52	0.12
Prostatectomy	0.49	0.12
Total, top 25 admission types, annual loss	$25.91 per capita	$6.22 billion

Source: Phelps and Mooney (1992, Table 3).

To develop practical estimates of CV, Phelps and Mooney (1992) used the residual variation derived from regressions of utilization rates on a set of variables representing population socioeconomic factors. They further assumed that inefficient use across market areas tends to average out, and that demand elasticities for all procedures equal 0.15. Based on these approximations, methods, and assumptions, Table 10.1 shows the estimated losses for the top 25 procedures ranked by welfare loss estimated for the United States. The estimated total for the United States for all these procedures amounted to over $6 billion for 1987.

Other Considerations

The estimates reported here suggest that these losses are greater than those associated with moral hazard and also greater than the cost of the research necessary to provide the needed information to determine the appropriate rates. They represent informed estimates of the potential value of medical research and the dissemination of the resulting medical technological information. However, it should be understood that such estimates may err either on the high or low side for any or all procedures. First, they may understate the true welfare costs if marginal costs of care are rising (not constant as they are in Figure 10.5) or if average inappropriate use across market areas in actuality is biased toward either high or low use.

Second, they may overstate the true welfare costs if the estimated value of CV has not successfully been purged of those legitimate sources of variation—that is, purged of all influences except that of the lack of medical technological information. The problem arises because the unexplained portion of variation in these multiple regression analyses cannot be attributed to practice style or any one cause with a known statistical level of confidence.

CONCLUSIONS

There are wide variations in the use of many medical and surgical procedures. The reasons for these variations, including the role of physician uncertainty and practice style, are not well understood. The notion that a scientifically correct use rate exists is modified in economic theory to recognize that an efficient use rate reflects the confluence not only of scientific information but also of patient preferences and other economic factors. Regardless of the extent to which practice style contributes to interarea variations, it is plausible and likely that inadequate clinical information about patient outcomes from alternative therapies tends to result in inappropriate care. This will cause welfare losses that may be substantial. The growing policy concern with informational inadequacies in the health care sector has quite naturally led to efforts intended to improve patient outcomes in cost-efficient ways. The resulting search for "what works" has necessitated a growing emphasis on cost-effectiveness analysis to evaluate alternative health care treatments and programs. This subject is taken up in Chapter 24.

Summary

1. The small area variations (SAV) phenomenon refers to the wide interarea variations in the per capita use rates found for many medical and surgical procedures.
2. Such variations have been found in the United States and many other countries.
3. The practice style hypothesis, which refers to physician uncertainty in diagnosis and treatment, has been proposed as the major explanatory factor.

4. Practice style can be modeled through differences among physicians in their beliefs about the marginal benefits of alternative treatments.

5. Most of the evidence for the practice style hypothesis is indirect, coming from studies showing the following:
   - changes in practice patterns following physician education and monitoring;
   - wide variations in utilization rates across small homogeneous areas;
   - high unexplained residuals in multiple regression analyses of interarea utilization rates.

6. The SAV phenomenon is often interpreted to suggest that considerable amounts of unnecessary care are being provided and that major savings are possible through elimination of that care. One estimate of the annual welfare loss resulting from inappropriate variations of the top 25 procedures (ranked by welfare loss) is $6 billion.

7. Substantial problems remain, however, in identifying inappropriate care and properly accounting for the role of patient preferences.

Discussion Questions

1. What is the SAV phenomenon? What are some economic forces that can help explain SAV? What are some demographic and other considerations? How might physician uncertainty lead to SAV? What evidence supports the practice style hypothesis?

2. How can two markets in which there are wide intra-area variations in physician practice style have the same per capita utilization rate?

3. What possible criticisms can you propose for the idea that areas with high utilization rates for a procedure indicate the provision of unnecessary care?

4. How would an economist define the correct rate of use? Using Figure 10.3, explain how areas can differ in their correct rates. Thus, what is wrong with the notion of a universally "correct rate"?

5. How does insurance lead to inefficiencies and to deviations from the economically correct rate?

6. Suppose you observed that there are no interarea variations in the use rates for some procedures. Can this be taken as evidence that good health care is being provided? If not, what other kinds of information would be useful?

7. If one cause of SAV is lack of information about various procedures, would you expect SAV to have increased, decreased, or stayed the same over time? Why?

8. As new technologies become available more rapidly for given procedures, would you expect an increased or decreased amount of small area variation?

9. Suppose there are large variations in average use rates per person within small areas as well as between small areas. Does this necessarily mean that the practice style hypothesis is incorrect? Suppose there are zero or small variations in average use rates between small areas. Does this necessarily mean that the practice style hypothesis is incorrect? Discuss.

Exercises

1. In comparing SAV across diseases and diagnoses, would more complicated diseases suggest greater or lesser variation?

2. Using Figure 10.5, what are the welfare gains to consumers in going from R_1 to R_2? What are the costs of the increased consumption? Show that the net gain corresponds to the area represented as A.

3. Consider the approximation of the welfare loss due to intra-area deviations from the correct rate of care. All else equal, which procedures would yield the largest welfare losses—those with low price elasticities or those with high price elasticities? Why is this the case?

CHAPTER

Insurance

The role of health insurance is paramount in the discussion of the health economy. Unlike the purchase of most other goods, average Americans, and indeed citizens of other countries, do not pay directly for the costs of their health care. Rather, much is paid indirectly through an insurance company or other program, with the consumer paying directly only a portion of the bill, or coinsurance. The insurance coverage is provided for by the payment of premiums or taxes. The premiums are often, although not always, purchased through the consumer's participation in the labor force.

While many economic decisions are made under conditions where the consumer knows fairly well the present and future prices, incomes, and other economic parameters, most people realize that for many economic decisions there is a substantial amount of uncertainty for future outcomes. Health care expenses, in particular, are uncertain.

Many illnesses occur fairly rarely and seemingly at random, but when they do, they entail substantial costs that could be financially troublesome to households. Moreover, it is conceivable that costs could be so high that, without outside financial help, treatment simply might not be available.

What Is Insurance?

For a clear picture of what insurance is, consider the demand for insurance without all of the detailed trappings (deductibles, premiums, coinsurance, etc.) that accompany modern insurance plans. Consider a club with 100 members. The members are about the same age, and they have about the same lifestyles. It seems that about once a year one of the 100 members gets sick, and incurs health care costs of $1,000. The incidence of illness seems to be random, not necessarily striking men, women, the old, or the young in any systematic fashion. The club members, worried about potential losses due to illness, decide to collect $10 from each member, and to put the $1,000 in the bank for safe keeping, and to earn a little interest. If a member becomes ill, the fund is then used to pay for the treatment. This, in a nutshell, is insurance. The members have paid $10 to avoid the risk or uncertainty, however small, of having to pay $1,000. The "firm" collects the money, tries to maintain and/or increase its value through investment, and pays claims when asked.

In general, insurance reduces the variability of the insureds' incomes by pooling a large number of units, and operating on the principle of the law of large numbers. That is, although outlays for a health event may be highly variable for any given unit in the pool, the average outlays for the group can be predicted fairly well. The law of large numbers shows that for a given probability of illness, the distribution of the average rate of illness in the group will collapse around the probability of illness, as the group size gets larger and larger.

This chapter considers the theory and the practice of health care insurance. It is necessary to quantify the idea of risk as well as attitudes toward risk. With those ideas, it is then possible to consider the structure of insurance policies, and how markets evolve to provide them. While markets will develop to provide insurance for the needs of many groups, we nevertheless also consider the possibility that insurance markets may not evolve for some groups of society.

Insurance Versus Social Insurance

It is useful at this point to distinguish between insurance, as is provided through the pooling of risk, and government programs (often referred to as social insurance) such as Social Security, Medicare, and Medicaid in the United States. The former is provided through markets in which buyers are protecting themselves against rare events whose probabilities can be statistically estimated. The government programs are insurance programs with the government as insurer, and are distinguished by two features:

1. Premiums (the amounts paid by purchasers) are heavily, and often completely (as in the case of Medicaid), subsidized.
2. Participation is constrained according to government-set eligibility rules.

In addition, government insurance programs often transfer income from one segment of society to another. Given the importance of such social insurance programs, we address an entire chapter (Chapter 21) to them later in the text.

Insurance Terminology

It is helpful to consider some terms that are used in the discussion of insurance. Although much of the analysis that we will consider is in the standard economic language of prices and quantities, the insurance industry has developed a set of definitions that should be understood. These include:

Premium Coverage   When people buy insurance policies, they typically pay an $X premium for $Y of coverage should the event occur.

Coinsurance and Copayment   Many insurance policies, particularly in the health insurance industry, require that when events occur, the insured person share the loss. This percentage paid *by the insured person* is the *coinsurance rate*. With a 20 percent coinsurance rate, an insured person, for example, would be liable (out of his or her own pocket) for a $10 *copayment* out of a $50 charge. The insurance company would pay the remainder, or 80 percent. Thus, coinsurance refers to the percentage paid by the insured; copayment refers to the amount paid by the insured (such as a fixed payment for a prescription).

Deductible   With many policies, it is often the case that there is some amount deducted from the payment to the insured person irrespective of coinsurance. In a sense, the insurance does not apply until the consumer pays the deductible. Deductibles may be applied toward individual claims, or, often in the case of health insurance, they may be applied only to a certain amount of total charges in any given year.

Coinsurance and *deductibles* are often used together. For example, an insurance policy may require that John pay the first $100 of his medical expenses out-of-pocket each year. It may then require that he pay 20 percent of each additional dollar in charges. This policy would then be said to have a deductible of $100, and a coinsurance rate of 20 percent.

Many feel that deductibles and coinsurance are simply ways that insurance companies "gouge" the consumers to make extra money. Economists, in contrast, have found that both deductibles and coinsurance may be used to design policies that lead to desirable economic consequences. The requirement that there be some copayment makes consumers more alert to differences in the true costs of the treatment they are purchasing. The charging of deductibles discourages frivolous claims or visits, and also makes the insured person more aware of the results of his or her actions. Both may serve to avoid claims and to reduce costs.

RISK AND INSURANCE

To this point in the book, we have assumed in our models that all decisions occur under conditions of certainty. That is, consumers know what the prices, incomes, and tastes are and will be. Clearly, however, many decisions are made in which the outcome is risky or uncertain.[1]

We begin by considering the insurance coverage of an event that occurs with the known probability p leading to a predictable loss and/or payment. This assumption will be used to characterize individuals' choices under uncertainty. We will then extend the general characterization to health insurance, which differs since the payment may be affected by the insurance. We address this difference once the basic points regarding risk are developed.

Expected Value

Suppose that Clyde asks John to play a game in which a coin will be flipped. If it comes up "heads," John will win one dollar; if it comes up "tails," he will win nothing. How much would John be willing to pay in order to play this game? Analysts find the concept of *expected value* to be useful in this analysis. With an honest coin, the probability of heads is one-half (0.5), as is the probability of tails. The expected value, sometimes called the expected return, then, is:

$$E = \text{(probability of heads)} \times \text{(return if heads, i.e., \$ 1)} + \text{(probability of tails)} \times \text{(return if tails, i.e., \$0)} \tag{11.1}$$

The expected value here is 50 cents, that is $(1/2 \times 1) + (1/2 \times 0)$. If he uses the decision criterion that he will play the game if the expected return exceeds the expected cost, John will play (pass) if it costs him less (more) than 50 cents.[2]

The special case where the price of the gamble is exactly 50 cents and is equal to the expected return is analogous to a situation in insurance where the expected benefits paid out by the insurance company are equal to the premiums taken in by the company. This equality of expected benefit payments and premiums is called an *actuarially fair* insurance policy. In reality, insurance companies will have additional administration and transaction costs that they will also have to cover to break even, but the definition of an actuarially fair policy is useful in talking about insurance.

Marginal Utility of Wealth and Risk Aversion

The foregoing example implies that John is indifferent to risk. That is, for him the incremental pleasure of winning 50 cents (one dollar less the amount he paid to play), is exactly balanced by the incremental displeasure of losing 50 cents. Suppose, however, the sizes of the bets were changed, so that the coin flip would now yield $100, or nothing, and that John was now asked to bet $50 to play. He may now refuse an actuarially

---

[1]Sometimes economists distinguish between *risk* and *uncertainty*. Risk refers to a situation in which we can list all outcomes and assign probabilities to them. Uncertainty refers to situations in which we may neither be able to list the outcomes nor assign the probabilities. Except where we make explicit distinctions, we will simplify our exposition by using the two terms interchangeably.

[2]More generally, with n outcomes, expected value E is written as follows:

$$E = p_1 R_1 + p_2 R_2 + \ldots + p_n R_n$$

where p_i is the probability of outcome i (i.e., p_1 or p_2 through p_n) and R_i is the return if outcome i occurs. The sum of the probabilities p_i equals 1.

fair bet—$50—on the grounds that he cannot afford to risk the $50 loss if the coin lands tails. This suggests that the disutility of losing money is larger than is the utility of winning a similar amount. This would be true, for example, if he felt that the utility of an extra dollar of wealth were worth more when he is relatively poorer than the utility of an extra dollar of wealth is worth when he is relatively richer. The utility from an extra dollar is called the marginal utility of wealth.[3]

It is useful to incorporate the individual's utility of wealth function into the analysis. To discuss utility in the context of analyzing the consumer's behavior toward risk, we must posit a degree of cardinality. Remember from Chapter 2 that when utility is treated as ordinal, we are assuming that the consumer can only rank consumer bundles but cannot compare magnitudes of satisfaction. To understand our utility model of risk behavior, we must further assume that the consumer cannot only rank alternatives but can also compare magnitudes, for example, assessing the sum of utilities of two outcomes weighted by their probabilities.

Consider the top panel of Figure 11.1. Suppose that John's wealth W is $ 10,000. That amount of wealth gives him a utility level $U_1 = 140$, and allows him to buy some basic necessities of life. This can be denoted as point A.

Suppose his wealth rises to $20,000. Will his utility double? While it is hard to know for certain what will happen, it is likely that the next $10,000 will not bring him the incremental utility that the first $10,000 brought. Thus, U_2 is likely to be less than twice that of U_1. Suppose, for example, that $U_2 = 200$. This is denoted as point B.

Do all of the points on the utility function between U_1 and U_2 lie on a straight line? If they do, this is equivalent to saying that the utility from the $10,001^{st}$ dollar is equal to the $19,999^{th}$ dollar and hence the marginal utility is constant. This is also unlikely. Since the marginal utility of earlier dollars is likely to be larger than that of later dollars, then the utility curve is likely to be bowed out, or concave, to the x-axis.

The marginal utility of wealth is the amount by which utility increases when wealth goes up by one dollar. This rise in utility, divided by the one dollar increase in wealth, is thus the slope of the utility function. The bowed shape of the utility function shows a slope that is getting smaller or flatter as wealth rises; thus, the marginal utility of wealth is diminishing. This is graphed in the bottom panel of Figure 11.1 as points A_1, F_1, and B_1. When the marginal utility of wealth is decreasing in wealth, the consumer is said to be risk averse.

Suppose that John's wealth increases to $20,000. He understands, however, that if he becomes ill, which may occur with probability 0.05, his expenses will cause his wealth to decline to $10,000. If this occurs, he can calculate his *expected utility, E:*

$$E = 0.95 \times (\text{utility of } \$20,000) + 0.05 \times (\text{utility of } \$10,000)$$
$$= 0.95 \times (200) + 0.05 \times (140) \qquad\qquad \textbf{(11.2)}$$
$$= 190 + 7 = 197.$$

---

[3]Wealth refers to the sum (or stock) of the consumer's net assets in money terms. It is related to income, which is the flow of additional funds in any given period. It may be sensible to refer to one or the other for certain discussions, but the substance of the insurance analysis refers to both.

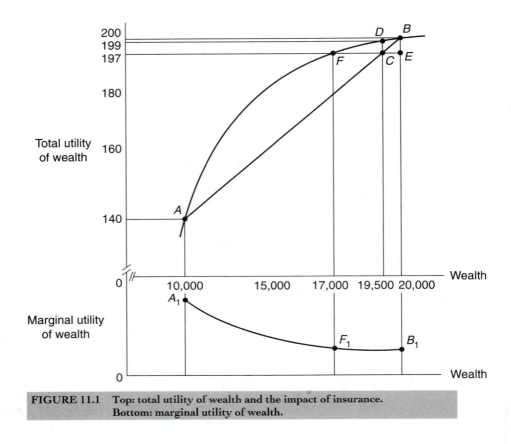

FIGURE 11.1   Top: total utility of wealth and the impact of insurance.
Bottom: marginal utility of wealth.

Thus, the expected utility is 197 or point *C* because of the risk of illness. Geometrically, this is the line segment between points *A* and *B,* evaluated at wealth level $19,500. It must be compared to the utility of 199 (point *D*), corresponding to the utility that he would receive if he were certain to have $19,500. Point *F* is sometimes referred to as the *certainty equivalent.* Clearly, the uncertainty leads to a loss of 2 units of utility, i.e., $199 - 197$.

Purchasing Insurance

Suppose that John is able to buy an insurance policy costing $500/year, such that his wealth would be guaranteed to be $20,000 irrespective of his health. Is it a good buy? We see that at net wealth of $19,500, which equals his initial wealth minus the insurance premium, his certainty utility is, in fact, 199. The consumer depicted is better off at point *D* than at point *C,* as shown by the fact that point *D* gives the higher utility. Thus, if insuring to get a certain wealth rather than facing the risky prospect makes this person better off, he will insure.

We can, in fact, use Figure 11.1 to calculate the maximum amount that John would be willing to pay for the insurance by moving "southwest" down the utility function to the level of $U = 197$, and reading the level of wealth (off the x-axis) to which it corresponds, or point F. The maximum amount he can spend on insurance, and still be better off than were he to go without insurance, is his wealth (here, $20,000) minus the amount (e.g., $17,000) that provides the same level of utility as point C (which represents his expected utility when not insuring). So, John would be willing to pay $3,000 for insurance, and still be as well off as if he had remained uninsured. This amount (distance FC) reflects John's aversion to risk. The difference between amount FE and the actual premium ($500) reflects his consumer surplus from having to pay only $500, rather than $3,000, to reduce his risk.

This analysis illustrates several facts:

1. Insurance can only be sold in circumstances where there is diminishing marginal utility of wealth or income—that is, when the consumer is risk averse. It can be seen that if marginal utility were constant, a requirement that the individuals pay an actuarially fair premium for insurance would leave them no better off than if they were uninsured.

2. Expected utility is an average measure; the individual either wins or loses the bet. Although the consumer will have an expected wealth and hence utility as indicated by point C on the graph each period, his actual wealth (utility) will be either $20,000 (200), or $10,000 (140). With the former, he would have lost $500 by paying the insurance premium; with the latter, he would get a check from his insurer for $10,000 (after paying the premium of $500).

3. If insurance companies charge more than the actuarially fair premium, people will have less expected wealth from insuring than from not insuring. Even though people will have less wealth as a result of the purchase of insurance, the increased well-being comes from the elimination of risk.

THE DEMAND FOR INSURANCE

The preceding section considered the circumstances under which a consumer might choose to purchase insurance, but it gave little guidance as to how much he would purchase. The next two sections present a model first provided by Mark Pauly (1968) to consider the fundamental demand and supply decisions regarding insurance. Within this discussion, we will again review the concept of actuarially fair insurance. We will also address the topic of optimal design of policies.

How Much Insurance?

We have discussed why John would choose to buy insurance. Now consider how much insurance he would choose. This consumer's expected utility involves his wealth under two possibilities, sickness (with a probability of 0.05, or p) or health (with a probability of 0.95, which would then be $1 - p$). First, if he becomes ill, his wealth will fall from level W (for example, $20,000) to level $W - L$ ($20,000 - 10,000$, meaning that his loss L is $10,000), with probability 0.05. If he stays healthy, his wealth will stay at W, which occurs with probability 0.95. John's expected utility is then as follows:

$$E = \text{(probability ill)} \times \text{utility if ill} + \text{(probability well)} \times \text{utility if well} \qquad \textbf{(11.3)}$$

or:

$$E = p \times \text{utility of (net wealth if ill)} + (1 - p) \times \text{utility of (net wealth if well)}$$
$$\text{or: } E = p \times \text{utility of } (W - L) + (1 - p) \times \text{utility of } (W) \tag{11.4}$$

If John is worried about the possibility of loss, he will want to buy an insurance policy that will pay him q dollars (as yet unknown) if he becomes ill. He must determine how much insurance to buy—that is, what value of q to choose. We will show that under certain circumstances it will be optimal to buy the amount of insurance q, such that q is exactly equal to his expected loss, L.

Suppose that in order to buy insurance coverage worth q, he must pay some fraction of that amount, which we call α, as a premium. Thus, if q equals $1,000, and $\alpha = 0.10$, then John must pay $\alpha q = 0.10 \times 1,000$, or $100 per year for an insurance policy from which he may collect $1,000. Thus, if he becomes ill, his wealth, with probability p, will now be:

$$\text{New wealth} = \text{Original wealth } (W) - \text{loss } (L) -$$
$$\text{insurance premium } (\alpha q) + \text{payment from insurance } (q)$$

or:

$$\text{Wealth (if ill)} = W - L - \alpha q + q = W - L + (1 - \alpha)q \tag{11.5}$$

If John remains well, which occurs with probability $(1 - p)$, his wealth will be:

$$\text{Wealth (if well)} = \text{Original wealth } (W) - \text{premium } (\alpha q) \tag{11.6}$$

As noted in the preceding section, not all people buy insurance. There are some who are not averse to the risk and, hence, are uninsured. There may also be incomplete markets for providing the insurance if the illness is not well known or understood (we address this in the next section). If John chooses to buy the insurance, however, he is choosing the amount of insurance q to maximize his expected utility. This means that he is weighing the expected marginal (utility) returns against the expected marginal (utility) costs of coverage. The returns stem from the added wealth when he is ill, and the costs from the decreased wealth when well. Thus, from equation (11.3):

$$E = p \times \text{utility of } (W - L + (1 - \alpha)q)$$
$$[1]$$
$$+ (1 - p) \times \text{utility of } (W - \alpha q) \tag{11.7}$$
$$[2]$$

A purchase of one extra dollar of insurance increases his utility in expression [1] of equation (11.7). This is because when he is ill (as he is under expression [1]) then the extra dollar of insurance q will net him a wealth increase of $(1 - \alpha)$, the dollar benefit payment less the premium of α dollars. The extra utility he gets from this extra money is equal to the $(1 - \alpha)$ dollars multiplied by the marginal utility (the utility gain per extra dollar). But this utility gain only occurs with a probability of p; thus, these terms must be multiplied by p.

Marginal Benefits and Marginal Costs— A Graphical Representation

John can buy additional insurance, that is, extra dollars of coverage. Each new extra dollar of coverage will yield a smaller expected marginal utility. This happens because as he buys more insurance, his wealth when he becomes ill gets larger and larger. Since marginal utility decreases as wealth increases, the expected marginal utility from extra dollars of insurance coverage (i.e., extra dollars of q) decreases with coverage (i.e., declines with q).

Figure 11.2 graphs this relationship. Although total utility rises with q, the marginal utility MU (if ill) of incremental level of wealth $(1 - \alpha)$ multiplied by the probability of illness will fall as q rises. Hence, the marginal return to insurance, $p \times (1 - \alpha) \times$ MU (if ill) falls as q increases. This is shown by the negatively sloped marginal return relationship MR.

If part [1] of equation (11.7) is related to marginal revenue if ill, then part [2] may be related to the foregone benefits if well, or marginal costs. As q rises, John's wealth, when he is well, falls by incremental amount α; that is, his wealth declines as he pays out premiums. Since the probability of his staying well is $(1 - p)$, then his expected marginal utility of coverage when he is well is $(1 - p) \times \alpha \times$ MU (if well). His marginal utility of wealth (the slope of the utility function) gets larger (steeper) as his wealth decreases. The foregone marginal utility (the lost premiums) if he stays well is a marginal cost, and it rises as q rises. This is shown by the positively sloped marginal cost relationship MC.

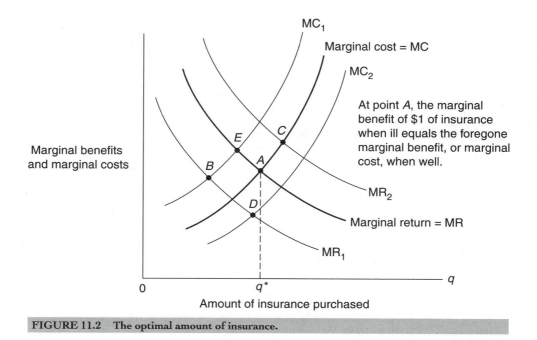

At point *A*, the marginal benefit of $1 of insurance when ill equals the foregone marginal benefit, or marginal cost, when well.

FIGURE 11.2   The optimal amount of insurance.

Looking at the graph, we see that John will choose to buy an extra dollar of coverage q as long as the expected marginal gain MR exceeds the expected marginal loss MC. He thus picks amount $q*$ such that marginal return equals marginal cost at point A.

Changes in Expected Loss, Premiums, or Wealth

It is useful to consider the impacts of changes in expected loss L, premiums α, or wealth W. Look first at α, the rate of premiums per dollar of coverage. An increase in α is an increase in the price that John must pay for amount q of insurance. Under most circumstances, this will shift downward his marginal return, say to MR_1. The increased premium also lowers his wealth if he stays healthy. Since lowered wealth is consistent with increased marginal utility of insurance at any value of q, his MC curve shifts back to MC_1. The new equilibrium at point B shows that John purchases less insurance as premiums increase.

Consider, instead, changes in expected loss L. This acts only on the marginal return side. If L increases at any level of q, then John's net wealth falls and, hence, his marginal utility of wealth rises. As a result, MR shifts outward to MR_2. It follows that an increase in expected loss L leads to the purchase of more insurance at point C.

Finally, starting again at point A, consider the impact of an increase in overall wealth W. On the one hand, with higher wealth, the marginal return if John is ill (for a fixed loss L) is decreased, so MR shifts downward, to MR_1. On the other hand (again, for any given loss), with increased wealth, the marginal cost shifts outward to MC_2. As a result, the new equilibrium value of q at point D may be higher or lower than the original value (as drawn in Figure 11.2, it is lower). If, however, increased wealth W implies increased losses L, then the marginal return curve may shift down less; in such cases, it may be shown that the amount of insurance will increase, since increased expected losses would make increased insurance more desirable.

We have shown how the consumer picks the optimal amount of insurance coverage given his or her utility function, probabilities, expected loss, and the premium rate. Note, however, that we still have not shown how the insurance companies choose a particular premium rate, α. To investigate this and related issues, we turn to the supply side of the market.

THE SUPPLY OF INSURANCE

Ultimately, to determine the amount of coverage an individual will buy, we must know the premium rate that companies will charge. To determine the premium rate (i.e., the value of α), it is necessary to have a model of how the insurance market works. Return to the example at the beginning of this chapter in which many people belonged to a club that paid the insurance in case of illness to one of its members. The officers of the club did not know, nor necessarily care, who would file the claim. All that was necessary was that revenues covered the costs.[4]

---

[4]It is, in fact, crucial for insurers to be able to recognize whether they are getting a nonrepresentative "slice" of the risk distribution. This is sometimes referred to as *adverse selection,* and can lead to financial losses for the insurer. It will be discussed later in the chapter.

Competition and Normal Profits

Under perfect competition, all firms earn zero excess, or normal, profits. In this example, the difference between benefits paid out and premiums received for a typical customer is $(\alpha q - q)$, the premium αq less the amount q to be paid out, with probability p, if he gets sick. Furthermore, the insurer earns αq dollars, the premium, with probability $(1 - p)$ if John stays healthy. The insurer's expected profit per transaction, then, is as follows:

$$\text{Expected profit} = -p(1 - \alpha)q + (1 - p)\alpha q - t \qquad (11.8)$$

where t is the cost of servicing each transaction. Such transactions or loading costs include the costs of determining the riskiness of policies, as well as the costs of running an office. Competition would suggest that over the long run these loading costs would be similar across types of insurers.

If there is perfect competition, then expected profits must equal 0, so:

$$-p(1 - \alpha)q + (1 - p)\alpha q - t = 0$$

We divide by term q, and multiply out the expression to give this result:

$$-p + p\alpha + \alpha - p\alpha - (t/q) = 0$$

This allows us to solve for α as:

$$\alpha = p + (t/q) \qquad (11.9)$$

This expression shows that the appropriate value of α equals the probability of illness p, plus the transactions cost as a percentage of policy value q, or t/q. Suppose that $p = 0.05$. Then $\alpha = 0.05 + (t/q)$. If transactions costs t are 10 percent of policy value q, then $(t/q) = 0.10$. Hence, in equilibrium $\alpha = (0.05 + 0.10)$ or 0.15. The premium for each dollar of insurance q is 15 cents. If firms charge less, they will not have enough money to pay the claims; if they charge more, there will be excess profits in the business, and other firms will bid down their rates in perfectly competitive markets.

Recall that in the discussion on the bearing of risk, we considered insurance policies that would compensate the individual against the loss based solely on the probability of the event's occurring. Such rates are referred to as actuarially fair rates. We see that the actuarially fair rates correspond to the case in which the transactions costs t approach 0 as a percentage of insurance coverage; hence:

$$\alpha = p + (t/q) \rightarrow \alpha = p + (0), \text{ or } \alpha = p \qquad (11.10)$$

Knowing the premium α that occurs under perfect competition, we can now solve for the optimal coverage. It can be shown that to maximize utility, an individual will insure such that his wealth will be the same whether he is ill or well. His wealth, if well, is his initial wealth W less his insurance payments αq, or:

$$\text{Wealth (well)} = W - \alpha q \qquad (11.11)$$

His wealth, if ill, is his initial wealth less his loss L plus his insurance payment (less premium) of $(1 - \alpha)q$, or:

$$\text{Wealth (ill)} = W - L + (1 - \alpha)q \qquad (11.12)$$

Equating the two yields:

$$\text{Wealth (well)} = W - \alpha q = W - L + (1 - \alpha)q = \text{Wealth (ill)} \qquad \textbf{(11.13)}$$

Subtracting W from both sides:

$$q^* = L \qquad \textbf{(11.14)}$$

The optimal insurance for John to buy if he expects a loss of $5,000 is $5,000. If the equilibrium price of insurance (premium α) exceeds the probability of event p due to loading costs, then John reacts to the higher price by insuring for less than the expected $5,000 loss. This is complete insurance against the expected loss. A more detailed derivation of this finding is found in the following section, which can be omitted without loss of continuity.

The Optimal Level of Coverage*

We have solved for the optimal value of α. We can now solve for the optimal value of q. We saw through the discussion of Figure 11.2 that the marginal return (MR) = marginal cost (MC) calculation leads to:

$$p(1 - \alpha)\,\text{MU (if ill)} = (1 - p)\alpha\,\text{MU (if well), or:}$$
$$p(1 - \alpha)\,\text{MU}\,(W - L + (1 - \alpha)q) = (1 - p)\alpha\,\text{MU}\,(W - \alpha q) \qquad \textbf{(11.15)}$$

From equation (11.8), competitive conditions in the insurance industry require that:

$$p(1 - \alpha) + t/q = (1 - p)\alpha \qquad \textbf{(11.16)}$$

Using (11.16), we can rewrite (11.15) as:

$$p(1 - \alpha)\,\text{MU}\,[W - L + (1 - \alpha)q] = [p(1 - \alpha) + t/q]\,\text{MU}\,(W - \alpha q) \qquad \textbf{(11.17)}$$

Now divide both sides by the term $p(1 - \alpha)$. This allows us to rewrite the equation as:

$$\text{MU}\,[W - L + (1 - \alpha)q] = (1 + Z)\,\text{MU}\,(W - \alpha q) \qquad \textbf{(11.18)}$$

Term Z equals $t/[qp(1 - \alpha)]$ and is positive if there are positive transactions or loading costs, t.

Thus, John must pick the insurance level such that equation (11.18) is satisfied. Assume first that $Z = 0$. When Z equals zero, equation (11.18) requires the marginal utility of wealth on the left-hand side to be equal to the marginal utility of wealth on the right-hand side. If there is constantly diminishing marginal utility of wealth, then the marginal utility of wealth on each side of the equation can be equal only if the two expressions for wealth are equal. Using Figure 11.2, the marginal return equals the marginal cost, when the net wealth is equal, or:

$$W - L + (1 - \alpha)q = W - \alpha q \qquad \textbf{(11.19)}$$

Subtracting W from both sides of the equation, we solve for q, which equals the expected loss, or $q^* = L$. The optimal amount of insurance for John to buy if he expects

---

*Can be omitted without loss of continuity.

a loss of $5,000 is, in fact, $5,000. He will insure himself completely against the expected loss.

If there are transactions or loading costs, then Z is positive. This implies that the marginal cost curve must be shifted up by the factor $(1 + Z)$. In Figure 11.2, the presence of loading costs implies that the new equilibrium is at point E, the intersection of MC_1 and MR. This indicates that the optimal amount of insurance q^* is less than the loss L. In other words, if premium α exceeds the probability of the event's occurring p, then the optimal q is less than L. If the premium exceeds the probability, John reacts to the increased price by covering himself against less than the full loss.

DEMAND FOR INSURANCE:
THE CASE OF MORAL HAZARD

To this point, we have discussed the theory of risk, as well as the demand and supply of insurance when the events and the expenditures are random. We now address the effects of the price system on the provision of insurance. In the foregoing section, we determined that the optimal insurance policy covers all the loss when there is zero transactions cost and less than the full loss in the realistic case when there are positive transactions costs.

In essence, the purchase of insurance lowers the price of the service at the time the services are purchased. However, in the analysis thus far, we have assumed that the amount of the loss was fixed, that it did not change merely because people bought insurance. If people purchase more service due to insurance, then many of the insurance propositions just presented must be modified.

Demand for Care and Moral Hazard

Suppose that John faces the probability $1 - p = 0.5$ that he will not be sick during a given time period, and so will demand no medical care, and also faces probability p, also equal to 0.5, that he will contract an illness which requires medical care. In Figure 11.3, panel A, we assume that the demand for medical services is perfectly inelastic; that is, it is unresponsive to the price of the services. We saw earlier (ignoring the transactions costs) that John would be willing to pay insurance for the amount of coverage P_1Q_1, which represents his expenditures should he need care. An actuarially fair insurance policy would then charge John $0.5P_1Q_1$, and he would purchase the policy because it insured him against the risk of illness.

Suppose instead that due to his income, his tastes for care, how ill he is—in short, all the factors that shape demand—John's demand curve is responsive to price (i.e., quantity demand varies inversely with price). This is noted in Figure 11.3, panel B. If he purchases insurance that pays his entire loss L, then this insurance makes treatment (ignoring time costs) free. Because the marginal price to John is 0, he would demand Q_2 units of care, for a total cost of care P_1Q_2 (shown as rectangle OP_1CQ_2), which is obviously larger than rectangle OP_1BQ_1.[5]

---

[5]Recall that even when the out-of-pocket price is 0, time costs generally keep the full price from being 0.

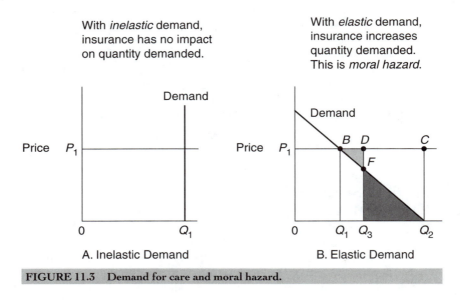

FIGURE 11.3   **Demand for care and moral hazard.**

This response to economic stimuli leads to one of two possibilities that was not a problem earlier:

1. If the insurance company charges the premium $0.5P_1Q_1$ for the insurance, the company will lose money. This occurs because the expected payments would be $0.5P_1Q_2$, which are larger.

2. If the insurance company charges the appropriate premium $0.5P_1Q_2$ for the insurance, John may not buy insurance. This amount may exceed the medical expenses that he would have spent on average had he chosen to self-insure. While John may be willing to pay more than $0.5P_1Q_1$ to avoid the risk, he may not be willing to pay as much as $0.5P_1Q_2$.

This rational response to economic incentives brought about by the elasticity of demand to the price of care is often termed *moral hazard*. Moral hazard refers to the increased usage of services when the pooling of risks leads to decreased marginal costs for the services.[6] Our analysis gives a simple measure of the costs of moral hazard— the excess of premiums over John's expected outlays had he not purchased insurance.[7]

Thus, John's insurance premium has two components. The first is the premium for protection against risk, assuming that no moral hazard exists. The second is the extra resource cost due to moral hazard. As before, John chooses insurance coverage $q*$ by weighing marginal costs against marginal returns, where as before the returns are the utility gains when John is ill. The twist here is that the costs now have two dimensions (the pure premium and the moral hazard). For some categories of care, the second may be quite important.

---

[6]Moral hazard may also refer to the disincentives created by insurance to reduce the probability of a loss.

[7]One would have to net out the transactions costs of servicing the insurance in this example, since they do not reflect increased use of services.

This analysis helps predict the types of insurance likely to be provided. It is clear that the optimal level of insurance is likely to increase relative to the expected loss as the degree of moral hazard decreases. Suppose we use demand price elasticity as an indicator of the potential for moral hazard, as we have estimates available from Chapter 6. Theory then suggests the following:

1. Deeper (more complete) coverage for more inelastic services.
2. Development of insurance first for those services that are most inelastic, and only later for more elastic services.

Data on current insurance coverage by area of service support the first hypothesis, and historical data support the second!

Effects of Coinsurance and Deductibles

This analysis also provides insight into the impacts of deductible provisions and coinsurance in insurance policies. Returning to Figure 11.3, Panel B, suppose that Q_1 reflects $500 of expenses (rectangle OP_1BQ_1) and that Q_2 is three times Q_1 (rectangle OP_1CQ_2), which reflects $1,500 of expenses. If insurance contains a deductible, John will compare the position he would attain if he covered the deductible and received level Q_2 free, with the position he would attain if he paid the market price for all the medical care he consumed.

Assume again that the probability of illness p equals 0.5. Consider first a policy containing a deductible, which requires John to pay the risk premium plus the first $500 of his medical care (rectangle OP_1BQ_1), after which all additional care is free. John will buy this policy because it protects him from risk and allows him to purchase Q_2 units of medical care for $500. His gain is the area under the demand curve Q_1BQ_2.

Suppose now that the insurance company raises the deductible from $500 to $700. Will John continue to buy the insurance? Recall that without insurance, John would have purchased amount Q_1 of health services; the $700 deductible yields amount Q_3. When ill, John is actually paying more for the amount $(Q_3 - Q_1)$ of incremental health care than he values the incremental care. The incremental costs are rectangle Q_1BDQ_3; the incremental benefits are the area under his demand curve (trapezoid Q_1BFQ_3). The difference is triangle BDF, and this represents a welfare loss to John.

However, after paying the deductible, he can get as much additional health care as he wants at zero cost, and he will buy quantity Q_2. This yields welfare gain triangle Q_3FQ_2 (incremental benefits less zero incremental costs). If Q_3FQ_2 (his welfare gain) is larger than BDF (his welfare loss), he buys the insurance, even with the $700 deductible. If BDF is larger than Q_3FQ_2, the loss exceeds the gain, and John is better off self-insuring and spending P_1Q_1 (in this example, $500) with probability 0.5.

Hence, the deductible has two possible impacts. A relatively small deductible will have no effect on the individual's usage. A large deductible makes it more likely that the individual will self-insure and consume the amount of care he would have purchased if he had no insurance.

A wide range of coinsurance coverages has been developed. Many analysts have considered how they may be formulated to lead to more economically efficient outcomes. We turn to that analysis next.

HEALTH INSURANCE AND THE EFFICIENT ALLOCATION OF RESOURCES

This section examines the impact of health insurance on the demand for health care. Economists are often concerned about the efficient allocation of resources, which occurs when the incremental cost of bringing the resources to market (marginal cost) equals the valuation in the market to those who are buying the resource (marginal benefit). If the marginal benefit is greater (less) than the marginal cost, one could improve the welfare of society by allocating more (fewer) resources to the sector, or individual, and less (more) resources to other sectors.

Consider Figure 11.4, which shows the marginal cost of care and the demand for care by a consumer under alternative conditions of insurance. If this consumer is not insured, then the optimal choice of health care is Q_0 units. The price (including travel time, parking, and the cost of bringing the service to market) reflects the cost to society of bringing the entire package to the market. Based on the consumer's (and the physician's) preferences, the marginal benefit, as described through the demand curve, equals the marginal cost. In economic terminology, this is an efficient allocation.

The Impact of Coinsurance

Consider now what happens when John pays only a fraction of the bill, say, at a 20 percent coinsurance rate. The demand curve rotates outward and a new equilibrium is reached with the new quantity demanded Q_1. The cost of bringing services to market has remained the same, at P_0. Services valued at P_0Q_1, rather than P_0Q_0, are now being provided. The incremental amount spent is $P_0 \times (Q_1 - Q_0)$, or the rectangle ABQ_1Q_0.

The incremental benefit can be measured by the area under John's original demand curve, ACQ_1Q_0. The remaining triangle ABC represents the loss in well-being

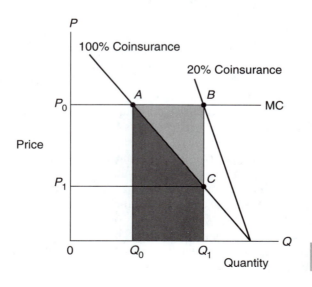

FIGURE 11.4   Health care demand with insurance.

that occurs because John is purchasing more health care than is optimal. It is a loss in well-being because the incremental resource cost ACQ_1Q_0 exceeds the incremental benefits ACQ_1Q_0 by triangle ABC.

What exactly does this mean? It means that John is led by insurance to act as if he were not aware of the true resource costs of the care he consumes. It also means that the insurance implicitly subsidizes insured types of care (often in organized health care settings) relative to other types of health care (e.g., good nutrition, exercise, uninsured types of care) that may be just as effective. It also subsidizes insured types of care relative to nonhealth goods. Although the degree of this distortion depends on the exact specification of the policy (that is, deductibles, maximum payments, rates of coinsurance), it is apparent that insurance can distort the allocation of resources among health care and other goods.

The losses may be even more significant in the market context as described by Figure 11.5. Clearly, as before, more services are used than are optimal. This has elements of both a redistribution of resources (from consumers and insurers to providers) and a *deadweight loss* (referring to a loss that comes from the misallocation of resources between types of goods). At the original price P_0 and quantity Q_0, producers were being paid the marginal cost to bring the products to market. Moving from Q_0 to Q_1 leads to an increase in total expenditures from P_0Q_0 (rectangle OP_0JQ_0) to P_1Q_1 (rectangle OP_1FQ_1).

The deadweight loss comes from a misallocation of resources among goods (i.e., more health care is provided than "should" be, according to consumer preferences). Incremental benefits induced by the establishment of a coinsurance regime (i.e., the area under the original demand curve) are measured by the trapezoid Q_0JKQ_1. Similarly, the additional resource costs of bringing the treatment level $(Q_1 - Q_0)$ to society is trapezoid Q_0JFQ_1. The deadweight loss to society from the overproduction of health

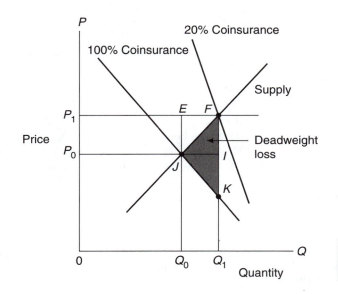

FIGURE 11.5 The effect of insurance cost sharing with upward sloping supply.

services due to insurance can thus be summarized as the difference in areas between the two trapezoids, or triangle *FKJ*.

The Welfare Loss of Excess Health Insurance

From the preceding discussion, one would ask why society would support policies that seem only to result in misallocations of resources. In fact, the foregoing analyses concentrate only on the costs. It is important to emphasize that people buy insurance, willingly taking on additional costs to themselves, to protect themselves against the risk of (possibly substantial) losses.[8] This protection provides major benefits through the protection against risk that offset the losses discussed here.

Many researchers have attempted to calculate the welfare losses of excess health insurance. One of the earliest and most prominent was Martin Feldstein (1973). In principle, Feldstein's method is straightforward, although the statistical challenges are substantial. The researcher measures the cost of the excess insurance by measuring the demand for health care and the coinsurance rate, and calculating the size of the loss polygons in Figure 11.5.

Measuring the benefits is also conceptually straightforward. Recall that in Figure 11.1, the horizontal difference between John's expected utility and his actual utility represented the dollar amount that he would have been willing to pay for insurance, over and above the amount that he was charged. Provision of insurance to John at the actuarially fair rate provides a utility gain to John through the reduction of uncertainty that can in principle be measured in money terms. Adding these gains across individuals provides a measure of net benefits to be compared to the costs of the excess insurance.

In plain terms, insurance policies lead to increased costs to society because they lead to increased expenditures on health services. These increased expenditures may occur in several ways:

- increased quantity of services purchased due to decreases in out-of-pocket costs for services that are already being purchased;
- increased prices for the services that are already being purchased;
- increased quantities purchased and prices paid for services that would not be purchased unless they were covered by insurance;
- increased quality in the services purchased, including expensive, technology-intensive services that again might not otherwise be purchased unless covered by insurance.

Any procedures that raise the coinsurance rate will tend to reduce the costs of excess insurance, but will also reduce the benefits from decreased risk bearing. Feldstein found that the average coinsurance rate was about one-third, or 0.33; that is, people paid 33 cents of every dollar of costs out of their pockets. Raising the coinsurance to 0.50 or to 0.67 would cut the amount of insurance purchased, reducing the excess insurance, but also increasing the amount of risk borne by the clients.

---

[8]One might ask about people whose employers pay the whole insurance bill. Most economists believe that employees choose the insurance in lieu of a compensating take-home wage. Hence, even in this case, the employee has "paid" for the insurance.

The welfare gains from changed coinsurance, then, are:

$$\text{Welfare gains} = \text{Change in benefits} - \text{change in costs} \qquad \textbf{(11.20)}$$

Feldstein's analysis considers the welfare gains from increasing the average coinsurance rate from 0.33 to 0.67. He discovers that the costs fall much more than do the benefits as coinsurance rates rise. He estimates the welfare gains to be approximately $27.8 billion per year (in $1984) under the "most likely" parameter values.

Feldman and Dowd (1991) update Feldstein's 1960s estimates by using 1980s parameters from the Rand Health Insurance Experiment (as discussed in Chapter 6) regarding both price elasticity of the demand curve and attitudes toward risk. They calculate that the lower bound for losses was approximately $33 billion per year (in $1984), and that the upper bound may be as high as $109 billion, depending on the exact parameters used. Although the exact values of these benefits depend crucially on the econometric estimates, the order of magnitude of these losses suggests an important role for the restructuring of insurance in the reduction of excess health care expenditures.

LOADING COSTS AND THE BEHAVIOR OF INSURANCE FIRMS

To this point, we have demonstrated that consumers can improve their well-being by sacrificing a (relatively) small certain premium to insure against the probability of a considerably larger loss. It is important now to demonstrate how the policies will be offered to specific groups and why, in fact, some groups will find it difficult to get insurance at all.

We have referred to the theory of a competitive industry, in which the firms will compete to where profits become zero, or normal. If profits are higher (lower), firms will enter (leave) the market. Only when profits have become zero, or normal, will entry and exit cease. In this model, the insurance carriers would collect money during the year and pay some of it out. In good years (for the carriers), they would pay out less than collected; in bad years, they would pay out more. Under this assumption, the good (and bad) years should be random. If firms have systematically good (bad) years, it suggests excess profits (losses), and the probability of entry into (exit from) the industry by other firms.

We have also shown how moral hazard can lead firms to offer certain types of coverage and not others. In particular, firms would shy away from covering conditions that are accompanied by price elastic demands for services.

Impacts of Loading Costs

Firms have additional costs of doing business, often referred to as *loading costs*. These costs are largely related to the numbers and types of customers and claims that they process. As a result, even in perfect competition these costs must be passed on to consumers or the firms will not be able to cover all costs and will be forced to leave the market. The incidence of these costs suggests that firms will shy away from covering events that occur very often, or those that seldom occur.

Consider again the consumer who behaves as though he had a utility of wealth function exhibiting diminishing marginal utility of wealth. Reproducing this idea from Figure 11.1, consider now Figure 11.6, in which we see that the amount that this consumer would be willing to pay over the actuarially fair amount is shown by the horizontal distance between his expected utility line and his (curved) utility function, measured in dollars. For example, at point *F,* this horizontal distance is *FG.* Clearly, the horizontal distance between the expected utility line and the utility function is zero if the event never occurs (i.e., if we are at point *A*). It increases up to some point as we move in a southwest direction, with increased probability of illness, and then decreases, as the illness becomes more certain, toward point *B*. This means that the extra premium people are willing to pay to avoid risk is smallest either for very rare events or for almost certain events.

Since insurance is taken against risk, then as probability of the uncertain event approaches either 0 or 1, insurance is less desirable. Near point *A,* the expected loss, that is the probability of the event, multiplied by the loss if the event occurs, is not big enough for John to bother. Near point *B*—since the event is almost certain—John might as well put away the money himself, and avoid the trouble of dealing with the insurer. For example, most people do not seek insurance against losses due to common colds.

Figure 11.6 addresses this issue graphically. The top portion of Figure 11.6 shows the utility function as we have just discussed. Moving "southwest" from the initial wealth (point *A*), we see that the gain from insurance increases initially, then eventually falls back to zero when the probability of illness becomes one. Below this graph, we plot the probability of the event on the *X*-axis, and the expected gain on the *Y*-axis. The lower *X*-axis is best understood as the probability of *not* filing a claim which decreases

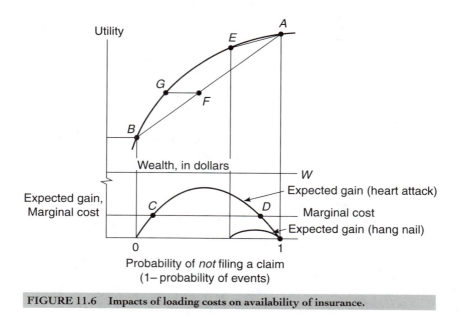

FIGURE 11.6 **Impacts of loading costs on availability of insurance.**

from 1 (under point A where the event never occurs) to 0 (under point B where the event always occurs). Thus at $p = 0$ (at A where there is no loss), or at $p = 1$ (at B where there is a certain loss), the expected gain from insurance is 0. Since the marginal benefits are positive in between, the marginal benefit curve has a hump in the middle.

Insurance for Heart Attacks and Hangnails

Comparing types of losses, at any value of $p,$ the larger the expected loss, the larger the gain from the insurance. This is easily seen from comparing the distances between the expected utility line, and the utility curve for a small loss (line segment EA) and for a large loss (line segment BA). The former shows a small distance; the latter, a larger one. Hence, if John has equal probabilities of a hangnail (small loss) and a heart attack (large loss), the expected gain from insurance for major (heart attack) coverage will be larger than for minor (hangnail) coverage.

Given the marginal benefits, consider the firms' decisions in providing insurance. Clearly, if the event is almost certain to happen, the costs of administering the policy may exceed the benefits. In other words, there are positive costs of administering claims. For simplicity, we have drawn these costs as constant marginal costs, a horizontal line.[9]

From probability 0 to point $C,$ it will not pay to insure claims because the marginal cost exceeds the expected marginal benefits. Between points C and $D,$ expected marginal benefits exceed marginal costs. To the right of point $D,$ again the marginal cost exceeds the expected marginal benefit, and no insurance will be provided. As the diagram is drawn, no firm could afford to offer hangnail coverage.

Loading Costs and the Uninsured

The analysis provides one avenue for addressing the problem of the uninsured. Health insurance in the United States is largely available through participation in the labor market. Those who do not participate in the labor market, and indeed those who are employed by small business, who are self-employed, or who are sporadically employed, may find it difficult to get insurance.

Although many explanations have been proposed, it is apparent that the costs of processing information and claims of people who are outside larger organizations (either companies or unions) may be higher. This would result in an increase in the marginal costs relative to the marginal benefits and would reduce or eliminate the range of services that may be offered.

The analysis also helps to address the impacts of entry and exit in the insurance market. More efficient processing and information handling presumably will lower the premiums that must be paid by customers in the market. If we again address Figure 11.6, we recognize that improved information handling and processing not only would lead to lowered prices, but would also permit firms to offer services (based on probability of occurrence) that had not previously been offered.

---

[9]All else equal, the higher the probability of claims, the more administration (forms filled out, or verification, for example). Hence, the marginal cost of processing the claims may rise the more claims there are, or the more complicated the claims become.

Consider points *C* or *D,* where the expected marginal benefit was previously just equal to (or possibly just below) the marginal cost. The ability of a firm to lower costs would allow that firm to offer insurance for types of events that previously were uncovered. Conversely, increased costs, either due to market forces or often due to mandated types of coverage, would force firms to cut back coverage on events for which the limited amount of consumer surplus would not allow the firms to pass the increased costs on to the customers.

EMPLOYER PROVISION OF HEALTH INSURANCE AND THE TAX SYSTEM

Unlike most other types of insurance, for the largest segment of the American population health insurance is provided through the workplace. The reason for this is almost an historical accident. During World War II, because of the booming economy and because of wartime shortages in consumer goods, there was not much to buy, and wage and price controls were imposed as anti-inflationary devices. Predictably, there was a need to change compensation in order to attract workers.[10] *Fringe benefits,* which were not legally considered as part of the wage package, were used to provide some flexibility in worker compensation, and hence to improve the allocation of workers among sectors of the economy. One of these fringe benefits was health insurance.

How the Tax System Influences Demand for Health Insurance

As federal marginal income tax rates rose in the post-World War II United States (to marginal rates as high as 91 percent in the 1950s), the incentive for workers to demand increased insurance grew. Consider the following example. Suppose John earns $1,000 per week and would like to buy health insurance. Ignoring state and local taxes, assume that he is in the 28 percent marginal tax bracket, so his take-home income is $720 per week. Suppose further that health insurance would cost him $50 per week. His net take-home pay would then be $670 net per week.

Suppose instead that John's employer purchases insurance for him, also at $50 per week. Although John's total compensation is still $1,000 per week, he is taxed only on the wage portion, or $950. His take-home pay will now be 72 percent of $950, or $684 per week. His $14 improvement in well-being occurs since he is purchasing the $50 of insurance with pretax dollars, which are 28 percent smaller than after-tax dollars. Clearly, with increased marginal tax rates, consumers have the incentive to increase employer health expenditures.[11]

---

[10]Wage controls in a full employment economy would prevent companies from raiding each other for workers; price controls would prevent consumers from bidding up prices of the scarce goods.

[11]Employers would also benefit from this arrangement because their levels of Social Security taxes would also fall. Currently, both employees and employers pay 6.20 percent for the Social Security portion and 1.45 percent for the Medicare portion. Since insurance is an expense to the employer rather than a factor payment, it is exempt from Social Security taxes.

The allocative problem within the economy is that certain goods, in particular health expenditures, have been chosen for special treatment. Consider Figure 11.7. This figure shows an entire wage package consisting of the sum of wages W and insurance I. Intercept M on the y-axis shows the amount of wages if there is no insurance in the package. Similarly, intercept N on the x-axis shows the amount of insurance, if the employee wanted his or her entire compensation as insurance benefits. If there is no special tax treatment, then the line has a 45° relationship to both the x- and y-axes, a slope of -1.0. In other words, a dollar of insurance trades for a dollar in wages.

The subsidy of health insurance through the government policies lowers the price of a dollar of insurance, relative to a dollar of wage remuneration. This causes the budget constraint line to rotate to N', leading to the purchase of more insurance, relative to wages, than otherwise. The subsidy rotates the budget line outward so that now one dollar of wages actually buys more than one dollar of insurance. Figure 11.7 shows that without special tax treatment John is consuming package A of I_0 and W_0. Thus, the tax system leads John to choose combination B with more insurance at the expense of less wages.[12]

Other Impacts of Employer Provision of Health Insurance

Employer provision of health insurance has other impacts as well. Because the employer is a large single buyer of coverage, the purchase of insurance through the employer provides scale economies of dealing with insurance providers that single purchasers could never enjoy. This tends to lower the effective price of coverage to the employees.

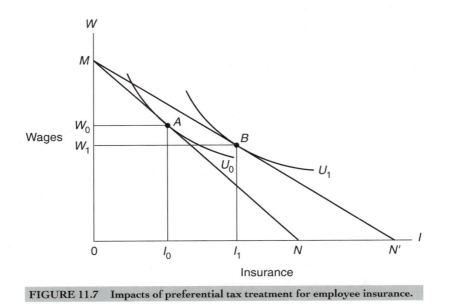

FIGURE 11.7 **Impacts of preferential tax treatment for employee insurance.**

---

[12]Not only will John buy more insurance, but the tax subsidy may encourage him to insure for the kinds of low- or high-probability events (e.g., routine dental care) that would otherwise be left uninsured. In terms of Figure 11.6, when the net cost of insurance is lowered, the range of probabilities over which the individual insures, as represented by distances such as *CD*, will increase.

In addition, group purchase by employers addresses the problem of adverse selection in the provision of insurance. Recall that at the beginning of this chapter we considered a club whose members participated in an insurance arrangement. The arrangement worked well because the contract provided a necessary service to the members. In particular, the probability of a claim was a random event that could be calculated, and that was independent of the actions of the members.

Central to this result is the proposition that the probability of usage is independent of the insurance plan. Suppose that the consumer "knows" that the probability of a claim is not the 5 percent that was assumed by the insurance company, but rather 10 percent. If he or she were able to convince an insurer that he or she indeed belonged to the less risky (5 percent) category, the consumer would be able to buy insurance at much less cost than the actuarially fair premium. This consumer would get a bargain; the insurer would lose money. The inability to identify probabilities, and hence their impacts on the insurance market, is often referred to as *adverse selection*.

As an example, consider an insurance plan that offers major hospitalization coverage. Consider also the fact that many heavy smokers may recognize their higher probabilities of lip, throat, or lung cancer and heart disease. If they can prevent the insurer from finding out about their smoking, then they can purchase insurance at much less than the appropriate premium, given their prior conditions.

It can be argued that the purchase of insurance by employers minimizes adverse selection by providing a more appropriate pool for the fixing of insurance rates. This is because most groups contain a broad mix of risks, by virtue of having been formed for some purpose other than insurance.

EMPLOYER-BASED HEALTH INSURANCE AND JOB MOBILITY

Since most private health insurance is obtained through employment and is typically not portable to different employers, researchers have sought to determine the extent to which health insurance may inhibit worker mobility. In particular, employees may fear losing coverage for preexisting conditions, which are generally defined as any medical problem that has been treated or diagnosed within the past six months to two years. This *job lock* may have several economic effects:

- The inability of workers to change jobs could lead to less productive workers staying at jobs for insurance reasons only; this would lead to decreased economic output since they would not be replaced by more productive workers.

- Even if all workers are equally productive, some workers may stay in jobs for fear of losing the health insurance benefits to the exclusion of those who would otherwise fill the jobs.

- Those who do change jobs may be denied coverage, face higher premiums, or only be able to obtain insurance subject to a waiver that excludes coverage of their health condition.

Both Cooper and Monheit (1993) and Madrian (1994) address the issue. We look more closely at Madrian's presentation.

Madrian uses a simple matrix of the probability of job mobility to consider the impact of job lock. She notes that because job lock is caused by the potential loss of health insurance coverage with changing jobs, one would not expect those with coverage through both their own employment and an outside job to face job lock:

	Employer-Provided Health Insurance	
	No	*Yes*
No Other Health Insurance	*a*	*b*
Other Health Insurance	*c*	*d*

A simple test for the magnitude of job lock is whether those workers with employer-provided health insurance and other coverage are more likely to change jobs than those without alternative coverage, or:

$$(\text{cell } d) - (\text{cell } b) > 0$$

However, if a man is in cell *d,* it may be due to the insurance provided by his wife, who may be providing income as well; all else equal, the additional income could lead to increased mobility. Hence, Madrian derives a second test: whether having other health insurance increases mobility more for those who have employment-based insurance than for those who do not, or $d - b > c - a$, which can be rewritten as $(d - b) - (c - a) > 0$. This test is referred to as *difference-in-difference,* referring to the difference between $(d - b)$ and $(c - a)$.

Madrian estimates several impacts, but her most general model looks at the probability of turnover of married men. The data come from the 1987 National Medical Expenditure Survey (NMES), which collected detailed information for 1987 about health insurance and medical care utilization, with several questions about employment, for approximately 14,000 households. Madrian estimates a probit model where the dependent variable is whether the married man changed jobs (1 if he did; 0 if he did not) during the 15-month survey period. Recall that the coefficients of a probit model determine the probabilities of job change.

The easiest way to present the results is to insert predicted job turnover probabilities into Madrian's matrix (Table 11.1).

The *raw estimate* indicates that job lock is responsible for a 26 percent reduction in mobility, calculated as $(0.115 - 0.085)/0.115$. The difference-in-difference estimates, attempting to account for any independent effect of other health insurance on mobility, give an alternative estimate of 31.1 percent.[13]

These results are consistent with anecdotal evidence of job lock as an unintended consequence of the system of employment-related coverage in the United States. It could be addressed through changes that are broadly consistent with prudent insurance practices. These include elimination of preexisting condition clauses and the develop-

[13]Cooper and Monheit, using slightly different methods to analyze the NMES database, calculate a 25 percent decline in the likelihood of job change when comparing those who are insured to those who are uninsured.

TABLE 11.1	Predicted Job Turnover Probabilities under the Possibility of Job Lock	
	Employer-Provided Health Insurance	
	No	*Yes*
No Other Health Insurance	0.256	0.085
Other Health Insurance	0.244	0.115
Estimates of job lock		
$(d - b)$		26.0% (13.8%)
$(d - b) - (c - a)$		31.1% (17.7%)

Standard errors are in parentheses.
Source: Madrian (1994).

ment of health insurance pooling mechanisms in local labor markets that might promote continuity of coverage across employers. Job lock must also be considered as a consequence of mandated approaches to health insurance benefits, both at state and national levels.

THE MARKET FOR INSURANCE—BLUE CROSS AND COMMERCIAL INSURERS

Although we have discussed the provision of insurance in the abstract, we now want to consider some institutional features of the market for health insurance. Such a discussion must address the roles of the Blue Cross insurers, which are nonprofit firms, and the commercial insurers, which are typically for-profit. (Once again, we note that programs such as Medicare and Medicaid will be discussed in detail in Chapter 21.) With increased competition in the health care sector, many distinctions have blurred. Nonetheless, to understand the current insurance market, it is helpful to consider how it has developed over time.

The Market for Private Insurance

The number of people privately insured in the United States has burgeoned since the pre-World War II period. From a base of 12 million insured in 1940, the number increased by over a factor of six by 1950 (to 76.6 million), and doubled again (to 158.8 million) by 1970. Table 11.2 provides a summary of insurance coverage.

Table 11.2 also divides the insurance coverage among private insurance companies, Blue Cross–Blue Shield plans, and other plans, which include self-insured and HMO plans. We can see that well into the 1970s most of the coverage was provided either by insurance companies (usually in group settings) or by Blue Cross–Blue Shield plans. Since the late 1970s there has been an increase in the use of other plans, with declines in both the shares and the absolute numbers of those covered both by the

TABLE 11.2 Number of Persons with Private Insurance by Type of Insurer (Millions)

End of Year	All Insurers*	Total Insurance Companies			Blue Cross/ Blue Shield	Self-insured and HMOs
		Total Persons	Group	Individual/ Family		
1940	12.0	3.7	2.5	1.2	6.0	2.3
1945	32.0	10.5	7.8	2.7	18.9	2.7
1950	76.6	37.0	22.3	17.3	38.8	4.4
1955	101.4	53.5	38.6	19.9	50.7	6.5
1960	122.5	69.2	54.4	22.2	58.1	6.0
1961	125.8	70.4	56.1	22.4	58.7	7.1
1962	129.4	72.2	58.1	23.1	60.1	6.9
1963	133.5	74.5	61.5	23.5	61.0	7.2
1964	136.3	75.8	63.1	34.0	62.1	6.8
1965	138.7	77.6	65.4	24.4	63.3	7.0
1966	142.4	80.4	67.8	24.9	54.3	6.6
1967	146.4	82.6	71.5	24.6	67.2	7.1
1968	151.9	85.7	74.1	25.3	70.1	7.3
1969	155.0	88.8	77.9	25.9	82.7	7.7
1970	158.8	89.7	80.5	26.7	85.1	8.1
1971	161.8	91.5	80.6	27.8	76.5	8.5
1972	164.1	93.7	81.5	29.1	78.2	8.1
1973	168.5	94.5	83.6	27.5	81.3	9.6
1974	173.1	97.0	85.4	28.8	83.8	11.1
1975	178.2	99.5	87.2	30.1	86.4	13.1
1976	176.9	97.0	86.8	27.0	86.6	14.9
1977	179.9	100.4	89.2	28.7	86.0	18.1
1978	185.7	106.0	92.5	36.1	85.8	21.5
1979	185.7	104.1	94.1	34.4	86.1	25.5
1980	187.4	105.5	97.4	33.8	86.7	33.2
1981	186.2	105.9	103.0	25.3	85.8	40.3
1982	188.3	109.6	103.9	29.4	82.0	48.2
1983	186.6	105.9	104.6	22.2	79.6	53.6
1984	184.4	103.1	103.0	20.4	79.4	54.4**
1985	181.3	100.4	99.5	21.2	78.7	55.1**
1986	180.9	98.2	106.6	12.1	78.0	64.9**
1987	179.7	96.7	106.1	10.4	76.9	66.9**
1988	182.3	92.6	100.5	10.7	74.0	71.3**
1989	182.5	88.9	98.7	10.0	72.5	78.6**
1990	181.7	83.1	88.7	10.2	70.9	86.2**
1991	181.0	78.0	83.3	9.9	68.1	93.5**
1992	180.7	76.6	82.1	8.5	67.5	97.9**
1993	180.9	74.7	80.9	7.4	65.9	105.7**

*The data in this column refer to the net total of persons protected, i.e., duplication among persons protected by more than one kind of insuring organization or more than one insurance company policy providing the same type of coverage has been eliminated. Excludes hospital indemnity coverage included in prior years. 1992 hospital indemnity count was 8.2 billion for group and 5.4 billion for individual policies.

**For 1984 and later, estimates of persons covered by 'other plans' have been developed by HIAA in the absence of other available data.

Note: The category entitled Self-insured and HMOs includes persons covered under ASO arrangements and MPPs. Some data were revised from previous editions. Data for 1978 and later have been adjusted downward because of new data on average family size. For 1975 and later, data include the number of persons covered in Puerto Rico and U.S. territories and possessions.

Note: Data for 1987 and 1988 reflect revised HIAA survey form. Data for 1989 and 1990 reflect a change in methodology.

Note: Data split is available for years 1990, 1991, 1992, and 1993 only.

Sources: Health Insurance Association of America; Group Health Association of America, Inc.; Blue Cross/Blue Shield Association.

insurance companies and the "Blues." This would suggest the movement toward self-insurance by large firms, as well as toward various types of alternative providers such as health maintenance organizations (HMOs). We discuss HMOs in Chapter 12.

Conflicts Between the Insured and the Insurer

There is often a conflict between insurers and the insured regarding the amounts of claims as well as whether the claims should be paid at all. From the earliest instances of health insurance, this type of conflict has existed. Providers, most particularly physicians, have argued that their judgments as providers must not be questioned on grounds of cost. Insurers, in contrast, have felt that they could increase their profits, and/or reduce premiums, by judiciously questioning treatments and/or costs.

One might ask why providers would ever consent to having someone second guess their decisions. Goldberg and Greenberg (1977) traced the growth of health insurance in Oregon in the 1930s. At that time physicians shared in the Great Depression with the larger population, and they saw acceptance of health insurance, even with its accompanying oversight, as a way of increasing earnings.[14] The authors provide colorful examples of reviews from the National Hospital Association, the insurer, that denied or reduced benefits to providers:

> It has come to my attention that several times recently you boys have performed operations without first taking the matter up with this Association as is required.

and:

> *Exceptions* are always made in *emergencies* [emphasis added] if, after investigation, it is shown that the person is eligible to care at the Association's expense. Will you please mention this to the other boys and let us have your cooperation in the future.

Insurance was attractive to physicians when times were difficult. There was considerable opposition, however, from physicians' groups, such as the Oregon State Medical Society. They threatened to expel physicians who participated in the plans, and to establish their own plans. The plans established by the physicians tended to be less strict in their cost reviews.

Blue Cross and Blue Shield plans were started by medical care providers. The "Blues" typically offer more complete and more comprehensive coverage, and they pay participating providers directly.[15] They are usually very generous in the payment of hospital care. The Blues are nonprofit corporations. Although the organizational distinction between nonprofit and profit-making firms may be fading, many feel that the lack of pressure to earn competitive profits may provide different managerial incentives.

---

[14]Wolinsky (1988) argues, from a sociological perspective, that similar pressures forced the acceptance of diagnostic related groups (DRGs), and their controlled payments, by hospitals.

[15]Sindelar (1988) provides an excellent discussion. Many points in this exposition are derived from her analysis and description.

We have seen that insurers must "rate" their clients. That is, they must determine a risk premium based on the experience of the group that they are insuring. When Blue Cross began, the method used was called *community rating*. All subscribers in a given location, irrespective of age or health experience, were charged the same premium. This contrasts with *experience rating* in which the insurer charges group premiums (to a company or a fraternal or service organization), based on its experience with the group.

Community rating leads to the overcharging of low-risk clients, and to a transfer from them to the higher-risk clients in the same pool. Advocates of community rating argue that this allows high-risk and/or low-income clients to buy insurance that would otherwise have been unavailable.

This cross-subsidization will also lead to the exit from the plans by lower-risk, lower-cost groups. Commercial insurers were able to "pick off" the lower-risk portions of the Blue Cross clientele. Many large firms chose either alternative carriers, or in fact, decided to self-insure. Clearly the extent to which community rating can survive is related to the amount of competition in the provision of the insurance.

Sales Taxes and Profits Taxes

Sindelar (1988) notes that insurance has not generally been regulated at the federal level, with most of the oversight occurring at state levels. All states tax insurance suppliers, typically in the form of a tax on premiums. That is, the tax is on sales rather than on profits. Domestic companies (those located within a state) are typically taxed at a rate of 1 to 2 percent; foreign insurers (those from outside the state) typically pay 2 to 3 percent. Since profits are small compared to sales, even a 1 or 2 percent tax on sales amounts to a much larger tax on profits.

An example of the distinction between profits taxes and sales taxes is helpful. Suppose that we define profits π, as sales S, minus costs, C:

$$\pi = S - C \tag{11.21}$$

Further define the total tax T, as fraction t of sales S, or

$$T = tS \tag{11.22}$$

Dividing (11.22) by (11.21) yields taxes as a fraction of profits:

$$T/\pi = t\,[S/\,(S - C)] \tag{11.23}$$

Thus, suppose that costs are 90 percent of sales. Equation (11.23) then reads:

$$T/\pi = t\,[S/\,(S - 0.9S)] = 10t$$

Here even a 1 percent sales tax ($t = 0.01$) is equivalent to a 10 percent ($10 \times 0.01 = 0.10$) tax on profits.

Because the Blues are nonprofit, they are typically exempted from such taxes. They are also exempted from property taxes and federal and state corporate taxes. Many analysts feel that such tax treatments are likely to give the Blues considerable competitive advantages.

Sindelar notes that even with such advantages, the Blues have not taken over the market; she discusses two views. The first is that because the Blues are not necessarily profit-maximizing firms, they may not have the same cost-minimizing incentives; hence, they tolerate inefficient managerial practices that cannot be tolerated in a competitive profit-making firm. Second, rather than lowering costs and prices, they may use their tax advantage to address other goals, such as increasing coverage.

A final comparison between the Blues and commercial insurance may involve possible cost advantages because of the typically large size of Blue Cross–Blue Shield operations, or because they hold monopsony power (i.e., the power to lower fees that can be exercised over providers by a large buyer). Several analysts have tried to determine whether these size advantages hold. The results have not been conclusive.

THE UNINSURED—AN ANALYTICAL FRAMEWORK

Given the high costs of health care and the inevitability of at least some expenses, it has become crucial for individuals to have access to health insurance. In the United States, health insurance availability has been linked to the workplace. Yet surveys have shown that as many as 40 million Americans have no health insurance at any moment in time, and that a large fraction of these people are employed.

Table 11.3 shows that not all firms offer health coverage and that the problem is particularly severe for both small firms and for certain sectors of the economy. Table 11.3 shows that only 33 percent of firms with fewer than 10 employees and only 60 percent of those with 10 to 24 employees offered benefits in 1993. This overstates the problem to some extent since over 92 percent of the employees in large firms (250 or more) had employer-provided coverage.

Certain sectors of the economy are also less likely to be covered. In 1990 (the most recent data available) only 68 percent of the employees in both the construction and the retail trade industries worked in firms offering coverage. Even in manufacturing, the sector with the highest coverage, 11 percent of the workers were in firms that did not offer coverage.

TABLE 11.3   Firms that Offer Health Benefits, by Size (1993)

Firm Size	Offer Health Benefits	Do Not Offer
Less than 10 Employees	33%	67%
10 to 24	60	40
25 to 49	75	25
50 to 99	60	40
100 to 249	75	25
250 to 499	60	40
500 to 999	75	25
1,000 or more	75	25

Source: Health Insurance Association of America (1994, Figure 2.12).

As we have noted, it is important for insurers to lower the loading factors—the costs of determining probabilities of claims and processing claims. The ability to insure through the workplace gives the opportunity to improve the experience rating. In principle, private insurers can insure those outside the workplace, and many do, particularly with relation to affinity groups such as organizations and clubs, or in terms of insuring the elderly. If high costs lead to onerous payments, then the problem may be poverty rather than high prices. This would suggest the need for governmental subsidies in a social insurance scheme.

The Working Uninsured

Consider now the working uninsured. Employees' remuneration may be considered as *net wage* w_n, an hourly sum which equals the sum of money wage w plus insurance i_o:

$$w_n = w + i_0 \tag{11.24}$$

Figure 11.8 shows the equilibrium employment point A for the profit-maximizing firm, where the value of the marginal product equals the net wage w_n that must be paid for benefit level i_0. At this equilibrium, L_0 workers are employed.

The literature (e.g., McLaughlin and Zellers, 1994) suggests that many businesses, especially small businesses, may have limited experience ratings; as a result, their loading costs may be quite high, as much as 10 to 40 percent higher than those paid by large firms. If the loading costs are high, then the small firms may be able to afford to pay only very small, or zero, i. To compete with other firms, they must match the w_n; hence it may be necessary that their w be larger than the wage level for other firms.

McLaughlin and Zellers summarize three major types of barriers to small business provision of health benefits. The first, affordability, is a price-related barrier, and is well summarized in Figure 11.8, leading to increased net wage w_n. Particularly in low-wage industries, a combination of low profit margins, low wages, and high premiums may make it difficult to provide health benefits.

There are two other broad categories of nonprice-related barriers to the offering of health benefits. Insurance *redlining* or preexisting-condition clauses may exclude specific individuals, or companies that employ them, from insurance coverage. McLaughlin and Zellers note that redlined industries typically employ older workers (over age 55), have high employee turnover, seasonal workforces, or workforces paid by commission or on the basis of other contractual terms. Lawyers' offices may be redlined because of fears of litigation, physicians' offices because of fears of high utilization of health care services.

A particular confluence of such factors occurs in the case of beauty shops, who have great difficulty buying group insurance for their employees (McLaughlin, 1993). Compared with the general population, there are three large groups of beauty shop employees who insurers find costly to insure:

1. Workers who work only intermittently. There is evidence that some workers enter the labor force when they need health care. Such adverse selection of the insured pool may lead to high costs for insurers.

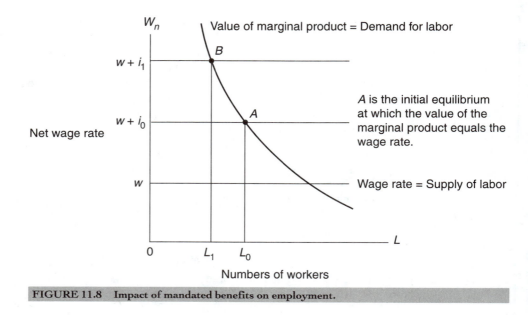

FIGURE 11.8   **Impact of mandated benefits on employment.**

2. Young women of child-bearing age who are likely to have children. This again leads to high insurance costs.

3. An apparently large homosexual workforce, whose members are at higher risk of exposure to AIDS, may also raise costs substantially.

In short, many nonprice barriers are placed before certain groups, including preexisting-condition clauses, long delays in processing applications, and, if the would-be client is persistent, extraordinarily high premiums, which make enrollment prohibitively expensive. As a result, many small businesses simply cannot obtain insurance.

A third barrier to the provision of coverage may be termed *attitudes.* Many firms are uninterested in offering insurance. Sometimes a large number of their employees can *piggyback* on health plans of spouses' or partners' employers. In such cases, employees prefer to be compensated in higher wages rather than in benefits.

The Impacts of Mandated Coverage

Many groups have advocated that the federal government or individual states mandate some, more, or particular types of coverage. Returning to Figure 11.8, if such coverage is provided through employer insurance, the mandates would raise the amount of *i*, as well as its costs. Firm responses to the increased marginal costs may result in two adverse impacts. The first is for the company to stop offering insurance entirely because it is too expensive.[16] Thus, rather than having modest health coverage with the benefits of whatever experience rating may exist within the workplace, there may be no

---

[16]Alternatively, *play or pay* proposals might require firms to provide a minimal level of insurance or to pay into an insurance pool which would insure the uninsured.

coverage at all. The firm may then have to raise the wage to keep employees, who would then have to buy their own insurance. This may allow for employee choice, but it also denies the employee workplace-related experience rating.

The second adverse impact may also be understood by examining Figure 11.8. The equilibrium of value of marginal product and net wage at point A represents a labor force of the appropriate size to maximize profits for the producer. To the extent that mandated coverage reflects increased worker benefits, that is to the extent that i_1 exceeds i_0, it must either increase gross wage w_n or decrease base wage w. If gross wage w_n rises, marginal workers now cost more than they are worth in terms of marginal productivity, and if firms are acting so as to maximize profits, some workers may be let go, leading to the new equilibrium point B. By this analysis, the result of mandated coverage, similar to the result of a binding minimum wage, is likely to be some additional unemployment amount $(L_0 - L_1)$, which, of course, means sharply curtailed insurance benefits.[17] How much the employment falls is related to the elasticity (or responsiveness) of the labor demand curve to the increased gross wage.

Alternatively, if base wage w falls to maintain gross wage w_n in the face of increased benefits, the workers have less money to spend on other goods; insurance has effectively crowded out other expenditures. Furthermore, the firm may lose workers to other firms that are willing to pay the increased w_n as a result of the mandated coverage.

To date insurance industry regulation has occurred mainly at the state level, and it is at this level that mandated insurance benefits have become popular. State health care mandates have grown from 48 in 1970 to about 1,000 in 1991, covering "heart transplants in Georgia, liver transplants in Illinois, hairpieces in Minnesota . . . and sperm-bank deposits in Massachusetts."[18]

Gabel and Jensen (1989) found that these requirements prevent insurers from offering lower-cost alternatives that exclude the mandated benefits. This effect could be substantial for many lower-income individuals who have been priced out of the market.

One response to this problem would be a total overhaul of the insurance system to separate it from the workplace. Although alternative systems exist in other countries, it is unlikely that they would be politically feasible in the United States. Governmental solutions within the current system (with workplace-provision of insurance) would be to subsidize at least a minimal standard of insurance for all who are working full-time. Purchase of insurance for nonworkers is more problematic and must be treated as an equity-based transfer program. We discuss this thorny problem in Chapter 20.

CONCLUSIONS

This chapter has concentrated on the unique role of insurance in the health care economy. No other good in people's day-to-day budgets is so explicitly tied to the arrangements for insurance as is health care. Such arrangements have an impact not only on

---

[17]Although a minimum wage may be in place, if employers must pay more due to local market conditions, then an increase in the minimum wage may have no impact on employment. Similarly, if employers are already offering more than the mandated coverage, broadening the mandates may have little or no impact.

[18]"Health Insurance: States Can Help," *The Wall Street Journal,* December 17, 1991, p. A14.

expenditures for serious illnesses and injuries, but also on plans for more routine expenditures such as childrens' well-care visits (for infants and toddlers), and for eye and dental care.

In this chapter, we have characterized risk and have shown why individuals will pay to insure against it. The result, under most insurance arrangements, is the purchase of more services than might otherwise have been desired by consumers and/or their health care providers. There is a considerable health care policy debate as to how insurance policies can be structured in order to reduce purchases and minimize insurance costs without compromising the health of the insured.

The chapter also has several implications about the uninsured. These are often people who may not be working; hence, they are not getting insurance. There are others whose health, employment, or lifestyle statuses may not permit commercial insurers to provide insurance profitably. Government mandates that employers must insure everyone if they insure anyone often lead employers to drop insurance plans entirely, thus leaving larger groups at risk. A "safety net" for those who are difficult to insure requires a social contract that only the government can provide.

Summary

1. Many illnesses occur fairly rarely and seemingly at random, but when they do, they entail substantial costs.

2. Insurance reduces variability of the insureds' assets by pooling a large number of units, and operating on the principle of the law of large numbers. Although outlays for a health event may be highly variable for any given unit in the pool, average outlays for the group can be predicted fairly well.

3. One should distinguish between insurance, as is provided through the pooling of risk, and government programs such as Social Security, Medicare, and Medicaid, which also redistribute wealth.

4. Insurance can only be sold in circumstances where there is diminishing marginal utility of wealth or income (i.e., when the consumer is risk averse). With constant marginal utility, requiring that individuals pay actuarially fair premiums would leave them no better off than if they were uninsured.

5. Expected utility is an average measure; the individual either wins or loses the bet.

6. If insurance companies charge more than the actuarially fair premium, people will have less expected wealth through insuring than through not insuring. Even though people will be less wealthy by purchasing insurance, the increased well-being comes from the elimination of risk.

7. In theory, the optimal amount of insurance in the absence of loading costs is to fully insure against the expected loss. With loading costs, the optimal coverage is less than the expected loss.

8. Moral hazard refers to the increased usage of services when the pooling of risks leads to decreased marginal price for the services. This suggests:
   - more complete coverage for price inelastic services,
   - earlier development of insurance for services that are most inelastic.

9. Insurance policies lead to increased costs to society because they lead to increased expenditures on health services. They provide increased benefits through the reduction of risks.

10. Losses due to excess insurance are estimated at between $33 and $109 billion ($1984) per year. This suggests the importance of restructuring insurance to reduce excess health care expenditures.

11. The higher costs of processing information and claims of people outside larger organizations (either companies or unions) may result in an increase in the marginal costs of insurance relative to the marginal benefits, and hence may reduce or eliminate the range of services offered.

12. Subsidizing health insurance through government tax policies lowers the price of a dollar of insurance premium relative to a dollar of wage remuneration. This leads to the purchase of more insurance relative to wages than otherwise.

13. Blue Cross and Blue Shield plans, as nonprofit firms, are typically exempted from profits taxes, property taxes, and federal and state corporate taxes. Many feel that such tax treatments give the Blues considerable competitive advantages.

14. Many groups have advocated that the federal government or individual states mandate either more, or various types of coverage. In reaction,
   - companies may stop offering insurance entirely because it is too expensive.
   - marginal workers may now cost more than they are worth, and some of them will be let go.

Discussion Questions

1. Discuss the difference between cardinal and ordinal utility. Why is cardinal utility necessary for the analysis of risk and insurance?

2. What does the term *moral hazard* mean? Give examples.

3. The deductible feature of an insurance policy can affect the impact of moral hazard. Explain this in the context either of probability of treatment and/or amount of treatment demanded.

4. Describe the benefits to society from purchasing insurance. Describe the costs. Define and discuss the welfare gains from changes in insurance coverage.

5. Consider groups of poor people or single people. Are they likely to buy more or less insurance than traditional households? Why? Would cash transfers to the poor tend to eliminate the uninsured problem?

6. In 1986, the U.S. Federal Income Tax system changed marginal tax rates so that the top marginal rate fell from 50 percent to 33 percent. Given the way fringe benefits are negotiated, what would you expect to happen to the demand for health insurance as a fringe benefit? Why?

7. Suppose that a company pays its workers $10 per hour, and provides an additional $1.50 per hour worth of fringe benefits, including a basic health insurance policy. Discuss the firm's reaction to a state mandate that requires it to expand the items

covered in the health care policy. What is likely to happen to the number of people employed? What is likely to happen to the firm's labor costs?

8. If only risk-averse people will buy health insurance, why do many people who buy health insurance also buy lottery tickets (an activity more consistent with risk taking)? Speculate on the differences and similarities.

9. Suppose that each person's health expenditures can be predicted with certainty by both the insured and the insurer. What are the implications for insurance markets? Explain the prevalence of insurance for highly predictable events such as routine dental services.

10. It is often advocated that health insurers be prevented from denying insurance to those with a preexisting condition such as cancer or AIDS at "reasonable" rates. Analyze the effects of such regulations on insurance markets.

11. Since health insurance tends inevitably to cause moral hazard, will the population necessarily be overinsured (in the sense that a reduction in insurance would improve welfare)? Are there beneficial factors that balance against the costs of welfare loss?

Exercises

1. Suppose that Nathan's employer provides a health insurance policy that pays 75 percent of each dollar over the first $50 spent. If Nathan incurs $500 in expenses, how much will he pay out-of-pocket? What percentage of his expenses will this be?

2. Suppose that rather than flipping a coin, one rolls a die. If the value is 1, 2, 3, or 4, the player wins a dollar. If it is 5 or 6, the player loses a dollar. Calculate the expected return.

3. We have discussed the role of utility functions in the purchase of insurance.
   a. Suppose Edward's utility function can be written as:

   $$U = 10Y, \text{ where } U \text{ is utility and } Y \text{ is income/month.}$$

   What is his marginal utility if income is $1,000 per month? $2,000 per month? Is Edward likely to insure against loss of income? Why?
   b. Suppose instead that Edward's utility function can be written as $U = 10Y^{0.5}$. What is his marginal utility if income is $1,000/month? $2,000/month? Is Edward likely to buy insurance against loss of income? Why?

4. Suppose, if ill, that Fred's demand for health services is summarized by the demand curve $Q = 50 - 2P$, where P is the price of services. How many services does he buy at a price of $20?

   Suppose that Fred's probability of illness is 0.3. What is the actuarially fair price of health insurance for Fred with a zero coinsurance rate?

5. In Exercise 4, if the insurance company pays Fred's entire loss, what will Fred's expenses be? How much will the company pay? Will it continue to offer him insurance at the actuarially fair rate? Why?

6. Suppose that the market demand for medical care is summarized by the demand function:

$$Q_d = 100 - 2p$$

and the market supply is summarized by the supply function:

$$Q_s = 20 + 2p$$

   a. Calculate the equilibrium quantity and price, assuming no health insurance is available.
   b. Suppose that health insurance is made available that provides for a 50 percent coinsurance rate. Calculate the new equilibrium price and quantity. (Hint: How does the demand curve shift?)
   c. Calculate the deadweight loss due to this insurance.

CHAPTER

Managed Care and Health Maintenance Organizations (HMOs)

12

- Managed Care

- HMOs and Their History

- Development and Growth of HMOs—Why Has It Taken So Long?

- Federal Policy Toward Managed Care

- Demand and Supply of HMOs

- Are HMO Costs Lower?

- HMOs and Growth in Spending

- Quality of Care in HMOs

- Competitive Effects of HMOs and PPOs

- Conclusions

We saw in Chapter 11 that insurance coverage will generally lead to overconsumption of health care by the individual insured. The insured individual considers only the out-of-pocket cost of care and not the true full cost at the point of service. Overconsumption here means that the insured person purchases health care beyond the point where the marginal benefit equals the full marginal cost. For insurance to be a net benefit to society, the costs of this overconsumption must be overcome by the benefits in the sense that risk has been reduced. Even with the risk-reduction benefits, however, it is clear that improved insurance coverage has led to increased costs to society.

It is tempting to suppose that insurance necessarily leads to higher costs and perhaps to waste. Many feel that various forms of *managed care* may address some of these problems. One might argue that physician practice must be managed in order to address high health care costs, and networks of providers, including health maintenance organizations (HMOs), preferred provider organizations (PPOs), and individual practice associations (IPAs), are widely seen as means to restore competition to the health care sector and as means to control expanding health care costs. We devote this chapter to managed care, with particular attention to the distinctive combination of insurance and care exemplified by HMOs and similar organizations. Unless distinguishing the individual types of institutions, we will refer to them as managed care. The prominent form, the HMO, receives special attention in this chapter both for its size and for the fact that much of the scholarly and policy research has focused on HMOs.

HMOs appear to overcome the information problems inherent in fee-for-service (FFS) health care markets; these problems may be exacerbated by ordinary insurance coverage. Reconsider the FFS system of remuneration. Under FFS, the provider both provides health care and advises the consumer on how much is needed. At first glance, it would appear that the consumer's imperfect information about medicine, when combined with FFS remuneration, would provide the incentives for substantial overconsumption. Overconsumption of this type—supplier-induced demand (SID)—was addressed in Chapter 8. It seems apparent here that the organizational form of HMOs eliminates the overconsumption incentives and replaces them with cost-control incentives and even possibly incentives toward *underconsumption.*

We begin the chapter with a general description of managed care and its cost-cutting potential. We then turn to HMOs as a form of health care organization in which the functions of insurance and provision of care are combined. We describe the HMO and its organizational relatives, and we assess the theory and evidence on the effects of HMOs. We investigate whether HMOs lead to cost savings and whether they increase competition in the insurance and health services markets.

MANAGED CARE

It is instructive to provide a general description of managed care, leading to a more specific discussion of HMOs, while recognizing that the concept of managed care is undergoing constant changes.[1] Most generally, analysts speak of an *organized delivery system* as a network of organizations (for example, hospitals, physicians, clinics, and hospices) that provides or arranges to provide a coordinated continuum (from well care to emergency surgery) of services to a defined population. This system is willing to be held clinically and fiscally accountable for the outcomes and the health status of the population served. It is tied together by its clinical (treatment) and fiscal (financial) accountability for the defined population. Most often the organized delivery system is defined by its association with an insurance product.

Shortell and his colleagues view the key feature of managed care as the provision of care to a defined number of enrollees at a capitated (fixed) rate per member per month. As a result, cost centers such as hospitals, physician groups, clinics, and nursing

---

[1]This discussion draws heavily from the work of Shortell, Gillies, and Anderson (1994).

homes must be managed under a fixed budget. Under traditional fee-for-service, since cost centers generate revenue, more volume means more profit. Under managed care, more volume means less profit.

Managed care creates incentives for keeping people well by emphasizing prevention and health promotion practices, and when people become sick, by treating them at the most cost-effective (least cost per unit care) location in the continuum of care. Clearly, there are also incentives to underuse services, and this may be harmful to patients. Through a more centralized management of services, the goal is to provide additional quality-enhancing features for a given price, or to provide a given set of quality attributes or outcomes for a lower price. The primary provider has a paramount role as the gatekeeper to limit further and more expensive services.

Figure 12.1 shows an integrated delivery system for an enrolled population with a predetermined set of benefits. A large continuum of services is assumed. Four broad categories of integrated structures can be considered:

1. *An existing hospital/health system.* This system is the most prevalent form because it combines financial, organizational, and leadership resources. Given the primacy of hospitals, however, there is a tendency to overuse the hospitals regardless of cost considerations.

2. *Physician groups.* These groups may potentially be the most responsive to consumer needs and to physician expertise. Disadvantages involve the problem that most physician groups are not large enough, nor expert enough, to run an integrated delivery system.

3. *Hybrid hospital/physician-led systems.* A combination of the preceding forms, such systems might combine the managerial strength and size of hospital-led systems with the closer consumer focus of the physician groups. Disadvantages involve the potential conflicts between the two groups. Further problems may exist when the physician component has a large specialist group rather than primary care physicians.

4. *Insurance companies.* They provide actuarial expertise, claims administration, and marketing expertise. However, by themselves, insurance companies may have little understanding of *how* to provide care.

An economic analysis of this model shows the importance of integrating the information among the various services. In Figure 12.1, information systems are the hub of the wheel; Shortell and his colleagues note that the "embryonic" development of most clinical information systems is a fundamental barrier to the success of managed care systems. Large health centers are budgeting $100 million or more apiece over the next several years to integrate systems that were often developed separately, and almost never "talk to each other."

A second feature of these systems is a studied de-emphasis of the acute care hospital model. Hospitals provide expensive care, and moving toward cost-effective models necessarily moves away from hospital care. As noted earlier, primary care physicians are the gatekeepers of managed care systems, directing patients to appropriate (i.e., cost-effective) treatment settings. If they are induced to "feed" patients into the hospital instead, this will lead to increased costs.

It is apparent that managed care seeks a vertical integration of what had previously been a generally unintegrated system of health care treatment. Through coordination of care and improved information, such integration has the potential to address the health care costs in a manner that would appear to address criteria of economic

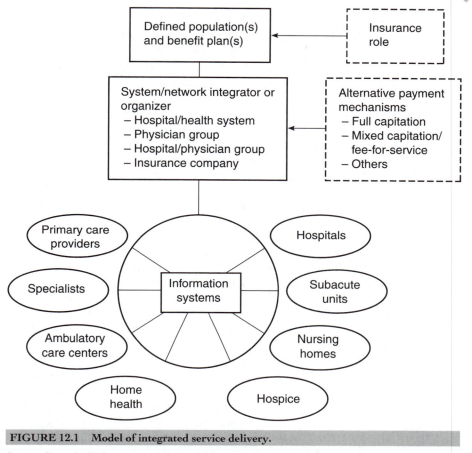

FIGURE 12.1   Model of integrated service delivery.

Source: Shortell, Gillies, and Anderson (1994).

efficiency. Yet the integration is costly, and the quality of the resulting care may not match all consumer preferences. A prime example of managed care on which there has been considerable research is the HMO. We begin with a description of HMOs and continue with their history and the rationale for a government policy that has promoted their development.

HMOs AND THEIR HISTORY

HMOs are not new in the United States. Kaiser-Permanente, the best known HMO, was formed in California in 1942. Although some prepaid group practices existed before that time, large nationwide enrollment in HMOs is a more recent phenomenon. Before we turn to the subject of HMO growth, we first define an HMO—a term that did not appear until the early 1970s.

Types and Functions of HMOs

An HMO is an organization that in return for a prepaid premium agrees to provide an enrollee with comprehensive health care over a given period of time. Patients receive care from a limited set of providers and at a limited selection of sites. Although there is considerable variety in the structure of HMOs and their remuneration of providers, there are a few general types of HMOs.[2] One important distinction is whether or not the physicians are employed (that is, salaried) by the HMO. An HMO which directly employs physicians is called a *staff model HMO*.

In contrast, some HMOs are primarily insurance providers who contract with physicians for the provision of the care, often on a capitation basis (that is, a fixed pre-arranged payment for each patient). When a group practice is contracted for the care, the HMO is identified as a *group model*. When a network of group practices is contracted, the HMO is identified as a *network model*. Independent practice associations (IPAs) consist of physicians in independent, either solo or small group, practices who contract to service an HMO's members.

An HMO integrates the insurance and provision functions in health care delivery. Contrast this to the traditional insurance contract under which a third-party (that is, insurer) is responsible only for reimbursing providers or the consumer for services that the patients have sought on their own. The integration of functions under the HMO structure appears to change provider incentives substantially. These changed incentives have caused many to predict that HMOs will be effective in constraining both utilization and cost of care.

The underlying logic behind this proposition is intuitive. When the provider agrees to handle all of a patient's health care needs for a fixed prearranged fee, that provider is accepting and bearing a substantial part of the financial risk. By bearing the risk of delivering services for a *fixed* premium, the HMO has a strong incentive to develop strategies for reducing excessive care and minimizing other inefficiencies. The fixed premium would also appear to provide the HMO with the incentive to offer the patient whatever forms of preventive care that are cost-effective. Such preventive care could decrease the need for more expensive curative care at a later stage. Whether, in fact, HMOs achieve these results is something we will return to later.

Preferred Provider Organizations (PPOs)

In defining and describing a variety of HMOs, it is also useful to describe other closely related arrangements such as preferred provider organizations. Some analysts use the term *alternative delivery systems* (ADSs) to describe arrangements such as HMOs and preferred provider organizations (PPOs).[3] The importance and role of PPOs is still evolving, and many have predicted that they will join HMOs as clearly defined alternative health delivery systems.

---

[2]This discussion is based on a review of the HMO industry by Christianson et al. (1991), and an evaluation of managed care performance by Miller and Luft (1994).

[3]A broad overview of PPOs is also found in Gabel and Ermann (1985), de Lissovoy et al. (1987), and Rolph, Ginsburg, and Hosek (1987).

Under a PPO beneficiaries (i.e., patients) are given financial incentives to receive care from a limited panel of physicians and hospitals with which the payer (as an agent for the consumer and/or the employer) has contracted. The financial incentives to use PPOs include lower coinsurance and deductibles and increased coverage. Premiums may also be lower.

Payers' interests are served when they select providers who may be known for their economical practice patterns and lower fees. Payment to providers is usually on a fee-for-service basis, but at negotiated rates. The possibility of extracting discounts is another advantage to the payer. Providers also often agree to submit themselves to some form of utilization review.

Preadmission certification, used by 88 percent of PPOs in 1992, concurrent utilization review (83 percent), and mandatory second-opinion surgery programs (47 percent) are the most widely used methods for restricting potentially unnecessary care. Despite these third-party restrictions on their practice styles, providers' (that is, physicians') interests are served because they gain access to a broader consumer market. The providers may also be guaranteed a certain volume of patients as well as prompt payment for services.

In 1994, there were 1107 PPOs. Some are sponsored by providers, others by insurers or entrepreneurs. Though we have described what is known as the generic PPO, in practice there is wide diversity in the specifics of the plans. For example, one PPO may be offered as an extension of a traditional insurance plan; another may be a completely distinct option. There is also potential diversity in paying providers through, for example, capitated arrangements, rather than through fee-for-service.

Though PPOs suggest advantages in theory, they also have problems. Can the PPO successfully identify those providers who have efficient practice styles? The answer is not easy. Simply using the claims histories of those providers to determine efficiency may reflect the characteristics and case-mixes of their patients rather than the providers' practice patterns.

There could also be legal obstacles to the implementation of PPOs. Many states have had laws, which although designed to protect consumers, also created problems for potential HMOs and PPOs. For example, freedom of choice laws have historically limited the ability of insurers to restrict patient choices (or, as some argue, to limit competition). Such laws would clearly limit the abilities of HMOs and PPOs to direct clients to specific providers. As a result of these legal obstacles, many states have changed their laws to enable PPOs to operate freely, but as of 1993, three states had severe restrictions (Idaho, Montana, and North Dakota).[4]

DEVELOPMENT AND GROWTH OF HMOs— WHY HAS IT TAKEN SO LONG?

If the HMO entity has so many apparently appealing characteristics, why has it taken so long for HMOs to become a force in the marketplace? A variety of institutional, economic, and political forces has influenced the pattern of their significant growth. HMO

---

[4]See Rolph, Ginsburg, and Hosek (1987) for further discussion.

enrollment jumped from approximately 3 million consumers in 1970 to about 47 million consumers in 1993.

The story of the development and growth of HMOs in the United States requires an account of the strenuous historical opposition from organized medicine. Early on, organized medicine fiercely opposed alternatives to free patient choice and particularly alternatives to fee-for-service (FFS). Kessel (1958) described the historic political actions of organized medicine and proposed the thesis that FFS enabled physicians to charge some patients a higher fee than others for essentially the same service, a pattern known as price discrimination.

The Economics of Price Discrimination

The ability to charge different prices to different consumers allows a seller to increase profits. Consider a market such as depicted in Figure 12.2, in which services can be provided at constant costs. That is, marginal cost MC equals average cost AC. If providers are perfect competitors, then each is a price taker, and each will charge a price P^* equal to marginal cost MC.

Suppose, however, that providers have some monopoly power such that they face the downward sloping demand curves shown in Figure 12.2. Suppose also that the providers can distinguish between two groups of consumers. Group H (Panel A) places a high value on health care, whereas Group L (Panel B) places a lower value. If providers can charge different consumers different amounts, above the average cost of providing services, they can earn additional profits.

As a monopolist, the provider faces a marginal revenue curve that lies below the demand curve (recall why this is the case). To maximize profits, he or she will provide services to the level where marginal revenue MR_H equals marginal costs, or Q_H, charging price P_H. This earns excess profits π_H by reducing the quantity sold from the competitive Q^* (at price P^*) to the monopoly Q_H (at price P_H).

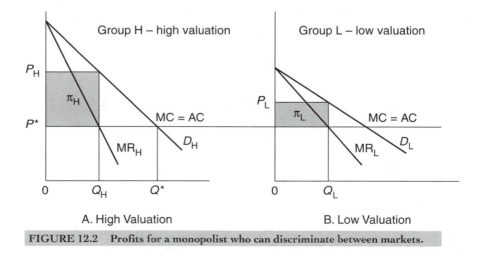

FIGURE 12.2   Profits for a monopolist who can discriminate between markets.

However, there is still a group of buyers (Group L) who would be willing to pay more than it costs (MC) to provide the services. These buyers generate marginal revenue MR_L, and the provider can provide quantity Q_L to them at price P_L. If health care were like other goods which could be resold, then Group L could purchase health care at price P_L and resell it at price P_H, negating the providers' attempt to practice price discrimination. However, one cannot purchase treatment for a broken arm and then sell it to someone else. Hence, the markets may remain separate with differing prices. In this case, otherwise similar individuals are charged different prices based on their valuations of the service.

Such price discrimination is difficult or impossible under the contracts that characterize prepayment-based organizations. First, providers will find it difficult to determine how much individual consumers value their services. Second, the prepayment-based organization may be able to shop among providers, thus limiting the providers' monopoly power.

It is also essential to examine the impacts of managed care at the individual consumer level. Recall that consumers may have the choice between fee-for-service and managed care options in employment-based insurance coverage. An analysis of consumer choice can provide insights into the cost impacts of managed care programs, and provide predictions as to changes in usage and in expenditures.

Figure 12.3 starts with consumer demand D_f under fee-for-service insurance. Assuming that the price is constant at P_f, total expenditures P_fQ_f are represented by the larger rectangle. These total expenditures would also represent the expected insurance component of the individual's wage package.

A managed care option by constraining choice of provider as well as various coverages is viable only if it reduces expenditures. By exerting market power over suppliers, by reducing inpatient care, and by limiting length of stay, HMO managers may lower prices from P_f to P_m.

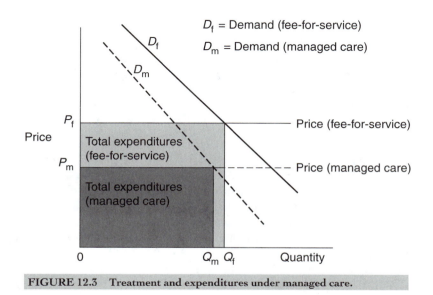

FIGURE 12.3 Treatment and expenditures under managed care.

Demand may also be reduced. HMO managers have incentives to minimize supplier-induced demand, thus shifting demand from D_f to D_m. Furthermore, a managed care option may appeal to consumers who are younger, healthier, or less concerned about risk—in short, those who would choose to demand less health care. The resulting expenditures are shown by the smaller rectangle representing total expenditures $P_m Q_m$.

It follows that managed care trades some constraint of consumer choices in return for lower per unit prices for care. As drawn in Figure 12.3, both decreased price per unit of care and decreased quantity of care contribute to decreased expenditures. Note, however, that a natural response to decreased prices is to increase quantity demanded. Total consumer expenditures will fall as long as the price decreases are not fully offset by increased quantity demanded.

Barriers to HMOs by Organized Medicine

Organized medicine has also posed barriers to HMO development. Organized medical groups opposed physicians' participation in plans and organizations that were not controlled by physicians and/or that were not offering a free choice of physician. Such restrictions were successfully challenged by the Federal Trade Commission in the 1970s.

FEATURE

Organized Medicine and Prepaid Group Practice

Rayack (1982) and others have documented organized medicine's resistance to prepaid group practice. Consider the following example:

> In 1937 employees of the Federal Home Owners' Loan Corporation in Washington, D.C., formed a nonprofit cooperative—the Group Health Association (GHA). Aided by a $40,000 grant from the loan corporation, the GHA equipped a clinic, engaged doctors, and assessed its members monthly prepayments to finance medical care and hospitalization for themselves and their families and sought members in other federal agencies. Almost immediately, the GHA was attacked on legal grounds by the District of Columbia Medical Society as being improperly engaged in the insurance business and in the "corporate practice of medicine" (p. 401).

This plan was not controlled by doctors. It restricted patient choice and was based on prepayment rather than FFS. Not surprisingly, the plan incurred the wrath of organized medicine to the point where GHA had difficulty recruiting physicians because they were threatened with expulsion from the local medical society and denial of hospital privileges. With an impaired ability to recruit physicians and gain access to hospitals, GHA and other similar plans would not be viable.

A landmark antitrust case ensued where ultimately the U.S. Supreme Court upheld a lower court ruling that organized medicine had engaged in an illegal conspiracy. Despite this decision in 1943, prepaid plans continued to meet resistance from the AMA and its affiliates.

FEDERAL POLICY TOWARD MANAGED CARE

The HMO Act of 1973 represented a turning point in federal policy. This policy promoted the development of alternative delivery systems as a cornerstone of its cost-containment strategy. The act enabled HMOs to become federally qualified if they provided enrollees with comprehensive benefits and met various other requirements. Loan guarantees and grants for startup costs were made available, but the main advantage accruing to a federally qualified HMO was that it could require firms in its area with 25 or more employees to offer the HMO as an option. Other regulatory barriers were subsequently reduced.

Despite these changes, the number of HMOs and their enrollees grew slowly. However, several changes in the 1980s accelerated HMO growth. These included a large increase in for-profit HMOs, after the program of loan guarantees was terminated and incentives to enroll Medicare and Medicaid recipients were improved. As a result, the number of HMOs grew from 235 in 1980 to 623 in 1986. Growth slowed in the late 1980s, and there was some consolidation in the number of HMOs, but the upward trend in enrollment resumed in the early 1990s. From 1990 to 1994, the number of plans fell from 572 to 540, but total enrollment increased from 36 million to 47 million persons.

It is also useful to consider the growth experience of preferred provider organizations (PPOs). Offering more flexibility in choosing providers, they have grown rapidly in recent years. In 1993, there were 1107 operating PPOs, covering 45 million eligible employees in the United States.

Though enrollments are largest in the Midwest and Pacific states (California alone accounted for over 25 percent of national HMO enrollment), HMOs and PPOs are

TABLE 12.1   Number of HMOs and HMO Enrollment (in millions) by Selected Characteristics, 1994

Characteristics	Plans		Enrollments	
	Number	*Percent*	*Number*	*Percent*
All Plans	540	100.0	47.3*	100.0
Model Type				
IPA	319	59.1	15.3	38.2
Group	117	21.7	15.4	32.2
Mixed	104	19.3	7.7	29.6

Geographic Region	*Number*	*Percent*	*Percent of Regional Population*
Total	540	100.0	
Northeast	101	18.7	19.5
Midwest	159	29.4	13.7
South	173	32.0	9.4
West	107	19.8	26.4

*Includes 5.1 million Medicare and Medicaid HMO members. They are not included in the other data.

Source: U.S. DHHS, *Health United States 1994*, Table 137.

common throughout the country and have increased their market penetration in other areas recently. The most recent figures regarding the structure of the industry (1994) indicate that group and IPA models dominate HMO membership and account for over 70 percent of enrollments. Table 12.1 provides additional information on the characteristics of HMOs and their enrollees.

DEMAND AND SUPPLY OF HMOs

The growth of managed care will be influenced by demand and supply considerations. Changes in professional and regulatory barriers, such as those described previously, largely influence the supply side. Also any exogenous changes that reduce the costs of starting and operating an HMO will increase supply. However, consider the demand side first.

The Demand for HMOs

An HMO typically provides a comprehensive set of ambulatory and inpatient services, including routine office visits and preventive care, most without coinsurance or a deductible. There is reduced paperwork and little uncertainty about coverage. These features make HMO membership attractive to consumers, especially to some who expect to be high users and who are concerned about out-of-pocket costs. Persons who are especially vulnerable to health care risks would seem to have extra incentives to join the HMO; hence, the HMO population may not be a random sample of the larger population. The possibilities of such biased selection (referring here to the variation of this sample from a random sample) of members as well as the impacts of the possible biases, are addressed later in this chapter.

In contrast to FFS arrangements, the HMO enrollee's choice of providers and access to hospitals (aside from emergency care) is limited. Also direct access to specialists usually requires a referral from the patient's gatekeeper—the primary care physician. To many, these are serious disadvantages.

In choosing between an HMO and traditional insurance, patients will be influenced by various factors. These include price (premiums and out-of-pocket costs), access to specific HMO sites involving various time and travel costs, the strength of any established physician–patient relationships, the patients' health status and expected use of care.

We saw in the previous chapter that wage packages include both money wages and fringe benefits. The rational consumer or union representative will recognize that any portion of insurance premiums paid by an employer has an opportunity cost in the form of other benefits and wages. Thus, even the employer-paid component of health insurance should be included in the full price because it reflects forgone wages. In addition, the probability that a given person will join an HMO may also depend on the person's education and income level.

To elaborate, a strong existing physician–patient relationship is likely to reduce someone's willingness to join an HMO. It is possible in this context that over time, the increasing mobility of the labor force, by weakening such long-term relationships, may have accounted for part of the recent growth of HMOs. For similar reasons, as traditional long-term patient–physician relationships become less common, patients will have less opportunity to monitor their physicians. It may be more difficult for patients to determine whether excessive or inappropriate services are being recommended. In such cases, membership in an HMO mitigates the information problem and helps reassure the patient that excessive or inappropriate care will not be provided.

There is possibly still another information problem that may cause bias in HMO membership. Consider that the potential HMO members probably know their own health care habits and can forecast their health care use better than the HMO itself. Do HMOs attract younger and healthier patients who are interested in minimizing out-of-pocket costs for routine, preventive care, but who are lower users of more expensive acute care services? This is the familiar issue of adverse selection, introduced in Chapter 11, which must be successfully addressed in order to identify correctly the causes and consequences of HMO cost savings, if any.

The Supply of HMOs

Consider next the supply of HMOs. The economic theory of the firm predicts that increased market demand should increase HMO premiums and profits, thereby encouraging entry of more HMOs or movement up the supply curve. Both the short-run and long-run supply relationships may also be influenced by subsidies to HMOs and their cost of providing care. Lower costs will increase the short-run supply and reduce long-run average costs, thus shifting out a supply curve.

Reconsider that an important determinant both of demand for HMOs and also for *growth* in demand for HMOs is the attractiveness of the prices that HMOs charge. HMOs can more easily attract consumers to the degree that they enjoy cost advantages over FFS. Since cost advantages are a key issue in membership growth, it is important to consider some of them:

HMOS MAY REDUCE THE QUANTITY AND INTENSITY OF CARE

This is perhaps the major potential cost advantage of the HMO form. Unlike with traditional third-party FFS reimbursement, HMOs have no inherent incentive to provide unnecessary or marginal ambulatory and inpatient care as well as unnecessary diagnostic procedures and tests. The incentive instead is to minimize utilization and perhaps even underprovide care. Furthermore, there is no apparent incentive to extend lengths-of-stay for patients who are hospitalized or to lengthen the treatment period for other patients.

HMOS MAY SUBSTITUTE LOWER-COST CARE
FOR HIGHER-COST CARE

To illustrate the general principle, consider two specific examples. Insurance coverage for inpatient care has traditionally been more comprehensive than coverage for outpatient care. Remuneration to providers for inpatient services has also often been greater, although many insurers have recently been changing this peculiar incentive structure. Thus, in contrast to HMO care, under FFS neither patient nor provider have had strong incentives to use the outpatient alternative.

In a second example, an HMO has an incentive to use less costly generic drugs during treatment, and to encourage patients to choose a generic drug when having a prescription filled. For many chronic and some acute conditions, drug costs can be a major component of total costs.

HMOS MAY ENJOY ECONOMIES IN THE PURCHASE OR USE OF INPUTS

There are several ways in which HMOs can reduce the cost of services. An HMO may be better able to make efficient use of its facilities and equipment. Through its larger size, an HMO may enjoy economies of scale. In addition, HMOs have incentives to contract with lower-cost hospitals and physicians. They may also be able to economize on the purchase of supplies and other inputs relative to individual physician groups.

Finally, HMOs have a strong incentive to improve productivity and to make better use of nonphysician inputs, such as nurse practitioners. Though there is still debate on the issue, it has been argued that physicians in private practice have tended to underutilize nonphysician personnel.

HMOS MAY BE QUICKER TO DEVELOP EFFECTIVE UTILIZATION REVIEW

HMOs have incentives to measure performance and to develop controls to monitor physicians. As part of the cost-control efforts, they will internalize so-called utilization review and other cost-control measures that the federal and state governments have imposed on the health care sector through regulation.

In the traditional FFS sectors, providers do not have incentives to review utilization. The incentives, in fact, would be for providers to evade those controls and to increase revenues. The issues of utilization review and other cost-control methods are important, and we consider them in more detail in Chapter 19.

HMOS MAY USE OR ADOPT NEW TECHNOLOGY MORE EFFICIENTLY

In theory, HMOs will not hurry to promote new technologies that are not efficient. As described in Chapter 14, the proliferation of new, expensive technologies is probably one of the major reasons for the rapid growth of health spending in the United States.

HMOS MAY ENCOURAGE THE USE OF COST-EFFECTIVE PREVENTIVE CARE

HMOs would logically have an incentive to provide cost-effective preventive care to reduce subsequent use of more expensive curative care. They will do so, however, only if there is reason to believe that enrollees will tend to stay as members over longer enough periods to warrant the preventive care effort.

HMOS MAY ENJOY ADMINISTRATIVE ECONOMIES

HMOs, particularly the larger ones, may be able to spread considerable fixed costs over a larger clientele, thus enjoying scale economies of administration. As vertically integrated groups, they may recognize the costs of paperwork and collection, and may strive harder to reduce them. These would imply administrative cost advantages over FFS plans.

Other Advantages and Differences

We have reviewed several possible avenues through which HMOs may develop cost advantages over FFS care. Harold Luft has been at the forefront of the analysis of HMOs. A more exhaustive list of possibilities for cost differences between the two types of care organization is found in Table 12.2, reproduced from Luft (1982). Luft recognizes medical care rationing factors for four types of care:

- Patient-initiated visits
- Physician-initiated visits
- Physician-initiated referrals
- Hospitalization

TABLE 12.2   Probable Effects on Utilization of Services of Various Factors in Different Practice Settings

Type of Medical Care Rationing Factors	Conventional Fee-for-Service and Insurance		PGP-HMOs	
Patient-Initiated Visits				
Price to consumer	Initial and preventive visits often not covered	–	Comprehensive coverage of all visits	+
Knowledge of provider	Often a local physician with a longstanding relationship	+	Often a local physician with no prior contact with patient	–
Appointment lag	Typically short, urgent visits "squeezed in"	+	Typically long, urgent visits routed to separate clinic	–
Accessibility to provider	Decentralized, likely one close to patient	+	Centralized, generally further from patient	–
Waiting time in office	Variable, often long because patients "squeezed in"	–	Typically short if appointment made in advance	+
Physician-Initiated Visits				
Physician incentives	Follow-up increases revenue	+	Follow-up reduces net income; substitute call-backs	–
Physician-Initiated Referrals				
Physician incentives	Reciprocal referrals among different specialists encouraged by professional network, discouraged by prohibitions on fee splitting	+	Referral attractive to "dump" a problem patient, but collegial and financial costs if frequent	–
Price to consumer	More likely covered than initial visit, still not complete	+/–	Comprehensive coverage of all visits	+
Accessibility of provider	Typically at different location	–	Centralized—"one-stop care"	+
Incentives to return patient to primary care physician	Depends on nature of referral network	+	Typically encouraged by the system	–
Hospitalization				
Price to patient	Often fairly comprehensive coverage but some copayments	–	Comprehensive coverage pays in full	+
Incentives for physician	Hourly income higher in hospital	+	No additional income, costs are borne by plan	–

+ = tends to increase utilization   – = tends to decrease utilization   +/– = mixed effects

Source: Luft (1982).

Consider, for example, the different effect of office waiting time in the FFS setting as opposed to the prepaid group practice HMO (PGP-HMO). FFS waiting time is variable, and often long, because patients are "squeezed in." This would tend to decrease utilization. In contrast, for PGP-HMOs, waiting times are typically short if appointments are made in advance. This would tend to increase utilization.

Regarding hospitalization, FFS plans lead to higher physician incomes, and hence to incentives for increased utilization. There is no additional income with a PGP-HMO since the costs are borne by the plan; the incentives are thus for decreased utilization. Table 12.2 indicates that some forces actually encourage utilization in HMOs. That is, not all the forces affecting HMOs will tend to discourage use of care.

ARE HMO COSTS LOWER?

In the previous section, we provided several reasons for predicting that HMOs will spend less per member. Policymakers have considerable interest as to whether this theoretical proposition is true. From early on, it has been reported that total costs—that is the sum of premiums and out-of-pocket expenses—were from 10 to 40 percent lower for HMOs. The cost differences were attributed largely to lower hospitalization rates, not to lower ambulatory care use rates.

An Introduction to the Data

An understanding of how these comparisons were made will help to make clear the research issues involved. In one study reported in 1978, Luft examined 26 pairs of patient groups. Each pair included an HMO group and a comparison FFS group. This pairing was done to control for population differences. The research question regarding these 26 pairs was whether HMOs tended to have different ambulatory care-use rates than FFS. In general, Luft found that HMO members in most cases had similar numbers of visits per period; however, IPA members had consistently higher rates.

Using a similar pairing procedure, Luft further investigated possible differences in hospital-use rates. Here he studied 51 pairs of HMO and non-HMO patient groups. HMO members tended to have lower utilization as measured by hospital days per capita, the product of admissions times length of stay. Contrary to the usual predictions, there were no clear differences in lengths of stay. The lower hospital-use rate was explained by a lower admission rate. The lower admission is consistent with theoretical predictions.

In a 1981 review, Luft reached the same general conclusion. HMO enrollees, especially prepaid group practice members, have lower hospitalization rates. Knowledge that HMOs have lower hospital use rates, however, still leaves many questions to answer. For example, there was no clear evidence that these lower rates were attributable to reductions in the less important, discretionary procedures. Furthermore, the evidence at hand could not dismiss the possibilities that biased self-selection of HMO membership or even underutilization in HMOs were responsible for the observed differences.

Reduction in use rates is only one way to reduce costs; cutting costs of producing services is another. Evidence on the service costs is even more limited. Are HMOs more efficient in production? Luft's 1978 study found that in examining eight types of discretionary procedures, contrary to expectations, there was no general pattern of differences in production costs favoring HMOs (except for lower rates of tonsillectomy in HMOs).

Arnould and colleagues (1984) examined both use and cost questions in a setting that helps to isolate the effect of the HMO from possible extraneous differences. They examined use rates and treatment costs for four surgical procedures—appendectomy, hysterectomy (surgical removal of the uterus), cholecystectomy (surgical excision of the gall bladder) and herniorrhaphy (hernia repair). Multiple regression was used to control for patient characteristics, and the data indicated whether any patient had already decided on surgery. HMO and other patients were treated at the same sites and by the same groups of physicians, which minimized the confounding problem of provider differences that plagued other comparison studies.

Arnould and colleagues confirmed Luft's conclusion that length-of-stay is not significantly different between the HMO and the FFS patients. They also found that the use of surgeon visits as well as lab charges per patient were lower for the HMO users (significantly lower for hysterectomy and appendectomy), although total hospital charges were significantly lower for the HMO patients only in the case of appendectomies. Thus, although there are differences in costs of elements of hospital care, there is not a strong case to conclude that HMOs produce hospital care more cheaply overall.

Miller and Luft (1994) update the analysis of cost differentials in a literature review through the 1980s and early 1990s. Compared with FFS, HMO plans generally had from 1 percent to 20 percent shorter hospital lengths-of-stay. HMOs have recently exhibited slightly higher rates of physician office visits than comparable FFS plans. HMO plans used an average of 22 percent fewer procedures, tests, or treatments that were expensive and/or had less costly alternative interventions for conditions including childbirth, heart disease, colon and colorectal cancer, and cardiovascular accident.

Miller and Luft provide the following evidence regarding bottom lines with respect to costs:

1. Inpatient services account for a higher percentage of total expenditures than do outpatient services.

2. HMO plans used fewer services that are expensive, and/or have less costly alternatives.

3. HMOs provided more comprehensive coverage than did indemnity plans.

These facts imply that HMOs provide care at lower cost than do indemnity (FFS) plans.

The Problem of Selection Bias

The lower overall costs for HMOs have been confirmed in many studies, and it is clear that HMO members tend to use less hospital care. What is less clear is whether HMOs encourage more efficient practice patterns or whether their savings result from favorable selection of enrollees. On the one hand, HMOs offer comprehensive benefits and so they may attract and retain sicker members. On the other hand, HMOs may attract disproportionately younger members and families who tend to be healthier and for whom the costs of care tend to be relatively lower.[5]

Two studies illustrate the potential importance of selection bias. One, by Strumwasser and colleagues (1989), examined a large firm that offered employees the option of retaining Blue Cross or switching either to an HMO or PPO. In the case examined, those employees who switched to the HMO or PPO plans were younger and had much lower utilization rates. In the year prior to switching, employees who later chose to switch to the HMO had incurred only 16 percent of the average expenditures of those who later chose to retain their traditional Blue Cross and Blue Shield coverage.

In a similarly relevant study, Lewis (1984) compared populations that leave an HMO with those that choose to continue. It was found that those who remained enrolled in the HMO used more services than those who left. Though the two studies suggest somewhat different implications, both emphasize the need to control for possible selection bias.

The Rand Study—A Randomized Experiment

Several studies investigate the problem of selection bias in studying differences in costs between HMOs and FFS populations. A more fruitful approach may be to ask whether it is possible to eliminate biased selection entirely before examining cost differences. The problem of biased selection can be understood as a common problem involved when one uses nonexperimental data. An appropriate solution may thus be to examine experimental data such as those produced in the Rand Health Insurance Experiment. There, patients were randomly assigned to different plans in a controlled experiment, thus apparently eliminating selection bias. Would HMO costs still be lower under such circumstances?

The Rand study compared HMO and FFS patients in the Puget Sound area where 1,580 individuals were assigned randomly to either an FFS physician of their choice or to the Group Health Cooperative (GHC) of Puget Sound—an HMO in Seattle, Washington.[6] The 431 FFS individuals were in one of four groups with the following coverages:

1. free care,
2. 25 percent of their expenses up to a maximum out-of-pocket liability of $1,000 per family,
3. 95 percent of their expenses up to a maximum out-of-pocket liability of $1,000 per family, or
4. 95 percent coinsurance on outpatient services, up to a limit of $150 per person ($450 per family).

In addition to the experimental GHC group of 1,149 persons, there was a control group consisting of a random sample of 733 GHC members who had previously been enrolled for at least one year.

---

[5]Luft (1981) reviews the extensive literature that compares the characteristics of HMO members versus other populations, including data on their relative health status and their attitudes toward health care.
[6]See Manning et al. (1984).

TABLE 12.3   Annual Rates of Admission and Face-to-Face Visits

Plan	Admission Rate	Hospital Days	Face-to-Face Visits	Preventive Visits
	per 100 Persons		per Person	
GHC experimental	8.4	49	4.3	0.55
	(0.67)	(9.6)	(0.14)	(0.02)
GHC control	8.3	38	4.7	0.60
	(1.01)	(9.0)	(0.17)	(0.02)
Fee-for-service				
Free	13.8	83	4.2	0.41
	(1.51)	(26)	(0.25)	(0.03)
25%	10.0	87	3.5	0.32
	(1.43)	(28)	(0.35)	(0.03)
95%	10.5	46	2.9	0.29
	(1.68)	(9.9)	(0.34)	(0.04)
Individual deductible	8.8	28	3.3	0.27
	(1.20)	(5.1)	(0.33)	(0.03)

(Standard errors in parentheses.)
Source: Manning et al. (1984).

Total expenditures per person were $439 for the experimental group, including out-of-plan use, compared to $609 for the free care (group 1) FFS group.[7] As seen from Table 12.3, ambulatory utilization, as indicated in the columns labeled "Face-to-Face Visits" and "Preventive Visits," was about the same. Thus, the 39 percent increased spending for FFS members (or 28 percent reduction for GHC) was due largely to a much higher admission rate and increased hospital days per person. The study could not pinpoint the reasons for GHC's lower hospital use.

To put the potential cost savings into better perspective, note that the use rates for the experimental HMO patients did not differ materially from the last two categories of FFS, the categories on "95 percent" coinsurance (group 3) and "Individual deductible" (group 4). Thus, for some population groups a shift to HMOs would not lead to savings, though the cost savings for other population groups might conceivably be important.

HMOs AND GROWTH IN SPENDING

There is a strong consensus that HMOs reduce utilization, especially of hospital care. A different but related question is whether HMOs also have lower growth rates in spending. If they do, a shift toward HMOs will result not only in reductions in spending

---

[7]Out-of-plan use can be substantial. Mott (1986) described numerous ways in which out-of-plan use by HMO members may be unrecorded. He suggests that even the Rand study, the best to date, may have missed some of that use.

levels, but also in the long-term rate of increase. If, instead, HMO spending is increasing at a faster rate than FFS, we could conclude that the cost advantage is eroding.

From a variety of time-series comparisons between HMOs and comparison groups, Luft (1981) tentatively concluded that HMOs have a "slightly slower growth rate." This phenomenon was attributed to slightly lower utilization rates rather than to a lower growth rate in costs per unit of service. With this question of growth, as with the question of differences in cost levels, we are nevertheless concerned about the problem of selection bias. Will this result hold up when it is clear that no confounding problem of biased selection exists?

Again, we appeal to the Rand study because its randomized experimental design controls for selection bias. The Rand study of GHC provided information on growth rates of HMO premiums between 1976 and 1981. Newhouse and colleagues (1985) found that the percent increase in premiums at GHC was very similar to the per capita increase nationally and to the increases in HMOs that enrolled federal employees. All were on the order of 75 percent. Also the increases under both arrangements were due to increases in the costs per unit of service.

Together with Luft's examination of the historical record, there is enough evidence to conclude that the growth rate of spending in HMOs is similar to the growth rate under FFS. The implications of this result, nevertheless, are important. First, over time, increases in the HMO market share would tend to increase the portion of the population receiving care at lower cost levels.

Second, and perhaps more important, if the percentage growth rates of FFS and HMOs are the same but they start out at different levels, then the absolute difference in costs between the two will tend to increase. Consider Table 12.4. Suppose FFS starts at $500 and HMO at $400, a difference of $100. If each increases at the rate of 10 percent, the absolute difference after one year will have increased from $100 to $110. Since all health care costs tend to inflate faster than general inflation, the difference between HMOs and FFS will also grow relative to other prices. The relative advantage of HMOs in this example will be still another measure adding to the cost attractiveness of HMOs to consumers.

QUALITY OF CARE IN HMOs

Do HMOs offer a quality of care that is comparable to care under FFS? Given the growth of HMO enrollments and the historical public policy encouragement of HMO growth, this question is of substantial policy interest. The HMO insurance arrangement

TABLE 12.4   HMO and FFS Rate Increases

	HMO	FFS	Difference
Year 1	400	500	100
10% Increase	40	50	10
Year 2	440	550	110

provides incentives to reduce the costs of care. Does it also provide incentives to cut corners by reducing the *quality* of care?

The answer to this question is by no means obvious. Cutting quality would likely lower costs in the short term, but it might increase the longer-term costs if patients required additional services later. Furthermore, if information about quality were available to consumers, lowering quality would tend to erode demand. Despite the importance of quality-of-care issues to health care analysis in general, and to analysis of HMOs in particular, quality issues are among the most difficult to resolve.[8]

A good place to begin is by identifying what quality means, and how it should be measured. Quality, in common usage, may range from consumer perceptions of the provider–patient relationship to the outcome effects of health care on health status. Most important for public policy are those aspects of quality that affect health status outcomes.

Quality measurement can be done at three conceptual stages of health care:[9]

- *Structure* refers to the quality and appropriateness of the available inputs and their organization.
- *Process* refers to the quality of the performance of the delivery of care.
- *Outcome* measures are the ultimate arbiter of quality of care, but they are the most difficult to assess scientifically.

We will follow this conceptual scheme in providing a synopsis of the evidence, concluding with a discussion of patient perceptions of HMO care.

In a nutshell, there is little evidence that HMO quality of care is inferior to that in an FFS system. Several items can be noted:

1. Regarding structure, Luft (1981) reports that HMOs tend to provide specialists as readily or more readily than FFS, and are more likely to have board-certified specialists.

2. Process assessment provides even a wider mix of evidence, though often some of the more established HMOs show up well on measures such as completeness of physical exams, appropriateness of referrals, and appropriateness of drug prescribing. There is little reason to conclude either in favor or against HMOs regarding process.[10]

3. With respect to outcome, Quick et al. (1981) found better infant mortality rates for prepaid group practice versus the general population. More general measures, such as disability days, have also sometimes favored HMOs.

4. Overall consumer satisfaction has been reported as comparable between the two settings. Other surveys show that relatively few members who voluntarily disenroll from HMOs cite dissatisfaction with the care they receive as the reason for their decisions.[11]

Once again, Miller and Luft (1994) provide an up-to-date summary of the most recent material on quality of care and customer satisfaction. Compared with FFS plans, HMO

---

[8]The discussion that follows is based largely on a thorough review of the literature by Luft (1981), a shorter review by Wyszewianski, Wheeler, and Donabedian (1982), and an updated review by Miller and Luft (1994).

[9]These terms follow a discussion from Donabedian (1980).

[10]Concerns have been raised by some; LoGerfo et al. (1979) suggest an undersupply of surgical care.

[11]For further detail, see Roemer and Shonick (1973), and Lewis (1984).

plan enrollees have recently received more preventative tests, procedures, and exami-nations (such as cancer screening, pelvic, rectal, and general physical examinations). Outcomes on a wide range of conditions (including congestive heart failure, colorectal cancer, diabetes, and hypertension) have been better or equivalent to FFS. HMO en-rollees were less satisfied with quality of care and physician–patient interactions but more satisfied with costs.

In summary, quality comparisons between HMO and FFS settings continue to be difficult, but it is hard to conclude that HMOs are either better or worse. This assess-ment of the literature is itself important, however, because HMO quality has been con-sistently questioned. It is surely unwarranted to conclude from the literature that HMOs provide inferior care.

COMPETITIVE EFFECTS OF HMOs AND PPOs

It is often argued that the spread of HMOs and PPOs will also reduce costs elsewhere by increasing competition in the provider and insurance markets. We will examine the evidence following a review of some theoretical issues.

Theoretical Issues

The spread of alternative delivery systems can elicit substantially greater competition in other sectors only if there is an absence of competition at the start. Otherwise, both providers and insurers would be operating at, or close to, their minimum costs of pro-duction. Though there is bound to be disagreement on the extent of the degree of mar-ket imperfections, most would agree that the insurance and provider markets are less than highly competitive.

Consider the consequences of having a larger number of products and competi-tors to an existing monopolistic seller. In Figure 12.4, D_1 is the current market demand and P_1 is the monopoly profit-maximizing price for each firm. The entry of other firms will have the following effects on each individual firm:

- shift the demand curve to the left to D_2
- shift the marginal revenue curve to the left to MR_2
- increase the elasticity of demand at any price because there are now more competitors.

With the same costs facing each firm, the new profit-maximizing price (where marginal revenue equals marginal cost) for each is reduced to P_2. If the decrease in firm demand is sufficiently large, it is possible that an individual firm will no longer be able to earn a competitive return at Q_2. This would occur if the demand curve shifts (due to the entry of competitors) so that it is everywhere below the firm's average cost curve.

The existing firm, say a Blue Cross–Blue Shield organization, may also respond in other ways. It may attempt to reduce its administrative costs. More important, it may try to court customers by attempting to market plans that limit utilization of services, and hence the costs of the services, through various devices. These include utilization review and the adoption of health care plans with increased cost sharing. Of course, it could establish its own HMOs and PPOs, further increasing competition. It could also

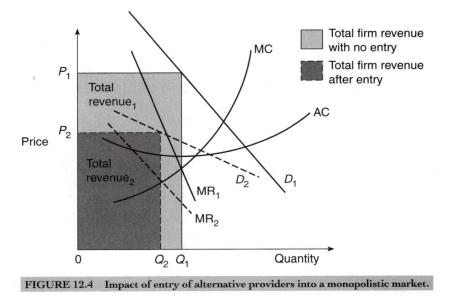

FIGURE 12.4 **Impact of entry of alternative providers into a monopolistic market.**

improve the quality of its service. Further, it may embrace forms of emerging nonprice competition such as advertising and marketing.

Is this theoretical scenario applicable? There are many items likely to be affected by the spread of HMOs and PPOs. These include the provider and health insurance markets, the phenomenon of biased selection, the roles of employers, and the rate of innovation and diffusion of technology.[12] To focus our discussion, we will limit it to two areas: (1) the impact of HMOs/PPOs on hospital markets; and (2) their impact on insurance markets.

HMO Competition in Hospital Markets

Much of the work on HMO effects on hospital markets has been conducted in the Minneapolis/St. Paul region, an area with a high HMO market share. There has been particular interest in the following:

- the degree of competitive bidding for HMO contracts,
- whether HMOs can get discounts,
- whether HMOs tend to rely on low-price hospitals.

Feldman and colleagues (1990) review some of the early evidence. Their review indicates that HMOs generally did not extract major discounts. In fact, price did not seem to be the major HMO consideration in the selection of hospitals with whom to affiliate. Rather, it was hospital location and the range of services that the hospital offered. There was no clear indication as to whether HMOs tend to affiliate with lower-priced hospitals.

---

[12]Many of these issues are reviewed by Frank and Welch (1985).

To update and to extend the evidence, the authors studied data from hospital markets in four cities. They explored and included various quality indicators. HMOs were distinguished solely on the basis of whether they followed IPA or staff–network models.

From statistical analysis, the authors found that hospital affiliation is not affected by prices. However, the estimated price elasticities of demand for hospital admissions were quite large in absolute value, indicating that consumer demand at a given hospital is responsive to price. Thus, although hospital affiliation is not affected by price, the elasticities show that use of services especially by staff–network plans is responsive to price. It was also found that these plans are able to concentrate patients at lower-priced hospitals more effectively than IPAs.

McLaughlin (1988) provides a different and more ominous interpretation of market responses to HMOs. She argues that the "providers are responding not with classical cost-containing price competition but, instead, with cost-increasing rivalry, characterized by increased expenditures to promote actual or perceived product differentiation" (p. 207). So although the increased presence of HMOs and PPOs has either indicated or projected greater hospital competition, it is still premature to draw definitive conclusions.

HMO Competition in Insurance Markets

Commensurate with the spread of HMOs, PPOs, and various forms of managed care, the health insurance industry is rapidly changing. Many have noted that health insurers were previously lethargic in introducing innovative insurance products and in their cost-containment efforts. In addition, we must consider the historic opposition by organized medicine, tax advantages, and provider control of the Blues, and the constraints imposed by state regulation and antitrust laws, all of which previously inhibited change in the insurance market.[13]

From a point in 1977, where the insurance market was divided about equally between the Blues and commercial insurers, Frech and Ginsburg (1988) identify the dramatic changes that have occurred. In addition to the growth of HMOs and PPOs, there have been the following:

- substantial increases in patient cost sharing,
- increased utilization review,
- self-insurance by many large firms.

Under self-insurance, a Blue Cross–Blue Shield or another organization will act only as a third party in processing claims. Thus, more competition is introduced because the self-insured firms will have more control over their health plans and more direct interest in cost-containment measures. Other changes since the mid-1970s include the removal of some of the tax advantages of the Blues and the increased willingness to use the antitrust laws.

Clearly, as measured by market shares or concentration and the availability and range of new insurance products, the health insurance markets have become more com-

---

[13]See, for example, Frech and Ginsburg (1988), and Havighurst (1988).

petitive. However, as a result of the many changes in addition to the presence of HMOs and PPOs, it is difficult to distinguish between cause and effect and to isolate the specific consequences of HMOs/PPOs. There is also concern that despite increases in competition in the insurance and other health care markets, it is difficult to discern their effects on the rate of growth of expenditures.

Nevertheless, events over the past 20 years indicate that major changes in health care delivery are possible. However, it is probably unwise to project the recent increase in managed care market penetration into the future. The managed care option was a major controversial feature of the 1993–1994 Clinton administration health care proposals. The demise of the proposals stemmed in part from opposition to the central role of managed care. Whether or not future reforms can overcome this opposition remains to be seen.

CONCLUSIONS

This chapter has considered HMOs and other similar health delivery systems, in which the functions of insurance and provision of care are combined. We began with a description of HMOs, their history, and the rationale for a government policy that has promoted their development.

Our discussion has emphasized that HMOs have incentives to curtail costs because they serve both as insurers and providers. Thus, the incentives for additional, less essential procedures are reduced. One key finding is that HMOs tend to reduce hospitalization, one of the most expensive of the health care services. While other findings are mixed, there is little evidence to suggest that the quality of the care provided in HMOs is inferior to FFS care.

The penetration of HMOs and PPOs into the health marketplace would seem to be a case of a "tug-of-war" between traditional providers who are fighting an erosion in their market power, and the sellers of a somewhat less costly, although also less personalized product. This competition suggests important roles for both types of service well into the future.

Summary

1. Managed care seeks to integrate what had previously been an unintegrated system of health care treatment. Such integration has the potential to reduce health care costs but the integration is costly and may limit choice of provider.
2. An HMO is a form of health care organization in which the functions of insurance and provision of care are combined. In return for a prepaid premium, an HMO agrees to provide an enrollee with comprehensive health care over a given period of time.
3. When a provider agrees to handle all of a patient's health care needs for a fixed prearranged fee, that provider is bearing a substantial part of the financial risk. By bearing such a risk, an HMO has a strong incentive to develop strategies for reducing excessive care and minimizing other inefficiencies.

4. A PPO is an arrangement under which patients are given financial incentives to receive care from a limited panel of physicians and hospitals with which the payer has contracted. The financial incentives to use PPOs include lower premiums, coinsurance and deductibles, and increased coverage.

5. If providers can charge different consumers different amounts, the providers can earn additional profits. Price discrimination is difficult or impossible under the contracts characterizing prepayment-based organizations because
   • providers will find it difficult to determine how much individual consumers value the services.
   • prepayment-based organizations may be able to shop among providers, thus limiting the providers' monopoly power.

6. An HMO typically provides a comprehensive set of ambulatory and inpatient services including routine office visits and preventive care, most without coinsurance or a deductible. There is reduced paperwork and little uncertainty over coverage. These features make HMO membership attractive to consumers, especially to some who are concerned about out-of-pocket costs.

7. In contrast to FFS arrangements, the HMO enrollee's choice of providers and access to hospitals (aside from emergency care) is limited. Also direct access to specialists usually requires a referral from the patient's gatekeeper—the primary care physician.

8. There is a strong consensus that HMOs reduce utilization, especially of hospital care, but there is little evidence that HMO quality of care is inferior to that in a FFS system.

9. HMOs generally do not extract major discounts from hospitals. Hospital location and the range of services that hospitals offer, rather than price, seem to be the major HMO considerations in the selection of hospitals with which to affiliate.

Discussion Questions

1. Compare staff model, group model, and network model HMOs.
2. What are the organizational differences between HMOs and PPOs?
3. Why would price discrimination in the provision of health care services be more prevalent than price discrimination in the purchase of food?
4. Why is selection bias such an important issue in measuring HMO performance?
5. Discuss ways that HMOs may be able to reduce costs of care to their clientele.
6. Why do some critics argue that HMOs provide lower-quality care than FFS plans? Evaluate this possibility from a societal perspective.
7. After a very large increase in membership, HMO enrollments "flattened" in the late 1980s, and many HMOs suffered financial difficulties. How might this be explained according to what is known about the supply and demand for HMOs?
8. If everyone chose to join an HMO, would average HMO expenditures per case tend to rise or fall? Would national health expenditures tend to rise or fall?

9. What features of HMOs tend to inhibit or discourage people from joining? What features tend to attract people? Discuss the advantages and disadvantages of HMO enrollment.

10. Why is the growth of HMOs a relatively recent phenomenon? Describe governmental policies and practices that have both encouraged HMOs and inhibited them.

11. In what ways can an HMO achieve economies?

12. If traditional FFS leads to demand inducement, what constrains the HMO from underproviding care?

13. Explain how the availability of alternative delivery systems is expected to produce competitive effects throughout the health economy.

Exercises

1. Consider an HMO with a demand curve of the following form:

$$Q = 100 - 2P$$

   Suppose that its marginal and average costs were $20. If the firm maximizes profits, determine its price, output, and profits.

2. In Exercise 1, if the firm must act as a perfect competitor, what will hapen to equilibrium price and equilibrium output?

3. Suppose, in Figure 12.4, that so many providers entered the health care market that individual demand curves fell below the average cost curves. Draw the new equilibrium. What would happen to short-run profits in the health care market?

4. Exercise 3 discusses a short-run equilibrium in the health care market. With entry and exit into and from the market, graph and discuss the long-run equilibrium.

Part Five: Technology

CHAPTER

13

The Production and Cost of Health Care

- ■ Substitution Between Health Care Inputs
- ■ The Cost Function and Economies of Scale and Scope
- ■ Empirical Cost Function Studies
- ■ The Survival Analysis Approach
- ■ Technical and Allocative Inefficiency
- ■ Conclusion: What Has Been Learned about the Production and Cost of Health Care?

Recognizing that health itself is the ultimate output in the health sector, we nevertheless take considerable interest in the production and cost of the intermediate output, health care. Despite some exceptions, politicians interested in cutting health costs usually do not propose cutting back on health care unless health care is perceived as unneeded. Yet there is a frequent perception that health care, even when needed, costs too much.

This chapter and Chapter 14 are devoted to economic issues of production, cost, technology, and efficiency. This chapter addresses three related issues. The first concerns the degree of flexibility we have in producing health care. Must physicians be used always for certain tasks, or can nurses and other less expensive inputs be substituted in some cases? Can we vary the combinations of types of nurses that are to be employed? Each such case is an issue of input substitution.

The second issue concerns the efficient size of health care firms. Economists commonly find that economies of scale exist in many industries. From the point of view of society at large, it would generally be best if firms were to choose the size at which their per-unit costs were at a minimum. In theory, the perfectly competitive industry achieves this in the long run without outside interference. Health care firms are generally not perfectly competitive, however, and we may wonder whether health firms in reality are producing at the optimal size.

We also treat the related issue of economies of scope, whether firms are producing an efficient combination of outputs. For example, it may or may not be more efficient to produce geriatric care and pediatric care jointly, rather than separately. We will examine more fully what this means, and we will study some attempts to gather evidence.

Choosing an appropriate scale or scope of activity is not the only threat to efficiency. Are health care firms producing as much as possible with their factor inputs and are they using the best combinations of inputs to achieve a given level of output? The third issue addresses these other forms of efficiency which are categorized under the headings of technical and allocative efficiencies.

SUBSTITUTION BETWEEN HEALTH CARE INPUTS

Economists often note that there are more than one, and often numerous, different techniques available to produce services. A single technique is a particular recipe for production, meaning a particular combination of inputs. To have numerous techniques available means that one has the advantage of choosing a relatively capital-intensive (labor-intensive) technique during times when capital (labor) is relatively cheap. It may also mean the ability to use cheaper forms of labor in substitution for some more expensive forms.

While it is a common finding in many industries that producers can use numerous alternative techniques, it is also common to hear health practitioners argue that there is basically only one correct way of treating a given illness. The belief that only one technique is possible or wise is what Victor Fuchs has called the monotechnic view.

Such a rigid view of the production process would mean that cost-saving substitutions are difficult if not impossible without reducing either output or quality. A more flexible production process could permit cost-saving improvements that may be beneficial, perhaps substantially so, to consumers. Economists potentially can perform an important service by challenging the monotechnic view and demonstrating, if it is indeed true of the real world, the possibility for flexibility.

The Concept of Substitution

Flexibility in production is essentially an issue of substitution of one input, such as capital, for an amount of another input, such as labor, while maintaining the level and quality of output. The possibility of substitution does not mean that the two inputs are equivalent, but rather that output can be produced using more than one technique.

The idea is illustrated by contrasting a case where no input substitution is possible with a case where an infinite number of combinations is possible. In Figure 13.1, panels A and B depict an example of the two cases illustrating the issue of whether nursing inputs can substitute for physician inputs.

In panel A, a single isoquant is shown, indicating the possible combinations of nurse hours and physician hours required to treat one patient case in a hospital; the isoquant is labeled $Q = 1$. Given this case, there is only one sensible production technique that combines the two inputs. Physicians and nurses must be combined in the ratio

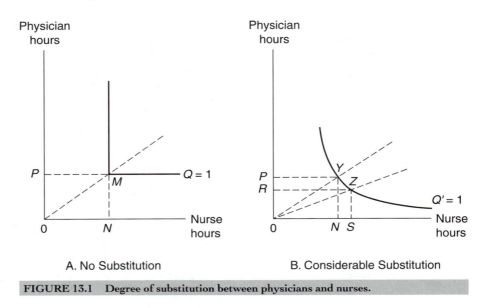

FIGURE 13.1 **Degree of substitution between physicians and nurses.**

given by $0P/0N$, the ratio of inputs used at the corner point M. Notice that $0P/0N$ is also the slope of line segment $0M$.

What does this mean? In panel A, $0P$ physician hours are required to produce one case, and the addition of nursing hours beyond $0N$ will not add to output unless physician hours are also increased. This is to imagine that the patient care requires certain professional physician tasks that only a physician is trained and competent to perform. To use nurses to perform these tasks would result in less care or at least lower-quality care.

It also follows from Figure 13.1 that if $0N$ nursing hours are required to treat one case, the addition of physician hours will not replace these minimum required nursing hours. The fact that the isoquant is flat, when moving rightward from M, means that adding nurses beyond the required combination produces no more output (i.e., it would be wasted). Likewise, the fact that the isoquant is vertical, when moving upward from M, means that additional physician hours beyond the required ratio combination are simply wasted resources.

How would the typical isoquant look if substitution were possible? Panel B, in contrast, illustrates a case where substitution is possible. Again a unit isoquant is depicted, but a smooth downward sloping convex curve illustrates that many different combinations of inputs could be chosen without necessarily being wasteful. In fact, an infinite number of possible techniques are implied by the graph. For example, one case can be treated with the $(0P, 0N)$ combination of inputs or equivalently with the $(0R, 0S)$ combination. Each point on the isoquant represents a different technique. The slope of any isoquant, such as the isoquant labeled $Q = 1$, is called the marginal rate of technical substitution (see Chapter 2), and it represents the rate at which nurse and physician hours can be exchanged while still maintaining output.

It should be emphasized again that even though substitution is possible in panel B, nurses and physicians are not equivalent. It is not even true of the graph that a fixed number of nurses can always replace a physician. Moving along the curve from point Y to point Z, the rate of substitution changes; that is, the slope becomes flatter, indicating a diminishing marginal rate of technical substitution. To replace one hour of physician time at point Y requires some number of nursing hours; however, at point Z, where fewer physician hours are being used, it requires a much greater number of nursing hours. That is, as physician time is more scarce relative to nursing hours, it becomes more difficult to replace. This retains the idea that, while substitution is possible, there are certain physician tasks that are very difficult, expensive, or unsafe to have nurses do, and vice versa. The curve may even become flat at some point, indicating that a minimum of required physician time has been reached.

What Degree of Substitution Is Possible?

The graphs in Figure 13.1 merely define terms; they do not tell us which of the two cases, or possibly a modified one, is true of the real world. From the 1970s on, economists addressed the question of whether and to what degree physician extenders were able to substitute for physicians. *Physician extenders* is an umbrella term referring to specially trained physician assistants or nurse practitioners who are utilized to perform certain tasks, including some that were formerly performed by the physician.

The estimates obtained at that time were equivalent to the measurement of a few points along an isoquant such as the ones depicted previously. This work suggested that physician extenders were able to substitute for physicians to a substantial degree. Depending on the amount of physician hours employed (recall that the rate of substitution may depend on the particular starting point on the isoquant), one physician extender could "replace" from 25 percent to over 50 percent of a physician's services.

Inasmuch as physician extenders represent a substantially lower cost of training, this degree of substitutability could mean a substantial savings in cost. Reports at the time suggested in fact that physicians were not employing sufficient numbers of assistants even in the sense that it would have been more profitable to the physician owners of the practice to employ more extenders. There is controversy over this question, and the issue is worth further investigation. We take up this further investigation, however, in Chapter 16, on physicians. The point at present is that physician extenders can substitute for physician labor inputs to an important degree, depending on the level of physician inputs.

ELASTICITY OF SUBSTITUTION

A second focus of production studies has been the hospital. One study of hospital production is worth detailed examination because it provides evidence of substitution among various categories of hospital inputs. It also illustrates a second and more convenient way to report on the possible degree of substitution between inputs. A convenient way to summarize the possibilities for substitution between any two inputs is the elasticity of substitution (E_S), a measure of the responsiveness of a cost-minimizing firm to changes in relative input prices. It is defined as the ratio of the percentage change in the factor input ratio to the percentage change in relative factor prices:

$$E_S = \frac{\text{Percentage change in factor input ratio}}{\text{Percentage change in factor price ratio}}$$

What does this elasticity mean? Consider that if a firm were a cost minimizer, then it would not be indifferent to changes in input prices. As long as it were possible to substitute between inputs, it would tend to respond to input price changes by shifting away from the now costlier input to the now relatively cheaper input. For example, suppose that a hospital is currently at combination Y in panel B of Figure 13.1 using $0P$ physician hours and $0N$ nursing hours to treat one case. Suppose also that physicians are paid $200,000 per year and nurses are paid $40,000 per year. Suppose, finally, that the hospital employs 100 physicians and 100 nurses. As a result of a 10 percent increase in the relative wage rate of physicians (from $200,000 to $220,000), the cost-minimizing hospital moves to combination Z, which substitutes NS nursing hours for PR physician hours. The relative physician input ratio decreases from the one shown by the slope of the line segment $0Y$ to the one shown by the slope of $0Z$.

Assume that the decrease in the slopes (i.e., relative factor inputs) is 6 percent. The elasticity of substitution is one way of measuring the degree of substitution. Here E_S has a value of 0.6 indicating that every 1 percent change in relative factor prices leads to a 0.6 percent change in the relative use of those factor inputs. Whereas the ratio of physicians to nurses was previously 1.00, a 10 percent increase in relative physician wages (from 5 to 5.5 times nurses' wages) would change the input ratio to 0.94 (a 6 percent decrease). This would represent the replacement of one physician ($220,000) with five nurses ($200,000), hence lowering costs by $20,000.[1] We will report E_S as positive numbers even though it is understood that firms respond to an increase in the relative price of one input by decreasing the relative use of that input.

The minimum value of E_S is zero. A firm with isoquants represented by the one shown in panel A of Figure 13.1 will have an elasticity of substitution equal to zero because it will always use the same input combination to produce a given level of output regardless of relative factor prices. Higher values of E_S indicate more substitutability for any 1 percent change in the factor price ratio.

ESTIMATES FOR HOSPITAL CARE

Jensen and Morrisey (1986) provide estimates of the elasticity of substitution for U.S. hospital care for both teaching and nonteaching hospitals. These authors used regression analysis to estimate the production function for hospital care, thus providing the information needed in principle to trace the isoquants and to calculate the elasticities of substitution between various pairs of inputs. They find the patterns in input use observed in a cross section of hospitals. The observed variation across hospitals is assumed to reflect the possibilities available in principle to any single hospital.

The Jensen–Morrisey study is especially illuminating because these authors correctly recognized that physicians (i.e., the medical staff of the hospital) are an important input in hospital care production, even though the medical staff is not hired and paid by the hospital. By including medical staff in the study, they have more correctly specified the production function. In addition, however, we gain estimates of the possibilities for substitution between physicians and other inputs.

Table 13.1 presents the estimated values for the elasticities of substitution between the indicated pairs of inputs. The numbers have, for example, the following literal

---

[1]The new ratio is 99 physicians to 105 nurses or 0.94.

TABLE 13.1   **Substitution Elasticities for Teaching and Nonteaching Hospitals Evaluated at the Mean**

Input Pair	Nonteaching Case-mix Adjusted Admissions	Teaching Case-mix Adjusted Admissions
1. Medical Staff with Nurses	0.547	0.159
2. Medical Staff with Beds	0.175	0.155
3. Nurses with Beds	0.124	0.211
4. Nurses with Residents	—	2.127
5. Medical Staff with Residents	—	0.292

Source: Jensen and Morrisey (1986).

interpretation. A 1 percent rise in the price of medical staff relative to nurses would result in a 0.547 percent drop in the ratio of medical staff to nurses.

How are we to judge the estimated degree of substitutability? The elasticities reported are sufficiently larger than zero to show that some significant substitutability exists between several categories of hospital inputs. In fact, the authors conclude that "all inputs in both teaching and nonteaching hospitals are substitutes for each other."

The smallest values for substitution reported here are between beds and categories of labor. *Beds* is a convenient measure of the various and often complex capital inputs used by a hospital. The data suggest that even in hospital care production, for which labor is often thought to be the critical input, capital can be substituted for labor.

Perhaps more important are the relatively high values for the elasticity of substitution between nurses and medical staff in ordinary nonteaching hospitals (0.547) and between nurses and residents (2.127) in teaching hospitals. These data reaffirm the substantial potential for substitution that exists between physicians and other professional health care labor.

THE COST FUNCTION AND ECONOMIES OF SCALE AND SCOPE

The production function, its isoquants, and the elasticities of substitution are important because they have consequences for costs. In this section, we will show what a cost function is and how it is derived in order to explain the meaning of the technical terms *economies of scale* and *scope.*

Deriving the Cost Function

While the production function describes the relationship between inputs and outputs, the cost function describes the relationship between outputs and costs. Production and cost functions are closely related, and under certain circumstances the two functions can be derived from one another. This close relationship can be described heuristically with the aid of Figure 13.2, panels A and B.

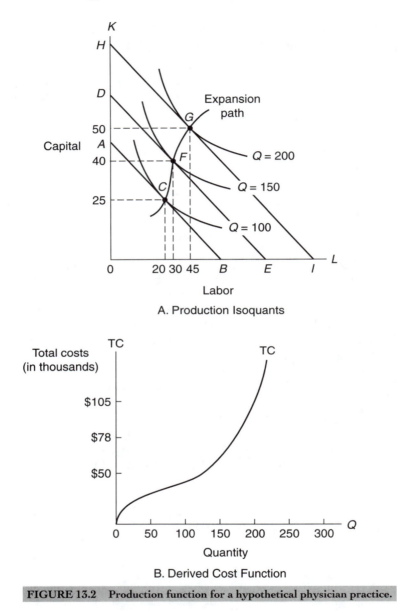

FIGURE 13.2   Production function for a hypothetical physician practice.

Panel A depicts several isoquants, collectively illustrating the production function for a hypothetical physician practice. Of the infinite number of different isoquants that exist in principle, we have chosen to show three. The first or lowest isoquant shown, for example, depicts the many different points or combinations of capital and labor that are capable of producing 100 physician office visits. The higher isoquants produce more as shown, 150 and 200 visits respectively.

COST MINIMIZATION

These isoquants show the many achievable combinations of inputs and outputs; they do not in themselves describe the cheapest choice of inputs to produce any given output choice. To understand how the firm can minimize its costs of producing a given level of output, we need also to introduce a second tool, the isocost curve. The downward sloping straight lines in the upper panel of Figure 13.2, lines such as *AB* and *DE,* depict isocost curves.

An isocost curve illustrates all combinations of capital and labor that cost the same amount. A given level of total cost, TC, can buy many possible different combinations of capital and labor, *K* and *L,* whose costs add up to TC = $rK + wL$ where *r* is the rental price of capital and *w* is the wage rate of labor. The rental price of capital here means the cost to the firm of using the capital for one period, regardless of whether it actually rents the capital or owns it. This particular isocost equation can be transformed algebraically so that *K* appears on the left-hand side, and all other terms appear on the right, yielding the equivalent equation, $K = TC/r - (w/r)L$, which is an isocost function.

The firm that wishes to produce a given output level, say 100 visits, will minimize its costs by choosing the lowest isocost curve that is tangent to the 100-visit isoquant. In the figure, least-cost production of 100 visits occurs at input combination ($L = 20$, $K = 25$) at point *C* on isocost curve *AB*. Given knowledge of the input prices, we can calculate the output cost. For example, let $r = \$1,200$ and $w = \$1,000$; then, least-cost production of 100 visits will cost $50,000. Alternatively, if the firm wishes to produce 150 visits, the least-cost production would occur at point *F,* which entails 30 units of labor and 40 units of capital for a total cost of $78,000. In this fashion, the combination of the production function represented by the isoquants, and the cost requirements represented by the isocost curves, together with the assumption of cost minimization, generate a set of outcomes or points *C, F,* and *G.* The set of all possible points of tangency is called the expansion path.

The expansion path supplies the information that associates a given level of output with its minimum cost. When these cost and output data are recorded in a graph, as in panel B, the result is the firm's total cost function. This cost function has a lazy S-shape that is thought to be typical of many firms in practice. It also goes through the origin, indicating that if the firm produces nothing it will incur no costs, meaning that the firm illustrated has no fixed costs. A period of time long enough for the firm to alter or avoid any of its commitments to input suppliers is called *the long run.* The implication is that the cost function shown is depicting the firm in the long run.

This cost function is a frontier in that it represents the minimum possible cost of producing a given output. Actual firms may operate somewhat inefficiently, and we will observe cost levels above the frontier. It is a contradiction in terms to say that one could observe a cost below the cost frontier. An important efficiency issue is to determine whether health care firms are operating on or above their cost frontier, and we will return to this efficiency issue later. At present we address a different sort of efficiency issue, the issue of whether a firm is operating at an economical *point* on the frontier from the point of view of society as a whole. In the terms we have introduced, we will address the issues of economies of scale and scope.

Economies of Scale and Scope

To simplify the exposition, we separate the issues of economies of scale and scope, treating scale economies first.

ECONOMIES OF SCALE

Consider a physician firm such as the one depicted in Figure 13.2. The long-run total cost function as shown in panel B can be transformed to express information about economies of scale. The average costs for this firm can be calculated by dividing the given cost level by the corresponding number of physician visits. The resulting long-run average cost (LRAC) function is shown in Figure 13.3. A firm is said to experience economies of scale when its long-run average cost curve is declining as output increases. Thus, the firm depicted exhibits economies of scale in, for example, the region AB. Conversely, the firm experiences diseconomies of scale if and only if the long-run average cost curve is increasing as output increases, such as occurs, for example, in the region BC.

What output level would a firm organized for profit choose in this case? It is tempting to suppose it would choose output Q_B at which its average costs are lowest (AC_B), but this is not necessarily the case. A firm is not in the business of minimizing its average costs and would do so only if coincidentally the output that minimized average costs also maximized profits.

ECONOMIES OF SCOPE

A related concept is economies of scope. By definition, economies of scope are possible only for a multiproduct firm; and inasmuch as many health care firms are

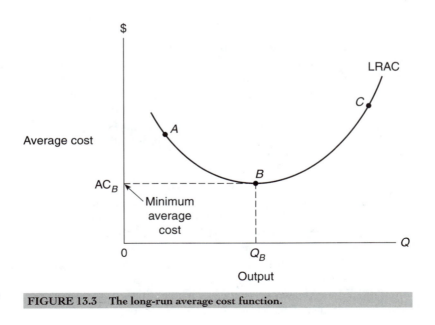

FIGURE 13.3   The long-run average cost function.

multiproduct in nature, the concept is highly relevant to health care. Economies of scope occur whenever it is possible to produce two or more outputs of different goods jointly more cheaply than they can be produced separately. As an illustration, consider the provision of pediatric hospital care (for children) and geriatric hospital care (for the elderly).

Suppose that there were two hospitals in town, one that provided only pediatric care and one that provided only geriatric care. Would the total cost of pediatric plus geriatric care be lower if one single hospital provided both? It may be cheaper to combine the two hospitals and achieve scale economies, but that is not the point at present. Conceivably, as well, it could be cheaper to combine them because the inputs needed for both types of care interact well together: Perhaps things learned in pediatrics have applications in geriatrics; perhaps the two together could support each other so that the result would be lower total costs. If so, we would say that by producing the two different outputs jointly we achieve economies of scope.

The concept of economies of scope is illustrated by equation (13.1). Here a cost function is depicted in mathematical notation. Two different outputs are shown, Q_1 and Q_2. For example, Q_1 may represent pediatric care and Q_2 may represent geriatric care. The example in equation (13.1) concerns the attempt to produce output levels $Q_1 = 100$ and $Q_2 = 150$ either jointly or separately. Economies of scope exist if the cost of producing the two outputs jointly, that is, TC $(Q_1 = 100, Q_2 = 150)$ is less than the sum of the costs of producing each quantity separately, that is, TC $(Q_1 = 100, Q_2 = 0) + $ TC $(Q_1 = 0, Q_2 = 150)$. That is, economies of scope occur in this example if the following inequality holds:

$$\text{TC}(Q_1 = 100, Q_2 = 150) < \text{TC}(Q_1 = 100, Q_2 = 0)$$
$$+ \text{TC}(Q_1 = 0, Q_2 = 150) \tag{13.1}$$

Why Would Economies of Scale and Scope Be Important?

Both of these concepts, economies of scale and scope, have been of considerable interest. We will illustrate their significance, using the idea of economies of scale, but similar arguments can be used to show the importance of economies of scope.

Recall that a profit-maximizing firm has no intrinsic interest in producing at that level of output at which average costs are at a minimum. It would do so if that output also coincidentally were profit maximizing, but this most often is not the case. From the consumer's point of view, it would be best for each firm to produce so that average costs were minimized, so long as these cost savings were passed on to the public. One of the reasons that the theory of perfect competition is so intriguing to economists is that competition forces the firm in the long run to operate so that it minimizes average costs. Though the competitive firm has no intrinsic interest in doing this, it is guided by competition, as if by an invisible hand, to serve society's interests in keeping costs low.

RELEVANCE TO HEALTH CARE FIRMS

Most health care firms, such as hospitals and physician practices, do not operate in perfectly competitive markets. Therefore, the forces of perfect competition will not necessarily force them to operate at the most efficient scale of operation. There may conceivably be too few of them or too many. If there are too many, some policy analysts will feel the need to intervene in health care markets to help to achieve the missing economies.

In recent history, areawide health planning efforts supported and backed by government have been applied under the belief that there are often too many hospital beds and equipment units such as CAT scanners in many markets. Much of government-backed areawide health planning controls on capital would make little sense if size and number of firms did not matter for average costs and if consumers' evaluations of the value of health care were to be accepted as valid.

The gain to society from successfully exploiting economies of scale is illustrated by the natural monopoly argument in economic theory. However, the essential idea can be seen from a simplified example. Consider Figure 13.4, which shows a hypothetical health care unit of a hospital that provides diagnostic services using a CAT scanner. If there are many such firms in the market area, such as the one in Figure 13.4, then it may be the case that no single CAT scanner is operating at the output level where it achieves lowest long-run average costs. Assume that because of this competition, the firm depicted in the figure is operating at point D, where average costs are found to be $0F$. Then it may be cost-saving from society's point of view if the number of CAT scanners in the market could be reduced so that the remaining ones could operate at higher capacity, achieving lower average costs, say at point B, with an average cost level of $0G$. In principle, it may be possible to see that the cost savings are passed on to the public. In this manner, the exploitation of economies of scale could benefit society as a whole.

The argument is valid as long as the cost function described in the figure represented all the costs that are relevant to society and so long as there really are economies of scale to be achieved. The average cost curve in Figure 13.4 records only costs incurred by the producing firm. From society's broader perspective, the costs incurred by patients and their visiting families and friends are also relevant. To switch the case

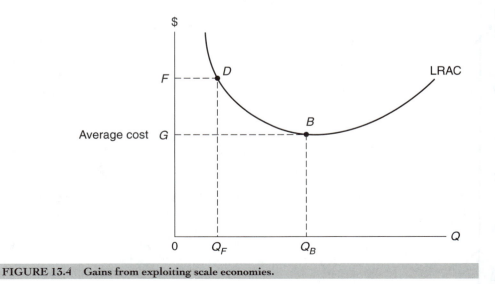

FIGURE 13.4   Gains from exploiting scale economies.

back to general hospital care, suppose we determined that minimal average hospital costs occurred for hospitals at the 500-bed size. Would rural areas of the country therefore be better off to build only one or two centrally located 500-bed hospitals? Rural residents would incur substantial additional costs under such a plan, costs in both travel expenditures and in delayed treatment of emergency cases.

Another use of information on economies of scale and scope involves proposed mergers in antitrust cases. Evidence of sufficiently strong economies of scale and scope provides a justification for allowing mergers if it can be established that the cost savings are likely to be passed on to patients.

EMPIRICAL COST FUNCTION STUDIES

Once the theoretical ideas are understood, the fundamental question becomes an empirical one. Are there, in fact, economies of scale and scope available to be exploited in real-world health care firms? At what level of output and for what combinations of outputs are these economies achieved?

Differences Among Hospital Cost Studies

Two major themes occur often and represent major differences in approach. We will describe long-run versus short-run studies, and behavioral versus structural cost functions.

LONG-RUN VERSUS SHORT-RUN STUDIES

The concept of economies of scale, as we have seen, is defined by the shape of the long-run average cost curve. The theoretical difference between the long run and the short run is clear. The long run is a period of time sufficiently long for the hospital to end any fixed commitments and to make any cost-saving adjustments that are possible. The short run is a period of time during which the hospital still has some fixed commitments that it cannot vary. An example is the number of beds set up for service.

While the distinction is clear in theoretical terms, it is more difficult to determine what we are actually observing in the data. Are hospitals that are being observed in cross section at a given point in time all achieving long-run cost minimization? Have they all adjusted their levels of capital, equipment, and other fixed commitments to their desired long-run levels? These assumptions seem doubtful, particularly when the data measurements are taken at points in time where our health system is in a state of flux.

Conversely, are the hospitals observed in cross section using capital and equipment levels that were determined as if without reference to the current state of their markets? This too seems an extreme view. Perhaps neither view is exactly correct, and it is understandable that analysts have taken either the long-run or the short-run approach to the study of existing data.

STRUCTURAL VERSUS BEHAVIORAL COST FUNCTIONS

Frequently a distinction is made between structural and behavioral cost functions. By structural cost function, we mean a cost function that is derived in a consistent manner from economic theory just as we have derived the cost function in the previous section. That is, the production function isoquants and the isocost curves are used to derive the cost-minimizing level of costs for each possible level of output.

A behavioral cost function[2] is one derived from analysis of the patterns in costs in actual data across hospitals. In such statistical analyses, variables are often included that distinguish real-world differences between hospitals. The variables matter for costs but often do not have a clear role in the theory of cost functions. Sometimes behavioral cost functions omit variables, like input prices, that are difficult to measure in the real world but that are theoretically important.[3]

Difficulties Faced by All Hospital Cost Studies

A central problem in hospital cost function studies is the measure of output, a problem that has at least two aspects. On the one hand, hospitals differ by the type of cases they treat; this is the *case-mix* problem. Medicare's Diagnosis Related Group (DRG) payment system identifies 495 diagnostic related groups; thus, the hospital can be understood as a multiproduct firm with potentially hundreds of different products. Studies of hospital cost functions have approached this problem in a variety of ways, ranging from virtual neglect to estimation of multiproduct cost functions including adjustments with case-mix indexes. Even the multiproduct approaches, which seem conceptually to be preferred, seldom incorporate more than five or six output categories due to data limitations, and no single set of case-mix variables completely does the job of accounting for hospital product heterogeneity.

A related output measurement problem concerns the question of how to treat quality differences. Unobserved or incorrectly measured variations in quality between hospitals may be mistaken in research for evidence of economies or diseconomies of scale. Research work to generate adequate measures of quality is ongoing, and much of our understanding of hospital costs may need to be amended when better-quality measures are incorporated into cost studies.

The case-mix issue is illustrated in Figure 13.5, and the quality issue, though not illustrated explicitly in the figure, is conceptually similar. In this figure, we have illustrated a case where the underlying true long-run average cost function is flat, exhibiting neither economies nor diseconomies of scale. Suppose that the three cost curves shown represent three hospitals, each with a distinct type of case treated. In order of ascending costs, these are Hospital 1 which treats uncomplicated medical cases, Hospital 2 which treats more complicated surgical cases, and Hospital 3 which treats the most highly complex level or *tertiary* cases.

Suppose that points *C, D,* and *E* represent the data observations available to the researcher for each hospital type for a given statistical study. If the underlying case-mix differences are inadequately controlled for by statistical methods, then the researcher may mistake the unobserved case-mix differences for diseconomies of scale; that is, the

---

[2]The term *behavioral cost function* is often attributed to Evans (1971).

[3]Cowing, Holtmann, and Powers (1983) have argued that omitting input prices is equivalent to assuming no substitution possibilities between inputs, which is an incorrect assumption.

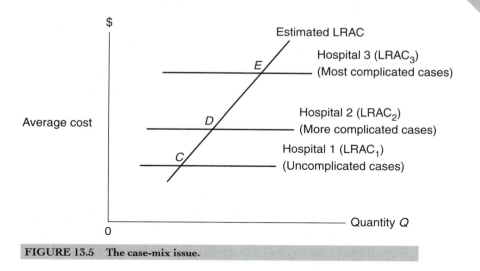

$

Estimated LRAC

E

Hospital 3 (LRAC$_3$)
(Most complicated cases)

Average cost

D

Hospital 2 (LRAC$_2$)
(More complicated cases)

Hospital 1 (LRAC$_1$)
(Uncomplicated cases)

C

Quantity Q

0

FIGURE 13.5   The case-mix issue.

researcher may mistakenly believe that the long-run average cost curve is rising as shown by the connecting line. This case is illustrative only, because the underlying patterns of case mix, quality, and size of output if unknown or not adequately controlled for could yield errors in either direction.

The effect of alternative statistical approaches to treating the case-mix problem on the results for economies of scale has been extensively investigated.[4] These studies show that case-mix differences between hospitals are materially important when estimating scale economies; thus, they cannot be overlooked.

Finally, another difficulty faced by most cost-function studies of hospitals is that they omit physician costs as well as physician input prices from statistical consideration. This practice is a natural result of the independence of the physician from hospital control and accounting, and the physician practice of billing the patient separately. Conceptually, physician costs are part of the total economic hospital cost of treating a case, but data on the physician side are often difficult or impossible to obtain. The omission of the physician, however, may bias the results.

Bays (1980) studied the issue of including physician costs by examining a sample of 41 nonteaching short-term general hospitals in California in 1971 and 1972. He devised an approximate measure for physician costs and showed that inclusion or exclusion of physician costs from the dependent variable caused a significant change in the measure of scale economies. He found that "with admitting physician cost excluded, the hospital exhibits constant or mildly decreasing average cost while the

---

[4]An example of an investigation of the importance of case mix is the study by Hornbrook and Monheit (1985). From data for 380 hospitals, they found that larger-scale hospitals in their sample tended to admit case mixes with relatively shorter lengths of stay. This study is one confirmation of the fact that the case-mix problem is materially important to the issue of estimating economies of scale.

addition of the value of the physician input implies that average cost increases with size" (p. 304).

The Evidence on Hospital Economies of Scale and Scope

Given the several differences between hospital cost studies and the imposing problems that they face, it is not surprising that results vary across the studies. The earliest studies in hospital economics yielded a bewildering array of results. Several found evidence of economies of scale with an optimum output level varying from 150 beds to as high as 900 beds.[5] Others reported either no economies of scale or very weak economies at best.

By the time of Carson Bays's study on the importance of physician cost data, the common consensus seemed to have emerged that hospitals achieve slight economies of scale up to a size of about 250 beds. The work of Bays and other studies conducted in the 1980s, however, brought more sophistication to hospital cost estimation at the same time as they discouraged any developing consensus. In view of the progress that has been made in addressing case-mix issues and other conceptual issues, we must place more credence on the more recent studies.

CONRAD AND STRAUSS

In the early 1980s, more attention was being paid to the task of estimating the structural cost function approach, as opposed to the behavioral approach, which some viewed as less rigorous.[6] Conrad and Strauss (1983) estimated a structural hospital cost function and used a multiple output approach to the case-mix problem. Their data represented North Carolina hospitals for the fiscal year 1978. Chief among their results was that these hospitals exhibited constant returns to scale, neither economies nor diseconomies of scale.

COWING AND HOLTMANN

Appearing in the same year, Cowing and Holtmann (1983) also introduced a structural cost model, but they also took the approach of estimating a short-run cost function and testing whether the data best represented the short run or the long run. Their findings suggest that their sample of 138 hospitals studied did not adequately represent the long run, and they argued that their short-run approach was better. In particular, they found that the sampled hospitals were using amounts of capital that would be excessive for the long run. Also, unlike in most previous studies, their approach permitted them to make estimates of economies of scope.

They found the existence of economies of scale, but their results for economies of scope were somewhat mixed. Their results suggested that pediatric care afforded

---

[5]For examples of differing early hospital cost function studies, see Cohen (1967); Carr and Feldstein (1967); M. S. Feldstein (1967); Ingbar and Taylor (1968); and Lave and Lave (1970).

[6]In 1983, a widely cited review of hospital cost studies (Cowing, Holtmann, and Powers) called upon the profession to make several improvements in the way hospital cost function analysis was done. High priority was given among other things to the use of more general and theoretically correct approaches.

economies of scope to the typical hospital but that emergency room services and several other services did not.[7]

GRANNEMANN, BROWN, AND PAULY

Some researchers argued that the push toward structural cost functions sacrificed too much real-world validity for the sake of theoretical consistency. The solution proposed by Grannemann, Brown, and Pauly (1986) was to "strike a balance between the two extremes." The result was a more extensive treatment of the case-mix issue than appears in structural approaches and in much previous work, for that matter. Even so, the authors suggested that they had not fully captured case-mix effects.

Their results indicate that hospitals with larger inpatient volumes tend to have higher average costs, suggesting diseconomies even after case mix is taken into account. However, the authors argued that the observed differences cannot be accounted for solely by scale-efficiency differences and instead asserted that they are probably the result of unobserved case-mix effects. More confidently, they argued that the emergency department exhibits fairly strong economies of scale though it affords the hospital diseconomies in terms of scope.

VITA

Vita (1990) made advances regarding the distinction between long-run and short-run costs and took a structural approach. An advance was to generate estimates of long-run scale phenomena from the short-run data. Applying his techniques to a 1983 sample of 296 short-term general care hospitals in California, Vita found that his sample tended to exhibit diseconomies of scale. Diseconomies are less pronounced for "hospitals operating at low levels of output . . . but are more severe for larger hospitals" (p. 17). His estimates found no evidence of cost complementarities, a precursor to economies of scope. He concluded that "While this by no means rules out the existence of long-run scope economies, it does make it difficult to establish their existence without further data" (p. 19). Furthermore, applying his methods to the previously cited study of Cowing and Holtmann, he found that their short-run evidence, when translated to the long run, also was consistent with slight diseconomies of scale. Unfortunately, the Vita study was somewhat less vigorous in addressing the case-mix problem than was Grannemann, Brown, and Pauly.

FOURNIER AND MITCHELL

As part of a broader study of the effects of market structure on hospital costs, Fournier and Mitchell (1992) examined 179 short-term general care hospitals in Florida. After controlling for case mix, competition, ownership, and other variables, the investigators determined that hospitals were not operating in long-run equilibrium but were employing too much capital and equipment.

---

[7]Dunn et al. (1995) introduce a different concept of economies of scope in examining selected multiple surgeries, defined as the performance of more than one procedure on the same day (e.g., excision of breast mass followed by modified radical mastectomy). Such multiple surgeries, which are becoming increasingly common, have important fee and third-party reimbursement aspects. The authors found that doing two procedures in one surgery reduces total work by 22% compared to separate surgeries.

Economies of scale were reported for specific product services such as outpatient, maternity, and emergency care, but the results were not statistically significant at usual standards. However, statistically significant economies of scope were estimated among various categories of services. The study suggests that, contrary to concerns that hospitals have excessively increased their scope of services, many hospitals have yet to take advantage of the economies associated with joint production.

SUMMARIZING THESE COST STUDIES

What can we conclude from this discussion of cost function analysis? Recall that at the end of the 1970s a consensus seemed to emerge that hospitals exhibited economies of scale with a moderate ideal size perhaps at about 250 beds. Instead of polishing this consensus and affirming it, the succeeding work brought it into question. The articles we have just reviewed do not provide evidence of scale economies. They even suggest diseconomies. We are left with a caution, however, that this result may itself be an artifact resulting from an inadequate accounting for the underlying heterogeneity of hospital output, which we have called the case-mix problem.

If a consensus is emerging, it is more to the recognition of the important underlying issues in hospital cost function analysis. The value of more sophisticated attention to problems is clearer. However, we may wonder whether some problems—such as the successful treatment of heterogenous output, quality,[8] and incorporation of physician costs and inputs—are even tractable. It is frustrating in social science not to have clear answers, but it is progress to see the problem more clearly.

THE SURVIVAL ANALYSIS APPROACH

The underlying difficulties of hospital cost function research lead to an alternative, related approach called survival analysis. With survival analysis, the focus of study is diverted from the hospital cost function to the changes in hospital size distribution over time. As noted by Bays (1986), "the analytical strength of the survivor technique is its simplicity: those size categories which grow relative to the rest of the industry are presumed to have some advantage over other sizes" (p. 362). Given the predominance of nonprofits among hospitals, the complex role of the physician in hospitals, and the regulatory environment of American hospitals, we cannot simply conclude that hospital size categories that have grown relative to others have done so because of scale economies. However, the data on relative growth are suggestive of the advantages of size in general.

Survival Analysis Applied to Hospitals

Bays studied the changing size distribution of U.S. hospitals over the period 1971 to 1977. Table 13.2 reports a selection of his findings and illustrates the approach. Market

---

[8]A study of nursing homes highlights the quality issue. When quality was ignored, Gertler and Waldman (1992) found scale economies. On the other hand, a quality-adjusted model showed scale economies only for low-quality nursing homes. Average-quality homes had constant costs while high-quality homes were associated with diseconomies of scale.

TABLE 13.2	Market Shares by Bed Size Categories: 1971–1977			
	Year			*Statistical*
Size Category	*1971*	*1974*	*1977*	*Significance?*
0–99 beds	54.9	50.9	46.7	Yes
100–199 beds	26.2	28.9	30.8	Yes
200–299 beds	11.5	13.1	14.5	Yes
300–349 beds	3.1	3.2	3.5	No
350–399 beds	1.8	1.5	2.0	No
400–449 beds	0.9	1.2	1.2	Yes
450–499 beds	0.4	0.5	0.5	No
500+ beds	1.1	0.7	0.9	No
Total number	3,274	3,282	3,215	

Source: Bays (1986).

shares are reported for each year. In addition, he tested the null hypothesis that the market share for a given size category has remained constant over these years. The test statistics calculated suggest that we can confidently reject the null hypothesis of constant market shares over time for four of the hospital size categories.

The only two size categories that have declined in market share in the sample are the categories 0–99 beds and 500+ beds. Combining both statistical significance and the material size of change, only the category 0–99 shows much of a decline. Within the context of the assumptions of survivor analysis, this small hospital category seems to show evidence of being uneconomical, perhaps in the sense of diseconomies of scale.

The complete story of hospital size category change is more complex than what has been illustrated here. Along with these reported results, Bays also found that the pattern of growth varied from nonprofit to for-profit hospitals and that the pattern varied across geographical regions.[9]

Survival Analysis Applied to Physician Group Practice

While most attention to scale phenomena has concerned hospitals, a significant literature and concern has also developed for economies of scale in physician group practices. The physician services industry, being typically a for-profit monopolistically competitive industry, is more approachable through survival analysis.

By the early 1970s, a substantial literature on group practice economies had developed with somewhat mixed results. A variety of methods had been used. Some evaluated correlations of physician income with practice size. Others examined cost functions as was commonly done in the hospital literature. Still others examined

---

[9]A sophisticated survivor analysis by Frech and Mobley (1995), which controls for quality and type of services rendered by hospitals, supports the existence of scale economies for sizes up to 370 beds.

productivity measures by size of practice. A useful alternative applied by Frech and Ginsburg (1974) seemed to account for the differences in previous studies and to provide some resolution of their differences.

Let us reconsider the underlying model of survival analysis and its application to physician group practice. We will assume that a physician manager or group of managers will tend to select a scale of practice that is most profitable to them. Under certain conditions, perhaps conditions that are close enough to being met in the physician care markets, the cost-efficient scale of practice will prove most profitable. If so, it follows that physician group practices will tend to gravitate in size toward this optimum:

> Over time, the size distribution of medical practices will tend toward an optimum where all sizes are equally efficient *at the margin.* Until this optimum is reached, those sizes that are growing most rapidly can be identified as most efficient at the margin (Frech and Ginsburg 1974, p. 26).

The authors applied this technique to changes in market share of physician practices between 1965 and 1969. Table 13.3 shows the ratio of market share in 1969 to market share in 1965 for physician practices of various sizes. As can be seen in the table, the market share of solo practitioners declined during the period, suggesting possibly that this form of practice was operating at a less efficient scale. The market share for all sizes of groups increased during the period. Note, however, that growth was slower in the group sizes of 7 to 25 physicians. Thus the data suggest that this lower middle range of groups was less able to capture certain scale advantages. In contrast, both relatively larger and relatively smaller groups were growing faster and thus appeared to be more efficient in scale. This result tended to incorporate previous

TABLE 13.3   Ratio of Market Share in 1969 to Market Share in 1965

Market Group Size # of Physicians	All in Office-Based Practice	Multispecialty	Fee-for-Service	Prepaid Practice
1–2	0.92	—	—	—
3	1.41	1.50	1.37	3.60
4	1.34	1.49	1.29	5.64
5	1.41	1.31	1.38	1.94
6	1.59	1.47	1.44	3.65
7	1.06	0.79	1.05	1.70
8–15	1.24	1.19	1.29	0.89
16–25	1.08	1.09	1.10	0.93
26–49	2.37	2.44	2.45	2.95
50–99	2.10	2.12	1.44	7.21
100+	1.62	1.62	1.68	1.58

Source: Frech and Ginsburg (1974).

TABLE 13.4	Distribution of Physicians in Practices of Different Sizes. Market Share in Percent				

	Size of Practice				
	1–2	*3–7*	*8–25*	*26–99*	*100+*
1965	84.69	8.37	4.30	1.33	1.31
1969	78.25	11.53	5.09	3.00	2.12
1975	68.67	13.31	8.53	5.08	4.42
1980	67.45	13.14	7.78	4.66	6.97

Source: Marder and Zuckerman (1985).

results in a single coherent pattern. Frech and Ginsburg accounted for their results by arguing that

> Standard industrial organization literature suggests that costs per unit of output increase after a point due to problems of coordination and control. However, the typical manner in which firms attempt to counteract these tendencies—hiring managers and varying labor remuneration—may not be available to the smaller medical groups (p. 33).

These results were more or less confirmed, and were extended to new time periods by a later study.[10] Table 13.4 shows the market share of physician practices of various size categories. It is notable that the size category 1–2 has declined substantially in market share, probably mostly indicating a decline in solo practice. All other size categories, however, have grown since 1965.

Confirming the earlier results, we see a decline in solo and dual practice for the period 1965–1969, and growth in market share, which occurred for all group practice sizes, was relatively smaller for the 8–25 size category. These later data, however, show a change in the growth pattern for the last interval studied. In this period, growth shifted more strongly to the very large groups.

TECHNICAL AND ALLOCATIVE INEFFICIENCY

There are two other forms of inefficiency that are of great concern to health care firms and policymakers. Economists categorize these forms generally under the headings of technical and allocative inefficiencies.

Technical Inefficiency

Technical inefficiency is illustrated in Figure 13.6, panels A and B. Panel A depicts a production process with one input, while panel B depicts a production process using two inputs, capital and labor.

---

[10]See in particular a 1985 study by Marder and Zuckerman. These authors identified market shares by group size for a somewhat smaller set of size categories, but the results are generally comparable.

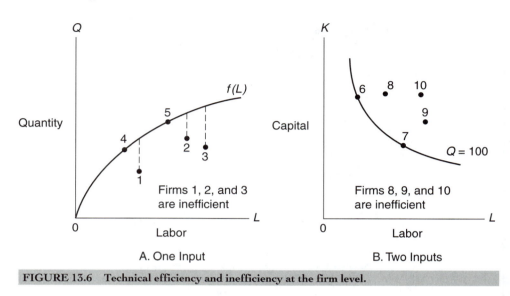

FIGURE 13.6   Technical efficiency and inefficiency at the firm level.

Technical inefficiency implies that the producer is not achieving a maximum amount of output from a given input combination. It is as if workers or machines were misused, not working at full capacity, or not cooperating well.

In both panels, each firm's actual experience is shown as a point indicated by a firm number. A technically inefficient firm is indicated by a firm that falls off its frontier. In panel A, the production frontier is shown as the production function labeled $f(L)$. Firms 4 and 5 are shown to be on the frontier; that is, they are currently technically efficient. In contrast, Firms 1, 2, and 3 are off the frontier and thus are currently technically inefficient. Inasmuch as the vertical axis measures output in panel A, the firm's relative vertical distance from the frontier is a measure of the degree of inefficiency.

In panel B, an isoquant for 100 cases treated is shown. This isoquant represents frontier practice for producing 100 cases. Suppose that the actual current output of all firms depicted in panel B is known to be 100 cases. Firms 6 and 7 in the panel are on the isoquant for 100 cases and thus are currently representing frontier practice and are technically efficient. Firms 8, 9, and 10 are off the isoquant, indicating that they have employed more input quantities than technically efficient production requires.

Allocative Inefficiency

Technical efficiency is a concept regarding production within a given firm. By contrast, allocative efficiency requires the efficient allocation of inputs between firms and between products. Essentially it requires that each type of capital and labor be put to its most rewarding use in society. Economic theorists have shown that allocative efficiency in production will result if each firm buys or hires inputs in competitive markets and if each firm minimizes production costs. Assuming competitive input markets—and thus fixed input prices common to all firms—permits us to describe allocative efficiency at the firm level. Here allocative efficiency requires that each firm respond optimally to input prices, and correspondingly, allocative *inefficiency* implies choosing an inappropriate combination of inputs in the sense that input prices have not been appropriately considered.

To illustrate, consider Figure 13.7. In this figure, the isoquant for 100 cases is illustrated as the curve labeled $Q = 100$. Assume that the firm being examined is currently producing its desired level of output and that the desired level happens to be 100 cases. Two isocost curves are also depicted, one indicating a cost level of $50,000 and the other a cost level of $42,000. Suppose that the firm in question were observed operating at point A. Since this firm is treating 100 cases using an input combination on the 100 cases isoquant, we can say this firm is technically efficient. However, it is not allocatively efficient.

To confirm this idea, consider that the firm in question could alternatively have produced 100 cases at point B. Inasmuch as point B lies on a lower and thus less costly isocost curve, the firm at B would incur less cost, and in this instance costs are reduced from $50,000 to $42,000 by moving from point A to point B. Point B entails a tangency of the desired isoquant with the lowest feasible isocost curve. Tangency in turn entails that the slope of the isoquant will equal the slope of the isocost curve. This condition implies the equality of the ratio of input prices to the ratio of marginal products for the inputs. This is the firm's appropriate response to input prices; that is, it results in allocative efficiency.

Though the conditions for efficiency of both types are well defined, several different empirical techniques have appeared to address them. These techniques can be grouped into two categories: *nonfrontier* and *frontier* studies. In the nonfrontier studies, actual output or cost experience for two or more groups of firms are compared while attempting to control for the effect of extraneous variables. In frontier studies, actual output or costs of firms are compared to the best possible experience. Presently we emphasize frontier, both because these studies can stand alone, and because they are conceptually closer to the definitions of technical and allocative efficiency.

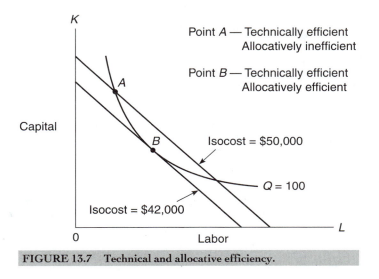

FIGURE 13.7 Technical and allocative efficiency.

There are two principal types of empirical frontier methods. One, the data envelopment method, has been extensively used to study hospitals. The other, the stochastic frontier method, has been applied to the health field only more recently.

THE DATA ENVELOPMENT METHOD

The data envelopment method is illustrated in Figure 13.8. In this case, the frontier production, initially unknown to the researcher, is found and the firm's relative distance from the frontier is measured. Numerous firms are shown and are represented by the points labeled 1 through 10, though in practice perhaps hundreds of firms will be analyzed at a time. The data envelopment method "finds" the frontier practice isoquant for a selected level of output (for example, $Q = 100$) underlying these observed production points by forming an envelope of the data. Researchers use computer programs to find this envelope, which can be thought of as an outer shell of the observed points. Figure 13.8 shows the estimated frontier isoquant as composed of linear segments. This reflects the method of estimation, which uses linear programming. Techniques also are available to reject certain points near or outside the envelope on statistical grounds that they represent outliers from common practice.

Once the frontier isoquant envelope is found, each firm not on the measured frontier is assumed to be technically inefficient, and the degree of inefficiency is measured by the relative distance to the frontier. For example, the efficiency level of firm 1 in Figure 13.8 is measured in percentage terms as the ratio $0B/0A$. Two examples of applications of the data envelopment method to the case of hospital efficiency are reported here.[11]

DATA ENVELOPMENT STUDIES OF HOSPITALS

Valdmanis (1990) applied the data envelopment technique to estimate technical inefficiency in two groups of hospitals in 1982, one representing 33 nonprofits and the

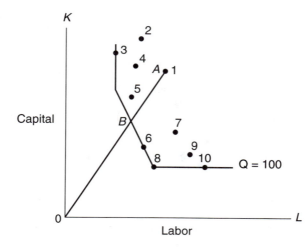

FIGURE 13.8   The data envelopment method.

---

[11]See Finkler and Wirtschafter (1993) for additional illustrations.

other 8 public hospitals in Michigan. Her measures indicated that the nonprofits achieved on average 86.6 percent of technically efficient use of inputs while the public hospitals performed better, achieving 98.5 percent or very near frontier efficiency.

Register and Bruning (1987) also applied the data envelopment method, in this case to a sample of U.S. hospitals including 300 nonprofits, 36 public, and 121 for-profit hospitals. These authors found a somewhat lower level of technical efficiency on average for the entire sample than did Valdmanis. Average efficiency for the Register and Bruning sample was 72.4 percent. These authors further found that there was no significant difference between hospitals by type of organization: nonprofits, for-profits, and government hospitals. They also found that competition levels, as measured by firm concentration ratios, had no significant effect on technical efficiency.

THE STOCHASTIC FRONTIER METHOD

The other principal frontier method, the stochastic frontier method, is well suited to countering one of the potential drawbacks of data envelopment approach, its sensitivity to unobserved shocks. Consider a hospital that is managed with technical and allocative efficiency. Suppose this hospital is affected during the year by the organization of a labor union and the calling of a work stoppage. Regardless of management's response to these events, the hospital's cost and output data for the year might be significantly affected. To the data envelopment analyst, this hospital might appear to be inefficient, attaining costs higher than the observed practice in other hospitals with the same number of cases treated. But by assumption, this hospital's management is efficient.

The point is that each firm may be affected during the period by random shocks that will affect its cost performance but that may not be related to efficiency of management. For an adversely affected firm, its best possible performance, its frontier, may itself be affected by these shocks. In such a case, the frontier will shift randomly. When a function is at least partly determined by a random process, it is called stochastic; hence the term *stochastic frontier.*

Techniques due originally to Aigner, Lovell, and Schmidt (1977) make it possible under certain conditions to estimate a stochastic frontier function. The concept of the stochastic frontier can be illustrated with the help of Figure 13.9. In the figure, a stochastic average cost process is shown. Here the mean frontier average cost curve is shown as a dark curve. This frontier curve is affected by random shocks whose distribution must be known. The two curves shown as broken lines illustrate shifted frontiers. Curve F_1 shows a firm affected by a helpful shock, whereas F_2 shows higher frontier average costs, higher than average because of a harmful shock. Thus, each hospital may have a unique frontier. By the Aigner, Lovell, and Schmidt approach, each firm's frontier can in principle be determined, while one simultaneously measures the firm's distance from the frontier, its inefficiency.

Stochastic Frontier Studies Wagstaff (1989) published a comparison of methods that includes the application of stochastic frontier techniques to the issue of hospital inefficiency. Using data for 49 Spanish hospitals, Wagstaff computed the variation in costs that were due to the random shock element and to inefficiency. He showed that 90 percent of the variation in hospital costs in his work was attributable to the random

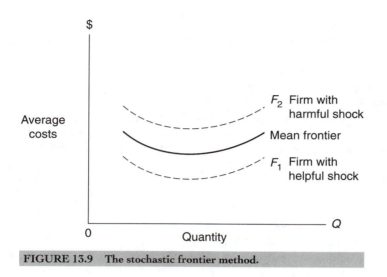

FIGURE 13.9   The stochastic frontier method.

shock element and that only 10 percent was due to inefficiency. He found further that the inefficiency element was not statistically significant; that is, he could not confidently reject the possibility that these Spanish hospitals were all operating on their frontier!

More recently, Zuckerman et al. (1994) have estimated stochastic frontier cost functions for hospitals in the United States and found efficiency levels typically between 80 and 88 percent depending on the types of hospitals considered. These inefficiency values are statistically significant and similar to the ones obtained by Valdmanis (1990) with the data envelopment method.

Before leaving the subject of stochastic frontier estimation, we examine an application of this method to physician group practice. Gaynor and Pauly (1990) developed stochastic frontier estimates for a sample of 905 physician group practices. They likewise measured production efficiency as a percentage of actual output to maximum attainable output. Their results indicate efficiency levels about 66 percent, which although appearing to be much lower than those found for hospitals are in a range common to studies of firms in other industries.

Currently, the viability of the frontier method is being disputed even as frontier studies are being published.[12] One central issue is the problem posed by complex outputs provided by the hospital or nursing home. If these complexities are not properly taken into account, unmeasured variations in the quality or other characteristics of output may end up as inefficiency statistics. For example, suppose one hospital provides double the nursing care so that nurses respond more quickly to patient problems and also provide more care time with the patient. If this extra "output" is not measured

---

[12]The October 1994 issue of the *Journal of Health Economics* featured arguments pro and con (Dor [1994], Hadley and Zuckerman [1994], Kooreman [1994], Newhouse [1994], Skinner [1994], and Vitaliano and Torren [1994]).

accurately, the hospital will show up under frontier analysis as inefficient. On the other hand, frontier analysts recognize these problems and are incorporating increasingly sophisticated measures of quality and output in their studies.

CONCLUSION: WHAT HAS BEEN LEARNED ABOUT THE PRODUCTION AND COST OF HEALTH CARE?

It will be useful to summarize some of the key ideas and results reported and explained in this chapter. The chapter has two main purposes: to explain the ideas and language of production and cost studies, and to report some of the key results of these studies. We began with the concept of substitution between inputs. Substitution describes the possibility of producing a given health care output with more than one, and perhaps many, alternative techniques. The degree of substitutability that is possible reflects the degree of flexibility available, which in turn provides a means to lower costs by choosing less expensive techniques from among those available.

The results of the study of substitution in health care contrast fairly strongly to the opposing view that there is only one possible way to produce health care, the monotechnic view. To the contrary, the data show that substitution is possible and indeed occurs to a considerable extent between health care inputs. This is reported for substitution between health care capital and labor, but also between various labor inputs including nurses, physicians and residents.

We then turned to the second major theme of the chapter, that of investigating possible economies of scale and scope in the production of health care. The result of examining the short and sometimes frustrating history of hospital cost studies is an understanding of the differences between studies and the difficulties faced by all such studies. The seeming consensus of past years suggesting slight economies of scale in hospitals has not been supported by more recent studies. It is more reflective of the recent literature to say that no clear consensus now exists.

Survivor analysis asks whether certain size categories of hospitals and physician group practices have better survival capability, perhaps evidencing underlying economies of scale. There is a variety of results for both hospitals and physician practices, but the clearest trends in both instances appear to be declines in the market share of the smallest size categories.

Finally, we explored the distinction between technical and allocative inefficiency. The former represents a situation in which a firm is not getting as much output as can be expected with its inputs, whereas the latter represents a situation in which a firm is not using the best combination of inputs relative to its costs. We have examined the two principle methods—data envelopment and stochastic frontier—used to estimate inefficiencies. The literature has not yet evolved to the point where there is a consensus on the extent of inefficiencies.

Throughout this chapter we have set aside certain production and cost issues for later discussion. These remaining issues, which have the themes of technology and technological change, are taken up in the next chapter.

Summary

1. Frequently, health care goods and services can be produced in different ways in the sense that they use different combinations of factor inputs.

2. Isoquants are used to represent the alternatives and to illustrate the possibilities for substitution. The marginal technical rate of substitution represents the amount of one factor that needs to be given up for a unit increase in another factor while maintaining the level and quality of output.

3. The elasticity of substitution is another way economists measure substitution. It represents the percentage change in the ratio of factor inputs resulting from a 1 percent change in relative factor prices.

4. Empirically, some substitution has been found not only between different kinds of medical staff but even between hospital beds and medical staff.

5. The principles of cost minimization, as represented by the locus of tangencies between the firm's isoquants and isocost curves, are used to derive the cost curves (total and average).

6. Economies of scale refer to a declining long-run average cost. Economies of scope represent situations where the cost of producing goods jointly is less than the sum of the costs of separate production. Both concepts are relevant to policies intended to promote efficient size and scope of hospitals.

7. There are important considerations in estimating hospital cost functions to determine economies of scale and scope. These include the handling of case-mix and quality differences and determining whether firms have made long-run adjustments.

8. Early empirical work on hospitals found evidence of economies of scale and an optimum size of about 250 beds. Several recent contributions suggest no economies or perhaps even some diseconomies of scale.

9. Survival analysis is an alternative to estimating cost functions. Inferences on optimum size are made from changes in the size distribution of firms over time.

10. Survival analysis for hospitals suggests diseconomies of scale for small hospitals, but no strong evidence for other size categories. For the physician firm, the decline in the market share of solo practitioners suggests diseconomies for this form of practice. Rapid growth of both relatively small and relatively large groups suggest scale advantages for those forms.

11. Technical inefficiency occurs when a firm fails to achieve the maximum potential output from a given set of inputs. It can be measured as a relative distance from the frontier production function surface or correspondingly as a distance from the isoquants of the frontier production function.

12. Allocative inefficiency arises in the case of competitive input markets when a firm fails to purchase inputs, given their prices, in a manner that minimizes costs.

13. Efficiency can be measured by recently developed frontier methods of two types. The data envelopment method estimates the frontier by statistically forming an envelope of data points representing production data. The stochastic frontier method estimates simultaneously a randomly shifting frontier and the firm's distance from that frontier.

Discussion Questions

1. Explain if there is any difference in trying to maximize output for a given cost or to minimize the cost of producing a given level of output.

2. Distinguish between the concept of economies of scale and economies of scope.

3. What is the relevance of economies of scale and scope to (A) health care providers; (B) policymakers and health care planners?

4. What are cross-sectional data? Why do economists find it so critical to control for case mix in studying health care cost functions? What are the analytical dangers if they do not?

5. Describe the technique of survival analysis and how it is used to make inferences about optimal scale and scope.

6. Are nurses and physicians likely to be perfect substitutes in production of health care? For what tasks can they easily substitute for each other? For what tasks is this difficult?

7. How do legal restrictions on practice for both nurses and physicians tend to affect the observed elasticities of substitution? Would they tend to be higher if legal restrictions were removed? Would quality of care be affected?

8. Given the cost function and economies of scale and scope information reviewed in this chapter, does a policy encouraging large centralized hospitals seem wise? Will market forces tend to reward centralization of hospital services?

9. Speculate on what types of services are more appropriate to large regional hospitals, and what types of services are more appropriate to small local hospitals?

10. Economists define the elasticity of substitution as the percentage change in the capital–labor ratio elicited by a 1 percent change in the factor–price (wages/capital costs, for example) ratio. Would you expect the elasticity of substitution to be positive or negative? What would be the elasticity of substitution of a set of right-angled isoquants? Why?

11. Contrast technical and allocative efficiency. How can technical and allocative inefficiency in health care firms affect patient welfare?

12. If the available data envelopment estimates of hospital inefficiency by Valdmanis are correct, can significant cost savings to the consumer be achieved through improved efficiency? What if the Register and Bruning estimates are correct?

13. What does *stochastic* mean in stochastic frontier efficiency estimation? Give several real-life examples of events that could shift the production frontier.

Exercises

1. Draw an isoquant that shows relatively little substitution between two factor inputs and one that shows relatively large substitution. Let the vertical axis represent capital and let the horizontal axis represent labor.

2. Draw isocost curves that are tangent to your isoquants in Exercise 1 and that have the same slope. Mark the points of tangency and note the capital–labor ratio. Draw

new, flatter isocost curves that are tangent, again each having the same new slope. Mark the points of tangency and note the capital–labor ratio. In which case is there a greater change in the capital–labor ratio? Which will have a higher elasticity of substitution?

3. Determine the elasticity of substitution in the case of the isoquant in panel A of Figure 13.1.

4. Explain why the isocost curves in panel A of Figure 13.2 have the same slope. What will happen to the slope if the price of capital decreases?

5. Suppose that a firm has the following production technology for Goods 1 and 2.

Good 1		Good 2		Both		
Q_1	Cost	Q_2	Cost	Q_1	Q_2	Cost
10	50	10	60	10	10	100
20	100	20	100	20	20	180
30	150	30	130	30	30	250

   a. Does Good 1 indicate economies of scale? Why?
   b. Does Good 2 indicate economies of scale? Why?
   c. Do the two goods indicate economies of scope? Why?

6. If any firm's price of labor and capital each double, what will happen to the expansion path (i.e., locus of tangencies between the isoquants and isocost curves)? What will happen to the firm's average cost curve?

7. Reproduce Figure 13.4, panel B, and draw in a family of isocost curves, choosing the common slope as you wish. As you have drawn these curves, show the point of least-cost production of 100 units of output. Are firms 8, 9, and 10 more costly producers than this? Are the technically efficient firms 6 and 7 either least-cost producers?

CHAPTER

Technology

■ Technological Change and Costs

■ Insurance, Technology, and Inflation: Looking Toward the Future

■ On the Diffusion of New Health Care Technologies

■ Conclusions

The rapid pace of technological change in the health care industry raises economic questions about the effects these changes will have. Technological change may be cost reducing, when it improves the productivity of health care resources, or it may be cost increasing, when it improves the quality of care or introduces new and costlier products. Because it often raises costs in the health sector, technological change is hypothesized to be the major contributor to health sector inflation. Deep and widespread insurance coverage in the health sector may induce technological innovations of the type that are cost increasing. The effects on costs and the improvements to quality of care will depend on the diffusion of these new technologies to providers. Thus, patterns of diffusion have become a critical subject of study. We investigate these issues in the present chapter.

TECHNOLOGICAL CHANGE AND COSTS

The production function, which embodies the technology available to the firm, shifts as technology changes. This change has consequences for costs, quality, and the availability of new products.

Technological Change: Cost Increasing or Decreasing?

Technological change necessarily entails an improvement either by providing less costly production methods for standard "old" products, or alternatively, by providing new or improved products. In either case, cost experience is improved in the sense that

321

it will be less expensive to produce a given output, holding quality constant. However, the mix of products and services sold may change in directions that raise the average cost of a patient day, a case treated, or a physician visit. In consequence, the total health care expenditure per capita may rise.

COST-REDUCING AND COST-INCREASING SHIFTS
IN THE ISOQUANTS

These concepts are illustrated in Figure 14.1. In panel A we hold quality of care constant and illustrate the isoquants representing 100 cases before and after a technological change. The technological improvement in panel A shifts the isoquant inward. The firm chooses an efficient combination of inputs at point *E* and after the change at point *E'*. This change results in the attainment of a lower isocost curve for treating the 100 cases.

Panel B illustrates the introduction of a new technology that makes it possible to treat 100 cases with better health status outcomes, thus providing a higher quality of care. Improvements entailing new products or, as shown in panel B, an improved quality of care, are beneficial to the consumer but they may be more costly. This is illustrated by a shift outward of the 100-case isoquant, resulting in production on a higher and costlier isocost curve. The typical patient treated will pay more for care. In some cases where patients are heavily insured, we may question whether the change is worth it to the patient when he or she pays increased insurance premiums, or to society as a whole.

THE CHANGE IN COSTS OF TREATMENT IN PALO ALTO

Has technological change in health care on average resulted in more costly or less costly treatment? This question is inevitably raised in efforts to develop a quality-constant

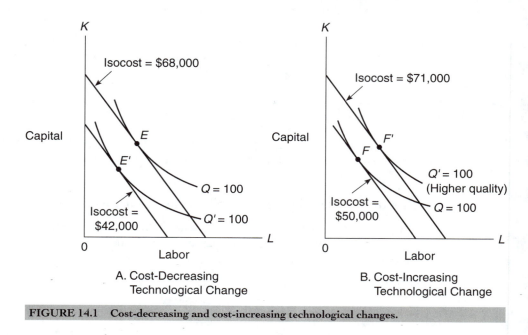

FIGURE 14.1   Cost-decreasing and cost-increasing technological changes.

index of health care prices and to assess the net impact of technological change. Researchers have approached the issue by examining the changing costs of treating a given illness at two or more points in time. Anne Scitovsky (1985) describes the methodology:

> The method involves selecting a number of specific illnesses that can be regarded as representative of illness in the population . . . obtaining detailed data on the number of and charges for specific services used in the treatment of these conditions . . . and comparing average charges for the episode of illness in the later year with average charges of treatment in the earlier year in the later year's prices (p. 1346).

Table 14.1 presents data from studies on clinic care conducted in Palo Alto, California. The table entries show percentage changes in the average cost of treatment for various conditions, holding prices of inputs constant. Thus, a positive (negative) percentage change represents an increase (decrease) in the number and qualities of the inputs that are used to treat an illness and that result in a cost-increasing (decreasing) change in the technology of treatment.

In the 1951–1964 period, changes in treatment tended to be cost increasing. The 1964–1971 period and the 1974–1981 period showed a more mixed pattern, but here too the majority of cases were cost increasing.

TABLE 14.1   Percentage Change in Average Cost of Treatment Measured in Constant Input Prices

Illness or Condition	1951–1964	1964–1971	1971–1981
Otitis media (children)	-17.8%	3.9%	-3.8%
Forearm fractures (child)			
Cast only	0.0%	3.2%	26.1%
Closed reduction, no general anesthetic	36.3%	23.3%	-6.1%
Closed reduction, general anesthetic or regional anesthetic	117.5%	-9.1%	12.8%
Pneumonia (nonhospital)*	NA	-14.1%	-8.7%
Duodenal ulcer (nonhospital)	-11.7%	9.1%	NA
Appendicitis			
Simple	3.6%	2.2%	19.0%
Perforated	7.9%	13.8%	16.7%
Maternity care*	-0.6%	-7.8%	1.6%
Myocardial infarction*	NA	33.3%	-4.1%
Breast cancer*	16.1%	-5.4%	3.4%

Notes: For column 1, both 1951 and 1964 input costs are calculated at 1964 prices; for column 2, both 1964 and 1971 input costs are calculated at 1971 prices; for column 3, both 1971 and 1981 input costs are calculated at 1981 prices. Percentage changes are calculated from data published in the cited sources.

*Pneumonia case data for 1971–1981 includes adult cases only, maternity care data excludes cesarean deliveries, myocardial infarction includes all cases, breast cancer includes all cases.

NA = Not Available

Source: Scitovsky and McCall (1977); Scitovsky (1985).

BIG-TICKET AND LITTLE-TICKET TECHNOLOGIES

Scitovsky characterizes the technological changes underlying these data as being of two types: little-ticket technologies, and big-ticket technologies. The former included primarily changes in the number of simple diagnostic procedures used, such as laboratory tests, diagnostic X-rays, and electrocardiograms. She found that cost-increasing uses of little-ticket technologies were characteristic of the years 1951–1964 and 1964–1971, especially during the earlier of these two periods. But during the 1971–1981 period, use of these small-cost technologies stabilized.

In contrast, the introduction of new big-ticket technologies was characteristic of the latter period studied, 1971–1981. These affected certain patient cases, particularly treatment of breast cancer and myocardial infarction. In addition, the use of cesarean section, itself a big-ticket technology, increased substantially during the latter period. The new big-ticket treatment technologies tended to raise costs per case substantially, but they were used by relatively few patients for the sample and period studied, so that average treatment costs for all cases rose only modestly for breast cancer and fell somewhat for myocardial infarction.

But the effect of the big-ticket technologies generally was to raise costs substantially, according to Scitovsky:

> This cost-of-illness study suggests that in the period 1971–1981, the rate of increase in the use of ancillary services appeared to have slowed down but that several new and expensive technologies came into use, which raised costs substantially (p. 1355).

Two examples illustrate how costly these new technologies are. During 1971–1981, new modes of treatment for myocardial infarction included streptokinase infusion, which cost $19,206 per case in 1981; and coronary bypass, which cost $47,564 per case—each compared to a mean cost of $10,094 for conventional care. However, lacking national data on the frequencies with which such technologies were used, Scitovsky could not extrapolate confidently their contributions to national costs.

TECHNOLOGICAL CHANGE AND HEALTH CARE INFLATION

These micro studies suggest that technological change has been cost increasing on average, but the data are mixed and it is difficult to draw macroeconomic conclusions from the approach. To make inferences about the contribution of technological change to health care inflation requires other data, and a characteristic method has developed, that of finding the residual change. Following Newhouse's (1992) exposition, we begin by identifying all logical contributors to health care inflation and make estimates of their contribution. The residual then is a candidate for interpretation as the effect of technological change. Newhouse identifies five factors that make potentially a significant contribution to health care inflation: aging, increased insurance, increased income, supplier-induced demand, and factor productivity problems in the service sector.

The proportion of the population over 65 increased from 8 percent in 1950 to 12 percent in 1987. Newhouse estimates the effect of this change by applying as weights the average expenditure of persons in each age group. He finds the effect to be only a

15 percent increase in expenditures. So this explains only a tiny fraction of inflation; during the period, average expenditure per person increased by a factor of five.

Newhouse (1988) shows that inflation due to insurance-induced demand increases can account for only a minority portion of the rise in expenditures. Evidence on the role of insurance from the Rand Health Insurance Experiment is useful because it isolates the role of insurance from that of technological change. By randomized assignment of insurance provisions to patients with access to essentially the same service facilities, the Rand study effectively held technology constant as it experimentally varied insurance coverage.

Applying the Rand estimates to the problem, one would expect the shift in average coinsurance rates from about 66 percent in 1950 to 28 percent in 1984 to have increased expenditures on the order of 50 to 100 percent, considerably less than the increase experienced. "Thus, it seems reasonable that the change in insurance (technology held constant) can only account for a small portion—perhaps a tenth—of the postwar increase in medical care expenditures" (Newhouse 1988, p. 274).

Income increased substantially during roughly this period. Looking at a slightly longer period, Newhouse (1992) finds per capita income rising by 180 percent from 1940 to 1990. With typical estimates of the income elasticity (0.2 to 0.4), this implies an inflationary impact of 35 to 70 percent, much lower than the 780 percent increase observed.

The effect of increased numbers of physicians on the demand for health care is also unlikely to have accounted for a substantial effect on costs roughly for this period. Health care expenditures have been inflating in real terms at about 4 percent per year since 1940. The increase in physicians came most strongly in the 1970–1990 period, yet the rate of inflation did not change. Recent estimates of the extent of supplier-induced demand also suggest a modest role.

It has also been argued that inflation is an endemic problem of service industries, which include the health care industries. The problem comes when service sector jobs, which are labor intensive, cannot be done more productively over time. How can you speed up a haircut, for example, without harming quality? As productivity and wages rise in other sectors, health, according to this theory, experiences the wage increases without the productivity increases. Hence, inflation ensues. A counterargument notes the many cases in health care where there has been substantial change both in diagnostics and treatment. Compare a haircut from 1940 with one given today; then compare the 1940 treatment for a heart attack with current methods. Clearly, the lack of productivity growth does not apply to the health sector, at least not across the board.

Newhouse also notes that health maintenance organizations have experienced rates of expenditure growth similar to fee-for-service care. HMOs have economic incentives to cut production costs. The fact that HMOs have experienced similar inflation rates to other parts of the health sector suggests that this inflation is not a result of growing inefficiency in the health care sector.

How much of the inflation in health care expenditures can these alternative hypotheses explain? Newhouse argues that it is difficult to measure largely because of the difficulty in measuring health sector productivity growth. However, his own view "is that they account for well under half—perhaps under a quarter—of the 50-year increase in medical care expenditure. Thus, we are left with trying to explain a large residual" (Newhouse, 1992, p. 11). Many analysts are "now inclined to emphasize technological change as the primary explanation of the historical increase in expenditure . . ." (Newhouse, 1988, p. 275).

Insurance and the Bias Toward Cost-Increasing Technological Change

If insurance is not the main contributor to inflation through its direct role in increasing demand, it may nevertheless play a major indirect role through its effect on technological change. It has been hypothesized that insurance coverage induces a bias in technological change toward the cost-increasing innovations versus the cost-reducing ones.

THE COST-INCREASING BIAS HYPOTHESIS

The argument can be understood at an intuitive level. Increases in health insurance coverage tend to reduce the portion of the bill that the patient pays out-of-pocket. Although the patient may realize that premiums will tend to rise if all patients act likewise, he or she will have the incentive to make use of the new expensive technology, and may use it when and to the extent that the marginal benefits do not fully outweigh the full marginal costs. Consequently, the payoff to owning a patent to new costly health care technology becomes higher.

Newhouse hypothesizes that insurance leads to a bias in the direction of cost-increasing technologies. He distinguished technologies between process innovations (which improve existing treatment processes, making them less costly) and product innovations (which introduce new products in the treatment process and are generally cost increasing). Newhouse proposes that insurance coverage tends to encourage new product types of innovations.

THE GODDEERIS MODEL

The elements of the relationship between insurance and innovation can be made more explicit (Goddeeris, 1984a). Figure 14.2 shows the theoretical relationship of improvements in health, Δh, to changes in health expenditures, Δm. As shown, this relationship is labeled $\Delta h(\Delta m)$. Health care innovations may be either cost increasing (entailing positive values of Δm) or cost reducing (entailing negative values of Δm.) It is hypothesized that innovations that tend toward cost-increasing change (higher values of Δm) also yield greater improvements in health status (higher values of Δh.) Thus, health improvements, Δh, are an increasing function of cost change, Δm. Here the function $\Delta h(\Delta m)$ is also hypothesized to be concave as shown.

Consider a model in which there is a health services provider who is also a potential innovator, and in which there is a consumer who maximizes utility. Let this consumer be insured so that he pays only a fraction, z, of the provider's bill out-of-pocket. Suppose that the market for this service is initially in equilibrium and that the provider considers undertaking the development of an innovation in treatment technology. Potential innovations may have consequences for the equilibrium health of the consumer and for the costs of treatment. The possibilities are summarized by the function we have just described, $\Delta h(\Delta m)$. For example, an innovation may be available that raises health by Δh_1 and reduces treatment costs by Δm_1; this example case results in the outcome indicated by point D_1 in panel A. An alternative innovation may result in a

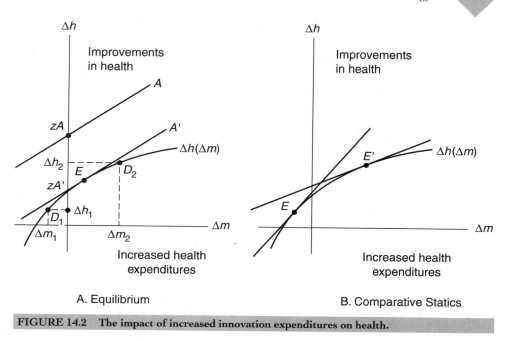

FIGURE 14.2 **The impact of increased innovation expenditures on health.**

rise in treatment costs, say by Δm_2, but substantially raises health, say by Δh_2, the outcome of which is shown by point D_2 in panel A. We shall assume that the innovations tend always to improve equilibrium health status.

By investing in a given innovation, the provider seeks to increase profits. We presume the provider will select innovations of the type that tend to give the highest potential profits. We can understand which innovations will provide the highest potential profits by the aid of the isoprofit curves. The provider's extra profit obtained through the innovation is equal to his extra revenue, minus the extra costs, Δm. The provider can charge the patient only as much and at least as much as the improvement in health is worth to the patient. Assume that the patient values each additional unit of health at a constant rate, and further let the changes in health be measured in units representing one dollar's worth to the consumer. Thus, the consumer is willing to pay at most $1 for each unit of increase in health status. But the provider can charge a full price per unit of health increase that is greater than $1 because the insured consumer only pays a fraction of the bill out-of-pocket, the coinsurance rate, z. Thus, the innovator-provider can charge $\Delta h/z$ for the innovation. His profits from the innovation are, thus,

$$\text{Extra profits} = \Delta h/z - \Delta m \qquad (14.1)$$

In Figure 14.2A, we represent these profit data by the isoprofit lines. An isoprofit line is defined as a collection of points $(\Delta m, \Delta h)$ that yields a given profit level. The isoprofit equation for profit level A is thus $A = \Delta h/z - \Delta m$. If we algebraically rearrange terms, the isoprofit equation can be written treating the dependent variable Δh as a function of the remaining terms. That is, the isoprofit equation is equivalently written as $\Delta h = z(A + \Delta m) = zA + z\Delta m$. This is a linear equation with intercept zA and slope z.

Two isoprofit lines are shown in panel A. The isoprofit line for an extra profit level of A dollars is so labeled in the graph. Its intercept is found by setting Δm equal to zero in the function $\Delta h = zA + z\Delta m$; thus, the intercept is zA. Similarly, the A' isoprofit line has an intercept of zA'. Since $zA > zA'$, it follows that $A > A'$. In general, higher isoprofit lines yield higher extra profit levels.

In panel A, the isoprofit line A is unattainable given the function $\Delta h\,(\Delta m)$ shown. In contrast, isoprofit line A' is just attainable. The equilibrium choice will be a point of tangency between the $\Delta h\,(\Delta m)$ function and the highest isoprofit curve attainable. Under the circumstances shown in panel A, the equilibrium will be at point E.

COMPARATIVE STATIC ANALYSIS

Comparative static analysis allows us to investigate the role of insurance and its effect on the incentives for innovation. Increased insurance coverage in this model is represented by a fall in the coinsurance rate, z. The slope of the isoprofit lines is z; thus, when z becomes smaller the isoprofit lines become flatter. In panel B, the innovator finds his optimal choice to have changed when the isoprofit curves became flatter. Assume that his optimal choice initially is point E, a point of tangency. When the insurance coverage increases, z falls, implying that the highest extra profit will be attained at a new point of tangency. This new equilibrium is shown as point E' in panel B.

Note that the equilibrium under greater insurance coverage entails a higher level of Δm than for the initial equilibrium. Thus, the presence of higher insurance coverage has induced the innovator to switch from an emphasis on cost-reducing innovations such as at point E, to cost-increasing innovations such as at point E', which now will have a higher profit.

INSURANCE COVERAGE AND THE TYPE OF TECHNOLOGY

When insurance increases the development of cost-increasing technologies, it may do so at the expense of "higher" technology. To explain this point, consider Thomas's (1975) categorization of health care technology as consisting of three types: *nontechnology,* representing care that is palliative but offers no real medical intervention to a disease that is poorly understood; *halfway technology,* representing often highly expensive complex treatments that prolong life but ultimately do not cure the disease, such as treatments for presently incurable cancers; and *high-technology* interventions for which medical theory is clear and that have a precise effectiveness, such as immunization and antibiotics. The highest technologies are often among the least expensive interventions. Thus, we may hypothesize that the bias induced by insurance may stimulate the advancement of halfway technologies, posing the question of whether there is a net welfare gain to society.[1]

THE EFFECT OF INNOVATION ON INSURANCE COVERAGE

Thus far we have described the relationship of insurance to technological change as one-directional, with insurance affecting innovation. Weisbrod (1991) notes that the

---

[1]Newhouse (1992) suggests that "There is reason to think that consumers want to pay for much of this change" (p. 18).

relationship in reality extends in both directions. First, as we examined, insurance coverage affects the desired types of innovations, thus affecting the choices made for investment in research and development. More generous insurance coverage typically tends to encourage investment in more cost-increasing technologies.

The existing state of technology, however, will also affect the definitions used by insurance companies and the technologies that are covered. If an effective new technology becomes available, there will be substantial pressure to develop insurance for it, and thus R&D generates a greater demand for insurance. Much of our insurance coverage is provided by government, and effective medical technologies are usually made available to that portion of the public that receives care through government either directly or indirectly. In either case, the availability of technology influences the demand for insurance.

EVIDENCE ON THE RELATIONSHIP OF INSURANCE, TECHNOLOGICAL CHANGE, AND INFLATION

Newhouse (1978b) proposed a test related to the hypothesis that insurance coverage induces cost-increasing innovations. He noted that if higher insurance coverage tends to induce technological change that increases costs, then we should observe higher inflation rates correlated with higher *levels* of insurance coverage.[2] If, on the contrary, insurance affects inflation primarily because it shifts the demand curve outward, then we should observe higher inflation rates associated with greater *increases* in the insurance coverage.

Newhouse examined these issues empirically in 1978 and then updated the study in 1988. He found a negative correlation between the inflation rate and the average *level* of coinsurance for hospital care, physician care, dental care, and drugs. This result supports the hypothesis that increased insurance coverage induces costly technological change. Similar correlations also were found in the updated versions, though the statistical significance levels weakened somewhat. This evidence generally supports the hypothesis, although the support is statistically weak.

THE NET EFFECT OF TECHNOLOGICAL CHANGE ON PATIENT WELFARE

A troubling aspect of the relationship of insurance coverage to innovation was pointed out by Goddeeris (1984b). As we have seen, health insurance coverage, which reduces the fraction of the bill paid by the patient out-of-pocket, may induce many patients to use new health technologies that are not worth their full cost. The average patient, of course, pays the full cost of new technologies through a rise in insurance premiums in addition to out-of-pocket costs. Goddeeris showed that the average patient may be worse off after the new technology was introduced than before it was invented; however, this issue of potential welfare gains or losses from innovation is complex to pursue.

---

[2]Newhouse also proposed a related hypothesis that higher insurance levels induce greater degrees of inefficiency. If inefficiency levels grow, then this hypothesis also accounts for a correlation between insurance levels and inflation rates.

One problem is that the current insurance system tends to provide the consumer with incentives so that what is good for him or her as an individual is bad for him or her as a member of society. The patient may fully understand that if everyone used the new expensive health technology, then costs would substantially rise for all. However, the individual may receive significant personal benefits and correctly ascertain that his personal contribution to higher premiums is quite small.

A second problem is that alternative insurance schemes with better incentive structures may never arise. Goddeeris shows that if insurance plans paid a flat lump sum per given diagnosis instead of a fraction of the charges, then the problem of "harmful" innovations would not arise. However, the transactions costs of providing such insurance policies are probably insurmountable.

Although this analysis does not prove that the recent pattern of technological change in health care has harmed patient welfare in net, it explains the possibility. It also shows that the possibility for "harmful" patterns of innovation is consistent with the existing incentive structure of insurance coverage.

INSURANCE, TECHNOLOGY, AND INFLATION: LOOKING TOWARD THE FUTURE

What about the future? In what direction are these relationships headed? Weisbrod identifies one factor that is already effecting changes toward cost-reducing technological change.

He notes that the recent major change in health insurance, from a retrospective cost-based system of payments to a prospective one, affects the incentives for innovation. Health insurance in the United States was largely retrospective until the early 1980s, meaning that payments by insurance companies were based on reports by hospitals looking backwards over the period to what their actual costs had been. With insurance companies paying for whatever technology was used, there was a strong built-in incentive for hospitals to adopt new, often cost-increasing technologies. Prospective payment, for example under Medicare's new system, pays a prearranged price and hospitals save money and increase net revenues by cutting costs. Available evidence suggests that the introduction of Medicare's prospective payment system in 1983 has in fact affected the adoption of hospital technologies.

Less well understood are the potential effects of market forces developing and expanding new insurance and delivery mechanisms under the general rubric of managed care. The HMO provides insurance and care under one roof, giving the HMO the incentive to control costs while maintaining quality. The pressure of businesses seeking better, cheaper packages for their workers and the pressure of individuals seeking attractive insurance/care packages enforce the cost discipline on the managed care providers. It suggests that this environment may encourage the careful scrutiny of new technologies to check their cost consequences (Goddeeris 1987).

Another way to ascertain something about the future effects of technological change in health care is to examine the technological changes that are in the pipeline. Schwartz (1994) reviewed the technological pipeline recently and suggested that we may be headed into a technological revolution. Autoimmune disorders (diabetes, multiple sclerosis, some hyperthyroidism, some kidney disorders, and rheumatoid arthritis) will have new treatments in the near future given continued success in the development of cell-specific blockers or destroyers of the errant lymphocytes. There are promising methods being studied in gene therapies for genetic diseases. Genetic screening for cancers, diabetes, hypertension, and other diseases may become routine. Gene research offers possibilities for cancer treatment. Advanced imaging techniques may soon provide noninvasive "biopsies."

Given this evidence of future "drastic" technological change in health care, what cost consequences will it have? Schwartz conceives of two very different scenarios. In one, dramatic curative therapies for some major diseases could develop which would reduce health care costs. What if we could cure cancer and heart disease with a pill? "The second and far more likely scenario envisions a future in which the historic pattern—cost increases driven in large part by new technology—continues for at least the next decade" (p. 78). Under this scenario, new therapies save lives but require costly chronic care. As a consequence of the many possibilities, we can only speculate on the future and try to understand the past.

ON THE DIFFUSION OF NEW HEALTH CARE TECHNOLOGIES

A new-product technology, often embodied in a new piece of capital equipment, is not automatically and simultaneously adopted by all providers. It is known from research in other industries that the adoption process takes time. The spread of a new technology through adoption by providers over time is called a diffusion process. From studies of other industries, it has been discovered that the diffusion process often follows a characteristic pattern described by the logistic function.

The logistic function describes a particular S-shaped pattern. Figure 14.3 illustrates a logistic function. The vertical axis measures the percent of potential users who have adopted the innovation. The horizontal axis measures the passage of time. The logistical diffusion process is one in which adoption begins slowly but at an increasing rate. At some point, the percentage of adopters continues to increase but at a decreasing rate, asymptotically approaching the maximum proportion of firms to adopt. This indicates the proportion who will have adopted the technology when diffusion is complete; here it is denoted by the proportion, K.

The Speed of Adoption

The S-shaped logistic function is described mathematically by equation (14.2). Here P_t is the proportion of firms that have adopted the innovation at a given point in time, a and b are parameters to be estimated from the data, and t is time:

$$P_t = K / (1 + e^{-(a+bt)}) \qquad (14.2)$$

The coefficient b measures the speed of adoption. Investigation of equation (14.2) will show that higher values of b imply higher proportions of adopters at any point in time; hence, the speed of adoption.

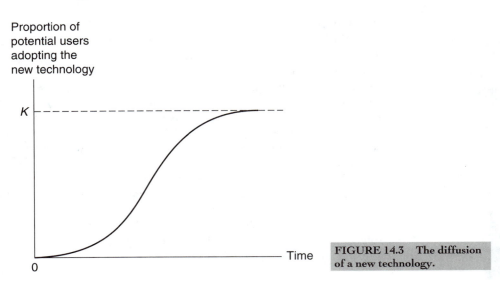

FIGURE 14.3 The diffusion of a new technology.

The speed of adoption has been estimated for five health care innovative technologies. These estimates are reported in Table 14.2, also with the estimated R^2 values for the regression equations that developed the estimates. The consistently high values of R^2 indicate that the logistic curve describes the pattern of diffusion of these health care technologies quite well. The speed of adoption was estimated for each of several hospital sizes in the study being cited. The pattern by size is clear and unsurprising. Larger hospitals tend to adopt all five of the technologies more quickly than smaller hospitals.

The rate of diffusion can be very rapid. A recent study of the diffusion of a new treatment for gallstones shows this. Escarce et al. (1995) studied the diffusion in the

TABLE 14.2 Estimated Speed of Adoption (parameter *b*) for Five New Health Care Technologies in Voluntary Hospitals by Size (R^2 in parentheses)

	Size Category			
Innovation	*< 100 beds*	*100–199 beds*	*200–299 beds*	*300+ beds*
Postoperative Recovery Room	0.131 (0.92)	0.318 (0.98)	0.420 (0.99)	0.484 (0.97)
Intensive Care Unit	0.183 (0.92)	0.307 (0.99)	0.347 (0.99)	0.411 (0.96)
Electroencephalograph	0.084 (0.76)	0.101 (0.97)	0.119 (0.98)	0.152 (0.97)
Diagnostic Radioisotopes	0.102 (0.93)	0.112 (0.87)	0.155 (0.91)	0.192 (0.96)
Respiratory Therapy	0.199 (0.94)	0.345 (0.99)	0.449 (0.98)	—

Source: Russell (1977).

United States of the surgical procedure called laparoscopic cholecystectomy. The procedure was first performed in France in 1987 with the first U.S. report coming in 1989. By 1992 about 80 percent of cholecystectomies in the United States were done using the laparoscopic technique. The pattern of adoptions shows the "S" pattern over time characteristic of the logistic function.

Why Adoption Rates Differ

What determines these patterns of diffusion? Why do firms not simply adopt a new technology immediately? The economic theory of innovation sheds some light on these issues.[3] The firm will tend to adopt an innovation when the present value of future profits due to the innovation is positive. However, firms may differ in their decisions on the timing of the adoption. Waiting too long may provide competitors with an advantageous share of the market, which may be permanently sustained. However, waiting has positive potentials in that one may take advantage of future advances and one may learn from the experience of others. Waiting thus may reduce risks, and more risk-averse firms may thus choose to wait somewhat longer. Small firms, which are less able to diversify, may tend to be more risk averse,[4] partially explaining the slower rate of adoption among small hospitals.

A study done in Norway sheds some light on the profitability issue (Klausen et al., 1992). The authors show that new dry chemical laboratory equipment was adopted sooner by physicians whose (later shown) profitability from the equipment was higher. The equipment allowed physicians to conduct tests on patient blood chemistry in their offices and be reimbursed for each analysis by the state. Alternatively, the physician could send the test away to a central laboratory and be reimbursed by the state. The reimbursement rates and rules differed and physicians would find one or the other approach more profitable depending on their practice characteristics. The profitability variable in this study was the strongest statistically and this serves to support the conventional economic theory. However, physicians also tended to adopt "too late" in the sense that marginal revenues from adoption were much higher than marginal costs. This latter point suggests that information issues probably also play a role in adoption.

DIFFUSION AND THE MEDICARE DRG SYSTEM

Regulatory factors may also help to explain adoption. Among factors that variously affect profitability and thus adoption, government cost-containment programs are perhaps of most interest, particularly the role of prospective payment systems.

Prospective payment methods of financing patient care in hospitals means that payers or government agencies set limits on the rates of payment. Medicare's Diagnosis Related Group (DRG) payment system, adopted in 1983, is a prospective system, and many states experimented with prospective systems prior to Medicare. The effect of a prospective payment system (PPS) on the diffusion of new health care technologies may be anticipated on theoretical grounds. A severe PPS program, one that sets

---

[3]See Kamien and Schwartz (1982); and Scherer (1984).
[4]See Sloan et al. (1986).

relatively low payment rates, will tend to lower the profitability of new costly technologies. PPS systems typically also are designed so that the hospital incurs all or part of the profits obtained from successfully controlling costs or the losses incurred when control efforts are unsuccessful. The PPS programs should thus also tend to encourage cost-reducing technologies versus cost-enhancing technologies.

This issue has been pursued empirically by several analysts. A study reports on the diffusion of five new hospital care technologies in six states, some of which are subject to PPS.[5] Among the hospitals studied, hospitals in New York experienced the most stringent state system of PPS. The data suggest that the New York program tended to retard significantly the diffusion of three cost-increasing technologies and tended to enhance diffusion of one of two cost-reducing technologies for the larger hospitals. The results for the other PPS states studied were less strong, but "taken broadly, these results are consistent with the incentive structures inherent in each program" (Romeo, Wagner, and Lee, 1984, p. 20).

Several other researchers found somewhat more mixed evidence. Sloan and colleagues (1986) found that mandatory rate-setting programs tended to retard diffusion of technology in *some* cases, particularly in the instances of coronary bypass surgery, morbid obesity surgery, and intraocular lens implants. However, the degree of slowing tended to be small. While Sloan and colleagues found somewhat mixed evidence, a recent contribution by Teplensky et al. (1995) concludes that restrictive rate-setting programs tend to significantly retard the adoption of new technology.

CONCLUSIONS

In the process of discussing technological change, we developed several issues. First was the issue of whether technological change has or has not been cost increasing. Scitovsky found that technology has been cost increasing in several eras. The most recent period has probably experienced cost-increasing change in the introduction of big-ticket technologies, though it is not possible to assess the impact nationally from her data on the Palo Alto clinic.

We then turned to the broader issue of whether insurance coverage tends to cause technological change to be biased toward cost-increasing changes. Finally, we investigated the diffusion of technology and found that it plausibly follows a logistical function pattern. Perhaps more importantly, we can show that diffusion of some technological innovation is impeded by regulation, though for many it is not.

Summary

1. Technological change in health care may be cost reducing, if it improves production technology of existing products, or cost increasing, if it emphasizes new products and higher-quality versions of old products.

---

[5]See Romeo, Wagner, and Lee (1984).

2. Evidence from the Palo Alto Clinic suggests that technological change has been cost increasing in many instances during the 1951–1981 period while it was cost decreasing in several. Recently there has been an emphasis on the introduction of new, costly, big-ticket technologies.

3. Technological change is a major suspected cause of the substantial inflation in health care since 1950. Other sources of inflation, such as increased insurance coverage, cannot explain the larger portion of inflation. Technological change is assumed to account for the unexplained residual.

4. The Goddeeris model shows how technological change can be influenced by insurance coverage. Greater insurance coverage increases the relative profitability of cost-increasing technological innovations versus cost-reducing ones.

5. In turn, the proliferation of health care innovations may induce changes in the prevalent forms of insurance coverage so as to expand insurance coverage.

6. New health care technologies are adopted gradually in an industry, and the pattern of adoption fits the logistic curve. Adoption patterns are influenced by regulation as evidenced in the instance of Medicare DRG legislation.

Discussion Questions

1. Which of the following types of technological change in health care are likely to be cost increasing? (A) threats of malpractice suits cause physicians to order more diagnostic tests on average for a given set of patient symptoms; (B) a new computer-assisted scanning device enables physicians to take much more detailed pictures of the brain; (C) the introduction of penicillin earlier in this century; (D) greater emphasis on preventive care. Discuss.

2. How can the net effect of technological change in the health care sector hypothetically harm average patient welfare? Discuss.

3. As technologies diffuse, why do some firms adopt them before others? What types of technologies would you expect to be adopted most quickly? Most slowly? What factors can slow the rate of diffusion of new medical technologies?

4. How do economists define technological change with respect to quantity of goods produced? With respect to quality of goods produced?

Exercises

1. For the evidence from Palo Alto described in Table 14.1, which illness/conditions showed a substantial cost increase in at least one of the periods with no offsetting reductions? Which illness/disease categories showed predominately a reduction in costs over the span of years 1951–1981?

2. What are big-ticket and little-ticket technologies? Which showed increases in the latter of the three periods studied at Palo Alto?

3. In the Goddeeris model in Figure 14.2, how would the equilibrium change in expenditure, Δm, be affected if there were a vertical parallel shift in the $\Delta h (\Delta m)$

curve, say caused by increased support of medical technological research? Show graphically the alternative possibility if support for research tended to emphasize cost-reducing innovations.

4. Technological change is often distinguished by whether it is labor saving, capital saving, or neutral. These are determined by the relative capital–labor ratios. For example, if the capital–labor ratio diminishes, the technological change is capital saving. Use isoquants as in panel A of Figure 14.1 to illustrate the three possibilities.

5. Use demand-and-supply analysis to show the effects of increased insurance on demand and costs and the indirect effect of insurance on costs through the induced effect on technological change.

C H A P T E R

Labor Markets and Professional Training

15

- The Importance of Labor in the Health Care Sector

- The Demand for and Supply of Health Care Labor

- The Human Capital Theory of Investment in Education

- Factor Productivity and Substitution Between Factors

- Health Manpower Availability

- Manpower Planning and the Meaning of Shortages

- Conclusions

Commensurate with its high component of GDP and the labor-intensive nature of its output, the health care economy employs a large number of workers. We use the term *labor* here in the general economic sense of an input in production that is distinct from capital and that is provided by human beings. Like other goods and services, the production of health services requires both labor and capital. Labor with various levels and types of skills, from hospital custodial personnel to brain surgeons, is needed in the production of health care.

While many health sector workers are relatively unskilled, the health sector also requires large numbers of highly trained professionals. Most physician specialists have years of postgraduate education past their medical school education. Labor issues in health economics thus range from general supply and demand, to labor theory and human capital theory, and to specialized topics regarding professionals. Issues include health manpower planning, medical school resources, physician location decisions, and shortages of professionals.[1] This chapter addresses general labor issues. Chapter 16 concentrates on issues pertaining to the training and location of physicians.

---

[1]Although regrettably sexist, the term *manpower* has evolved as the standard term for planning health care labor needs.

THE IMPORTANCE OF LABOR
IN THE HEALTH CARE SECTOR

To emphasize the importance of labor to the health sector, and the importance of health sector labor to the economy, we refer to Table 1.3a in Chapter 1. The table shows the magnitude and variety of health care occupations. In 1993, over 10 million people, about 9 percent of the U.S. labor force, were employed at health services sites.

These data do not include millions of other workers in the health economy. Those that are not shown include workers in the pharmaceutical industry, as well as those in industries providing supplies, capital goods, and services for people providing direct patient care. Workers in some other health-related occupations such as pharmacists employed in drugstores are also not shown.

Many of these numbers have also been increasing as health care spending has increased. Between 1970 and 1992 the number of active physicians rose from 291,000 to 614,000, or over 110 percent; the number of registered nurses increased from 750,000 to 1,893,000, or over 150 percent. The per-capita ratios are shown in Table 1.3b. In other cases the growth rates are more modest, but growth is the common finding. Thus, the labor component in the health sector is large, important, and growing.

THE DEMAND FOR
AND SUPPLY OF HEALTH CARE LABOR

How labor is used—and how it is combined with other factors of production—helps to determine both the amount of health care provided and the wages and salaries of the providers. The productivity and training of health care providers are important to the working of labor markets and to the demands and supplies of labor.

We begin by describing the factors that determine demand for labor. Demand for a factor of production, either labor or capital, is a derived demand. We demand health care providers because we demand health care, and in turn we demand health care because we demand health.

Production Functions and Isoquants

Recall that we use the production function to describe the relationship of factors of production (the inputs) to the resulting ultimate goods produced (the outputs). The production function shows the maximum sustainable output that can be obtained from the possible combinations of inputs such as labor, materials, and machinery, with existing technology and know-how.

For convenience, we express the production relationship as follows:

$$Q = f(X_1, X_2, \ldots, X_n) \tag{15.1}$$

where Q represents output and X_1, X_2, and so on are quantities of the various inputs, again various types of labor, materials, and/or machinery. Figure 15.1 (panels A and B) describes the isoquants with labor and capital.

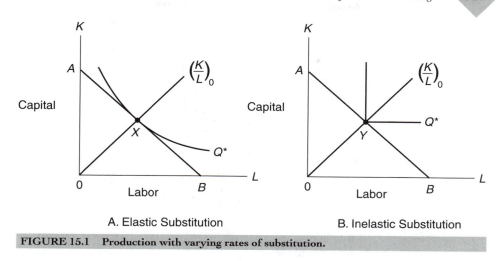

FIGURE 15.1 **Production with varying rates of substitution.**

In panel A, the isoquant shows a technology in which labor and capital are fairly good substitutes for each other; to be more exact, labor and capital can be combined in many different proportions to produce output. The budget line, *AB,* reflects the trade-off of the costs of capital and labor, and point *X* is the location at which the costs of producing *Q** units of output are minimized.

With the given set of factor prices (wages and payments to capital) the equilibrium capital–labor ratio $(K/L)_0$ is the slope of a ray from the origin through point *X*. Due to the curvature of the isoquant (reflecting the elasticity of substitution of production), a change in relative prices leads to a change in the capital–labor ratio. Here labor and capital are good substitutes as we move along a given isoquant. Lower prices of labor (i.e., a flatter budget line) will lead to a relatively large substitution of labor for capital, and vice versa.

In contrast, panel B shows a technology in which labor and capital are not good substitutes; as drawn, they must be used in fixed proportions to one another. Although point *Y* represents the same (K/L) ratio as point *X,* changes in the factor prices will not change the capital–labor ratio. Specialized surgeries, for example, may require specific ratios of labor to capital with little substitution available. The degree to which substitution between inputs is possible, either between health care labor and capital, or between different types of health care labor, is a key issue in manpower planning and in determining the efficiency of production exhibited by health care firms. The demand for any type of health care labor depends in part on these substitution possibilities.

The demand for a factor of production also depends on the price of the output. Consider an example. Suppose you were working as a skilled worker in a bicycle manufacturing plant, and suppose that bicycle riding was becoming more popular. The increase in demand would result, at least temporarily, in a higher price for bicycles. Bicycle workers would be more in demand as a consequence.

Marginal Productivity of Labor

Finally, consider that the demand for a factor, and consequently the wage paid to the factor, will depend at least in part on the factor's productivity. This is one explanation as to why college-educated workers earn more money than others. If college-educated workers are more productive than others, then the demand for them will be greater. While this is only one theory that explains earnings advantages of college graduates, it illustrates the premise that more productive laborers will be in greater demand.

Reconsider the idea of marginal product, the increase in output when an input is increased by one unit. Suppose that input X_1 in production function (15.1) represented the number of laboratory technicians employed. If we added one lab technician to the production process, holding constant the available lab equipment and materials, we would probably increase lab output. This increase would be the marginal product of lab technicians.

While additional lab technicians in the production process are likely to add to output, they will likely add incrementally less output. As we increase an input, holding all others constant, output will tend to increase, but at a decreasing rate. This illustrates the law of diminishing returns.

The number of lab technicians that one should hire depends also on the price of output. Suppose that the units of output of the laboratory in question sell for $50 per unit. Suppose also that an additional technician would increase lab output by four tests per day. If these tests sell for $50 each, the technician is bringing in an additional $200 in revenue. The extra revenue generated is called the marginal revenue product (MRP).

Would it pay to hire this extra technician? Clearly, the answer depends on the wage per day. If the technician earns $100 per day, then he or she nets the hospital a $100 gain ($200 marginal revenue product less $100 wage), and it thus pays to hire the technician. It always pays to hire a laborer whose marginal revenue product exceeds his or her wage.

Would it pay to hire still another technician if he or she has a marginal product of three tests per day? Since output (the tests) sells for $50 each, this next technician is netting the hospital $50 because the marginal revenue product, $150 in this case, exceeds the wage, $100. It will pay the firm to continue to hire more workers up until the point where the marginal revenue product equals the wage.

Figure 15.2 represents the marginal revenue product curve for lab technicians. The curve is downward sloping, illustrating the law of diminishing marginal returns. Assuming competitive markets, the MRP curve in Figure 15.2 is found by multiplying the marginal product curve (not shown) by the price of output. The optimal number of lab technicians depends on the wage rate. At wage W_1, the optimal input demand at point A is L_1; in contrast, at a higher wage, W_2, the firm would demand fewer technicians, L_2, at point B.

This analysis shows that the demand for labor is precisely the marginal revenue product of labor curve. It is closely related to the production function for the laboratory test and is directly related to the price of the output laboratory tests. If the price of the lab tests rises, then the marginal revenue product $P \cdot MP_L$ rises, and more labor is demanded. If better machines are made available, then the technicians might become even more productive, also raising the demand for their services.

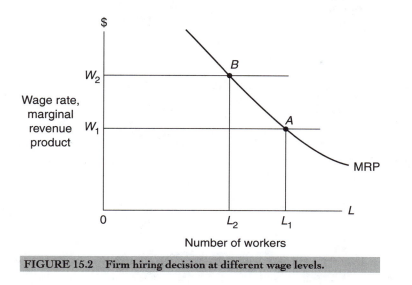

FIGURE 15.2   Firm hiring decision at different wage levels.

Factor Substitution and Labor Demand

At this point, recall the meaning and importance of the substitutability of one input for another. Suppose, for example, a new machine is invented that allows lab technicians to perform certain functions that were formerly done by radiologists. This makes the technician a better substitute for the radiologist. As a result, the demand for technicians will tend to increase. Furthermore, this change will also tend to shift the demand for radiologists and probably make it more elastic—that is, flatter and more responsive to the wage rate. As a result, if the firm finds it can substitute more easily between inputs, then it will tend to become more resistant to input price changes, replacing increasingly expensive inputs with cheaper substitutes.

In recent decades, firms and policymakers have become especially interested in substitution possibilities because of the impetus to turn to physician extenders in efforts to control health care costs. To the extent that nonphysician providers can substitute for physicians, they allow firms to hire lower-cost workers, hence cutting costs and possibly increasing the amount of the service provided. We address this issue in more detail later in the chapter.

The market demand for various occupations is determined by the combined labor demands of all firms. The market demand is determined by horizontally summing the demands of the individual firms. The market demand for laboratory technicians is illustrated in Figure 15.3 by the downward sloping curve labeled D_1. Under competitive conditions, the determination of a labor market equilibrium, and consequently of the equilibrium wage, depends on the interaction of both demand and supply.

The Supply of Labor

The supply of labor tends to slope upward. This implies that the higher the wage rate in a given market, the more workers would be forthcoming. First, those workers currently employed may choose to work more hours if higher wages are offered. Second, similar

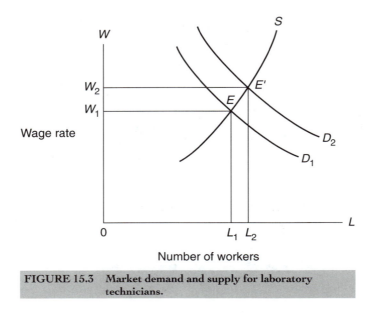

FIGURE 15.3   Market demand and supply for laboratory technicians.

workers may be attracted into the market from elsewhere by the higher wages. The labor supply curve for lab technicians is shown in Figure 15.3 as *S*.

The equilibrium market wage W_1 for technicians, along with the market clearing number of technicians, L_1, is determined by the intersection of the supply and demand curves. Consider that the market equilibrium wage will tend to rise in response to any demand-increasing event. These include increases in the firms' desires to substitute lab technicians for other laborers, increased productivity of the technicians, and increases in the price of the lab outputs. Here demand increases to D_2, with resulting increases in equilibrium wage to W_2 and number employed to L_2.

Similarly, the market wage will tend to fall in response to events that increase the labor supply. These include increased graduations of trained technicians or influxes of technicians into the market from other professions or other locations.

THE HUMAN CAPITAL THEORY
OF INVESTMENT IN EDUCATION

A major concern of manpower planning specialists is the availability of new graduates. To have an appropriate number of graduates at any given time requires that an appropriate number of applicants had entered school years before. Thus, the number of graduates depends importantly on the individual decision of the potential health professional to go to school and get the required education.

Professional Training as an Investment

Consider the issues behind choosing whether or not to go to medical school. Suppose that Janet Miller, who has just graduated with a B.S. degree in biology, has an academic record that would qualify her to become a physician. She has a choice of going to work for a pharmaceutical company, or going to medical school.

Her decision to become a physician is essentially an investment decision. In Chapter 5 we introduced the theory of investment that suggested that people will at least in part base their investment decisions on the potential net returns from the investment.[2] Since investment decisions usually deliver their payoffs over time, we must consider the entire stream of costs and benefits that Janet will incur over the life of the investment.

What are the costs of an investment in medical school to Janet? There are two categories of costs:

- The opportunity costs of forgone earnings because Janet cannot work while going to school.

- The out-of-pocket costs for the medical education.

Medical education takes a considerable amount of time: four years of medical school plus several years of residency. During at least part of this time Janet will earn less than she would have earned had she gone directly to work with her B.S. degree. These forgone earnings are a cost like any other. In addition, medical school is costly in itself.

Also consider her potential earnings stream. By investing in a medical education, Janet can expect to have an earnings advantage, in most countries a very substantial one, over a worker who has a B.S. degree. As we have noted, this advantage comes only after many years, but then it likely continues throughout her working life.

Notice that the largest costs come in the early years, while the largest payoffs come in later years. Thus, Janet needs to consider the value of a given dollar today in comparison to her valuation today of a given dollar that she will receive only many years from now. Most people will tend to value dollars paid in the distant future as less valuable or less important.[3]

Discounting and the Internal Rate of Return

Discounting future values is done by dividing future dollars by a discount factor that equals $(1 + r)^t$ where r is the discount rate and t represents the year, starting with $t = 1$ to represent the first year. Suppose that the costs Janet incurs through time are C_t, where t refers to each period of time. Recall that her costs in the early years, C_1, C_2, C_3, and so on, will be fairly high because of medical school costs and forgone earnings, but the

---

[2]This, of course, is a simplification. Physicians are likely to get utility out of doing good for other people. To the extent that this is the case, then part of the investment in medical school does in fact provide utility.

[3]We present fundamental aspects of discounting in the appendix to Chapter 2.

costs in later years, such as C_{12}, C_{13}, C_{14}, and so on, will be small. Similarly, the income she earns, R_t, will be small in early years and then larger in later years. If Janet were to discount future values at 4 percent, then the present discounted value (PDV) of the investment would be:

$$\text{PDV} = \frac{R_1 - C_1}{(1 + .04)^1} + \frac{R_2 - C_2}{(1 + .04)^2} + \frac{R_3 - C_3}{(1 + .04)^3} + \cdots + \frac{R_n - C_n}{(1 + .04)^n}$$

$$= \sum_{t=1}^{t=n} \frac{R_t - C_t}{(1 + .04)^t}$$

(15.2)

If the present value is positive, then this is a good investment. Consider the fact, however, that the present value will depend critically on the rate at which she discounts the future. If she cares little about the distant future, she will choose a very high discount rate. In the present example, if she chooses a rate higher than 4 percent, the present value calculated for this investment will tend to become smaller.

We might also ask what is her rate of gain, so that we can compare the rate of gain or rate of return to that of her other investment opportunities. A common choice among economists is to calculate the internal rate of return. This is equivalent to that discount rate which would yield a net present value of zero. The internal rate of rate is defined as i, such that:

$$\text{PDV} = \sum_{t=1}^{t=n} \frac{R_t - C_t}{(1 + i)^t} = 0$$

(15.3)

Higher internal rates of return imply better returns on investment. Among investment opportunities, Janet will tend to choose the one with the highest internal rate of return. If this rate of return is sufficiently high, she will go to medical school because in time, the increased skills will earn not only more than she had invested, but also will make her wealthier in the long term than she would have been otherwise.

An Example

Table 15.1 demonstrates this issue by example. Suppose that Janet could begin her work for a pharmaceutical company at a salary of $30,000, and could increase her earnings by 3 percent each year over 40 years, after which she would retire (in this analysis we assume no inflation, so that all of the figures are in "real" dollars). Column (b) shows Janet's salary from Years 1 through 40.[4] This is a *cost* of her education since she is giving up job earnings to go to medical school. The second cost in this admittedly simplified example is medical school tuition, which we assume starts at $20,000 and rises by $2,000 each year, from Year 1 to Year 4. Total costs are noted in column (d), which adds columns (b) and (c).

---

[4]One might argue that Janet actually took her biology degree as an investment to get into medical school. If this is the case, then this portion of her education should also be treated as a capital investment.

TABLE 15.1   Net Present Value of a Medical School Education (dollars)

(a) Year	(b) Job Earnings	(c) Medical Tuition	(d) Total Costs (b) + (c)	(e) Returns	(f) Net Returns 0%	(g) Net Returns 10%	(h) Net Returns 8.2%
1	30,000	20,000	50,000	0	−50,000	−45,455	−46,210
2	30,900	22,000	52,900	0	−52,900	−43,719	−45,184
3	31,827	24,000	55,827	0	−55,827	−41,944	−44,070
4	32,782	26,000	58,782	0	−58,782	−40,149	−42,885
5	33,765	0	33,765	20,000	−13,765	−8,547	−9,281
6	34,778	0	34,778	23,000	−11,778	−6,648	−7,339
7	35,822	0	35,822	26,000	−9,822	−5,040	−5,657
8	36,896	0	36,896	29,000	−7,896	−3,684	−4,203
End of Formal Training							
9	38,003	0	38,003	50,000	11,997	5,088	5,901
10	39,143	0	39,143	52,500	13,357	5,150	6,072
11	40,317	0	40,317	55,125	14,808	5,190	6,222
.	.	.	.	.	.	.	.
.	.	.	.	.	.	.	.
25	60,984	0	60,984	109,144	48,160	4,445	6,712
26	62,813	0	62,813	114,601	51,788	4,345	6,670
.	.	.	.	.	.	.	.
.	.	.	.	.	.	.	.
39	92,244	0	92,244	216,097	123,854	3,010	5,725
40	95,011	0	95,011	226,902	131,891	2,914	5,634
Sum	2,262,037	92,000	2,354,037	3,862,942	1,508,905	−56,337	0

What is the return to this investment in human capital? Returns to the education involve the salary that is earned because of the training. In this example, salary begins in Year 5 at $20,000, and increases by $3,000 per year each year to Year 8. In Year 9, Janet begins practice at a salary of $50,000 per year, which will increase at a rate of 5 percent each year through Year 40, at which point it will be $226,902. Column (f) shows the net return each year, which equals the gross return (column e) less the total cost (column d). Over the 8 years of medical school the net return (total returns less total costs) is −$260,770. Continuing down column (f), we discover that the net return per year once Janet begins practice rises from $11,997 in Year 9 to $131,891 in Year 40.

   Is this a good investment? If *r* is very small or 0, this implies the ability to lend or borrow at 0 percent interest. As a result, the big future returns have a big present value. The denominators of the terms referring to future returns stay close to 1, and PDV becomes very large. As noted in Table 15.1, if the rate of interest were 0 percent, the net present value (sum or the returns less the costs) of the investment would be $1,508,905. It would be a good investment indeed.

What if it cost 10 percent to borrow money? The denominators of the terms referring to future returns would get very large (evaluate 1.10^{40} for yourself to see), discounting the future improvements in income very severely. Calculating the net present value at an interest rate of 10 percent would lead to a net present value of –$56,337. Janet would be better off working in the pharmaceutical industry.

As it turns out, net present value equals 0 at a discount rate of 8.2 percent. If Janet can borrow money at a rate of less than 8.2 percent, it will pay by our investment criteria for her to invest in being a physician.

Clearly, the higher the wage level for health providers (in this case physicians), the higher the rate of return will be for training in medical education. As a result, higher wages should lead to an increased supply of health care providers. This analysis implies the upward sloping supply of labor curve, as we have assumed.

Creation of Human Capital

Because Janet is investing in capital stock of knowledge for herself, economists term such an investment as the creation of *human capital.* Human capital investment consists not only of paid schooling but also of:

- explicit on-the-job training programs.
- improved skills from actually doing the work, which economists call *learning by doing.*

Surgeons are taught procedures with the slogan, "see one, do one, teach one." The formation of human capital in all fields varies from job to job, depending on the combination of these factors. Here we emphasize the types of human capital formation achieved through education. We realize, however, that there are substantive differences among types of education.

Information regarding the rate of return to a medical education is also useful to the policy analyst. Suppose we were to discover that the average rate of return to medical education was very high and rising. This information might suggest that physicians were increasingly scarce, thus suggesting a shortage. There have been numerous studies that have attempted to estimate the rate of return to a medical education. We examine such studies in Chapter 16.

FACTOR PRODUCTIVITY AND SUBSTITUTION BETWEEN FACTORS

The supply of health services, and consequently health care prices, clearly depends on the number of workers. However, a critical determinant of supply is the productivity of labor inputs. Productivity improvements increase output: Alternatively, the same output can be produced with fewer inputs. In a macroeconomic sense, general improvements in productivity represent a major source of economic growth and rising standards of living. At a microeconomic level, productivity gains in an industry can lead to lower prices for the goods and services produced in that industry and possibly also to higher rates of remuneration for workers.

The productivity of a factor of production can be measured as the average product of the factor—that is, the ratio of total output (Q) to the amount of a particular labor input (L):

$$\text{Average product of labor} = Q/L \qquad (15.4)$$

This definition corresponds to the concept of average product used in microeconomics and is distinguished from marginal product, which is defined as the change in output associated with a one-unit increase in the input, holding all others constant.

Despite the simplicity of the concept of average product, there are difficult problems involved in measuring it. Output may be heterogeneous, consisting of many very different outputs. In such cases, one often uses the dollar value of output for the numerator Q. Similarly, many different kinds of labor are used in the production process. In such cases, a weighted sum of related inputs is often used in the denominator term L.

Measurement of Physician Productivity

The classic study of physician productivity was undertaken by Reinhardt (1972). He examined general practitioners in private practice for three measures of output: total patient visits, office visits, and patient billings. In addition to physician time, he considered the use of various auxiliary personnel. Reinhardt estimated the marginal product of physician time, the increment to output resulting when one extra hour of physician time is added to the production process.

Reinhardt found that the physician's marginal product tends to increase up until the point that the physician is working a total of about 25 hours per week; the marginal product eventually declines to zero at about 110 hours per week. He found that starting from a base of 60 hours per week, a 1.0 percent increase of physician input will result in an increase of 0.8 percent in the number of patient visits produced.

In addition to studying the physician's productivity, Reinhardt examined the substitution possibilities between physician and other labor inputs. Consider physician aides. He found that the aides' marginal products were highest when approximately one aide was present per physician. Reinhardt found that physicians could improve productivity of their practices and increase profits if they doubled the number of aides from the average he found of two aides per physician.

The Efficient Utilization of Physician Assistants — Substitution Among Inputs

The possibility that physicians were underutilizing aides was a provocative one. In 1988, Brown reexamined this issue and refined Reinhardt's work. Brown's estimates of the marginal products of physician time and other inputs, calculated at mean values of the variables, are shown in Table 15.2. The marginal products of auxiliary workers are shown in the columns labeled MP for data from physician offices of various categories: These include all physicians, solo physicians, and group practice physicians.

The columns labeled MP/W are of special interest. By dividing MP by the wage rate of each input to get the marginal product per dollar spent on each factor, we can draw inferences about whether physicians are underutilizing or overutilizing various

TABLE 15.2 Marginal Products and Efficiency of Input Use

Input	All Physicians		Solo Physicians		Group Physicians	
	MP	MP/W	MP	MP/W	MP	MP/W
Physician	2.967	0.114	2.686	0.102	2.793	0.110
Secretary	0.192	0.043	0.253	0.058	0.105	0.023
Registered Nurse	0.585	0.104	0.628	0.109	0.625	0.114
Practical Nurse	0.542	0.129	0.533	0.132	0.485	0.109
Technician	0.320	0.067	0.321	0.059	0.278	0.057
Physician Assistant	0.231	0.040	-0.014	-0.003	1.082	0.192

MP = Marginal product

MP/W = Marginal product per dollar wages spent on input

Source: D. Brown (1988).

categories of workers. The marginal product per dollar is the relevant measure when determining which input to increase. To increase profits, one should hire the extra input that has the greatest MP/W. If this marginal product per dollar is not equal for each category of worker, the firm can always save money by trading a lesser producing worker per dollar for a higher producing one.

Brown concluded from these data that physicians were underutilizing nursing inputs. Consider, for example, the data for practical nurses in all physicians' offices. These practical nurses have a higher marginal product per dollar, 0.129, than do physicians, 0.114; thus, the offices would become more profitable if one substituted practical nurses for physicians.

In addition, Brown found that physicians in group practices were on average 22 percent more productive than those in solo practices. He suggested that this figure, much higher than the 5 percent estimated by Reinhardt, resulted from advantages that group practices have in employing physician assistants. From Table 15.2, we can see that the marginal product of physician assistants (PAs) for solo practices was actually estimated to be negative; in contrast, PAs are very productive on the margin in group practices. Even so, group practices are underutilizing PAs.

HEALTH MANPOWER AVAILABILITY

A recurrent policy concern in twentieth-century America has been the availability of various critical categories of health manpower. The issue usually hangs on whether we have or will have enough of these people, whether there will be shortages or surpluses. Before addressing such questions, we first examine the data, asking how many health care laborers of various kinds there are, and how these numbers have been changing.

Table 1.3a presented data on a selection of health manpower groups. In each category, the total number of professionals has increased, often quite substantially, since

1970. The population of ordinary citizens (the potential consumers) also increased during the period. Table 1.3b, however, made clear that the professionals in each case have been increasing more rapidly, so that the number of professionals per 100,000 population has also increased. In fact, the rate of increase for physicians and registered nurses per capita has been very sharp.

Availability of Physicians

In the following sections, we will use the example of physicians to explore manpower planning, and nurses to examine concepts of shortages. Since allopathic physicians have a substantial degree of control over input use in the U.S. health care system, we will consider this critical group in some detail. An important consideration in manpower availability analysis is the availability of personnel to provide needed or demanded patient care. Many federal physicians (approximately 19,000, or 3 percent of the total) provide services only to the portion of the population eligible, such as veterans. Furthermore, many physicians are in nonpatient care employment. Since the portion providing office-based patient care to the public has not changed much over recent decades, the rapid increase in physicians per capita has also meant a greater number of patient care physicians per capita.

Of the 559,000 active medical doctors (M.D.s) in the United States in 1992, about 92 percent provided direct patient care. Of those, nearly three-fourths were office-based and the rest were hospital-based, including residents. As we noted previously, the pattern of the portion of physicians available for patient care has not been changing very rapidly.[5]

TABLE 15.3   Physicians by Type of Practice: 1970–1992

Type of Practice	Number in 1,000s				Percent		
	1970	1980	1990	1992	1970	1980	1992
All Physicians	348	487	646	687	100	100	100
M.D.s	334	468	615	653	96	96	95
Active Nonfederal	281	397	527	559	81	82	81
Patient Care	255	362	480	513	73	74	75
Other	26	35	47	46	8	7	7
Federal	30	18	21	19	7	3	3
Inactive/Unknown Address	23	53	68	75	7	11	11
Doctors of Osteopathy	14	19	31	34	4	4	5

Source: Statistical Abstract of the United States (1994).

---

[5]Active Doctors of Osteopathy (D.O.s) numbered less than 33,000 in 1993. Though it is often useful to combine osteopaths with M.D.s when considering physician supply and access to physician care, there have been major differences in the historical development and organization of the two groups. Thus, unless otherwise indicated, our discussion will focus specifically on M.D.s.

Physicians do not form a homogeneous group. Instead they form a large number of specialties. About 40 percent of physicians practice in primary care and 25 percent are in the surgical specialties. The remainder have other specialties. Concerns about increased specialization with corresponding declines in primary care providers, as well as about uneven distributions between rural and urban areas, have long been heard in the United States.

Physician Specialties and Licensure

Physicians must be licensed by a state in order to practice in that state. Requirements for licensure include graduation from an accredited medical school, passing a licensure examination, and completing one to two years of internship or residency in an accredited graduate medical education program. Many graduates, nevertheless, complete three- to four-year residency programs. Many physicians also become board certified specialists. The requirements typically include advanced residency training for periods of three to six years, practice in the specialty, and passing of the board examination.

Like the decision to become a physician in the first place, the decision to seek board certification plausibly will respond to economic incentives. Wilensky and Rossiter (1983) suggest that board certification tends to increase the typical physician's annual income by nearly $13,000 on average but varies from specialty to specialty. Against these substantial future income gains, the physician considering whether or not to seek board certification would have to weigh the opportunity costs, as in any human capital investment decision.

MANPOWER PLANNING AND THE MEANING OF SHORTAGES

In one sense, planning, or looking ahead and preparing for the future, speaks for itself. What is somewhat more at issue, at least in America, is whether someone else, such as a government body, must, should, or can plan effectively on behalf of society as a whole.

The Role of Health Manpower Planning

In the case of health manpower, the long time lags between entering a professional school and becoming a practicing professional suggest the need for forethought, and invite the question of whether market forces alone will suffice. Thus, health manpower planning, at least in the further sense of investigating whether or not market forces are adequate, also seems eminently sensible.

What market forces exist that would tend to ensure that a sufficient number of health professionals will complete their training at the time when they are needed? The market relies on certain information signals to achieve this spontaneous coordination.

Recall the human capital investment decision of the potential health professional. She must investigate whether the stream of costs and benefits over time of this particular career provides a sufficient rate of return, a sufficient reward. In doing this analysis, she inherently must guess at the salary levels she could attain as a professional. A physician's future salaries, for example, will depend on the supply and demand of physicians in the future. If physicians are in "short supply"—one sense in which we would say they are "needed"—then physician salaries will tend to be "high," thus sending the right signal to potential physicians.

Will these information signals and the thousands of individual decisions suffice to provide adequately for future needs? They seem to work for other forms of professional education, such as for law schools. One way in which they may do poorly is in a case where the information available to potential professionals is weak or otherwise faulty. One role for manpower planning is to provide potential professionals with better information.

Often, however, we act through our government agencies to use other devices to ensure that adequate manpower is available. One common device is the government subsidization of professional education, sometimes to the point where the government virtually controls access to education. In fact, the present level of subsidization for education of all kinds is so substantial that the argument comes full circle. One may well argue that if the government controls access to health manpower training already, then it must do health manpower planning.

Nevertheless, a lesser government role is required to the extent that market forces—perhaps with the aid of increased information and existing government involvement—will lead to adequate availability of manpower in future years. We must ask, regardless of one's preferences for governmental involvement, what *is* an adequate quantity of health manpower?

Need-Based Approaches to Health Manpower Planning

The lay public may see different possible answers to the question of an adequate quantity of health manpower. Much of the confusion can be resolved through an analysis of the various reasons for the many determinations of manpower requirements, including necessarily the many definitions of health manpower shortages.

There are basically two types of shortages described in the literature: need shortages and economic shortages. Need shortages, for the present purpose, will be identified as determinations of manpower shortages that use a nonmarket, or noneconomic, definition of shortage. In some cases, determinations of need shortages in the health literature represent an inappropriate ignoring of economics and economic laws. In other cases, need determinations represent either an implicit or explicit rejection of the market as the arbiter of how much health care people will get.

SHORTAGES BASED ON MEDICAL GROUNDS

One common method of determining health manpower requirements is to base these calculations on purely medical grounds. Health care professionals and providers will recognize a far different standard of needed health manpower than will others, such as politicians, economists, or perhaps the public at large. The most important early work that employed a medical determination of health manpower needs was a study by Lee and Jones (1933). Their method calculated the number of physicians necessary to perform the needed number of medical procedures. The needed number of medical procedures, in turn, was based on the incidence of a morbidity (illness) in the population.

Consider, for example, condition A, which strikes 1 percent of the population in a given county. Suppose further that its treatment requires 6 hours of physician time, and that there are 250,000 residents in the county. How many physicians are needed, if a physician works 2,000 hours per year? The answer is fairly easy to analyze:

- 250,000 persons $\times$ (1 morbidity/100 persons) = 2,500 morbidities
- 2,500 morbidities $\times$ (6 hours/ morbidity) = 15,000 hours
- 15,000 hours $\times$ (1 physician/2,000 hours) = 7.5 physicians

Whether this involves seven full-time physicians and one part-time physician, or some larger number of providers who also do other things, is not important for this discussion, although it will be important as a practical problem. For the present, it may be concluded that 7.5 full-time equivalent physicians are needed based on the Lee–Jones style of need determination.

Suppose that the county currently has 7.5 physicians, and that the county's population is projected to rise from 250,000 to 400,000. Without any adjustment for the morbidity rate, or for the technology of care, the need would be projected to rise to (400,000/250,000) $\times$ 7.5, or 12.0 physicians. If the projected (actual) total is less than 12.0, then a projected (actual) shortage is said to exist.

This type of analysis entails some very severe assumptions. Even if we supposed that there are only two factors of production, physicians L and some amount of capital or machinery K, the Lee–Jones approach tends to ignore the possibilities for substitution between inputs. That is, the presumption that a constant number of physicians is necessary to give a certain amount of care implies the following assumptions:

1. There is no substitution of other inputs for physician inputs.
2. There is no projected technological change in the production of health care services.
3. There is a single, unique answer to the question of how many medical procedures are appropriate given the illness data for a population.
4. Manpower provided to the public will be demanded by the public or otherwise paid for.
5. Medical doctors are the appropriate body of people to determine population needs.
6. Prices and costs of various inputs are safely ignored.

Are these implicit assumptions realistic, and is this planning scenario realistic? As we have shown here and elsewhere, there are, in fact, substitution possibilities in the provision of health care. Thus, there is reason to challenge Assumption 1.

Assumption 2 can also be challenged, as new technologies are constantly changing the answer to the question of what is the best combination of the various inputs for producing health care. Both Assumptions 1 and 2 imply falsely that there is a fixed single technique for producing health care, what Fuchs (1974) has criticized as the "monotechnic" approach.

There are also possibilities for substituting alternative medical techniques or procedures in treating a given illness; the best choice of technique will depend in part on the patient's value system. Furthermore, medically determined needs, even if they were to reflect a consensus of the medical profession, may not represent a consensus of the public, given the multiple public and private objectives involved in setting national as well as personal priorities. Also, even some people who are not usually cynical might question the wisdom of asking the physicians to determine the "needed" number of physicians. Finally, the medically determined needs approach suggests by omission that one can ignore costs in determining national priorities, a proposition that could be true only if there were no scarcity.[6]

FEATURE

Work Force Planning Versus the Power of Markets

The rapid growth of managed care in the 1990s has led to the popular view that there are too many specialists and physicians overall though probably not enough primary care physicians. HMOs and other managed care organizations are under intense pressure to control their costs by eliminating unnecessary care, improving physician productivity, and by substituting cheaper inputs for more expensive inputs (e.g., primary care providers for specialists; nonphysician providers for physicians). These trends are expected to reduce the demand for physicians, especially specialists. Various projections of the "correct" supply of physicians have been based on HMO ratios.

Can we rely on the marketplace to make these and other adjustments? Support for planning and regulating the health care work force is based in part on the idea of supplier-induced demand; that is, the demand–supply model just does not apply to physician markets. Reinhardt (1994b) summarizes the two main weaknesses of health care markets as follows:

> First, . . . our medical schools and teaching hospitals can dictate the size and composition of the physician supply with virtual autonomy. Second, . . . once trained, physicians enjoy almost total discretion in dictating the volume and composition of the health care they render patients. Combined with considerable discretion in setting their own fees, the physicians' ability to control the volume of their services "demanded" by the patients allows physicians to extract from society very high "target incomes," virtually regardless of the local physician–population ratio. [pp. 252–253]

On the other hand, some experts suggest that the aging population, new diseases, and new technologies requiring additional physician inputs invalidate existing projections of physician surpluses. The questionable historical record of regulation in the United States coupled with the public's distrust of government and its preference for market solutions are also powerful arguments for relying on market forces. Finally, Moore (1994) describes how markets are already working (e.g., through higher salaries and benefits for primary care physicians in HMOs) to meet the transition to managed care.

---

[6]See Pauly (1971) for further discussion on this issue.

ASSESSING NEED-BASED APPROACHES

Rejection of so many of the premises underlying the medically determined needs approach cannot easily be extended into a rejection of *all* need-based approaches. Need determinations need not be solely medically determined. Consideration of the public's preferences can in principle be incorporated in setting health goals. We can recognize that health manpower need determinations must operate within the context of markets and must obey economic laws. After all, the expression by an informed group within the public at large might reasonably argue that many people in America are not getting the health care they need.

If we accept the health manpower need determination of any group of concerned citizens as being an expression of their informed opinions and their values, much of the mystery surrounding need determinations disappears. To treat health manpower need determinations as expressions of needs derived from legitimate health goals is not to trivialize them. To recognize that different groups will plausibly make different statements about how much health care the country needs is not to say we should ignore them all. The alarms sent by such groups, while perhaps not as "objective" as some scientific determination, may be important to society's well-being. However, a recognition that need determinations inherently reflect people's values explains the multiplicity of reported needs, because people's values differ.

This account of need shortages—that is, accounts of health manpower requirements based at least partly on nonmarket criteria—inevitably leads to many questions. For example, is there a best way to determine these needs? Is there a fair way? Such questions lie in the realm of normative economics, discussed in Chapter 20.

Economic Definitions of Shortages of Health Professionals

Economic definitions of manpower shortages are usually quite different from those based solely on medical grounds. Economists often apply definitions based on considerations of how a given market for professionals deviates from an ideal, efficient market.

One can expect that economic definitions of shortages will be somewhat more objective, inasmuch as the concept of an efficient market can be objectively defined. Consequently, one might expect that there would be a single, clear definition of an economic shortage of health manpower. Unfortunately, there are several economic definitions.

EXCESS DEMAND

Consider as a starting point the conventional economic definition of a shortage: the excess of the quantity demanded over the quantity supplied at market prices. Figure 15.4 depicts a shortage defined in this way: The health manpower shortage at the wage W_1 is equal to $L_{d1} - L_{s1}$. If the wage instead had been W_2, there would have been no shortage. This is because at the higher wage, less labor services would have been demanded, and more would have been supplied.

This definition, though valid, raises critical questions in the case of health manpower. The main question is why the wage does not rise to equilibrium, thus automatically eliminating the shortage. In the usual case of persistent excess demand, the

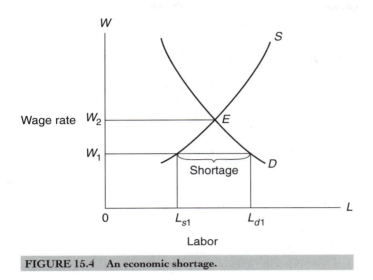

FIGURE 15.4   An economic shortage.

stickiness in wages is imposed by law or regulation. A common example of such regulation is rent control, which is sometimes found in the market for rental housing.

What would cause wage stickiness in health manpower markets? It seems doubtful that health manpower wages are sticky in this sense, or that health manpower shortages in terms of excess demand are a serious policy problem. Some analysts have argued, in fact, that excess demand shortages are not serious concerns for most categories of professionals.

RELATIVELY RAPID INCREASES IN WAGES: DYNAMIC SHORTAGES

An unnecessary focus on excess demand also obscures the fact that economically meaningful shortages of professionals may well exist even when supply and demand are in short-term equilibrium. In particular, a shortage may occur when demand and supply conditions change over time. Suppose, for example, that demand for a category of health professionals expands over time, and that the supply of these professionals is slow to respond or even perhaps faces barriers in responding. The result may be a rise in the wage that is large relative to the wage gains of other professionals.[7]

To illustrate, consider Figure 15.5, which depicts the demand for physicians at two points in time: an initial Period 1 and a subsequent Period 2. We compare the equilibrium (supply equal to demand) in Period 1 with that in Period 2. The wage increase from W_1 to W_2 may indicate a shortage, even though supply equals demand (at L_1 and L_2) in both periods. We would say there is a shortage if the relative wage of physicians has risen sharply relative to that of other professionals. The measure of shortage under this approach is the relative wage and the direction of its movement.

---

[7]See Blank and Stigler (1957) for further discussion.

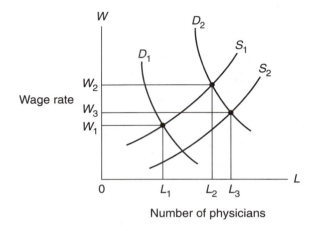

FIGURE 15.5 **Change in equilibrium wage over time depending on supply adjustments.**

. Several variations on this general approach have been described. The pattern of wages over time may be more complex than the movement described from equilibrium at W_1 to an equilibrium at W_2. We might find, for example, that the initial market response to increased demand for the professionals would be to raise wages to W_2; only after these very high wages had induced the expansion of supply to S_2 would we observe market wages adjusting to W_3 (and supply L_3). Under this scenario, the professional's wage for a time falls, here from W_2 to W_3. Thus, a decline in relative wage during a given period may reflect a long-run adjustment offsetting a shortage and not necessarily an indication of excessive supply.

RELATIVE RATES OF RETURN

How should we measure the monetary gains from professional training?[8] Hansen (1962) provides a measurement approach that is both plausible and consistent with the theory we have developed. He proposes that the relevant measure of monetary gains to a given health professional group must take into account the various opportunity costs incurred by the professional in obtaining his or her training. As we have seen, a measure that attempts to accomplish this conceptual task is the internal rate of return.

Since the internal rate of return to education is the rate of discount that equates the present value of the stream of costs and benefits of education to zero, the higher the rate of return, the greater the financial rewards to investment in the human capital attained through education. Thus, to determine whether a given health professional group was in relatively short supply, we would compare the internal rate of return to that of other professionals, and examine the pattern of these comparative data over time.

High, even excessive rates of return, may occur whenever the supply of labor fails to respond quickly to changes in demand. In some instances, the underlying reason for this slowness in response may be barriers to entry faced by potential health professionals.

---

[8]Yett (1975) provides a detailed discussion of the problems of the alternative approaches to measurement.

A barrier to entry exists, in this case, when a potential health professional faces higher entry costs than incumbents faced.

This definition certainly includes cases where potential entrants are completely barred from entry. Such barriers would occur if controls on slots in health professional schools limited entry. They also occur to some degree whenever entry to the profession is limited by licensure laws. The issue of licensure laws is of special interest here because it is common in the health professions. Because of this connection, we treat the empirical literature on rates of return to physician education in the discussion of licensure in Chapter 16.

The Role of Monopsony Power — Shortages of Registered Nurses

Practitioners who describe health manpower availability often rely on reported percentages of unfilled budgeted positions. One explanation of this measure (using Figure 15.4) is excess demand. Excess demand, however, is generally a temporary phenomenon; as long as prices are not rigid, price rises will tend to cure the problem. More plausibly, the analyst will focus on changes in the percentage of unfilled budgeted positions, analogous to dynamic definitions of manpower shortages. First, however, we must address the problem of interpreting reported data for markets that are monopsonistic.

MONOPSONISTIC LABOR MARKETS

Under monopsony, a firm may report unfilled budgeted positions, for example, for registered nurses, even when actually in equilibrium. A *monopsony* is a market that in theory has only one buyer; for example, a monopsony would be one hospital that hires virtually all registered nurses in the market. The paradox is that such a monopsony firm may announce that it wishes to hire more nurses, when it actually is unlikely to take the necessary steps to do so.

The paradox is explained by the monopsony firm's upward sloping supply curve. Because it is a big employer, it has the power to influence nurses' wages and thus to induce more nurses to work by raising the average nurse wage level. The monopsony firm is willing to hire more nurses *at the current wage,* but it has no intention of paying a higher wage in order to hire more nurses.

These ideas can be illustrated with the help of Figure 15.6. Here we imagine that there is one hospital that is the only demander of nurse labor in the market. The hospital's demand curve for nurse labor, labeled *D,* represents the marginal revenue product curve for nurses employed at that hospital.

What the monopsony element brings to the analysis is the fact that the supply curve for labor will no longer represent the marginal labor cost, MLC, to this hospital. Contrast what would have happened had this hospital been a competitive hirer, one firm among many. Competition would have meant that the hospital could have hired as many nurses as it wanted at any given wage. In a competitive market, N_d workers will be hired at wage W_1. In contrast, the monopsonist will hire fewer, and at a lower wage.

Consider the monopsonist's marginal labor cost curve, MLC. When the monopsonist hospital seeks to add one nurse to its labor force, it must pay a higher wage than before in order to induce this marginal (extra) nurse to work. But it then must pay *all* of

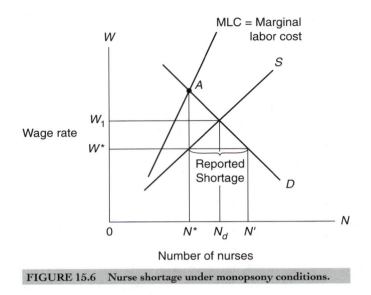

FIGURE 15.6 **Nurse shortage under monopsony conditions.**

its employed nurses a higher wage. The problem arises entirely because the labor supply curve faced by this firm is rising, as is typical under monopsony, instead of being flat, as is typical under competition.

The extra (marginal) labor cost incurred for that one nurse is not just the wage it pays him or her, but it also includes the extra wages it must pay all its other nurses. As a result, the marginal labor cost curve, MLC, will lie above the labor supply curve, *S*.

REPORTED SHORTAGES

Suppose now that the hospital acts to maximize its profits. It would find it profitable to hire an additional nurse so long as the extra revenue he or she brought in, the marginal revenue product, is greater than the extra cost he or she caused the hospital, the marginal labor cost. Thus, as long as the demand curve (the marginal revenue product) lies above the marginal labor cost curve for a given level of nurse employment, it will always pay to hire more nurses. The hospital achieves its profit-maximizing complement of nurses where $D = MLC$, an employment level of N^* nurses in Figure 15.6. The equilibrium wage is found on the corresponding point of the labor supply curve; here it is W^*.

At this equilibrium wage W^*, the hospital would desire to hire N' nurses. It may well budget for these nurses and effectively report a shortage of $(N' - N^*)$. The hospital acts as if it did not realize that if it wants more nurses to work it must pay its nurses more. At any rate, a shortage in this case has a limited meaning; it only means additional nurses being desired *at the current wage level*.

This theoretical point suggests the hazards of interpreting data on unfilled budget positions. The existence of monopsony power in labor markets suggests that unfilled positions data may overstate the problems of nursing availability. The problem is somewhat mitigated by the fact that these data typically represent unfilled *budgeted*

FEATURE

Are Nursing Markets Monopsonistic?

Do nursing labor markets, in fact, tend to be monopsonistic? The question has been approached by many empirical researchers, but there are generally two approaches. Some have examined the relationship between market concentration measures and measures of nursing wages. If markets are more like monopsonies (having higher levels of market concentration), then the typical firm labor supply is more likely to be upward sloping (reflecting the monopsony power). Thus, nurse wages will tend to be depressed below their marginal revenue product. Studies of this type have often found a negative relationship as expected by the theory. Higher concentration levels were statistically associated with lower wages.[9]

A somewhat more direct measure of the theoretical constructs was reported by Sullivan (1989). Instead of estimating the association between concentration and wages, he developed estimates of the typical firm's labor supply curve. This is a more direct approach because the essential problem is that the monopsonist's labor supply curve is upward sloping.

Sullivan found that the typical hospital's labor supply appeared to be upward sloping to a degree that suggested considerable monopsony power. The Sullivan results support the several previous studies that reported the existence of a significant degree of monopsony power in the nursing labor markets.

---

positions because a hospital is unlikely actually to budget for all the positions it theoretically desires at the current wage.[10] Furthermore, the analyst might in any case be interested in changes in the percentage of unfilled budgeted positions. If unfilled positions were rising rapidly, it would suggest increasing relative scarcity of nurses.

CONCLUSIONS

In this chapter we have discussed the training and utilization of labor in the health sector of the economy. We have shown how some fairly elementary tools of economic analysis can provide important insights into the demand and supply of labor in the health sector.

Perhaps the most controversial aspect is the discussion of manpower planning, as it challenges some venerable traditions of health services research. The implications are not trivial. The training of health professionals is costly and time-consuming. Appropriate measures of the need, and of the productivity of the trained professionals and their substitutes, could save millions of dollars that might be more productively used elsewhere.

---

[9]See, for example, Hurd (1973), Link and Landon (1975), and Feldman and Scheffler (1982). However, Adamache and Sloan (1982) found no evidence of association between wages and concentration.

[10]See Yett (1975) for further discussion.

The training and location of physicians are two of the most important aspects of health sector manpower analysis, given their importance in the provision of health care. We turn to this issue in Chapter 16.

Summary

1. In 1993, over 10 million people, about 9 percent of the U.S. labor force, were employed at health services sites.
2. The demand for labor is precisely the marginal revenue product of labor curve. It is closely related to the production function, and is directly related to the price of the output.
3. The supply of labor tends to slope upward, implying that the higher the wage rate in a given market, the more laborers would be forthcoming. Workers currently employed may choose to work more hours if higher wages are offered; other workers may be attracted from elsewhere by the higher wages.
4. The higher the wage rate for health providers such as physicians, the higher the rate of return for medical education. As a result, higher wages should lead to an increased supply of health care providers.
5. Reinhardt found that the physician's marginal product tends to increase up until the point that the physician is working a total of about 25 hours per week; the marginal product eventually declines to zero at about 110 hours per week.
6. Reinhardt also found that physicians could improve productivity of their practices and increase profits by doubling the number of aides from the average of two aides per physician.
7. There are basically two types of shortages: need shortages and economic shortages. Need shortages use a nonmarket, or noneconomic, definition of shortage.
8. One definition of an economic shortage is the excess of quantity demanded over the quantity supplied at the market wage rate. Stickiness in wages helps explain why the wage does not rise to equilibrium, thus automatically eliminating the shortage.
9. Meaningful shortages of professionals may exist even when supply and demand are in short-term equilibrium. If demand for a category of health professional expands over time, and supply is slow to respond, the result may be a rise in the wage that is large relative to wage gains of other professionals.
10. Under labor monopsony conditions, a firm may report unfilled budgeted positions, for example, for registered nurses, even when actually in equilibrium. A monopsony firm may announce that it wishes to hire more nurses, when it actually is unlikely to take the necessary steps to do so.

Discussion Questions

1. Give examples of ways in which labor and capital can be substituted for each other in the production of health services.
2. What is the meaning of the term *internal rate of return?*

3. In the text we considered only forgone income and tuition as costs to medical school. Enumerate other monetary and nonmonetary opportunity costs to medical school.

4. What is "learning by doing" for physicians and other health care professionals? How does this differ from formal education?

5. Why might demand for nurse labor by hospitals or other organized health providers be monopsonistic?

6. What is the marginal product of an input? Marginal revenue product? Why does the demand for a factor correspond to the marginal revenue product curve? What will determine whether the demand for a factor will be elastic or inelastic?

7. Why will a profit-maximizing physician firm want to equalize the marginal product per dollar spent across all inputs?

8. What are the key assumptions of the needs-based approach to manpower planning in the Lee–Jones study? Is there evidence to invalidate one or more of the assumptions?

9. What is meant by the term *barriers to entry*? What are some entry barriers for someone who wants to be an obstetrician? For someone who wants to be a nurse's aide or orderly?

10. If barriers to entry into a profession were absolute so that entry would not be possible, what would the supply curve look like? What would the supply curve look like if there were free and easy entry into an occupation? Thus, what role do barriers to entry play in explaining relative rates of return to an occupation?

11. Define monopsony and marginal labor cost. Why is the marginal labor cost in the case of monopsony above the supply (average labor cost) curve? What is the nature of the inefficiency or misallocation associated with monopsony power? Is there any inefficiency when the supply curve facing the monopsonist is perfectly elastic?

Exercises

1. Consider the firm's demand for labor, such as in Figure 15.2. If the demand elasticity is -0.5, what will be the effect of increased wages on total labor earnings?

2. For Exercise 1, graph and analyze the impact of an increase in the price of lab tests on the labor market.

3. Consider the market for highly skilled laboratory technicians. Graph the impacts on market wages if limitations on immigration were lifted. Would more or fewer services be provided? What would happen to the price?

4. In this chapter we discuss how physicians' marginal products rise up to 25 hours, and then slowly fall to zero at 110 hours. Graph both marginal and total products from this statement.

5. In Table 15.1, Janet Miller's wage is assumed to rise by 5 percent per year, once she graduates from medical school. What would happen to the net present value of her investment in medical education if her wage rose by 4 percent instead of 5 percent? What would happen to the internal rate of return to her investment?

6. Suppose that the demand for labor curve is summarized by the function
$$L = 500 - 5W,$$
and the supply of labor is
$$L = 100 + 5W.$$
What would be the equilibrium supply and wage in a competitive market?

7. (For students with calculus.) Using the information in Exercise 6, how much labor would a monopsonistic hospital hire, and at what wage?

CHAPTER

The Training and Practice of Physicians

16

- ■ Medical Education Issues and the Question of Control

- ■ Licensure and Monopoly Rents

- ■ Physician Pricing and Behavior

- ■ Geographic Location of Physicians

- ■ Conclusions

I n Chapter 15, we discussed several issues regarding labor training and market analysis. These issues could be generalized to the many different types of health care workers, including physicians, nurses, aides, and technicians, and we chose examples among various health care fields.

The physician is the primary provider within the health economy. There are several issues in physician training and practice that merit particular attention. We explore four that provide both particular insight as well as the use of important economic analytical tools:

- *Medical Education.* Physicians must generally attend four years of medical school, an additional three to four years of residency training, and often after that, an additional amount of specialist training. They thus postpone their main earning years well past the age of 30. This training process clearly limits both short- and long-term responses to any sort of market conditions.

- *Licensure.* Physicians must be licensed at the state level in order to practice medicine. We will address the motives for licensure laws as well as the effects of entry restrictions on rates of return to medical education and the quality of care.

- *Pricing of Services.* Physicians have traditionally held some monopoly power over their clienteles. The ability to discriminate by price has allowed physicians to segment the market, and this has many implications.

363

- *Geographic Location of Physicians.* There have been many accounts of towns losing their doctor, or not having one to begin with, while developers in major cities with large numbers of doctors may be building new clinics to accommodate still more doctors who wish to work there. We address the economic aspects of geographic location that may account for the patterns that have emerged over time.

MEDICAL EDUCATION ISSUES AND THE QUESTION OF CONTROL

Many professions require a considerable length of time for education and training, but the time period for formal training of physicians is among the longest. In addition, medical education poses the question of who has control. Does the medical profession itself exercise control over access to medical education in order to improve its own profitability? It is helpful to study medical schools and their funding, as well as information about the supply of potential medical students.

Sources of Medical School Revenues

Medical school education is heavily subsidized by government. This situation is an outcome of public concern for the adequacy of the supply of physician labor. The rapid growth in medical school enrollments did not arise by accident. Several actions by Congress, beginning with the Health Professions Educational Assistance Act in 1963, provided grants to medical schools and financial assistance to students. Some of this federal support hinged on enrollment increases. In 1971, however, federal support to medical schools was substantially increased and came in the form of capitation grants, grants that rewarded the medical schools for expanding their enrollments by giving money on a per-student basis, initially about $3,000 per year per student (Newhouse 1978a). With fears of physician surpluses emerging by the late 1970s, assistance under the Health Professions Educational Assistance Act was phased out and enrollments stabilized.

Nevertheless, medical education is still heavily subsidized. Table 16.1 shows the sources of revenue for U.S. medical schools during various years. Tuition represents a relatively small source of revenues; thus, the student pays only a small portion of the true costs of the investment in education. Note that governmental support comes both as support for operating revenues, and through grants and contracts. Total government support for medical schools in the 1989–1990 school year was almost 40 percent of total revenues.

Capital Market Imperfections Justify Subsidies

The policy that students pay for a relatively small share of their training raises questions in light of the fact that physicians earn high incomes and receive relatively high rates of return to their investment. However, at least part of this subsidy can be understood as a policy that attempts to overcome imperfections in capital markets. The capital markets at issue are those markets where potential medical students would have to go to get the loans needed to pay for their education. The imperfections at issue are

TABLE 16.1   United States Medical School Revenues

	Academic Year		
	1960–1961	*1980–1981*	*1989–1990*
Number of schools reporting	87	119	126
	Percentage from Operating Revenues		
Federal/state/local appropriations	15.8	21.8	14.6
Other government support	4.4	6.9	6.8
Practice plans	3.0	15.6	29.8
Tuition and fees	6.4	5.4	4.3
Endowment and gifts	7.3	1.9	3.9
Parent university support	4.1	1.6	0.9
Reimbursement from hospitals		9.2	9.9
Miscellaneous	9.2	3.6	4.5
Total General Operating Revenues	50.2	65.9	74.7
	Percentages from Grants and Contracts		
Research	37.4	20.8	17.0
Federal	27.3	17.1	13.0
Nonfederal	10.1	3.7	4.0
Teaching and training	11.3	6.5	2.5
Federal	9.9	4.3	1.4
Nonfederal	1.4	2.3	1.1
Other	1.4	6.8	5.8
Total grants and contracts	50.0	34.1	25.3
Total Revenues	100.0	100.0	100.0

Source: Jolin et al. (1991).

economic imperfections stemming from the difficulty to get these markets to lend up to the full value of the investment.

Even though it is clear that a medical education pays off handsomely, it is difficult for a potential lender to secure the loan adequately. The investment in education, as we have seen, is an investment in human capital. Human capital cannot be bought and sold in the same way as physical capital.

To make the point plain, one cannot repossess a human being. While the bank knows that the typical medical graduate can easily afford to repay the loan, it is difficult to guarantee this repayment in an individual case. Thus potential medical students may not get the needed loans even though the investment is well worthwhile. From society's point of view, this problem may result in insufficient numbers of medical students.

Leffler and Lindsay (1981) conclude that with such capital market imperfections, reliance on private markets leads to an underinvestment in medical education. Thus, government support can be justified on economic grounds. These authors estimated that an optimal level of support would be about 36 percent of the costs of medical education, a substantial figure.

Teaching Hospitals, Medical Schools, and Joint Production

Medical education is a good example of joint production. That is, medical schools produce at least three products jointly:

- Medical education.
- Patient care.
- Research.

To reimburse for patient care or to fund medical education appropriately, it is necessary to determine the pure costs and the joint costs of these activities. An example taken from Newhouse (1978a) illustrates these terms.

In Table 16.2, the total annual cost for a medical school that produces only education and patient care is shown to be $6 million. If the school produced only education, with only the minimum patient care needed to do this, its costs would be $5 million. If it produced only its present volume of patient care and no medical education, its costs would be $3 million.

Incrementally, the cost of patient care raises the school's budget from $5 to $6 million. Thus, the *pure cost* of patient care is the extra $1 million. Reasoning in a similar fashion, adding education to the cost of patient care raises the budget from $3 million to $6 million. Thus, the pure cost of education is $3 million.

Notice that the difference between total cost of this hypothetical medical school and all the pure costs is $2 million. This $2 million is called the *joint cost*. It follows that if the school were reimbursed only for pure costs, it would run a deficit. Much of the controversy with respect to funding revolves around the problem of who will pay for the joint costs.

The issue of joint production has centered on the teaching hospital, which also jointly produces patient care and medical education through its provision of internship, residency, and medical research. In particular, with the substantial cost differences

TABLE 16.2 Hypothetical Example of Joint Production at a Medical School	
	Millions of Dollars
Total cost of school	6
Cost if school produced only patient care	3
Cost if school produced only education	5
"Pure" cost of education*	3
"Pure" cost of patient care*	1
Joint costs*	2

*The pure cost of education is total cost (6) less the cost of producing only patient care (3). The pure cost of patient care is total cost (6) less the cost of producing only education (5). Joint costs are total costs (6) less all pure costs (3 + 1).
Source: Newhouse (1978a).

between teaching and nonteaching hospitals, third-party payers are concerned about whether they are unnecessarily subsidizing medical education. The conventional wisdom in the 1970s was that the cost of education and affiliation with a medical school was substantial.

An examination of the cost differences between teaching and nonteaching hospitals shows that nonphysician costs per day are 21 percent higher in teaching hospitals. However, sorting out the causes for cost differences and making appropriate statistical adjustments, refine these data. After this is done, nonphysician costs, though still higher in teaching hospitals, show a difference that is typically less than 10 percent.[1]

Foreign Medical School Graduates (FMGs)

Physician supply in the United States is dependent to a significant degree on foreign medical school graduates (FMGs). Nearly one-fourth of all physicians are graduates of foreign medical schools. Furthermore, the relative reliance on foreign medical school graduates has changed considerably. As a portion of the total number of physicians, foreign medical school graduates increased from less than 14 percent of the total in 1963 to 23 percent in 1992.

The availability of physicians from other countries can have important policy and planning implications, especially now that the reliance on FMGs has grown. Politzer and colleagues (1989) have estimated that the growth in their numbers has exceeded the projections by the Department of Health and Human Services. The availability of foreign national FMGs can increase the responsiveness of physician supply in the United States to changes in the physician wage.

Rapid increases in physician wages send a market signal to potential physicians; this increases the estimated rate of return to an investment in medical education. It takes a very long time, however, for new applicants among American college graduates to get to medical school, get trained, and get into practice. Thus, the supply of new American physicians will respond slowly to the wage signal. However, foreign national FMGs, already trained but currently practicing elsewhere, can respond more quickly than this. Therefore, the availability of foreign national FMGs makes total physician supply in the United States, in principle, more elastic.

These facts about FMGs can be used by policymakers during periods of shortages and rising fees. Immigration policy can be relaxed to admit more foreign national FMGs during periods of physician shortages, and vice versa during periods of perceived physician surpluses. This in fact is what happened during the 1960s, when preferential treatment was given to foreign national FMGs. Requirements were subsequently tightened by a 1976 act once shortages were no longer perceived.

In addition to immigration policy, the number of FMGs, including U.S. graduates of foreign medical schools, is influenced by certification and licensure requirements. All FMGs must take certification examinations required for admission into an approved graduate medical education program. The 1976 act also placed restrictions on the access of FMGs to graduate medical education.

---

[1]See Sloan, Feldman, and Steinwald (1983) for more detail.

A frequent concern about FMGs is quality of care. Arguments for tightening standards for FMGs are usually justified on the basis of claims that these graduates are inferior in quality to those of U.S. and Canadian medical schools. Such conclusions are often based on comparisons of examination performance and other measures of the credentials and personal attributes of FMGs and their U.S. counterparts.

Studies of the quality of the care provided by FMGs, however, find little difference between the two groups. Some have argued that differences are more likely to arise, if they exist, in ambulatory care settings because of a much lower level of organizational control than in hospital settings. A study that examined over 14,000 patient episodes by nearly 1,200 physicians in three specialty groups, however, found little difference in performance. FMGs, in fact, sometimes outperformed U.S. medical graduates.[2]

The Control of Medical Education

In 1974, Victor Fuchs wrote that "most economists believe that part [of physicians' high incomes] represents a 'monopoly' return to physicians resulting from restrictions on entry to the profession and other barriers to competition" (p. 58). What Fuchs refers to is the claim that physicians restrict entry to their profession in order to drive up prices for their services and thus themselves make larger incomes.

Do physicians control entry to their professions in order to earn above normal returns on their investment? This question can be asked in two steps, taking first the issue of whether physicians do, in fact, earn above normal returns. Historically, physicians have often earned above normal returns. Distinguished economists found this to be the case using data from early in this century, and it was suggested that control of entry was the cause. More recent studies find high returns in at least some recent historical periods.[3]

How is it that physicians could control entry? Our present ideas and beliefs about the role of organized medicine in controlling entry owe much to the writing of Kessel (1958). Kessel argued that monopoly power was attained by organized medicine in several ways, two of the most important being (1) licensure of physicians, and (2) control of access to medical education. The first, licensure, is explored later in this chapter. At present, consider Kessel's account of the control over medical education exerted by physicians primarily through the American Medical Association.

Control over Entry

Early after the founding of the American Medical Association in 1847, the organization campaigned state by state to get the medical profession controlled through licensure. Having largely achieved this goal by the turn of the century, the AMA turned its attention to the control of medical schools, which had proliferated in number. In 1906, the Council on Medical Education of the AMA inspected the 160 medical schools existing

---

[2]See Rhee et al. (1986)

[3]See Burstein and Cromwell (1985). For earlier work, see Friedman and Kuznets (1945) and Leffler (1978).

at that time, declaring only slightly more than half of them to be acceptable. The council sought support for this position through the Carnegie Foundation, which in 1910 issued the Flexner Report calling for both substantial reductions in the number of medical schools and control on their quality. Kessel argued:

> If impact on public policy is the criterion of importance, the Flexner Report must be regarded as one of the most important reports ever written. It convinced legislators that only the graduates of first class medical schools ought to be permitted to practice medicine and led to the delegation to the AMA of the task of determining what was and what was not a first class medical school (p. 28).

Following this report, the number of medical schools fell to 85 by 1920 and to 69 by 1944. Kessel pointed out that giving the AMA charge over determining the supply of physicians was like "giving the American Iron and Steel Institute the power to determine the output of steel" (p. 29). The AMA was also able to gain control over the internship/residency process through its ability to certify hospitals for such training. It also maintained control over the process through which physicians become board certified. The picture is one of significant power and means to control entry.

The AMA was also able to exercise control over substitute providers (e.g., optometrists, podiatrists, chiropractors) by influencing licensure to limit their scope of practice and later to limit third-party reimbursement for their services. Starr (1982) wrote of a survey of 9,000 families conducted between 1928 and 1931, which found that nonphysician providers treated only 5.1 percent of all attended cases of illness. He concluded that "physicians had medical practice pretty much to themselves" (p. 127).

Kessel's argument is historical and written near mid-century, yet many analysts point to anomalies in recent medical school data as continuing evidence of control of entry by the medical profession. The large excess demand for medical school slots by qualified applicants to medical schools has been used to support the claims. Table 16.3 shows that historically large fractions of medical school applicants in the United States are rejected; that is, there appears to be a substantial excess demand for medical school slots. Is this evidence of monopolizing control by the medical profession? Kessel's view certainly suggests that it is.

Another View—The Donor Preference Hypothesis

This simple story of professional control can be challenged on several grounds. Hall and Lindsay (1980) argue that medical schools do not take larger proportions of applicants and medical school enrollments respond only partially to applicant demand because the administrators of medical schools are responding rationally to their economic incentives. As we have seen, medical school revenues come not so much from tuition paid by students but from "donors"—that is, sources such as government agencies, alumni, businesses, research organizations, and so on. For the most part, it is these donors who are the true demanders of the output of medical schools, trained physicians.

The donors, however, are often interested only in some of the many potential graduates, those with specific attributes in terms of personal characteristics, and performance and professional goals. For example, medical schools discriminate among applicants by test scores, and they also discriminate among applicants by selecting

	Total	Total Percent Accepted	Men Applied	Total Accepted	Percent Accepted	Women Applied	Total Accepted	Percent Accepted
1968	21,118	47.8	19,021	N/A	N/A	2,097	N/A	N/A
1978	36,636	45.1	27,075	12,352	45.6	9,561	4,175	43.7
1983	35,200	48.9	23,239	11,577	49.8	11,961	5,632	47.1
1984	35,944	47.8	23,468	11,463	48.8	12,476	5,731	45.9
1985	32,893	52.4	21,331	11,370	53.3	11,562	5,858	50.7
1986	31,323	54.6	20,056	11,159	55.6	11,267	5,933	52.7
1987	28,123	60.5	17,712	10,822	61.1	10,411	6,205	59.6
1988	26,721	64.0	16,457	10,785	65.5	10,264	6,323	61.6

TABLE 16.3   Excess Demand for Medical School Slots

Source: U.S. Department of Health and Human Services (March 1990, Table VI-A-5 and VI-A-6).

younger ones, those with specific specialization interests, and those who indicate a willingness to return to "shortage areas." These attributes reflect the preferences of the donors. That is, to ensure that donations and financial support continue, medical schools establish a selection process to recruit the "appropriately qualified" students. Thus, the data on excess medical school applicants should not be viewed as true excess demand when we see that the true demander is the medical school donor.

In addition to providing an explanation for the apparent excess demand for medical school slots, Hall and Lindsay show that medical school enrollments rise in response to both applicant demand and the more important demand for trained physician graduates by the donors. These results tend to contradict the view that medical school enrollments are controlled by the AMA to maximize the returns to its members.

Other evidence also supports this new view. If medical schools are artificially keeping their enrollments small to benefit organized medicine, then why don't these schools also raise their tuition charges to clear the market? The fact that tuition is only a small fraction of the true costs of education tends to support the Hall and Lindsay hypothesis.

In summary, we may say that organized medicine historically exerted considerable influence over the supply of trained physicians. Such influence is consistent with a view of the profession as one seeking above normal returns by trying to control entry of new physicians. However, data in recent decades indicate that medical school enrollments are responsive to market forces. These data further suggest that continuing to view medical education as controlled by a monolithic or conspiratorial medical profession is somewhat implausible.

LICENSURE AND MONOPOLY RENTS

Licensure is not unique to the health care professions. However, licensure of physicians has received unparalleled attention. The first licensure requirements (though they had little effect and were minimally enforced) for prospective doctors were passed in

New York City in 1760.[4] Subsequently, many states introduced licensing, often through state medical societies. After the 1820s, however, many of the same states modified or abolished licensure. It was not until after the founding of the AMA in 1847 and the last decades of the nineteenth century that stronger licensure laws were widely promulgated.

The primary controversies with respect to licensure are its role in limiting competition and the role of professional societies on state licensure boards. The conventional view held by many economists is that organized medicine has used control of licensure for self-interest by limiting entry (and by influencing the licensure requirements of potential competitor providers to the advantage of physicians). Some, however, have advanced a public interest argument for licensure—that is, as a result of information imperfections, the public demands quality controls. Licensure and certification help fill these information gaps.

Many economists believe that licensure and professional control over medical education ensure that physicians earn economic rents, payments to factors over and above those necessary to induce them to provide their services. These views have been heavily influenced by the early work of Friedman and Kuznets (1945) and Kessel (1956). Friedman and Kuznets examined the relative return of physicians and dentists. After adjusting for training differentials, they estimated that about half of the 33 percent excess earnings of physicians between 1928 and 1934 represented economic rents.

Much has changed in the health industry since the publication of these earlier articles. However, the broader issues of monopoly rents and motivation for licensure remain controversial. Despite other empirical estimates supporting the rent hypotheses, several critiques of these studies have appeared. Leffler (1978) argued that many earlier studies failed to take into account some important economic considerations that tend to reduce estimates of the return. These adjustments include the high number of hours worked by physicians, their expected mortality rates, and the progressive income tax structure.

Leffler's work includes these adjustments. His estimates of the net present value to general practitioners who served a one-year residency were sometimes negative until the 1960s, especially when they were discounted at 10 or 12 percent.[5] Leffler concluded that the relatively high net returns in the late 1960s and early 1970s reflected a temporary disequilibrium situation resulting from the passage of Medicare and Medicaid in 1965.[6]

On the other hand, a subsequent study undertaken by Burstein and Cromwell (1985) compared the internal rates of return[7] of physicians to dentists and lawyers. The authors incorporate many adjustments into their estimates including length of physician

---

[4]Starr (1982, p. 44). Starr provides a fascinating history of licensure legislation in the United States.

[5]Many economists would question Leffler's use of such high discount rates in the low-inflation period studied.

[6]In addition to the adjustments suggested by Leffler, Headen (1986) separated the labor from entrepreneurial returns for self-employed physicians in family practice. He found that about 16 percent of the reported incomes are associated with their entrepreneurship.

[7]The rate that equates the present value of the returns with the present value of outlays.

training, length of working life, and the earnings of medical residents. These data, adjusted for hours of work, or r_a, as well as unadjusted, or r_u, are shown in Table 16.4.

The rates of return are high as compared to lawyers and, not given in this table, for specialization based on board certification requirements. This was true despite the rapid growth in physician supplies and the constraints imposed by third-party payers to contain costs over the study period. The authors therefore concluded that "the conventional picture of medicine as a financially attractive profession is strongly confirmed" (p. 76).

Public Interest or Self-Interest

The specific issue of licensure is but a part of the broader issue of regulation reflecting the two competing theories: public interest versus self-interest motives.

PUBLIC INTEREST AND SELF-INTEREST THEORIES OF REGULATION

The *public interest* motive is based on theories of market failure such as information failure. According to the public interest view, there is a demand for regulatory measures such as licensure due to the limited information patients have about quality and the relatively high costs of obtaining information. Drawing on Akerlof's lemons model introduced in Chapter 7, Leffler (1978) argued that costly information will lower quality. Thus, with asymmetric information about the quality of care, a "state-

TABLE 16.4 Internal Rates of Return,[a] 1967–1980

Year	All Physicians		General Practitioners		Dentists		Lawyers[b]
	r_a	r_u	r_a	r_u	r_a	r_u	r_u
1980	12.1%	14.0%	14.2%	16.7%	—	—	7.2%
1979	11.6	13.7	14.5	17.2	—	—	7.2
1978	11.0	13.2	13.0	16.3	16.3%	14.9%	6.8
1977	10.2	12.6	13.3	17.0	—	—	6.8
1976	10.5	13.3	12.4	16.4	15.8	14.9	7.1
1975	11.6	14.2	12.3	16.7	—	—	7.1
1974	12.0	14.3	14.5	18.2	14.9	14.8	7.1
1973	10.8	13.8	12.5	17.4	—	—	6.7
1972	10.7	14.2	12.2	17.8	14.4	14.8	5.7
1971	11.6	15.1	13.2	18.9	—	—	6.6
1970	11.8	14.7	12.1	16.8	16.1	15.7	7.0
1969	11.3	14.3	12.5	17.2	—	—	4.7
1967	11.7	15.5	13.2	19.0	13.5	15.4	7.7

[a] r_a is the hours adjusted rate of return, and r_u is the unadjusted rate.
[b] No r_a was calculated for lawyers due to lack of data on hours of work for this group.
Source: Burstein and Cromwell (1985, Table 3).

FEATURE

A View from the Medical Profession

More recently, Weeks and medical physician colleagues (1994) computed the returns to education for primary care and specialist physicians and for other professionals. To seek comparably talented groups, they focused on undergraduate academic performance and selected, for comparison to physicians, graduates of the top 20 business schools and those of law and dental schools. The annual yield to educational investment beyond the high school level was measured by the hours-adjusted internal rate of return. The estimated rates of return were: 15.9 percent for primary care physicians; 20.9 percent for specialists; 25.4 percent for attorneys; 20.7 percent for dentists; and 29 percent for businesspersons.

Some of the implications seem clear. The returns to physicians in this analysis are not high relative to other comparable professions. As for physician payment reform, an increase in primary care providers relative to specialists will be unlikely without a narrowing of the gap in payment levels between those groups. Also, if the returns to specialists are reduced to the levels of primary care providers, a larger proportion of qualified undergraduates will be encouraged to enter other professions.

---

enforced minimum quality standard is claimed to be an efficient response to costly quality information" (p. 173).

In contrast, the *self-interest* motives for licensure and other forms of regulation to reduce competition have long been accepted in economics but have only relatively recently been formalized.[8] In this theory, regulation is the result of special interests who provide financial and political support in return for favored legislation. There is thus a demand for political favors arising from the rent-seeking behavior of special interest groups. The effort and amount of resources expended by a special interest group are limited by the rents that would accrue from the favored legislation.

EVIDENCE OF PUBLIC VERSUS SELF-INTERESTS

Paul (1984) tested the public versus self-interest theories using data on the initial decisions by states to license physicians and rejected the public interest theory. His findings show a strong negative association between the year of initial licensure and the per capita number of AMA associated physicians in a state.

Graddy (1991) also tested the competing hypotheses by estimating the probability (and type) of regulation by states of six health care professions. Variables representing the public interest view included the profession's educational requirements in years (to capture the complexity of the service) and professional liability insurance rates (to represent the potential risk to consumers in the absence of regulation). The legislative

---

[8]See Stigler (1971) and Peltzman (1976).

environment was represented by variables such as the strength of the majority party and the rates of turnover of legislators. Variables such as the size of the occupation and its proportion of members belonging to a professional association represented private interests.

The statistical approach was made possible through the fact that there is substantial variation across states in licensure practices for many professions. The professions and type of regulation across the states are summarized in Table 16.5. Graddy found important roles for each of the categories of explanatory variables in determining the kinds of regulation. His findings indicate a higher probability of a stricter form of regulation as the profession's educational requirements are higher—a finding consistent with a public interest motive. The overriding conclusion, though, is that there is no single dominant motive for regulation. Legislators respond to organized interests, the public interest, and their own legislative environments.

Licensure and Quality

The Graddy evidence supports, in part, a public demand for regulation. We also know that physician board certification, or even board eligibility, increases remuneration, meaning that consumers are willing to pay more for those with additional training and credentials.[9]

However, does licensure actually improve the quality of care? Gaumer's (1984) review of the empirical evidence questions whether the goals of protecting the public and ensuring minimal standards of competency are being achieved. He found (1) that in spite of licensure there is a substantial amount of deficient care being rendered, (2) that quality of care would not be impaired if the scope of practice of secondary (nonphysician/dentist) providers were increased, (3) that the licensing process may "not accurately assess the practice competence of applicants" (p. 397), and (4) that there are higher fees and provider incomes in states with more restrictive licensure requirements (supporting the self-interests motive for regulation).

More specifically, with respect to the quality of physician care, he cites studies indicating that 5 percent are "unfit to practice," 8 to 22 percent of obstetrics patients

TABLE 16.5 Number of States Regulating Occupations by Type of Regulation, 1984

Occupation	Unregulated	Registration	Certification	Licensure
Dietician	40	0	4	6
Occupational therapist	23	0	0	27
Psychologist	0	0	5	45
Social worker	17	5	3	25
Physician assistant	5	14	28	3
Nurse-midwife	8	0	17	25

Source: Graddy (1991, Table 1).

---

[9]Wilensky and Rossiter (1983).

and 61–65 percent of well-care patients received deficient care, and that 7.5 percent of all cases in two hospitals indicated physician-inflicted injury (p. 395).

Brennan and colleagues (1991) provide additional evidence on the quality of medical care in hospitals. Licensure is just one of many regulatory requirements intended to ensure that standards are being met. From a large number of randomly selected admissions, the researchers found that nearly 4 percent produced "adverse events," defined as injuries caused by medical management. Nearly 14 percent of these injuries led to death. The authors concluded that "there is a substantial amount of injury to patients from medical management, and many injuries are the result of substandard care" (p. 370).

Though no one is suggesting that eliminating licensure and other requirements will reduce such negative outcomes, it is clear that regulation does not ensure quality care. Will tighter regulation help? From his review, Gaumer concludes as follows:

> Research evidence does not inspire confidence that wide-ranging systems for regulating health professionals have served the public interest. Though researchers have not been able to observe the consequences of a totally unregulated environment, observation of *incremental* variations in regulatory practices generally supports the view that tighter controls do not lead to improvements in quality of service (p. 406).

As a result of the questionable effects of licensure on quality, changes in the health care environment, and the anticompetitive effects of restrictions on entry and restrictions on the scope of practice of potential competitors (e.g., podiatrists, nurse practitioners), the benefits of licensure are being reexamined. Svorny (1992) suggests that the benefits have been weakened by, among other reasons, the added liability that courts have placed on hospitals and HMOs for the negligent conduct of independent physicians and by the increased use of salaried physicians. In a stronger attack, Safriet (1994) concludes:

> Clearly these barriers serve no useful purpose, and in fact contribute to our health care problems by preventing the full deployment of competent and cost-effective providers who can meet the needs of a substantial number of consumers (p. 315).

PHYSICIAN PRICING AND BEHAVIOR

Closely related to the returns to physician education is the manner in which physicians have charged for their services. In this section, we briefly review the models of pricing that allow price discrimination to occur. We follow with a discussion of the history of payment to physicians. We then discuss *assignment,* the acceptance by physicians of fixed payments for their services by Medicare and other third-party payers.

Physician Pricing

It is useful to review the manner in which firms price their goods. We have established elsewhere that if a market is perfectly competitive, the value on the margin of the resources to the consumers, or the price, will just equal the value of the resources in production, or the marginal cost. Further, free entry and exit will ensure that firms will not earn larger than normal economic profits over the long run.

It is also clear that this model has not been truly valid for physician services. Why? Most observers would agree that physicians face downward sloping demand curves. In other words, physicians who raise prices may lose some but not all of their customers. As a result, physicians have some control over the price charged. We have also seen that entry into the medical profession has been limited by educational and licensure requirements. As a result, a monopoly type of model is appropriate for considering pricing. We present such a model here, and then modify it to consider recent developments in policy toward physician pricing.

Under monopoly the marginal revenue curve lies below the demand curve, since lowering the price to one customer requires lowering the price to all of the others. Hence, marginal revenue is less than price. Here we use the monopoly model to illustrate the possibility of price discrimination, although the market is actually monopolistically competitive.

In this simple model, as noted in Figure 16.1, the physician produces quantity *C*, at which the marginal cost curve MC intersects marginal revenue curve MR, or point *F*. At quantity *C*, the demand curve indicates that price *A* can be charged, and the total revenues equal 0*ABC*. The physician's profits equal total revenues less total costs, which are indicated by the average costs and quantity *C*, or box 0*CDE*. Hence, profits are equal to the remainder, or box *ABDE*.

An important feature of the pricing policies of the medical profession is the ability of the physician to discriminate among customers. In economic terms, discrimination means treating different customers differently. Consider a storekeeper who sells candy. He likes adults more than teenagers, so he charges the adults less for boxes of candy than he charges teenagers. Can this practice persist?

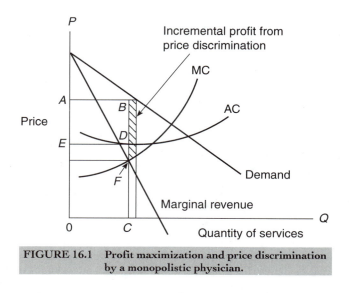

FIGURE 16.1 **Profit maximization and price discrimination by a monopolistic physician.**

Certainly not over time. Teenagers who wish to have the candy will simply ask adults to buy the candy for them. Alternatively, adults who buy candy could resell the candy to teenagers for at least the price that they paid. Competition among adults, in this example, would bid down the price of the candy to where the adults would be making normal, or zero profits, in selling the candy at the same price that it was sold to them.

Health services cannot be resold in this manner. Suppose that a rich person needs knee surgery, and the physician knows that the rich person could pay considerably more than a poor person for the surgery. The rich person cannot have a poor person buy knee surgery and resell it to him. This simple example suggests that there is considerable leeway for physicians to charge different prices to different customers.

Returning to Figure 16.1, even after the physician has chosen to charge fee A for the service, there is still room for price discrimination. Suppose that one more customer, who was not quite willing to pay price A, but instead $(A - 1)$, comes to the office. Suppose it costs $(F + 1)$ to provide the service to that customer. As long as $(A - 1)$ exceeds $(F + 1)$, the physician will increase profits by $(MR - MC)$, or:

$$\text{Increased profits} = (A - 1) - (F + 1)$$
$$= A - F - 2$$

Thus, even if the physician is charging this customer less than before, she may still increase her profits.

FEATURE

Price Discrimination by Physicians Under a Charity Hypothesis

Kessel's (1958) theory of profit-motivated price discrimination among physicians is not without detractors. Ruffin and Leigh (1973) develop a competitive model of physician pricing that features, in contrast, a charitable motivation. They show that prices will vary with the patient's income in a model where physicians gain in marginal utility from serving the poor, after considering the compensating reduction in services for the rich. Thus, the pattern of price discrimination observed in the twentieth-century United States can be alternatively explained.

Furthermore, these authors argue that the charity model is more consistent with certain observed facts, two of which we note here. First, physician price discrimination existed prior to 1910, the approximate point at which organized medicine, according to Kessel, achieved sufficient power over hospital staffing privileges to maintain profit-motivated price discrimination. Second, price discrimination by income has been observed in physician office care as well as in hospital care, where staff privileges are important and provide more power to organized medicine. On the force of Ruffin and Leigh's theory and discussion, it becomes clear that charitable motivations cannot be ruled out, and in fact, the hypothesis performs well.

We have already seen how a substantial portion of physician care is paid by third-party sources, private as well as government. Important concerns relating to third-party coverage, such as moral hazard, were also discussed. In this section, we describe alternative mechanisms under which providers can be reimbursed, though we concentrate on the dominant usual, customary, and reasonable (UCR) method. We then take up some of the concerns that arise from UCR reimbursement.

History of Physician Payment

Traditionally, physicians in the United States have been paid on a fee-for-service (FFS) basis. Although there has been rapid growth of capitation and other payment methods over the past two decades, our focus will be on FFS. Under FFS, each physician has a schedule of fees and expects to be reimbursed for each unit of service provided.

In the days when insurance was less prevalent, many physicians charged less to lower-income patients or even provided some free care. Price discrimination was widespread. Physicians explained this phenomenon by stressing a charitable motive. That is, the profits that were made on those who were able to pay large amounts for care enabled physicians to provide care for those who were less able to pay.

On the other hand, many economists attribute this behavior to more selfish motives. As we discussed earlier, price discrimination is also consistent with profit maximization. Today, however, price discrimination based on physician perceptions of patient income is no longer thought to be common.

As commercial insurance proliferated with the growth of the Blues and other private insurance following World War II, benefit schedules were generally used to determine reimbursement. These schedules contained the maximum amounts that the insurers would pay for a particular service. If the provider charged less, the lower amount would be paid. Typically, also, individuals paid the providers' charges and were reimbursed (indemnified) by insurers according to the benefit schedule. Indemnity plans are still common in the for-profit insurance market.

UCR Reimbursement, Assignment, and Alternative Payment Mechanisms

Following the introduction of Medicare in 1965, another system for reimbursing providers became more prevalent. It uses fee screens and is commonly called the usual, customary, and reasonable (UCR) payment mechanism. Under UCR, the maximum reimbursement is the lowest of the actual charge or the two fee screens.

The fee screens are determined by the maximum of the doctor's median charge (i.e., usual charge) and the customary fees charged by the other physicians in the area. Some criterion, such as the 80th percentile of the distribution of charges, may be selected for this cutoff. In addition, higher charges may be allowed if they are deemed reasonable in light of any unusual circumstances that would justify the higher payment.

Clearly, the UCR method is far more complicated and difficult to administer than the benefit schedule because it involves data collection on every provider. Supporters of this approach argue, however, that it is flexible and fair because it allows for differences across different specialty groups and market areas. Once Medicare adopted

UCR, the Blues and many other third-party payers followed. In 1975 it was estimated that approximately 130 million of 169 million persons with private coverage for physician care were subject to UCR methods.[10]

However, several concerns with UCR soon became apparent. Many critics argued that UCR is inflationary. Providers have incentives to raise their charges in order that the usual and customary screens increase, so that their future payments will increase. Furthermore, there is no incentive to compete by charging less than the screens. Studies of UCR generally support this view. To deal with this problem, Medicare and many Blue Shield plans introduced various mechanisms to limit the increases in the screens.

Limiting maximum payment levels can create other complications, however. It has been argued that providers will induce increases in demand to circumvent the fee controls. This is supplier-induced demand, or SID, which is discussed in Chapter 8. Others point out that existing inequities will tend to be locked in. Perhaps, more importantly, Medicare and the Blues, unlike other commercial indemnity plans, encourage providers to enter into agreements in which they will accept the insurance payment as payment in full. This is commonly called a *participation agreement.* The choice of the physician to accept the insurance payment as payment in full is called accepting *assignment.* Under Medicare, the patient will be liable only for the deductible and 20 percent of the reasonable fee.

Physicians do not have to participate or to accept assignment. If they do not, patients are billed for the services and are reimbursed by their insurance carrier. Patients are thus liable for the full difference between reimbursement and physician charges (though stringent limits on "balance billing" were introduced for Medicare patients in 1991).

Both the Blues and Medicare are concerned about participation. High physician participation rates make the Blues attractive by assuring patients that there will not be additional liabilities. Participation can be attractive to providers because it eliminates collection problems and does not place providers at a competitive disadvantage with others who have agreed to participate. Thus, many of the Blues have achieved high participation rates.

Two reasons exist for concern about assignment within the Medicare program. A low assignment rate not only increases patient payments, but reduces access for those unwilling or unable to incur the additional liabilities.

Not surprisingly, the lower the Medicare allowable charge, the lower the participation rate. The reason for this is that physicians take on their most profitable patients, those providing the greatest marginal revenues, first. Lower Medicare fees lead to a substitution of other patients and nonassigned Medicare patients for patients with assigned reimbursements.

The empirical evidence provides interesting patterns. Until 1984, physicians were able to accept assignment of all patients, no patients, or were able to decide on a case-by-case basis. From a survey conducted in 1976, Mitchell and Cromwell (1982) found that 28 percent never took assignment, 19 percent always did, and 53 percent

---

[10]See Showstack et al. (1979).

sometimes took assignment. Because assignment rates over all cases were dropping markedly, Medicare in 1984 provided physicians with incentives to enter a participation agreement under which they would take all Medicare patients on assignment. Subsequently, the rate of assigned cases increased. The rate further increased after Medicare introduced a new payment system that increased payments to primary care providers. These changes are reviewed later in the chapter.

An Analytical Model of Assignment

To study all of these effects, let us examine the decision to accept assignment on an all-or-nothing basis. To simplify the task, we assume two markets: Medicare, and a private market. Whether the physician takes assignment depends on whether he or she can earn higher profits by accepting it or refusing it.

In Figure 16.2, a physician who will take no cases on assignment will face a marginal revenue curve taken from a combined Medicare and non-Medicare demand. This is shown by MR_1. Profit-maximization occurs at Q_1, at the intersection of marginal revenue and marginal cost. To keep the diagram uncluttered, we omit the underlying demand curve but assume that the resulting price is high enough to provide necessary profits to the physician.

Suppose instead that the physician accepts assignment for all cases. The marginal revenue schedule becomes more complicated. Assume a Medicare reasonable fee of R. When Medicare patients leave the private market, the underlying demand, and hence, the MR schedule, shifts to the left, as shown by segment AB. The physician will first service all patients in the private market whose marginal revenue exceeds R. This will be followed by Medicare patients generating marginal revenue R shown by the horizontal segment BC, and then all private market patients whose marginal revenue is less than R.

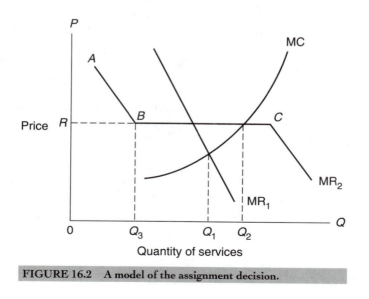

FIGURE 16.2   A model of the assignment decision.

In this model, then, the relevant marginal revenue is shown by MR_2, and the profit-maximizing level is Q_2. The physician would service Q_3 patients in the private market, at a fee determined from private demand, and $(Q_2 - Q_3)$ Medicare patients. Whether the physician accepts assignment is determined by the regime in which profits are higher.

It is critical, then, to examine those factors that influence profits, and thus influence the decision to accept assignment. These include marginal cost, the private demand, and the reimbursement rate. Assume that the physician accepts assignment. Suppose that private demand rises, hence shifting out the marginal revenue curve. The physician is likely to supplant (increase Q_3, thus reducing $Q_2 - Q_3$) assigned patients (with their fixed reimbursement) for those patients who can pay more.

Suppose instead that the marginal cost curve shifts upward due, for example, to increased labor costs. Here the physician is likely to reduce the number of assigned patients $(Q_2 - Q_3)$ whose fees do not now cover the newly increased costs or may choose to stop accepting assignment. Conversely, if the reasonable fee is increased, the relative profitability of accepting assignment, the relative number of Medicare patients, and the total number of patients served will all increase.

The effects of raising the reasonable charge can be substantial. Mitchell and Cromwell (1982) estimated that a 10 percent increase in the allowable charge would raise the assignment rate by 15 percent.

The real and perceived difficulties with managing UCR fee-for-service payment systems have stimulated proposals for a large number of alternatives. Problems with UCR include administrative difficulty, incentives to overconsume, possible inflationary effects, and manipulation of the fee schedules. The alternatives propose different units for payment rather than the service or the procedure.

The main options include payments based on an episode of illness or some form of capitation.[11] With fixed payment for an episode (defined by the length of the illness rather than the number of treatments), the incentives will be to cure the illness rather than to increase the level of service. With capitation, as in HMOs, there will be no incentive to overutilize. However, a physician-based case or episode payment system, like DRG hospital reimbursement, contains an incentive to increase the number of cases. Thus, the monitoring and administrative costs are likely to be substantial.

Relative Value Scales

As the complexity of medical practice increases, providers are faced with the need to establish fees for an increasingly large number of services. Currently, the Medicare procedure code manual for physicians lists thousands of distinct procedures. Both providers and payers seek guidance on the amounts to charge or the amounts to pay.

In response to these needs, relative value scales (RVSs) were developed by state medical societies and other organizations (the California RVS, developed in 1969, was one of the most widely used). An RVS is a guide that establishes a weight (or multiple) for each procedure. The weight may reflect the time to perform a procedure and its

---

[11]See, for example, Langwell and Nelson (1986).

complexity. Though the RVS does not provide fee information, if a provider adheres to the guide, the price he or she sets for any one procedure will determine the prices charged for all other procedures.

One should recognize that any system of relative value scales depends on a set of given technologies. For example, when the method of treating heart disease changes, the relative value scale for that category must also change in order to be valid. If the technological advance causes the treatment to become cheaper, the treatment may become very profitable to the provider as long as the treatment retains its old place in the relative value scale.

Over the years, perceived inequities in Medicare's UCR system between primary care and surgical specialties were a major reason behind attempts to change Medicare's physician payment system. Researchers at Harvard University, led by William Hsiao, undertook the task of developing a "resource-based" RVS, or RBRVS, as an alternative method of reimbursing physicians. These researchers developed an index based on the inputs needed to provide a procedure. The input is determined by "time spent, intensity of time, practice costs, and costs for advanced training."[12] As a result of their work, a new Medicare physician payment system was to be phased in over a five-year period beginning in 1992.

The system introduced a major restructuring of fees away from specialists and toward primary care providers. This development is supported by many in the health care community who feel that health care in the United States is improperly skewed toward the provision of specialized care. However, many who encourage the use of market-based mechanisms generally believe that the new system will reduce competition among providers.

The new RBRVS will produce substantial redistributions among providers. Consider the fee changes scheduled for implementation under Medicare over the five-year period beginning January 1992. Table 16.6 shows projected comparisons of payments per service, as well as total payments, compared to the previous method, for a number of specialties.

Total Medicare payments per service for all physician specialties were expected to diminish by 6 percent in 1996 compared to the payments found in the previous method. However, payments to family and general practitioners were expected to rise by about 28 percent per service, and payments to optometrists by even more. Payments to some specialty groups were expected to drop sharply, up to 22 percent for radiology and 27 percent for anesthesiology.

Preliminary data support these projections. Between 1991 and 1993, payments per service for family and general practitioners rose by 16 percent with corresponding decreases for surgeons, radiologists, and various subspecialists.[13] During this period participation rates rose as the Medicare payment reforms also limited the amounts physicians could charge Medicare patients to no more than 115 percent of the fee schedule amount. The percentage of physicians signing participation agreements rose from 70 percent in 1991 to 83 percent in 1993.

---

[12]See Hsiao (1987) and Hsiao, Dunn, and Verrilli (1993).
[13]Prospective Payment Review Commission (1995).

Specialty	Payments per Service	Total Payments
All Physician Specialties	−6%	0%
Family Practice	+28	+30
General Practice	+27	+29
Cardiology	−17	−8
Radiology	−22	−11
Anesthesiology	−27	−14
General Surgery	−13	−7
Ophthalmology	−21	−11
Optometry	+41	+43
Podiatry	+14	+16

TABLE 16.6   Projected (1996) Impact of RBRVS Compared to Previous System

Source: Commerce Clearing House (1992, Chart 2).

GEOGRAPHIC LOCATION OF PHYSICIANS

Given the importance of access to highly trained health professionals, we discuss where providers, especially physicians, choose to practice. There is considerable public concern when rural residents must travel miles to see a physician at the same time that new facilities are constructed in already well-served urban areas. There is also public concern if inner-city residents must wait longer for clinic appointments than their suburban counterparts.

To address this dilemma, we consider two aspects of geographical distribution of people and activities:

- How health-related activities will cluster, given the technology of production.
- How physicians will respond to the clustering of activities in choosing where to practice.

Location of Facilities and Providers

Consider a society in which all workers are self-sufficient in providing for their everyday needs. Physicians in this society are all trained as general practitioners, using their educations and small amounts of capital to treat others. In fact, at the limit in this model, each person has a small portion of physician training, and cares for his or her family. The geographic distribution of people in this society would be flat, as no place would be much different from any place else.[14]

---

[14]Mills (1972, Chapter 1) presents a classic and elegant discussion of this type of location theory. Mills and Hamilton (1994) discuss the implications in more detail.

Suppose now that many types of workers discover that it pays for them to specialize, that being geographically close to each other makes each more productive. These are components of increasing returns to scale, and this presents an economic explanation for the establishment of towns and cities. In the model, physicians, as other workers, discover that it pays for them to specialize, to be close to other physicians, and to share facilities. That is, the output of physicians increases by a larger proportion than the number. One might recognize this specialization in the construction of laboratories, clinics, and hospitals.

Moving a step further, it is easy to see that there may be some specialties such as major surgery that require large numbers of providers to work together and, since demand per customer is small, that require large market areas. As Starr (1982) has noted, the improvement in transportation in the early twentieth century fundamentally changed the way that physicians and patients interacted. Physicians and hospitals could now expect patients to come to them. The more specialized the provider, the farther patients can be expected to travel.

Because of the gains from agglomeration of activities, we note that large cities may have specialty clinics or hospitals that are not available in smaller cities. They will also have specialists, and probably some general practitioners. The smaller cities will not have the major clinics, but will have specialists who are not available in the towns. The towns may have general practitioners or no one at all. Thus, the distribution of resources within regions is not equal; it should therefore not be surprising to see more physicians and specialists in large cities than in small ones.

Other economic aspects of the specialization in the region can be described. The regional market area is defined by the patients' ability to travel to the location where care is needed. Since people in smaller towns must travel farther for care, the value of the land on which they live must compensate them for the increased travel. Land rents must be lower than in the larger cities. Since suburban and rural commuters must commute smaller distances to get to their jobs, and to procure the goods and services that they need, wages may be less in these locations than they are closer to the larger cities in the region. The differences in wages and rents serve to equalize well-being among residents of small and large cities in the regional system.

Implications of Regional Analysis

The size of a city, as well as the size of the surrounding region, is related in part to the incomes of the residents, since increased incomes imply the desire to buy more land, and more land (in the aggregate) can be acquired only by increasing the size of the city and the region. Thus central cities, and especially suburban areas, must grow. This tendency has been bolstered by constant improvements in transportation, from horse carts to streetcars, to automobiles. These, once again, allow residents to disperse within an area.

Increases in income and decreases in transportation costs also explain dispersion of medical providers. As populations have grown, the shares of central cities' populations have fallen. As populations have decentralized, so have the providers who serve them.

This regional economic model is helpful in explaining why physicians may choose to locate in one part of a region rather than another. If all regions were then the same, the story would end, because what would explain location in one region would explain it in all of them. However, regions may also vary by climate, social values, or cultural amenities.

Consider a specialist trying to decide whether to live in Detroit or San Francisco, and assume that the hospital facilities are identical. It is likely that the climate, recreational amenities, and possibly social values available in San Francisco would require would-be Detroit employers to make higher offers than would-be San Francisco employers.

Many economic models have tried to explain physician location by concentrating on differences among regions. The simplest model would argue that as long as income is higher in Ohio than in Mississippi, then physicians should migrate from Mississippi to Ohio. We have seen, however, that the income or earnings differences may be compensated by lower costs of living, different amenities, or different social values. Most studies have not addressed this issue well, and as a result there is a wide range of findings that, in sum, have been inconclusive.

Empirical Findings

There are two types of implications of the regional model. One is that there will be migration toward locations that are considered to be more desirable. The second implication is that location theory can predict existing patterns of physician location.

Many studies have tried to link location and migration of physicians to attributes of various regions. Ernst and Yett (1985) note that regression analyses of physicians' location patterns show the patterns not to be sensitive to physicians' net practice incomes, yet they are sensitive to proxies such as population size or per capita income. These findings are broadly consistent with the findings from location theory that there will be more location in population centers and that location will be correlated with the higher per capita income that occurs there. A major problem with these types of studies is that the theoretically correct income measure, expected lifetime income, is very difficult to model.

Similarly, patterns are sensitive to variables that proxy for "quality of life" in the specific area. Variables that are used for this include population size, educational attainment, or racial composition of the population. While there seems to be some consensus that these variables explain the stock of physicians in an area, they are much less successful in explaining the flow of physicians to the area.

The explanation, in part, is that if differences in prices and incomes are necessary to define a locational equilibrium, then we will not see migration as a response to these differences. It is apparent that more careful modeling of physician incentives is the answer.

One study explicitly integrates location theory into its analysis. The results are theoretically appealing and provocative, with respect to location of physicians within regions.

Location Patterns and Availability of Physicians

Newhouse and colleagues (1982) seek to investigate physicians' location decisions. Framing their hypotheses in the location theory discussed previously, they provide strong tests of two hypotheses:

- Within a given specialty, larger towns have higher probabilities of having one or more specialists.
- As a specialty grows, its members disperse into smaller towns. As a result, smaller towns (which had fewer or no specialists) gain specialists at a higher rate than do large towns.

The researchers obtained data for all physicians from the American Medical Association for 1970 and 1979 for selected states, and they divided physicians into 17 specialty categories. They first investigated location of general plus family practitioners. In both 1970 and 1979, nearly all towns with populations of 5,000 or more included a general or family practitioner, and over 85 percent of towns between 2,500 and 5,000 were also represented. This compared, for example, to the distribution of neurosurgeons, which showed that only 28 (56) percent of the communities with populations between 30,000 and 50,000 people in 1970 (1979) had a neurosurgeon. These findings are quite consistent with the location theory that suggests the appropriate market sizes for specialties.

Recall that location theory predicts that the more specialized practitioners would locate in the biggest market areas, the large cities. It would follow that as more were trained there would be more competition, and that some would diffuse into the smaller cities and towns. This would suggest that over time there would be larger percentage increases in smaller towns than in larger ones. Consider Table 16.7, which reproduces summary results from the study.

In Table 16.7, the authors calculate the ratio of specialists per person in 1979 to specialists per person in 1970. If the hypothesis is to be supported, the ratio for smaller markets should be higher (where there is more infusion of physicians) than for larger markets. We see that in almost all cases, the hypothesis is indeed supported. Consider pediatrics, for example. The ratio in towns of 2.5–5 thousand population was 2.66. It fell to 1.62 in the next group (5–10 thousand), and settled down to between 1.35 and 1.45 for the remaining categories. Other specialties yield similar results.

TABLE 16.7   **Ratio of Specialists Per Person in 1979 to Specialists Per Person in 1970**

Size of Town (thousands)	2.5–5	5–10	10–20	20–30	30–50	50–200	200+
Specialty							
Internal medicine	1.79	1.56	1.64	1.54	1.62	1.68	1.65
General surgery	1.08	1.00	1.04	1.08	1.06	1.02	1.08
Obstetrics/Gynecology	1.50	1.27	1.23	1.42	1.25	1.21	1.22
Pediatrics	2.66	1.62	1.36	1.43	1.38	1.35	1.35
Psychiatry	—	1.29	1.30	1.56	1.42	1.34	1.50
Radiology	2.19[a]	1.50	1.34	1.38	1.44	1.39	1.56
Anesthesiology	1.01	1.01	1.40	1.46	1.44	1.28	1.42
Orthopedic surgery	—	3.46[a]	1.92	1.95	1.70	1.51	1.47
Ophthalmology	—	1.18	1.39	1.29	1.39	1.17	1.26
Pathology	—	2.06[a]	1.52	1.45	1.49	1.31	1.57
Dermatology	—	—	1.44	1.79	1.56	1.31	1.33
Neurosurgery	—	—	—	2.71[a]	2.57	1.44	1.28
Plastic surgery	—	—	—	—	2.47	2.19	1.69

[a]Only 5 to 10 percent of the towns in this population range had a specialist in 1970.
Source: Newhouse et al. (1982).

Geographic Location — Some Equity Considerations

Two major groups of geographically defined consumers may be particularly influenced by physicians' location decisions. Consumers in sparsely populated rural areas are likely to have to travel longer distances, at greater costs, to obtain certain types of treatments. Consumers in disadvantaged (by socioeconomic income, race, or class criteria) urban neighborhoods may have to travel relatively far, at relatively high costs compared to other residents, because physicians have chosen to locate closer to their more affluent clientele.

One can conceive of incentives on both the supply and the demand sides to address this problem. On the supply side, initiatives to increase overall physician supply might also be expected to reduce maldistribution as market forces draw physicians to underserved areas.[15] (This was the U.S. policy until the mid-1970s when it became increasingly apparent that there was no longer an overall shortage of physicians.) As for more specific strategies targeting spatial inequalities, sponsors (either governmental or private groups) may offer student loans that are "forgiven" if the recipient practices in a shortage area. Agencies may finance and/or subsidize clinics and/or practices that would otherwise not be economically viable. Ultimately, in some cases government may choose to employ providers at shortage locations. Many of these strategies have been adopted.

On the demand side, policymakers must recognize that lack of physicians and/or facilities stems from the inability of would-be patients to pay for services. This is a problem of poverty and insurance. As with other social insurance programs, this problem requires redistribution of resources from the more affluent to those in need.

If the disadvantaged were equally distributed throughout a city or a region, the uneven distribution of physicians would be less problematic. The geographic aspect of such shortages is related to the fact that many of the poor and needy live near each other, making it unprofitable for physicians to locate nearby. We have already considered supply possibilities regarding the location of physicians. Programs to provide income, and to pool risks for health insurance, may increase purchasing power for health care, and thus demand, such that more might be provided by physicians in a market setting.

CONCLUSIONS

This chapter has addressed several analytical issues in the training, pricing, and location of physicians. It is apparent that the long and arduous training procedures tend to reduce the responsiveness of physician supply to short-term changes in economic conditions. People can be trained to do simple procedures as nurses, assistants, or medics and, in many less developed countries, simple examinations are administered by nonphysicians with limited training. The lore of World War II, for example, is replete with

---

[15]Federal government policies and their effects on the geographic diffusion of physicians are analyzed by Foster and Gorr (1992).

examples of medics who were trained to do emergency battlefield medical procedures. The barriers to entry to the physician profession would lead one to expect higher than normal rates of return to physician training, and this is borne out in empirical studies.

Our discussion of physician pricing again suggests that physicians, like other entrepreneurs, respond to market signals. Given their monopoly power, and the inability of patients to resell medical care, the ability to discriminate among patients by price has long been a factor in the pricing of physician services. Insurers, in turn, have used their market power to negotiate charges for procedures. The relative power of the bargaining groups will depend on the underlying demand and cost (supply) conditions.

The location of physicians represents our final specialized discussion. We note that the agglomeration economies of cities can be quite appropriately applied to the health care sectors. There are cost-reduction benefits in being close to other providers. More specialized physicians have larger market areas and are hence located in larger urban areas.

Summary

1. Many professions require a considerable length of time in education and training. The time period for physicians is among the longest.

2. Medical education is heavily subsidized. Tuition is a relatively small source of revenues; thus, the student pays only a small portion of the true costs of the investment in education.

3. Medical education is a good example of joint production. Medical schools produce medical education, patient care, and research.

4. Immigration policy can be relaxed to admit more foreign medical school graduates (FMGs) during periods of perceived physician shortages, and vice versa during periods of surpluses. This happened during the 1960s, when preferential treatment was given to foreign national FMGs. Requirements were subsequently tightened in 1976, once shortages were no longer perceived.

5. Kessel argued that monopoly power was attained by organized medicine through (1) licensure of physicians, and (2) control of access to medical education.

6. According to an alternative view of medical education, the donor-preference hypothesis, medical school revenues come not so much from tuition paid by students, but from "donors," such as government agencies, alumni, businesses, and research organizations. For the most part, it is these donors who demand and control the output of medical schools: trained physicians.

7. Licensure is a prominent example of the controversy of self-interest versus public-interest views of regulation.

8. It is generally believed that licensure has given physicians economic rents. Licensure has not led to obvious improvements in quality and there are growing calls for reform of licensure laws.

9. The UCR payment mechanism uses fee screens. The fee screens are determined by the maximum of the doctor's median charge (i.e., usual charge) and the customary fees charged by the other physicians in the area.

10. Factors that influence profits, and thus the decision to accept assignment, include marginal cost, the private demand, and the reimbursement rate. With an increase in demand, for example, the physician is likely to supplant assigned patients (with their fixed reimbursement) for those patients who can pay more.

11. Relative value scales (RVSs) were originally developed by state medical societies and other organizations as guides in establishing physician fees and reimbursement rates. The weights under the resource-based RVS (RBRVS) introduced under Medicare's physician payment reforms are determined by the inputs needed to provide a procedure. These include time spent, intensity of time, practice costs, and costs for advanced training.

12. In regional economic analysis, physicians discover that it pays to specialize, to be close to other physicians, and to share facilities. That is, the output of physicians increases by a larger proportion than the number. One might recognize this specialization as the construction of laboratories, clinics, and hospitals.

13. Location theory predicts that the more specialized practitioners would locate in the biggest market areas, the large cities. It would follow that as more were trained there would be more competition, and that some would diffuse into the smaller cities and towns; this hypothesis is borne out empirically.

Discussion Questions

1. It is argued that imperfect capital markets constitute one reason for subsidizing medical education. Discuss why the market for human capital differs from, say, the market for housing capital (that is, buying a house).

2. If there were no subsidy for medical education, would classes be larger or smaller? Would the return to medical education be larger or smaller? If physician education were not subsidized, would the economically warranted supply of physicians tend to emerge?

3. What are the social benefits and costs behind regulating the number of medical schools?

4. What is joint production? What does the term *joint production costs* mean? Given that medical schools engage in joint production of education, patient care, and research, what inferences can be drawn about the economies of scope in producing these three outputs?

5. In contrast to medical education, there have been numerous night and part-time law schools established. Compare and contrast the various aspects of training that have led to these very different educational systems.

6. What is a participation agreement? What would encourage a physician to enter such an agreement?

7. Regional analysts refer to the gains from agglomeration of activities at central locations. Discuss such gains in the context of the provision of health services.

8. Suppose that an analyst determines that the number of physicians in Cleveland is decreasing, and the number in Atlanta is increasing, even though wages in Cleveland are higher than in Atlanta. How might the analyst explain this phenomenon?

9. The rate of return to investment in medical education exceeds that for other professions. What are arguments for and against government subsidies?

10. What is price discrimination? What conditions are necessary for price discrimination to exist? Are these conditions satisfied in the markets for professional care? What developments in recent decades have made price discrimination less prevalent?

Exercises

1. Using supply-and-demand analysis, model the equilibrium level of physicians' incomes. What would be the impact on physicians' incomes of more stringent policies on the employment of foreign medical school graduates?

2. Suppose that a medical school provides three outputs—patient care, education, and research—and that the total cost of the school was $10 million per year. If the school produced only education, its costs would be $6 million. If the school produced only patient care, its costs would be $3 million. If it produced only research, the costs would be $2 million. Joint costs for each pair would be $1 million.
   a. What are the pure costs of education, patient care, and research?
   b. What are the joint costs?

3. Suppose that in Figure 16.2 there is a cost-cutting technology improvement that would lower the marginal cost curve. How will this affect the likelihood that a physician not currently accepting assignment will accept assignment?

4. Suppose that the licensure requirements for health care providers were eliminated. Use supply and demand analysis to predict what may happen to the price and quantity of health care services. Are there other considerations—in particular, mechanisms—that could evolve to replace licensure?

C H A P T E R

17

Hospitals and Long-Term Care

- ■ Background And Overview of Hospitals

- ■ Hospital Utilization and Costs

- ■ Long-Term Care

- ■ Conclusions

In 1992, there were 6,066 hospitals with 1.14 million beds in the United States (Table 17.1). Hospital care dominates total health care spending and the hospital remains at the center of a rapidly changing health economy. At the same time, the aging of the population has created a major challenge for the adequate provision of long-term care. This chapter provides an overview of the hospital and long-term care sectors. It also examines several issues that have led to some surprising and controversial results. These issues include the "medical arms race" and cost shifting for hospitals, and various quality, demand, and cost themes in the nursing home literature. Other areas of study relating especially to hospitals but also to nursing homes are found in the next two chapters.

BACKGROUND AND OVERVIEW OF HOSPITALS[1]

It is often helpful to distinguish among the many hospitals by using four criteria: length of stay, type, ownership, and size. Hospitals are categorized as short stay (usually less than 30 days) or long term (usually over 30 days). The *community hospital* is the type with which the general public is most familiar. It consists of all nonfederal general

---

[1]More extensive discussions of many of the topics in this section are found in Starr (1982), Temin (1988), Jonas (1992), and Raffel and Raffel (1994).

TABLE 17.1   Short-Stay and Long-Term Hospital Data

	1970	*1980*	*1992*
All Hospitals (beds)	7,030 (1,599,229)	6,787 (1,346,228)	6,066 (1,135,350)
Short-Stay Hospitals (beds)	6,193 (935,724)	6,229 (1,080,164)	5,619 (996,112)
Federal	334 (87,492)	325 (88,144)	298 (73,370)
Nonfederal	5,859 (848,232)	5,904 (992,020)	5,321 (922,742)
Nonprofit	3,386 (591,937)	3,339 (692,929)	3,182 (656,355)
Proprietary	769 (52,739)	730 (87,033)	723 (98,760)
State-local government	1,704 (203,556)	1,835 (212,058)	1,416 (167,627)
Size			
6–199 beds	—	4,389 (358,282)	3,861 (325,317)
200–499 beds	—	1,466 (456,248)	1,421 (434,734)
500 or more beds	—	374 (265,634)	337 (236,061)
Occupancy Rate (percent)	77.9	75.6	66.2
Admissions (thousands)	30,706	38,140	32,640
Average Length of Stay (days)	8.7	7.8	7.4
Outpatient Visits (thousands)	173,058	255,320	408,507
Outpatient Surgeries (% of total)	—	16.4	53.6
Long-Term Hospitals (beds)	837 (663,505)	558 (266,064)	447 (139,238)
Federal	72 (73,260)	33 (28,433)	26 (17,220)
Nonfederal	662 (570,308)	515 (236,131)	418 (121,713)
Nonprofit	166 (21,530)	113 (16,683)	78 (9,545)
Proprietary	41 (3,500)	68 (7,233)	67 (5,442)
State-local government	418 (534,112)	326 (211,167)	257 (104,561)
Tuberculosis	103 (19,937)	10 (1,500)	3 (305)
Occupancy Rate (percent)	81.2	85.5	87.0

Numbers in parentheses are number of beds.

Source: U.S. DHHS, *Health United States 1994* (Tables 90, 108, and 109).

hospitals that provide acute, short-term care. Community hospitals employed 3.6 million personnel in 1993.

Many community hospitals are also teaching hospitals. These are hospitals that have residency programs approved by the Accreditation Council for Graduate Medical Education. Other hospital types are: mental, including those treating alcoholism and other chemical dependencies; tuberculosis and other respiratory diseases; and other special (e.g., maternity, orthopedic, and rehabilitation).

Hospital ownership can be private or public (federal, state, county, or local). The former category consists of either nonprofit or proprietary (for-profit) hospitals.

Table 17.1 indicates that there are 1,714 public short-stay hospitals, mainly state or local. Nonprofits dominate the remainder, accounting for about 81 percent of the nearly 4,000 short-stay nonpublic hospitals.

Most short-stay hospitals are relatively small with less than 200 beds. However, the categories consisting of hospitals that have over 200 beds account for 67 percent of all beds. The largest hospitals are usually affiliated with university medical schools and provide tertiary care in addition to primary and secondary care. Tertiary care consists of the most complex procedures such as organ transplant surgery and open heart procedures. The typical community hospital is limited to secondary care consisting of the more common surgical and medical procedures. Primary care consists of the kinds of preventive and curative care received by patients who are not hospitalized.

History

The history of hospitals dates back to the Egyptian and Greek periods. From that time, places of healing in many countries were organized by religious establishments. Illness was closely associated with a lack of faith or superstition and care was administered by priests. Even today, it is not unusual for the afflicted to believe that they are being punished or cursed and, in some parts of the world, shamans and other "medicine men" are called upon to exorcise evil spirits.

Early hospitals in the United States were associated with the poor or with mental and infectious diseases, and medicine was practiced mainly at the home. This picture changed as more effective surgery became possible following scientific and technological advances in the last half of the nineteenth century. The modern U.S. hospital emerged at the turn of the twentieth century. In particular, important advances in antisepsis to help fight off infections greatly increased the probability of surgical success. Major advances in anesthesia, anatomy, and physiology, and the invention of the X-ray were also important contributors.

Two nonscientific factors helped accelerate the process. One was the rapid pace of urbanization resulting from industrialization. Sophisticated hospitals could not be supported by rural areas because of transportation problems and low population densities. Urbanization also created health problems, such as outbreaks of infectious disease that were much less common in rural areas, and that required hospitalization. The second factor was a financial one. Early hospitals relied on philanthropic contributions or state and local government funds. These alone would have been inadequate to support the growing numbers and costs associated with the modern hospital. The rise of an urban middle class led to a greater ability to pay as well as third-party payment through private insurance and workers' compensation, which originated shortly after the turn of the century.

The opening of The John Hopkins Hospital in Baltimore in 1885 was a significant milestone. Though few other hospitals would ultimately be able to emulate or compete with its international reputation, The Johns Hopkins Hospital introduced the latest advances in medical technology and hospital design. Through its affiliation with The Johns Hopkins University, it became a model of the teaching and research hospital.

Organization

The typical nonprofit community hospital is governed by a board of trustees that selects the president and is responsible for approving most major decisions. The members of the board are often leading members of the community known for their ability to contribute or raise funds.[2] The president and other administrative staff are regular employees who manage the hospital.

A distinguishing feature of the hospital arises from claims that the hospital's decision-making power rests with the medical staff rather than the administrators or the board. To appreciate the significance of this phenomenon, consider that the medical staff in most hospitals is composed of admitting physicians who are not employees of the hospital. Physicians apply for staff privileges to admit patients and perform certain procedures. Because it is the physician who often has admitting privileges at many hospitals and who brings patients to the hospital, admitting physicians have considerable influence on hospital decision making by serving on many committees relating to hospital governance and patient care. Because of these arrangements, the hospital has been referred to as the physician's "rent-free workshop" where the physician can direct substantial resources for patient care but is not directly held accountable for those resources. The physician also bills separately for his or her services.

To deal with the conflicts and cost pressures created by the traditional system, more hospitals are now relying on permanent physician-employees who are paid salaries or combinations of salaries and bonuses, the latter driven by various incentives. As these staff physicians are no longer the driving force to admit patients, hospitals with permanent staff physicians must have other means to attract patients. The source of patients for such hospitals is often affiliation with or ownership of HMOs. Direct advertising through the broadcast or print media and purchases of physician practices are also becoming important sources of patients.

The hospital industry is going through a period of rapid change. As a result of declining inpatient utilization, many smaller hospitals have closed while others have merged or reorganized. Hospitals face considerable pressure to join networks of providers in order to participate in managed care plans and to become diversified health care centers with expanded primary care facilities. Many hospitals are concentrating resources on free-standing outpatient surgery units and other outpatient programs such as cardiac rehabilitation. Table 17.1 reveals the extent of these changes. Inpatient admissions in 1992 were substantially below the levels of 1980 and the occupancy rate fell to 66 percent. On the other hand, outpatient visits increased by 60 percent over the same period while outpatient surgeries increased to 54 percent of all hospital surgeries, from just 16 percent in 1980.

Despite this dramatic shift to outpatient care, it is likely that the pace of hospital closings will increase and that hospitals will continuously reorganize, especially as Medicare and Medicaid budgets tighten. Governments provide over 50 percent of hospital revenues, although this figure can go higher than 75 percent for many urban and

---

[2]These are evolving into boards with business backgrounds. Also the roles of boards have been changing as they become more concerned with community health in managed care settings.

small hospitals that rely heavily on poor and elderly patients. Proposals to reform Medicare and Medicaid tend also to be directed at reducing the federal deficit and invariably include reductions in hospital reimbursement rates. Thus, hospitals that disproportionately depend on Medicare and Medicaid are especially vulnerable.

Nevertheless, in an increasingly competitive, cost-conscious environment, all hospitals are under considerable pressure to respond quickly to new incentives and opportunities. For example, one legislative proposal developed in 1995 creates opportunities that would enable hospitals to form networks that could bypass insurance companies completely by selling Medicare plans directly to beneficiaries.

Regulation and Accreditation

Hospitals are subject to a wide variety of state and federal regulations designed to deal with quality, costs, and reimbursement. They are licensed at the state level, although licensure is often focused on the adequacy of the hospital's physical plant and other inputs. Hospitals have their own quality assurance programs but, of greater policy significance, Professional Standards Review Organizations (PSROs) were established in 1971 under federal legislation to monitor quality while limiting utilization. After considerable controversy regarding their effectiveness, these agencies were replaced in 1984 by Peer Review Organizations (PROs). PROs are awarded contracts by the Health Care Financing Administration (HCFA) to perform case-by-case peer review and to monitor Medicare utilization in hospitals and other facilities. Because PROs are often dominated by physicians and hospitals, the impact of PROs has been questioned. In the mid-1990s, HCFA adopted the position that case-by-case inspection brings only marginal improvements in quality. As a result, PROs' funding and responsibilities were substantially reduced.

Hospitals are also subject to numerous other regulations and requirements. Many of these relate to reimbursement such as Medicare's Prospective Payments System (PPS) and various forms of state rate regulation. Certificate-of-need (CON) laws have been used to limit capital spending and hospitals are subject to antitrust laws intended to promote competition. Given their importance, the next chapter is devoted entirely to these regulatory measures.

In addition to meeting licensure and regulatory requirements, most hospitals and many other health care facilities seek accreditation from the Joint Commission on the Accreditation of Healthcare Organizations (JCAHO). The JCAHO is a private not-for-profit organization that was founded in 1952 and has a board dominated by representatives from physician and hospital associations. Its goal is to set standards for patient safety and quality of care. Hospitals seeking accreditation are evaluated by a visitation team, which examines hospital compliance with JCAHO standards. To maintain accreditation, the hospital must undergo an on-site review every three years. A recent survey of 300 hospital CEOs found that 59 percent indicated that hospitals should seek accreditation to validate and measure quality and safety; 25 percent indicated that they seek accreditation to improve quality.[3]

---

[3]*American Hospital Association, AHA News,* September 25, 1995.

Many third-party payers reimburse only for care provided in accredited hospitals. Though hospitals can be evaluated by federal inspectors to qualify for Medicare and Medicaid reimbursement, JCAHO accreditation also satisfies the federal requirement. As a result of the importance of JCAHO accreditation and concerns about the accreditation process, the JCAHO has been described as "one of the most powerful and secretive groups in all of health care."[4] The potential for conflict between professional self-interests and public interests is evident. The influence of the JCAHO can be used to limit hospital competition and to protect physicians against other groups of providers by denying them access to hospitals or influence within hospitals. An example of the former emerged in one antitrust case in which osteopathic doctors successfully sued a hospital over discrimination in the awarding of staff privileges.[5]

HOSPITAL UTILIZATION AND COSTS

The relentless and rapid growth of hospital costs has served as the impetus for many forms of regulation and other policy initiatives. Table 17.2 shows the extent of the increases in total hospital costs as well as costs per day and costs per admission. Hospital costs account for 40 percent of total health expenditures and have increased at an annual rate of 11.4 percent since 1960. Table 17.2 also shows that a minimal and dwindling share has been paid out-of-pocket, especially after Medicare and Medicaid were introduced in 1965. Governments now pay for over one-half of all hospital costs.

The increase in costs is not the result of more inpatient admissions despite a growing and aging population. As previously noted in Table 17.1, the number of hospital beds and occupancy rates have actually been declining. Rather, the cost per day and cost per admission and the shift to outpatient services (leaving hospitals with high fixed costs) are the main driving forces. The influence of these determinants of hospital costs is closely intertwined with numerous features of health care markets including changes in technology and reimbursement methods. These issues and many others relating to hospital costs and health system reform are developed in other chapters. In this section, we address two of the many other concerns relevant to the growth of hospital costs. The first concerns the effect of competition on costs and the second deals with cost shifting.

Competition and Costs

Is hospital competition inefficient and has it led to, as many analysts contend, an unproductive and costly medical arms race (MAR)? Intuitively it would appear that having a larger number of hospitals in a given market would lead to unnecessary duplication of expensive capital equipment and unnecessary expenditures on advertising in order to attract doctors and their patients. It may also create pressure to fill beds through questionable admissions.

---

[4]"Prized by Hospitals, Accreditation Hides Perils Patients Face," *The Wall Street Journal,* October 12, 1988, p. 1.
[5]*Weiss* v. *New York Hospital,* 745 F.2d 786, 814 (3rd Cir. 1984).

TABLE 17.2 Hospital and Nursing Home Costs				
	1960	*1970*	*1980*	*1993*
Health Care Spending ($ billion)	27.1	74.3	251.1	884.2
Hospital Care ($ billion)	9.3	28.0	102.7	326.6
% of total spending	34.3	37.7	40.9	36.9
Percent of Hospital Care Paid by				
Out-of-pocket	20.7	9.0	5.2	2.8
Private health insurance and other private	36.8	37.5	42.6	41.3
Government	42.5	53.5	52.3	56.0
Average Cost ($)				
Per day	—	74	245	881
Per stay	—	605	1,851	6,132
Nursing Home Care ($ billion)	1.0	4.9	20.5	69.6
% of total spending	3.7	6.6	8.2	7.9
Percent of Nursing Home Care Paid by				
Out-of-pocket	80.0	48.1	38.3	33.0
Private health insurance and other private	6.4	5.2	4.2	4.4
Government	13.6	46.6	57.6	62.6

Sources: U.S. DHHS, *Health United States 1994* (Table 125) and *Statistical Abstract of the United States 1995* (Table 186).

Such concerns with the potential adverse consequences of hospital competition are interesting and unique. With the exception of natural monopolies, resulting from economies of scale, economists usually endorse competition as being in the best interests of consumers. There is substantial evidence that higher levels of seller concentration in most markets lead to higher prices and reduced choices. Indeed, this is the premise behind federal and state antitrust laws, though the relevance of these laws to the hospital sector has also been questioned by those who support the MAR hypothesis.

Are there any features of the hospital industry that might negate the conventional wisdom? With hospitals enjoying only limited economies of scale (Chapter 13), the economies of scale justification is not well supported. Instead hospital reimbursement methods probably hold the key. Traditionally, hospitals were reimbursed by third parties on a retrospective cost basis. Higher costs generally meant higher payments to hospitals. Unlike other industries, where sellers must compete on the basis of price for customers, retrospective reimbursement meant that hospitals were largely immune from the discipline exerted by the competitive process.

FEATURE

Game Theory and the Medical Arms Race (MAR)

Game theory is a powerful analytical tool that is being used increasingly in economics and other disciplines. The theory of games can be used to show why it may be in the best interests for each hospital to engage in a MAR even when hospitals as a whole are negatively affected. Game theory begins with a payoff matrix of the type shown in Figure 17.1. Suppose there are two large hospitals, A and B, in a market, each facing the decision of whether or not to add an expensive heart transplant unit without knowing what its rival will do. The payoff matrix shows the total profit for each hospital (with values for A's profit shown first) resulting from the four combinations of strategies. For example, if both adopt (the "northwest" cell), each hospital will have a total profit of $100 (million). If A alone adopts (the "northeast" cell), assume that it will have a significant advantage resulting in a profit of $200, while B loses $50.

Game theory tries to predict a solution, that is, the strategy chosen by each participant. It is clear that both hospitals with a combined profit of $300 will be better off if neither introduces the unit. However, if the hospitals cannot agree (for example, they may not trust each other or they may believe that antitrust laws preclude cooperation), game theory predicts a solution in which each hospital will adopt the unit and combined profits will be $200. Why? Given the payoff matrix, each hospital has a dominant strategy. That is, regardless of what Hospital B does, A will always have a higher profit by adopting rather than not adopting, that is, $100 versus –$50 if B adopts and $200 versus $100 if B does not adopt. Similarly B's dominant strategy is to adopt and, hence, a scenario results consistent with the MAR hypothesis.[6] In addition to decisions involving the acquisition of technology and introduction of new services, game theory can provide insight into hospital advertising and other forms of nonprice competition.

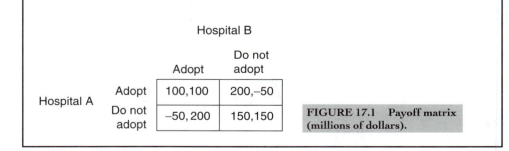

FIGURE 17.1 Payoff matrix (millions of dollars).

		Hospital B	
		Adopt	Do not adopt
Hospital A	Adopt	100, 100	200, –50
	Do not adopt	–50, 200	150, 150

---

[6]Students of game theory will recognize this as an example of the prisoner's dilemma and the solution as a Nash equilibrium. See McKay (1994) for other health care applications.

This situation has changed in recent years. Hospitals as well as insurance companies must compete for their managed care business through price and quality. Hospitals are also now reimbursed by many major third-party payers on a prospective basis at rates that are independent of their actual costs. It would thus appear that hospitals have a strong financial stake in being efficient and in avoiding capital investments that are not profitable.

Economists have begun to look at the MAR hypothesis in this increasingly competitive environment. Dranove and colleagues (1992) developed and estimated a theoretical model of the number of specialized hospital services in a market. They found that increased competition increases the number of services offered, but the MAR effect is dominated by economies of scale and scope as well as other demand and supply considerations.

Mobley and Frech (1994) also provide insight into the role of competition, although they do not directly deal with the MAR hypothesis. In their study of California hospitals over the 1980s, the authors found that demand is an important determinant of growth and survival and that increased competition forces smaller, low-quality hospitals to exit.

Hospital Cost Shifting

Hospitals provide substantial amounts of uncompensated care.[7] Most of this care is provided to uninsured indigents, but uncollectibles from incompletely insured patients are also considerable. In addition, many third-party payers place stringent limits on reimbursement rates, and proposals to reduce Medicare and Medicaid expenditures typically call for further reductions. After an initial period of generous payments under PPS, by 1993 Medicare paid only 89 percent of hospitals' costs to treat its patients, compared to 93 percent for Medicaid and 129 percent for private patients.[8]

A vital policy issue is whether or not the costs of uncompensated care and "discounts" to some third-party payers are passed on by hospitals to other patients as is often claimed. Thus, if Medicare and Medicaid cuts are passed on to others, there would be no savings to society but merely a shifting of the hospital cost burden. The burden would be similarly shifted, if the number of uninsured or poorly insured increases because of an increase in part-time employment in the services sector and cutbacks in fringe benefits by some employers.

Intuition suggests that these costs are shifted. After all, services must be paid for and it stands to reason that the burden for those who are not paying must be picked up by others. However, the issue may not be as simple as it first appears. To see why, we develop a model of hospital fee determination.

A variety of models of hospital behavior is examined in Chapter 18 but, for simplicity, assume that hospitals maximize profits (or the undistributed residual in the case

---

[7]There are many legal and ethical reasons why hospitals provide uncompensated care. A good review is found in Duncan (1992).

[8]Prospective Payment Assessment Commission (1995, Table 1–8).

of nonprofits). Suppose also for simplicity that there are just two groups of patients: private (insured or self-pay) and Medicare. The downward sloping demand curve for the private sector and the constant Medicare hospital reimbursement rate (R_1) per patient are shown in Figure 17.2. The private demand curve (panel A) is negatively sloped because at least some patients economize or substitute other services as their out-of-pocket obligations increase, and hospitals that raise fees lose patients to other hospitals. Assume further that R_1 covers the average variable cost (C_1) for a fixed number of Medicare patients seeking admission (i.e., Q_2 Medicare patients in panel B) but that the rate does not necessarily cover all costs. Finally, assume that the hospital is operating below capacity and that C_1 is constant over the relevant range and equal to marginal cost.[9]

If the hospital is unable to price discriminate in the private sector, it will accept Q_1 private patients (the quantity where marginal revenue equals marginal cost) and charge the price P_1.[10] It will also accept all Medicare patients (Q_2) at the

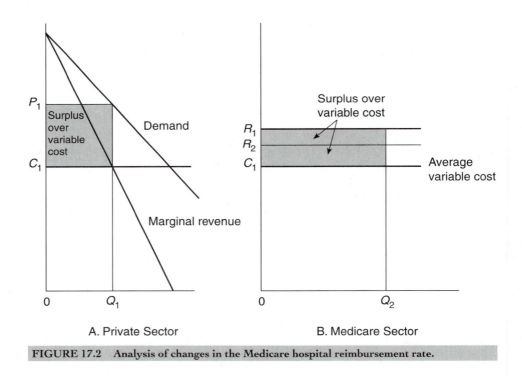

FIGURE 17.2   **Analysis of changes in the Medicare hospital reimbursement rate.**

---

[9]With considerable excess capacity in the U.S. hospital industry, this assumption is plausible. It is made only for convenience and does not affect the results.

[10]Ideally, the hospital would like to perfectly price discriminate by charging each private patient the highest he or she is willing to pay. In this ideal case, it will admit private patients up to the intersection of the demand curve and cost curves in panel A with prices to some patients falling as low as C_1. The hospital will then capture the entire consumers' surplus consisting of the area under the demand curve and above the cost curve.

Medicare rate[11] so that the hospital treats a total of $(Q_1 + Q_2)$ patients. Total revenues of $(P_1Q_1 + R_1Q_2)$ produce a surplus over variable cost equal to $(P_1 - C_1)Q_1 + (R_1 - C_1)Q_2$.

Suppose that the Medicare reimbursement rate is lowered to R_2 but that the rate still covers the average variable and marginal costs so that the hospital continues to accept Q_2 Medicare patients. Contrary to intuition, it makes no sense to increase price in the private sector. Hospital surpluses diminish at prices above P_1 because it will lose private sector patients whose marginal revenue exceeds marginal cost. The optimal private rate remains at P_1 for the Q_1 private patients and there is no cost shifting.[12]

But this is not the end of the story because the hospital's revenues are reduced. In the long run, revenues must cover all costs; otherwise the hospital could not survive. If revenues exceed costs for the hospital in Figure 17.2 after the lower Medicare rate, then there may be no effect on the private rate in the long run as well. Suppose, however, that the hospital's revenues now fall short of total costs. If it cannot reduce costs, the hospital and others in the same situation may be forced out of business or forced to merge. As this happens, demand will increase for the remaining hospitals and, as a result, the private rate could also rise.

Determining the burden of lower public reimbursement is thus quite complex. The burden can ultimately be borne by many groups through reductions in the number of hospitals, lower compensation to hospital employees as the demand for their services diminishes, reduced access to care for those with public insurance or those receiving uncompensated care, and higher fees to the private paying groups.

A review of the limited evidence on cost shifting by Morrisey (1995) indicates that cost shifting through higher prices has taken place but that it is far from complete. One study included in his review shows that California hospitals reduced the amount of uncompensated care by 53 cents for every $1 decrease in their discounts to third parties. This would have been unnecessary if the hospitals could have shifted the costs to others. Other studies showed partial cost shifting through higher fees.

LONG-TERM CARE

The rapid growth of the elderly population in many countries has led to considerable interest in the problems associated with long-term care. Long-term care encompasses a wide variety of services and arrangements used to care for the elderly and others with serious functional impairments. There are several types of long-term hospitals (Table 17.1), although the number of hospitals and patients has markedly declined since 1970.

In this section, we concentrate on the nursing home rather than attempt to examine also other arrangements such as home care or day care. Numerous economic issues

---

[11]With capacity limitations, it will first raise the price to eliminate those private patients whose marginal revenue is below the Medicare rate.

[12]Cost shifting could certainly arise if the hospital was not previously maximizing profit and accepting "unprofitable" patients whose marginal revenue fell short of marginal cost. The lower Medicare rate would encourage the hospital to reduce the number of these patients by raising the private rate.

have been investigated in the nursing home literature. Following some background information, we will focus on issues involving quality, cost shifting, and financing the care.

Background and Costs

Traditionally, the elderly were cared for until death by their families. Hence, the nursing home is a relatively recent phenomenon. Raffel and Raffel (1994) trace its origins. The first "nursing homes" in the United States were the county poorhouses of the eighteenth and nineteenth centuries established for invalids and those without families. Most of the patients were elderly and the conditions were dreadful. Other state and local facilities evolved and some, usually with higher standards, were sponsored by religious and fraternal groups. The Social Security Act of 1935 provided funds for patients in private nursing homes but the major increase in funding and nursing industry growth came after the passage of Medicare and Medicaid in 1965.

In 1960, nursing home care amounted to just $1.0 billion with 80 percent coming out-of-pocket (Table 17.2). Just 15 years later in 1975, spending reached $10 billion with Medicaid's share at 48 percent and only 42 percent coming out-of-pocket. By 1993, spending had grown to $69.6 billion with Medicaid contributing 52 percent (another 9 percent came from Medicare) and patients or their families paying just 33 percent. Between 1963 and 1991, the nursing home population grew from 491,000 to 1.73 million. About 75 percent of the beds are in for-profit facilities.

As suggested by these data, the burgeoning nursing home population and growth of costs are closely connected to Medicare and Medicaid. Medicare typically covers beneficiaries who are discharged from a hospital and require skilled nursing care to help recover from an acute illness. A skilled nursing facility (SNF) provides round-the-clock nursing care and close medical supervision. Medicaid, on the other hand, pays for the long-term care of the poor including the nonelderly as well as the elderly.[13] It covers both skilled nursing care and intermediate (custodial) care. Many nursing homes provide both types of care.

A 1987 legislative change created new standards that drove costs higher. All nursing homes participating in federal programs, including Medicaid-only facilities, must now meet the same standards as Medicare SNFs. Also nursing homes participating in federal programs must evaluate each resident's needs and "provide services and activities to attain or maintain the 'highest practicable level' of function (physical, mental, and psychosocial well-being)."[14] These requirements led to large increases in staffing and the use of rehabilitation services.

Quality of Care

Despite increasingly stringent state and federal requirements, the issue of quality is undoubtedly the one with which the public is most concerned. To many, nursing homes evoke powerful images of neglected and poorly treated patients. It is thus natural that

---

[13]Medicaid is administered by the states subject to federal requirements so that the eligibility requirements can vary across the states. Generally, individuals must have minimal assets or have depleted their assets before qualifying.

[14]*Health Care Financing Review,* Medicare and Medicaid Supplement, 1995, p. 84.

health economists and other scholars have concentrated their efforts on nursing home quality.

As we have seen from those chapters that deal with quality issues, the researcher must deal with the formidable challenge of defining and measuring quality. Regulatory standards for nursing homes tend to focus on *structure,* that is, the quantity and categories of inputs used to provide care, rather than on evaluating how the care is delivered (*process*) or on outcome indicators such as patients' satisfaction or their quality of life.

It follows that the most comprehensive and readily available information on nursing homes and other health care institutions is in the form of input data—their types and costs. Scholars have used these data to examine the relationship between quality and nursing home size, ownership, expenditures, and source of payment.[15]

One would expect, other factors held constant, that there would be some positive association between size and quality as a result of economies of scale and scope. If such economies occur over some range of output, larger institutions would be able to provide the same quality of care at a lower cost, or a higher quality for a given level of spending per patient. Davis's (1991) review of a large number of studies including those that used process and structure measures of quality suggests that there is no clear relationship.

A more important issue involves quality and cost or expenditure per patient. Do "you get what you pay for" in nursing care? Using structure measures of quality, not surprisingly, most analysts find a positive relationship, but these results are not meaningful unless they are supported by studies using process or outcome measures. (If inputs represent quality, one expects a close relationship between various measures of input and quality.) Of the 18 process and outcome studies included in Davis's review of the literature, only 6 indicate a positive relationship between quality and cost or inputs, while the results in 11 are insignificant (one is negative). The failure to consistently find positive relationships is troubling. It indicates that improvements are needed in measuring quality as well as in formulating the statistical models used to estimate the relationships.

A third area of interest is in the relationship between type of ownership and quality. The next chapter will discuss further the concept of contract failure within the context of nursing homes. Put simply, contract failure arises when quality is not easily observable. In the case of nursing homes, the patient may believe that nonprofit organizations are more likely to serve his or her interests than one motivated by profits. Is this view justified by the evidence? Nursing home costs per patient are higher for nonprofits so that structure measures are clear on this point. However, since analysts have not been able to detect an unambiguous positive relationship between quality and costs, it follows that they would have great difficulty in detecting any relationship between type of ownership and process or outcome measures of quality. Davis's review confirms this conclusion.

Finally, Davis also reviews the literature on quality and the proportion of public pay (Medicaid) patients. There are wide perceptions that nursing homes dominated by Medicaid patients are inferior. Expenditures per resident are lower in homes with

---

[15]The 1987 requirements are also creating a valuable source of information through the instruments used to collect the resident assessment data. See Zimmerman et al. (1995) for use of these data to test nursing home quality.

higher proportions of Medicaid patients so that structure measures unequivocally support a negative relationship between quality and the proportion of Medicaid residents in a nursing home. However, with few studies that have used process or outcome measures, further work is needed to help settle the issue.

Excess Demand

It has been widely held for many years that the nursing home industry is characterized by excess demand and that this excess demand is one of the reasons for the allegedly inferior quality of care provided to public pay patients. Economists are naturally intrigued by, and at the same time skeptical of, claims of persistent shortages of any commodity. Put simply, they believe that prices or supply will increase to eliminate the excess demand. On the other hand, Chapter 15 explored the same idea within the context of shortages of nurses, and several possibilities that could explain the claim of persistent nursing shortages were examined.

To examine the possibility of excess demand for nursing home care, Figure 17.3 shows the demand and cost conditions for a representative nursing home.[16] The demand curve reflects only the private demand (self-pay or insured), while R_1 represents the Medicaid reimbursement rate. The segment AC along R_1 shows the number of Medicaid patients seeking admission. For simplicity, assume a constant (horizontal) marginal and average variable cost (C_1) up to the capacity level (Q_C patients) where it becomes vertical.

Under the conditions represented here, the profit-maximizing nursing home will first select all private patients whose marginal revenue exceeds R_1 and then fill

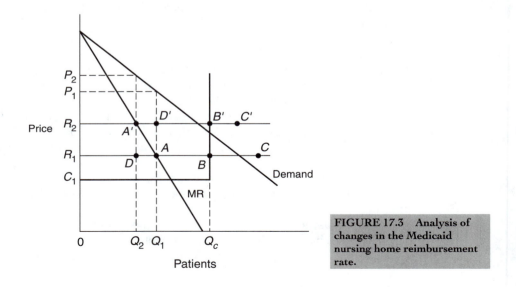

FIGURE 17.3   Analysis of changes in the Medicaid nursing home reimbursement rate.

---

[16]The model is a variant of one developed by Scanlon (1980).

the remainder of beds with Medicaid patients. The nursing home admits R_1A private patients paying a price P_1 and AB Medicaid patients, leaving an excess demand of BC Medicaid patients.

The shortage can be reduced or even eliminated by raising the Medicaid rate. At R_2, nursing homes will raise the private fee to P_2 and substitute $A'D'$ Medicaid for AD private patients. The excess demand is reduced to $B'C'$ from BC.[17] Conversely, reductions in the Medicaid rate will lower Medicaid admissions and the private fee but increase the excess demand. Similarly, an increase in private demand resulting from higher incomes or more prevalent private long-term insurance will reduce Medicaid admissions and increase the excess demand.

There is one additional aspect to consider. If the nursing home industry is profitable, and evidence suggests that it is, one would expect entry to reduce the excess demand. However, nursing homes are also subject to Certificate-of-Need (CON) and it has been argued that legislators have intentionally used CON and other restrictions to limit nursing home entry as a way of limiting Medicaid spending.[18] There is a similar theme of legislative aversion to policies that would raise the Medicaid rate which, as shown earlier, increase public spending while squeezing out private patients.

Various tests have been proposed to test the shortage hypothesis. For example, in our model, changes in reimbursement rates do not affect total utilization, just the composition between private and Medicaid patients. Any new beds are more likely to be filled by Medicaid than by private patients because that is the population for which there is excess demand. Using national data for 1969 and 1973, Scanlon's (1980) empirical tests indicate considerable excess demand for Medicaid patients. However, there may be wide variation among states in their willingness to fund public patients as well as changes that have taken place in more recent years that may have reduced the shortages. For example, Nyman's (1993) estimates for 1988 for Minnesota, Oregon, and Wisconsin generally do not support the shortage hypothesis.

Financing Long-Term Care

The continuous growth of the population that will need nursing home care, the requirement that patients must meet income and asset tests to qualify for Medicaid, and the budgetary problems created by the growth of Medicaid spending have led to many proposals to reform Medicaid. The need to deplete one's assets is especially irksome to the middle class. The sore point is that after paying a lifetime of taxes to support Medicaid and other welfare programs, one has to become poor ("spend down") to qualify for Medicaid. As a result, a variety of proposals has been introduced to help resolve this contentious issue. These range from proposals allowing individuals to have higher incomes and retain a higher proportion of their wealth to qualify for public assistance, to proposals which would cover everyone who meets certain medical requirements.

---

[17]The rate that would eliminate the Medicaid excess demand is found by sliding the segment $A'C'$ further up the marginal revenue curve until the quantities such as $B'C'$ are eliminated. Clearly the rate must be above R_2.

[18]CON was federally mandated until 1987 and then left to the states, many of which have retained some form of CON.

Short and Kemper (1994) estimate the effects of a variety of plans. The least costly are proposals that create a front-end entitlement covering everyone for a limited period, for example, three to six months of care. Back-end entitlements that cover everyone after a certain waiting period of, say, one or two years of nursing home care are more costly. The most expensive are proposals without limitations even if they have cost-sharing provisions. Short and Kemper estimate that full entitlement with a 30 percent coinsurance rate would increase overall nursing home expenditures by nearly 20 percent and public expenditures by about 80 percent (due to the overall increase in utilization and the substitution of public spending for private spending).

The alternative to greater public spending, especially in an era where many government programs are being downsized, is a strategy to encourage more private long-term coverage. The market for such insurance is growing and subsidies or tax incentives could be used to encourage further growth. Allowing for tax-deductible contributions to long-term care accounts, similar to retirement plans, is one of the ideas that has been advanced.

CONCLUSIONS

Following a discussion of the history and organization of hospitals and hospital costs, we examined two economic and policy issues—the medical arms race hypothesis and cost shifting. Careful analysis indicates that both issues are far more complex than they first appear. The existing literature confirms this analysis by indicating that the common perceptions of a wasteful MAR and complete cost shifting do not accurately represent how hospital markets function.

We also examined the long-term care sector focusing on nursing homes. Three issues are emphasized: quality, especially for Medicaid patients; shortages; and financing nursing home care. We found that economic theory and empirical evidence can provide useful and sometimes surprising results. For example, there is no clear relationship between costs and quality. It is also possible to have a persistent shortage of nursing home beds without any mechanism, such as price, that would alleviate the shortage.

Chapters 18 and 19 continue with a comparison of the behavior of profit and nonprofit institutions and regulation of hospitals. There are also many other topics that could not be accommodated in this text but are found in a growing interdisciplinary literature on hospitals and long-term care.

Summary

1. The modern hospital evolved at the turn of the twentieth century following the invention of the X-ray and significant advances in antisepsis, anesthesia, and the biological sciences.
2. Hospital spending has grown rapidly in recent decades as a result of the growth of private and public insurance and other factors. It accounts for about 40 percent of health expenditures.

3. The hospital industry is experiencing rapid change including reductions in the number of hospital beds and inpatient utilization and significant growth of outpatient services. There is competitive pressure on hospitals to further diversify and to introduce or participate in managed care arrangements.

4. Hospitals are licensed and subject to a wide range of state and federal regulation.

5. Many analysts believe that the hospital industry is in a medical arms race resulting in unnecessary duplication of expensive technology. The limited empirical evidence does not support this view.

6. Intuitive reasoning suggests that the costs of discounts or uncompensated care to some patient groups must be passed on to other paying groups. More formal analysis leads to a richer set of results including situations where costs cannot be shifted. The empirical literature indicates that cost shifting is far from complete.

7. The nursing home population has grown dramatically since the introduction of Medicare and Medicaid. Governments pay over 60 percent of all nursing home costs.

8. Nursing home quality has been examined through structure, process, and outcome indicators. Surprisingly, there is no conclusive evidence relating cost to quality or supporting the view that nursing homes with higher proportions of Medicaid patients produce lower-quality care.

9. A familiar theme in the nursing home literature is one of persistent excess demand by Medicaid patients. A model of chronic excess demand is plausible, although recent evidence indicates that excess demand is not a universal phenomenon.

10. Financing the growing nursing home population is a great social challenge. Many proposals would reduce the need for patients to "spend down" their assets to qualify for public coverage.

Discussion Questions

1. Explain why it is often claimed that hospitals compete for doctors rather than patients. What are some of the implications of this phenomenon assuming that it is true?

2. Even not-for-profit hospitals must earn a "profit." Evaluate this statement.

3. What is the medical arms race (MAR) hypothesis? What features of hospital markets make the presence of an unproductive MAR possible?

4. Suppose that the Medicare rate of hospital reimbursement is reduced. Explain why the costs may not be shifted to other patients in the short run. Under what circumstances will the costs for other patients actually be reduced?

5. How can the JCAHO limit competition?

6. Hospital costs have grown following growth of private and public insurance. Describe other factors that could account for some of the growth.

7. Explain how excess demand for nursing home beds may persist over long periods of time. How can the hypothesis be tested?

8. Nonprofits are dominant in the hospital industry while for-profits dominate the nursing home industry. Develop some possible explanations for this difference.

Exercises

1. What is a dominant strategy in game theory? Using Figure 17.1, replace the entry in the first row and second column with (125, –50). Does A have a dominant strategy? Does B? What is the solution to this game?

2. Assume that there are three groups of hospital patients (instead of two as shown in Figure 17.2): private, Medicare, and Medicaid (which has a lower fixed rate of reimbursement than Medicare). Explain how a hospital would select patients in order to maximize profits.

3. Suppose that the Medicaid reimbursement rate does not cover the variable costs of patient care. Will a profit-maximizing hospital accept Medicaid patients? If not, under what circumstances will the hospital accept such patients?

CHAPTER

The Role of Nonprofit Firms

18

- ■ An Introduction to Nonprofits
- ■ Why Nonprofits Exist and Why They Are Prevalent in Health Care
- ■ Models of Nonprofit Hospital Behavior
- ■ The Relative Efficiency of Nonprofits Versus For-Profits
- ■ Conclusions

Nonprofit firms account for less than 5 percent of the GDP, but they make up a significant portion of the health care sector. They care for 70 percent of all inpatient cases in acute care hospitals, and for half of the market for inpatient specialty mental health treatment and substance abuse treatment. Frank and Salkever (1994) note that for 1989 health sector nonprofits earned $191.4 billion in revenues. This was 31.8 percent of total U.S. health spending for that year.

Inasmuch as nonprofits are prominent in health care, especially in the important hospital industry, they pose questions of considerable interest. Will the economic behavior of nonprofits be distinctly different from that of the more common for-profit firm or from government enterprise? A growing literature on nonprofits addresses such questions and adds to our understanding of many health-related firms. Studies within the field of health economics are also important, and they share our focus on health care institutions.

AN INTRODUCTION TO NONPROFITS

What is the nonprofit firm? People commonly presume that nonprofits are firms organized to provide some charitable good or community service and that they obtain their incomes significantly from donations. While it is true that several fit this category, such a definition does not serve well conceptually, nor does it make an important economic distinction. On one hand, many profit-making firms provide important services to the community, and many provide basic goods such as food and housing to the poor. On the other hand, many nonprofit firms serve the well-to-do, many serve in competition with for-profits, and many obtain nearly the lion's share of their revenues from the sale of goods and services. To the present point, health care nonprofits obtain over 90 percent of their revenues from the revenue category called sales and receipts.

In economic terms, the most important distinction of the nonprofit firm is the *nondistribution constraint*. This concept means that the laws either explicitly or implicitly allow no one a legal claim on the nonprofit's residual. Residual, in this sense, means the difference between the nonprofit's revenues and its costs, or what an ordinary firm would call its profits. Since there is no residual claimant, there is a possibility that the nonprofit's objectives will differ from profit making. Two secondary distinctions between nonprofits and for-profits are also consequential. First, nonprofits are exempt from corporate income taxes and often from property and sales taxes. Second, donations to nonprofits receive favorable tax treatment. These three distinctions make the nonprofit a potentially different economic entity.[1]

WHY NONPROFITS EXIST AND WHY THEY ARE PREVALENT IN HEALTH CARE

In a country like the United States, there are essentially three different types of firms: private profit-making enterprises; government enterprises; and voluntary nonprofit enterprises. Why do each of these types of firms exist? To trivialize the answer to this question, these firms exist because our laws have specified their existence. But in a deeper sense, society's economic institutions are not created at random; they must reflect some basic economic incentives, some unmet economic needs that these firms and the laws accommodating them were created to satisfy.

Nonprofits as Providers of Unmet Demands for Public Goods

Burton Weisbrod (1975) has formulated a noteworthy account of the existence of nonprofits, and his analysis guides the following exposition. In the United States and other Western economies, a natural presumption favors for-profit competitive enterprises. Economists learn that a perfectly competitive industry under certain circumstances is economically efficient, and they often presume that profit incentives foster growth. Government enterprises, under this account, are needed only in cases where competitive markets fail. As this theory further unfolds, nonprofits in turn are needed in cases where government enterprise also fails. It is useful to begin by reviewing the standard explanation for the role of government enterprise, and then to introduce Weisbrod's explanation of the unsatisfied demands that nonprofit firms may help to meet.

---

[1]For further discussion on the nature of nonprofit firms, see Weisbrod (1988).

Under the standard economic explanation, government enterprise might possibly—though it need not necessarily—have a role in improving market efficiency in cases where competitive markets tend to fail. The most prominent cases of market failure involve public goods and externalities. Two examples will enlighten this issue.

MARKET FAILURE: EXTERNALITIES

Most consumer goods entail private benefits and zero, or at least insignificant, externalities. An externality is an uncompensated direct effect of the production or consumption of a good on persons other than the producers or consumers. Consider a good with no externality. When one enjoys a hamburger at a local fast-food restaurant, the pleasure is primarily private, and the benefit goes to the one who consumes. There is likely no effect on parties external to the market—that is, to parties other than the producer or consumer. However, consider the case where one purchases a vaccination for influenza. This good entails a private benefit to be sure: The purchaser will less likely suffer from influenza. In addition, however, there is an external benefit to others because the purchaser will less likely be a carrier of the disease and is less likely to infect others.

Free markets will tend to underproduce goods for which there exist significant external benefits. This economic reasoning takes the following pattern: The purchaser of the vaccination will tend to consider primarily the private benefits and will ignore the external benefits to the community. The benefit to society is the sum of the private benefits and the external benefits to the community. Since demand will represent only the private benefits, it will understate society's benefits and give a false or inadequate signal to the market. The market then produces less than the amount that would maximize net social benefits. This is economically inefficient, and we call this situation a case of market failure.

Generally economists on all sides of the political spectrum recognize the existence of such externalities—both the beneficial and detrimental kinds—but they argue over their relative importance and the appropriate remedy. The existence of an externality of significant size raises the possibility of a role for government. This is only a possibility because the inefficiencies entailed in governmental activity may more than cancel the potential gains. If we recognize that markets may fail, we must recognize that governments too may fail to act efficiently. The mainstream Western approach, however, usually recognizes that in some cases governmental activity will improve the net benefits to society.

MARKET FAILURE: PUBLIC GOODS

The vaccination is a private good with an external benefit. The external benefit of this good itself entails certain public good aspects. To understand this fully, let us first introduce the case of a pure public good. A public good in economics is defined as a good that is both nonexcludable and nonrival. *Nonexcludable* means that people cannot be economically excluded from consuming the good even if they refuse to pay for it. *Nonrival* means that one person can consume the good without depleting it for others. Our hamburger is an example of a private good, not a public good. The hamburger is excludable because McDonald's can easily refuse the hamburger to someone who refuses to pay. Likewise, the hamburger is a rival good, because the act of one person consuming the burger causes it to be depleted; it is eaten up.

Contrast the hamburger with a classic, though occasionally disputed, example of a pure public good: national defense. Imagine an antimissile system that effectively puts a defensive umbrella over a country. This defense system would be nonexcludable because any person living in the country would benefit even if he or she individually refused to pay for it. It would be impossible, let alone costly, to allow the nonpayer alone to be subject to an enemy missile strike. Likewise, the defense system is nonrival because the protection one individual receives (that is, consumes), arguably does not diminish the defense enjoyed by others in the country.

Public goods like this are often provided by government enterprise. Private enterprise may tend to provide too little of a public good or even none at all, if hypothetically it were given the responsibility. Remember that a public good like defense is nonexcludable. Therefore, if private enterprise were to attempt to provide defense it could well find many or most citizens choosing to be *free riders*. A free rider is a person who consumes the public good but refuses to pay. Private enterprise does not have the power to tax or otherwise force consumers to pay. And it cannot resort to the standard means of private enterprise in inducing payment; that is, it cannot refuse or exclude service to nonpayers.

THE PUBLIC GOOD ASPECT OF DONATIONS

Now consider an example of a public good that is conceptually more difficult: charitable donations. A charitable donation to the health of others in the community has the character of a public good. Suppose, for example, a donor gives money to a shelter for abused women. This donation helps provide shelter, food, and perhaps some health care. The benefits to the donor are the good feelings he or she incurs in knowing that a recipient is provided for. That is, the consumption by the ultimate recipient of the donation entails an external benefit, an aura of good feeling, to the donor. But these benefits cannot be confined to the donor; they are available to anyone who perceives the external benefit of feeling good about the consumption of someone in need. That is, these benefits are nonexcludable as well as nonrival, giving the benefits the character of a public good.

Now consider a case where the government provides a public good. This case will enable one to understand Weisbrod's explanation of the kind of government failure that provides a rationale for the existence of nonprofits. In Figure 18.1, let the curves D_1 through D_5 represent the demand curves of five different voting individuals for a public good to be provided by the government. Let the demand curves represent the external benefits to these different groups of taxpayers. These demand curves thus represent the marginal benefits to the taxpayer donors.

To pay for this public good, assume that these five different taxpayers are to be equally taxed at a per-unit tax rate of MT, which is the marginal tax. Since the five individuals are being equally taxed, the marginal tax for each will be exactly one-fifth of the marginal cost to society. Thus, if the government were to provide output 0C, then each of the five taxpayers would be charged 0C × MT, and the total tax receipts would exactly pay for the project. If the output were 0B, then 0B × MT would be collected from each individual, and so on.

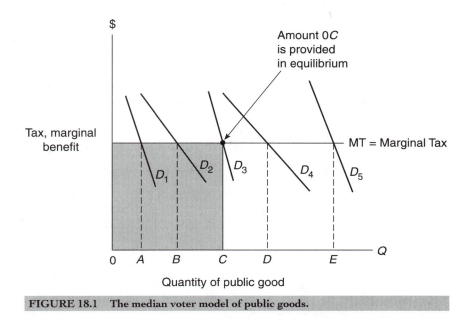

FIGURE 18.1 The median voter model of public goods.

What output level will government choose to provide if the outcome is left to the democratic political process? Economists find it convenient to imagine that there is an elected manager, whose continued term in office is determined by his or her ability to provide the "right" level. If level 0A is proposed, four of the five voters would prefer more (why?), and would vote against it. If level 0B is proposed, three of the five would prefer more, and would vote against that level. In contrast, level 0D would provide too much public good for three of the five voters, and similarly for level 0E. Only level 0C will gain a majority vote. This majority is made up of Voter 3, who is exactly satisfied since her marginal benefits equal the marginal tax, and Voters 4 and 5, who would like to see more but are satisfied with level 0C. Suppose that the manager proposed just a little more than 0C. This is too much for Voter 3, who now votes against the manager in favor of someone else who would reduce the public good level back to 0C.

Weisbrod's point is illustrated in this example. The government enterprise level chosen entails dissatisfied voters on the margin, whose demands are not exactly satisfied. The marginal tax rate is perfectly tailored only to Voter 3, the median person. For this person, the marginal benefit just equals the marginal tax rate at the provided output. It is theoretically possible to design a tax system so that for each person the marginal tax is equal to his or her marginal benefit. However, it is difficult to accomplish this in practice. Without such a tax system, some voters will prefer less of the public good and some will prefer more of it. For those who would prefer more, the government enterprise will have failed to satisfy their demands. Such unsatisfied voters will have the incentive to form a nonprofit enterprise and provide the good themselves.

It follows from Weisbrod's theory that nonprofits arise because private profit-motivated markets will tend to underproduce goods or services entailing beneficial externalities. In turn, government may also underprovide such goods and services in the eyes of a significant minority of voters. These citizens will tend to include those who perceive the external benefit to the community most keenly. Such citizens (here, Voters 4 and 5) become the founders of nonprofit corporations.

Weisbrod's analysis applies to health care when it is not a pure private good. The health care provided to the indigent is itself private because the indigent person could have been excluded had we wished. The care is also rival, as it is consumed by the recipient. Nevertheless, the health care provided to the indigent entails a beneficial externality to any charitably minded person. It is this external benefit that is a public good, and it is in this sense that health care is not a pure private good.

RELEVANCE TO HEALTH CARE MARKETS

Hospital services, nursing home services, and kidney dialysis services are probably not pure private goods. The Weisbrod analysis will be applicable in principle to any such services that provide external benefits to the community at large. Thus, nonprofit health care enterprises may arise where a sufficient minority of voters are dissatisfied with the quantity or quality of such services provided by the for-profit sector or government.

The theory provides a plausible account of the historical rise of nonprofit hospitals. Hospitals in the United States and in many countries began as charitable institutions, providing care primarily to the poor and relying heavily on donations.[2] Even today, nonprofit hospitals operating in states where substantial numbers of for-profits also exist tend to provide significantly greater charitable or "uncompensated" care than their nearby for-profit counterparts.[3]

Furthermore, the theory encompasses a broader range of external benefits than are involved in the provision of indigent, uncompensated care. High-quality prestigious hospitals may enhance a community's sense of pride and well-being. They may indirectly provide benefits to local business. Their excess capacity also provides an insurance for the currently healthy citizens in that a bed will be available should they need one.

However, the purely charitable aspects of hospital care have become less important. During this century, improvements in medical technology transformed hospitals into workshops for doctors, places for treating all patients, both rich and poor. Modern hospitals tend to get only very small portions of their revenues from donations. Sloan and colleagues (1990) report that donations account for only $33 per admission on average. The demise of hospital donations has been attributed to the growth of hospital insurance coverage, especially since the advent of Medicare and Medicaid. The decline in donations is consistent with the Weisbrod theory: Individual demands have stayed fairly stable while increases in public sector provision or financing have occurred.[4]

With the decline in cash donations, other forms of donations as well as other forms of nonprofit hospital advantages have become relatively more important. Donations of time and energy for board members and other individuals may, for example, now be relatively more important. To be sure, cash donations still play an important role in

---

[2]The history of hospitals and the relative importance of nonprofit versus for-profit status are further explored, for example, in Bays (1983), Frech (1990), and Temin (1988).

[3]See Lewin, Eckels, and Miller (1988).

[4]Burton Weisbrod in personal communication, November 1991.

certain capital fund drives. But in the present day, the financial advantages enjoyed by nonprofit hospitals stem more importantly from the subsidization of nonprofits by the government through tax exemptions.

Nonprofits as a Response to Contract Failure

A related theory of the role of nonprofit firms is complementary to Weisbrod's ideas. Hansmann (1980) theorizes that the nonprofit sector has a useful role in cases of a particular type of contract failure. The contract failure in point occurs when the quantity or quality of output is not easily observable by the purchaser. The asymmetry of information between the firm and the buyer of services becomes important (as noted in Chapter 7) in explaining the nonprofit role.

A classic example of the contract failure illustrates the problem. Suppose that you are motivated to contribute food and clothing to suffering people in Ethiopia. You can find a firm to deliver the care; however, it would be prohibitively costly to verify that the firm is actually delivering the desired goods to the designated population. You would hardly fly to Ethiopia just to check on this. Under these circumstances, you may prefer to employ a nonprofit firm.

As a deliverer of the aid packages, a for-profit firm will be perceived to have a conflict of interest. Such a firm could increase its profits by reneging on its promise. Inasmuch as the nonprofit cannot distribute its residual, it would have less incentive to renege. In this case, the nonprofit, by better serving the donor's interests, also serves the market more efficiently.

APPLICATIONS OF CONTRACT FAILURE TO NURSING HOME CARE

Contract failure is not confined to the issues of donated goods and services, as it can exist even when the purchaser is close at hand. Contrast the management of hotels and nursing homes. Hotels are profit-seeking enterprises, which provide rooms and suites along with housekeeping services, dining, and recreation to travelers and residents. Nursing homes also provide rooms and suites, dining, and recreation along with housekeeping services and, of course, specialized nursing services largely to an older and often infirm population. In fact, many nursing homes began as hotels.

What is the difference? Hotel patrons are assumed to be utility-maximizing consumers who compare benefits and costs in deciding whether to stay at the hotel. Nursing home patients may not be able to assess the quality of the facility and the care they receive accurately, perhaps because of their health impairments. Relatives or friends may obtain only limited impressions upon visiting and may not be sophisticated assessors of the quality of long-term care. A for-profit home, in contrast to a for-profit hotel, may appear to have a conflict of interest in the eyes of some demanders.

Whether for-profit nursing homes in practice provide lower quality is a matter of dispute. A survey of studies comparing quality in for-profits and nonprofits, published in 1983, reported mixed results with several noteworthy instances finding no significant difference.[5] The measurement of quality is itself an issue of dispute. Outcome measures,

---

[5]See O'Brien, Saxberg, and Smith (1983).

such as changes in patient health status, are best in principle, but reliable outcome measures are difficult to obtain. Analysts are often forced to rely on input data instead, but input data, such as the number of registered nurses per patient, while more readily available, can easily be misinterpreted.

For example, does a nursing home with more nurses per patient provide higher quality or is it simply less efficient? In practice, nursing homes with more personnel per patient do tend to have better patient outcomes, but it is difficult to sort out efficiency and quality.[6] Gertler (1989) attempts to take account of these problems and finds a somewhat higher-quality level in nonprofit homes.[7] Many analysts, however, would probably reserve judgment on this point.

RELEVANCE OF CONTRACT FAILURE
TO HOSPITALS AND OTHER FIRMS

If contract failure theory may apply to nursing home care, it does not appear to be appropriate for hospitals, a point noted by Hansmann (1980). Hospital patients are under the close supervision of the physician acting as the patient's agent. The physician has little incentive to misinform the patient by overstating the quality of care. More likely, the physician's incentives would cause him or her to encourage the patient to choose the highest quality available. Thus, the physician as agent of the patient may eliminate the potential contract failure.

The applicability of contract failure to the health care sector in general has been questioned by Sloan (1988), who notes that physician services are nearly entirely provided on a for-profit basis in the United States. Consumers would likely find it difficult to judge the quality of physician care; the physician as agent of the consumer at least superficially has a conflict of interest.

Interest Group Theory of the Role of Nonprofit Hospitals

The theories we have examined featuring the role of externalities in one case and the role of contract failure in the other have become standard in the nonprofit literature. These theories potentially account for the presence of nonprofit institutions of all kinds. Bays (1983) offers a special theory for the rise of nonprofit hospitals. His account may be called the *interest group theory,* and it provides a useful counterpoint.

THE ROLE OF PHYSICIANS IN THE HOSPITAL INDUSTRY

Bays begins his analysis with attention to the history of U.S. hospitals and their nature as institutions. He notes that in the nineteenth century U.S. hospitals were usually charitable institutions where physicians largely donated their time. Notably, medical technology had not yet developed to the point where hospitals were important to the physician either technologically or economically. As rapid population growth and expansion of hospitals occurred in the early twentieth century, for-profit

---

[6]See Linn, Gurel, and Linn (1977).
[7]Gertler (1989).

hospitals flourished, accounting for about half of existing hospitals in 1910 and reaching their zenith by 1930. These for-profit hospitals were generally quite small.

As medical technology was revolutionized, hospitals became the workshops of doctors; holding admitting privileges at one or more hospitals was crucial to a physician's practice. Hospitals also rapidly grew in size. With greater interest in the operation of hospitals, physicians increasingly developed and used their influence as an interest group to exert some control over them. By controlling hospital admitting privileges, organized physicians gained a degree of market power including the ability to exercise discipline over physicians whose practices tended to erode the market power of the organized group. For example, the affiliation by some physicians with prepaid group practice was treated as "unprofessional conduct."

Under this theory, physicians prefer nonprofit hospitals because they have greater power within them. Power over decision making permits the physician to enhance his or her income. The physician can order hospital services complementary to his or her own services, ordering hospital services perhaps well past the extent that would be profitable to the hospital. This account, Bays points out, is consistent with the policy stand of the AMA in support of Hill-Burton, a federal act that provided construction aid and loan subsidies to nonprofit hospitals. Furthermore, under this account, the favored tax treatment and private and public subsidies to nonprofit hospitals arise in part through physicians' political support, support that ultimately benefits the physician through the provision of lower-cost complementary hospital inputs.

How then can we theoretically account for public acquiescence in supporting the nonprofit mode? If the theory were correct, the subsidies (both tax relief and dollar subsidies) to nonprofit hospitals in effect tax the general public majority to support the narrower interests of the physician minority. To account for this anomaly, Bays appeals to interest group theory.

Under interest group theory, small groups may become more powerful than a majority when their interests are highly concentrated and their membership is homogeneous. It will be worthwhile in such case for the physician to support lobbying on behalf of measures that result in significant benefits to him or her, whereas the loss to the general public is diffused. While the individual consumer may benefit by challenging the status quo, the personal gains are small relative to the personal costs. The theoretical situation depicted by Bays, a situation that substantially and lopsidedly favors the physician at the expense of the general public, may nevertheless represent a regulatory equilibrium.

Summary on the Reasons for the Prevalence of Nonprofits

Several theories explain the existence of nonprofits. In some cases, these theories are complementary; in other cases there are sharp contrasts. Weisbrod accounts for the existence of nonprofit firms in an economy with three sectors: for-profits, government, and nonprofits. In his view, nonprofits arise to provide for unmet demands for public goods, most notably in cases where there are significant external benefits to the provision of a good.

Hansmann's view is complementary to this account, emphasizing the special role for nonprofit firms in cases of contract failure (cases where it is difficult to observe the provision or quality of the good in question). These two theories provide insights into the prevalence of nonprofit firms in the provision of hospital care and nursing home care. Under either of these two accounts, the public deference to nonprofit firms (such as in allowing for special tax provisions favoring them) makes some sense.

In contrast, Bays offers an interest group theory of the preference of physicians for nonprofit hospitals. In his account, physicians prefer nonprofits and use their influence to further the role of nonprofits at least partly, if not primarily, out of interest for personal gain. Under Bays's account, favored treatment of nonprofit hospitals is not so clearly in the public interest. This multiplicity of theories regarding the existence of nonprofit firms, particularly of hospitals, is mirrored in a multiplicity of theories of hospital behavior.

MODELS OF NONPROFIT HOSPITAL BEHAVIOR

The literature of health economics offers numerous descriptions of hospital behavior. Three models represent the distinctive classes of hospital behavior. We begin with an account of nonprofit behavior that is theoretically applicable to the entire class of nonprofit firms. We then follow with two economic theories that are specific to nonprofit hospitals.

The Quantity–Quality Nonprofit Theory

When economists analyze issues involving nonprofit hospital responses to policy change, they often begin by positing an objective of the hospital decision makers. Most frequently, the analyst chooses either a utility-maximization type of model or a profit-maximization type. Of the utility-maximizing type, one prominent example is the theory proposed by Joseph Newhouse (1970) to describe nonprofit firms of all kinds.

Under this account, the objective of the hospital is to maximize utility. Utility here has a similar meaning to consumer utility in consumer theory; that is, utility is an index of the decision maker's preferences, with higher utility numbers given to preferred bundles. Utility is thus a measure of satisfaction.

The special difficulty for the case of hospitals is to describe the complex elements and interactions of the set of hospital decision makers. Nonprofit hospitals in the United States tend to have three parties with considerable decision-making authority. The trustees are nominally in charge of the hospital, but boards of trustees may include people with widely varying backgrounds, knowledge of health care, and management expertise. The trustees' decision-making agent is the hospital administrator or CEO. This manager may have varying degrees of actual power and authority. Finally, the arbiters of medical decision making are the physician staff. These physicians may also exercise considerable decision-making authority over administrative decisions. We assume that this complex decision-making apparatus resolves into a single utility function and describes a set of well-behaved indifference curves.

THE UTILITY FUNCTION

Under Newhouse's construction, the hospital's preferences are defined over quantity and quality of output. Quantity of output could be measured in several ways, but in the graphical treatment we assume that it is measured by the number of cases treated by the hospital over a given time period. We further assume that there is only one type of case to be treated, though in principle there could be hundreds. Quality of output can entail many different characteristics of the care provided. Some top decision makers may value the quality or beauty of the hospital structure; others may emphasize expertise of the physician or nursing staff; others may emphasize prestige in the medical community; and still others stress the quality of mercy or the tender loving care provided. Graphically, we shall suppose that there is just one index of quality.

This conception of the nonprofit hospital is consistent with the external-benefits account of the role of nonprofit firms. The utility derived from producing quantity and quality *could* be construed as arising because care to these patients entails an external benefit to the community at large and to the hospital decision makers in particular. The external benefit could take on many forms, being purely charitable in some cases or purely concerned with personal prestige and influence in others. Nevertheless, the objective of the hospital could be construed as to maximize the external benefit.

THE QUANTITY–QUALITY FRONTIER

In any case, the hospital does not simply maximize quantity or maximize quality, but instead selects a combination of quantity and quality that maximizes utility. The hospital faces a budget constraint: It must pay its bills and cannot run a negative net revenue as a general rule. Furthermore, the nondistribution constraint on all nonprofits entails that this hospital has no incentive to choose positive net revenues as a general rule. Thus, the budget constraint effectively requires that the sum of patient-generated revenues plus donations equal the hospital's costs.

Following Newhouse, assume that all revenue sources, which are primarily patient-generated revenues, are summarized in an average revenue curve labeled $D(q_1)$ in Figure 18.2. This curve is the demand curve facing the hospital. This demand curve would in general depend on the level of quality q_1; higher quality of care would translate into a higher demand for care. Thus, for example, $D(q_2)$ would represent the demand curve for a higher-quality level. Inasmuch as quality is costly to produce, we can assume that higher-quality levels will entail higher average costs. For example, average cost curve $AC(q_2)$ represents the average cost curve for quality level 2, a higher-quality level than for average cost curve $AC(q_1)$, the average cost curve for quality level 1.

The budget constraint requires that the hospital produce where average revenue equals average cost. For example, output Q_1 satisfies the budget constraint for quality level 1. If consumers place a higher marginal valuation on the incremental quality than it costs to produce, then $D(q_2)$ will shift up by more than will $AC(q_2)$, and incremental quality will be accompanied by incremental quantity. Eventually, however, it is likely that the cost of incremental quality will increase by more than consumers' willingness to pay for it ($AC(q_3)$ constitutes a much bigger rise than $D(q_3)$). When this happens, it becomes clear that incremental quality comes at the expense of quantity of services (fewer people can afford the high-quality services). Thus, although Q_2 exceeded Q_1, quantity Q_3 (and all further quantities) represents decreases in equilibrium quantity as trade-offs with increased quality. Tracing out all these possibilities generates the quality–quantity frontier of the hospital in Figure 18.3.

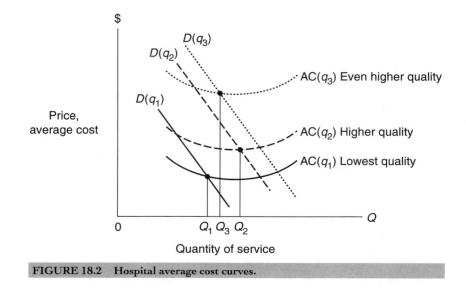

FIGURE 18.2   Hospital average cost curves.

MAXIMIZATION OF UTILITY

Given the possibility frontier, the hospital decision makers choose the point that maximizes utility. The constrained utility maximization point occurs at a point of tangency between the frontier and the highest indifference curve attainable. In Figure 18.3, utility maximization occurs at point A. The quantity provided in equilibrium is Q_2 at quality level 2, labeled q_2.

The model also illustrates two other prior theories as special cases. On the one hand, let the hospital preferences place sole weight on quantity. Then the hospital would behave like a constrained quantity maximizer and produce at point B. This special case is similar to a theory of hospital-quantity maximization proposed earlier by

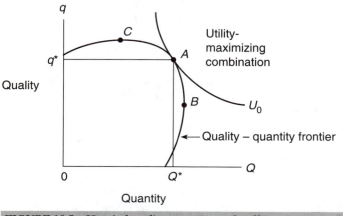

FIGURE 18.3   Hospital quality–quantity trade-offs.

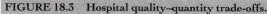

Long (1964). On the other hand, let the hospital primarily value quality, and further let quality as perceived by the top decision makers be primarily the prestige of the hospital as compared to its peers. It would produce at point *C*. This special case is similar to a model of the hospital as a conspicuous producer as proposed by Lee (1971). A unique feature of Lee's approach, however, is that the hospital chooses production technologies that are conspicuously prestigious, such as for open heart surgery or transplants. The hospital's search for prestige may lead to socially inefficient production technologies or output qualities.

The Hospital as a Physicians' Cooperative

A very different account of the nonprofit hospital is provided in theories that posit the objective of the hospital as the maximization of some pecuniary gain to the decisive set of decision makers. A prime example of this type of model is proposed by Mark Pauly and Michael Redisch (1973), who describe the not-for-profit hospital as a "physicians' cooperative." Here we begin with the assumption that the hospital is de facto controlled by the physician staff who operate the hospital so as to maximize their net incomes.

In this view of the hospital, the focus is on the "full price" of the hospital care, meaning the total charges to the patient by both the hospital and the physician. Assume that the patient pays a single bill representing the full price of the care; let donations be zero. The full price of care will be determined by consumer demand, and depends on the total quantity of care offered by the physicians' cooperative. The amount of care produced and offered to patients depends in turn on the quantity of inputs chosen by the top decision makers, here the physicians. Summarize hospital inputs as capital, K, and labor, L. Let the physician input be M, which is fixed if the hospital selects a "closed staff."

MAXIMIZING NET REVENUE PER PHYSICIAN

The hospital is then run so as to maximize the net revenue (NR) per physician (M), or NR/M. The net revenue is the sum of all of the revenue less factor payments to nonphysician labor and payments to capital. The net revenue per physician divides that revenue over the total number of physicians M. An increase in the number of physicians M initially increases revenues per physician. Eventually, revenues per physician must fall because (due to the fixed levels of nonphysician labor and capital) the percent increase in revenues (in the numerator) will be smaller than the percent change in number of physicians (in the denominator).

Figure 18.4 shows the optimal size of the staff if the physicians can limit the size of the staff, or "close" the staff. Here dollar values are on the vertical axis and the number of physicians on staff, M, on the horizontal. The curve N denotes average physician income. The N curve starts at the origin point A (no revenue), rises to a maximum at point B, and then falls. Curve s depicts the supply curve of physicians, which is infinitely elastic, representing plausibly a case in an urban, physician-dense environment. For physicians who are on the staff, the optimal staff size would be M^*, where curve N reaches its maximum.[8]

---

[8]The authors state that this model is similar to models used to explain the economic behavior of the former Soviet collective farm.

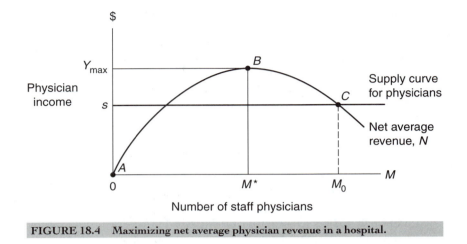

FIGURE 18.4   Maximizing net average physician revenue in a hospital.

In contrast, if the hospital has an open staff, physicians are free to enter as long as their resulting average income N equals or exceeds their supply price s. The open-staff equilibrium, hence, occurs at point C, where net revenue (the demand for physicians) equals supply s, with M_0 physicians hired. Regardless of the number of physicians on staff (either a closed-staff or an open-staff equilibrium), the hospital inputs are chosen to maximize residual income for the medical staff. If the Newhouse model can be viewed as resulting from the maximization of external benefit perceived to accrue to the community, then the Pauly–Redisch objective is the complete antithesis.

A Comparison of the Quantity–Quality and the Physicians' Cooperative Theories*

It should be apparent that these two models are conceptually very different. It is useful to contrast the two by comparing them on the same graph. To do so, we must make simplifying assumptions to ensure that the two models are described in a comparable context. Applying the Pauly–Redisch idea of full price to both models, we represent combined (physician and hospital) revenues as a single function, $R = R(K, L, M_0)$. The combined revenues depend on the quantity and quality of care produced, which in turn depend on the amounts of the inputs used. Like Newhouse, assume that the hospital/physician care is produced efficiently so that a higher quality of care requires necessarily a higher level and hence cost of inputs. Let us add that the hospital may receive additional revenues in the form of donations, D_0, and government subsidies, G_0. Let physician supply be perfectly elastic at a constant supply price, s. Constant input prices, r for capital and w for labor, complete the description. Finally, define the hospital residual, HR, revenues as the following equation:

$$\text{HR} = R(K, L, M_0) - wL - rK - sM_0 + D_0 + G_0 \qquad (18.1)$$

*May be omitted without loss of continuity.

Under the Pauly–Redisch model, the hospital residual, HR, is "usurped" by the physicians on the staff. For a given level of physicians on the staff, M_0, the physicians will maximize their average incomes by maximizing HR itself.

In contrast, the Newhouse hospital will maximize utility of quantity, Q, and quality, q, subject to the constraint that the hospital residual is zero; that is, the hospital breaks even. To simplify the graphical representation, let the hospital residual function, HR, form a rounded hill.[9] The contours of that hill are shown in Figure 18.5 in a graph with quantity and quality of care on the axes. The contours have a meaning analogous to contour lines on a topographical map. For example, the contour line labeled HR = 1 represents the collection of all combinations of quality and quantity of care that yield a hospital residual of $1 million. Contours farther away from the maximum residual point, HR = HR_{max}, yield successively lower levels of hospital residual. The contour curve labeled HR = 0 indicates the combinations of quality and quantity that yield a zero residual.

Let us begin with the Pauly–Redisch analysis of a closed hospital staff. Let the hospital physician staff be fixed at some level M_0. The Pauly–Redisch hospital chooses the quantity–quality combination that maximizes the hospital residual, point HR = HR_{max}. The hospital residual then goes to the staff physicians, and these physicians will thus have maximized their average incomes. In contrast, the Newhouse hospital maximizes utility at point A, the point of tangency between the HR = 0 contour, representing the Newhouse budget constraint, and the highest indifference curve attainable. Thus, in the closed-staff case, the models yield very different results. As depicted, the Newhouse hospital tends to produce more quantity and quality of care. Perhaps more disturbing, under the Pauly–Redisch behavior, the physicians indirectly

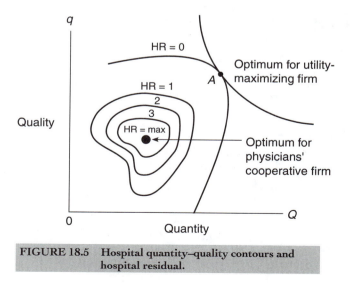

FIGURE 18.5 Hospital quantity–quality contours and hospital residual.

[9]For further understanding of the shapes of these isoprofit contours, see Spence (1973).

usurp the hospital-care residual, and this entails the donations and government subsidy as well! It is as if the nonprofit hospital is a for-profit firm in disguise. If we believe that the nonprofit hospitals behave like this, we would likely call for an end to government tax exemptions for this nonprofit status. This helps to explain the arguments for the end of nonprofit subsidies as made strongly, for example, by Clark (1980).

EFFECTS OF INCREASED COMPETITION

Before leaving the comparison of models, examine an effect of increased competition in the hospital sector. If there were free entry, then all potential firms that may want to compete for hospital care patients are free to do so. Potential competitors could include alternative delivery systems as well as other hospitals. As more competitors enter the market and compete for business, the demand for care at any existing hospital will tend to fall. For our purposes, this means that competition will tend to shrink the hospital residual hill in size.

Figure 18.6 depicts a case where competition has continued until the maximum hospital residual attainable is zero. As we move away from the top of the hospital residual hill in any direction, the contours reflect negative and successively more negative residuals. The result is that the Newhouse and the Pauly–Redisch nonprofit hospital in this end result will converge in their choices of quantity and quality.

It is often agreed that the hospital industry experienced increasing competition in the 1980s. Especially noteworthy are the competition from alternative delivery systems and the competitive incentives introduced under Medicare's prospective payment system. A tendency for nonprofit hospitals to converge toward for-profitlike behavior has long been noted in theory (Newhouse, 1970), and more recently it has been proposed as a probable result of competition in the 1980s and beyond.

However, many analysts have emphasized the tendency for incumbent nonprofit hospitals to help foster barriers to entry against competitors. Certificate-of-Need laws

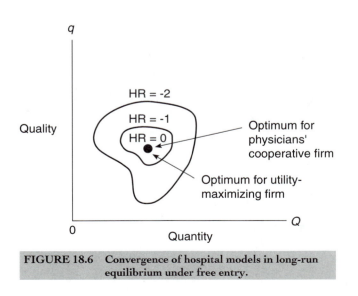

FIGURE 18.6   Convergence of hospital models in long-run equilibrium under free entry.

that restrict capital investments in hospitals are sometimes viewed in this light. With barriers to entry, the two nonprofit models will diverge.[10]

The Harris Model

The two hospital models strongly contrast the roles of the two principal power groups in the modern hospital, the physician staff group and the trustee–administrator group. The utility-maximizing models posit this power distribution to be resolved somehow into a coherent utility function, and it is tempting to view the utility function as representing the top management as constrained by the realities of physician behavior. The Pauly–Redisch model posits the de facto control by the physicians. In either case, there is presumably a resolution of power that occurs perhaps even harmoniously. The hospital theory proposed by Jeffrey Harris (1977) represents an entirely different approach. The hospital, under Harris's account, is the scene of continual conflict within an organization inherently split into two parts, what Harris describes as a noncooperative oligopoly game.

The Harris model is noteworthy for two additional reasons. On the one hand, Harris is a physician with a Ph.D. in economics. He devised his account after experience as a physician in an urban hospital. As an economist, he is trained in economic organizational theories. On the other hand, Harris presents his work more informally in words and images describing experience within a hospital. Without equations or graphs, students often find the model to be simpler as well as more realistic. To theoreticians, it may well be seen as more complex.

THE HOSPITAL AS TWO FIRMS

Harris proposes that the hospital's internal organization is really two separate firms interacting in a complex way. The structure of a hospital has two main parts, the trustee–administrator group that serves as the supplier of inputs, and the physician staff that serves as the demanders. Like an automobile parts-and-service shop, the hospital has technical experts providing the actual service and requesting supplies from the organization. Unlike the auto shop, the physician's loyalties lie almost entirely with the patient. The physician is the patient's "hired gun."

Rather than having a predictable technological and inventory problem, the administrator has the problem of providing inputs to the physician-agent during a complicated, uncertain sequence of events. Consider Harris's account of a hypothetical case history:

> Mr. X comes to Dr. A with a fever and a cough. A chest X-ray reveals a density. He is hospitalized. Penicillin is administered. Although the fever subsides with this treatment, a repeat X-ray shows that the density has not disappeared. A sputum cytological examination is performed and lung cancer is diagnosed. Further studies suggest that the cancer can be removed surgically. An operation is performed. Unfortunately, massive postoperative bleeding occurs. Matched whole blood is administered. Despite this treatment, a cardiac

---

[10]For an interesting account of hospital behavior emphasizing the cartellike hospital behavior toward inhibiting competition by other firms, see Shalit (1977). Certificate-of-Need laws are examined in detail in Chapter 19.

arrest ensues and an emergency resuscitation (code call) is announced. Mr. X is transferred to Intensive Care with chest tubes and a respirator. A special contrast study
(angiogram) reveals the site of bleeding. A repeat operation is performed (p. 469).

The moral of this account is that rather than being a predictable assembly procedure, the hospital service is unique and customized for each patient; it plays out in an
unpredictable way. The physician hurries to various supply centers, demanding services
on behalf of his patient: He is like a "fire-fighter." The administrator is the supplier of
these services. Under the circumstances, marketlike negotiations between the supplier
and demander are impossible, as are lengthy determinations of an exact price for the
patient prior to treatment. The problem is not merely that the patient is usually heavily
insured; instead it is the unusual agency relationship that requires the physician to make
noneconomic decisions on the patient's behalf. As Harris states,

> There is a special negative externality in an arrangement in which one makes repeated
> marginal decisions about life and death. This externality is so important that the physi-
> cian's participation in the "market" for angiograms and code calls is explicitly foreclosed.
> Whether or not it is justified, this notion has an important influence on the way the hospi-
> tal is organized (p. 473).

The hospital, according to Harris, solves the rationing problem with a variety of
nonprice-related decision rules. "There are loosely enforced standards, rules of thumb,
side bargains, cajoling, negotiations, special contingency plans, and in some cases literally shouting and screaming" (p. 478). Furthermore, the physicians are often not organized collusively as a group; rather, each is vying to establish his or her own empire.

IMPLICATIONS

There are three implications to this model. First, given the role of physicians, we
can expect that the hospital's preferences for new technology will be driven by the preferences of the physician demanders. The physician-agent will tend to prefer technologies that are complementary to existing capacity and that are thus quality enhancing.
Second, hospital regulation aimed primarily at the trustee–administrator group may
have little effect. That is, regulation to limit hospital costs must establish incentives for
and constraints on the physician-agent as well as the administrator. Third, reorganiza-
tion of the hospital along product lines might make it a more effective organization. For
example, reorganizing departments by cardiology, neurology, and so on, may better
help to integrate the physician into the decision-making apparatus.

Summary on Models of Hospital Behavior

While many theories of nonprofit hospital behavior exist, we have described three main
types. Most commonly, hospitals are depicted in research as being either utility maximizers or profit maximizers. Of the utility-maximizing type, the Newhouse model is
a prominent example, and it depicts the top hospital decision makers as choosing a
best combination of quantity and quality of care. Of the profit-maximizing models, the
Pauly–Redisch physicians' cooperative version is perhaps most prominent. The key
feature in this type of approach is that the nonprofit hospital is depicted as effectively

making choices that serve to maximize the pecuniary gain to physicians—the decisive set of decision makers. The Harris model forms a distinctive alternative, depicting the hospital as really two firms representing somewhat opposing interests who interact in ways similar to what professional economists would term a noncooperative oligopolistic game.

The attempt to distinguish the theoretical models will remain a serious interest for policy if only for the importance of this issue to the nonprofit's favored status. For example, would we continue to extend tax-exempt status to the Pauly–Redisch type of nonprofit? Ironically, if we become successful in identifying nonprofit hospitals by behavioral type, we may find that hospitals of all types coexist. At present, we must be content in finding many ideas about nonprofits contained in the various theories.

THE RELATIVE EFFICIENCY OF NONPROFITS VERSUS FOR-PROFITS

Inasmuch as nonprofit and for-profit firms coexist in the health sector, it has become a focus of interest for policy to determine which of the two forms is relatively more efficient in producing care. It is often presumed that the for-profit is the more efficient. A theoretical rationale for this hypothesis has been derived from property rights theory, and it is instructive to examine the elements of this theory. In developing the application of property rights theory to nonprofit health-related firms, we will follow the exposition of Frech (1976).

Property Rights Theory and Its Application to Nonprofits

Private property rights are important to the functioning of the firm organized for profit. This is becoming even more evident as the former Soviet Union and other former Eastern Bloc countries struggle toward market economies. The key property rights entail the right of the owner to decide on the employment of the firm's resources, the right to keep the residual, and the right to sell the value of any wealth gains (that is, to sell the property rights). The firm's wealth is understood as the current market value of its assets. In standard theory, the market value of a firm's assets will tend to equal the present value of all future dividends.

In any for-profit firm, the day-to-day managers will make decisions for the owners. These agents for the owners in reality probably acquire some independence and have the opportunity to act as imperfect agents. It is costly for the owners to monitor perfectly the managers, and the owners may accept some degree of departure from pure profit-maximizing behavior. The manager may find it rewarding to seek nonpecuniary gains as well as profits in any given period.

Nonpecuniary benefits could include anything other than money rewards that the manager enjoys: pleasant office space, extra staff, the firm's prestige, or even the prestige of producing high-quality and high-quantity output. Since profit making is what creates firm wealth, this behavior means that the firm will behave as if the top decision makers valued two goals, both wealth and nonpecuniary benefits. Thus the firm is a utility maximizer, but here the indifference curves are described over firm wealth and nonpecuniary benefits. The curves U_1 and U_2 in Figure 18.7 represent examples of these indifference curves for the top decision makers of the firm.

The production of nonpecuniary benefits will affect the wealth attainable by the firm. For example, if the hospital introduces an unprofitable open heart surgery capability for prestige reasons, it will find that its current profits and hence its wealth are reduced. This idea suggests that the firm will face a constraint on its choices, the constraint being the trade-off between maximum possible wealth and the level of nonpecuniary benefits. This wealth–benefits possibility frontier is shown in Figure 18.7 as curve *FF*.

THE FOR-PROFIT AND NONPROFIT EQUILIBRIA

The for-profit firm, as managed by the top decision makers, is thus really a utility maximizer over wealth and nonpecuniary benefits. The utility will be maximized in a manner common to all constrained maximization problems at a solution where the highest attainable indifference curve is reached. The for-profit utility maximization occurs in Figure 18.7 at the point of tangency labeled *A*.

In contrast, the nonprofit firm experiences a radical attenuation of property rights. There is no property right attaching to the residual and hence to wealth. Only the manager or administrator, and perhaps some other employees, are in a position to attach or usurp the firm's wealth by funneling this wealth to themselves in subtler forms. When this occurs in money terms, we can term the payments a form of salary. Nonprofits in any industry are usually limited in the degree of salary that can be paid to managers, so that unreasonably large salaries are discouraged by regulatory agents. Thus, the most wealth a nonprofit firm can or will accrue is limited to the present value of this implied salary limit. In graphical terms, the nonprofit faces a second constraint in that wealth may not exceed that salary limit, *LL,* in Figure 18.7.

A nonprofit firm with similar preferences as the for-profit firm depicted will therefore maximize utility at the corner solution point labeled *B*. Note that at *B* the nonprofit reaches the highest indifference curve attainable given its constraints—that is, indifference curve U_1. The implication of Frech's analysis is that the nonprofit will tend

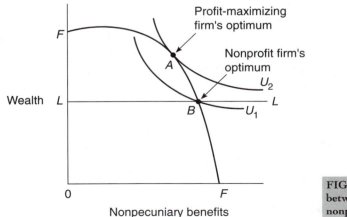

FIGURE 18.7 Optimization between wealth and nonpecuniary benefits.

to choose a higher level of nonpecuniary benefits than the for-profit. If these nonpecuniary benefits entail things that are not productive, then the nonprofit will tend to be a more costly and inefficient producer than the for-profit firm.

IMPLICATIONS OF FRECH'S MODEL

Frech's model offers a contrast to the nonprofit behavioral models we have just examined. In particular, it introduces the idea that firms are often not perfect profit maximizers because managers are imperfect agents. Furthermore, since nonprofits lack the usual profit incentives, they will likely be even worse at attaining goals that increase firm wealth and are likely to be worse in terms of production efficiency. Although not depicted by Figure 18.7, it has been argued that the fact that nonprofit assets cannot be sold for profit in the market also inhibits the nonprofit's incentives to produce efficiently.[11]

However, alternative theories exist. Consider, for example, that the Newhouse nonprofit and the Pauly–Redisch nonprofit hospital, alternatives to the Frech construction, are cost-efficient. If nonprofit hospitals tend to be of either type, then we should not find any efficiency advantage of the for-profit firms among hospitals.

Nevertheless, Frech's argument contains an important insight. On the face of it, nonprofit firms appear to lack a key element behind the drive toward efficiency of the for-profit. This key element is the missing property right, the right to claim the residual gains of the firm. Let us consider the available empirical evidence on the relative efficiency of nonprofits in the health industry, both for hospitals and nursing homes.

Are Nonprofit Health Care Firms in Fact Less Efficient?

Cost-efficiency comparisons of nonprofit and for-profit hospitals have been mainly of three types: comparisons of matched samples, regression studies, and frontier studies.

HOSPITAL STUDIES

The simplest types are the *matched sample* studies. In this approach, the researcher chooses samples of nonprofits and for-profits matched pairwise for a set of confounding factors that affect costs but that are unrelated to efficiency. The remaining cost differences per unit of output are then presumed to be attributable to efficiency.

Two studies of this type illustrate the approach. One study examined matched pairs of hospitals from three states: California, Florida, and Texas.[12] The study reported that Medicare patients' average costs were 4 percent higher in the for-profits. This small difference is in the "wrong" direction, and it was not statistically significant. A similar result was obtained for a different study that grouped samples of California hospitals on the basis of several factors, including size, location, teaching status, and service mix.[13] This time, total operating expenses per admission were studied, and it was reported that costs were 2 percent higher in for-profit chain-owned hospitals than in nonprofit voluntary hospitals, while independent for-profits reported costs that were

---

[11]See Alchian and Demsetz (1972).
[12]Lewin, Derzon, and Margulies (1981).
[13]Pattison and Katz (1982).

3 percent lower than those for nonprofits. Thus, very little difference is noticeable in the matched-pair studies.

In contrast, the *regression* studies were designed to estimate the cost function of the hospital and to test for any cost differences attributable to ownership status. One of the earlier studies of this type found that for-profit, chain-owned hospitals were significantly less costly than nonprofits.[14] However, the study contained relatively few chain-owned hospitals.

On the other hand, several regression studies published in the 1980s tended to find no significant cost differences. In what is perhaps the most thorough of these studies in controlling for extraneous factors, Becker and Sloan (1985) reported regression studies of hospital cost functions estimated on 1979 data in which chain ownership was broken down into old and new chains. This was done to control for the possibility that newly acquired hospitals may have been targeted for acquisition based on their inefficient management. Becker and Sloan found that total costs per admission were lower in free-standing for-profit institutions than in free-standing nonprofits, but were higher in for-profit chains. Neither result, however, was statistically significant. Thus, the regression studies of hospital cost functions tend to find no significant difference between hospital ownership types.

The frontier approach attempts to identify those firms in the sample that are the best producers. It categorizes a firm as being inefficient when the firm falls short of best possible production practice, the frontier. Frontier methods are described in more detail in Chapter 14.

Wilson and Jadlow (1982) compare nuclear medicine services in nonprofit and for-profit hospitals. By focusing on nuclear medicine services, they avoid the complications that are caused because hospitals have heterogeneous outputs. They found for-profit hospitals to be significantly more efficient at providing nuclear medicine services than were the private not-for-profit hospitals in the sample.

What should we conclude about the relative efficiency of for-profit and nonprofit hospitals? We must recommend caution on several counts.[15] First, most studies use accounting costs rather than economic costs (in particular, return on owners' equity is not counted). Second, accounting practices differ between ownership types. Third, many studies do not remove for-profit tax payments from the cost figures. Fourth, studies vary in their success in holding constant factors, other than ownership, that affect cost variations. Finally, the presence of nearly complete insurance, often on a cost-reimbursement basis in the case of hospitals, may have tended to cause the for-profits effectively to face a nonprofit constraint, thus confounding their economic behavior. These are some of the key conceptual difficulties that warrant caution in assessing the cost-comparison issue. Can anything be concluded? We would conclude with Sloan (1988) who considers the evidence in light of the inherent difficulties and says that

> Considering results from all of the studies, it appears that efficiency differences between private not-for-profit and for-profit hospitals are small, at most (p. 132).

---

[14]Bays (1979).

[15]See Sloan (1988) for a discussion of the potential drawbacks of the variety of hospital cost studies. Sloan specifically addresses the issue of the relative cost-efficiency of nonprofit versus for-profit health care firms.

Why Are RNs' Wages Higher in Nonprofit Nursing Homes?

Holtmann and Idson (1993) provide recent evidence to explain why registered nurses (RNs) are paid higher wages by nonprofit than by for-profit nursing homes. As described previously, nonprofits are formed in response to patients' informational limitations in assessing quality. Specifically, because of patients' difficulties in distinguishing among nursing homes of varying quality, the market will fail to produce high-quality nursing homes. (Why? Recall the lemons problem in Chapter 7.)

Holtmann and Idson observe, as have others, the differentially higher wages that RNs receive in the nonprofit nursing home sector. Earlier studies (for example, Borjas, Frech, and Ginsburg, 1983) attributed these differentials to the premise that since nonprofits do not distribute the residuals (the revenues less the costs), they are less interested in minimizing the costs. Holtmann and Idson propose an alternative hypothesis, that nonprofits pay nurses higher wages to get higher quality.

Using sophisticated econometric analyses, the authors discover that the differential wages reflect quality-enhancing characteristics of the nurses, such as years of experience and length of tenure on the current job. Both of these reflect higher quality of care, since the provision of such care may require more stable employment relationships.

The authors then compare the quality and the property rights hypotheses. According to the property rights hypothesis employees in nonprofit homes are paid higher wages than they could command in for-profit homes; this implies a higher return to their productivity-related attributes than in for-profit homes. However, the authors' methods show that workers in nonprofit facilities are generally compensated at a lower rate for their productivity-related attributes, and it is the fact that they have *more* of these attributes that leads to the wage differences. They view these distinctions as "strong evidence against the property-rights hypothesis that nonprofits are paying wasteful, inefficient wage premiums" (p. 73).

Such a conclusion does not warrant rejection of property rights theory or of the Frech hypothesis per se, but it does raise the question of the theory's applicability to the hospital sector. The possibility that nonprofit hospitals are of the Pauly–Redisch type is sufficient to account for this result. Cost-efficiency in production may be the somewhat ironic side benefit of de facto physician control. But if the theory does not appear to apply to nonprofit hospitals, it is nevertheless natural to ask in turn whether for-profit nursing homes differ in cost-efficiency from nonprofit homes.

NURSING HOME STUDIES

The nursing home cost studies tend to concur that for-profit homes have lower costs per patient day than the nonprofit homes. Bishop (1980) concluded that "Cost studies have consistently found that facilities owned and operated by nonprofit voluntary and government organizations have higher costs than for-profit nursing homes by at least several dollars per day" (p. 50). A slightly later study conducted a total of 11 separate cost analyses on 20 sets of nursing home data spanning single-state samples as well as a national sample.[16] The authors found consistently higher costs in nonprofit homes.

Finally, several studies of nursing homes conducted by Frech and several colleagues focused on the applicability of the property rights hypothesis.[17] These confirmed earlier work in finding nonprofits to be more expensive than for-profits. Also consistent with the property rights theory, they found that nonprofit nursing homes were paying significantly higher wages than for-profit homes.

Thus, the nursing home studies clearly support the property rights hypothesis of lower costs in the for-profit firms. Even so, as we have noted in another context, caution is warranted in concluding about the reasons for nursing home cost differentials because of the difficulty in controlling for quality differences. However, in this case at least, we see a clear difference in costs in the predicted direction.

CONCLUSIONS

This chapter has surveyed several issues regarding nonprofit firms in the health care sector. We began with a description of the nonprofit firm, noting the importance of the nonprofit constraint (the rule that no one has a legal claim on the firm's residual). We then examined theories of why nonprofit firms exist and applied them to health care firms.

Weisbrod's theory, which applies to nonprofits in all industries, reasons that the nonprofit arises to provide for demands for public goods that are not adequately provided either by government or the private for-profit sector. Hansmann's theory complements this view, emphasizing that people will tend to put more trust in nonprofit firms in cases where the output or its quality is difficult to monitor. Bays provides an application of interest group theory to explain the special case of why hospitals are commonly nonprofit in the United States.

Focusing on hospitals, we have described multiple theories of the economic behavior of nonprofit hospitals. The Newhouse utility-maximizing theory poses the top decision makers as choosing the best combination of quantity and quality of care. Pauly and Redisch, in contrast, view the nonprofit hospital as a physicians' cooperative run de facto for the benefit of physician decision makers. Harris, quite differently, offers a hospital model devised from experience in a large urban hospital. Here the administration and the physicians constitute noncooperative separate firms. These three models represent the main types of the many hospital models in use. We find that it is difficult to distinguish between the models empirically, though each offers insights to hospital behavior.

Finally, we have posed the nonprofit versus the for-profit health care firm in terms of economic efficiency. Frech's application of property rights theory argues that non-

---

[16]Birnbaum et al. (1981).

[17]See Frech and Ginsburg (1981), Borjas, Frech, and Ginsburg (1983), and Frech (1985).

profit firms lack the economic discipline found in for-profit firms where someone or some group has a legal pecuniary interest in the efficiency and profitability of the firm. The theory does not seem to apply to nonprofit versus for-profit hospitals, perhaps for reasons peculiar to the hospital industry. In contrast, studies of the nursing home industry in the United States have consistently found lower costs among the homes organized for-profit.

It is instructive to speculate on the future of the nonprofit portion of the health care system in the United States given the move toward universality of insurance coverage and a decline in the importance of public hospitals. Frank and Salkever offer three predictions.

First, with improved information available regarding the quality of health care, the role of nonprofit organizations is likely to decline. The trust that people may have in nonprofit organizations may become relatively less important; hence, the organizations may become less competitive relative to the for-profit sector.

Second, to the extent that improved insurance enables people to purchase for-profit services, the nonprofit sector will specialize to a greater extent in public goods. Rather than competing directly, nonprofit organizations will offer service to those with chronic health problems, and will offer other health-related services on the boundaries between health and social or educational services, like nutrition programs.

Third, the authors believe that continued concern about government finances will lead to a closer scrutiny to ensure the government and its taxpayers that nonprofits are providing social benefits in exchange for their tax breaks. Those that are not may face challenges to their nonprofit and tax-exempt status. It is likely that this evolving sector will continue to undergo substantive changes in an era of health care reform.

Summary

1. The defining characteristic of a nonprofit firm is the nondistribution constraint. Furthermore, nonprofits are typically tax exempt and donations to nonprofit firms receive favorable tax treatment.

2. The Weisbrod theory for the existence of nonprofits proposes that nonprofit firms arise to fulfill unmet demands for public goods.

3. The contract failure theory for the existence of nonprofits proposes that nonprofit firms are advantageous under circumstances where it is difficult or impossible for the purchaser of the good to verify the delivery and the quality of the good.

4. The interest group theory for the existence of nonprofit hospitals proposes that physicians favor the nonprofit hospital organizations because they can exercise greater economic control within them.

5. Utility-maximizing models of nonprofit firms are exemplified by the Newhouse model in which the hospital decision makers choose preferred combinations of quality and quantity of care subject to a breakeven constraint.

6. The physicians' cooperative model in contrast depicts the hospital under de facto physician control exercised so as to maximize average physician income.

7. The Harris hospital model is distinct from both the utility-maximizing type and the income-maximizing type. Harris depicts the nonprofit hospital as the outcome of two noncooperative interacting firms represented by administrators, on one side, and physicians, on the other. These groups must often employ nonmarket decision making in life-or-death situations.

8. Under property rights theory, the nonprofit health care firm is less efficient than its for-profit counterpart because the incentive to maximize firm wealth is attenuated by the nondistribution constraint.

9. Evidence suggests that nonprofit hospitals in the United States are not very different in economic efficiency from for-profit hospitals. Evidence on nursing homes in contrast shows clearly higher costs in nonprofit homes.

Discussion Questions

1. What is the nondistribution constraint? In what way is the nondistribution constraint circumvented in the Pauly–Redisch model? What implication does this have for the efficiency of the Pauly–Redisch nonprofit hospital?

2. If the delivery and quality of care by health care firms could be cheaply and accurately monitored by a monitoring agency, would there be any contract failure in health care remaining? Would there be any need for nonprofits in health care? Would any arise?

3. If the interest group theory applies to hospitals, why doesn't it also apply to nursing homes? Would a doctor-owned, for-profit hospital be as attractive to physicians as a nonprofit hospital?

4. Suppose that population growth expands the quality–quantity frontier of a Newhouse utility-maximizing nonprofit hospital. How would its choice of quantity and quality change? In your view, is a for-profit hospital likely to respond more quickly to population growth? Discuss.

5. Under which of the three models of hospital behavior described in this chapter does the tax-exempt status of nonprofit hospitals make the most sense? Under which the least?

6. Can we say which are the most efficient hospitals—nonprofits or for-profits? Which the most efficient nursing homes? What qualifications apply to our present knowledge in each case? What is your view?

7. Why might information problems lead to consumer preferences for nonprofit provision of some goods and services? Reconcile your answer with the observation that most physician care, drug products, and many other services are provided by for-profit firms.

8. In what sense do nonprofits earn "profits" and need to earn "profits" to survive?

9. What are some cost advantages that nonprofits have over for-profits? Are there any disadvantages?

10. Explain the logic behind the argument that donations have characteristics of a public good.

Exercises

1. In Figure 18.1, if two additional voters had demand curves equal to D_5, what amount of the public good would tend to be provided by the democratic government? Which voters would be unlikely to promote a nonprofit? Which likely?

2. In Figure 18.1, suppose that Voter 5 decides that he values the public good even more than before. Will there be an increase in the amount provided through the median voter model of the voting process? Why or why not?

   Suppose that Voter 5 can bribe one of the voters to change his or her preferences. Which one will Voter 5 approach?

3. Under the physicians' cooperative model, if the supply price of physicians were to rise, how would this affect the equilibrium staff size in the open-staff case? How would it affect the optimal staff size in the closed-staff case?

4. Of the Newhouse and the physicians' cooperative models, which nonprofit hospital is likely to produce more quantity and quality in equilibrium with barriers to entry? In long-run equilibrium with free entry and exit?

5. In the property rights model graph in Figure 18.7, if strenuous regulatory activity were to lower the maximum salary level LL of nonprofits, how would this affect the nonprofit efficiency level?

6. Weisbrod, Bays, and Hansmann present three different theories on the existence of nonprofit organizations. Compare and contrast them with regard to the types of firms, and the ways that they are financed.

7. Consider Figures 18.2 and 18.3. Suppose that technological improvements allow hospitals to produce quality at lower average costs. What will happen to the average cost curves in Figure 18.2? What will happen to equilibrium quality and quantity in Figure 18.3?

CHAPTER
19

Government Intervention in Health Care Markets and an Introduction to Regulation

- ■ Economic Rationale for Government Intervention
- ■ Government Involvement in Health Care Markets
- ■ Introduction to Regulation
- ■ Regulation of the Hospital Sector
- ■ Prospective Payment
- ■ Competitive Strategies
- ■ Conclusions

The material in previous chapters has partially revealed the scope of government involvement in health care delivery. We have seen that (1) government spending accounts for a substantial portion of all health care spending, (2) governments are deeply involved in producing as well as financing health care services, and (3) governments regulate the health care industries. Also we have found that governments are at the center of most contemporary health care issues. These include both major policy issues such as national health insurance and initiatives intended to control costs and increase access to care, but also less publicized issues such as those involving federal government support for education and research.

The purpose of this chapter is to provide a framework for assessing the role of governments in health care markets. We begin with the conventional approach favored by economists that emphasizes market failure as the rationale for government intervention. This is followed by a historical review, including examples of federal, state, and local involvement in the health economy. We continue with a more general introduction to regulation that provides a framework for evaluating some of the major instruments used to regulate hospitals. As an alternative to regulation, we also address competitive strategies to improve health care delivery and to meet this nation's policy goals.

ECONOMIC RATIONALE
FOR GOVERNMENT INTERVENTION

Efficiency is a common standard for evaluating the desirability of economic allocations.[1] Inefficient allocations are associated with various distortions that lead to market failure.

Monopoly Power

The classic example of market failure is monopoly power. A profit-maximizing monopolist produces to the level at which marginal revenue equals marginal cost. Because the marginal revenue curve lies below the demand curve, the price charged by the monopolist will exceed the marginal cost of production. It is this price–marginal cost gap that creates the welfare loss.

However, monopoly power need not be associated solely with pure monopoly. The monopoly model is commonly applied to markets in which one or a small number of sellers are dominant. Several health care markets seem to hold a potential for the exercise of monopoly power in health care. Examples include hospital services in markets with few hospitals, pharmaceutical products that are protected by patents, and some health insurance markets dominated by Blue Cross and Blue Shield associations.

The potential for monopoly power exists even in markets characterized by a large number of sellers, as in the markets for doctor and dental services. Licensure laws and other forms of regulation restrict entry into some professions. Furthermore, professional associations may be able to reduce price competition by setting minimum fee schedules or by inhibiting the flow of information to buyers.

Note several issues regarding monopoly power. First, some of the barriers to entry and competition result from government intervention itself. These include licensure and patent laws. Licensure is intended to ensure minimal standards of quality; patent laws are intended to promote innovative activity.

Second, monopoly power may be inevitable in some situations and does not necessarily lead to economic profits. In a small market, for example, demand may be sufficient for only one hospital to survive while it just covers costs. If, in fact, demand were to diminish, even the one existing hospital would not be able to survive unless it received subsidies or donations or it could cut its costs.

Third, the proposed cure to monopoly inefficiencies may be worse than the problems posed by the existence and exercise of monopoly power. Some have argued that direct intervention through public provision or price controls could worsen the situation because of government failure. These critics suggest that countervailing forces and

---

[1]The concept of (Pareto) efficient allocations is formally developed in Chapter 20.

other constraints on the full exercise of monopoly power will tend to arise in private markets, especially where there is vigorous enforcement of antitrust laws.

In the simplest case, and in the absence of government failure, price controls can theoretically reduce the welfare loss caused by monopoly. Figure 19.1 illustrates a hospital monopolist with constant long-run average costs (equal to long-run marginal costs) of production. The profit-maximizing price–quantity combination (P_1, Q_1), found by equating marginal revenue with marginal cost, results in a welfare loss shown by area *ABC*. In theory, fee controls could reduce the welfare loss and drive the monopolist toward marginal cost pricing.

Suppose a maximum fee control of P_2 is established. The monopolist's marginal revenue is constant, equal to the price P_2, up to an output of Q_2. Because marginal revenue exceeds marginal cost up until output Q_2, the monopolist will produce at least to Q_2. Beyond, Q_2, the marginal revenue is found from the usual MR curve since the monopolist would have to lower prices to attract more buyers. Marginal revenue then will be below marginal cost and will eventually become negative. The profit-maximizing output is Q_2, and the welfare loss is now reduced from area *ABC* to area *DEC*. While it thus appears in this case that price regulation can be an effective instrument in reducing prices, monopoly profits, and welfare losses, consider that a typical hospital or physician provider may produce many different services. Consider also that demand and technology are constantly changing and that it may be difficult to monitor quality. As we will discuss later, price regulation under such circumstances becomes a far more difficult task.

Public Goods

A public good should not be confused with the public provision of a good. The postal service and garbage collection service are examples of public provision of private goods. Such goods may be provided by government because of natural monopoly or a

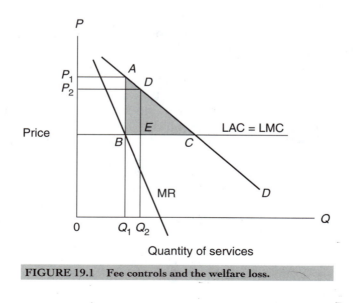

FIGURE 19.1   Fee controls and the welfare loss.

desire to subsidize certain users (e.g., rural postal customers). In contrast, a pure public good is one for which consumption is nonrival (i.e., consumption by one individual does not reduce someone else's consumption) and nonexcludable (i.e., a consumer cannot be excluded from consuming the good either by having to pay or through some other mechanism). National defense is often used as an example of a pure public good. Other examples of goods having some degree of publicness include highways, bridges, and parks.[2]

Market failure arises because only an inefficiently small quantity of pure public goods will be provided in private markets. Many people will become *free riders* (i.e., make no contributions) because they cannot be excluded from consuming the commodity. They may have no economic incentive to contribute voluntarily because the impact of their own contributions to the availability of the public good will be small. The predicted undersupply of public goods in private markets has led many to conclude that governments should provide these goods.

But are health care services public goods? Health services provided to *you* are not at the same time consumed by others. Also, those who do not pay can be excluded from receiving care. Health care services, therefore, are private goods even though they may involve public provision (e.g., through the Veterans Administration) or public financing (e.g., through Medicare and Medicaid). Thus, the public goods rationale for government provision of health care is not immediately apparent.

Despite this caveat, economic theories of public goods are highly relevant to certain health care issues. Consider the following cases:

INFORMATION

Information can be thought of as an economic good that has a high degree of publicness. By obtaining information, one consumer does not reduce the information available to another. Although those who do not pay can often be excluded from receiving information, the marginal cost of providing information to another individual is often relatively small. It can thus be argued that information will be underproduced in private markets and that government intervention is needed to increase its availability.

There are two distinct roles that government may take on. The first is to help disseminate existing knowledge to the public. This can be achieved either through direct provision or through subsidizing private sector activities. Second, governments may also expand the stock of knowledge by taking an active role in scientific research, again by direct provision or through subsidizing private sector research. The federal government has pursued both strategies.

REDISTRIBUTION

There is also a public goods dimension to voluntary giving. Donations help to raise lower-income persons' standards of consumption, including their consumption of health care. By letting others donate, and knowing that one's contribution will have little impact on total contributions, individuals often become free riders. To help offset

---

[2]Consumption of such goods tends to be nonrival but only up to some congestion point. Also these goods are not consumed equally and it may be feasible to exclude those who do not pay for their use.

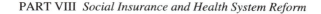

this effect, it can be argued that mandatory programs are needed to correct the under-supply of voluntary giving.

There can be, however, considerable disagreement over the form of the redistribution. Should it be done through cash transfers to let recipients spend their additional incomes as they see fit? Or should some programs take the form of in-kind transfers (e.g., Medicaid) where the transfers must be used to purchase health care services? The many issues relating to equity and mechanisms for redistributing income will be taken up in Chapters 20 (Equity, Efficiency, and Need) and 21 (Social Insurance).

Externalities

In contrast to pure or nearly pure public goods, another group of goods has a varying degree of publicness to it. This group is composed of those goods that have third-party effects, also known as externalities, Recall that externalities arise when a third party is affected by another party's consumption or production of a good. If a neighbor's loud music or smoke from leaves burning bothers you, a negative externality has been created.

Moreover, to be considered an externality, the effects must be transmitted outside the price system. Thus, a situation where an increase in demand for lower cholesterol meats raises their prices, adversely affecting consumers of these products, is not an externality. The higher prices ration the supply of low-cholesterol products.

The major problem with many negative or positive externalities is that the externalities may not be fully reflected in the prices of the goods and services with which they are associated. Thus, even where competitive forces drive prices to the marginal cost of production, social efficiency requires that price equal the marginal social cost, consisting of both marginal production costs and external costs.

With a negative externality, there will be a tendency toward overproduction in competitive markets. The marginal social cost will exceed the marginal benefit. Conversely, positive externalities will lead to underproduction and higher-than-optimum prices. The marginal social benefits will exceed the marginal cost. Positive externalities can be important in health care, as when a charitably minded person derives satisfaction from knowing that the sick, poor, or uninsured consume more health care. More tangible externalities are created when others are inoculated against communicable diseases.

The extent of the role of positive externalities should not be confused with health benefits that are largely private. Subsidies that lead to improved health are often supported on the grounds that recipients will benefit society by being more productive. But the gains from an individual's increased productivity are largely private. Thus, the effects of the consumption of health care on productivity are not externalities.

Other Rationales for Government Intervention

There are also several other arguments for government intervention. An important responsibility of the federal government is to stabilize the economy through macroeconomic policies. Although macroeconomics does not usually focus on specific sectors of the economy, changes in monetary, fiscal, and debt policy can have major effects both on federal and state health care programs as well as on private health care spending through changes in taxes and interest rates.

Another distinct category involves government's role in promoting the consumption of merit goods. Merit goods are commodities thought to be good for someone regardless of the person's own preferences. Support for the arts, compulsory education, and mandated consumption of other goods are in part supported by arguments that individuals do not always know what is in their best interests. Undoubtedly, to some extent, public policy with respect to seat belts, alcohol, tobacco and drug use, and other public health issues has reflected the merit goods idea.

A final role for government involves incomplete markets. These are situations in which private markets fail to meet an existing demand. Certain insurance markets, such as those for patients with cancer, AIDS, or other preexisting conditions who seek new insurance, are sometimes suggested as examples of incomplete markets in the sense that such patients may not be able to buy insurance at *any* price. It has been proposed that government has a role in filling these gaps by providing insurance or requiring insurers to do so.

Care is needed, however, to determine whether some of these markets are truly incomplete. Is there sufficient demand by those willing to pay actuarially fair rates so that a market would emerge? Since premiums would, on average, match insurance payments, they would be very high. Are such patients actually seeking subsidies by having legislation guaranteeing access to insurance at lower than actuarially fair rates?

GOVERNMENT INVOLVEMENT IN HEALTH CARE MARKETS

Hardly any economic activity is free of government intervention. Intervention comes mainly through three activities: provision of goods and services, redistribution, and regulation. Governments have pursued each of these activities in the health economy. Through public hospitals, the Veterans Administration, and other programs, they provide substantial amounts of health care, though this activity is overshadowed by social insurance programs for the elderly and many poor. The provision of health care and of health insurance is also the major means used to redistribute income to lower-income groups from higher-income groups. Less obvious to many is governments' role as a regulator. At the federal level, the Securities and Exchange Commission (SEC), the Environmental Protection Agency (EPA), and the Occupational Safety and Health Administration (OSHA) are among the numerous regulatory agencies that affect nearly every business and working individual. In addition, various state and local requirements, such as those governing building and safety codes, may have to be met.

However, when economists and others speak of regulating or deregulating the health care industries, they are not referring to the kinds of social and commercial controls cited earlier. Rather, they are concerned with regulations that are targeted specifically at the health care industries. Government involvement in the health economy takes on many forms, some of which are developed elsewhere in this text. At this point, we only provide several examples to highlight the variety and scope of government intervention in health care markets.

Support of Hospitals

As described in Chapter 17, the modern hospital did not begin to emerge until the confluence of several developments in the late nineteenth century such as major improvements in anesthesia, antisepsis, and in the invention of X-rays. Temin (1988) characterizes hospitals prior to this period as being more like municipal almshouses funded by taxes or voluntary contributions. Hospitals "existed for the care of marginal members of society, whether old, poor, or medically or psychologically deviant" (pp. 78–79).

In retrospect, one can argue that public support for hospitals was based on a redistribution motive and by a desire to deal with the negative externalities associated with the insane and those harboring communicable diseases such as tuberculosis. With the improvements in physicians' abilities to diagnose and to treat patients surgically, hospitals grew rapidly in the first decades of the twentieth century. Public hospitals continued to serve the poor but also focused their attention on the growing middle classes. Ultimately, patient payments and insurance became the primary sources of funds for many of these institutions.

The Hill-Burton Act

Federal support for private hospitals was minimal until the passage of the Hill-Burton Act in 1946. The program was designed to expand rural health facilities by providing for matching grants to nonprofit institutions. Temin found that the Hill-Burton program contributed substantially to the rise in per capita hospital beds between 1947 and 1970.

The Hill-Burton Act, however, also required states "to survey its hospital needs, to develop a statewide plan for the construction of public hospitals and health centers, and, finally, to construct needed hospitals and health centers."[3] This process of planning was carried a step further with the enactment of other health-planning legislation. As governments increasingly emphasized cost issues in the late 1960s, the health planning agencies that were created turned to capital expenditures controls to limit hospital growth and costs. The resulting Certificate-of-Need requirements represented a major turning point toward an increasingly regulated health care system.

The Veterans Administration and CHAMPUS

In addition to direct subsidies for hospital construction, governments are also major providers of health care. State, county, and municipal hospitals account for approximately 20 percent of total hospital beds in the United States. The largest public provider is the Veterans Administration (VA). In 1994, the VA spent $14.6 billion for providing, among other services, hospital care for 920,000 patients and over 24 million outpatient visits.[4] The ostensible purpose of the VA is to provide care for service-related injuries through institutions that specialize in providing and undertaking research for such care. However, a veteran may be treated for other conditions unrelated

---

[3]Hochban et al. (1981, p. 61).
[4]U.S. Department of Health and Human Services (1995).

to service injuries if facilities are available and the veteran indicates that he or she cannot afford treatment from other sources. As a result, most patients in VA hospitals are lower-income people, treated for conditions not related to their military injuries.[5]

In addition to direct care provided by the VA, the federal government finances care for retired military personnel and dependents of active-duty, deceased, and retired military personnel through CHAMPUS (Civilian Health and Medical Program for the Uniformed Services). The program has a large number of potential beneficiaries and is similar in its scope of service coverage and administration to Medicare. Because beneficiaries are encouraged to use on-base facilities with low charges, CHAMPUS finances only a relatively small portion of care for eligible beneficiaries.[6]

Food and Drug Administration

Various pieces of drug legislation have been promulgated, beginning with the Food and Drug Act of 1906. The 1962 amendments to the act required considerably more testing and evidence of efficacy and, in general, gave the Food and Drug Administration (FDA) considerably more control over the introduction of new products than previously. The pharmaceutical industry's concerns are that regulatory requirements lengthen the period to FDA approval to about 10 to 12 years, and raise the cost of introducing new drug products, estimated to average over $200 million to the point of marketing.[7]

The economic issues of drug regulation pit the relative gains in drug safety and efficacy against the discouragement to innovation and the delays in availability attributable to the approval process. Benefit–cost analysis, presented in Chapter 24, is well suited to evaluate such trade-offs.

Mandated Health Insurance Benefits

The insurance industry is regulated mainly at the state level. The state's traditional role here is to ensure financial solvency of insurance companies. However, in both auto and health insurance, the states have considerably expanded their roles. One relatively recent phenomenon in health insurance is exhibited by the proliferation of mandated insurance benefits. Such laws have grown from 48 in 1970 to about 1,000 in 1991, covering "heart transplants in Georgia, liver transplants in Illinois, hairpieces in Minnesota . . . and sperm-bank deposits in Massachusetts."[8] Such laws are often promulgated after lobbying by special interest groups who have traditionally been excluded, or after highly publicized cases involving persons who find they are not covered for heart transplants or certain expensive experimental therapies.

Gabel and Jensen (1989) found that these requirements prevent insurers from offering lower-cost alternatives that exclude the mandated benefits. This effect could be substantial for many lower-income individuals who have been priced out of the market.

---

[5]P. Feldstein (1988, p. 522).

[6]Krizay and Wilson (1974, p. 85).

[7]DiMasi et al. (1991). See also Pharmaceutical Manufacturers Association (1987) for extensive data on the industry and new drug product approval.

[8]"Health Insurance: States Can Help," *The Wall Street Journal,* December 17, 1991, p. A14.

Tax Policy

As noted in Chapter 11, federal and state governments provide substantial tax subsidies for the consumption of health care and purchases of insurance. In particular, employer contributions to group health plans are not included in an individual's taxable income (escaping federal, state, and Social Security taxes). Individual payments for health insurance as well as many health care expenses can be itemized if they exceed threshold levels (7.5 percent of adjusted gross income in 1995).

Some have argued that the substantial reductions in the marginal cost of insurance and health care represent a major reason for the growth of insurance and consequent growth of health care spending that occurred in the 1960s and 1970s. Thus, a proposed cost-containment strategy is to reduce such subsidies. Without discussing the merits of this argument here, we wish only to point out that there seems to be little justification for the extensive tax subsidies. Ironically, the tax advantages are greatest to those in the highest marginal tax rates, meaning that the subsidies do not promote equity.

Public Health

We have thus far focused largely on the study of personal health and health care decisions. Public health, on the other hand, deals with areas such as communicable diseases, epidemics, environmental health issues, and other activities with significant third-party health effects such as smoking and the use of drug and alcohol.

Until the latter part of the nineteenth century, public health was a state and local responsibility. However, in 1878, the U.S. government created the Marine Hospital Service, which became the U.S. Public Health Service in 1912.[9] Despite the federal responsibilities, state and local governments spent almost 87 percent of the $25 billion spent on public health in 1993.

Other Government Programs

Numerous other channels for government involvement exist. Some are quite apparent—such as support for medical education and medical schools, which will influence the supply of providers. Similarly, support for health care research undertaken directly by a government agency such as the National Cancer Institutes, or undertaken by other public and private organizations, can have a substantial impact on the spread of technology and the direction of the health care system. For example, critics of the U.S. system claim that it has excessively emphasized high-tech medicine at the expense of preventive medicine and that this bias stems in part from the kinds of research projects that are supported. We are hearing concerns that while there was insufficient support for AIDS-related research in the early years after the discovery of the disease, there is now excessive support to the detriment of those afflicted with other conditions.

Other forms of intervention are less obvious. Changes in immigration policy can affect the supply of health care personnel. Also easily overlooked is the role of the federal government as the nation's largest employer in providing fringe benefits to its

---

[9]See O. Anderson (1990) for a history of public health in the United States.

employees. The Federal Employees Health Benefits Program (FEHBP) offers about 400 different insurance plans to employees and their dependents. Because of its size and its ability to experiment with alternatives, the FEHBP has the potential to influence and serve as a model for the private sector.[10]

To summarize, governments at all levels have heavily intervened in the health care sector. The intervention has taken the forms of direct provision of care, financing of health insurance (especially of Medicare and Medicaid), subsidizing of medical education and the construction of health facilities, subsidizing of purchases of health insurance through the tax structure, and the regulation of health care industries. This intervention has major effects on the total resources devoted to health care as well as on the distribution of resources within the health care industries.

Table 19.1 indicates the scope of public spending in 1993, overall as well as across health care industries. Government spending accounts for about 44 percent of total health

TABLE 19.1   National Health Expenditures, by Source of Funds and Type of Expenditure: 1993

Type of Expenditure	Total	All Private Funds	Private				Government		
			Consumer						*State and Local*
			Total	Out of Pocket	Private Insurance	Other	Total	Federal	
1993				Amount in Billions					
National health expenditures	884.2	496.4	453.6	157.5	296.1	42.8	387.8	280.6	107.3
Health services and supplies	855.2	484.3	453.6	157.5	296.1	30.7	370.9	268.6	102.4
Personal health care	782.5	445.5	415.5	157.5	258.0	30.0	337.0	259.0	78.1
Hospital care	326.6	143.7	126.9	9.1	117.8	16.8	182.9	149.2	33.7
Physician services	171.2	113.1	110.3	26.2	84.1	2.7	58.1	45.0	13.1
Dental services	37.4	35.6	35.5	18.7	16.8	0.2	1.7	1.0	0.8
Other professional services	51.2	40.6	37.0	21.2	15.8	3.6	10.6	7.3	3.3
Home health care	20.8	9.4	6.9	4.3	2.5	2.5	11.4	9.8	1.5
Drugs and other medical nondurables	75.0	65.8	65.8	47.4	18.4	—	9.2	4.7	4.4
Vision products and other medical durables	12.6	8.5	8.5	7.6	0.9	—	4.2	4.0	0.2
Nursing home care	69.6	26.0	24.7	23.0	1.7	1.3	43.6	28.3	15.3
Other personal health care	18.2	2.8	—	—	—	2.8	15.3	9.5	5.8
Program administration and net cost of private health insurance	48.0	38.8	38.1	—	38.1	0.7	9.2	6.3	2.8
Government public health activities	24.7	—	—	—	—	—	24.7	3.3	21.4
Research and construction	29.0	12.1	—	—	—	12.1	16.9	12.0	4.9
Research	14.4	1.2	—	—	—	1.2	13.1	11.1	2.1
Construction	14.6	10.9	—	—	—	10.9	3.8	0.9	2.8

Source: Levitt et al. (1994, Table 13).

---

[10]Moffit (1992) considers choice and competition the elements that make FEHBP a government program that works.

care spending and is concentrated on expenditures on hospital, physician, and nursing home care. However, these amounts understate the impact of public programs. By influencing levels of competition, purchases of health insurance and the innovation and spread of technology, government activities also have substantial effects on private spending.

INTRODUCTION TO REGULATION

Economists in the United States typically favor market solutions to the problem of resources allocation. However, when there is reason to believe that market forces in an industry are not strong, many among the same groups are likely to consider alternatives such as regulation and public provision. These alternatives are even more likely to be pursued when the goods in question are considered necessities and account for substantial consumer expenditures.

Historical Background

The early focus on regulation in the United States was found in the transportation and utilities sectors. In those sectors, concern with excessive monopoly power and natural monopoly arising from economies of scale and high capital expenditures led to the establishment of the Interstate Commerce Commission in 1888, which regulated railroads and shipping. Subsequently, other federal and state regulatory commissions were formed to regulate a variety of commodities including electricity, gas, telephone service, oil pipelines, airlines, and broadcasting.[11] The overriding objective in regulation was, and continues to be, on rate setting. Its primary goal is to limit the high price–cost margins that would otherwise be expected.

Despite concerns with possible abuse of monopoly power in certain health care markets, those favoring increased regulation do not rely on the traditional monopoly power argument. They focus on the absence of discipline in markets brought on by a lack of consumer information and the prevalence of comprehensive fee-for-service insurance.

Lack of consumer information, as discussed elsewhere, has been used to justify licensure and other quality controls as means to ensure minimal standards of care. Similarly, the role of insurance as a source of market failure was discussed earlier, emphasizing the lack of incentives to both patient and provider to shop around or otherwise conserve resources. Perhaps more importantly we emphasized the role of traditional forms of insurance in contributing to moral hazard. Unlike other sources of market failure, market failure associated with insurance has led to regulation of fees and also to regulation of hospital revenues and costs.

Health Regulatory Policy: An Introduction

Regulation refers to the use of nonmarket means to address the quantity, price, or quality of the good brought to market. Since regulations typically address the quantity of services used, the quality of the services, or the amount that payers (either individuals or insurers) are charged, consider total expenditures in a given health care market.

---

[11]Some of these industries have since been deregulated.

By definition, expenditures E equal the price of health care P multiplied by the quantity of services Q or $E = PQ$. Price of care P also depends on quality of care, q. Quality of care in this framework can be thought of as any aspect of a service for which someone is willing to pay extra. An example may be a private, rather than a shared, room in a hospital. Under most circumstances, the private room does not make the patient recover more quickly. However, the patient may be more comfortable with the privacy, and hence be willing to pay more for it.

The key feature of this framework is the idea that within the health economy, regulation uses nonmarket means to affect P, Q, or q, or, of course, combinations. For example, licensure requirements may raise q, which is likely to raise P. If they also restrict the supply of providers, they are further likely to raise P. Other regulations such as the Medicare Prospective Payment System may tend to decrease the amount of services Q used, lowering expenditures. We will address these aspects elsewhere in this chapter. The point here is that most regulations are directed toward changing price, quantity, or quality.

However, the objective of regulation is not merely to reduce spending; otherwise rationing or even prohibiting certain services may successfully meet this objective. Rather, its goals are to promote minimal quality levels while eliminating the inefficient components of spending. The inefficiencies include technical inefficiency, allocative inefficiency, and the inefficiencies associated with economies of scale and scope. These arise for various reasons, which we have already studied.

Regulatory Instruments in Health Care

A variety of price, quantity, and quality controls have been introduced. Here we provide a brief overview of these controls, leaving more detailed analyses of hospital regulation for the next section.

FEE CONTROLS AND RATE REGULATION

Physician fees under Medicaid are controlled, and those under Medicare have been subject to UCR constraints (see Chapter 16). The UCR method of physician reimbursement is also important because it has been emulated by private insurers.

It is the hospital sector, however, that has been the main object of rate regulation. In his review of this subject, Sloan (1983, p. 195) defines *rate regulation* as establishing "the terms under which public and/or private insurers pay hospitals." In the 1960s and 1970s, many states adopted various mandatory or advisory forms of regulation. State approval of rate changes was generally based on hospital costs per day, per admission, or on a hospital's overall costs.

Reimbursement for hospital care was usually on a retrospective basis, determined by allowable costs that were incurred. A number of states, however, adopted prospective forms of reimbursement beginning in the 1970s. Some have been mandated at the state level while other programs are voluntary.[12] The goal of these arrangements is to remove the disincentives hospitals have both to be efficient producers under cost-based retrospective reimbursement and to limit the amount of care they provide patients who are hospitalized.

---

[12]Gaumer et al. (1989) describe many of these arrangements.

Prospective reimbursement, especially once it was adopted by Medicare in 1983, marked an important turning point in regulatory efforts to contain the growth of hospital costs. Medicare's Prospective Payment System (PPS) limits hospital revenues per patient. Under PPS, hospitals are reimbursed a fixed amount per admission, determined by the patient's diagnostic condition, regardless of the hospital's actual costs. The strategy behind PPS is simple. By limiting revenues, it provides hospitals with strong disincentives to extend lengths-of-stay and provide unnecessary or marginal care. A detailed discussion of PPS and its effects is found later in this chapter.

QUANTITY AND CAPACITY CONTROLS

The controls on quantity tend to be indirect rather than direct, with the most prominent example being Certificate-of-Need (CON) laws. These laws required hospitals to obtain approval from planning agencies for capital expenditures in excess of various threshold levels. The rationale was embedded in views that unnecessary duplication of facilities as well as the mere availability of facilities lead to higher costs (i.e., fixed costs spread out over fewer users) and to higher rates of utilization (due to access and/or physician discretion).

Utilization review (UR), although primarily directed at quality, has also been supported on the basis of its expected negative effects on quantity. To the extent that third parties choose not to reimburse for services determined to be inappropriate, UR could have a deterrent effect on the provision of questionable services.

Quality Controls

Apart from licensure and accreditation requirements, utilization review is the primary quality assurance mechanism. Utilization review is conducted by hospitals and by Peer Review Organizations (PROs).[13] Under UR, the main questions are whether the admission and length-of-stay were appropriate and whether the patient had received appropriate care. However, most of the work of evaluating UR has focused on costs rather than quality, so that there is little evidence on quality effects.

REGULATION OF THE HOSPITAL SECTOR

Given its large and growing share of the U.S. health economy, policymakers have addressed cost inflation by regulating the hospital industry. The previous section provided a general introduction to regulation. In this section, we focus on the three major forms of hospital regulation: rate regulation, utilization review, and Certificate-of-Need. These are administered mainly at the state level.

---

[13]See Chapter 17 for further discussion of PROs and their predecessor, Professional Standards Review Organizations (PSROs).

Rate Regulation, Utilization Review, and Certificate-of-Need

As described previously, rate regulation defines the terms under which hospitals are reimbursed. The underlying premise has been that, due to market power, hospitals may charge rates that vary from the cost of providing the services. Prospective forms of reimbursement are also intended to deal with hospital inefficiency and incentives to overprovide care that exist under retrospective reimbursement.

Rate regulation (RR) may occur by type of service provided, on a daily (or per diem basis), or on a per patient or per admission basis. The goal of rate regulation is to lower costs, or at least to reduce the rate of hospital cost inflation.

Utilization review (UR) programs seek to determine whether specific services are medically necessary, and whether they are delivered at an appropriate level of intensity and cost. Ermann (1988) identifies three general types of utilization review:

- *Preadmission review* examines the necessity of hospital admission, before admission occurs, to determine if inpatient care is necessary.
- *Concurrent review* ascertains whether patients need continuing care, by means of record review.
- *Retrospective review* attempts to identify questionable patterns of care.

Another form of UR is second-opinion surgery review. This either requires or encourages patients who are contemplating elective surgery to seek advice from a second physician. One of the key questions in analyzing the impacts of any form of utilization review is the extent to which "truly" unnecessary procedures are eliminated, as opposed to the extent that the quality of care suffers.

Certificate-of-Need (CON) regulation addresses capital expenditure (either beds or other expensive hospital equipment). The general aim is to reduce excess capacity, or to eliminate costly duplication of resources. An unintended impact occurs, however, if this review process reduces competition in the provision of the services. This reduction of competition, of course, could lead to increased monopoly power and to higher prices.

Empirical Findings on Regulation

UTILIZATION REVIEW

The premise behind UR is to reduce unnecessary costs without adversely affecting patient health. The results of UR have been mixed. Much of the work has reviewed the Professional Standards Review Organizations (PSROs) that were established at local levels under federal laws in 1972. Two factors have led to difficulties. First, there has been a wide variation among PSROs. Some may have been quite effective, while others were not. Looking across a whole group may not provide much guidance.

Second, the PSRO program had two mandates. Cost was to be contained and quality was to be ensured. It is clear that if quality-related aspects of health care provision cost money, then these two goals may conflict with each other. Not surprisingly, empirical results have generally been inconclusive. Rosko and Broyles (1988, Chapter 12) provide a review of earlier studies.

More recently, Wickizer, Wheeler, and Feldstein (1989) found that UR reduced admissions by 13 percent, inpatient days by 11 percent, expenditures on routine hospital inpatient service by 7 percent, expenditures on hospital ancillary services by 9 percent, and total medical expenditures by 6 percent. The same authors (1991) also find that the adoption of UR implies substitution of outpatient care for inpatient care. The small magnitude of these substitution effects (approximately $9 per insured person per year) suggests a limited, although measurable effect.

As for concerns that patients will get less care and with less certain (and possibly less positive) outcomes, Ermann (1988) cites the lack of conclusive evidence. Dranove (1991) nevertheless argues that price competition may force those who engage in UR to focus on cost savings "at the expense of appropriateness." He concludes that "cost cutting through UR is easy. Improving the health care product through UR is not" (p. 26).

RATE REGULATION

Much of the research investigating the impact of RR has centered around the states of Connecticut, Massachusetts, New Jersey, New York, Maryland, and Washington, which had or adopted rate regulation through the 1970s and early 1980s. Studies investigating the impacts of RR have typically looked at costs, or changes in costs, in these states, or in hospitals within these states. The typical method is to estimate a regression such that

$$\log C_t - \log C_{t-1} = b(X_t - X_{t-1}) + dD + \epsilon$$

where the left-hand side reflects the change in the logarithm of hospital expenses (or the logarithm of the percent change in expenses), as a function of changes in explanatory variables X, and the imposition of rate regulation D. If coefficient d is negative, then, all else being equal, the imposition of regulation D reduces the growth in costs.

Dranove and Cone (1985) present an interesting discussion of the impacts of rate regulation. They carefully examine the possibility of *regression to the mean*. Suppose in examining hospital costs over time, at a given point some states have unusually high or unusually low costs. If these differences are transient, due to jumps in energy or insurance costs, or some form of natural disaster, then total costs would be expected to return to the mean as the transient events disappeared. Laws enacted in high-cost states may appear to be successful because the effects attributed to the laws are really caused by regression of the state to the overall mean of all states. The reverse, of course, is also possible. States that were below the mean could see rising costs, even with effective regulation.

Although their correction for regression to the mean is technical in nature, it is useful nonetheless to examine their regression results. They estimated the foregoing difference equation, with the following explanatory variables:

- Income—median family income
- Education—population percent with high school diploma
- Age—population percent over age 65
- Insurance—population percent insured against physician expenses
- Metro—population percent living in an urban area
- Union—population percent who are union members

and the following policy variable:

- Law—number of years the law has been in effect

The variables that they sought to explain were (1) expenses per admission, (2) expenses per day, and (3) expenses per person.

The regression results are presented in Table 19.2. Multiplying each coefficient of the law variable by 100 approximates (due to the logarithmic transformation of the dependent variable) the law's percentage impact. For example, those states with a regulation law exhibited approximately a 1.32 percent smaller increase in expenses per admission than other states; a 1.41 percent smaller increase in expenses/day; and a 1.04 percent smaller increase in expenses per person.

Regression to the mean does occur. Dranove and Cone suggest that mean regression made laws in New York and Massachusetts look more effective than they actually were (costs would have decreased anyhow). Conversely, mean regression made laws in Connecticut, New Jersey, and Washington look less effective. New Jersey, in fact, moved from 4 percentage points worse than the average rate-setting state to 4 percentage points better.

Rosko and Broyles (1988) summarize findings of restraint of cost inflation per year:

- Costs per admission rose by 1.4 to 8.7 percent less.
- Costs per patient day rose by 1.2 to 10.5 percent less.
- Expenditures per capita rose by 2.0 to 7.6 percent less.

CERTIFICATE-OF-NEED

Certificate-of-Need (CON) legislation has been studied in a variety of contexts. Salkever and Bice (1979) provided early and useful analyses of the programs. Their

TABLE 19.2   Percentage Change in Hospital Costs

Variable	Expenses per Admission	Expenses per Day	Expenses per Person
Constant	0.70[a]	0.72[a]	0.46[a]
Income	0.66[a]	1.13[a]	0.79[a]
Education	−0.63[b]	−0.69[b]	0.30
Age	0.35[b]	0.28	0.83[a]
Insurance	−0.094	−0.26[b]	−0.67
Metro	−0.016	−0.70[b]	−0.33
Union	−0.11	−0.33[a]	−0.57
Law	**−0.0132[a]**	**−0.0141[a]**	**−0.0104[b]**
Adjustment	−0.20[b]	−0.005	−0.33[a]
Adjusted R^2	0.46	0.50	0.52

[a]Significant at 1 percent level.
[b]Significant at 10 percent level.
Source: Dranove and Cone (1985, Table 4).

methods, as with others, were to predict costs, using binary variables to represent the presence, comprehensiveness, and maturity of programs designed to regulate capital formation. Almost all of the studies found that there was essentially no impact of CON on total expenditures.

Nevertheless, it is plausible to expect that other hospital inputs may increase to substitute for limits on capital expenditures. Salkever and Bice note that hospitals appear to have substituted investment for new services in place of investment in beds. Another study reported similar results, as well as increased ratios of registered nurses per bed, and licensed practical nurses per bed.[14]

Recognizing the problem of characterizing CON across states, Mayo and McFarland (1989) present a theoretically appealing examination over time within a single state. Recall that the goal of CON is to reduce capital expenditures, and thus prevent costly duplication of facilities.

One can posit three impacts of CON:

1. The intended impact on capital costs, which reduces cost by reducing capital expenditures.

2. The substitution effect in which the hospitals substitute nonregulated inputs for the regulated ones. This may offset capital cost reductions.[15]

3. The increased monopoly power of existing hospitals. If competitors are prevented from engaging in capital expenditures, then existing hospitals have increased monopoly power. Some economists also argue that incentives to innovate, and hence lower production costs, may be lost if competition is lessened.

Mayo and McFarland, in data for the state of Tennessee, find the direct effects of CON to lower hospital costs, and the indirect substitution and market concentration effects to raise them. While many studies in other states indicate no significant effect of CON, the newer theoretical and empirical models suggest the importance of modeling cost-containment policies at the hospital rather than at the regional level. Hospitals react to cost-containment policies not only by changing the costs of the services, but by adjusting the amounts of the services, and the inputs into the services.

PROSPECTIVE PAYMENT

The enactment of Medicare and Medicaid got the federal government into the reimbursement of services in a big way. There have been substantial increases in the costs of these programs over the years, and as costs have grown, so has interest in cost-containment policies.

In this section, we focus on the Medicare program that converted the financing of Medicare hospital care to a prospective payment system based on diagnosis-related groups (DRGs). We discuss the system in the present context because its widespread

---

[14]See Sloan and Steinwald (1980).

[15]Mayo and McFarland (1989) do not address this issue. In response to an insightful comment by K. Anderson (1991), they reestimate their cost equation (Mayo and McFarland, 1991) to allow for such a cost adjustment. Our discussion uses the reestimated 1991 equation.

use stems from its adoption by the Medicare program. However, the PPS system under DRGs has wider significance both to other segments of the health sector as well as to the regulation of industry in general.

Description of PPS

Understanding PPS under DRGs requires knowing what prospective payment means, and what DRGs are. Prospective payment is best seen in contrast to the former retrospective reimbursement system under Medicare. Under retrospective payment, a hospital submits its bill to Medicare after the care has been given and the costs to the hospital are known. Retrospective payment allowed the hospitals to recover their expenses, as allowed by Medicare rules, regardless of whether these expenses were high or low, excessive or efficient. Under retrospective reimbursement, there were questionable incentives for cost-efficiency.

Prospective payment sets payment rates prior to the period for which care is given. By setting a fixed reimbursement level per admission, prospective payment provides economic incentives to conserve on the use of input resources. Hospitals that use more resources than covered by the flat rate lose the difference. Those with costs below that rate retain the difference.

The rates themselves are determined by DRGs. Under PPS, patients are admitted according to their condition under one of 495 DRGs. Each DRG attempts to represent a case type that identifies patients with similar conditions and processes of care. Some of the most common DRGs, based upon hospital discharges for Medicare patients, are shown in Table 19.3.

Each DRG is given a flat payment rate calculated in part on the basis of costs incurred for that DRG nationally. These rates are modified somewhat, in practice, to account for differences in local wages, urban versus rural location, and other factors such as whether the hospital is a teaching hospital. The rates are flat in the important sense that they are not varied or softened for hospitals that spend more than the rate, or for that matter less.

TABLE 19.3   Five Leading DRGs for Medicare Hospital Discharges: 1992

Rank	DRG Code	Description
1	127	Heart failure and shock
2	89	Simple pneumonia and pleurisy, age greater than 17 and with complications and/or comorbidities
3	140	Angina pectoris
4	14	Specific cerebrovascular disorders except transient ischemic attack
5	209	Major joint and limb reattachment procedures of lower extremity

Source: Health Care Financing Review, Medicare and Medicaid Statistical Supplement (February 1995).

The Theory of Yardstick Competition and DRGs

Shleifer (1985) has described the theory of a payment system he calls *yardstick competition,* which is a close approximation of the Prospective Payment System under DRGs. We can think of yardstick competition as the ideal form of such a system, while the actual Medicare payment system is a real-life approximation. As such, it is helpful to consider the economics behind it.

Shleifer describes yardstick competition in the context of markets where firms are monopolists or at least have some monopoly power. Since most medical providers face downward sloping demand curves, they possess some degree of monopoly power. This characterizes the hospital care market reasonably well.

Recall that under monopoly, firms reduce production to below what a competitive firm would offer, and correspondingly charge higher prices. This behavior is harmful to the consumer and causes losses in consumer welfare. Sometimes, the government regulates firms with monopoly power, and when it does, the appropriate regulation of prices must address the goals of cost control, waste prevention, and the promotion of cost-reducing innovation. Left to its own devices, the secure monopoly firm lacks some of the incentives to be cost-efficient that rigorous competition would provide. In hospital markets in the United States prior to PPS, the most important source of disincentives was the retrospective payment system that we have discussed. Shleifer describes a regulatory scheme, in this case simply a payment scheme much like Medicare's PPS, that restores cost-consciousness incentives.

The context in which yardstick competition is effective requires that existing firms be less cost-efficient than they might. Shleifer assumes that firms could reduce costs with suitable investments. Consider an example in which a hospital knows it could be more cost-efficient if it would hire a team of efficiency experts (which is costly) and carry out their advice (which also is costly). An optimal scheme would lead the firm to invest so as to reduce costs. The problem for yardstick competition is to set up a payment scheme so that these firms have the incentives to expend just the right amount of money and effort on reducing production costs.

We must at this point ask the following question: What is just the right amount of expense to incur in the effort to reduce production costs? Suppose that a firm discovers by its own research that it could most likely reduce its marginal costs of production (for simplicity, assume they are constant) by $1 per unit of output if it were to spend a total of $1,500 on cost-reduction efforts. Suppose this firm is a hospital that produces 5,000 cases treated per year, or 5,000 units of output. Would the cost-reduction effort be worth it? The example is shown in the first line of the following schedule.

	Marginal cost of efficiency effort		*Marginal revenue generated*
(1)	$1,500	<	$1 × 5,000
(2)	$3,500	<	$1 × 5,000
(3)	$4,985	<	$1 × 5,000
(4)	$6,850	>	$1 × 5,000

Row (1) represents the first of four possible steps in cost reduction. Each step, let us assume, will reduce costs per case by $1. Thus, in row (1), reducing per-unit costs by one dollar costs the firm a total of $1,500 dollars in cost-efficiency efforts. The extra dollar saved for every case treated generates a total of $1 × 5,000 dollars in extra revenue. In this example, the $1,500 is called the marginal cost of efficiency effort, not to be confused with the marginal cost of producing the cases.

Clearly, this step of cost saving is worthwhile: It costs less ($1,500) than it saves ($5,000). By similar reasoning, one more step of cost saving would also be worthwhile, costing $3,500 but saving another $5,000. Step (3) is worthwhile too, but that is where we would stop. Unregulated monopolists or the retrospectively reimbursed firms will not necessarily have the built-in incentives to take these three steps. It would be good to have a payment system that would induce them to do so.

The efficient level of efficiency effort can be shown graphically. Consider Figure 19.2. The marginal cost of cases treated by the hospital is shown on the x-axis. The marginal cost of the efficiency efforts is shown on the y-axis. For simplicity, this is shown not in discrete steps but as a continuous downward sloping curve. Notice by following MC_E backward that the more effort expended to reduce production costs by another dollar, the more expensive is the efficiency effort.

In contrast, the benefit of each step of cost reduction—the extra revenue generated (which would correspond to the $5,000 in the numerical example)—is shown as line MB_E. At point A, the increased profits to the firm from the efficiency effort are equal to ($5,000 − MC_E); if MC_E equals $4,000, the incremental profits are $1,000. Starting at point A and working backward, we would ideally continue to reduce production costs as long as the marginal benefit of doing so exceeded the marginal efficiency costs—that is, as long as line MB_E is higher than line MC_E. The best choice, where one stops further cost-reduction efforts, thus occurs at point B.

The yardstick competition system induces firms to choose point B. It works as follows. Prices at which the firm is reimbursed are set *beforehand* at fixed rates. These

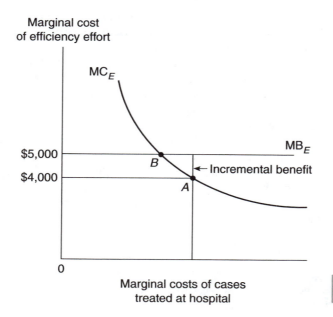

FIGURE 19.2   Efficient level of efficiency effort.

rates—that is, these regulated prices—are set equal to the averages of the marginal costs of all *other* firms in the market.

In addition, under Shleifer's scheme the firms are given a yardstick lump-sum subsidy equal to the costs they incur from efficiency efforts. Suppose the regulator is able to determine the marginal cost of each hospital. Consider, then, Hospital 1. Hospital 1 is assigned both the price of services and the breakeven subsidy, equal to the average of all of its competitors, Hospitals 2 through *N*. With its revenue per patient now fixed prospectively, Hospital 1 now wants to maximize its profits (or at least break even) given this price. Clearly, Hospital 1's incentive is to invest in cost-cutting technologies or practices.

Why does this work? By fixing the price as a yardstick, yardstick competition and breakeven subsidies prevent a hospital's inefficient choice from affecting the price (and subsidy) that the hospital receives. By using the costs of other hospitals, the regulator is ensuring that sector-specific cost conditions are addressed. By omitting the hospital's own costs in setting the rate, the regulator keeps the hospital from influencing the price by inflating its own costs.

In addition, we recognize that yardstick competition imposes a horizontal marginal revenue curve on the hospital. Recalling the welfare losses that accompany monopoly power, we would also expect output to rise.

In this model, hospitals are not subsidized for inefficient behavior. Hospitals compete, and this competition leads to the optimum solution discussed earlier.[16] Shleifer notes that it is

> essential for the regulator to commit himself not to pay attention to the firms' complaints and to be prepared to let the firms go bankrupt if they choose inefficient cost levels. Unless the regulator can credibly threaten to make inefficient firms lose money . . . cost reduction cannot be enforced (p. 327).

The model presented implicitly assumes that all firms, in this case hospitals, are the same. Shleifer, however, shows how one could construct a multiple regression model that would help to generate a similar solution in the more realistic case where firms are different from each other. Furthermore, he demonstrates a closely related scheme of pricing based on average industry costs that leads to virtually the same results in the realistic case where the theoretically needed lump-sum subsidies would be difficult to calculate or difficult to pass politically.

Let us return now to DRGs as practiced. It is important to note that, consistent with Shleifer's formulation, a hospital's actual costs do not enter into the formula for its payment rate. As a result, the hospital must become a price taker in the strictest sense. If it costs the hospital more to provide the service than the DRGs allow, the hospital either loses money on the service and is forced to stop offering it, or is forced to cross-subsidize the service from other services that may be produced at costs lower than their DRGs. Thus, the cost-cutting incentives are strong.

---

[16]This process is known as a Nash equilibrium. It refers to a market solution in which each firm does the best it can, given the decision of others. It is an equilibrium since once the choices are made, no firm has any motive to change its action.

Predictably, the inception of DRGs raised major concerns among hospitals. Those familiar with diagnoses will recognize that even as many as 495 categories imply that the thousands of diagnoses must be lumped into groupings that offer single payments appropriate to some, but not to all, conditions handled in a given DRG. This would suggest the necessity of refining the DRG categories.

Shleifer, in fact, notes that some of the problems with DRGs result from the fact that not all of the sources of cost variation are considered. Medicare does not adjust payment for severity of illness. Although it would seem that average severity of illness might be the same among hospitals, those hospitals getting the more severely ill patients might suffer financially.

On the Effects of Medicare's Prospective Payment System

It is clear that yardstick competition in theory and the actual Medicare Prospective Payment System in practice change firms' economic incentives considerably.[17] Results to date show some clear impacts, as well as some remaining ambiguities. We examine briefly here several categories of possible effects.

AVERAGE HOSPITAL LENGTH-OF-STAY

One method of cutting costs available to hospitals, in theory, is to reduce the number of days of care taken to treat a patient case. In fact, average length-of-stay did drop after the advent of PPS. It dropped 9 percent in the first year of PPS, and a total of 14.6 percent between 1982 and 1985.[18] The effect of PPS on length-of-stay is both plausible and clearly established in the data. However, Newhouse and Byrne (1988) point out that this effect is found in short-term acute general care hospitals that are subject to PPS. When considering the effects of increased length-of-stay in other, exempted longer-stay institutions, the net result is that overall health system length-of-stay actually rose between 1981 and 1984. Even so, net cost savings are possible systemwide because exempted institutions tend to have lower daily costs.

A related item is the admission rate to short-term hospitals. Although the effect of PPS on admissions is theoretically ambiguous, several analysts had expected PPS to increase admissions to hospitals. However, since the onset of Medicare's PPS, admission rates have tended to fall rather than rise.

ACCESS AND QUALITY

A number of people have been concerned that the Prospective Payment System under DRGs would induce hospitals to save on costs by cutting corners, reducing quality, refusing to treat costly patients, or closing treatment units. That is, the system would reduce access to care and the quality of care. Research has addressed these issues to some extent.

---

[17]Hodgkin and McGuire (1994) develop a model in which the level of prospective payment affects the hospital's choice of intensity of care, which affects the demand for admissions. The model suggests that both the average payment level and the incentives created by changes in the marginal rate affect hospital utilization.

[18]See Guterman and Dobson (1986), and Feinglass and Holloway (1991).

One study found that use of intensive care units did not fall after PPS, allaying fears about access to needed care. Use of many diagnostic and treatment technologies did fall after PPS started, but these also fell for non-Medicare patients. A second study used statistical techniques to estimate quality changes in a sample of 729 U.S. short-term general care hospitals following Medicare's PPS. The results were negative, meaning that no evidence of quality reduction was found.[19]

DesHarnais and colleagues (1988) found no evidence of quality reductions for a sample of 646 U.S. hospitals. Also relevant to quality issues, Carroll and Erwin (1987) showed no significant difference in several major health status measures for patients being transferred from hospitals to nursing homes before and after PPS. In surveying the available evidence as of 1991, Feinglass and Holloway (1991) conclude that while there is evidence of individual instances where access or quality has been limited because of PPS,

> to date, there is *little direct, generalizable evidence* [emphasis added] that PPS has reduced the quality of care for Medicare patients. Hospital use and mortality rates for potentially unprofitable patients such as the oldest old, minorities, self-paying, uninsured, or nursing home patients covered by both Medicare and Medicaid have decreased at the same rate as the rest of the population (p. 107).

SEVERITY OF THE CASE MIX

Another observed change following the onset of Medicare's PPS has been the increase in common *case-mix indexes.* A case-mix index is a numerical measure of the assortment of patient cases treated by a given hospital, so that a higher value for the index indicates a greater average degree of complexity of the cases and consequently a greater need for input resources. Some of the increase in the indexes has probably occurred because hospitals are being more careful about which diagnosis they pick (for patients with multiple diagnoses) to categorize the patient for Medicare payment purposes. This maneuver is sometimes called "DRG-Creep."

It is difficult, however, to distinguish this as the cause of increased case complexity. In any case, it seems clear that there has been a change in hospital treatment practice patterns following PPS. Also it is reported that average severity of the cases treated on an inpatient basis in hospitals has increased subsequent to PPS,[20] suggesting that less severe cases are now assigned to outpatient treatment.

FINANCIAL CONDITION OF HOSPITALS

Most agree that PPS puts a degree of financial stress on hospitals, particularly on those that have higher than usual costs. This, after all, is the way in which PPS alters financial incentives. However, hospitals that are run on the principles of yardstick competition might well increase their wealth position subsequent to PPS. In any case, at the beginning of Medicare's PPS, the fixed payment rates proved sufficiently generous so

---

[19]For the two studies cited, see Sloan, Morrisey, and Valvona (1988a), and DesHarnais et al. (1987).

[20]See Steinwald and Dummit (1989), Feinglass and Holloway (1991), and Sloan, Morrisey, and Valvona (1988a).

that average operating margins of hospitals were substantial, thus reducing the cost-saving incentives. Payment rates did not subsequently keep up with inflation, perhaps due to Congressional concern about hospital windfall profits, and operating margins fell steadily. By the late 1980s and extending through the early 1990s, average operating margins for the Medicare segment of patients tended to be negative.[21]

EFFECT ON COSTS

The point of this program, from Medicare's point of view, was to control costs. So the ultimate question is whether PPS succeeded. This question, however, can be addressed from at least three perspectives.[22] First, did individual hospitals respond by reducing their expenditures? There is evidence that they did so, at least in the first year. Zwanziger and Metnick (1988) observed that for a sample of California hospitals, those under the strongest pressure from PPS responded by reducing expenditures.

Second, did PPS reduce expenditures in Medicare's budget? Hospital savings seem likely. Medicare outlays for hospital care increased at an annual rate of 3.5 percent in 1984–1987 compared to 7.1 percent in 1977–1982, and hospital care fell as a proportion of the Medicare budget from 70 percent to 57 percent by 1988. Subsequently, PPS payments per case rose only slightly faster than the consumer price index so that by 1993, after the first ten years of PPS, Medicare's share of hospital payments remained at 28 percent despite a 23 percent growth in Medicare enrollments.

Lastly, did per capita expenditures for society as a whole fall as a result of Medicare's PPS? This is a much more difficult question to answer. Feinglass and Holloway (1991) argue that the savings from PPS were one-time-only events, occurring in the early years of PPS. This possibility is evidenced by increasing inflation rates in the late 1980s for U.S. health care expenditures, which in real terms were outstripping the inflation rates of 1980–1985.

In a statistical study of the issue, Sloan, Morrisey, and Valvona (1988a) find a significant reduction in hospital patient generated revenues per capita subsequent to PPS, but they note that the savings are found primarily in reductions in admissions, a category PPS does not provide specific incentives to reduce. They note the possibility that utilization review under Peer Review Organizations (PROs)—a utilization review effort begun along with Medicare's Prospective Payment System—could conceivably be the actual source of per capita cost reductions for hospital care.[23]

Thus, on the principal question of the three, we are left somewhat in doubt. Feinglass and Holloway argue that Medicare's PPS may actually have had an ambiguous or negligible effect on overall societal health care costs. Many economists and policy analysts have found that when you squeeze a balloon in one place, it expands in others.

---

[21]For further references, see Folland and Kleiman (1990), Dobson and Hoy (1988), Bromberg and Goodwin (1988), and Prospective Payment Assessment Commission (1995).

[22]For discussion, see Hadley, Zuckerman, and Feder (1989), Feinglass and Holloway (1991), Guterman and Dobson (1986), and Prospective Payment Assessment Commission (1995).

[23]Shifts to outpatient care, which similarly does not provide specific cost-reduction incentives, may also occur.

COMPETITIVE STRATEGIES

Regardless of any changes in the direction of U.S. health care policy, governments will remain heavily involved in the financing and delivery of health care. Nevertheless, as a result of unprecedented concerns with access and costs, policymakers are in the middle of "one of the biggest ideological battles of the 1990s: a fight over the future of the ailing American health-care system."[24] The battle is over the superiority of: (1) increased government involvement through both expanded regulation and additional government programs to provide or finance health care, or (2) an increased emphasis on market mechanisms and market forces with corresponding decreases in the use of regulatory instruments.

This controversy is not new to the academic and policymaking communities, where it is referred to as the debate over competition versus regulation. Yet, in the afterword to a special issue of the *Journal of Health Politics, Policy and Law* devoted to the controversy, editor Lawrence Brown (1988) wrote:

> it is striking that . . . fifteen years after the first flush of enthusiasm in Washington for a competitive approach, there still seems to be little agreement on what we *mean* by "competition" or a "market approach" to containing health costs (p. 361).

Those who deny the applicability of the competitive framework are most likely to favor regulatory strategies. Proponents of further regulation tend to argue that information imperfections, flawed agency relationships, and other distortions cannot be readily corrected by attempts to promote partial forms of competition. Proponents of regulation have also been strongly influenced by the rapid growth in overall health spending and in spending on Medicare, Medicaid, and other public programs. The spending record in the United States, as compared to other more highly regulated systems, has reinforced beliefs among many that health care markets do not work like most other markets. Especially widely accepted are beliefs that increases in supplies of hospital beds and physicians increase utilization of marginally necessary or even unnecessary services. There are widespread views that physicians can and do create demand and that empty beds in hospitals will be filled through physicians' discretionary decisions to admit patients.

The logical strategy to those who share these views is to increase controls limiting hospital capacity and physician supplies, and to increase monitoring of services that are being provided. We have outlined the general forms of these controls. At this point, we digress from further study of regulation to return to the question raised by Brown: What is competition in health care? Pauly (1988a) defines competition through the conditions of "free entry and potential entrants willing[ness] to offer goods and services to consumers, with no one firm large enough to have an important influence on levels of and quality" (p. 35).

---

[24]"Health Care Choices: A Bigger Federal Role or a Market Approach," *The Wall Street Journal,* January 15, 1992, p. 1.

From this definition, we would expect the following in a competitive health care industry: (1) elastic demands facing providers, (2) a tendency toward marginal cost pricing, (3) efficiency in production—allocative as well as technical efficiency, and (4) the availability of alternatives in terms of price, quality, and form of delivery.

Others see competition in a more limited way, largely through the form of government policy rather than the structure or performance of health care markets. A competitive health care policy is one that relies primarily on financial incentives rather than controls to achieve goals. The theoretical underpinning of this approach is the view that market participants respond to changes in prices in a predictable and substantial way. Supporters of competitive approaches also argue that even imperfections in their strategies are preferable to the distortions caused by imperfect regulation.

Under either view of competition, most forms of government intervention such as CON laws, utilization review, and mandated benefits are anticompetitive—they compel. To be more specific in the distinction between competition and regulation, consider the uninsured. From the competitive point of view, many of the uninsured are seen largely as having insufficient income to purchase insurance. Their dilemma is aggravated by mandated benefits and other requirements that drive up insurance prices. A competitive solution is to subsidize purchases of insurance for lower-income uninsured through tax credits, and to deregulate insurers so that lower-priced options become available. Programs, on the other hand, that would provide insurance for the uninsured are seen as lacking in incentives for efficient consumer search. Bearing in mind these distinctions, we turn to several broad competitive strategies for reforming the U.S. health care system.

Increased Cost Sharing

Martin Feldstein was the earliest and the best-known advocate of using increased cost sharing to overcome the incentives to overinsure. Furthermore, he argued that the prevalence of "first-dollar insurance" up to certain limits (often inadequate for catastrophic events), is the result of the tax preferences described previously for purchases of insurance, especially of employer-provided group insurance. He and others have advocated a variety of plans that would involve reducing the tax subsidies and increasing patients' out-of-pocket costs to approximately 10 percent of income.[25] This would be achieved through high coinsurance rates on initial health care expenditures, but with declining coinsurance until the maximum out-of-pocket liability is reached.

The effects of coinsurance on moral hazard and demand elasticities have been described in our chapters on demand and insurance. Findings from the Rand Health Insurance Experiment support the hypotheses that consumers respond in a significant and substantial way to changes in their share of costs.

However, we have not previously considered Feldstein's hypothesis that taxes and other distortions in the insurance market have skewed purchases toward comprehensive first-dollar coverage. On this issue, Hershey and colleagues (1984) administered a questionnaire to a random sample of 480 nonunion employees of a university to see how they would choose among actuarially fair policies. Their findings indicated a

---

[25]For example, see M. Feldstein (1977).

preference for coverage with higher limits. But respondents were also as likely to select policies with cost-sharing features (which reduce price) as they were to select policies without those features.

Thus, to summarize, there is evidence that consumers will behave differently in circumstances where there are no tax subsidies and where there are wider choices than those usually available under group health insurance. Some consumers would opt for plans with greater cost sharing when the premiums for these plans are sufficiently reduced.

Development of Alternative Delivery Systems

The dominant competitive strategy, which evolved in the 1970s, has been the promotion of delivery systems that can provide an alternative to traditional fee-for-service with its comprehensive first-dollar insurance coverage. The cornerstone of this strategy has been the promotion of health maintenance organizations (HMOs), preferred provider organizations (PPOs), and other forms of managed care.

As described in Chapter 12, HMOs and other capitated health plans provide a comprehensive set of services for a fixed monthly premium. Typically there is minimal (or no) cost sharing for covered ambulatory services. In exchange for expanded coverage, a patient's choice is restricted to specific providers and hospitals. Furthermore, the patient's primary care physician serves as the gatekeeper in that this physician's approval is required for referral to most specialists and nonemergency hospital admissions.

Expansion of the population covered by HMOs has been a major policy goal. The primary motive behind the HMO strategy is the view among many policymakers that the traditional form of health care delivery was the primary culprit in rising costs and unnecessary care.

HMOs tend to reduce costs primarily by reducing the rate of hospital utilization. However, the rates of increases in HMO costs have paralleled the rates of increases elsewhere—a phenomenon that limits the overall potential for cost containment. Nevertheless, federal policy continues to emphasize the HMO strategy by proposing expanded incentives for those who select prepaid, managed care systems, especially Medicare and Medicaid beneficiaries. This dichotomy between health care policy and results suggests that it is worth examining Medicare's HMO experience.

Medicare Managed Care

Though the possibility of some HMO involvement was included early in the Medicare program, the Tax Equity and Fiscal Responsibility Act (TEFRA), implemented in 1985, marked an important turning point. Under TEFRA, an HMO can contract with the Health Care Financing Administration (HCFA) to enroll Medicare beneficiaries on a prepaid capitation rate determined by 95 percent of its area's AAPCC (the average adjusted per capita cost). This payment is based on the amount HCFA expected to pay on behalf of a beneficiary if he or she had remained in the fee-for-service sector.

This type of contract is called a TEFRA risk contract because it places the HMO at risk for costs that exceed its receipts. Though some limited risk contracts were available prior to 1985, and 52 HMOs participated in the demonstration period, most HMOs entered into cost contracts. These provided capitated payments based on actual costs up to 100 percent of AAPCC.

Immediately after TEFRA, there was a sharp increase in HMO enrollments and HMO beneficiaries. Medicare enrollments nearly doubled between June 1985 and July 1987, and the number of Medicare HMOs increased from 102 to 179.[26] Most were TEFRA risk contracts.

Using data from the demonstration period, Adamache and Rossiter (1986) found that market entry was mainly influenced by the AAPCC rate. However, despite a 14 percent increase in the AAPCC rate, 21 HMOs did not renew their risk contracts in 1988; also, HMO enrollments dropped slightly.[27]

As of March 1995, 8.7 percent of all beneficiaries selected a managed care plan.[28] Of these, 76 percent were enrolled in risk-based plans. Enrollments in managed care plans have grown 11 percent annually since 1990 and 16 percent between 1993 and 1994, possibly because HMO enrollments in managed care plans tend to be highly correlated with overall HMO enrollments, which have increased rapidly.

A Republican bill introduced in 1995 to control the growth of Medicare spending calls for new incentives for beneficiaries to join managed care plans. These include extra patient liabilities for those who retain fee-for-service coverage. As noted previously, it is not clear that such a policy, even if it is successful in moving large numbers into managed care plans, will have any substantial impact on the rate of growth of spending.

Antitrust

The goal of U.S. antitrust laws is to promote competition. The Sherman Act passed in 1890 and several successive acts constitute the federal laws. These laws attempt to define the practices that constitute anticompetitive behavior and create the agencies, Department of Justice (DOJ) and Federal Trade Commission (FTC), to enforce the laws.

Until recent decades, antitrust was used sparingly in the health care sector, in part because of perceptions that the "learned professions" were immune from the federal laws. Several landmark decisions handed down by the U.S Supreme Court in the 1970s forcefully rejected this view and led to a flurry of antitrust activity, especially cases dealing with the granting or termination of hospital staff privileges. Arrangements involving physician control over Blue Cross and Blue Shield plans, the use of relative value scales, AMA restrictions on advertising, and AMA restrictions that limited competition from other providers such as chiropractors were successfully challenged. There is general agreement that antitrust enforcement has benefited the consumer by raising the level of competition in many health care markets.

Nevertheless, the growth of managed care and this nation's preoccupation with costs and efficiency have led to many changes in the health care sector. These changes are reflected in the increasing number of hospital mergers and cooperative activities including information sharing among providers, hospital joint ventures involving expensive capital equipment, and hospital purchasing agreements. Such activities could certainly lead to more monopoly power to the detriment of the public.

---

[26]Pitt (1988).

[27]Ibid.

[28]Medicare managed care data are taken from Prospective Payment Assessment Commission (1995) and Physician Payment Review Commission (1995).

On the other hand, policymakers are concerned that many cooperative arrangements that may lower health care costs are being discouraged by the uncertainty over antitrust enforcement. As a result, the U.S. Department of Justice and the Federal Trade Commission (1994) have issued statements intended to clarify their enforcement policies. These statements establish "antitrust safety zones" that "describe the circumstances under which [they] will not challenge certain collaborative activities by hospitals, doctors, and other health care providers." The statements deal with the areas just described above and others such as physician joint networks. It is still too early to determine what the effects of these new policies will be.

Medical Savings Accounts

Individual medical savings accounts (MSAs) represent a unique strategy to encourage more efficient health care utilization. Under the MSA scheme, employers or public payers would make contributions to an individual's MSA enabling the person to buy relatively low-cost insurance with high deductibles or copayments. Balances in an MSA could then be used to pay out-of-pocket costs, or the unused portion could be distributed to the individual.

Those who support MSAs argue that comprehensive, tax-subsidized insurance creates substantial moral hazard and ineffective incentives for efficient consumption of care. On the other hand, the lure of a potential distribution from an MSA provides the individual with an incentive to become a prudent user of care. In principle, patients will be less likely to consume unnecessary or marginally beneficial care, and stronger market forces will help restrain prices.

A 1995 Republican bill illustrates one such proposal.[29] It would allow Medicare beneficiaries to set up MSAs in which Medicare would provide each recipient with a fixed annual dollar amount (e.g., $5,100 in 1996) to buy insurance from a company offering MSA coverage. Part of the money would pay for catastrophic coverage with the remainder going into an MSA. Those who have MSA funds left over at the end of the year after paying out-of-pocket costs will be able to keep at least a part of the balance.

Though one can foresee a possible adverse selection problem (i.e., healthier people set up MSAs because they are more likely to have funds left over), the MSA scheme is theoretically appealing. But will it work? Fortunately, health care reforms introduced in Singapore in 1984 provide an example where theory has been put to the test.

Singapore requires all workers and the self-employed to contribute a portion of earnings to Medisave accounts.[30] The Medisave account is used to pay for hospital care and a limited amount of outpatient care (the remainder is paid out-of-pocket). Once Medisave balances reach a certain level, funds can be transferred for other approved uses. At death, balances become part of the deceased's estate.

---

[29]Originally developed by Stano (1981), many variations of the basic MSA concept have been proposed. Another alternative, introduced by Pauly and Goodman (1995), would provide tax credits to those who voluntarily choose a combination of catastrophic coverage and an MSA. This proposal is also discussed in Chapter 23, which deals with health care reform.

[30]The material on Singapore is taken from Hsiao (1995) and Massaro and Wong (1995).

Evidence indicates that hospitals have become more productive and efficient and that patients are satisfied with the quality of care. The record on cost containment is unclear. Expenditures continued to rise rapidly, although not as much as in other Asian countries.

Representation of the Competitive Approach

The shortcomings of the existing system of health care delivery, together with the goals of the competitive approach, can be illustrated with the help of Figure 19.3. At the risk of neglecting the various market imperfections and resulting inefficiencies that we have studied, we rely on the simplicity of the demand–supply paradigm. Let S_1 and D_1 represent the existing demand and supply curves for health care. The equilibrium quantity is Q_1, and total spending is represented by the rectangle $0P_1EQ_1$.

Competitive strategies have two broad goals. The first is to reduce demand by increasing the number of patients in managed care settings who are sensitive to price and the diminishing marginal benefit associated with health care. By encouraging the use of managed care and reducing the tax subsidy for employer-provided health insurance, it is expected that demand for health services, especially the relatively less beneficial services, will diminish to D_2. The equilibrium quantity will decrease, as will prices, and expenditures, though the price effect will be small where the elasticity of supply is large.

However, there is another important role for competitive strategies, which operates through effects on the supply side. Here a relaxation of regulatory, entry, and capacity controls is seen as reducing producer costs and increasing the supply of providers. At the same time, competitive pressure introduced through consumer search will push providers to become more efficient producers of care so that any given quantity of care can be provided at lower cost. These effects are represented by a rightward movement in supply to S_2.

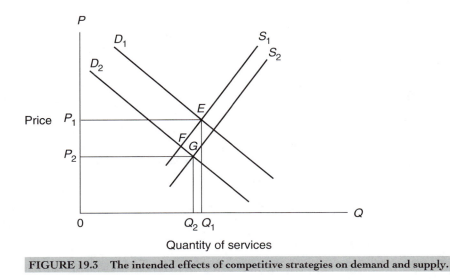

FIGURE 19.3 **The intended effects of competitive strategies on demand and supply.**

The combined effects, if they are substantial, would lead to large decreases (from $0P_1EQ_1$ to $0P_2GQ_2$) in health care spending, as illustrated in Figure 19.3, or to reduced growth rates in spending. Of course, the predicted effects must materialize. Otherwise, the strategies would be ineffective and might even backfire. For instance, if supply does increase, but prices remain rigid and large amounts of supplier-induced demand (SID)

FEATURE

Do the Laws of Demand and Supply Apply to Health Care Markets?

We have devoted much of this text to the idea that conventional economic tools can play a powerful role in explaining how health care markets work. Certainly, great care is needed to account for the special features of the health economy and, where appropriate, to modify the analysis. Overall, we have found considerable empirical evidence attesting to the rationality of decision makers. Supporters of competitive strategies have faith in the power of market forces to allocate resources to their best uses, both between health care and other goods and within the health care markets.

However, it would be unwise to ignore concerns about the strength of market forces. Consider the following taken from *The Wall Street Journal,* one of this nation's most respected publications, known for its strong resistance to government intervention in the marketplace.[31]

> In a conventional market, a high-cost, low-quality producer would be doomed, or, at the very least, worried. But the laws of economics have been repealed in the health business. Consumers don't comparison-shop and often lack the information to do so. Many hospitals compete to buy the latest technology rather than provide the lowest-cost quality care. And providers resist outsiders' attempts to gauge quality. The result: a seemingly unstoppable increase in the cost of health care.

To support this argument, the article compared cost and outcome data for coronary bypass surgery at two Pennsylvania hospitals located 38 miles apart. One hospital charged about 50 percent more than the other in 1989, but its death rate considerably exceeded the expected death rate as determined by the age and health of patients. The death rate at the lower-priced hospital was below the expected rate.

A lack of access to such information about both price and quality, lack of incentives to patients, and provider resistance to releasing mortality data were singled out as culprits. To help correct these deficiencies, a Pennsylvania agency planned to release such data on individual physician performance. The agency was quoted by *The Wall Street Journal* as saying that "making such information public and encouraging employers and patients to use it is essential if the health care market is to work without major government intervention."

---

[31]"Laws of Economics Often Don't Apply in Health Care Field," *The Wall Street Journal,* January 22, 1992, p. A1.

follow, then both demand and supply may increase, thereby aggravating the utilization and spending problems. For this reason, the issues of SID and the existence of independent demands that are responsive to financial incentives are seen by economists as being at the heart of the controversy.

CONCLUSIONS

Governments are major players in the health economy as producers, redistributors, and regulators. We have provided various examples of government involvement that are often justified on the basis of some form of market failure. This chapter introduces and emphasizes governments' regulatory functions. It establishes a framework to study regulation and examines various regulatory instruments, including the Medicare Prospective Payment System.

There is no doubt that the health economy will continue to be heavily regulated. At the same time, federal policy is promoting competitive strategies to deal especially with the cost and access concerns. The emphasis in this policy has been on an expansion of health care delivery by HMOs and other forms of managed care. With the strong political pressure to downsize the role of government, there is likely also to be continuing interest in market-driven changes to Medicare and Medicaid such as MSAs and the shifting of recipients into managed care. It remains to be seen whether such changes can break the "stalemate between halfway competition and ineffective regulation"[32] to bring meaningful reforms to the health economy.

Summary

1. Government spending accounts for about 44 percent of total health care expenditures.
2. The traditional rationale for government intervention is market failure. Sources of market failure include monopoly power, externalities, and public goods.
3. There is a public goods aspect to information and redistribution that can be used to justify a role for government in health care.
4. Governments have been involved in a wide variety of activities, including the direct provision of health care, subsidizing the production of health care, the provision of social insurance, public health, and regulation of health care products and providers.
5. Regulation refers to the use of nonmarket means to affect the quality, price, or quantity of a good or service. The principal categories of regulation include fee controls and rate regulation, quantity and capacity controls, and quality controls.
6. Empirical findings on utilization review have tended to be inconclusive. A study by Wickizer, Wheeler, and Feldstein finds that utilization review reduces admissions, inpatient days, and expenditures.

---

[32]Altman and Rodwin (1988, p. 323). As a result of this stalemate, they predicted that health care spending, as a share of GNP, would continue to rise through the 1990s.

7. Studies of rate regulation suggest that this regulatory device is effective in reducing expenses per admissions, per day, and per capita.

8. Studies of CON have tended to find it ineffective. Mayo and McFarland, in contrast, find that CON significantly lowered the number of beds and consequently costs in a single state studied.

9. The Medicare Prospective Payment System (PPS), based on diagnosis-related groups, predetermines a flat fee per case. Hospitals that exceed this rate suffer the loss while hospitals with case costs below the rate receive the profit.

10. Medicare's PPS approximates yardstick competition. By setting the payment rates according to industry average marginal costs, yardstick competition induces the firms to choose the socially efficient level of cost-containment expenditure.

11. Medicare's PPS has led to reduced average length-of-stay in hospitals subject to the regulation. It is doubtful that the regulation has led to a reduction in quality of care or access to care. Case-mix severity has increased post-PPS. Finally, while it is likely that the system has helped to control Medicare's budget, it is unclear whether there has been a reduction in per capita costs.

12. The past two decades have witnessed a major debate over whether to rely increasingly on regulatory strategies to achieve health policy objectives or to rely increasingly on competitive strategies.

13. Competitive strategies include increased cost sharing, the promotion of alternative delivery systems, more aggressive enforcement of antitrust laws, and the establishment of medical savings accounts.

Discussion Questions

1. What is meant by market failure? For the cases of market failure found in the health care sector, what is the potential role of government in each instance?

2. In what sense can information and redistribution be thought of as public goods? Explain whether private markets will oversupply or undersupply these goods.

3. What are some examples of government providing health care? Of subsidizing the production or consumption of health care? Of providing insurance for health care? Of regulating health care markets?

4. Describe the major regulatory strategies that have been adopted in the United States.

5. How does prospective payment change the incentive to hospitals as compared to retrospective reimbursement? What predictions would one make as a result of the adoption of reimbursement based on DRGs?

6. Some argue that controls on some payers lead to a shift in cost to other payers (and that a one-payer system is needed). What evidence would suggest cost shifting to other third-party payers? What evidence suggests that not all the costs are shifted?

7. What is *regression to the mean*? How might this affect our evaluation of the efficacy of rate regulation?

8. CON legislation is designed to control costs by limiting capital expenditures. However, CON may also influence competition in the hospital market. Discuss at least two ways in which this might occur.

9. Under Shleifer's theory of yardstick competition, why does the firm have an incentive to reduce its costs? If all firms respond by reducing their costs, will the payment rate also subsequently fall?

10. What is the Medicare PPS program under DRGs? How has the Medicare PPS payment under DRGs affected hospital practices? Length-of-stay? Quality of care? Financial condition?

11. Does the Medicare PPS payment under DRGs reduce costs? Discuss.

12. What are the major competitive strategies proposed by economists? How, for example, would elimination of the tax subsidy for employer-provided health insurance, reduce spending on health care?

13. The pharmaceutical industry has been subject to considerable regulation in bringing drugs to the marketplace. Discuss the benefits and the costs to society that accrue from such a policy.

Exercises

1. Using the demand–supply framework, explain how increased cost sharing could lead to lower utilization and spending on health care.

2. What is a deadweight loss of monopoly? Who bears this loss?

3. Suppose that the government taxes air polluters in order to reduce pollution. What is the impact of the tax on producers? On consumers? Is it necessary that the government use the tax to clean up the air?

4. Suppose that a hospital has a production function of the type:

$$Q = S^\alpha B^\beta$$

where Q is quantity of output, S is level of services, and B is number of beds, with α and β as parameters. The hospital buys S at price p_s and B at price p_b.
   a. If regulators force the hospital to decrease the amount of B by 10 percent, what must the hospital do to maintain quantity Q?
   b. If the hospital maintains quantity Q, what will be the effect of the regulation on total hospital expenditures? Why?

5. Suppose that Hospitals A through E have the following marginal cost for a given procedure:

   Hospital A—$1,000
   Hospital B—$1,200
   Hospital C—$ 800
   Hospital D—$1,700
   Hospital E—$1,300

   Calculate the yardstick prices that would be assigned to each hospital. Which two hospitals will be assigned yardstick prices that do not cover their current marginal costs?

CHAPTER

Equity, Efficiency, and Need

20

A re health care markets efficient, and are people getting the care that they need? These two questions occupy the minds of the many people who study or simply think about the state of health care in America. Efficiency questions arise because of the high costs people must pay for health care. Are these costs too high? Likewise, equity questions are raised because of the experiences of many people, certainly including the uninsured, who face barriers in obtaining health care.

Compared to Canadians and many Europeans, Americans are more likely to find experts and analysts who favor competitive market solutions to health care system problems, though many here as elsewhere argue that this approach is ill-suited to the nature of health care markets. Among Canadians and Europeans, there is a greater willingness to use government interventions such as social insurance programs in addressing health care problems. Proposals to expand social insurance for health care died in Congress in the United States in 1994. Medicare reform remains an issue, however, and for many Americans basic issues of equity and efficiency in the health care system remain important.

A solid grounding in these issues requires an understanding of the economics of efficiency, the departures of many health care markets from the competitive model, the role of equity concerns, and issues of social justice theory. Because of the central role of the concept of need within the realm of the health system, it also requires an investigation into the meaning of health care need. These subjects are the themes of the present chapter.

We begin by developing the simple analytics of welfare economics within the context of the Edgeworth box for exchange. We will discover that competitive, efficient, well-functioning markets can leave many in economic need. This chapter and the three following describe this issue and address its resolution.

Following an exposition of the theoretical efficiency of competition, we then identify the departures of health care markets from the model of perfect competition, and we investigate a possible efficiency rationale for social programs in health care. The nature of health care need is then featured, including some approaches found in this literature. This is followed by a discussion of three contrasting theories of social justice.

EFFICIENCY AND COMPETITIVE MARKETS

The meaning of economic efficiency can be made fairly clear within the context of the Edgeworth box for exchange. This approach is a useful way of showing theorems that are developed in more sophisticated mathematical models.

The analysis here generates the First Fundamental Theorem of Welfare Economics and illustrates the Second Fundamental Theorem as well. The First Theorem demonstrates that competitive markets under certain conditions are economically efficient. The second establishes the idea that any desired economically efficient outcome could in principle be achieved by competitive markets given appropriate initial endowments.

The Concept of Pareto Efficiency (Optimality)

To establish these ideas, we must rigorously define the concept of efficiency. Nearly a century ago, the economist Vilfredo Pareto defined the concept of efficiency as it is most frequently used by economists today. According to Pareto, an economically efficient (optimal) outcome in society is one under which it is impossible to improve the lot of any person without hurting someone else. Pareto efficiency also implies that no further exchanges would be found that could in principle improve the lot of everyone to some degree. An efficient economy would necessarily have exhausted all means for mutual gains.

The Edgeworth box, using a hypothetical two-person economy and showing exchanges between these two people, provides a context in which to make the idea of Pareto efficiency clear. Consider the Edgeworth box depicted in Figure 20.1. In the two-person economy depicted here, there is a fixed total quantity of the goods available. We assume that only two goods are available: medical care, M, and food, F. The total available quantities are $0_A M$ and $0_A F$ respectively.

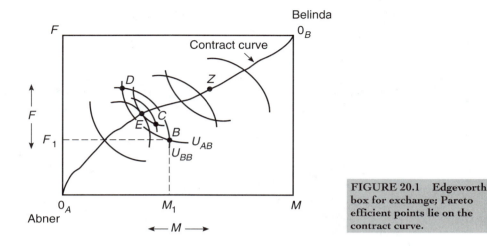

FIGURE 20.1   Edgeworth box for exchange; Pareto efficient points lie on the contract curve.

Abner has preferences over food and medical care, preferences that are represented by the indifference curves sloping downward and convex to the origin, 0_A. In contrast, the indifference curves for Belinda have been inverted so that her origin is point 0_B and higher indifference curves for her are ones to the southwest.

To identify the concept of efficiency in this context, consider the arbitrary starting point B. Point B, like any point in the box, represents a complete distribution of the two goods between the two persons. B identifies a situation where Abner has $0_A M_1$ units of medical care and $0_A F_1$ units of food. As an exercise, identify the quantities of food and medical products owned by Belinda at point B. With this orientation, we ask the following question: Is point B an economically efficient distribution?

The answer to this question must be no. To see this fact, examine by comparison point C. Point C lies on an indifference curve that is above (to the northeast of) indifference curve U_{AB} and, therefore, C is superior to B in Abner's view. Similarly, point C lies on an indifference curve that is above (to the southwest of) indifference curve U_{BB} and, therefore, C is superior to B from Belinda's view. Since point C is attainable and improves the lot of both persons while harming neither, it follows that the original point B is not economically efficient.

Geometrically, the analysis just completed regarding point B can be repeated for any point that forms a "lens" from the indifference curves passing through it. A lens is formed by the indifference curves U_{AB} and U_{BB} from point B to point D. Whenever such a lens can be found, it will be possible to identify one or more other points superior to the initial point.

Reapplying this method of reasoning, point C is also not Pareto efficient. Pareto superior moves, where the welfare of both improves, can be made from point C. In contrast, a Pareto efficient point in the box is a point of tangency between two indifference curves, such as point E. It is impossible to move from a point of tangency without harming the lot of one of the two persons.

Each of Abner's indifference curves will have a point of tangency with one of Belinda's indifference curves. The collection of all Pareto efficient points in the box is called the *contract curve,* which is so labeled in the figure. For example, at point 0_A, Belinda has all of both goods, and even if this may be considered inequitable by many or most people, it *is* Pareto efficient.

The Idea of Trading Along the Budget Line

Having defined efficiency in the context of the Edgeworth box, we next ask whether the competitive market generates an efficient equilibrium in exchange. In a competitive market, each person treats prices as given and responds to prices by choosing the utility-maximizing bundle subject to his or her resource constraint. The resource constraint in the present context depends on the person's initial endowment of food and medical care. Let the initial endowment for this two-person economy be represented by ω in Figure 20.2. Either person may trade away from his or her initial endowment at the market prices. Thus, Abner's resource constraint will be represented by a budget line that passes through point ω. As with any budget line, the slope of this line is the negative of the ratio of the price of medical care to food.

Inasmuch as the slope of the budget line represents the rate at which one can trade one good for another at market prices, the steeper the budget line in Figure 20.2 the greater the price of medical care relative to food. For example, budget line *AB* represents a relatively lower price of medical care relative to food than does budget line *CD*.

The Competitive Equilibrium

To find the competitive equilibrium, we must identify the offer curves of both persons. Abner's offer curve, for example, is the collection of points representing his offer for trade at each possible set of prices. To illustrate, let the prices be such that budget line *AB* obtains. Given budget line *AB*, Abner is willing to stay at point ω, the point of tangency between budget line *AB* and the highest indifference curve that is attainable.

To complete Abner's offer curve, find his desired trades at other possible prices. For example, suppose the price of medical care were higher relative to food so that the steeper budget line *CD* obtained. Given budget line *CD*, Abner's optimal trade would

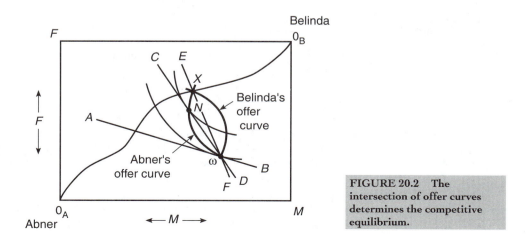

FIGURE 20.2 The intersection of offer curves determines the competitive equilibrium.

be from point ω to point *N*. With budget line *EF* Abner's optimal trade is to point *X*. Connecting all such points generates *Abner's offer curve.*

The figure also shows Belinda's offer curve, beginning at endowment point ω. This offer curve is found in a similar manner and is labeled *Belinda's offer curve.* The two heavily shaded offer curves represent voluntary trades for the two parties. For trade, as in a competitive market, to be mutually voluntary, the offers of the two persons must agree. The offer curves agree only at their point of intersection labeled point *X* in the figure. Point *X* thus constitutes the competitive market equilibrium in exchange for this two-person economy, given an endowment of ω.

The First Fundamental Theorem of Welfare Economics

Is the competitive equilibrium, *X,* Pareto efficient? This is so, and it must be so of every competitive equilibrium in this context for the following reasons. The intersection of two offer curves is reached by a single price line from point ω. By construction of each offer curve, each person is at a point of tangency between the budget line and the highest attainable indifference curve. At point *X,* Abner's indifference curve (not shown) is tangent to the budget line. Likewise, at point *X,* Belinda's indifference curve (also not shown) is tangent to the budget line. Since these indifference curves are tangent to the same budget line at the same point, they must be tangent to each other. Since they are tangent to each other at point *X,* this point is Pareto efficient. The same argument applies for any competitive equilibrium; therefore, we have shown the First Fundamental Theorem in this context, namely that the perfectly competitive market equilibrium is Pareto efficient.

The theorem makes the competitive market solution attractive. If perfect competition can be achieved, then the market forces left to their own workings will generate an efficient outcome, an invisible hand solution. However, the theorem evokes several serious questions: Can competitive markets be achieved in health care? Is the context of this theorem appropriate for health care? Would the competitive market solution be equitable or would it leave too many people without adequate health care? We will address each of these questions. However, we begin this process by exploring the issue of equity within the context of the Second Fundamental Theorem.

Redistribution of the Endowment

The applicability of the First Fundamental Theorem is extended somewhat by the second. The Second Fundamental Theorem states that any Pareto efficient outcome can in principle be achieved by a competitive market, given an appropriate endowment. Figure 20.3 illustrates the significance of this theorem.

In Figure 20.3, suppose that the initial endowment is ω, and suppose that this endowment results in the competitive outcome represented by point *E*. Point *E* is only one of an infinite number of Pareto efficient points. It may be an outcome that is viewed as inequitable by some members of the society. In real life, the society may have millions of members, and the analogous market outcome may even be perceived as inequitable by a majority of people.

The Second Theorem, however, defines a central role for competitive markets even in cases where some competitive outcomes are considered inequitable. This idea

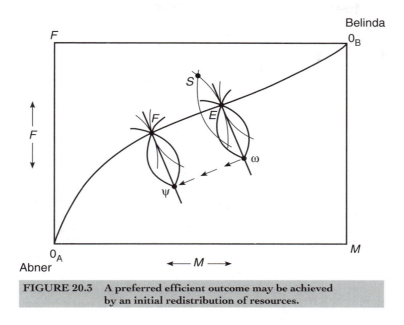

FIGURE 20.3 A preferred efficient outcome may be achieved by an initial redistribution of resources.

is illustrated in the figure. Suppose, for example, that society determines that outcome *E* is inequitable and thus rejects this particular market solution. It prefers outcomes in the vicinity of point *F*. By the Second Theorem, the desired outcome can be achieved by a competitive market, but it requires a different initial endowment from point ω. As shown, the endowment point Ψ is a suitable point from which to achieve an equitable market outcome, point *F*. Seen this way, redistribution combined with competitive markets generates an outcome that is both efficient and equitable. This is in contrast to command systems that eschew free markets and in contrast to alternative solutions such as price discrimination.

Price Discrimination

An alternative method often proposed for achieving a more equitable outcome is to provide certain services to the poor at reduced, subsidized prices. It may be surprising to learn that such systems are not consistent with Pareto efficiency. Consider the proof of the efficiency of competitive markets. Here it was crucial that both parties optimizing with a given budget line achieve a point of tangency to the same budget line. If different prices for medical care are charged to the poorer person than to the richer, then the two face different slopes of their budget lines. The result would be a position such as *S* in Figure 20.3, a point that is not Pareto efficient.

The inefficiency of price discrimination can be understood intuitively as well as through the geometry. Consider, for example, a situation where the poor are subsidized in the purchase of bread. The poor would adapt to the subsidized price until the rate at which they were willing to trade bread for other goods were equal to the rate at which they could exchange the goods at the subsidized price. The result is that the poor would undervalue bread in comparison to the wealthy. It would be more efficient for the poor then to buy up bread and sell it to the rich. Such a side market, which would improve efficiency in the bread example, is not possible for medical care, which is not easily transferable. Thus, subsidized prices for medical care would generate an inefficient equilibrium.

The two theorems, plus the facts regarding the inefficiency of price discrimination, suggest the superiority of income transfers as a solution to equity problems in health care markets. In Figure 20.3, the following situation takes place: by transferring initial resources between the two persons, the market is then allowed to achieve an efficient outcome within the equitable range.

Okun's Leaky Bucket

The theoretical superiority of redistribution of income to programs such as price subsidies has led many analysts to favor income maintenance programs as policy tools to offset the problems of poverty, including the problems of access to health care. Income maintenance programs are government programs designed to provide cash subsidies to the poor so as to maintain their incomes at or above a preset floor. Despite continuing interest in such programs, policymakers have often hesitated to use large-scale income redistribution.

The major criticism of income maintenance can be summarized by appealing to Arthur Okun's (1975) analogy of the leaky bucket. The problem is that the act of transferring wealth from one group to another in society generates disincentives that discourage productive effort. The tax-paying group incurs a tax burden that may reduce work incentives, and the recipient group receives subsidies that may reduce incentives to work and to self-help. By analogy, when we transfer income our task is similar to transferring water in a leaky bucket. The amount of income available to be redistributed will decline as a result.

In recent decades, the federal government sponsored large-scale experiments to investigate in part the degree of work loss induced by the incentives inherent in income maintenance programs. These experiments reported reductions in work effort on average between 5 and 10 percent. However, the work reduction estimates were considerably higher for certain subgroups such as "male nonheads" (meaning nonheads of families) and women. Also, results generated in an experimental situation make it difficult to predict the results if the program were to become universal and permanent.

DEVIATIONS FROM THE COMPETITIVE MODEL IN THE HEALTH CARE SECTOR

Another major criticism of the applicability of our theoretical analysis concerns the question of whether health care markets are sufficiently competitive or whether they can be made to be sufficiently competitive for competitive outcomes to obtain. There are clearly substantial differences between most health care markets and the theoretical model of competition.

The results of the First and Second Theorems have been extended to larger and more complete models that include production. These models increase the number of commodities and individuals, and they identify optimal results for competition in production and exchange. For the results to hold, several assumptions must apply.

The Assumptions Under Perfect Competition

First of all, the theorems apply to competitive markets. Consider the assumptions necessary for a market to be perfectly competitive: It must have free entry and exit, perfect information, a homogeneous product, and numerous buyers and sellers, each with no power over price. Furthermore, the efficiency of competitive markets is derived under conditions where there are no significant externalities, public goods, or natural monopolies. Finally, the actors in the competitive markets are alternatively consumers maximizing their utility or producers maximizing their profits.

DEVIATIONS FROM THE COMPETITIVE ASSUMPTIONS

Many have criticized the applicability of the theorems to the health care sector, claiming that health care markets are typically not perfectly competitive. The health care markets depart from competition in several ways:

1. Barriers to entry exist in health care markets. Such barriers include licensure laws and health planning controls on prices and facility construction.
2. Information problems exist.
3. Often firms are few enough in number so that they have some degree of monopoly power.
4. Health care services are not uniform in quality or character.
5. Externalities are prevalent in health care.
6. Motivations other than pure profit are common in health care.
7. The model depicts the operation of markets under conditions of certainty. However, health events entail a considerable degree of uncertainty.

THE ROLE OF UNCERTAINTY

Several of the seven listed deviations need little further explanation. However, we consider three of them for extended discussion: the role of uncertainty, the role of information, and the role of externalities.

As we have seen, the uncertain nature of health status gives rise to the demand for insurance coverage among persons who are risk averse. In the present context, insurance creates problems for the efficient functioning of health care markets. Four issues should be noted: (1) Insurance changes the price of care to the insured person, which in turn leads to the distortions described under price discrimination; (2) insurance causes the price paid to suppliers to differ from the price paid by the consumer, and this distorts the efficient matching of production to consumption; (3) large insurance companies and government programs have historically negotiated payment rates on a retrospective cost basis, thus removing price determination, at least in part, from the market; and (4) in some health care markets the average insurance coverage is so complete as to distort substantially the producer's incentives to be efficient.

THE ROLE OF INFORMATION

The efficiency results for competitive markets depend on all parties' having complete information available. As we have shown elsewhere, it is particularly problematic for market functioning when information is imperfect and asymmetrically available to the parties in the market, whether it be the consumer or the provider who is relatively less informed. Potential problems of information and efficiency arise both when the physician is much more informed about the appropriateness and effectiveness of treatments and techniques than the consumer, and also when the consumer has more knowledge of his or her health status and health habits than the potential insurer.

THE ROLE OF EXTERNALITIES

Finally, health care markets are subject to prevalent externalities. A prominent externality will occur whenever participants in the market are significantly concerned about the health care received by others, not just their own health care. This externality may be difficult to internalize in private charity markets, and it arguably causes health care markets to be inefficient. Because externalities have been identified by some analysts as the most important efficiency argument for social insurance programs in health care, we develop an extended discussion in this chapter.

PROMOTING COMPETITION IN THE HEALTH CARE SECTOR

If we could manipulate real-world markets as easily as we can change the assumptions of theory, then it would seem to follow from our theoretical discussion that we should promote competition in health care markets whenever possible. Often the promotion of competitive elements in health care markets will prove useful. However, further theoretical grounds exist to qualify our statements.

The Theorem of the Second Best

One qualification involves the *Theorem of the Second Best* in welfare economics. In informal terms, consider an economy in which there is more than one departure from the conditions of perfect competition. Consider further any policy that corrects one or more of these departures from perfect competition but does not correct all of them. It has been shown under the Theorem of the Second Best that such a policy will not necessarily improve society's welfare.

An intuitive understanding of why this result obtains can be gained by considering a frequently used example. Consider a market where there exists a pure monopolist (a departure from the conditions of perfect competition) who is also a polluter (a departure from the conditions under which competition is efficient). Basic theory shows that a monopolist will produce less output than a competitive industry would have under otherwise similar conditions. A policy that hypothetically converts the industry to perfect competition would resolve one discrepancy but not both. Such a policy would not necessarily improve the well-being of society because both output and pollution would increase. Societal valuations of the extra output versus the extra pollution could in principle determine whether the change worsened society's well-being. Thus, correcting some economic "wrongs" but not all of them will not necessarily improve welfare.

This classic example of the monopolist polluter illustrates the idea of the theorem, but it does not make clear its applicability to the health sector. Consider a somewhat more controversial example that applies to health. Physician licensure laws grant licensed physicians a degree of monopoly power, a distortion from the competitive conditions. At the same time, however, consumers in health have imperfect information on therapies and prices, and information asymmetrically favors the physician; this too is a departure from competitive conditions. If one eliminated the imperfection caused by licensure but did not simultaneously address the information problem, patient welfare could be worsened.

The Wisdom of Promoting Competition in Health Care Markets

It would be a misapplication of the Theorem of the Second Best, however, to conclude that all policies that improve competitive elements in health care markets are incorrect. More properly, it means that we cannot assume such policies will improve welfare. Instead, we are operating in a world of second best. We are necessarily in the world of second best because it will be impossible to convert all health care markets into the model of perfect competition. It is nevertheless the case, however, that a given competitive policy may improve the functioning of health care markets in a manner that improves society's well-being. Each policy must be considered on its own merits, not on the grounds per se that it promotes competition.

AN ECONOMIC EFFICIENCY RATIONALE FOR SOCIAL PROGRAMS IN HEALTH CARE BASED ON EXTERNALITIES

An externality occurs when someone external to the market transaction—that is, someone who is neither the buyer nor the seller—is directly affected by the transaction and not compensated. A common example in health care occurs in the case of immunization for contagious diseases. Here people outside the market transaction—people who are not presently being immunized—are affected by the immunization. This occurs because the immunized person is less likely to become a carrier of the disease. This situation is an example of a beneficial consumption externality.

In the presence of a beneficial externality, the competitive market will tend to produce an inefficiently low level of output. The Pareto efficiency definition can be transformed in terms of a single market as the condition that marginal benefits equal marginal costs in equilibrium. Individuals in a well-functioning, perfectly competitive market in theory will, for example, use medical care until the marginal benefits, measured through the demand curve, equal marginal costs, which in equilibrium will equal the price. In Figure 20.4, this leads to an efficient level of consumption, Q_m, in the absence of externalities.

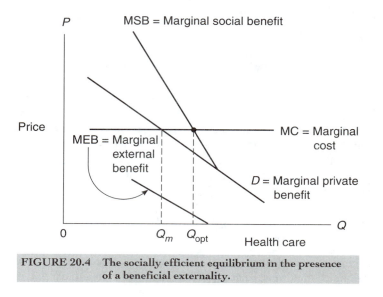

FIGURE 20.4 **The socially efficient equilibrium in the presence of a beneficial externality.**

When there exists a marginal external benefit to people in society, then this external benefit must be added to the marginal private benefit, which is measured by the demand curve, to determine marginal social benefit. In Figure 20.4, the marginal external benefit curve is shown as MEB. The marginal benefit to society as a whole is the vertical sum of the MEB curve and the demand curve. The result is the marginal social benefit curve, MSB. Efficiency for society occurs at output level Q_{opt}, whereas the market would achieve an inefficiently low level of output, Q_m. Thus, on efficiency grounds alone, society may be justified in subsidizing immunizations in some way.

While the case of immunization for contagious diseases illustrates the logic and role of beneficial consumption externalities in justifying subsidies for (or possibly public provision of) care, such as the polio immunizations of the 1950s and 1960s, it represents a fairly minor problem and could not in itself be used to justify large social insurance programs. However, an alternative health care externality, one which we have identified elsewhere as a charitable externality, can in principle be sufficiently important to justify such programs.

This externality would occur, for example, whenever people feel that some segment of society is receiving insufficient care in the sense that the charitably minded person would be willing to pay to help these people get care. *Willing to pay* here means that they would pay if it were so arranged that their contribution would be perceived as helping the poor to acquire health care.

Such charitable feelings are probably widespread in most societies. As Pauly (1971) argued:

> The desire to eliminate the diseconomy that the presence of curable but uncured disease or injury may exert on others does appear, in general terms, to be a common characteristic of human beings. At least at some levels, most of us would be willing to give up some of our income to help a suffering fellow. Some may, of course, be immune to such feelings,

but individuals may also be immune to contagious disease, and this should cause no insurmountable theoretical problems (pp.10–11).

Although this externality has a different source than the case of immunization and is probably of more substantial importance, the economic argument is of the same form. In Figure 20.4, consider the curve MEB to measure this charitable externality. Then, as before, the efficient level of output, Q_{opt}, is greater than the market output, Q_m. Under certain circumstances, this efficiency may be sufficient grounds to intervene, for example, by providing a program of social insurance.

NEED AND NEED-BASED DISTRIBUTIONS

If we can accurately identify the efficient allocation of health care, we nevertheless may find many people in society dissatisfied with the outcome. That is, there may be additional concerns, over and above efficiency concerns, regarding equity. In the health care literature, the concerns for equity most often center on the question of whether people are getting the health care that they need. Thus, health care needs must be addressed.[1]

The task of treating the concept of health care need analytically is made difficult by the fact that need is often either undefined or variously defined. The definitions employed may take either extreme, need being defined maximally or minimally. For example, when a medical definition is used, it may appear as a technical maximum. Jeffers et al. (1971), seeking to distill the implicit definitions then current, proposed to define health care need as

> That quantity of medical services which expert medical opinion believes ought to be consumed over a relevant period of time in order for its members to remain or become as 'healthy' as is permitted by existing medical knowledge (pp. 46–47).

In this case, need is maximal!

In contrast, common usage of need often implies a minimal requirement or a standard of adequacy. This was the spirit of federal health planning efforts in the 1970s, which sought to control the perceived proliferation of health care in order to control costs. Health planners argued at least implicitly that consumers were often getting more health care than they really needed.

Often the discussion of needs gets disconnected from the fact that the output of health care and the distribution of health care to meet people's needs are chosen in the context of society's choices of all its public goals. We present a construction of need that brings this to mind.

Let health care needs be defined within the context of the choice of society's goals for population health status as well as in the contexts of other goals like education and defense. To illustrate, we identify in Figure 20.5 the production function for health defined over the levels of a variable input, health care, given the conditions of

---

[1] This discussion and interpretation of need follow Folland (1986).

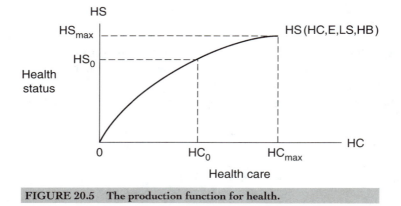

FIGURE 20.5   The production function for health.

environment, E, lifestyle, LS, and human biological endowment, HB. Here the technically maximal health status is HS_{max}. To achieve this health status level, a health care level of HC_{max} is needed. However, society may choose a lesser health status goal than the maximum achievable, using the savings to further other goals. For example, if society through its choice processes selects health status goal HS_0, then health care level HC_0 is needed.

Health Care Needs and the Social Welfare Function

How, then, is the health status goal selected? We depict this choice using the concept of a social welfare function.

THE UTILITY-POSSIBILITY FRONTIER

The Edgeworth box shows the efficient choices available to society in allocating resources between people. Yet it is also apparent that at many points on the contract curve, Abner or Belinda may be allocated little or no resources. These points are unquestionably economically efficient; yet they may be indefensible within any definition of a humane society.

Economic theory suggests that a social welfare function reflecting society's overall preferences is necessary to determine which of the efficient points is chosen.[2] We can trace out a utility-possibility frontier UU from the points in the Edgeworth box in Figure 20.1. Begin at the allocation where Belinda has everything and Abner has nothing. In Figure 20.6, we can assign Abner a utility of 0, and evaluate Belinda's utility as the intercept of the y-axis.

We can then draw a UU curve, by reallocating resources to Abner from Belinda, as we move along the contract curve in Figure 20.1. Recall that the fundamental prop-

---

[2]The classic discussion of this problem is Bator (1957). Since our discussion concerns exchange only, we have simplified his exposition.

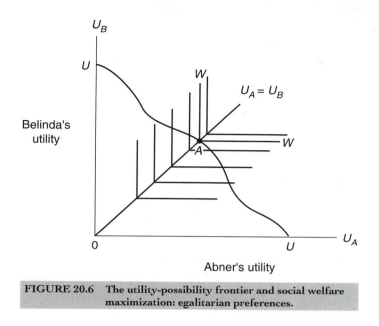

FIGURE 20.6 The utility-possibility frontier and social welfare maximization: egalitarian preferences.

erty of Pareto efficient distributions is that Abner's utility can come only at the expense of Belinda's utility. Therefore, the *UU* curve in Figure 20.6 must be downward sloping. The *x*-axis intercept summarizes the point at which Abner has all of the resources.

THE SOCIAL WELFARE FUNCTION

It is now up to society to decide which of the points on *UU* to choose. This decision must be made according to the rules by which societies operate: through debate, consensus, and maybe even dictatorial power. Economists define this as a *social welfare function.* Consider, for example, a society in which the consensus was that everyone's utility level should be exactly the same, with no variations tolerated. We would recognize this as a set of right-angled social indifference curves along a 45-degree line from the origin. The optimum allocation would be at point *A,* which is a tangency between the *WW* curve and the *UU* curve. This would indicate equal utility levels for Abner and Belinda. From point *A,* we can then return to the one point on the contract curve in Figure 20.1, in which the utility levels are equal, denoted *Z.* Picking this point leads to the unique allocation of the two goods to Abner and Belinda (although not necessarily the same amounts to each, as shown in Figure 20.1).

Many would argue that the specific social welfare function (with equal levels of utility) discussed previously would be highly questionable. Humane societies might agree that everyone should be provided with enough resources for at least a minimal standard of living; for Abner this would be U^A_{min}, and for Belinda this would be U^B_{min}. This can be characterized as two constraints on the *UU* curve in Figure 20.7. Such societies would consider no utility functions that would provide Abner with less utility than U^A_{min}; similarly for Belinda regarding U^B_{min}. Even here, however, the answer depends on

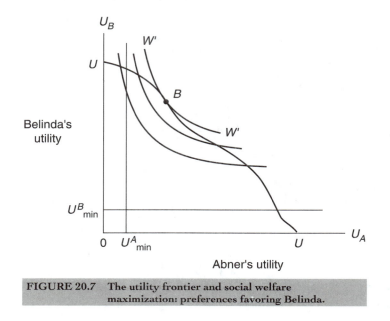

FIGURE 20.7 The utility frontier and social welfare maximization: preferences favoring Belinda.

the exact social welfare function chosen. Societies in which people like Belinda are most influential may have social welfare functions with social indifference curves like $W'W'$. In this case, people like Belinda would get larger shares of the resources than people like Abner. The optimum at point B, although providing subsistence living for citizens like Abner, would leave citizens like Belinda better off than the optimum in Figure 20.6.

THE SOCIAL WELFARE FUNCTION AND HEALTH CARE NEEDS

Within this framework we now discuss the various social choice processes that scholars and policymakers have proposed for the equitable provision of health care. Let the social welfare function of society (SW) represent the preferences of society as a whole. The function in a commonly used form may be written as follows:

$$SW = f(U_1, U_2, \ldots U_n) \tag{20.1}$$

where social welfare is characterized as a function of the utility levels of each of the n persons in the society. Utility for each person as usual depends on his or her consumption of the available goods in society, including health care. In addition, we may suppose that each individual to some degree perceives an external benefit from the consumption of health care by others.

Society may be perceived to be efficient when it acts as if it were choosing among its choice variables to maximize the social welfare function. The choice process may be conceived graphically in Figure 20.7 as choosing the highest social indifference curve attainable given the utility-possibility frontier. The level of health care needed can be defined within this context. The health care needed by each person in society is that which maximizes SW. Social welfare will be maximized when society chooses its optimal health status goals in conjunction with optimal levels of other goals.

Norman Daniels's Concept of Health Care Need

To assume that health care need is determined by the same social choice mechanism by which society makes all its choices of social goals is to treat health status like all other goals. Some analysts argue in fact that health is special and that the health care needs have a more objective independent basis. Norman Daniels (1985) has developed one such argument and we provide an outline of his approach here. There are three main elements to Daniels's concept of health care need.

1. *Health care is special.* Under this view, health care can be separated from other goals. To make this separation plausible, health care must be viewed as a primary good that is special because it is central to the task of attaining or restoring a fair equality of opportunity. In this sense, it comes prior to other considerations.

2. *Species-typical functioning.* It is further argued that the human species has a range of functioning that is typical and appropriate to it. Disease here means the absence of health; health is defined as the ability to attain a functioning level typical to the species.

3. *Fair equality of opportunity.* Given the nature of society and the human species, there is a range of behavior opportunity that every person in society should have available. The range will vary somewhat from person to person inasmuch as we each have different endowments of skills and abilities. But all are entitled to their fair share.

To use the *fair equality of opportunity* standard of health care need, we must imagine that there is a degree of objectivity behind its construction, and that need so constructed would be observable in common by most people. We do not solve this matter here, but instead point out what Daniels's project entails. If Daniels's view were accepted as correct, then health care need could be identified separately from the context in which other goals for society are chosen. We leave as a discussion question the issue of whether this is possible. The issue can be pursued further beginning with Daniels's stimulating and controversial book (1985) and articles (1981, 1982).[3]

ECONOMIC CRITICISMS OF NEED-BASED DISTRIBUTIONS

The ideas of mainstream economics often clash with need-based conceptions of the appropriate distribution of health care resources. The economic criticisms that have been leveled do not necessarily apply to each existing conception of need. The criticisms are each directed to particular conceptions of need. They can be understood as criticisms of the form "if by need you mean *X,* then the following criticism applies. . . ." Several criticisms of this sort are found in the literature.

1. *The bottomless pit.* Health is undoubtedly subject to diminishing marginal returns in production. Thus, if the technical maximum health status goal is chosen, the marginal unit of health care will have nearly zero effect on health status. Since it is doubtful that all societal goals can be maximally attained, social welfare would generally be improved if

---

[3]For a critique of Daniels's book on economic grounds, see Folland (1990).

society would reduce health care use somewhat and use the freed resources for other goals. For that matter, health care needs at or close to the technical maximum could also exhaust most of society's resources, and thus constitute a bottomless pit.

2. *Needs should not be chosen independent of costs.* Society's health status goals should depend in part on the costs of health and thus on the price of health care. This is so because the costs of health care resources determine the amounts of other goods that must be given up to attain health goals. No society is wealthy enough to attain the maximum amounts of all goals, and thus there are opportunity costs to health.

3. *The role of scientific medicine in determining needs.* From similar reasoning, it follows that health needs cannot be determined solely on the basis of scientific medical knowledge. The role of medical experts is critical in needs analysis, inasmuch as scientific data are certainly required to determine the medical inputs needed to attain a given health goal. However, the appropriate health status goals themselves must be chosen with knowledge of society's economic constraints and its values. In some form, the political process is required to identify the trade-offs that society is willing to incur to attain any given goal.

4. *Monotechnic needs.* Finally, Fuchs (1974) has pointed out that when needs analyses are stated in terms of needed health resources per capita, they often implicitly falsely assume that only one available technique exists for pursuing a health status goal. More plausibly, there are many opportunities for substitution, not only between health care inputs but also between health care inputs and other inputs into the production function of health.

HORIZONTAL EQUITY AND NEED

Health care need is also a central focus in recent research attempting to answer questions about the equitable treatment of people with equal needs. Equal treatment of equals is known as *horizontal equity*. To understand the issues and findings, we draw on the work of van Doorslaer and Wagstaff (1992).

These authors define inequity by beginning with the following equation:

$$m_i = a_p + b_p h_i \qquad \text{if poor}$$
$$m_i = a_r + b_r h_i \qquad \text{if rich}$$

(20.2)

In this equation, m is medical expenditure, a_p and a_r are constant levels of expenditure when healthy for the poor and the rich respectively, b_p and b_r are constant coefficients of health status, h_i, which equals 0 when the person is healthy and 1 when sick. (We omit random error terms depicting the minor characteristics of individuals that affect medical expenditure irrespective of need.)

Horizontal equity occurs when $a_p = a_r$ and $b_p = b_r$, that is, when the expected average spending of the rich and poor are equal both when well $(h_i = 0)$ and when sick $(h_i = 1)$. Does this square with your own sense of what equity means?[4]

---

[4]Mooney et al. (1991, 1992) question whether equity means equal expenditure. An individual may differ from another because of different preferences, so even with equal access the amount of expenditures on care will differ. Culyer, van Doorslaer, and Wagstaff (1992) respond to this objection. The interested reader is recommended these original sources.

How to Compare Horizontal Equity Between Countries

To generate a measure of the degree of inequity, the authors then calculate the standardized expenditure shares, based on equation (20.2), which are the groups' shares of total expenditure reflected by their spending. The final result is described graphically in Figure 20.8. Here the curve labeled *g* measures the cumulative standardized shares against the cumulative population arranged by income level. As shown in this hypothetical example, the poorest 20 percent of the population accounts for about 5 percent of medical expenditure, the poorest 40 percent accounts for about 11 percent of the expenditure, and so on.

If spending favors the rich, the curve will lie below the diagonal, as in this case. When spending favors the poor, the curve will lie above the diagonal. The degree of inequality is measured as the ratio of the area of the ellipsoid *A* to the total area under the diagonal.[5]

The Results

The van Doorslaer and Wagstaff results for inequity across countries are shown in Table 20.1. These data suggest that unequal use by people and income groups given health status is the common rule, not the exception. However, the negative numbers in

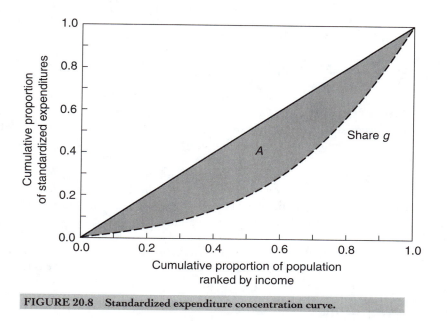

FIGURE 20.8   Standardized expenditure concentration curve.

---

[5]If the curve lies above the diagonal, then the inequality is measured as the ratio of the negative area of the ellipsoid to the total area under the diagonal.

TABLE 20.1 Tests of Inequality Across Countries

Country	Measure of Inequality*	Statistically Significant
Denmark	–0.055	Yes
Ireland	–0.076	Yes
Italy	–0.036	Yes
Netherlands	0.025	No
Spain	0.146	Yes
Switzerland	–0.043	No
United Kingdom	0.013	Yes
United States	0.028	Yes

*Measured at the 1 percent level of statistical significance.
Source: van Doorslaer and Wagstaff (1992).

the table show countries where the estimated inequality is in favor of the poorer people. Only in the Netherlands, Spain, the United Kingdom, and the United States is the distribution tending to favor the rich, although in the Netherlands the result is not statistically significant. When the elderly are left out of consideration in the United States, then the authors report the distribution even in the United States favors the poor. While measurement and definition issues of horizontal equity may elicit disagreement, these numbers representing unequal use for a given health status across income groups are clearly defined and tell an important part of the story.

THEORIES OF SOCIAL JUSTICE

Inevitably, a treatment of what health care distribution is equitable, and of what health care needs should be met in a society, depends on ethical theory. An ethical theory serves to identify a context and reasoning to determine what ought to be done, as opposed to mere positive analysis of what is the case. Ethical theories that serve to determine a fair or just distribution of economic resources are sometimes called theories of social justice. Seen this way, any notion of equity or need in health care, in order to be complete, must be connected to an ethical theory or perhaps to a theory of social justice.

Several theories of social justice have been proposed. It cannot be said that we have a consensus-accepted theory of social justice. Even without a consensus, however, an examination of several examples of theories of social justice helps to illuminate the issues that must be addressed if a consensus is to be achieved. We offer a brief overview of three social justice theories, along with a selection of criticisms of each theory.

Utilitarianism

Utilitarianism became prominent in the nineteenth century and is still current in modified forms. It can be understood as an interpretation of the social optimum as those choices that provide for the greatest good for the greatest number. In its classical form, it identified the social optimum as those social choices that maximized the sum of utilities of all persons in society. Using the concept of the social welfare function, classical utilitarianism in effect defines the social welfare function as the sum of individual utilities.

In the form of utilitarianism promoted by Jeremy Bentham in the nineteenth century, an individual's utility was conceived of as cardinally measurable, at least in principle, and comparable between individuals. The utilitarian ethic thus originally was conceived somewhat literally as maximization of society's total satisfaction level.

Utilitarianism captures the idea of trade-offs between goals. Under this construction, society may choose to accept some harm for a few members in return for a greater good for the many. As such, it avoids the bottomless pit criticisms mentioned earlier. Health status would generally not be maximized for every individual in society under this view.

SOME CRITICISMS OF UTILITARIANISM

Classical utilitarianism came to be criticized within the economics profession early in this century. Economists generally rejected the idea that utility could be cardinally measurable and comparable between people. It is viewed as unscientific to suppose that one individual's level of satisfaction could somehow be added to that of another person. Modern social welfare theory in economics has proceeded along ordinal utility lines. Utility in these theories retains the role of ranking preferences among alternatives, but the notion of a fixed quantitative measure of happiness was discarded in most modern theory.

Two other criticisms of utilitarianism help to illustrate some of the weaknesses that have been identified in the theory. One is the question of domain—that is, whose utilities are to count? Utilitarianism does not itself identify where to draw the boundaries of membership in the society. Are foreign people or noncitizens to count? If not, why not? Are animals to count? Unborn future generations? Is the utility of the fetus to count or only that of the already born?

A second criticism raised by Robert Nozick (1974) poses a similar question regarding possibly malevolent individuals in society. For example, suppose an individual, because of bigotry or sheer malevolence, gets satisfaction out of the suffering of some other group in society. Is the malevolent utility of such a person also to count?

Rawls and Justice as Fairness

John Rawls (1971) has approached the concept of social justice from a different viewpoint. Here a primary principle of justice is that social choices must be fair. It is unfair, according to Rawls, for social choices to be dominated by people with economic or political power who often have vested interests because of their circumstances in society. Instead, to be fair we should make our choices from a position divorced from arbitrary special interestedness. Such a position, it is proposed, is one from behind the "veil of ignorance."

The Rawlsian veil of ignorance is a hypothetical situation in which we can think rationally but for which our particularities of self and economic situation are as yet unknown. It is as if we could somehow contemplate life in society before we are born and before we know whether we will be rich or poor, black or white, male or female, tall or short, and so on. Rawls's idea is that, so divorced from our vested interests of life, we would generally come to a consensus about principles of social justice, and specifically we would agree to the Rawlsian *maximin* principle.

Under the maximin principle, we would each reason that without knowing who we were to become in society we would presume that we could be the person worst off. Under such circumstances, we would agree, argues Rawls, only to a system of justice in society that maximized the position of the worst off. This need not result in complete equality of incomes and resources including health care, but departures from equality would be permitted only if the lot of the worst off would improve. Health care under a Rawlsian system of social justice would presumably also be provided if the needs of the worst off were regarded as a priority.

SOME CRITICISMS OF RAWLSIAN JUSTICE

Rawls's theory of justice has also drawn criticism, and we illustrate some of these criticisms. It has been pointed out that Rawls assumes that each of us behind the veil of ignorance is extremely risk averse. Suppose that an alternative situation, A, offered everyone an income of $10,000, while alternative B offered one person $9,000 but everyone else $100,000. Under the maximin principle, persons behind the veil would choose alternative A, the alternative with the higher income for the worst off. Would people really be so risk averse as to forgo even extremely good odds of a large gain?

The Rawlsian theory of justice also appears subject to the bottomless pit argument. The instance of health care provides a good example of the problem in the views of Arrow (1973):

> Thus there could easily exist medical procedures which serve to keep people barely alive but with little satisfaction and which are yet so expensive as to reduce the rest of the population to poverty (p. 251).

Despite the criticisms, Rawlsian justice provides a prominent example of a theory of social justice that entails a strong presumption in favor of equality, a presumption that permits inequalities to arise only if they contribute to the lot of the worst off.

Nozick and Entitlement Theory

Finally, we describe a theory of justice that puts a premium on liberty. Robert Nozick (1974) offers a conception of justice that begins by proposing that natural rights suggest the necessity for a libertarian constraint. By a libertarian constraint he means that any system of social organization should prohibit the coercion of others. All persons are entitled to enter into voluntary transactions, free from coercion. Property rights are acknowledged and people are entitled to keep any property received through a voluntary transaction.

From these principles, Nozick develops a justification for the existence of a minimal state. He argues that these principles of justice necessarily limit the role of the state, and in consequence social programs beyond the minimal functions of government in providing public police protection services would not be warranted. It follows that social programs providing for health care would also not be warranted, and the health care needs of one person would not place obligations on any other person other than for what he or she voluntarily is willing to accept.

SOME CRITICISMS OF ENTITLEMENT THEORY

A central focus of criticism is the assumed libertarian constraint itself. For those who do not accept the constraint as an implication or necessity of natural rights, it will be hard to see why we are not free to trade off some degree of liberty in order to make gains in efficiency. For example, the Food and Drug Administration restrictions on the availability of certain drugs represent restrictions on liberty, but at least in some cases they may be supportable on efficiency grounds. Pauly (1978) has argued, for example, that if the costs of conveying information to the public are sufficiently large, substantial efficiency gains may accrue simply by restricting access to a potentially dangerous drug. The restriction of access may in some cases require a physician's prescription; in other cases it may require banning the drug from the market.

Members of society frequently accept rules that are expected to improve outcomes yet that restrict liberty somewhat. Wittman (1982) has discussed the potential efficiency of simple rules in day-to-day life and in sports. A traffic light restricts liberty somewhat but promotes the efficient and safe flow of traffic. If we accept the principle that liberties can be traded off to gain certain efficiencies, this raises the question of whether we must accept the libertarian constraint.

CONCLUSIONS

The three theories of social justice described here attempt to ground our understanding of the distribution of goods and services—including importantly health care—in a system of ethics. The brief review of these theories cannot account for all arguments and rebuttals and cannot resolve controversies. Those interested in ethics, as it concerns economic distribution, should consult the original sources.

The theories, however, serve to show how widely people's understanding of appropriate distributions of health care differ, and their consideration suggests that we have as yet no consensus. Nevertheless, these issues of justice are raised whenever society wishes to modify the distribution of health resources on grounds of need and equity. The issues are no less important because there is disagreement.

The meaning of efficiency is more sharply defined. Here the issues of controversy involve the degree of efficiency attainable either with existing health care markets or with health care markets as modified by new policies. The theoretical model of perfect competition generates a Pareto efficient outcome. Health care markets in practice, however, differ in many respects from those that have perfect competition. Perhaps the most notable discrepancies of actual health care markets from the theoretical model arise because of the role of uncertainty, the problems of information, and the presence of externalities.

Perfection in either direction is not attainable. We must inevitably accept approaches to health care distribution that are second best, evaluating each proposal on its merits. While perfect competition is unattainable, proposals that improve the degree of competition in health care markets may nevertheless improve society's well-being. On the other hand, proposals for providing social insurance programs to at least some segments of the population can be supported in principle on efficiency grounds whenever substantial charitable externalities are present. Alternatively, social insurance programs may be justified on the basis of one or more systems of social justice.

Summary

1. Pareto efficiency defines a situation where it is no longer possible to make mutually beneficial changes. It is Pareto efficient to exhaust all avenues for gains that benefit someone and harm no one.

2. Under theoretical conditions of perfect competition, the competitive market is Pareto efficient. In the Edgeworth box for exchange, regardless of the initial endowment position, a competitive free exchange will lead to a Pareto efficient point, a point on the contract curve. This is the First Fundamental Theorem of Welfare Economics.

3. The Second Fundamental Theorem of Welfare Economics is also illustrated by the Edgeworth box for exchange. The theorem holds that any Pareto efficient outcome can in principle be achieved by a competitive market, given a suitable initial distribution of resources.

4. Price discrimination is Pareto inefficient. This result includes that form of price discrimination arising when a favored segment of the population is provided reduced prices for health care so as to improve access.

5. The health care sector deviates from the conditions of perfect competition in many respects. These include major issues of the role of uncertainty, the role of information, and the role of externalities.

6. The Theorem of the Second Best suggests that promoting competitive features in health care markets is not welfare enhancing per se. Nevertheless, many competitive proposals in practice may be welfare enhancing.

7. Social programs for the subsidization or provision of health care can be theoretically rationalized on grounds of efficiency as well as equity. The usual efficiency argument posits the existence of a charitable externality in health care. The presence of externalities may in principle justify market interventions.

8. Need-based distributions of health care resources tend to be based on equity grounds and usually imply a rejection of market outcomes. Health care need may be understood as health care resources required to attain a given health goal chosen by society.

9. Society's optimal choice of goals may be summarized by the social welfare function, defined over all possible combinations of the individual utilities of society members. This leads to the optimal choice by selecting the point on the utility-possibility frontier that maximizes social welfare.

10. Norman Daniels's concept of health care need is based on the fair equality of opportunity. It argues that health care needs may be identified separately from other social decisions.

11. Several need-based distributions can be criticized on economic grounds. These grounds argue that health care needs should not be (1) the technical maximum, (2) independent of cost, (3) chosen solely on technical medical criteria, or (4) monotechnic.

12. A philosophical theory of justice is needed to provide an ethical grounding for a proposed distribution. There is no present consensus on such a theory of justice.

Discussion Questions

1. At point 0_A in Figure 20.1, Belinda has all of both goods. Is this point Pareto efficient? Is it equitable? Discuss.

2. If society could clearly choose an equitable point reflecting a distribution of the two goods, is this point inevitably going to lie on the contract curve?

3. Choose an example of a health care market, and identify ways in which it differs from the perfectly competitive model. Do you think that these deviations from competition could be each repaired by appropriate policies? Discuss.

4. We describe several economic criticisms of need-based distributions. Do any of these criticisms apply to Norman Daniels's conception of health care need?

5. Speculate on how each of the three described theories of social justice would view government programs designed to provide infant and child care to the poor using tax dollars.

6. Under utilitarianism, one maximizes the total utility of society. What does this imply about the marginal utility for each person? What does it imply about the total utility for each person?

7. Suppose that society determined that it must provide a minimal sustained level of health to everyone. What would this imply regarding society's expenditures on health?

8. Insufficient health care for some is often seen as a problem of insufficient income to purchase health care. Discuss two alternatives to social programs that provide health care.

Exercises

1. Prove that point *B* in Figure 20.1 is not Pareto efficient.

2. Draw an Edgeworth box of the type in Figure 20.2 but with only these details inside: the point ω and budget line *AB* through ω. Using indifference curves, depict the utility-maximizing choice for Abner. Now let the budget line rotate to *CD*, drawn to reflect a higher relative price of medical care. Again identify the utility-maximizing choice for Abner.

3. Is it possible to find a point on the contract curve that is not a competitive equilibrium?

4. Let Q_{opt} in Figure 20.4 represent the optimal level of health care in society under the external benefits rationale for social health care programs. Would members of society necessarily view Q_{opt} as the equitable amount of health care?

5. If all tax-paying members of society became "hard hearted," feeling no external benefit in the health care provided others, then what would be the optimal health care output under the external benefit rationale in Figure 20.4?

6. In Figure 20.7, depicting the utility-possibility frontier, would society ever choose an inefficient point (inside UU) as the optimal point?

7. Suppose Fred has an income of $5,000 per year, and Harry has an income of $105,000 per year. If we tax $50,000 from Harry to give to Fred, will this represent a Pareto improvement for society? Why or why not? Would this improve society under some other criteria?

CHAPTER

Social Insurance

- Social Insurance Policies and Social Programs
- Historical Roots of Social Insurance
- Medicare and Medicaid in the United States
- The Effects of Medicare and Medicaid
- National Health Insurance
- Conclusions

Throughout this book, we have emphasized the role that markets can play in providing health care. We have also generally taken economic efficiency, provided in theory by perfectly competitive markets, as a standard against which to judge the costs and benefits of policies. In this chapter, we address instead the issues that arise when a society considers providing for health care by offering health insurance, to some significant degree, at the public's expense. Such insurance programs provided through taxes or regulations are called *social insurance programs*. Having provided an overview of the rationales for social insurance in health care in the previous chapter, we now turn to an examination of social insurance. We begin by considering the history of health care social insurance throughout the world, with some emphasis on the United States. In this section we also analyze the demise of the Clinton health plan in 1994. We then examine Medicaid and Medicare and their effects, and close by examining prospects and issues for national health insurance in the United States.

SOCIAL INSURANCE POLICIES AND SOCIAL PROGRAMS

We begin with a review of the types and characteristics of social insurance programs in both health-related and other contexts. Social insurance programs can be usefully discussed under five categories. While not mutually exclusive, these categories suggest distinctive aspects of the various programs. Programs of the following five types exist both in the United States and in other countries.

Types of Programs

1. *Poverty.* The individual lacks purchasing power to buy the amounts of goods that are considered to provide the minimal standards of decent life. Programs that are directed toward persons experiencing poverty involve either the provision of cash, or more often the subsidized provisions of goods "in kind," such as rent vouchers or food stamps.

2. *Old Age.* The individual has attained a certain age, generally coinciding with his or her retirement from active employment. Programs that are directed toward the elderly include income maintenance, such as Social Security, as well as services and considerations (such as old-age housing, Meals-on-Wheels) that may address the generally decreased mobility of the elderly.

3. *Disability.* The person has either a temporary or permanent inability to work because of illness, or has a work-related injury. Programs generally provide cash benefits. Disability programs were among the earliest social insurance programs available.

4. *Health.* Programs cover illness or well-care financing and/or provide facilities for various segments of populations. In the United States, most programs are addressed to the elderly and/or poor. The individual's health care is financed either entirely or in part by the government. In other countries, governments have more direct involvement in the financing and delivery of health services for larger segments (or all) of the population.

5. *Unemployment.* The person receives assistance because of a temporary loss of work due to economic considerations. Programs generally provide short-term cash benefits. In many countries, longer-term unemployment may lead into poverty-related welfare programs.

Several other definitions are useful in considering social insurance programs. Some programs, termed *entitlements,* are available to all who qualify. Food stamps, for example, are available to all households whose incomes fall below specified levels.[1] Medicaid, or financed health care for the poor (to be discussed in considerable detail later in this chapter), is also an entitlement program. Housing programs in the United States, in contrast, are not entitlements. There are only limited numbers of subsidized units (on the supply side) or vouchers (on the demand side) available.

Many programs are *means-tested.* That is, they are available only to individuals or households who meet certain income criteria. Households who receive aid for poverty-related problems may lose some or all of it if their incomes pass certain levels. Such means testing is not confined solely to poverty programs. In the United States, Social Security benefits for the elderly were formerly untaxed. The sight of already well-off individuals receiving still more income from the government led to the partial taxation of Social Security income for those above certain threshold levels of income. This change also serves to raise revenues.

Finally, the aid may take various forms. Often it is tied to the purchase of certain items, such as food or housing. This procedure ensures that the people use the aid to buy items that the legislators have deemed important. Under certain circumstances it may be

---

[1]The determination of these specified levels may depend on income, family size, and geographic location. Such determinations are often related to political considerations.

more efficient to provide a cash subsidy rather than one in kind. Economists have long felt that it is cheaper, and therefore more efficient, to provide cash instead. Generally, such cash programs would make the recipient better off in his or her own eyes: Which would you prefer, $100 in cash, or $100 worth of physician care? Legislators and the voting public, however, seem often to prefer that the subsidies be made in kind rather than in cash to control the purchases of those receiving the subsidies.

Program Features

To characterize health-related social insurance programs, both in the United States and elsewhere, we discuss certain common features:

1. Contributions. These include taxes, deductibles, and coinsurance.
2. Benefits. There are various benefit aspects to be discussed, including how much, who is included, and what types of treatment are included.
3. Length of coverage.
4. Means of reimbursement to providers.
5. Methods of determining payment levels to providers.

The first three items are related fundamentally to the receipt of care. The last two are related both to the provision of care, as well as to the political problems involved in initiating plans.

Although supported by government, most social insurance plans are not costless to the recipients. Many are funded by tax collections, and recipients of care often are also taxpayers. In some cases, the taxes in question may be regressive. A regressive tax is one for which lower-income people pay higher portions of their incomes to the tax than do richer people. In contrast, a progressive tax is one in which lower-income people pay lower portions of their incomes to the tax than do richer people.

Tax payments into the Social Security program have been somewhat regressive. Throughout most of the life of the program, the tax has been a constant percentage of wage income, up to some ceiling, at which point the marginal tax rate becomes zero. This means that on average people in higher income groups pay a smaller proportion of their income in payroll taxes; thus, the tax is regressive.[2]

To determine whether a social insurance program is redistributive in net—that is, whether it in net causes a transfer of money from the rich to the poor—one must consider not just the tax payments made but also the benefits received. For example, data for the Social Security program in the United States tend to show that Social Security is redistributive, that the poorer people in a given age group tend to gain more in net than the rich.

In addition to tax payments, eligible recipients must also often pay deductibles or coinsurance. Time costs with respect to paperwork, or waiting time for appointments or treatment, must also be considered.

---

[2]The Medicare tax rate is now 1.45% of all wage income. For 1996, the wage base for Social Security Old Age and Disability will be 6.20 percent on a base salary of $62,700.

Levels of benefits and length of coverage are fairly similar in description to the workings of private insurance. Given the equity considerations of social insurance, political considerations may affect both. The determination of who and which treatments are covered is also important. Coverage of individuals may involve children and spouses. Coverage of treatments may mandate coverage of certain diseases (i.e., end-stage kidney disease), and exclude others (i.e., optometric or chiropractic services).

Health-related social insurance also has supply-related characteristics. Some expenses may be paid directly by the patient, and may be reimbursed; others may be paid directly by the government to the provider. In some countries, all physicians who participate in the national health care program are government employees.

HISTORICAL ROOTS OF SOCIAL INSURANCE

European Beginnings

The United States and South Africa are often characterized as the only industrialized countries that lack a comprehensive health-related social insurance system. Experts identify the pioneering legislation for a system of compulsory national health insurance as that which started in Germany in 1883. National health insurance spread to other European countries at the end of the nineteenth and the early part of the twentieth centuries.

The German system and the other European systems were extensions of already existing voluntary associations, often guild or mutual aid groups whose benefits to members included the pooling of insurable risks.[3] The political impetus for converting or merging voluntary local groups in a system of national coverage was often its usefulness as a stabilizing influence:

> Political discontent precipitated the introduction of social insurance in both Germany and England. . . . In Germany, Bismarck introduced social rights to avoid granting wider political rights; in Britain, Lloyd George sought social rights within the context of existing rights to political participation. But both were basically defensive efforts to stabilize the political order. . . . (Starr, 1982, p. 239).

The German laws of 1883 set up a highly decentralized program covering workers in mining, transportation, construction, manufacturing, mechanical trades, and establishments using power machinery. Other countries followed. Austria (1888), Hungary (1891), Sweden (1891), Denmark (1892), and Belgium (1894), were early adopters of health insurance. With Spain's adoption of a plan in 1929, nearly every European country had enacted health insurance laws. Some were compulsory, as in Germany, but other countries, such as Belgium, Denmark, Sweden, and Switzerland, provided government subsidies to voluntary mutual funds.

The United Kingdom established its first social health insurance system in 1911. The 1911 legislation creating social insurance in Britain is of special interest because it

---

[3]For more discussion, see Starr (1982) and Jensen and Cotter (1987).

helped to prepare for the British National Health Service that was adopted in 1946. Governmental provision of health care through a national health service system is most prominently exemplified in the Western countries by the United Kingdom. Government provision was common in Eastern European countries and the former Soviet Union, which began its system in 1926. A more detailed examination and comparison of health insurance systems across countries are discussed in Chapter 22.[4]

Early Experience in the United States

Compared with the European countries, the United States was a latecomer to the provision of social insurance, and to the provision of governmental health insurance in particular. In the late nineteenth century and early twentieth century, the American experience was similar to that of Europe in that voluntary group purchasing arrangements, mutual benefit associations, and the like were common. However, in America the funding of these voluntary societies was not taken up by government, and from the advent of the German system in 1883 to the beginnings of the British system in 1911, governmental compulsory insurance for health care was not really an issue in the United States.

In the early years of the twentieth century, health insurance plans began to gain supporters. The American Association for Labor Legislation (AALL) supported such a plan, and the American Medical Association initially responded positively to health insurance proposals.[5] But a political consensus was lacking, as evidenced by the fact that Samuel Gompers, president of the American Federation of Labor, opposed compulsory health insurance.

As the Great Depression approached, public attention to health issues was focused by the activities of the privately funded Committee on the Cost of Medical Care (CCMC). The most prominent recommendations of the committee supported group practice in the provision of medical care and the use of insurance, either private or tax supported, to pay for its costs. The flurry of minority reports and opposition by other groups indicated problems in achieving consensus, as stronger alliances both pro and con were apparently forming.

The major advent of social insurance legislation in the United States occurred in the midst of the Depression during the 1930s, through the Social Security program that began in 1935. Despite the social insurance thrust of the program and the reform-minded support for it, the legislation evidenced concessions to political opposition to the New Deal, including the omission of governmental health insurance. Starr notes the following:

> The omission of health insurance from the Social Security Act was by no means the Act's only conservative feature. It relied on a regressive tax and gave no coverage to some of the very poor, such as farm laborers and domestics (p. 269).

The Roosevelt administration in the late 1930s investigated the needs for a national program in health care through the work of the Technical Committee on Medical

---

[4]Gordon (1988, p. 201) provides a good overview of this topic.
[5]Much of the following material is treated in more detail by Starr (1982).

Care. The committee recommended support of state-funded programs instead of a single national health insurance program. Though support seemed to gather for compulsory health insurance through the work of this committee and the succeeding National Health Conference, opposition, in part from the American Medical Association, convinced President Franklin Roosevelt to step back from such a plan.

Proponents of compulsory health insurance plans were not successful through the 1940s and 1950s. President Truman called for another national conference on health issues.[6] Truman proposed "a single health insurance system that would include all classes of the society, even those . . . not covered by Social Security" (Starr, p. 282). During the public debate over these issues, compulsory health insurance was often called *socialized medicine,* a term that greatly weakened its support during the political climate of the early years of the Cold War. Though Truman won the election in 1948, his success was never translated into a health insurance program.

The Establishment of Medicare and Medicaid

Throughout this time, however, there was also substantial and perhaps growing support for health insurance, in particular for governmental insurance aimed to support the health needs of the elderly. A compromise program sponsored by Senator Robert Kerr and Representative Wilbur Mills was passed in 1960; Kerr-Mills responded to the growing concern for unmet health insurance needs but was directed solely at the aged poor. Kerr-Mills used federal dollars to support state-based programs, but many states did not respond; three years after its passage, Kerr-Mills funding was not evenly spread because five large industrial states were receiving 90 percent of the funds.

The major social insurance programs for health care in the United States, Medicare and Medicaid, were passed during the Johnson administration. Johnson had supported health care for the aged, and by winning a landslide victory in the 1964 election, he was able to push for these programs. The political climate had also shifted somewhat in favor of such programs. Even so, the passage of the Medicare bill, in a form apparently more extensive than the President had even initially asked for, is a story of individuals interacting in a complex way. As Anderson (1990) says:

> How the bill that finally passed was put together is difficult to determine. It is unlikely that the chain of events and decisions could be reconstructed, even by the principals (p. 177).

The social insurance debate in the United States often ranged between those who believed in *voluntarism* and voluntary insurance, as won in negotiations between self-reliant industries and unions, and those who believed that only a compulsory insurance program would provide the insurance that was necessary for the larger population. The resolution of the debate in the form of Medicare and Medicaid can be said to have achieved widespread political support since the 1960s.

The fundamental concerns about Medicare and Medicaid stem from their rising costs. In the mid-1990s, with growing elderly and poor populations as well as contin-

---

[6]See O. Anderson (1990) for further discussion.

ual health care cost inflation, the total costs of the social insurance programs are perceived by many to have gone out of control. Politicians seek to ensure that Medicare will have a sufficient trust fund to meet future needs, while balancing these needs against the increased taxes and payments for services necessary to support them.

The wider issue of social health insurance for the population as a whole cannot be said to be decided at this writing. The experience of 1993–1994 with the Clinton health plan, however, was a "massive political upheaval"[7] that must be studied in order to sketch possibilities for the future. The Clinton plan began with fairly positive reviews and public interest. Clinton was elected in 1992 on a plurality with a campaign promising health system reform. There had been signs of growing interest among the electorate in health system reform including social health insurance. The Clinton plan was drafted during January–May 1993 by a large task force made up of government officials, health policy experts, congressional staffers, and others. Many perceived the task force to be secretive. During the remainder of the year a coalition of interests failed to form around clearly defined features of reform, while substantial interests, such as insurers, lobbied and advertised against the plan. During 1994 the plan was reworked to respond to critics. The public, however, seemed increasingly to believe that Clinton's plan would entail huge government bureaucracy, cost, and inefficiency. By the end of summer 1994, we had witnessed the resounding demise of the plan.

Will the U.S. government pass health reform including social health insurance in the near future? It can be said that many of the same cost and insurance issues are still with us. Insuring the uninsured is costly, and the present antispending sentiment augurs against this. However, while there are new efforts for an incremental approach, the "whole cloth" approach of the early Clinton plan seems impossible for the foreseeable future.

MEDICARE AND MEDICAID
IN THE UNITED STATES

The two major health-related social insurance programs in the United States, Medicare and Medicaid, were enacted in 1965 after years of debate. Medicare is a national program that primarily provides compulsory hospital insurance to the elderly plus optional medical coverage to which nearly all elderly subscribe. In contrast, Medicaid is a program operated by the states with matching federal dollars, a program that primarily provides health care coverage to categories of the poor.

Medicare

Although originally targeted solely toward the elderly, Medicare has been expanded through the years. It now includes those under age 65 who have been receiving federal disability insurance benefits for at least 24 months, as well as to childhood disability

---

[7]The account in this paragraph comes from Skocpol (1995).

beneficiaries, and people suffering from end-stage kidney failure. Nevertheless, the beneficiary group still consists primarily of the elderly.

Medicare is financed by a payroll tax as part of the Social Security package of 1.45 percent each on employers and employees. Medicare comes in two parts. Part A provides for compulsory hospital insurance for virtually all persons aged 65 and older. Part B provides supplementary medical insurance which, although voluntary, is purchased by some 97 percent of eligible persons aged 65 and over. This supplementary medical insurance receives about three-quarters of its revenue from federal revenues, and the rest from a monthly premium, which is deducted from the monthly benefits of those receiving cash Social Security benefits. Even with these two coverages, many elderly feel the need for additional health insurance to cover the gaps left by Medicare; some 70 percent of the elderly purchase such "Medigap" coverage.

The Part A hospital insurance under Medicare provides 90 days of hospital care for each episode of illness, with an additional 60 days available over a beneficiary's lifetime. There is provision also for home health care. In addition, there are 100 days of skilled nursing home care per spell of illness, available following a hospitalization of at least three days. With its limitations in coverage, the nursing home portion of Medicare is designed to supplement hospital care and is not really a nursing home insurance. Medicaid is far more important to nursing home financing (Chapter 17).

The health care provided for under Medicare is not free to recipients. Beside the taxes they have paid, recipients must pay both deductibles and coinsurance. The deductible portion means that the beneficiary must pay an amount, in practice equal to about the cost of a day of hospital care, before receiving Medicare benefits. The coinsurance requirements mean that the beneficiary pays a portion of the remaining bill. In practice, the coinsurance for Medicare is one-fourth of the deductible amount for days 61 to 90 of hospital care, and more thereafter. The structure of coverage, including these coinsurance features, has not changed much in real terms over the last two decades.

Medicaid

In contrast to Medicare, the Medicaid programs are run by individual states to finance health services for certain categories of the needy whose economic status is seen as largely beyond their control. These eligible poor include dependent children, the elderly, the blind, and the disabled. The states, in return for conforming to federal requirements, receive federal matching grants to underwrite their costs. Because programs are initiated at the state level, there is considerable variation throughout the country.

Following the exposition by Gordon (1988), we describe the program in some additional detail. Medicaid allows states to cover four needy groups:

1. Those receiving benefits under the Aid to Families with Dependent Children (AFDC) program.

2. Most people receiving benefits under the Supplemental Security Income (SSI) program.

3. Persons who qualify for cash assistance but who do not actually receive it.

4. The "medically needy," that is, persons meeting all of the categorical requirements for Medicaid eligibility and whose income, after the deducting of medical expenses, is less than the state's "medically needy" income standard.

Medicaid benefits cover hospital and physician services, in addition to other services. Medicaid is far more liberal in the financing of nursing home services, since their coverage is not restricted to recovery from serious illnesses. In consequence, Medicaid is one of the major payers of nursing home care.

THE EFFECTS OF MEDICARE AND MEDICAID

Though we can be certain about the provisions of Medicare and Medicaid, we are necessarily less certain about their effects. The effects are actually the more important research concern. Research has narrowed the range of uncertainty to a considerable degree. We consider here a selection of what is known about the effects of Medicare and Medicaid on the following:

- Health care costs
- Access to health care
- Health status

We examine health care costs first.

Costs and Inflation

The implementation of Medicare and Medicaid in 1965 coincided with a considerable increase in health care costs in the United States. While health care costs had been rising before 1965, both in simple percentage terms and as well in comparison to the general rate of inflation, the hospital care inflation rate increased somewhat after the implementation of Medicare and Medicaid.[8]

The level of expenditures on the two programs increased much more rapidly than most people had expected. Table 21.1 shows the pattern of expenditures over time. As shown, the percentage increases in expenditures on both programs has been in double digits for most of the years. Even accounting for the substantial rate of inflation since the late 1960s, Medicare outlays increased by a factor of 6, and Medicaid outlays by a factor of 8. Ginsburg (1988) notes that charges per Medicare discharge increased at an annual rate of 11.2 percent for the 1970–1981 period. This inflation exceeded the general inflation by 2.9 percentage points per year, and it came in spite of a decline of 2.2 percent per year in average length of hospital stay.

Clearly also, the populations at risk grew for both Medicare and Medicaid. The number of Medicare enrollees grew at an average annual rate of 3.3 percent, a number that included disabled enrollees beginning in 1973. This is a rate that far exceeded population growth and can be attributed in large part to the aging of the population. Growth in the enrollee population is often cited as the primary reason for growth in Medicaid payments. Responding to the availability of Medicaid, which provided cost sharing for many programs, many states changed their need standards for AFDC, thus enabling

---

[8]See P. Feldstein (1977) for further discussion.

TABLE 21.1   Personal Health Care Expenditures Under Medicare and Medicaid: 1966–1994

Year	Enrollees (millions)	Medicare Spending (billions)	Increase (%)	Recipients (millions)	Medicaid Spending (billions)	Increase (%)
1966	19.1	$ 1.6		—	$1.3	
1967	19.5	4.9	206.3*	—	3.0	130.8*
1968	19.8	5.9	20.4	—	3.4	13.3
1969	20.1	6.8	15.3	—	4.0	17.6
1970	20.5	7.2	5.9	—	5.1	27.5
1971	20.9	8.1	12.5	—	6.4	25.5
1972	21.3	8.8	8.6	17.6	8.0	25.0
1973	23.5	10.2	15.9	19.6	9.1	13.8
1974	24.2	12.8	25.5	21.5	10.6	16.5
1975	25.0	15.7	22.7	22.0	12.9	21.7
1976	25.7	18.9	20.4	22.8	14.5	12.4
1977	26.5	22.1	16.9	22.8	16.6	14.5
1978	27.2	25.8	16.7	22.0	18.5	11.4
1979	27.9	30.1	16.7	21.5	21.2	14.6
1980	28.5	36.4	20.9	21.6	24.8	17.0
1981	29.0	43.8	20.3	22.0	28.9	16.5
1982	29.5	51.4	17.4	21.6	30.6	5.9
1983	30.0	58.5	13.8	21.6	33.6	9.8
1984	30.5	64.3	9.9	21.6	36.0	7.1
1985	31.1	70.1	9.0	21.8	39.7	10.3
1986	31.7	75.4	7.6	22.5	42.9	8.1
1987	32.4	81.7	8.4	23.2	48.2	12.4
1988	33.0	89.7	9.8	22.9	52.3	8.5
1989	33.5	99.8	12.8	NA	NA	NA
1990	34.1	109.0	9.2	NA	69.0	NA
1991	34.8	121.2	11.2	NA	87.4	26.7
1992	35.5	134.2	10.7	NA	112.5	28.7
1993	36.2	149.1	11.1	32.1	124.9	11.0
1994	36.9	166.1	11.4	NA	NA	NA

Note: The percentage increases for 1967 may be misleading. They are so large only because 1966 was a partial year for the beginning of the programs.

Note: NA means not available.

Source (1966–1988): Office of National Cost Estimates (1990, Table 12).

Source (1989–1994): Prospective Payment Assessment Commission, *Medicare and Medicaid Guide, Medicare and the American Health Care System,* June 15, 1995, Tables 3-1, 3-3, and 3-11, and Figure 3-3.

more families to qualify for cash assistance. There was additional publicity for Medicaid programs, and additional states initiated Medicaid programs.

WHY SPENDING HAS RISEN—INCREASED COVERAGE, TECHNOLOGICAL IMPROVEMENT, AND INCREASED INEFFICIENCY

The role of the increased population that is eligible and covered by Medicare and Medicaid clearly helps to explain why program expenditures have risen, but it does not fully account for the inflationary effects that these programs could have. Newhouse (1978) suggests three ways through which insurance programs such as these could affect prices and costs, even without growth in the population served.

First, Medicare and Medicaid both tended to increase the insurance coverage of the populations eligible. An increase in insurance has expansionary effects on the demand for care, as we have discussed in Chapter 11.

Figure 21.1 reviews this theoretical effect. Start at point A, where quantity of service Q_0 is provided at price (or cost) P_0. When the increase in insurance coverage reduces the portion of the bill paid by the eligible recipient, the demand for care rotates outward to the right from D_1 to D_2. In Figure 21.1, price rises to P_1 and quantity consumed increases to Q_1, or point B. Total expenditures rise from $P_0 Q_0$ to $P_1 Q_1$.

Newhouse explains, however, that these social insurance programs may have additional effects. He proposes that insurance coverage may induce technological improvements. If more costly technological improvements are induced by these social insurance programs, then the cost per unit of care may rise.

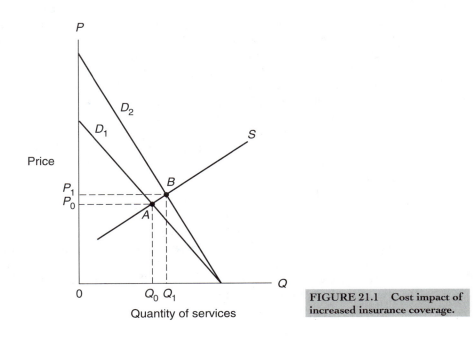

FIGURE 21.1 Cost impact of increased insurance coverage.

Finally, Newhouse proposes a third theory for the effect of insurance on costs and quantity used. This may be called the "increased inefficiency" theory. The idea is that when insurance covers a very substantial portion of the health care bill, institutions such as hospitals have less incentive to control costs. It is not clear from this theory that the advent of Medicare and Medicaid, for example, would cause the level of inefficiency in hospitals to increase over time, but such a pattern is at least consistent with the theory.

THE EVIDENCE

What do we know of the patterns of inflation subsequent to the adoption of Medicare and Medicaid, and what do we know about the sources of this inflation? One approach is to partition the observed rise in expenditures into its logical components. As noted in the 1985 *Economic Report of the President,*

> The factors responsible for rising medical care expenditures can be attributed either to changes in price or in quantity. Price changes can be subdivided further into general inflation and increases unique to the medical sector. Quantity changes can be partitioned into three elements: *changes in population,* in *quantity per capita,* and in the *nature of services provided* per visit or per admission [emphasis added] (p. 134).

The report asserts that general inflation was responsible for slightly over half of the inflation in hospital spending between 1971 and 1981, but hospital input prices increased an additional 11.7 percent more than general inflation. Population growth was a lesser factor, contributing 7.2 percent during that period, whereas growth in admissions per capita contributed 8.6 percent and, importantly, real expenses per admission, 20.8 percent. The growth in real expenses per admission is especially noteworthy because it tends to reflect technological changes, or more generally, all changes in the nature of hospital care.

Similar figures are available for physicians' services. Here the *Economic Report* says that 58 percent of the inflation in this category is due to general inflation between 1971 and 1981. In addition, the physicians' price index increased faster than general inflation by about 10 percent. Other factors included an increase in the quantity of visits, 5 percent, and a substantial increase in the real expenses per visit, 27 percent.

These data are consistent with the Newhouse theories, but they do not address the theories directly.[9] It seems likely that technological change has played a substantial role. However, the evidence is not precise, and we must conclude that while we have a fairly clear understanding of how social insurance programs like these could affect prices and use rates, we are not equally certain about the magnitudes of the effects.

Access to Health Care

Irrespective of the considerable costs, the predominant evidence seems to suggest that both Medicare and Medicaid have succeeded in addressing the problems of access to which they have been directed. That there was a change in health care use rates among the lower-income groups in the years directly following the beginning of Medicare and Medicaid is evident from the data.

---

[9]See Newhouse's own (1978b, 1988) econometric studies for further detail.

Table 21.2 suggests how Medicare and Medicaid have affected the use of physicians' services among the population since their inception. Most relevantly, these data show that the gap in the use rates between the low-income and the high-income groups was narrowed, though the effect is most noticeable in the "All Ages" category.

We can also learn something about the effects of the two programs by examining data on the out-of-pocket expenditures of eligible recipients. Table 21.3 reports these figures, comparing 1964 (pre-Medicare and Medicaid) and 1984. As shown in Subtable A, out-of-pocket expenditures were reduced sharply after the programs as a percentage of total expenditure. However, expenditures out-of-pocket by persons age 65 or over as a percentage of income, and beneficiary liabilities as a share of total health expenditures have been held fairly constant since the beginning of the programs (Subtables B and C).

These data on use rates and financial access to care, however, leave at least one question unanswered. Would we find that these social insurance programs increased access to care in a study that controlled, among other things, for the level of health status or health care need, rather than just comparing data before and after the event?

The answer to this question appears to be yes. Davis and Reynolds (1976) examine the effect of access to these public assistance programs in a statistical context that controlled for other factors. For people with the same health status, they compare average health care use by those eligible for assistance, with those low-income people not receiving assistance. Examine Table 21.4 excerpted from their study. These data indicate a fairly strong impact of improved financial access on care.

These data, however, do not resolve a perhaps more important question: Have the inequalities in use rates between the low-income and the high-income groups been reduced? The difficulty in assessing inequalities in use rates between the low-income and high-income groups lies in the fact that lower-income groups tend to be sicker. Are use rates equal after adjusting for health status?

TABLE 21.2 Physician Visits Per Capita by Age and Family-Income Group, Fiscal Year 1964, Calendar Year 1971

Age and Income Group	1964	1971
All Ages	4.5	5.0
Low income	4.3	5.6
Middle income	4.5	4.7
High income	5.1	4.9
Ratio, High Income to Low Income	1.19	0.88
65 Years and Older		
Low income	6.3	6.7
Middle income	7.0	6.4
High income	7.3	7.5
Ratio, High Income to Low Income	1.16	1.12

Source: Davis and Reynolds (1976, p. 393).

TABLE 21.3   Three Ways to Measure the Health Care Expenditure Burden for the Elderly Under Medicare

Subtable A: Per Capita Personal Health Care Expenditures for Persons 65 Years or Over, by Source of Funds: Fiscal Year 1966 and Calendar Year 1984

	1966		1984	
Source of Funds	*Amount*	*Percent*	*Amount*	*Percent*
Per capita	$445	100.0	$4,202	100.0
Out-of-pocket	237	53.2	1,059	25.2
Private insurance	71	15.9	304	7.2
Other private	5	11.1	16	0.4
Medicare	—	—	2,051	48.8
Medicaid	—	—	536	12.8
Other government	133	29.8	236	5.6

Source: Gornick et al. (1985).

Subtable B: Mean Out-of Pocket Health Costs as a Percent of Income for Persons 65 Years of Age or Over, Selected Years, 1966–1984

Year	Mean Out-of-Pocket Expenditures	Mean Personal Income	Out-of-Pocket as a Percent of Income
1966	$300	$2,000	15
1977	690	5,592	12
1981	1,187	8,639	14
1984	1,575	10,615	15

Source: Gornick et al. (1985).

Subtable C: Estimated Beneficiary Liabilities 1985–1994

Year	Beneficiary Liability ($ billion)	Program Payments ($ billion)	Beneficiary Share of Total Payments
1985	$13.5	$70.3	16.2%
1986	15.4	75.7	16.9
1987	16.8	80.5	17.2
1988	18.0	88.5	16.9
1989	17.4	99.8	14.8
1990	21.4	109.0	16.4
1991	22.7	121.2	15.8
1992	23.4	134.2	14.8
1993	30.6	149.1	17.0
1994	31.4	166.1	15.9

Source: Medicare and Medicaid Guide, No. 858, June 15, 1995, Table 3-4, p. 67.

TABLE 21.4 Annual Predicted Utilization for Low-Income Persons by Health Status and Welfare Eligibility, Adjusted for Other Characteristics, 1969

| | Health Status | | | | | |
| | Public Assistance Recipients | | | Other Low-Income Persons | | |
	Good	Average	Poor	Good	Average	Poor
Physician visits	4.09	4.95	7.10	2.29	3.36	5.12
Hospital admissions	0.14	0.16	0.21	0.09	0.11	0.15
Hospital days	2.40	2.72	3.47	1.18	1.42	2.04

Source: Davis and Reynolds (1976).

This issue is disputed in the literature, but the relevant evidence has been reviewed by Starr (1986).[10] He concludes as follows:

> The poor show significantly lower levels of physician use at comparable levels of health and disability, and the age-adjusted number of physician visits per hundred bed-disability days proved to be 80 percent higher among higher income whites than among whites below the poverty level (pp. 117–118).

Before concluding this discussion of access to health care, we should identify a characteristic of access specific to the Medicaid program. Because Medicaid is state operated, as we have noted, characteristics vary somewhat across the nation. In addition, the coverage of the population of poverty families has varied over time. Oberg and Polich (1988) note these salient features:

> In 1972, Medicaid included 32 percent of those at or below the poverty level. The program reached its peak in 1975, when 63 percent of low-income individuals were eligible for Medicaid. As the government began efforts to contain the program's budget, the percentage started to fall. In 1980, 50 percent of the poor and near-poor were eligible for Medicaid. In 1985, it was estimated that the program served only 46 percent (p. 90).

We can conclude from these data that a substantial portion of the poor or near-poor are not covered by Medicaid and that the coverage of the poor and near-poor did not keep pace with the rise in the numbers of people in these income groups during the 1980s.

Health Status

The ultimate question regarding Medicare and Medicaid is whether or not these programs improve the health status of the eligible populations. This question is a specific application of an earlier question we addressed, regarding the production function of

---

[10]See also Davis and Reynolds (1976), Aday, Anderson, and Fleming (1980), and Kleinman, Gold, and Makue (1981).

health. Early econometric studies of the effects of health care on mortality rates suggested a small and insignificant effect. Studies of health care effects on morbidity rates tend to come up with similar results. Most striking, the Rand Health Insurance Experiments investigated the issue with the use of a randomized controlled experiment and found little or no effect on health status in most cases for the increased health care consumed by people with better insurance coverage.[11] At least up until the mid-1980s, the evidence seemed to weigh against the belief that health care made a significant difference in the health status of populations generally, and the insured populations in particular.

However, studies that began to appear in the mid-1980s have found important counterevidence. Hadley's studies (1982, 1988) focus on the role of Medicare expenditures. He finds a significant effect of Medicare on mortality rates, and this health care is sufficiently effective to be cost-beneficial. Hadley also finds a stronger effect of Medicare expenditures for population subgroups including blacks, whose lower than average health status has been of public concern.

NATIONAL HEALTH INSURANCE

Return now to the question of broader social insurance for health care. We have noted that the United States is one of two industrialized nations without a comprehensive social insurance program for health care. Should the United States adopt national health insurance? It would seem that this issue is dead with the demise of the Clinton plan. Steps toward universal coverage might be taken with limited goals in mind. Steps toward cost containment may be more palatable in the current climate. Nevertheless, health system reform is still on the agenda in the United States and many other countries. It is wise to be acquainted with the possible features of such plans.

Different Kinds of Possible National Health Insurance (NHI) Plans

It should be clear from the discussion that there are several desirable aspects of a national health insurance scheme:

- It should provide a health "safety net" for all residents, irrespective of age or employment status.
- It should provide choice for providers and patients.
- It should provide market incentives for cost containment.
- It should be relatively easy to administer.

Unfortunately, even within the list of presumable noncontroversial goals noted previously, there is considerable room for controversy. To illustrate, the *Journal of the American Medical Association* (May 1991) asked health care experts to formulate plans for health insurance reform. Over 80 proposals were submitted, and after rigorous review, the journal published 13 of them. During the 1993–1994 national debate on

---

[11]See, for example, Brook et al. (1983), and Valdez et al. (1985).

health reform, counting plans and versions of plans, there were at least as many plans before Congress.

Particular bills at particular times will vary considerably, especially when one considers the options across countries. Several features of the bills considered by Congress in 1993–1994 address questions posed by most reform efforts. Table 21.5 lists several features that appeared in the various bills including the Clinton plan. A quandary among the plans was whether to fund national health insurance coverage by individual mandate, employer/employee mandate, or general revenues. An individual mandate is a law that requires individuals to buy health insurance for themselves, with subsidies for those who can't afford it. The subsidies would usually be funded out of general revenues. The employer/employee mandates require a tax on wages for the employee's share. The employer's share may actually fall on the employee in the form of lower wages. Subsidies out of general revenues would provide for the unemployed.

People advocating a Canadian system seek a single-payer system with government revenues providing all of the national health insurance. A final alternative is the medical savings accounts method of payment that would allow people to set up a tax-free savings account out of which they can pay the out-of-pocket costs of their health care. Usually these systems entail health insurance with high deductibles and coinsurance.

Some plans would define a minimum acceptable level of insurance, with people allowed to purchase more extensive coverage if desired and if they can afford it. Others would define one plan to fit all. At the beginning of the debates many plans featured

TABLE 21.5	Alternative Features of a National Health Insurance Reform
Financing:	employer/employee mandate
	individual mandate
	general tax revenues
	medical savings accounts
Coverage of Services:	a minimum plan defined
	a standard plan for all
Coverage of People:	universal
	limited
Insurer:	private insurance companies retained
	government insurance
Managed Care:	encouraged or mandated
	not encouraged or mandated
Purchasing Cooperative:	alliances mandated
	no alliances mandated

universal coverage. As support for this waned in Congress, more plans offered lesser goals for reaching the population.

Single-payer systems tend to eliminate the private insurance function and feature government as the single payer. Managed care, which we have discussed at length in Chapter 12, was a central feature of the health debate since the Clinton plan featured it. Managed care is promoted under health insurance reform as a cost-saving mechanism. Finally, Congress debates whether to feature purchasing cooperatives for health insurance, compulsory or voluntary. These cooperatives are viewed as a way to provide people with a choice of health plan, whether or not their employer offers it, and whether or not the person is employed.

The Costs of NHI

National health insurance programs certainly cost a great deal of money, but it is important to distinguish which costs are actually incremental. In other words, what are the additional costs to society from the imposition of NHI?

From society's point of view, the incremental cost of NHI in the United States is the extra total expenditure on health care that would be incurred if we switched to national health insurance. Inasmuch as most people are already insured for almost all hospital care and most physician care, the extra cost of NHI would be much smaller than many people expect.

The truly incremental costs stem from several sources. First, the major reason for switching to a national health insurance plan is to extend coverage to the uninsured, perhaps some 40 million people. Pauly and colleagues (1991) estimate the incremental costs of this newly covered population at roughly $17 billion, about $459 per person, or about 3 percent of health care spending. If this amount seems low, it should be understood that the uninsured already consume over half as much care as the insured population on average; that is, uninsured does *not* necessarily mean zero care.

Second, there will be some incremental cost for the insured population to the extent that the national health insurance proposal chosen provides greater typical coverage than people already choose to buy or have provided to them by other sources. Third, any tax-supported system of financing care necessarily entails a deadweight loss to society, as noted in Chapter 11. This is true even if the program is of the employer-mandated type because a law forcing employers to incur expense is really a tax. The deadweight loss of a tax means that there is some efficiency loss caused by the disincentives to work and invest.[12]

These sources of incremental costs to society are probably the most significant. In one sense, the incremental costs are the real costs to society, whereas differences in financing methods are not as economically meaningful. It may be politically more palatable to choose a plan that does not greatly expand the government budget; employment-mandated plans may be attractive politically for this reason. It should be made clear, however, that society incurs the cost irrespective of whether it is financed through the government or mandated to employers by law.

---

[12]See Browning and Johnson (1980) for a more complete discussion.

CONCLUSIONS

In this chapter, we have presented a general discussion of social insurance, and its application to the health care sector. We noted that almost all modern industrialized countries provide fairly comprehensive health care social insurance, and we have reviewed the history of these developments and the pattern in the United States.

Today, the major health care social insurance programs in the United States are Medicare and Medicaid. These programs increase costs in theory and have been increasingly costly in practice. It is clear that they have had a beneficial effect on access to care among the elderly and low-income groups, and recent studies suggest that they have a beneficial effect on health status. They leave, however, a fairly large number of the poor or uninsured without health care coverage.

Finally, whether the United States should move to a national health insurance must reflect the values of the public. This is true both of efficiency and equity rationales. The efficiency rationales depend on individual values expressed in willingness to pay. The equity rationales, in contrast, are directly an expression of values. Comprehensive social insurance for health care in the United States would directly address and presumably solve the widely perceived problem of providing for the uninsured, who often include people in the poverty, near-poverty, and other lower-income groups.

There are many ways to address these problems. We have noted the salient policy features or decision issues in the plans considered by Congress in 1993–1994. What can economics say about these features whose ultimate choice or the choice of no change depends on the values of the voting public? There are areas of theory and evidence in economics that shed light on these questions. It is also useful, however, to look at health reform beyond the borders of the United States. We learn from each other's experience and research. We begin such an effort by first comparing the features of health systems across countries in the next chapter.

Summary

1. There are different types of social insurance policies and social programs. These include poverty programs, old age assistance, disability, health, and unemployment programs.

2. Program features variously include contributions, benefits, length of coverage, means of reimbursement to providers, and methods of determining payment levels to providers.

3. Social insurance originated in nineteenth-century Europe. Groups in the United States have supported health care social insurance programs throughout the twentieth century. This history culminated in the adoption of Medicare and Medicaid in 1965. Since then, however, the United States remains one of the few developed countries that has not adopted a comprehensive health care social insurance program.

4. Medicare is a national program that provides hospital insurance to the elderly, along with optional supplemental physician care insurance. Medicaid programs are state run and provide health care to certain categories of the needy.

5. Medicare and Medicaid expenditures have increased rapidly since the programs began, due to increases in medical care prices, in the population covered, in the quantity of care per capita consumed by the population, and due to changes in the nature of the services provided.

6. Medicare and Medicaid preceded a clear improvement in access to care by the lower-income population, as evidenced by increased use rates by lower-income groups both absolutely and relative to the higher-income groups.

7. National health insurance proposals include compulsory private insurance programs through employers and tax credits for the purchase of private insurance, as well as proposals for an all-government system.

8. From society's viewpoint, the cost of NHI is the incremental cost of additional health care purchased by people due to improved insurance coverage. These costs may be offset by savings from successful cost controls.

Discussion Questions

1. How does social insurance differ from private insurance? Of the five types of social insurance programs described, Medicare and Medicaid form combinations of types. Which types describe Medicare? Which types describe Medicaid? What are the similarities between Medicare and Medicaid? What are the differences?

2. What factors contributed to the growth in Medicare spending historically?

3. Describe how Medicare has affected access to care for the elderly.

4. Is health status affected by the access to health care provided through social insurance programs? Discuss the evidence.

5. What are some possible reasons that other industrially advanced countries have far more comprehensive social insurance programs for health care than the United States?

Exercises

1. Historically in the United States, what groups have supported social insurance for health care, and what groups have opposed it?

2. Suppose that an analyst considers the data in Table 21.2 regarding the number of patient visits before and after the inception of Medicare and Medicaid. The analyst wishes to see whether the programs improve poor people's access to health care.
   a. Is it likely that the poor's health has been improved?
   b. How else might access be improved other than by paying for office visits?

3. Do public assistance programs result in better access for low-income people when controlling for health status?

4. What proportion of the poor is covered by Medicaid? How has this proportion changed over time?

5. Describe the major types of national health insurance proposals.

CHAPTER

22

Comparative Health Care Systems

- Criticisms of the American Health Care System

- Contemporary Health Care Systems

- National Health Programs: Three Examples

- The Canadian Health Care System

- Differences in Health Care Spending Across Countries

- Conclusions

We will now consider the experiences of other countries in providing large-scale health care. We undertake this study for two reasons. First, many European countries have constructed programs that predate U.S. programs by decades. There is a rich variation in programs and experiences that in itself is worth discovering. Second, and more important, the U.S. system has some gaping holes compared with the coverage extended by many other systems. Understanding the approaches used by other countries may provide important clues to assessing our own system.

CRITICISMS OF THE AMERICAN HEALTH CARE SYSTEM

Rashi Fein is one of the major critics of the Medicare and Medicaid delivery systems. He and others have expressed concern about the sizable personal liabilities involved for individuals entering hospitals under Medicare.

Gaps in Medicare and Medicaid

Here are some examples of uncovered expenditures under Medicare and Medicaid. In 1996, the inpatient hospital deductible under Medicare was $736. Subscribers to Part B Medicare were required to pay the following:

- the monthly premium of $42.50 in 1996, plus
- a $100 annual deductible, plus
- coinsurance payments of 20 percent of the Medicare-approved charge, *and*
- the difference between the approved and actual charge, subject to limits.

Overall, beneficiaries were liable for 16 percent of Medicare expenditures in 1994 (Prospective Payment Assessment Commission 1995).[1] In addition, services such as drugs, dental care, eyeglasses, and most long-term care are not covered. Are these personal liabilities under Medicare too burdensome? Certainly some Americans like Fein think so.

Regarding Medicaid, approximately 70 percent of the individuals receiving Medicaid are poor, but most of the poor do not receive Medicaid assistance. States also have wide latitudes in setting eligibility requirements and benefit levels.[2]

The Uninsured

Many, however, would characterize the main weakness in the American system as the problem of the uninsured. By some estimates, 40 million people, at any point in time, go without health insurance. While this does not mean that they go entirely without care, the uninsured consume only half as much health care on average as the insured.

While lack of insurance is a matter of choice for some, the freedom to choose for many of the uninsured is severely constrained. Often the uninsured are the poor and the near-poor who do not receive Medicaid. Other uninsured people often work at jobs that typically do not offer health insurance fringe benefits, or are people who do not qualify for benefits on the job.

Still other Americans want to control health care cost inflation. There is considerable political pressure to contain costs for public programs. In Chapter 19 we have discussed specific strategies, such as the Medicare Prospective Payment System under DRGs.

If the United States is to move to a national health care program, what sort of system should it be? We provide both an introduction to cross-national data on health care spending and a typology of the various systems that have been put into place.

We then examine the United Kingdom, Germany, and South Korea in more detail because their health care systems are perceived to be successful. Because of the similarities between the United States and Canada, we devote an entire section to Canada's national health program, and compare its performance with that of the United States. We then present a framework for comparing different spending rates across countries.

---

[1]However, about 77 percent of beneficiaries purchase private supplemental insurance or Medigap coverage. Another 13 percent receive various forms of public assistance.

[2]Fein (1986, p. 77 and p. 110). Although this volume takes a rather liberal political slant, it describes well the evolution, economics, and politics of national health care policy development in the United States.

CONTEMPORARY HEALTH CARE SYSTEMS

Many industrialized countries either provide health care directly through the government or provide publicly funded health insurance with comprehensive coverage. The origins of government programs for health care, particularly for social insurance programs, were explored in Chapter 21. Rather than describe details about the health care programs of dozens of countries, we prefer to characterize the basic types of systems employed, and to develop a few examples in greater detail.

A Typology of Contemporary Health Care Systems

Consider a broad framework for describing different approaches. For this purpose, Gordon (1988) develops a useful typology of four health benefit systems. Table 22.1 lists countries representative of each category:

1. *Traditional Sickness Insurance.* This is fundamentally the private insurance market approach, with state subsidy. Coverage is basically employment related. This type of system originated in Germany and other countries that pioneered health care insurance.

2. *National Health Insurance.* The state establishes a national-level health insurance system. Canada has the most immediate experience with this organization.

3. *National Health Service.* The state provides the health care. The United Kingdom is a prime example of this approach.

4. *Mixed System.* The country exhibits mixed elements of the above programs. Several countries, including the United States, fall into this group.

Comparing Expenditures Across Countries and Systems

In comparing economic data across countries and systems, Table 22.2 shows per capita health expenditures expressed in U.S. dollars in many Western countries for 1993. These

TABLE 22.1	Basic Structure of Health Benefit Systems, 1985, Selected Industrial Countries		
Traditional Sickness Insurance	*National Health Insurance*	*National Health Service*	*Mixed System*
Austria	Canada	Czechoslovakia	Australia
Belgium	East Germany	Denmark	Ireland
France	Finland	Greece	Japan
Netherlands	Norway	Hungary	South Korea
West Germany	Spain	Italy	Switzerland
Yugoslavia	Sweden	New Zealand	United States
		Poland	
		Romania	
		United Kingdom	
		USSR	

Source: Gordon (1988, p. 204). South Korea has been added.

TABLE 22.2	1993 Per Capita Health Expenditures in OECD Countries in U.S. Dollars—Adjusted for Purchasing Power Parity		
Country	*Amount*	*GDP*	*Ratio*
Australia	$1,493	$17,555	8.5%
Austria	1,777	19,126	9.3
Belgium	1,601	19,373	8.3
Canada	1,971	19,271	10.2
Denmark	1,296	19,340	6.7
Finland	1,363	15,530	8.8
France	1,835	18,764	9.8
Germany	1,815	21,163	8.6
Greece	500	8,782	5.7
Iceland	1,564	18,931	8.3
Ireland	922	13,847	6.7
Italy	1,523	17,865	8.5
Japan	1,495	20,550	7.3
Luxembourg	1,993	28,741	6.9
Netherlands	1,531	17,602	8.7
New Zealand	1,179	15,409	7.7
Norway	1,592	19,467	8.2
Portugal	866	11,800	7.3
Spain	972	13,330	7.3
Sweden	1,266	16,828	7.5
Switzerland	2,283	23,033	9.9
Turkey	146	5,376	2.7
United Kingdom	1,213	17,152	7.1
United States	3,299	23,358	14.1

Source: Organization for Economic Cooperation and Development Health Data, 1995.

figures have been adjusted for the purchasing powers of the local currencies (known as purchasing power parity). The second column shows each country's gross domestic product. The final column shows health care spending as a percent of GDP.[3]

The United States is by far the biggest spender in absolute per capita terms ($3,299). It is also the biggest spender as a share of GDP (14.1 percent). These, as well as concerns about access to health care, are the sorts of indicators that have led many to question what Americans are getting for their spending. However, high expenditures may have three meanings:

---

[3]We show 1993 data because the GDPs and spending levels have been adjusted for purchasing power parity.

- High average level of services.
- High resource costs of services.
- Inefficient provision of services.

In looking at cross-country differences, we keep these points in mind. A high level of services reflects at least the possibility that the populations have chosen to spend their incomes in this fashion. We have noted previously that higher income levels are reflected in higher consumption levels of all normal goods, including health care. Cross-national studies indicate a fairly substantial income elasticity for health care. U.S. expenditure levels thus reflect in part the high per capita income level in the United States.

NATIONAL HEALTH PROGRAMS: THREE EXAMPLES

In this section, we examine the national health systems of three countries: the United Kingdom, Germany, and South Korea. In the next section, we will contrast Canada's plan, an example of a national health insurance system, with that of the United States, an example of a mixed system.

The United Kingdom is featured as an example of a national health service. Germany is important as the birthplace of compulsory insurance schemes, and it represents an example of the traditional sickness insurance. South Korea is a newcomer to the community of nations that have universal health insurance. Though that country's program has received little publicity, its mandated approach offers important insights to other countries, including the United States, that have considered or are considering a plan based on mandatory employer coverage.

The United Kingdom — The National Health Service

Great Britain's National Health Service (NHS) was established in 1946 and provides health care to all British residents.[4] It is financed largely (about 85 percent) through general revenues, with capital and current budget filtering from the national level down to the regional, and then to the district level. The plan pays general practitioners on a capitation basis and hospital physicians largely on a salaried basis. In addition to the NHS, there is also a private sector health system. About 10 percent of Britains purchase private health insurance.

Services are not entirely free. Patients desiring private rooms pay extra, and there is a small surcharge for drug prescriptions filled outside the hospital. Dental care and eyeglasses also require patient copayments.

The general practitioner, or GP, serves as the gatekeeper to the health care system. Contrary to U.S. perceptions, GPs are not government employees. Rather, they are self-employed and receive about half their incomes from capitation contracts with a Family

---

[4]The descriptive material here is taken largely from Gordon (1988) and Maynard (1990).

Practitioner Committee. They typically treat routine conditions and will refer patients to hospitals for more specialized care. The referral will usually be to a district hospital. Once at the hospital, the patients are under the care of physicians (consultants) who are allocated staffed beds and junior hospital staff to work under their direction.

The United States has 27 percent fewer hospital beds per capita than is provided in the United Kingdom, but it has 60 percent more physicians. The United States has also 30 percent fewer nurses. Germany by comparison has 40 percent more beds than the United Kingdom, 85 percent more physicians, but 59 percent fewer nurses. Thus, the resources used by these systems vary widely (Culyer and Meads, 1992).

Referring to Table 22.2, we can see that per capita spending ($1,213) in the United Kingdom in 1993 was less than 40 percent of the rate in the United States ($3,045) and just a little less than half when expressed as a ratio to GDP (7.1 percent as opposed to 14.1 percent). How does the United Kingdom keep its health care expenditures this much lower while providing universal access to health care? Though patients have relatively easy access to primary and emergency care, specialty care is rationed through long waiting lists and a limit on the availability of new technologies. A relatively simple model is useful to illustrate this phenomenon.

A MODEL OF RATIONED HEALTH CARE AND PRIVATE MARKETS

We can consider the practices of an NHS-type of organization diagrammatically. In panel A of Figure 22.1, we treat the supply of health services as totally price inelastic. That is, the supply curve, being a reflection of what is provided by the government, is a vertical line. This indicates that the quantity supplied is unresponsive to the price of the services.

Furthermore, the money price of the services is set by the government at P^*, which is less than the market clearing price of P_c. Predictably, there is excess demand

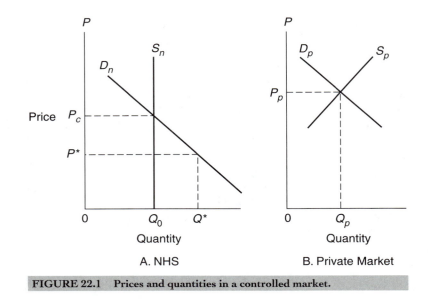

A. NHS   B. Private Market

FIGURE 22.1   Prices and quantities in a controlled market.

$(Q^* - Q_0)$ at the administered price P^*. Since most health care cannot be bought and resold, other forms of rationing, largely time related, become important. There is a legendary list of ailments for which waiting periods for treatment by the NHS are for months, or even for years.

Again, as might be predicted, a small private market for services has developed for those who choose to enter the private market without governmental aid, either due to strong preferences for private care, or to the ability to pay more than the NHS price. Since there is excess demand at P^*, that excess demand, in part, represents people who are queued and who may wish to pay in the private sector to avoid the long waits. Those who participate in the private market, shown in panel B, will pay P_p for the quantity of services Q_p.

PERFORMANCE UNDER THE NHS

On the one hand, the effect of a system such as the NHS that depends on queuing for access to care is often to postpone, or simply not provide, certain services. On the other hand, the NHS devotes considerable resources to such high-return services as prenatal and infant care. To these populations served, and to the larger public concerned with equitable provision of care to these segments of the population, the universal nature of the service is particularly beneficial.

Over the years, the United Kingdom has spent considerably less on health care than the United States and many other countries. Expenditures through the 1980s have held at about 6 percent of GDP, while U.S. expenditures have not been that low since 1965. By most measures of mortality and morbidity, the United Kingdom does about as well. Certainly, there are many nonmedical factors that are involved in determining disease and death rates in a population, and these factors will also vary across countries.

In addition, despite universal access to care in the United Kingdom, historically there have been considerable regional disparities in funding and in the use of health care. There is evidence showing that upper-class patients have received substantially more care for a given illness than have lower-class patients.[5] Thus, even where access is universal, the results are not necessarily equal.

The NHS is extremely popular with the public and is probably the most valued piece of the British welfare state. Nevertheless, in response to perceived inefficiencies (Enthoven, 1985), 1989 reforms promoted market incentives to seek the best bargains for care. Early reports are somewhat mixed—for example, the reforms have not reduced an overbedding in the London area—and the success of market incentives will depend on the responses of politicians (Culyer and Meads, 1992). However, it is significant to see that even the NHS, with its worldwide reputation, is trying to install elements of competition.

The experience of the United Kingdom's National Health Service in the area of cost containment, however, seems fairly clear. Rationed care cuts money costs! We should inquire whether their observed ability to keep costs lower holds some opportunities for the United States.

---

[5]See Maynard (1990) for further details.

Germany

The German health care system is rooted in the programs laid out by Bismarck in 1883. Legislation was introduced to require workers in various occupations to enroll in sickness insurance funds. The original legislation covered only a small fraction of the population. Nevertheless, the basic approach of mandatory enrollment in autonomous sickness funds, financed by payroll taxes, expanded and today lies at the heart of the German social insurance program.

Also at the heart of the German health system is a sense of solidarity, a sense of all citizens concerned with the provision of equal access to health care. Germans and many Europeans speak of this as the solidarity goal (v.d. Schulenburg, 1992). Despite the many Americans who support such a goal, the base of support is not similar, so that Uwe Reinhardt (1994) has spoken of Germany's health system as "not the American way" (p. 22).

STRUCTURE OF THE SYSTEM

In the German system, all working persons are required to have health insurance with costs divided equally between employer and employee.[6] The employee's share is collected as a payroll tax at a rate proportional to his or her gross wages. The average contribution rate to sickness funds in 1995 was 13.2 percent in West Germany and 13 percent in East Germany. Individuals with income beyond a given ceiling were eligible to choose the private health system, which handles about 10 percent of the population. The ceiling in 1995 was about 70,000 DM (approximately $47,000)[7] (Hinrichs, 1995). Contributions for pensioners, the unemployed, and disabled come from other social insurance funds (though, since 1987, pensioners also contribute on their own behalf).

Approximately 88 percent of Germans have social health insurance, 10 percent have private insurance, and the remaining 2 percent, for various reasons, receive free care. The social insurance component is organized around some 1,152 localized sickness funds. These funds are independent and self-regulating. They pay providers directly for services provided to their members at rates that they negotiate with individual hospitals. Regional groups of funds negotiate with regional doctors' and dentists' associations for payments for ambulatory and dental care. Payment from these funds represents about 70 percent of health care spending in West Germany.

The sickness funds are required by law to provide a comprehensive set of benefits. These include physician ambulatory care provided by physicians in private practice, hospital care, home nursing care, and a wide range of preventive services. There is minimal patient cost sharing. The funds, like disability insurance, also provide additional cash payments to those who are unemployed as a result of illness.

As for reimbursement, ambulatory providers are paid on a fee-for-service basis, hospitals on a prospective basis. There are both public and private (including for-profit) hospitals, though the public hospitals account for about half the beds. Hospitals tend to use salaried physicians, and, unlike the United States, physicians in private practice

---

[6]The following material is based largely on Henke (1990) and special reports by Hurst and by Schneider in the Spring 1991 issue of *Health Care Financing Review*.

[7]The conversion to dollars was done at the February 1996 exchange rate of 1.48 DM per dollar.

generally do not have admitting privileges. Thus, many doctors have invested in elaborately equipped clinics to compete with hospitals by being able to provide a wide range of procedures.

The German experience is especially relevant to the United States. Coverage is provided through a large number of relatively small and independent plans. In this sense, the delivery of health care is similar to that found in the United States where, for the most part, large numbers of employee groups, independent insurers, and providers reach agreements without direct government intervention. Many Americans propose mandated coverage for the working uninsured. Germany relies on a mandated approach, where coverage for certain conditions is required by law. Germany also introduced cost controls similar in principle to prospective payment under the U.S. DRG mechanism.

THE ROLE OF GOVERNMENT

Each level of government has specific responsibilities in the German system.

- The central government passes legislation on policy and jurisdiction.
- State governments are responsible for hospital planning, managing state hospitals, and supervising the sickness funds and physician associations.
- Local governments manage local hospitals and public health programs.

Within this framework, there is considerable decentralization. As we have noted, the sickness funds and physician associations have considerable administrative autonomy.

Despite this autonomy, it is apparent that government intervention is extensive and that is has been steadily increasing. Expenditures of the sickness funds grew rapidly in the 1960s and early 1970s. As a result, the Cost Containment Act of 1977 introduced a fixed budget for payments by the sickness funds to the physician associations. In essence, this program is similar to prospective payment schemes developed in the United States. However, because hospitals were excluded from this act, a series of additional acts was introduced between 1981 and 1986. Here, too, prospective budgets were required to be negotiated between the sickness funds and hospitals.

The Health Care Reform Act of 1989 introduced more major changes. These were directed at attempts to further reduce the growth of health expenditures through means familiar to those in the United States. These include increased cost sharing and attempts to control hospital costs through reductions in hospital capacity, hospital inpatient admissions, and hospital expenditures on capital equipment.

As costs continued to rise for the sickness funds at a rate faster than the rise in incomes, there was continued call for reform. Figure 22.2 shows this pattern of increased expenditures. This concern led to the 1993 Health Care Reform Act. These reforms capped physician expenditures at the growth rate of incomes of members of the sickness funds. They gave members the freedom to choose among the sickness funds and changed the hospital payment system from a per diem payment to a prospective payment basis (Henke, Murray, and Ade, 1994).

PERFORMANCE

Despite the frequent calls for reform in Germany, as well as the recurrent complaints that the system is in crisis, the German health system has been relatively successful at controlling costs. Preceding the period of reforms, 1970–1977, spending increased

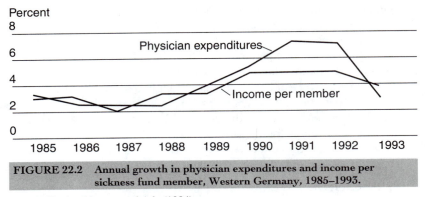

FIGURE 22.2   Annual growth in physician expenditures and income per sickness fund member, Western Germany, 1985–1993.

Source: Henke, Murray, and Ade (1994).

at a 14.4 percent annual rate, but this dropped to 6.5 percent from 1977–1983 and to 5.1 percent between 1983–1989. The contribution rate of payment to the sickness funds was 13.2 percent in 1995 compared to 10.5 percent in 1975. The public health expenditure as a percent of GDP has hovered around 6 percent (6.1 in 1992) since 1975 (Hinrichs, 1995).

For a better perspective of the relative success of the German, British, Canadian, and U.S. systems in controlling inflation, examine Figure 22.3. Again, the data describe only country average trends in share of GDP spent on health care and do not identify causes. However, the data are suggestive. One notices that the upward trends in expenditures continued throughout the period for the United States, but the rate of increase was noticeably moderated in the other three systems.

Germany has achieved a favorable record along other criteria as well. It has a publicly funded system with virtually universal coverage but has avoided queues and extensive government intrusion. Both patient and provider have considerable autonomy.

After examining the performance of the German system, we may question whether it is the United States or Germany that has the better system. A recent survey of public opinion in these two countries (Table 22.3) plus Canada helps to answer the subjective side of this question. While Canadians and Germans are still more satisfied with their systems, public opinion has been changing, so that more Canadians and Germans are finding fault with their systems, whereas Americans have become somewhat more favorable.

The German health system faces many challenges. The German population is aging rapidly, causing a demographic change that will place severe pressure on its social security and health care programs. Hurst (1991) claims that there is an overemphasis on "high-tech" medicine at the expense of preventive and long-term care. Those who have private insurance have more choice than those in the statutory programs, and similarly situated individuals may contribute different amounts to their sickness funds because the membership profiles of their respective funds are different. Hurst is also concerned about excessive regulation of the funds and lack of incentive for the funds to become efficient buyers of services.

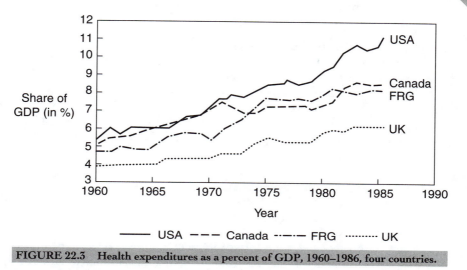

FIGURE 22.3 Health expenditures as a percent of GDP, 1960–1986, four countries.

Source: Pfaff (1991, Figure 1).

Reunified Germany also has the problem of integrating the former East Germany into the system. The current plan has sought to apply the West German model of sickness funds. However, Hurst speculates that the East's traditional reliance on salaried providers practicing in polyclinics may result in a more pluralistic system of health care than that which prevailed in West Germany.

TABLE 22.3 Ratings of Health Care Systems in the United States, Canada, and Western Germany, 1988, 1990, 1994

	United States		Canada		Western Germany	
	1988	*1994*	*1988*	*1994*	*1990*	*1994*
On the whole, the health care system works pretty well, and only minor changes are necessary to make it work better	10%	18%	56%	29%	41%	30%
There are some good things in our health care system, but fundamental changes are needed to make it work better	60	53	38	59	35	55
Our health care system has so much wrong with it that we need to completely rebuild it	29	28	5	12	13	11
Not sure	1	2	1	—[a]	11	4

[a]Less than 0.5 percent.

Sources: Blendon et al. (1995).

South Korea

Unlike the two other examples we have examined, South Korea has received little attention either in the scholarly literature or by policymakers.[8] However, the South Korean experience may provide an important example to other countries without universal health care coverage, including the United States. As recently as 1977, less than 10 percent of the South Korean population had insurance. By July 1989, however, South Korea completed the final phase of a program that introduced universal coverage to a system that maintained private provision of health care with fee-for-service reimbursement.

STRUCTURE OF THE SYSTEM

In 1977, South Korea required all firms with more than 500 employees to establish insurance societies to provide specific health care benefits. The employee threshold was reduced in stages so that by January 1988, it included firms with less than five employees.

A second scheme for government employees, teachers, dependents of soldiers, and pensioners was phased in under another law. Similarly, the self-employed, farmers, fishermen, and other occupational groups were phased in under a third program. Finally, low-income individuals were covered by public insurance similar to Medicaid.

The insurance is provided by insurance societies and is financed by employer contributions and payroll deductions. For example, for the employee program (class I), deductions are taken as percentages of wages or salaries. These are shared equally between employers and employees at rates ranging from 3 percent to 8 percent. The insurance societies also determine the benefits and cover a broad range of inpatient and outpatient services. The system is characterized by a relatively high coinsurance rate of 20 percent for hospital inpatient care and 30 percent to 55 percent for outpatient care.

Commensurate with the expansion of insurance and the rapid growth of South Korea's economy has been a rapid increase in utilization and costs. For example, annual outpatient visits per person for class I beneficiaries increased from 1.3 in 1977 to 6.2 in 1987; hospital inpatient cases increased from 3.0 to 6.2 per 100 persons. Spending as a share of GDP rose from 2.8 percent of GDP in 1978 to nearly 7.1 percent in 1991 despite some of the highest coinsurance rates in the industrialized world.

PERFORMANCE

South Korea's cost-containment strategies rest mainly with high coinsurance rates and fee controls. Because of rapidly increasing standards of living, spending continues to increase rapidly, and it is difficult to isolate the effects of the cost-containment measures.

There are also inequities resulting from a concentration of health resources around major urban areas. Nevertheless, the South Korean experience demonstrates to the United States, and especially to other emerging industrial countries, that it may be possible to phase in a mandated employment-based insurance without serious adverse effects to a nation's economy.

---

[8]For more detail, see Moon (1989), G. F. Anderson (1989), Flynn and Chung (1990), and Peabody, Lee, and Bickel (1995).

THE CANADIAN HEALTH CARE SYSTEM

As a result of the rapid increases in U.S. health care costs, and growing concern over the large number of uninsured, many in the United States look at Canada's health system as a possible model for reform in this country. There is a widespread perception in the United States that Canada has successfully developed a comprehensive and universal national health insurance program that is both cost-effective and highly popular.

Background

The Canadian system of financing and delivering health care is known as Medicare, although it should not be confused with the U.S. Medicare program that has been developed for the elderly. In Canada, each of the ten provinces and two territories administers a comprehensive and universal program that is partially supported by grants from the federal government.[9] Various criteria established by the federal government with respect to coverage must be met. Coverage must be universal, comprehensive, and portable, meaning that individuals can transfer their coverage to other provinces as they migrate across the country. There are no financial barriers to access, and patients have free choice in the selection of providers.

Canada's Medicare should also be distinguished from Britain's National Health Service. Most Canadian physicians are in private practice and have hospital admitting privileges. They are reimbursed by the provinces on a fee-for-service basis under fee schedules negotiated by the provinces and physician organizations. Hospitals are also private institutions, although their budgets are approved and largely funded by the provinces.

The Canadian system originated in the 1930s when compulsory health insurance programs were introduced by some provinces.[10] The main impetus, however, came from two sources: the federal legislation adopted in 1957 that provided cost sharing for inpatient hospital services, and the Medical Care Act of 1966 that provided cost sharing for physician care. Since 1971, every province and territory have provided universal coverage for both hospital and physician care.

The extraordinary U.S. interest in Canada's approach is attributable to the fact that Canada and the United States share a long border and similar heritage in terms of language and culture, and have similar economic institutions. The health care systems also evolved similarly until the 1960s. Even as recently as 1971, both countries spent approximately 7.5 percent of their GNPs on health care.

---

[9]Good overviews are found in Coyte (1990) and Rakich (1991).

[10]There was considerable support for national health insurance in both the U.S. and Canada up to the late 1940s, with much of it coming from organized labor. President Truman even proposed compulsory prepaid insurance among other health reforms but he could never put together a successful political coalition. Organized medicine in both countries was strongly opposed to the proposal and, with the start of the Cold War, the AMA was more successful than its Canadian counterpart in linking national health insurance to "socialized medicine" and the communist threat, and hence preventing its adoption. Maioni (1995) provides further discussion of this fascinating history.

Since 1971, however, the health care systems have moved in very different directions. While Canada has had publicly funded national health insurance, the United States has relied largely on private financing and delivery (although governments have been heavily involved through Medicare, Medicaid, and numerous regulatory programs). During this period, spending in the United States has grown much more rapidly despite large groups that are either uninsured or minimally insured.

Table 22.4 provides comparative data on the two countries for 1988. The data indicate a substantially lower per capita spending and share of GNP for Canada, despite physician and bed-population ratios that are greater than those found in the United States. After adjusting for exchange rate differences, the table indicates that Americans spent about 27 percent more per capita than Canadians even while 13 percent of the U.S. population had no insurance. Despite lower spending, common health status indicators—such as life expectancy and infant mortality—are more favorable in Canada than in the United States. Finally, public opinion polls indicate that Canadians support their

TABLE 22.4 Comparative Data: Canada and the United States

Selected Data	Canada ($CN)	United States ($US)
GNP (billion)		
CN 1986/87; US 1986/87	$493.0	$4,526.7
Federal budget (billion)		
CN 1986/87; US 1986/87	$116.4	$1,004.6
Population 1986 (million)	25.3	241.6
Percent 65 and older	10.6	12.1
Population with no insurance 1985		
Number (million) (%)	0.0 (0.0)	31.3 (13.3)
Number physicians 1985	52,000	577,000
Population/physician	486	418
Beds/1,000 population	7.1	5.4
Occupancy rate	83.8%	68.4%
Total health care expenditures		
(billions) CN 1987/88; US 1987	$50.4 [$40.3]	$496.6
Percent of GNP	8.7	11.2
Per capita	$1,945 [$1,556]	$1,973
Publicly funded (1985)	75.9%	41.1%
Physician sector (1985)	15.7%	19.6%
Hospital sector (1985)	40.4%	39.6%
Hospitals CN 1986/87; US 1986		
Occupancy rate	73.9%	64.3%
Length-of-stay (days)	8.1	7.1
Expense/sep.-stay	$2,797 [$2,014]	$3,532
Expense/day	$337 [$243]	$500

Source: Rakich (1991, Table 1). Conversions at $1 Canadian/$0.72 U.S. shown in brackets.

system much more than Americans support theirs, and are very concerned about any threats to it.

Given the Canadian record, health care scholars, policymakers, and politicians have shown great interest in determining the sources for its apparent success. In particular, health researchers have focused on the sources of the "savings" under the Canadian plan. One study of expenditures for physician care is especially revealing.

Physician Fees and Quantity

Table 22.5A provides further data on spending per capita in the United States and Canada in U.S. dollars. The data are from an interesting study by Fuchs and Hahn (1990). Total figures are provided for both countries. In addition, the U.S. state of Iowa is compared with the Canadian province of Manitoba. Both have largely rural areas, with relatively homogeneous populations. The data have again been adjusted to reflect purchasing power parity. Fuchs and Hahn estimated that per capita spending was 38 percent higher in the United States in 1985. More striking was the disparity in spending on physician services; it was 72 percent higher in the United States, and 178 percent higher for the procedures component.

Since spending is the product of prices and quantities, it seems logical to pursue differences in fees (prices) and utilization per capita (quantities). Comparative fee data for various services are shown in Table 22.5B. Overall, fees were 239 percent higher in the United States for 1985. Though there are variations in the ratios, U.S. fees were considerably higher in each category. The net incomes of U.S. doctors were also substantially higher than were their Canadian counterparts.

Perhaps more surprising than the fee differentials are estimates of the service volume, shown in Table 22.5C. Despite the much higher spending per capita for physician care, the quantity of care per capita is actually considerably lower in the United States. Thus, the savings in Canada, at least for physician care, do not come from reduced volume of care.

Why Are Fees and Hospital Costs Lower in Canada?

This section discusses the reasons for lower fees and hospital costs in Canada. Tables 22.4 and 22.5 provide evidence on the lower costs of Canadian hospital care. Patients in Canada have longer lengths of stay, in part because of the greater use of Canadian hospitals for chronic long-term care. Nonetheless, after adjusting for differences in case mix between the two countries, researchers found that the cost per case-mix adjusted unit was roughly 50 percent higher in the United States.[11] Several reasons can be proposed for this phenomenon.

In Canada, unlike the United States, physician fees result from negotiation between physicians' organizations and the provincial governments, as well as from other limits on total spending. Physicians cannot evade the fee controls by charging extra (sometimes called *balance billing*) to patients who can afford it.

---

[11]See Newhouse, Anderson, and Roos (1988).

TABLE 22.5   Health Care Indicators per Capita: Canada and the United States

Subtable A.   Health Expenditures per Capita, According to Type of Expenditure, 1985

Expenditures	United States	Canada	Ratio of United States to Canada	Iowa	Manitoba	Ratio of Iowa to Manitoba
	U.S. dollars			U.S. dollars		
Total	1,780	1,286	1.38	1,432	1,326	1.08
Physicians	347	202	1.72	240	159	1.51
Procedures	193	69	2.78	130	51	2.54
Evaluation and						
management	154	133	1.16	110	107	1.02
Hospitals	698	520	1.34	541	519	1.04
All other	735	564	1.30	651	648	1.01

Subtable B.   Physicians' Fees, 1985

Service	Ratio of United States to Canada	Ratio of Iowa to Manitoba
Surgery	3.21	2.76
Anesthesiology	3.73	2.86
Radiology	3.59	4.19
Procedures (weighted average)	3.34	2.99
Moderate office visit	1.56	1.44
Extensive office visit	1.55	1.50
Moderate hospital visit	4.77	3.56
Extensive hospital visit	2.57	2.70
Consultation	1.60	1.64
Evaluation and management (weighted average)	1.82	1.72
All services	2.39	2.18

Subtable C.   Estimation of the Ratios of Quantity of Physicians' Services per Capita, 1985

Service	Ratio of United States to Canada	Ratio of Iowa to Manitoba
Procedures		
Expenditures per capita	2.78	2.54
Fees	3.34	2.99
Quantity of services per capita	0.83	0.85
Evaluation and management		
Expenditures per capita	1.16	1.02
Fees	1.82	1.72
Quantity of services per capita	0.64	0.60
All services		
Expenditures per capita	1.72	1.51
Fees	2.39	2.18
Quantity of services per capita	0.72	0.69

Source: Fuchs and Hahn (1990, Tables 2–4).

TABLE 22.6   Availability of Selected Technologies: Canada, West Germany, and the United States

	Comparative Availability of Selected Medical Technologies					
	Canada (1993)		*Germany (1993)*		*United States (1992)*	
	Number of Units	*Units per Million Persons*	*Number of Units*	*Units per Million Persons*	*Number of Units*	*Units per Million Persons*
Open heart surgery	36	1.3	61	0.8	945	3.7
Cardiac catheterization	78	2.8	277	3.4	1,631	6.4
Organ transplantation	34	1.2	39	0.5	612	2.4
Radiation therapy	132	4.8	373	4.6	2,637	10.3
Extracorporeal shock wave lithotripsy	13	0.5	117	1.4	480	1.9
Magnetic resonance imaging	30	1.1	296	3.7	2,900	11.2

Source: Rublee (1994).

Hospital costs are similarly regulated by the provinces through approval of hospital budgets. Hospitals and provinces negotiate operating budgets financed by the provincial governments. The capital budget may include other sources of funding, but provinces must still approve capital expenditures. Thus, there is a centralized mechanism to allocate resources to the hospital sector and to determine the distribution of resources among hospitals.

Occupancy rates are higher in Canadian hospitals, as indicated in Table 22.4. Also the provinces have limited the capital costs associated with expensive new technologies.

Table 22.6 provides comparisons on the availability of several relatively recent and expensive technologies among Canada, the United States, and the former West Germany. The United States has greater availability of each technology. This is particularly true for procedures such as lithotripsy and magnetic resonance imaging (MRI). Whether the data suggest overutilization in the United States, or rationing in Canada or Germany, is a subject to which we will return.

Administrative Costs

The centralized system of health care control in Canada has led to theories about the possible economies associated with administrative and other overhead expenses. Almost all patients in the United States are familiar with extensive paperwork and complex billing practices. For providers and third-party payers, the paperwork is more than an inconvenience; it involves major administrative expenses. Table 22.7 contains estimates of various categories of administrative expenses for 1987. The total expenses were approximately $300 more per capita in the United States than in Canada. This figure accounts for a substantial portion of the difference in per capita spending between the countries.

Even more provocative is the direction of the trends. Woolhandler and Himmelstein (1991) note that the increases since 1983 were especially severe. For example, the authors found that administrative costs in the United States increased from 21.9 to 23.9 percent of health care spending between 1983 and 1987, while similar costs declined in Canada from 13.7 percent to 11 percent.

TABLE 22.7 Costs of Health Care Administration per Capita: Canada and the United States, 1987		
	Spending per Capita	
Cost Category	*U.S.*	*Canada*
Insurance administration	106	17
Hospital administration	162	50
Nursing home administration	26	9
Physicians' overhead and billing expenses		
Expense-based estimate	203	80
Personnel-based estimate	106	41
Total costs of health care administration		
High estimate	497	156
Low estimate	400	117

Note: All costs are expressed in U.S. dollars.

Source: Woolhandler and Himmelstein (1991, Table 1).

A Critical Comparison

The foregoing data suggest that the Canadian system appears to be more effective than the U.S. system in several respects. Costs are lower, more services are provided, financial barriers do not exist, and health status as measured by mortality rates is superior. Canadians have higher life expectancies and lower infant mortality rates than do U.S. residents.

However, the comparisons tell neither the whole story nor do they necessarily imply that the United States should adopt the Canadian approach. Some have argued that a system that is manageable for a population of 30 million cannot be easily adapted to a more pluralistic country with a population ten times that level.

Others point out that many Canadians are no longer confident that the provinces will be able to afford their current systems. As a result of unprecedented federal deficits, the Canadian government has substantially reduced its cash transfers to the provinces. The provinces are thus faced with the following options to cope with their increased burdens: find new sources of tax revenue, impose more stringent fee and budgetary controls on health providers, find ways to increase efficiency in health care delivery, scale back on benefits by no longer insuring some previously covered services, and impose user fees (Rathwell 1994). It is clear that Canada, like many other countries, is facing difficult choices. But, aside from these problems, there are some serious economic considerations that we have not addressed.

Critics of the Canadian system charge that health care is rationed in the sense that all the care that patients demand, or would be provided to meet their best interests, cannot be supplied on a timely basis. As noted in the model on the British National Health Service, rationing below market price leaves some people, who would be willing to pay more, unable to purchase *any* of the good at all. Though specific estimates of such shortages are not available, there is a consensus that the limits on capacity and on new

---

FEATURE

How Is Health Care "Rationed" in Canada?

Though there have been many claims that health care is "rationed" in Canada through longer waiting times and reduced access to services, more recent studies help identify specific differences between the U.S. and Canadian systems. The following are prominent examples of this research emphasis.

Coyte and colleagues (1994) examined waiting times for patients undergoing knee-replacement surgery in Ontario and the United States. The median waiting time after the surgery had been planned was eight weeks in Ontario versus three weeks in the United States. Overall satisfaction with the surgery was comparable at about 85 percent in both countries.

On the issue of access to technology and aggressive medical intervention, G. M. Anderson et al. (1993) compared use of coronary artery bypass surgery among several U.S. and Canadian regions. The combined age-adjusted rate for three Canadian provinces was 62 per 100,000 population, far below the rates of 113 for California and 88 for New York.

To study possible differences in inpatient physician practice patterns, Katz, McMahon, and Manning (1996) examined the use of diagnostic tests for comparable patients admitted to U.S. and Canadian hospitals with similar availability of technology. Despite the similar technologies, U.S. medical patients received 22 percent more tests (there was little difference among surgical patients) and the differences were greatest among the most expensive tests.

Elsewhere, Rouleau et al. (1993) examined patients admitted to a coronary care unit in 19 Canadian and 93 U.S. hospitals. Fifty-one percent of the Canadian patients had acute myocardial infarction (MI) compared with 35 percent of U.S. patients. This suggests that somewhat more serious cases were being treated in the Canadian hospitals. Coronary arteriography and other procedures were performed at much higher rates in the United States. Interestingly, these differences in treatment patterns had no effect on mortality or rate of reinfarction but there was a slightly higher rate of activity-limiting angina in Canada.[12] From this evidence, the authors conclude that there may be a higher threshold in Canada for hospital admission and for performing expensive diagnostic and therapeutic procedures.

These studies leave little doubt that in some instances Canadians get less health care or have to wait longer. But with little observable effects on mortality and other outcome indicators, Canadian practice patterns and case management can provide useful information to U.S. providers and third-party payers on strategies to reduce utilization and costs.

---

[12]On the other hand, Marks et al. (1994) found that patients in both countries had the same functional status after 30 days but U.S. patients showed more improvement after a year.

technology result in longer waiting periods for hospital services.[13] The "safety valve" of a private system, as in the United Kingdom, for those who are willing to pay more, is not readily available, although some Canadians (particularly those near large U.S. border cities such as Buffalo and Detroit) use the U.S. facilities for this purpose.

Defenders of the U.S. approach claim that the waiting and queues found in Canada would be unacceptable to many U.S. patients. There is a greater level of amenities in the United States and the greater availability of specialized care, together with high-tech medicine, is often taken as an indicator of superior quality. Certain population health status indicators, when used to compare the health levels of the United States and Canada, do not support this claim of higher quality in the United States, but additional quality comparison data would be useful.

Furthermore, some analysts believe that the difference in health care spending between the two countries is not nearly as great as it appears. Krasny and Ferrier (1991) suggest that the following three factors represent much of the gap:

- The failure to account for capital costs in Canadian hospitals.
- The larger proportion of elderly in the United States.
- The higher level of spending on research and development in the United States.

It is of some interest to review the polled opinions of U.S. and Canadian economists on the matter (see also Chapter 1). A survey found that almost all of the Canadian respondents believed that their system is far superior; U.S. respondents were divided on this issue. The Canadian economists are much more willing to accept a government solution to the question of health care allocation. In contrast, many U.S. health economists argue in favor of freedom of choice for patients. They are also more likely to advocate a health system that seems both to be more responsive to patient preferences, and in which the patient is given incentives to choose wisely.

Though the current U.S. system has failed to achieve comparable performance to other systems in many respects, many believe that appropriate changes can be made. These changes would allow the United States to maintain a largely private system of finance and delivery, while it would preserve flexibility, choice, and higher levels of efficiency. The degree to which a synthesis of the two systems may be possible is an important health policy question.

DIFFERENCES IN HEALTH CARE SPENDING ACROSS COUNTRIES

We have noted that different countries have different incentive systems, and, in fact, have differing shares of national product in the health care sector. Having described the systems, and having examined briefly the shares of national product in the health sector, it is appropriate now to explore why the shares differ.

---

[13]See Rakich (1991), and Krasny and Ferrier (1991) for good discussions on this issue.

A Simple Model of Health Expenditures Shares

Consider a model of health expenditures. Let us call total expenditures on health care E. By definition, these expenditures equal the price of health care multiplied by the quantity of health care consumed, or $E = PQ$. Defining the share of national income spent on health care as s, we calculate s as the ratio of E to national income, Y, or:

$$s = PQ/Y \qquad (22.1)$$

In this accounting framework the share, s, can rise because either the price or quantity has risen, or because the national product has fallen. In fact, mathematically it can be shown that

$$(\% \text{ Change}) \, s = (\% \text{ Change}) \, P + (\% \text{ Change}) \, Q - (\% \text{ Change}) \, Y \qquad (22.2)$$

The preceding expression is an identity, mathematically true *by definition*. Even so, it can provide useful insights. If the price of health care, P, rises by the same rate as the price of all other goods, so that Y rises at that same rate, then the health care share of national income does not change.

Applying the Model

Rather than looking just at the percentage changes that occur, we try to examine *why* they occur. Consider, for example, that prices of health care may be related to the kind of health system the country has or to the social insurance scheme. Also consider that the quantity of health care used, Q, tends to increase when national income, Y, increases. Note also that the quantity of health care, Q, tends to be negatively related to the price of health care, P, through the demand relationship.

Consider several ideas in turn:

1. An increase in the price of health care would increase the share, if there were no consumer response. The extent to which consumers reduce demand (in response to price changes) will offset the increase in prices.

2. An increase in the number of people in the population who use health care would tend to increase health care expenditures.

3. An increase in national income, Y, that is unaccompanied by an increase in demand for health care would decrease the share. However, this effect would be offset to the degree that increased national income leads to increased demand; the effect depends on the income elasticity of demand. If, in fact, a 1 percent increase in national product leads to a 1 percent increase in expenditures (that is, the income elasticity at the national level is one), then the share will be constant.

Abel-Smith (1984) suggests factors that account for the continuing increases in health expenditures. Several can be well understood, within our present context, as factors that tend to increase Q:

- Expansion in the coverage of health insurance and/or in the scope of benefits provided.

- Demographic change—particularly the increasing proportion of elderly, with their higher health care costs.

- Expansion of providers (including physicians and dentists) per 1,000 population, leading to larger numbers of services authorized.

- Increases in hospital beds and the rebuilding of hospitals, thus reducing or removing bottlenecks and supply restrictions.

- Financial incentives to authorize the use of more resources per patient.

Other changes in share s work through changes in price P, including the following:

- Higher relative remuneration for health sector workers, due to equal pay for women and growing unionization.

- Introduction of new technologies involving both higher capital expenditures and running costs.

Cross-National Comparisons: Private Versus Public Financing Systems

Pfaff (1990) examines the comparative growth of health care budget shares in the period 1960–1985. He notes that health care spending grew rapidly in nearly all of the Western industrialized countries until about 1975. Starting in the mid-1970s, however, the health care budget shares of most countries have tended to flatten out; that is, they remain constant over time. The United States, however, has seen significant increases in its health care cost share.

Pfaff attempts to relate expenditures and budget shares across countries for the years 1975, 1980, and 1983, to numerous variables reflecting incomes, prices, costs, and demographics. Any systematic relationships between spending and these variables would provide evidence to explain changes in budget shares.

When Pfaff groups countries on the basis of their health care system, he finds that countries financed primarily by private payments, most particularly the United States, emerge with the highest expenditures, and this is not explained solely by a higher level of per capita income. In the context of a larger study, he concludes that the dominant differences between countries in shares and expenditures are found in the mode of public or private financing. He argues that centrally funded health care systems offer more countervailing power to providers' abilities to increase P and Q than do privately funded health care systems. He also finds that copayment variables tend to be insignificant and argues that this factor casts serious doubt on the ability of market-based methods to reduce costs.

Pfaff concludes as follows:

> If this line of reasoning is accepted, a further conclusion may also be inescapable. As countries characterized by a national health service generally show lower health expenditures than those financed by contributions, and as there are no striking differences evident in the health status of the population either, the former may also be more cost-effective than the latter. Such a conclusion would *not necessarily hold* [emphasis added], however, if health status and benefits were measured not only in terms of morbidity or mortality indicators but also in terms of waiting times in ambulatory practices, delays in hospital admission, individual satisfaction of patients, etc. (p. 23).

A careful reading of Pfaff's statement here emphasizes that there are additional factors to consider in choosing a health care system. A careful analyst must impute the extra time costs, as well as the possibly lower quality of care in national health service systems, before deciding conclusively on the full costs of alternative systems. The analyst must also decide whether a consumer, or a country, expresses a willingness to pay more for higher quality. Nonetheless, Pfaff's findings offer provocative evidence and encourage continued attempts to compare alternative health care delivery systems.

CONCLUSIONS

In this chapter we have examined a variety of health care systems found elsewhere. Variation exists in terms of financing, provider payment mechanisms, and the role of government, including the degree of centralization. The United States stands out as the country with the highest expenditures on health care.

It would appear that systems that ration their care by government provision or government insurance incur lower per capita costs. On the other hand, in the largely private system in the United States, there tends to be lower waiting times than in rationed systems, a conclusion that follows simply from theory as well as from observation. Americans, who historically have been more dissatisfied with their health system than Canadians or Europeans have been of theirs, have recently come to view it more favorably. Canadians and Germans, in contrast, are viewing their systems less favorably. Blendon et al. (1995) who surveyed opinion in these countries in the late 1980s and again in 1994, note this convergence of opinion. Which system then is best? Study of comparative systems helps to clarify the real differences and advantages from what is just opinion. The study of comparative systems suggests several features of other systems that may be worth adopting. It also suggests that cultural differences among countries may dictate that systems tailored to the local culture be different even in the long run.

Summary

1. Many characterize the main gap in the American system as the problem of the uninsured, as many as 40 million people. While this does not mean that they go entirely without care, the uninsured consume only half as much health care on average as the insured. Experiences of other countries might lend useful guidance in formulating new policies.

2. A useful typology of health benefit systems provides four categories:
   - *Traditional Sickness Insurance:* the private insurance market approach, with state subsidy.
   - *National Health Insurance:* the state establishes a national-level health insurance system.
   - *National Health Service:* the state provides the health care.
   - *Mixed System:* mixed elements of the above.

3. Among all countries, the United States is by far the biggest spender in absolute per capita terms. It is also the biggest spender as a share of GDP.

4. The United Kingdom's NHS provides relatively easy access to primary and emergency care, while elective services are rationed either through long waiting lists or by limiting the availability of new technologies. The NHS devotes considerable resources to high-return services such as prenatal and infant care.

5. The United Kingdom reformed its health system in 1989 to include elements of competition. The United States has fewer hospital beds per capita than the United Kingdom, and fewer nurses per capita as well. Health care spending per capita in the United Kingdom, however, is only 40 percent of the U.S. level.

6. Germany manages to provide a health system that delivers virtually universal health insurance while avoiding the queues that often trouble governmental systems. However, costs per capita have been increasing faster than the incomes per capita, a problem leading to strenuous 1993 reforms.

7. From 1977 to 1989, South Korea jumped from having just 10 percent of the population covered to universal health coverage. South Korea's cost-containment strategies rest mainly with high coinsurance rates and fee controls.

8. Inequities in South Korea result from concentration of health resources around major urban areas. Nevertheless, the South Korean experience demonstrates that it is possible to phase in a mandated employment-based insurance without serious adverse effects to a nation's economy.

9. Many Americans feel that Canada has successfully developed a comprehensive and universal national health insurance program that is both cost-effective and popular.

10. Compared to the U.S. system, the Canadian system has lower costs, more services, universal access to health care without financial barriers, and superior health status. Canadians have higher life expectancies and lower infant mortality rates than do U.S. residents.

11. Part of the gap between U.S. and Canadian health care costs may be explained by a
    - failure to account for Canadian hospitals' capital costs,
    - larger proportion of elderly in the United States,
    - higher level of spending on research and development in the United States.

12. Careful analysis across alternative health care systems must impute the additional time costs, as well as the possibly lower quality of care in national health service systems, before deciding conclusively on the full costs of alternative systems.

Discussion Questions

1. Discuss the factors that may lead one nation to spend more per person on health care than another nation might spend. What are the implications of finding health care to be income elastic in cross-national studies? When health care is income

elastic, will richer countries tend to have a higher or lower proportion of GDP spent on health care?

2. In countries in which there is nonprice rationing for care, there may be substantial waiting time costs. How could you evaluate the economic costs of the waiting time?

3. Periodically, some analysts look at diagrams such as Figure 22.3 and predict that if expenditures continue to rise at the same rate, the United States will soon be paying 20 percent or more of the gross domestic product for health care costs. Consider the components of health care costs. How would you address such conjectures?

4. Create a table comparing the British, German, and South Korean health care systems with respect to financing, availability, and costs of care. How do they compare with the system in the United States?

5. Suppose that the price of health care services rises, and the quantity demanded falls. Under what conditions might the health care share of GDP fall? Rise?

6. It is important to compare items, under the rubric of all else equal. What are some of the crucial factors that must be adjusted when comparing health expenditures across countries?

7. Distinguish between a national health insurance system and a national health service. Provide examples of each. What kind of a system does the United States have?

8. Americans are more dissatisfied with their health care system than are people in other countries. Discuss whether this a useful indicator of the performance of a health care system.

9. A common thesis in economics is that markets are efficient unless there are characteristics that lead to market failure. What sorts of market failure in the health economy can be used to justify adoption of universal national health insurance? What kinds of government failure can be used to argue against this proposal?

10. Do countries with more comprehensive national programs for the provision of health care tend to have lower average costs than the United States? Do they have lower rates of growth in costs? Discuss.

11. Speculate on the level of technology available across countries. Do you think that better health care is available in the United States than in Canada? Do international health indices suggest this? What are the complicating issues?

Exercises

1. Consider the allocation of services in the United Kingdom's NHS, as noted in Figure 22.1. If the government raises the administered price up from P^*, trace what would happen to expenditures in the NHS and in the private sectors.

2. Define income elasticity of health care demand. If income rises by 1 percent and the income elasticity of health care demand is 0.5, does the share of income going to health care rise or fall? Why?

3. Suppose the price elasticity of health services is −0.5. What will happen to the share of health care expenditures, given a 10 percent drop in health care prices?

4. For more advanced students, Table 22.2 provides data for at least rudimentary estimates of income elasticity of health care expenditures. Estimate a regression equation of the following form:

$$\log \text{Exp} = a + b \log \text{GDP}$$

What is the implied income elasticity of expenditures across countries?

CHAPTER

Health System Reform

- ◼ International Perspective: Health System Reform
  in Selected Countries
- ◼ Financing
- ◼ Insurance Issues
- ◼ Conclusions

H ealth care reform is an international issue tieing together countries that lack universal social insurance for health with countries that cover everyone. It unites countries with competitive elements and pluralistic health systems with countries that have highly centralized and bureaucratic systems. There are two major themes to health care reform:

- the attainment of lower costs, or lower growth rates of costs.
- the provision of equitable access to care for all citizens or residents.

All countries favor lower costs, and more recently even countries with traditional and substantial welfare states have examined the possibility of market reform in their health systems to address the cost issue. Equity of access interests many Americans who supported some form of universal coverage during the 1993–1994 debate over the Clinton plan. Over time, equity has dominated costs in the policy arena, but the recently rising costs across all countries of all types have made cost containment a major concern.

Reform issues across nations feature both the particular and the general. Local features of the health system must be known and addressed by the reformers, and in the previous chapter we have described particulars of selected health systems. There are also general issues faced in common by most systems undergoing the process of reform.

In this chapter, we address a substantial selection of such general issues. Health care must be financed, and social insurance systems must be funded by some form of taxation. These facts imply that issues of tax incidence and employer versus individual mandates have wide relevance beyond the U.S. health debate.[1] Cost control is a common concern, and we address issues of managed care. We also discuss insurance reform to ensure coverage of those with preexisting conditions and people who have left employment. These and other related issues are treated under the categories of Financing and Insurance Issues.

INTERNATIONAL PERSPECTIVE: HEALTH SYSTEM REFORM IN SELECTED COUNTRIES

We begin by reviewing reform efforts and problems in three selected countries: the United Kingdom, the Netherlands, and Germany. In most of Europe health insurance is provided with universal coverage. However, one would be wrong to expect no urge to reform the system. European countries have responded to climbing health care costs with waves of reform campaigns. These include both governmental controls on budgets and prices, a regulatory approach, as well as efforts to install more elements of competition, with an emphasis on managed competition. Reform is sometimes accompanied by political turmoil, a condition familiar to U.S. observers.

The United Kingdom

The recent reform effort in the United Kingdom began with Margaret Thatcher's call for a review of the health system, which was completed and published in 1989 as *Working for Patients.* The British National Health Service, which is government operated and bureaucratically managed, was to have elements of competition. The system would remain funded out of general taxes and available free to citizens, but hospital and community health services became self-governing trusts, and district authorities became purchasers of care. This separation of purchaser and provider roles created what were called internal markets. A hospital would now survive only if it could attract sufficient patients.[2]

As this market for supply developed, hospitals began to analyze their own costs and productivity more carefully. Also they began setting prices for their services that would be paid by the district hospital authorities as purchasers, and in some cases, huge disparities in prices appeared between hospitals. The purchasing authorities had even stronger financial incentives to choose the cheaper hospitals when it proved that these were also closer to patients' homes.

In London, the changes were particularly evident and unsettling. Hospitals that had been in operation for 800 years, revered by patients and physicians alike, began to show deficits.

The results of these reforms were not left up solely to a free market, and the public took up debate of the issue. The government put the matter to an inquiry, chaired by

---

[1]Tax incidence analysis is the study of who ultimately pays the tax.
[2]For further study see Ham and Brommels (1994).

Professor Sir Bernard Tomlinson, which published its recommendations in October 1992. This report claimed that London had 2,500 too many acute hospital beds. The government kicked this reform effort into gear, and it established a "London implementation group" to oversee the cuts in beds.[3]

The issue of whether London was overbedded created a wave of protest led by an educator and general practitioner, Professor Brian Jarman, who in 1994 published a rebuttal to the government's position. He argued that, while inner London was overbedded, London as a whole was not. He pointed to the relatively low bed rates in the United Kingdom compared to other OECD countries. The continuing contention over the reforms makes clear that efforts to reform the health system, for good or bad, generate turmoil not only in the United States but in other countries as well. The United Kingdom moved very quickly with its reform efforts. The speed may have contributed to the discontent it stirred up. In contrast, the Netherlands, by culture and politics, moves very slowly to change.

The Netherlands

The health reforms in the Netherlands build on a system of social insurance that covers the entire population for serious and prolonged disability and sickness. In 1987, the Dekker Report led to reform efforts intended to introduce universal insurance for "virtually all health services and administered by competing insurance organizations" (Hamm and Brommels, 1994, p. 108). The other key feature of the Dekker reform proposals was to introduce "selective contracting," where insurance companies selectively shop around for the best deals from hospitals, clinics, and other health providers. Thus, a central feature of the Dutch reform efforts has been to introduce elements of competition into the health care marketplace.

Compared to the United Kingdom, competition has developed much more slowly in the Netherlands. "This reflects the more cautious Dutch approach to health care reform, the limited scope of competition in many parts of the country, and prevailing cultural characteristics" (Hamm and Brommels, 1994, p. 112). As of this writing, there has been very little competition reported in the Netherlands health system.

Germany

> While Germany has been viewed for many years by American health care policymakers as a country that can control costs and maintain universal access, German policymakers are increasingly worried about their ability to provide all desired services to the entire population. As the German population ages and as medical progress and medical technology become even more widespread, the Germans . . . are searching for new ways to control costs (Henke, Murray, and Ade, 1994, pp. 19–20).

In response to a perceived cost-control problem, Germans created a wave of reforms in 1987. Though cost controls had been used in the past, this was the first instance of expenditure caps. These are limitations that tie the rate of growth in physician

---

[3]This paragraph is based on an article by James (1995).

expenditures to the rate of growth in the incomes of the insurance group members. Restrictions like this on the entire budget of the sickness fund (the insurance organization for a group of insureds in Germany) are called global budgets.

When physician expenditures continued to grow at a high rate, the government passed a major health reform law that took effect in 1993. The law controlled both the price and the volume of physician services and pharmaceuticals. It also changed hospital payment to a prospective payment basis. To protect against unfavorable physician reaction, it even limited the rights of physicians to strike.

The law was considered revolutionary. But it is clear that the German reforms described here are more regulatory than competitive, and probably more regulatory than would prove tolerable or politically feasible in the United States. Nevertheless, global budgets were featured in an early version of the Clinton plan; the global budgets were activated if other plan features failed to control costs.

In the short term, the German reforms have had a clear effect on expenditures. Physician expenditures grew by 3 percent in 1993, less than the 3.9 percent growth in member incomes. Dentistry expenditures grew by 2.2 percent in 1993, down from 9.6 percent the year before. Most dramatic of all, pharmaceutical expenditures declined for the first six months of 1993. Will these short-term gains prove lasting?

Health Reform Internationally

The pattern of health reform we see in these countries reflects concern for costs. Universal access to care through social insurance is widely found in developed countries, and the issue of improving coverage is to a considerable extent a U.S. issue. However, most countries are concerned about costs, and prominent among concerns is the interest in fostering elements of competition. Many of the individual issues raised have relevance across systems. These include reforms of financing mechanisms and insurance markets, as well as managed care and managed competition. Some features of competition and regulation were discussed in Chapter 19. We develop several salient reform issues here beginning with financing reforms.

FINANCING

Individual Versus Employer Mandates

The country that wishes to provide universal coverage for health care must choose one scheme or another to extract tax payments from its households. It should be understood that schemes for employers or government to pay the bills are only mechanisms by which households ultimately pay. In the U.S. health debate, two mechanisms were prominently featured in proposals and thus contrasted: individual versus employer mandates.

Employer mandates form the backbone of the health systems in Europe, Latin America, and Asia (Krueger and Reinhardt, 1994). Under the employer mandate, the employer must procure health insurance for its employees and their dependents. While the employer nominally pays, the firm will undoubtedly pass on as much of this cost as it can to customers (if possible) in the form of higher prices, and to employees in the form of lower wages. Under the individual mandate, each person is obligated to purchase health insurance for himself and his family either from private insurance (individually purchased) or through a group such as work groups, professional organizations, or religious groups. The poor are subsidized in their purchase through government taxation of the relatively well-to-do.

The issue of who pays can be developed graphically. Figure 23.1A shows the demand and supply of labor in a market in which firms do not provide their employees with insurance. The equilibrium before the employer mandate is wage, W_0, and employment level, L_0. Suppose the health insurance premium for each worker is $\$H$. By forcing the employer to pay this premium, we are adding $\$H$ to the wage bill; employers would likely subtract this from the wage they are willing to pay. To keep the problem simple, let us also assume that workers do not value this fringe benefit as something inherent in this work alone. They are also covered when they are not working. The effect of the mandate then is to shift the demand curve downward by the amount of the premium.

The new demand for labor, the dotted line in Figure 23.1A, forms a new equilibrium at wage W_1 and employment level L_1. Thus, the result is a job loss of $(L_0 - L_1)$ and a reduction in wages of $(W_0 - W_1)$. The employee thus faces a substantial part of the burden of the mandate. The loss in wages here is less than the premium because part of the premium shock has been absorbed in a reduction in employment.

Business leaders often complain that employer mandates will either reduce profits or force firms out of business. Such responses seem often to be made, however, under the assumption that the one firm is the only one affected by the mandate. If all firms were made to bear the same labor costs, it is doubtful that closings would result. In the short run, firms would pay workers less, take less in profits, and raise prices to consumers. "Economists are convinced, however, that in the longer run more and more of the cost of the employer mandate would likely be shifted backward to employees . . . through smaller real (inflation adjusted) increases in wages than would have been warranted by long-run productivity gain" (Krueger and Reinhardt, 1994, p. 44).

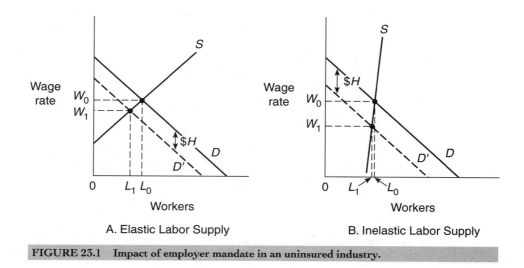

A. Elastic Labor Supply   **B. Inelastic Labor Supply**

FIGURE 23.1   Impact of employer mandate in an uninsured industry.

It appears that the individual mandate would accomplish much the same result with a clearer pathway. The cost would fall ultimately on the one to whom it is assessed. Pauly (1994b) describes an individual mandate with the payments enforced by the employer and subsidies for the nonworking poor to purchase their own insurance. He notes that "It seems desirable, for rational political decision making, for citizens to be aware of what taxes they are paying to obtain benefits" (p. 23). Under this principle, the individual mandate is attractive.

The reasoning behind this proposition requires the assumption, generally true but with exceptions, that the employer mandate ultimately falls entirely on the worker. Given this assumption, there is no difference in the long run in the sense of who pays between the individual and employer mandate. Under Pauly's version of an individual mandate, the worker pays 100 percent of the health insurance cost out of his or her wages. Since the fraction paid by employee/employer is irrelevant to who finally pays (the worker pays by assumption), the two schemes have the same result. But, as we noted, the individual mandate is a clearer, perhaps more honest, connection between the ostensible payer and the true payer.

The long-run effects of employer payment versus individual payment also pose the question of clarity and perhaps honesty. During the U.S. debate of 1993–1994, there was frequent dispute over the fraction that the employer pays versus the fraction paid by the individual. The presumption in these arguments is that the chosen fraction reflects the burden. Economists, however, tend to agree that the particular fractions chosen ultimately do not matter. What matters is the actual burden, not the legal burden. Some may argue that it is a political necessity to overlook the economics, an approach that Pauly suggests is Machiavellian. It is also plausible that honest public discussion of the economic issues would improve the quality of the national debate.

Pauly further argues that it is always true that regardless of where the cost of the mandate falls, it will be no different between the individual and the employer mandate. Because of this similarity, we ask what benefits other than "truth in advertising" are provided by the individual mandate.

The advantages of an individual mandate include fine-tuning so that the subsidies could be based on low income rather than on wage. Not all low-wage families will have low income because of multiple jobs or nonwage (such as interest or dividends) income. Also the individual mandate does not require reductions in wages. Wage reductions are difficult for firms to propose and for employees to accept, so some employers may resort to layoffs in the intermediate term when employer mandates are used. Also there would be no problems with part-time workers or two-worker families.

If all other things were equal, and individual versus employer mandates were the societal choice, most health economists would probably agree with Pauly that the individual mandate is to be preferred. But things are not equal. Many voters either ignore or reject economic ideas about where the cost of a tax—and mandates of either kind *are* taxes—will ultimately fall. Also there may be unexpected sharp cost effects in the short run for either choice.

In addition some, including President Clinton, have questioned whether individual mandates would destroy the relationship of employers and employee health insurance. Presently most Americans get their health insurance through their jobs. Would employers still be willing to provide health insurance if the individual were mandated to purchase it? The group coverage that an employer could present (though not pay for) would likely be advantageous to the employee. Employees would probably view a lower-cost plan offered at work to be a benefit of working at the firm.[4] To compete with other employers, the firm would probably make plans available to purchase. If employers had previously paid (at least part of) the insurance premium, ceasing to do so would make them less competitive in attracting employees. For individuals who do not presently have coverage at work, the individual mandate would give them the incentive to bargain with their employers for it in a trade-off with wages. Under these scenarios, it would seem likely that coverage at work would grow rather than wither away with the individual mandate (Pauly, 1994). This, however, is a contentious issue and a worry regarding the individual mandate.

Another criticism of the individual mandate is that it requires that very high marginal tax rates be levied on low-income families. Suppose, for example, that low-income families are subsidized with the subsidy beginning at the poverty level and then the subsidy is phased out as income rises to double the poverty rate. This gradual loss of a subsidy, worth about $5,000 for a family of four, is essentially a marginal tax. Krueger and Reinhardt (1994) argue that this marginal tax rate, which they calculate to be about 35 percent, added to other tax rates paid by the poor or near-poor would generate a marginal tax rate of about 75 percent. This would reduce the individual incentives to work.

Unemployment is an issue under either type of plan. Will either plan create unemployment? Suppose that an individual mandate is passed. Firms that were providing a package of $8 per hour in money wages plus $2 per hour in health benefits, or $10, would now offer the entire $10 package as wages (firms that did not would lose workers to others that did). Hence, the individual mandate places no new burden on firms, so it is not likely to result in unemployment.

In contrast, the employer mandate appears to create unemployment. Assume that an employer was originally paying $10 per hour, without benefits, and that a $2 per hour benefits package is mandated. Costs to the employer then rise to $12 per hour, inducing the employer to cut back on the number of workers, unless the money wage package is reduced. Clearly, for firms that did not previously provide insurance, wages must either decrease, or rise more slowly than would have otherwise occurred. For workers at the minimum wage, wage reduction is impossible, and it is likely that some will be laid off. Will the layoffs be widespread?

Economists argue that widespread layoffs are unlikely for essentially the same reasons that they believe that the cost of the tax falls mainly on the worker. Consider Figure 23.1B, where the labor supply curve is very inelastic. This reflects the fact that while the supply of labor to a firm may be very elastic, the supply of labor to the economy (for example, the country as a whole) is quite inelastic. Again, the employer mandate shifts the demand for the labor curve downward. The equilibrium wage will be reduced by approximately the entire tax, illustrating the proposition that the burden

---

[4]Currently fringe benefits provided by the firm are exempt from taxation in the United States. If this remained the case under the individual mandate, there would be an inducement for firms to continue to offer health insurance as a fringe benefit, provided that wages were adjusted correspondingly downward.

falls largely on the worker. Second, notice that the employment level stays approximately the same, illustrating the point at hand.

Single Insurer Versus Multiple Insurers

A move in the United States toward universal coverage also entails the option of a single insurer, presumably the federal government. The option of multiple insurers retains part of the status quo in the United States where many private insurance companies provide the majority of insurance with government providing about 40 percent. The most prominent single-payer proposal discussed in the U.S. debates was a version of the Canadian system, which the Canadians call Medicare.

In principle, costs can be reduced by consolidating insurers if there are economies of scale in administration or if there are gains to be made from pooling the insureds. It is popular to argue that the U.S. health system has excessive administrative costs. Assuming administrative savings by switching to government is somewhat risky, however. The same technology is available to the private sector, and if further economies were possible, it is likely that further mergers and growth of firms would have occurred to provide it. In addition, the profits that private firm insurers gain are not a waste to the economy, but rather a payment for capital that government must incur.

Theoretically a single-payer system reduces costs by eliminating the multiple forms and policy rules that face hospitals, clinics, and nursing homes. There are some 1,500 different insurers at present in the United States (Gauthier et al., 1992). The difficulty of coordinating many different policies falls on hospitals and physicians and it is external to the insurance company. Nevertheless, it is a real economic cost to society, and it could be reduced when the government as single payer offers fewer forms and some standardization. In a sense, these are costs that increase with decentralization.

There is speculation, however, that these costs of decentralization can be reduced by improvements in computer technology. As claims handling becomes computerized, there is increased potential for solving the problem with software that establishes interfaces between the forms and protocols of different companies. Electronic data interchange technology can link "the entire health care administration and delivery systems" (Gauthier, p. 314) through the use of cards with a magnetic strip similar to ATM cards. Common formats and standards will be widespread.

The operation of government enterprise also raises the question of incentives. Government may fail to reduce costs because government, in most cases, lacks the discipline of the profit incentive and the discipline of market competition. The result would be higher costs rather than lower costs.

The question of saved administrative costs is ultimately an empirical one, and Table 23.1 presents some estimates assuming a Canadian-style system is adopted in the United States. These estimates, ranging from $78–$95 billion in savings from one source to $31 billion in extra costs from another source, reflect the difficulties of making this kind of comparison.

These estimates are based on accounting definitions and allocations of administrative costs, which differ among firms and between the United States and Canada. It is also true that the United States tends to pay its health workers, including administrative personnel, substantially more. The problem is further complicated by the fact that the

TABLE 23.1 **Estimated Savings in U.S. Administrative Costs If a Canadian-Style System Were Adopted (1991 billions of dollars)**

	Woolhandler and Himmelstein	Physicians for a National Health Policy	GAO	Lewin/ICF
Total	78 to 95	80	67	47
Insurance administration/overhead	26	32	34	23
Physician administration/overhead	19 to 36	11	14	11
Hospital administration/overhead	32	37	18	13
Estimate of offsetting costs	Not estimated	14	64	78
Estimate of net savings (added costs)	78 to 95	66	3	(31)

Note: Estimates that originally appeared in 1987 dollars have been adjusted to 1991 rates using the ratio of the overall CPI for 1987 and 1991, respectively. Figures are in billions of dollars.
Source: Gauthier et al. (1992, p. 311).

health sector of each country produces a different set of health care and health insurance products. Furthermore, administrative costs include fixed costs that must be arbitrarily allocated across these multiple outputs. These costs will depend on the type of output. For example, some policies provide complete insurance for risk while some share the risk with the insured. The administrative costs may well be different between these two types of policies.

These problems suggest another qualification. In public debates, there is the implicit assumption that the lower the administrative costs, the better. This approach wrongly treats higher administrative costs as wasteful, whereas they represent an input cost. Gauthier et al. explain that "in health care as in other areas, 'overhead' does not automatically signal waste" (1992, p. 318). Administrative costs may also incur benefits to insureds and to society by controlling total system costs.

We have identified areas for potential savings and also presented best estimates of the savings possible by switching to a Canadian type of system. We have discussed the conceptual and practical difficulties in making these comparisons. These difficulties should encourage the reader to examine very cautiously strong claims regarding the supremacy of one plan or another in terms of administrative costs.

In any case, the switch to a single-payer system would require the biggest change since the insurance industry would largely be eliminated. Do the problems of the health care system warrant this radical change? Others prefer more modest changes to address specific problems. For example, the problem of the uninsured may be addressed by subsidies for the poor under some programs as opposed to the assumption of all insured under the government program. In another example, the problem of insurance companies not accepting insureds with preexisting conditions might be solved by legislation.

Another potential drawback of a single-payer system is the effect on innovation in the insurance industry. Consider as an example the rapidly changing and developing computer industry. Would change have come as quickly if it were not for the many small startup companies? In health care insurance, would a single payer innovate rapidly? While many analysts would answer that pluralism is best for innovation, there is little empirical data to confirm it, just informed speculation.

A potential benefit of the single-payer system lies with the common coverage that is possible. We may worry now that some insured people have inadequate policies in terms of the depth and breadth of coverage. In contrast, the single payer could offer one policy or just a few, regulated so that each one is deemed adequate by policymakers representing the public. In contrast, the availability of many policies from many companies offers variety, tailoring policies to the individual preferences for cost-sharing features and coverage. Here the policyholder determines adequacy, not the government official. Under a pluralistic system, some standardization could be maintained by regulation or by government certification of policies offered. The government subsidy or outright purchase could be limited to only those policies certified to meet a minimum standard. Presumably, HMOs and related organizations could flourish in a pluralistic system.

In summary, there are issues and questions surrounding the choice of a single-payer versus a pluralistic system that cannot be answered with confidence. Even the claim that a single-payer Canadian-style system would have lower administrative costs is controversial. To eliminate the insurance industry on the basis of existing knowledge would be more of a political choice and an indictment of the insurance industry than an economic choice.

Health Care Reform and International Competitiveness

A frequently raised issue in the debate on health care reform was whether universal health care "paid for" by the employer would tend to make the United States uncompetitive internationally. The auto executive was widely heard arguing that the high cost of health care adds hundreds of dollars to the price of a new American car. How can we compete? The answer to this question is derived from an analysis of the incidence of a health tax and borrows from some analysis we have already done.

First, take the issue of the price of cars. In theory, the health insurance paid by the firm is just part of the total compensation. The worker and employer can bargain regarding the fraction of compensation paid in wages versus the fraction paid as health insurance premiums. Under our tax laws, the portion paid as health insurance is not taxed, and this "tax subsidy" implies that the cost of health insurance is cheaper to the worker if paid as a pretax fringe benefit. So most workers will prefer it. Of course there will also be workers who do not perceive the trade-off between wages and health insurance.

When health insurance costs rise or employer-based universal coverage is mandated, the adjustments will come to wages, profits, or the price of cars. The degree to which it falls on reduced wages in theory depends on the elasticities of labor supply and demand. We will discuss that side shortly, but first suppose that it fell entirely on the employer. To consider the ability of the firm to pass along this cost to the buyer, panels A and B of Figure 23.2 depict the demand, marginal revenue, and marginal cost curves for the firm under the alternative assumptions that, A, it has some monopoly power, and, B, that it faces considerable competition.

In panel A the demand curve is downward sloping and the marginal revenue curve lies below the demand curve. If health costs cause the firm's wage bill to rise, this

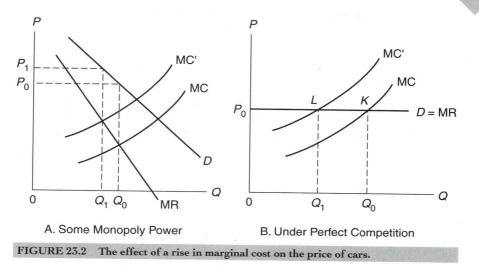

FIGURE 23.2 **The effect of a rise in marginal cost on the price of cars.**

will affect the marginal cost of producing cars, shifting the curve MC upward to MC'. In response the equilibrium price will rise from P_0 to P_1. In this sense, part of the rise in marginal costs has been passed on to the consumer. However, suppose that the firm faces substantial competition from other U.S. car companies and from abroad so that its demand curve is flatter. The more elastic demand curve implies that the firm will lose substantial business if it raises its price. In this case, the demand curve and marginal revenue are very close together. We have drawn the limiting case in Panel B where they are identical. Now note that as marginal cost rises, the price of cars does not rise. The equilibria to compare are points K and L.

The implication of these analyses is that the ability of the firm to pass on its health costs to the consumer depends on its elasticity of demand. If the increased car price includes hundreds of dollars of increased health costs, it is only because the firm had the power to pass these hundreds on. The more vulnerable our firms are to competition, the less ability they have to pass extra costs along to consumers. If not consumers, then who pays for them? We turn our attention now to the market for labor.

Refer back to Figure 23.1, A and B, and assume that each panel depicts the market for labor for auto workers, under alternative assumptions about labor supply. The demand curves represent the auto firm's willingness to hire workers; the supply curves represent the laborers' willingness to work. In panel A, the supply of labor is shown as relatively elastic suggesting that laborers are very responsive to wage offers in determining their decision of whether or not to work. Here the imposition of higher health care costs as incurred by a firm required by contract or by law to pay the costs has the effect of shifting the demand curve downward by the amount of the tax. At the new equilibrium, the wage has dropped by $W_0 - W_1$. The health care tax is the total vertical distance between D and D'. Thus, portion $W_0 - W_1$ is the incidence (where the tax, H, ultimately falls) on the laborer; the remainder (the tax minus the laborer incidence) is the incidence on the firm.

Contrast what happens in panel B where the laborer is inflexible in his decision to work; that is, he has to work. As before, the change in health premium costs, which are like a tax if the firm has to pay them, shifts the demand curve down by the amount of the tax. At the new equilibrium, the wage has fallen by $W_0 - W_1$, virtually the amount of the tax.

In real life, how can firms lower worker wages considering the strong antipathy of people to accept lower wages? One practice available is to hold back on raises so that over time the real value of the wages becomes a lower fraction of compensation.

Economists, reviewing the empirical evidence, tend to find that the labor supply curve for the whole economy is quite inelastic.[5] The general implication of this finding is—as per our analysis—that the cost of universal health insurance mandated to be paid by the employer will fall mainly on the worker. Thus, a universal coverage plan is like a national tax—borne by the worker. As such, it will have little effect on the competitiveness of our products internationally.

Medical Savings Accounts

Some lessons seem clear in the United States with the demise of the major health care reform legislation in 1994. One is that sweeping comprehensive reform is unlikely to win support politically in the near future. This reality has led some researchers and policy analysts to search for incremental steps toward reform, steps that will address some of the key problems but without doing harm or changing the system substantially. One such proposal, which calls for the creation of medical savings accounts and tax credits, was proposed by Pauly and Goodman (1995).[6]

They address several problems. The first problem is the distortion caused by the current tax treatment of health insurance on the job. Since employer-provided health insurance is not taxed, the insurance is effectively subsidized. Furthermore, the subsidy increases with the employee's marginal tax rate. Second, the subsidy is available only to those who work for someone else, and the employer must be one that provides health insurance. Third, the bigger the insurance policy one buys, the larger the subsidy. Finally, the subsidy also violates the principle of horizontal equity (similarly situated persons should be treated similarly), since it varies in size for people at the same income level due to the amount of insurance they buy.

The present system with these problems creates distortions for economic choice. The distortions occur because the tax provisions create gaps between the true costs and benefits of insurance and health, and the costs after taxes to the individual. These distortions result in inefficiencies. In addition, insurance that offers first-dollar coverage leads to the problem of moral hazard (discussed in Chapter 11) in which the provision of insurance increases the amount of health care purchased. The Pauly/Goodman proposal is designed to encourage insurance coverage while removing some of these distortions. First consider analytically the inefficiencies under the present system.

---

[5]The labor supply for a firm or for an industry may be quite elastic, but for the whole economy workers will have to work and are relatively unresponsive to wage, though elasticities for women tend to be larger than those for men.

[6]Medical savings accounts were first discussed in Chapter 19. See that section for further development of the ideas.

In Figure 23.3A, the market demand curve for health insurance is drawn as curve *D*. The supply of insurance available is labeled *S*. With no tax subsidy, the equilibrium will occur at point *E*, with a price P_0 and a quantity Q_0. For the employee working at a firm that offers health insurance, the insurance policy is paid for ultimately by the employee with pretax dollars. The market price is then reduced to the employee at the rate of the employee's marginal tax rate, the reduction in price being greater the higher one's income tax bracket. Panel A shows this effect as a rotation of the demand curve to *D'* with a new equilibrium of *K*. Insurance purchased above Q_0 incurs marginal costs measured on *S* that exceed marginal benefits measured on the true demand curve *D*. The inefficiency is measured as the welfare loss triangle of *EKL*.

Panel B shows that similar analysis applies to the issue of moral hazard under insurance. Curve D_1 represents the market demand curve for health care without insurance. Curve *S* shows the supply curve facing this consumer. When the individual is insured, the policy may reduce the fraction of the health care bill he has to pay, and this rotates the demand curve clockwise to D_2. The consumer will purchase care without full regard to its costs, which is usually paid for in the form of premiums. The new equilibrium is at *X*, and the welfare loss is represented by the area of triangle *XYZ*.

The Pauly/Goodman proposal is designed to reduce or eliminate these inefficiencies. They propose to replace the current tax subsidy for health insurance with a tax credit for the purchase of insurance. The amount of the credit would be fixed irrespective of the size of the policy purchased. They also propose medical savings accounts (MSAs) and the purchase of catastrophic insurance with high deductibles.

The MSAs are savings accounts earmarked for payments of out-of-pocket expenditures for health care. The idea of MSAs is that instead of buying expensive full-coverage policies, consumers would seek to save money by buying cheaper, high-deductible catastrophic care coverage and then choose how to spend their leftover dollars for out-of-pocket costs under the deductible. Any money remaining in the MSA at

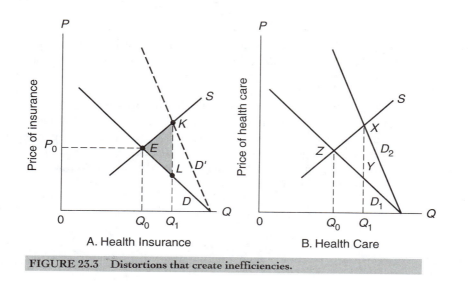

A. Health Insurance B. Health Care

FIGURE 23.3 Distortions that create inefficiencies.

year's end could be withdrawn and spent in any way the consumer sees fit. This feature means that the account holder has a strong incentive to buy wisely and conserve MSA money.

The tax credit would be a fixed dollar amount contingent only on securing a basic catastrophic plan or more coverage. The credit does not increase if consumers choose to buy more extensive policies. If people choose a more expensive plan, the dollars come out of their own money. A further feature of the tax credit is that it is available to all citizens regardless of whether they are employees or not.

The proposed MSA contribution would occur with after-tax income; hence, it would be subject to tax just like wages and most other forms of income. Since the employee fringe health benefit at work is currently tax free, this feature of the proposal poses a problem both to encourage people to adopt the new policy of catastrophic insurance and MSAs and to remove the inefficiencies of the tax subsidy under the old policy. It would probably be politically difficult to eliminate the tax subsidy. The subsidy is worth about $100 billion a year, and people have not only come to rely on it but they have made their decisions about work with this subsidy assumed.[7]

INSURANCE ISSUES

Managed Care and Cost Containment

It is clear by now that managed care, as provided by HMOs and PPOs, delivers medical service at a lower cost than fee-for-service care, the savings being achieved primarily through lower hospital use rates. Here, at least, the managed care arrangements have clearly changed the economic incentives of the decision makers. If managed care savings can be transformed into savings in per capita costs and if managed care arrangements can be translated to work in other countries and cultures, then managed care poses a significant potential for health system cost containment. But it is exactly at these key points that managed care has come to be questioned.

Alain Enthoven (1993) has addressed the first issue of why managed care has failed to contain national health costs. A vigorous advocate of managed care, Enthoven nevertheless bases his admission of its failure to control health care spending on the grounds that health spending as a percent of GDP has increased rapidly. From 1980 to 1992 this percentage increased from 9.1 to 14.1 in the United States. This came despite the proliferation of HMOs and PPOs; during this time membership in HMOs grew from approximately 9 million to 44 million. Enthoven sees this lack of cost control as a result of a lack of price competition and argues in favor of plans to promote price competition among managed care groups, that is, "managed competition."

One problem with the current system, according to Enthoven, is that certain market features have limited the growth of managed care. For example, about half of employees work for firms with fewer than 25 employees. Offering a choice of plans to this employee group may not be economically feasible because the member firms do

---

[7]For a proposal that might encourage many to opt out of the tax subsidy voluntarily, see Pauly and Goodman (1995).

not offer the large size that allows pooling of risks to lower costs. To address the diffi-culties of small-size firms, he promotes the development of purchasing cooperatives that combine or pool large numbers of employees from small firms. The idea of purchasing cooperatives became reflected in the Clinton plan as the "health alliances." Despite the demise of the Clinton plan, the idea of purchasing cooperatives seems a good idea in the sense that a voluntary, perhaps commercial, form might meet a market test.

A second problem with managed care is that employers who offered an HMO to their employees often paid the premium as long as the HMO premium was not higher than the fee-for-service premium. This behavior by employers creates distorted incen-tives for the HMO in controlling its cost in order to lower the premium. In Figure 23.4, the HMO's demand curve is essentially vertical up to the point of the fee-for-service premium and quantity of care Q_0, at point A. The HMO has an incentive to control costs (as noted by average cost curves C_1, C_2, and C_3), but only such that they are lower than the fee-for-service premium P_f.

Enthoven suggests that this incentive distortion could be corrected if employers would offer better policies for making their employer contributions. To increase cost awareness, the employer could contribute a fixed dollar amount for the health insurance with the employee paying the full difference between plans. The greater the portion of the marginal premium paid by the employees, the stronger the incentive to choose lower-cost plans. For example, if the employer pays 80 percent of the premium and the employee the remainder, then the employee only pays 20 percent of the difference between the low (let's presume here) HMO premium and the higher fee-for-service premium.

The tax code also distorts economic incentives. Since the health insurance fringe benefit is not treated as taxable income, it is effectively offered at a reduced price. For example, many people face a marginal tax rate (combining federal and state rates) of

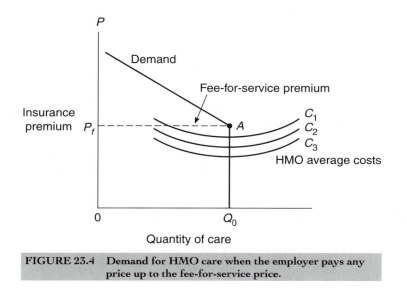

FIGURE 23.4 Demand for HMO care when the employer pays any price up to the fee-for-service price.

around 40 percent. When considering how to handle extra income of, say, $100, they can choose to take it as income, yielding a net $60, or they can take it as a fringe benefit, yielding the full $100 to spend on whatever health benefit they can get for it. In other words, $100 will bring more in health benefits, at market prices, than it will in cars, groceries, or most other goods that are bought with after-tax dollars. This tax benefit is a subsidy that removes part of the consumer's incentive to shop for health insurance at low cost. In Enthoven's words, "the tax code is, in effect, a heavy tax on cost containment, and its effect is to reduce significantly the demand for HMO membership" (p. 37).

Another potentially important factor in explaining the apparent failure of managed care to reduce health care costs in the population is adverse selection. In some cases, younger and healthier people tend to be attracted to the HMO, which offers lower-cost care, and from their perspective, adequate lower levels of care. In other words, the HMO offers cost containment and the younger, healthier person contracts for it. As a result some HMOs will have an unrepresentative healthy population to serve. The members fulfill their own prophecy because of their lower health care needs, and the HMO reports annually that it has lowered costs. As such, the HMO is not necessarily reducing costs for the population as a whole because the non-HMO population will tend to represent poorer health risks and thus have more costly care. The sum of HMO and non-HMO patient care may thus yield no cost savings.

Does managed care save the population money? Yes and no. First, it is true that the HMO structure of incentives leads to reductions in costs in study populations chosen by randomized experiment (see Chapter 12). Second, cost savings on a wide scale and across the population will require both the wide adoption of managed care by the public and the practical solution to the problems Enthoven describes. Most particularly, it must present people with the full incentives to choose between higher-cost and lower-cost plans.

International Perspective

We have so far addressed the issue of whether managed care savings reported in some studies can be transformed into cost savings for the population as a whole. But can the managed care structure be translated as well to other cultures and other countries? This is a question addressed by Harold Luft (1991).

Health care costs have been rising around the world, and there is increasing interest worldwide in potential cost-reducing changes to the health system, including an interest in managed care. Borrowing strategies from the United States, a highly recognized big spender when it comes to health care, may seem unwise. But on a case-by-case basis, elements of the U.S. system may prove effective cost containers. Can our experience with HMOs be translated to other health systems?

Luft warns that HMOs are not simple, homogeneous organizations: ". . . each HMO is a highly complex combination of economic incentives, bureaucratic structures, and personalities" (p. 172). What we know about them is limited. Economists have carefully studied a number of cases, but applying this knowledge to the broader population of HMOs may be difficult.

There is a wide variety of HMOs, organizations that contract to deliver a range of health services to an enrolled population on the basis of a prearranged premium. For example, an HMO could contract with physicians in several ways: It could hire them at a salary, contract with a preexisting group practice of physicians, or contract with physicians who maintain a substantial fee-for-service practice (the IPA form or Individual Practice Association). According to Luft, "Because specific social, legal, historical, political, and economic aspects of the medical care environment have shaped delivery systems such as the HMO, it is not reasonable to expect that the typical HMO could be transplanted intact to another country" (p. 173). Nevertheless, Luft feels that some general points can be made.

First, public risk taking can be limited somewhat with HMOs. When the public accepts the responsibility for seeing that health care is provided to some segment (or all) of the population, it may do so on an entitlement basis. An entitlement program requires the government to spend without limit, bearing the risk that costs will be unusually high. Some of this risk could be transferred to the HMO, which makes a flat charge per patient.

Second, some ideas may be drawn from our experience with varying alternatives of physician payment. Though widely used, fee-for-service payment gives physicians the most incentive to increase the services provided. Straight salaried physicians, however, have little incentive to improve productivity. Capitation payment might be most effective when the capitation rate is paid to a group of physicians who pool the risks of cost variation.

Third, there is a difference in the work division between primary care and specialist physicians between the United States and Europe, which may make it hard to simply import the classic HMO structure. Generalists and specialists share responsibilities, make referrals to one another, and the generalists can have hospital privileges and see patients through their hospital care. In Europe, the generalists' duties end at the hospital door. Luft argues, however, that some HMOs have developed in such environments. He cites cases where an HMO primary care group contracts with medical school affiliated specialists, who are essentially salaried physicians taking over when appropriate at the specialist level.

Fourth, the key to HMO cost savings is that the organization provides the wide range of medical services, both inpatient and outpatient. In this way, the HMO can receive the cost savings implied by reduced hospital use, a common feature of HMO cost saving. The shift of expenditures may be difficult to manage in systems where there are separate financing mechanisms for primary care physicians and inpatient care, as is the case in many countries. As Luft (1991, p. 180) remarks, "If there were no way to shift funds from the 'hospital side' to the 'physician side,' it would be difficult to reward clinical decisionmakers for the development of more cost-effective practice styles."

In summary, managed care, exemplified at least by the HMO, has an incentive structure capable of shifting health expenditures from expensive inpatient settings to less expensive physician outpatient settings. There are, however, important limitations in existing organizations and practices of employers that may hinder the HMO from providing cost savings to the population as a whole. Enthoven argues that many of these limitations and design flaws can be corrected by some form of managed competition. Whether or not an effective form can be put in practice here and also exported to other countries is questioned by Luft, who illustrates several characteristics of HMO arrangements in the United States that may be difficult to install in other countries.

What can we say overall? Managed care has exhibited solid potential for changing incentives, lowering costs, and maintaining quality. Generalizing from the existing studies to the broad array of managed care arrangements in the United States is not yet possible. The potential for other countries is one additional step removed in that U.S. forms are not directly transplantable. Managed care nevertheless remains an intriguing if uncertain possibility for future cost containment through the reform of insurance organizations.

Separation of Health Insurance from Employment

In designing reforms for the U.S. health system, a good argument can be made for revising or replacing the predominance of health insurance provided by the employer. The "benefits" of employer provision are largely a result of a deception, which is possibly well-meaning in many cases but causes economic distortions.

The historical relationship of the two reveals a distortive beginning. During World War II, the U.S. government instituted price and wage controls with the result that wages were frozen. Firms and markets are nevertheless dynamic and resistant to such a freeze. To compete for laborers, firms that wished to expand found it effective to provide larger amounts of fringe benefits, which were not subject to the freeze. It was at this time that U.S. firms began to offer health insurance as a fringe benefit. In the postwar years, employer contributions to health insurance were and continue to be tax exempt. Thus, purchasing health insurance through the employer could be done at a substantial discount, encouraging overinsurance for many employees.

The tax-exempt status of employer-provided health insurance is the root of just one of the distortions caused by employer-provided health insurance. The tax subsidy leads the consumer to purchase insurance beyond the point where the marginal benefits of health care equal the marginal costs of health care. Meanwhile, many of the unemployed and those employed at low wages go without health insurance. The U.S. system seems to have overinsurance for some and underinsurance for others.

A final example of distortions involves the problem of job mobility, that is, the ability of the insured consumer to move from one job to another and still maintain the insurance. At present, it is common for mobile people to have difficulties in maintaining coverage. When leaving a job, a new individual policy could be purchased, but these tend to be more expensive than group policies. Also insurance companies frequently require a waiting period before accepting a new policyholder, and some individuals may have preexisting conditions that make it almost impossible to buy coverage.

To deal with these and other distortions, some recommend radical changes in the tax system including the severing of insurance from employment. As Fuchs (1994, p. 111) says: "It is certainly true that if government imposes enough mandates, enough subsidies, enough surcharges, and enough controls and regulations, the tie to employment can be severed. But such a complex system invites evasion, gaming, and litigation. Why pursue such a tortured path when there are more effective mechanisms available?" His recommendation—a value-added tax to finance universal coverage of health insurance—like most in this arena, is not without some controversy. But it does suggest an alternative system where health insurance is not tied to a job.

Ethical Values and Reform

Economists most often compare positive analysis (what *is*) with normative analysis (what *ought* to be). The difficulty of distinguishing between normative and positive statements illustrates the difficulty of economics as a science to make a difference in determining real-world policy. In his 1996 presidential address to the American Economics Association, Victor Fuchs addressed these issues systematically. Fuchs considered the U.S. debate over health care reform in 1993–1994 to be "shallow and inconclusive." Why does the health policy debate not have more solid economic content?

Fuchs (1996) considers three possibilities: (1) The research itself was inconclusive. (2) Economists and others did not disseminate this research to a wide enough audience. (3) The debate foundered on differences in people's ethical values. To pursue these issues, he developed and sent a questionnaire to leading health economists (46, or 88 percent, responded), leading economic theorists (44, or 63 percent, responded), and practicing physicians (42, or 89 percent, responded). The 20 statements in the questionnaire were identified by positive or normative contents by three experts who were not participants in the survey. Seven were identified as relatively value-free "positive" questions and the remaining 13 as relatively value-laden "policy-value" questions.

The responses were then tested to see if the responder groups tended to have within-group agreement. The result is that health economists were in agreement significantly for all positive questions and exhibited differences for 7 out of 13 policy-value questions. Clearly, economists differ often about issues of value.

Fuchs found the health economists' agreement on positive questions to be very high, higher than economists in other fields found in another recent survey, and these responses were significantly different from random chance on all seven positive questions. But on normative questions, as is the case in many countries, health economists disagree frequently. Why is this so?

Disagreement on policy-value questions among health economists could conceivably reflect underlying disagreement on factual aspects of the policy-value questions. For example, the question "The United States should now enact some plan (national health insurance) to cover the entire population" elicited a 62–38 split among health economists. This disagreement could result from different personal estimates of the degree of inefficiency resulting from the requirement that everyone have the same health insurance. Also plausible, however, is underlying disagreement on values, with those who agree placing a higher value on everyone having a right to care.

Fuchs's work suggests a fruitful area for future research. Its purpose would be to determine the possibilities for increasing the degree of agreement on policy issues based on further agreement on underlying positive issues. His own view is that values are the key, that the problem is not so much that the health economists disagree about the embedded questions as that they are uncertain about them.

This insight suggests that the health policy debate in this country could improve if we are more explicit and open about value differences. Economists can help by identifying the factual bases of policy issues and providing answers to positive questions of health economics. A further research question is to study the formation of ethical values and differences among people. Fuchs's inquiry improves our understanding of past policy debacles and poses some optimism for the future.

CONCLUSIONS

We have considered several reform issues relevant to U.S. health policy and to the many countries that continue in the reform process. Theory and empirical evidence help to clarify some of these, but it remains clear that most policy issues have a substantial normative component. Economics can estimate what it will cost to extend health insurance universally, but only one's values determine whether or not it should be done.

Summary

1. A common theme of health system reform across countries is the attempt to instill elements of competition.
2. Economic theory suggests that individual mandates and employer mandates will have similar tax incidence.
3. Advantages of the individual mandate include fine-tuning so that the subsidies could be based on low income rather than on wage.
4. Switching from the current U.S. health system to a single-payer system may save money by saving administrative work. However, such projections are risky and a recent review of the literature produced mixed results.
5. For the entire country, labor supply is thought to be very inelastic. Assuming very inelastic supply, the incidence of a mandated health insurance falls mainly on the laborer. International competitiveness in product markets in this case is not affected.
6. A plan for encouraging medical savings accounts with tax credits poses the possibility of eliminating the inefficiency now caused by the tax treatment of employer-provided health insurance.
7. The ability of managed care to control per capita costs depends on whether consumers face incentives to choose the lower-cost plans. Managed care systems, such as HMOs, vary considerably, and they may not easily translate to other countries and other cultures.
8. Some recommend the separation of health insurance from employment in order to eliminate the inefficiency caused by the tax-exempt status of employer-provided health insurance.
9. Public disagreement on health system reform issues may often be caused by the confusion of positive issues with issues of ethical values. An opinion poll analysis suggests that differences in ethical values may be an important problem.

Discussion Questions

1. What issues are prominent in health system reforms internationally?
2. Would individual mandates for health insurance be more burdensome to the poor than employer mandates? Would lower-income groups be wise to favor one plan over the other?

3. If the national labor supply curve were elastic instead of very inelastic, how would an employer-mandated health insurance plan affect the country's international competitiveness?

4. How could a single-insurer health insurance system provide cost savings over a multiple-insurer system like that in the United States? What are the likely savings?

5. How does the medical savings account give incentives for the insured to save on care?

6. What ideas discussed in this chapter would be suitable to recommend to a country just now revising its health system? To pursue equity? To pursue cost containment?

7. What potential has managed care to control per capita health costs in the United States? In other countries?

Exercises

1. In Figure 23.1A, find the full per-unit cost of labor to the employer under an employer mandate. When labor supply is very inelastic, as in panel B, find the full per-unit cost of labor. Which of the two results is more likely in fact?

2. Suppose that a firm faces a downward sloping demand curve and offers no health insurance to its employees. Let an employer mandate for health insurance be enacted. If this causes the firm's marginal costs to rise, will the firm pay the full cost of the health insurance out of profits? Is the mandate in fact likely to raise the firm's marginal costs?

3. In Figure 23.4, suppose the HMO sets price equal to its average cost. What is the effect on the HMO if its average cost were to rise from C_3 to C_2? What if its demand curve were to shift to the right?

CHAPTER

24

Cost–Benefit Analysis and Applications to Health Care

- Cost–Benefit Analysis: Basic Principles

- The Valuation of Benefits and Costs

- Cost–Benefit Analysis in Health Care

- Quality-Adjusted Life Years (QALYs)

- Cost-Effectiveness Analysis

- Conclusions

In health economics, as in other areas of economics involving public policy, we must frequently evaluate policy alternatives systematically. Just as the rational individual would want to choose efficiently among attainable possibilities, governments similarly face budget constraints. Legislators and policymakers must similarly choose among alternatives such as spending more on preventive care versus giving additional support for acute care facilities versus choosing additional investment in medical research. Even in cases of regulatory action, where government expenditures may be relatively small, rational decision makers will recognize society's resource limitations and will want to evaluate the effects of the regulatory actions on resource use. Social cost–benefit analysis (CBA) is a method for evaluating the desirability of a proposal as well as for comparing alternative proposals. It is designed to promote efficient use of scarce resources.

A presentation of CBA by economists, particularly as related to the health care sector, must recognize the particular aspects of that sector. Health practitioners have traditionally resisted placing a dollar value on life in calculating benefits. As such, they have emphasized the practice of determining the least-cost alternative regardless of the benefits; this is known as cost-effectiveness analysis. Alternatively, benefits have often been defined in quality-adjusted life years (QALYs) without dollar values attached. It is

562

Is the United States Spending Too Much on AIDS Research?

The need to focus on rational decision making was forcefully brought out in an article titled, "Is Too Much Being Spent on AIDS?" by economist Joel Hay (1989). Because it was published in *The Wall Street Journal,* the controversial article received considerable public attention.[1] Hay questioned the $2 spent on AIDS research for every dollar of AIDS patient care versus a few cents per dollar of treatment costs on many other fatal conditions. He also noted that the amount spent by the Centers for Disease Control for HIV/AIDS exceeded federal spending on research, education, and prevention for each of diabetes, stroke, hypertension, Alzheimer's disease, and premature birth.

Clearly, such data do not reflect the marginal gains from increased research on other diseases. The marginal gains from research on AIDS, a relatively new disease, could well be greater than the marginal benefits of additional spending on established diseases. At this time, we just do not know the answer. And this is the major point of Hay's article. Rational decisions are needed if we are to allocate public spending both within health care and across categories of public spending. As Hay concluded, there is an urgent need "to begin the painful process of determining which lines of biomedical research, prevention, education and patient care activities are cost-effective and then using these guidelines to make tough choices about allocating resources."

incumbent both on health analysts and economists alike to recognize the assumptions that underlie the differing analyses.

The primary goals of this chapter are to develop the basic principles of cost–benefit analysis and to illustrate the principles through applications in health care. As part of our discussion, we will address the valuation of life and other challenges that limit the use of CBA, and we will consider alternative methods such as cost-effectiveness analysis and QALY analysis.

COST–BENEFIT ANALYSIS: BASIC PRINCIPLES

The fundamental rationale behind CBA reflects the need to determine an efficient allocation of resources when an underlying market is not readily available. In standard economic analysis, individuals and firms consume goods to the point at which marginal benefits equal marginal costs. Since the marginal benefits exceed marginal costs until the last unit, then it follows that the total benefits exceed the total costs, and any additional cost–benefit analysis is unnecessary.

---

[1] A collection of articles on the economics of AIDS is found in the Fall 1991 issue of *Inquiry.*

There are several circumstances, however, for which this scenario does not hold. Decisions to build bridges, parks, or athletic stadiums are not easily analyzed with standard supply-and-demand analyses. In the health care sector, public health decisions with regard to pollution control or water treatment and private decisions, including screening for disease or appropriate treatment modalities, do not provide comfortable market indicators as to their desirability.

The rationale for a formal CBA rests on the premise that a project or policy will improve social welfare if the benefits associated with the project or policy exceed the costs. The benefits and costs include not only direct benefits and costs to individuals and organizations but also any indirect benefits or costs through externalities or third-party effects. Thus, CBA requires evaluation of social benefits and social costs.

Applying Analysis at the Margin

To clarify these terms and the underlying efficiency concept, consider the example of pollution abatement. Pollution is a classic problem involving externalities, an indirect (third-party) effect of a market activity of either the buyers or the sellers that falls upon someone outside of the market relationship. Also the third party is neither compensated nor required to pay for the external cost or benefit received. Thus, the market price of the transaction does not reflect the external costs and benefits.

For example, factories that discharge contaminants into the air or water create external costs by damaging the environment and adversely affecting third parties (residents downwind or downstream) who are not involved in the consumption or production of the good. In the absence of successful litigation or other agreements, the third parties are not compensated for the damages they suffer so that the prices of the goods produced do not reflect the external effects. Conversely, pollution abatement by a firm that needs clean water for its production process creates external benefits to others (e.g., boaters and homeowners) who are not directly involved in the firm's decisions. They typically do not pay for the benefits they receive.

Figure 24.1 illustrates the principle for efficient use of resources when the marginal social benefits (MSB) and marginal social costs (MSC) of reducing discharges into the environment for a hypothetical effluent are known. The MSB curve represents the sum of all marginal benefits, both private and third party. For many pollutants, these marginal benefits will include the benefits of improved health as well as other benefits. For example, the incidence of cancer and respiratory disease has been linked to various forms of air pollution. The benefits of reduced morbidity and mortality will be included. Other benefits to be considered include the slower deterioration rates of property, improvements in the yields and quality of agricultural production, and the recreational and aesthetic enjoyment resulting from a cleaner environment.

In Figure 24.1, the MSB is negatively sloped to reflect the likelihood that incremental reductions in discharges result in a diminishing marginal benefit. The MSC curve, which shows the marginal cost of reducing discharges and would include external costs where applicable, is positively sloped to reflect the increasing amount of resources often needed for incremental reductions in discharge levels. After some level of abatement, it is likely to be very steep. That is, the marginal cost will be very large.

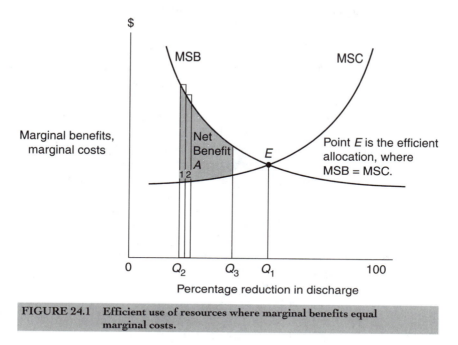

FIGURE 24.1   Efficient use of resources where marginal benefits equal
marginal costs.

The Social Optimum

The social optimum is at point E, where MSB = MSC, and Q_1 is the desired level of abatement. If the current standards for discharge result in a level of abatement shown by Q_2, the gap between MSB and MSC indicates an inefficiency and the desirability of further reducing discharge levels. The gains in welfare by moving toward Q_1 are similar to those described in the partial equilibrium discussion of monopoly and Pareto efficiency in other chapters. In monopoly, a gap is created between price, an indicator of marginal benefits to buyers, and the marginal cost of production. The level of production is inefficiently low.

Despite its apparent simplicity, the approach described through Figure 24.1 is sufficient to reveal the foremost problem facing public decision makers. The information underlying the MSB and MSC curves, and thus the optimum level, is unknown. CBA represents an attempt to get at some of that information and thus help in decision making. To illustrate, suppose the current level of discharge at Q_2 can be observed and that a project or legislation requiring Q_3 is proposed. If MSB and MSC are the true but unknown relationships, an accurate estimate of the project benefits will determine a value that corresponds to the area under the MSB curve between Q_2 and Q_3 and similarly for costs by the area under the MSC curve. The study will reveal a net benefit equal to area A in Figure 24.1.

Before such an estimation process can proceed, significant practical and conceptual problems must be resolved. First, we must identify all the relevant benefits and costs and measure them in pecuniary terms.[2] In light of the task, it is often impractical and sometimes impossible to evaluate marginal increases in the scope of a project. This occurs when the project cannot be broken down into small parts even conceptually so as to evaluate the incremental costs or benefits of each part. Thus, discrete changes such as the one from Q_2 to Q_3 in Figure 24.1 are usually considered.

Second, many projects involve outlays and benefits that accrue over long periods of time. These benefits and costs must be both estimated and discounted to present values. Closely related to the long life of a project is the considerable uncertainty in the estimates of benefits and costs. Third, even where total benefits exceed total cost, not everyone's benefit will exceed cost. There are bound to be winners and losers associated with any project, and consideration will have to be given to equity as well as to efficiency.

Choice becomes even more difficult when, in principle, there are many alternatives for achieving the social optimum. In the pollution abatement example considered above, a variety of instruments are available to help reduce discharge rates. These include regulatory methods and incentive approaches through the use of taxes and subsidies or the auctioning of pollution rights. There could be substantial differences in the distributional effects of these alternatives.

Cost–Benefit Criteria

To examine many of the issues we have raised, we begin with a formal statement of the net benefits (NB) of a proposed project:

$$\mathrm{NB} = \sum_{t=1}^{t=T} \frac{(B_t - C_t)}{(1 + r)^t} \tag{24.1}$$

where B_t and C_t represent the social benefits and costs in year t, r is the discount rate, and T is the life of the project in years. Thus, net benefits represent the sum of a future stream of discounted values. Projects that have positive net benefits improve efficiency and are candidates for adoption.[3]

It is not uncommon to find the cost–benefit criterion expressed as a ratio of discounted benefits to costs. Here,

$$B/C = \sum_{t=1}^{t=T} \frac{B_t}{(1 + r)^t} \bigg/ \sum_{t=1}^{T} \frac{C_t}{(1 + r)^t} \tag{24.2}$$

---

[2]For those unfamiliar with these relationships, consider a one-unit increase in Q. The social benefit associated with that increase is given by the marginal benefit that can be approximated by the rectangle labeled as 1. Another one-unit increase will increase social benefits by rectangle 2, and so on until level Q_3 is reached. By making the units arbitrarily small, the total social benefits associated with the project will be represented by the area lying under MSB between Q_2 and Q_3. Similarly, the total cost of the project will be given by the area under MSC between Q_2 and Q_3.

[3]Those who have studied business investment criteria will see the similarity between equation (24.1) and the net present value criterion that replaces social benefits with revenues in equation (24.1). Projects that have a positive net present value raise the total profits of the firm and are candidates for selection.

Ratios greater than one indicate that the present value of social benefits exceeds the present value of social costs and that the project has a positive net benefit. In comparing projects, however, the benefit–cost ratio can be very misleading because it does not reflect the scale of a project. Thus, even though a small-scale project could have a very high benefit–cost ratio, it may be less attractive than another mutually exclusive larger-scale project that has a lower benefit–cost ratio but a much higher level of net benefits.

The benefit–cost ratio can also be misleading in applications involving averted costs. These are costs that will not be borne in future periods because of the project. Such applications are common in health care, in that the primary goal of many proposals (e.g., increased emphasis on preventive care) is to improve health and reduce subsequent costs of medical treatment. These averted costs can be viewed either as reductions in costs or as benefits. The method chosen to handle averted costs has no effect on net benefits, but can play havoc with the benefit–cost ratio.

Consider the following example in which total benefits excluding averted costs are 10, total costs are 6, and averted costs are 2. The net benefits are 6, calculated either as:

$$NB = (\text{Total Benefits} + \text{Averted Costs}) - \text{Total Costs}$$
$$= (10 + 2) - 6$$

or:

$$NB = \text{Total Benefits} - (\text{Total Costs} - \text{Averted Costs})$$
$$= 10 - (6 - 2)$$

However, in the first case, the benefit–cost ratio is $12/6 = 2.0$, while in the second, the benefit–cost ratio is $10/4 = 2.5$. This example shows that care must be given in comparing analyses with differing benefit–cost ratios.

Which Benefits and Costs?

The task of identifying relevant benefits and costs as well as delineating between them is not a trivial one. The previous section has already described how external benefits and costs need to be included. When a large number of third parties are involved, the challenge of preparing accurate estimates could be very formidable. However, apart from practical considerations, it is important to sort out some conceptual issues that are often distorted in deliberations over the merits of a project. Perhaps the greatest source of confusion is found in the common practice of counting some costs as benefits and double counting some benefits.

To illustrate the former flaw, those who support the use of government funds to subsidize or build a major sports stadium will invariably and incorrectly argue that jobs will be created. Even where new jobs on balance are created, the wages paid to workers both during the construction phase as well as during the operations phase are costs, not benefits.

The benefits are measured by the value that the public places on the activities held in the stadium. Similarly, the jobs that may be created by multiplier effects originating from the initial expenditures should not be counted as benefits. Multiplier effects can result from the respending of income. Often, though, these effects are overestimated by a failure to recognize the diversion of expenditures from other activities. Finally, even if net unemployment is reduced by the project, the opportunity costs of the previously unemployed resources cannot be ignored. Thus, the general practice is to exclude employment effects except in areas of chronic unemployment.[4]

As for double counting, the value of land and commercial enterprises (e.g., parking lots, restaurants) situated close to the stadium may increase. It would be incorrect to include this added value as well as the additional business generated at those sites. The higher property values incorporate the capitalized value of the additional business. Thus, the same benefit would be counted twice.

A more direct application of double counting in health care involves the value of life and productivity. More specifically, some studies may try to estimate a value for the increased length of life or improvement in the quality of life. These estimates are often closely related to the additional incomes that can be earned by the individuals who are treated. If the study also includes the additional productivity from the reduced morbidity and mortality, there is a double counting. The two concepts are different sides of the same benefit.

THE VALUATION OF BENEFITS AND COSTS

As difficult as it can be to determine clearly the relevant benefits and costs, their valuation is perhaps a greater challenge. A prime reason for this difficulty lies in the absence of markets and corresponding prices for the goods and services resulting from the proposed project. This is particularly true for projects that involve public goods (e.g., national defense) and others that are intended to improve the quality of life, or where the benefits are intangible. In some cases, ingenious methods have been proposed to overcome the problem. For example, environmental improvements would be expected to raise property values or to reduce the compensation necessary to attract workers to the area that is being cleaned up. These are magnitudes that can often be estimated.

Assigning Monetary Values

However, even where private markets exist, the task of assigning monetary values is not always simple. Market prices and factor costs will not represent marginal social benefits and marginal social costs in cases of monopoly (monopsony) power and where

---

[4]This view is based on the idea that the opportunity cost of labor in areas with chronic unemployment is zero so that the jobs created do represent a benefit. However, Hyman (1990) stresses that those hired for the project will not necessarily come from those who were unemployed and also that there is always an opportunity cost associated with the funds used for the project. Thus, it would be unwise to ignore or minimize the labor opportunity costs even where unemployment rates are high.

there are significant third-party effects. For example, the MSB of a commodity that generates substantial external benefits will exceed its price. Here, the use of market prices will underestimate the MSB unless the third-party effects are also properly evaluated. Or consider the case where some of the inputs for a project are provided by monopoly sellers. From the standard monopoly model, it follows that the prices paid for such goods and services exceed the marginal cost of producing those goods or services. And it is the marginal costs that represent the opportunity costs of the resources needed for the project. These opportunity costs are the relevant costs for CBA.

We make one final observation with respect to the valuation of social projects. Suppose that Figure 24.2 represents the demand for flu inoculations, and that there are no external costs or benefits. If each vaccination is priced at $1, and 10,000 people choose to get inoculated, total spending and therefore revenues will be equal to $10,000, as shown by rectangle A. This rectangle, however, does not represent total benefits.

There is a justification also for including the *consumer surplus*. This is the amount consumers are willing to pay for a commodity over and above the amount they have to pay. The consumer surplus is measured by area B under the demand curve and above the price line. The social benefits consist of the sum of A and B, which is the area under the demand curve, and this value should be compared to the total cost of the project. Thus, apart from revealing the inadequacy of using projected revenues as a measure of total benefits, the correct concept points to the even more difficult task of estimating consumer demand to derive a measure of consumer surplus.

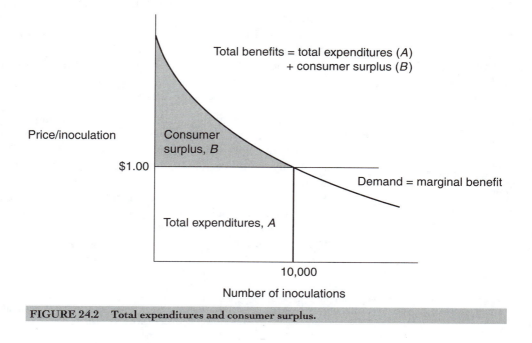

FIGURE 24.2   Total expenditures and consumer surplus.

The Life of the Project and the Discount Rate

Social projects involving capital expenditures, such as public hospitals and bridges, tend to have a long life. This does not affect the validity of CBA, but it does create difficulties. Clearly, benefits and cost have to be calculated far into the future. Thus, all the caveats described in the previous section apply for each year of the project's life.

Second, in some cases the selection of current projects may affect the kind and feasibility of future projects. For example, regulations that require firms to adopt a particular technology to control pollution may preclude the adoption of new, more efficient technologies that are subsequently available. Third, because future values have to be discounted, multiperiod analysis calls for a determination of the correct discount rate.

In the riskless, perfectly competitive, perfect information world of neoclassical economics, there is a single interest rate equal to the rate of return on private investment. This rate is also equal to the rate earned by savers. It reflects the rate at which they are willing to give up current consumption for future consumption (known as time preference). The appropriate discount rate for both private and public investment decisions would be this single interest rate.

In the real world of private investment decisions, the relevant rate is the rate at which the financial community is willing to supply funds for the project—that is, the rate the borrower pays for the funds.[5] The rate will typically vary with the life of the project as well as its riskiness in terms of the probability of default (i.e., a longer life and more risk require higher rates). How do these considerations of the borrowing rate and risk apply to social projects?

Though there remains ongoing controversy over this matter, it is widely accepted that the appropriate social discount rate is determined by the opportunities that are forgone in the private sector as a result of the social project.[6] The forgone opportunities reflect reduced private investment and consumption. Two crucial questions are whether the rate at which governments are able to borrow is the appropriate rate and whether adjustments to the rate are needed to account for the riskiness of the social project.

What Is the Appropriate Discount Rate?

Aside from rates paid by financial intermediaries, the cost of borrowing to the U.S. Treasury is the lowest interest rate for borrowers because there is no practical possibility of default. This risk-free rate certainly does not account for the riskiness of the project itself as measured by the degree to which benefits and costs are projected to vary around expected levels. Further, the risk-free rate certainly does not necessarily correspond to the opportunity cost of the private sector investment or consumption that is displaced by the government spending. The opportunity cost of displaced investment will be considerably higher, as reflected by pretax returns as well as by the risk premiums found in the private sector.

---

[5]Where one's own funds are used, the appropriate rate is the opportunity cost (i.e., rate of return on the next best alternative). Because the financing of individual projects cannot be separated in many organizations, the financial literature also emphasizes the weighted average cost of debt and equity capital.

[6]Baumol (1968) is often credited with providing the clearest rationale for this view.

For example, assume a risk-free rate of 5 percent, a risk premium of 1 percent on the one kind of risky corporate investment available, and a 50 percent corporate tax rate. Corporate investment must earn $2 \times (5 + 1)$ or 12 percent in order to provide investors with an after-tax rate of return of 6 percent.[7] The opportunity cost of displaced consumption will also be 12 percent because consumers forgo current consumption through a net return of 6 percent as well as a tax collection of 6 percent that could be used for the provision of social goods.

In actual practice, a variety of private activities with different opportunity costs will be displaced by the social project. Unless these displaced activities and their returns are actually determined, there is little guidance to the decision maker. Nevertheless, agencies of the federal government have recognized that the appropriate discount rate will exceed the government's borrowing rate.

Should this rate also reflect the riskiness of the social project? Stiglitz (1988) argues that it would be inappropriate to adjust the discount rate to account for higher risk because, for example, projects with high but uncertain costs in the latter stages are actually made relatively more attractive when a higher discount rate is used. Conversely, projects with high but uncertain benefits in later years are made relatively unattractive compared to projects with higher near-term benefits. These results arise because higher discount rates disproportionately reduce the present values of sums to be received well into the future as compared to discounting at lower rates.[8]

Stiglitz proposes introducing certainty equivalents to eliminate the biases that result from including a risk-adjustment factor in the discount rate. Under the certainty equivalent method, the uncertain net benefit in any period, often represented by a probability distribution of outcomes, is replaced by its equivalent, in the sense that the decision makers are indifferent between the former and a value to be received with certainty. The more risky the project, the lower will be the certainty equivalent to someone who is risk averse. The cost–benefit criterion represented by equation (24.1) is then applied using the certainty equivalents for each period.

Other Considerations

Though cost–benefit analysis is primarily intended to improve efficiency, as some of our examples have shown, changes in the distribution of income often result from a project. In cases of narrowly focused projects, there will tend to be a relatively small number of large gainers and perhaps many small losers. To the extent that society is concerned about equity, the distribution of the gainers and losers by income group should be a consideration. At the practical level, after projects are ranked according to their net benefits, decision makers could invoke informal judgments as to the relative effects on the distribution of income, and then adjust their rankings. More formally, Stiglitz proposes distributional weights through which the net benefits or losses of

---

[7]This reasoning follows the exposition found in Sassone and Schaffer (1978). The authors also describe the alternative arguments in favor of adopting social discount rates that are lower than opportunity costs.

[8]Compare the present values of $1 million to be received in 20 years at 5 percent and at 10 percent. An actual example of what happens to the net benefits as the discount rate changes in a project with a long life is found in Hanke and Walker (1974).

lower-income groups are given more weight than other groups. Of course, the method will still be subjective in that the weights themselves will necessarily reflect the judgments of the decision makers.

A second concern deals with the treatment of inflation. Conceptually, macroeconomic inflation is not a problem. Since estimates of the inflation rate often turn out to be incorrect, it is best to measure both benefits and cost in current or real terms and then discount at the real (inflation-free) discount rate. If an inflation factor is introduced, then the discount rate should be increased by that inflation rate to get the nominal rate.[9] It is important, though, that the discount rate reflect that inflation factor and not some other rate.

Apart from the treatment of the overall inflation rate in the economy, it is important to determine if there will be changes in the relative prices (real prices and costs) for the goods related to the project. For example, the real cost of health care services has increased markedly in the last 30 years. Projections of real price changes can be problematic, but they would have to be made.

COST–BENEFIT ANALYSIS IN HEALTH CARE

The usefulness of CBA to evaluate health care programs can be especially troublesome because of the need, in many instances, to place values on human life, increased longevity, and improvements in health status. In addition, a major benefit of a proposed program can be the averted hospital, physician, and other health care costs. With wide variations in treatment costs for some conditions, these costs can be difficult to estimate, especially for those conditions requiring long-term care and where rapid changes in medical technology are also taking place.

Valuing Human Life

One of the most difficult but often unavoidable tasks in health care CBA is to place a value on human life. There are two widely used approaches. The first, known as the human capital approach, estimates the present value of an individual's future earnings. This approach has been especially favored in legal applications that require estimates of damages. It also measures the loss of national output from mortality and morbidity or the production gains from saving and extending life.[10] On the other hand, the human capital approach is flawed as a welfare measure in that it does not directly measure an individual's willingness to pay to avoid death, injury, or illness. It is this willingness to pay—the second major method—that corresponds to the welfare losses or gains used by economists in efficiency criteria.

Though measuring willingness to pay may look like a formidable if not impossible task, various ingenious approaches have been developed. These include estimates of wage differentials among occupations that vary by likelihood of death and injury,

---

[9]There is actually a divergence between the two methods. A correct statement of the relationship between real (r) and nominal (n) rates is that $(1 + n) = (1 + r)(1 + f)$ where f is the expected inflation rate. If the cross-product term rf is ignored, as it is previously, the two methods will be equal.

[10]Blomquist's (1981) review of several studies found a range of $330,000 to $2.5 million in 1979 dollars.

since individuals must be compensated (bribed) for undertaking more risky work. The objective is to measure the additional compensation for the expected decrease in mortality and increased probabilities of injury and morbidity. Similar applications are found through estimates of willingness to pay for safety, as with automobile air bags and antilock brakes.[11] Table 24.1 illustrates the wide range of estimates that one investigator has found from various applications of the willingness to pay approach. The wide range calls for explanations. Do households underestimate or overestimate risks for some activities? Are there inadequacies in the underlying data and methods? Until such questions are answered, the valuation of benefits will remain problematic and will therefore limit the role of CBA.[12]

Apart from the need for future research that will further refine these estimates, the recent literature also focuses on the relationship between the human capital, willingness to pay, and other approaches.[13] Will there be systematic relationships between the measures? Though there are still no definitive answers, it is believed that value of life, as measured by willingness to pay, exceeds the discounted value of future earnings because the latter ignores the value of nonmarket activities.

TABLE 24.1   How Much Is One Life Worth?

Range of implied values of a human life, extrapolated from what people pay for various products, services, or regulations that can change the risk of death

Basis for Calculation	Value of Life (1987 dollars)
Desire for prompt coronary care	$ 66,000
Automobile air bag purchases	360,000
Smoke detector purchases	373,000
EPA requirement for sulfur scrubbers	500,000
Seat belt usage	541,000
Wage premiums for dangerous police work	850,000
EPA regulation of radium content in water	2,500,000
Wage premiums for dangerous factory jobs	3,200,000
OSHA rules for workplace safety	3,500,000
Premium tire usage	3,600,000
Desire for safer airline travel	11,800,000

Source: The Wall Street Journal, December 12, 1988, p. A7.

---

[11]There is actually a distinction between willingness to avoid risks and the bribe needed to incur risks. The former is constrained by a person's income, and thus willingness to pay can be highly income dependent. There is no such constraint with a bribe in that the needed bribe can exceed a person's income.

[12]Cropper and colleagues (1992) determined that the EPA weighed benefits and costs in decisions to ban pesticide use. However, they estimated that the implicit value placed on a life was $35 million for applicators of a pesticide but only $60,000 for consumers who expose themselves through pesticide residues on food.

[13]See, for example, Linnerooth (1979), Blomquist (1981), and Berger et al. (1987).

Cost–Benefit Analyses of Disease-Screening Programs

Notwithstanding the shortcomings of CBA, one can find exemplary studies in the literature. To illustrate such a study,[14] as well as to highlight methods that have been used to value benefits (including intangibles), we examine a CBA of various screening tests used to detect gonorrhea in asymptomatic women. The study was published by Goddeeris and Bronken (GB) in 1985. Screening for various forms of cancer, sexually transmitted diseases, and other conditions is commonly endorsed or proposed. The GB example provides a framework that is helpful to a consideration of the broader issue of screening programs.

Screening will result in four possibilities: true positive, true negative, false positive, false negative. By considering the probabilities that individuals with positives (including false positives) return for treatment and that some may have adverse reactions, the GB study developed an expression for the expected net benefit per individual screened. The costs include screening costs, time costs, and treatment costs, including those for adverse reactions, and subsequent treatment costs that are averted.

The benefits consist of three components: the improvement in treatment quality resulting from early detection, the value of reassurance from negative test results, and the external benefit that earlier detection has in limiting the spread of the disease.[15] For the first component, GB distinguishes among benefits representing future medical costs that are averted, greater productivity, and other subjective benefits.

With regard to future medical costs, the study concentrated on pelvic inflammatory disease, the main complication avoided by early detection. The authors estimated that this condition is prevented in 15 percent of the true positive cases. For this condition, lost productivity was determined to be two weeks for those treated on an outpatient basis and six weeks for those who are hospitalized. A consensus method involving a panel of physicians and social workers was used to provide a simple majority consensus estimate of the benefit of pain and suffering per case ($15,000) and the benefits of avoiding other possible conditions ($350) such as infertility. Consensus methods were also used to place values on reassurance ($10), mild adverse reaction ($15), and a false positive case ($4,500).

Table 24.2 shows the per-case net benefits of three alternatives for the estimated values of the parameters. These consist of the modified Thayer-Martin (TM) test; the Gonozyme immunoassay; and a slower, but less expensive, Gonozyme immunoassay. Only the TM test, the most common test, produced positive net benefits per patient screened at the baseline parameter values. In general, the results were not very sensitive to other estimates of the parameters. Thus, the authors concluded that TM is both worthwhile and superior to the alternatives considered (although there are many more alternatives that were not considered).

The analysis in Table 24.2 reflects a larger policy debate with respect to disease screening. The major categories of positive benefits from screening programs accrue from the treatment of disease for people who were unaware that they had a disease.

---

[14]See also Weisbrod (1971) for an early, but classic, cost–benefit study involving research on poliomyelitis.

[15]The study did not attempt to estimate the third-party effects. All monetary values are measured in 1983 dollars.

TABLE 24.2   Net Benefits of Gonorrhea Screening

| | | Screening Alternative | |
	TM	Gonozyme Fast	Gonozyme Slow
Dollar values			
S (screening cost)	10	20	13
T (treatment cost)	28.5	21	28.5
R (reassurance)	10	10	10
B (benefit from early treatment)	2,869	2,869	2,869
A (adverse reaction cost)	15	15	15
F (false positive cost)	4,500	4,500	4,500
Net benefits V	18.6	−124.7	−118.7

Source: Goddeeris and Bronken (1985, Table 3).

This is directly related to the *prevalence* of the disease. The major costs of the screening program are related to the unneeded treatments that accrue to patients who are incorrectly judged to have a disease, reflected by the *false positive* rate.

Russell (1994) looks at three major screening initiatives: (1) the Pap smear for cervical cancer (for women); (2) screening tests for prostate cancer (for men); (3) high blood cholesterol. She notes that in many cases the probability of a false positive result from the screen (yielding major costs) is greater than the probability of disease prevalence (treatment of which provides major benefits). Thus, cost–benefit analysis of screening programs in which false positives rates are high may indicate net economic losses due to the unnecessary treatment, even though the diseases that they address may be life-threatening.

QUALITY-ADJUSTED LIFE YEARS (QALYs)

The health care community has often resisted placing dollar values on the benefits of health care. As a result, alternative methods of evaluating these benefits have been derived, and one of the most prominent is the calculation of quality-adjusted life years (QALYs).

Following Wagstaff (1991), a QALY score is calculated by weighting each remaining year of an individual's life by the expected quality of life in the year in question. The expected quality is a probability-weighted average of quality-of-life scores associated with each of the possible health states the individual might find himself or herself in. Consider a man at age 70 who may be expected to live 20 more years. From age 70 to 80, we expect his health to be perfect, but due to a variety of illness possibilities between the ages of 80 to 90, we expect each of these years to provide only half the quality of life of the previous ten. Thus, although he will be expected to live for 20 more years, he has only 15 QALYs left, or:

$$15 = (10 \text{ years} \cdot 1 \text{ QALY/year}) + (10 \text{ year} \cdot 0.5 \text{ QALY/year})$$

Analysts frequently refer to the quality-of-life score as a utility score. It can be linked to the costs through *cost–utility analysis* in the following manner. Consider treatments for two different diseases. The treatment for Disease C would improve the quality of life by 0.1 QALY per year, while the treatment for Disease D would improve the quality of life by 0.2 QALY per year. Comparing costs per QALY for the different treatments would provide insights into which treatment is more cost-effective per QALY. One decision rule would be to choose those treatments with the lowest cost per QALY.

Wagstaff provides a useful discussion of resource allocation under QALYs. Consider two types of individuals, some like Alex (type A) and some like Betty (type B). In Figure 24.3, in the absence of treatment, both Alex and Betty enjoy the same number of QALYs, $A_1 = B_1$, at point M. Additional societal resources could be used to improve their health to A^* and B^*, respectively, on the health frontier. The location and shape of the health frontier, the bowed-out curve in Figure 24.3, depend on the resources available, the capacity of Alex and Betty to benefit from health care, and the costs to society of that health care. The frontier's bowed-out shape assumes that health care is subject to a diminishing marginal product. Any point on the frontier, including A^* or B^*, represents a feasible result from a given increment of societal resources.

Society's health may be defined as the sum of QALYs, or $A^* + B^*$. There are several points of interest in this graph. As drawn, the frontier in Figure 24.3 implies that Betty can be treated at lower cost than Alex. Alternatively, the same resources will provide more additional QALYs to Betty than to Alex; that is, B_{max} is greater than A_{max}. The sum of A^* and B^* is greatest at point R. This is determined as the point where a line with a slope of -1.0 is tangent to the frontier. We can verify this by realizing that going southeast (northwest) from R, along the frontier, an additional 1 QALY for Alex (Betty) reduces Betty's (Alex's) QALYs by *more than* 1, thus reducing the sum.

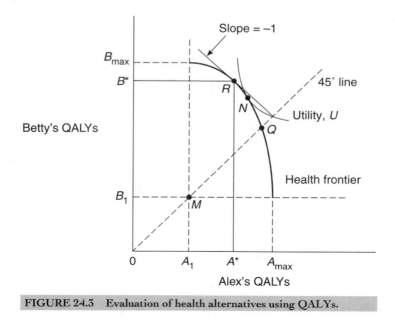

FIGURE 24.3   Evaluation of health alternatives using QALYs.

Point *R* is the most cost-efficient point for society (i.e., Alex and Betty) in terms of QALYs per dollar, but it provides more QALYs for Betty than for Alex. An allocation in which Alex and Betty have the same level of QALYs (but where relatively more resources are provided to Alex) is determined at point *Q*. This point is defined through the intersection of a 45-degree line, which by definition provides equal numbers of QALYs to both, with the health frontier. Alternatively, society may decide through a social welfare function (as defined in Chapter 20) that some level of inequality is appropriate, as defined by the tangency at point *N* of the health frontier and social indifference curve *U*.

Economists' criticism of the QALY method is that it assigns the same quality-of-life scores to everyone. Furthermore, these scores are typically derived by groups of clinical experts in experimental settings with little relationship to market parameters. In resource allocation discussion using QALYs, people in the same health state by definition receive identical utilities. This is certainly at odds with the fundamental premise behind market willingness to pay curves that underlie cost–benefit analysis.

However, one must criticize many cost–benefit studies as well in that they assign mean values (to the "average person") to benefits. This practice essentially treats all individuals as identical. It is necessary to derive better methods of measuring the health improvements that accompany health care initiatives, assigning monetary values to these improvements, and considering the distributional aspects of the initiatives and health improvements.

Cost–Benefit Analysis and Treatment Efficacy

The analysis from Goddeeris and Bronken indicates an important distinction between cost–benefit analysis and the traditional clinical measures of treatment efficacy. Note that there were three fundamental benefits from a medical procedure.

1. The patient would be more productive at his or her job.
2. Regardless of productivity on a job, the person would feel better.
3. The person would live longer, which would allow him or her either to be more productive on the job, or to feel better.

All three of these benefits are ones that individuals in principle would be willing to pay for and should, therefore, be included as economic benefits. Moreover, it is quite possible that a procedure could be pronounced as economically beneficial, even if the person lived no longer than without it but the quality of life was improved dramatically.

Clinicians focus almost entirely on the third criterion, whether or not a person lives longer. Treatment efficacy refers to the probability of extended life and the quality of life in the extended period. Treatments that do not extend life are not considered to pass a treatment efficacy criterion.

This issue has arisen in the analysis of prostate cancer screening. In contrast to the analysis of gonorrhea screening, where there is a menu of treatments with proven efficacy for those who test positive, prostate cancer treatment is less certain. It has not been proven to extend life and can in fact lead to impotence and incontinence. Moreover, there are some forms of prostate cancer that might progress so slowly that "watchful waiting" is preferred to surgical or other treatments. Littrup, Goodman, and Mettlin (1993) find that in the hands of skilled urologists, prostate cancer screening provides net benefits of the same order of magnitude as mammography. These benefits occur from the sum of increased productivity and improved quality of life.

In contrast, Krahn et al. (1994) assert that widespread prostate cancer screening should not be supported because it decreases quality-adjusted life expectancy (related to QALYs) regardless of monetary benefits. The multidimensional nature of the economic benefits contrasts with more limited clinical measures and may support policies that would be opposed on treatment efficacy grounds alone.

COST-EFFECTIVENESS ANALYSIS

In light of the practical limitations of CBA, especially when a program has widespread third-party benefits that are largely in the form of intangibles, cost-effectiveness analysis (CEA) represents a more modest approach to program evaluation. The goal of CEA is to minimize costs in achieving a particular objective. In cost-effectiveness analysis, one assumes that the objective is desirable even though the benefits cannot be evaluated in monetary terms (so that, strictly speaking, none of the alternative projects may actually yield positive net benefits were it feasible to compute the net benefits). Though the valuation of benefits is not considered, all of the problems in determining costs remain.

Advantages of CEA

The task under CEA is conceptually similar to the production decision of the firm, which is to produce a given level of output from among alternative production methods at the lowest possible cost. Also, as in the firm-production decision, the objective must be quantifiable and similar across projects. Otherwise, a clear relationship between costs and output cannot be determined, and programs cannot be compared and evaluated because their outputs are not similar.

Cost-effectiveness analysis has been widely applied by the Department of Defense to determine, for example, the most cost-efficient means of achieving a particular level of military preparedness. Objectives can be quantified, say, in terms of ability to deploy forces, and the most efficient means of achieving the objectives is estimated. Note that CBA is not feasible in such cases because the benefits of the military capability cannot readily be evaluated in monetary terms. Or, to take another example, there is considerable current interest in many communities in recycling to the point where mandatory recycling is becoming more widespread. Assuming that a community has decided on the goal of reducing garbage, cost-effectiveness analysis can be used to compare recycling with incineration and other waste management strategies.

Finally, CEA can be a useful first step toward undertaking a cost–benefit study.[16] If the analysts run into significant problems in undertaking a CEA, there is little likelihood that a CBA will be feasible. Conversely, good progress in developing a CEA can

---

[16]See Klarman (1982).

often determine whether it is possible to take the next step and extend the CEA into a cost–benefit study.

An Application: The Sixth Stool Guaiac Test

We earlier described the problems of valuing human life and other benefits. CEA completely sidesteps this issue. Nevertheless, CEA can provide extremely helpful evidence for improving medical practice through the evaluation of treatment techniques that have a homogeneous measure of output such as saving a human life or detecting an illness. The lengthy debate over the sixth stool guaiac test for colonic cancer illustrates both the strengths and weaknesses of CEA.

In 1975, Neuhauser and Lewicki studied a protocol recommended for screening cancer of the colon. The protocol consisted of six sequential stool tests for occult blood. These are called guaiac tests. A barium-enema procedure is administered if any of the tests are positive. From other sources, the authors assumed that 72 persons out of a population of 10,000 who are screened have colonic cancer and that the probability of detection is 91.66 from any single test, with a false positive rate of 36.51 percent.

The authors calculated that the second test will detect 99.3 percent of the cancer cases $(91.67 + 91.67 (100 - 91.67))$. Using similar computations, Table 24.3 shows the number of cases detected in a population of 10,000, the incremental gain in detection, and the associated total and incremental costs for each test. The total and incremental screening costs assume values of $4 for the initial guaiac test, $1 for each additional test, and $100 for a barium-enema procedure. The last two columns in the table show the marginal and average cost per case detected. These figures are determined by dividing the incremental and total screening costs by the incremental gain in cases detected and the number of cases detected, respectively.

The results are startling. The average cost per case detected is small and increases relatively slowly to $2,451 after six tests. Based on average costs, the recommended

TABLE 24.3   Cancer Detection and Screening Costs with Sequential Guaiac Tests

No. of Tests	Cancer Detection		Screening Costs ($)			
	No. of Cases	Incremental Gain	Total[a]	Incremental	Marginal[b]	Average[c]
1	65.9469	65.9469	77,511	77,511	1,175	1,175
2	71.4424	5.4956	107,690	30,179	5,492	1,507
3	71.9004	0.4580	130,199	22,509	49,150	1,810
4	71.9385	0.0382	148,116	17,917	469,534	2,059
5	71.9417	0.0032	163,141	15,024	4,724,695	2,268
6	71.9420	0.0003	176,331	13,190	47,107,214	2,451

[a]Calculated by addition of cost of guaiac stool testing on 10,000 people and cost of barium-enema examination on all of those with positive tests.

[b]Calculated by division of incremental cost by incremental gain for cancer detected.

[c]Calculated by division of total cost by no. of true positive results detected.

Source: Neuhauser and Lewicki (1975, Table 2).

protocol seems more than reasonable. However, the point of the article is to focus on marginal costs as a basis for decisions. The marginal cost rises rapidly and exceeds $47 million for the sixth test. Even though no monetary value is placed on the benefits of detection (this is not a cost–benefit study), by almost any reasonable standard, the sixth test is not worthwhile.

This investigation has been regarded by some as a model of CEA and the application of marginal analysis. Perhaps, as a result of its standing, it has been the object of justifiable criticism. Among other oversights, recent articles point out that the assumed true positive and false positive values are based on limited information and have been improperly calculated.[17] Even small changes in these rates could have large impacts on the marginal cost of detection, although marginal costs may still run to the thousands of dollars.

CONCLUSIONS

Cost–benefit analysis is a methodology intended to improve the efficient use of resources allocated through the public sector. The efficiency concept is a social welfare concept in that the value of the social project to users and third parties is compared with the opportunity costs of providing the project.

The high level of government involvement in the health economy suggests an extensive role for CBA through a wide variety of applications. These would include screening programs, evaluating alternative treatment procedures and new technology, and medical research. Cost–benefit analysis can also be applied to regulatory measures, such as those affecting the costs and length of time of new drug product development.

Despite its potential, CBA applications in health care are still less prevalent than one would expect. Difficulties in evaluating benefits, especially the value of life and improved quality of life, place limits on CBA and its usefulness to decision makers. As a result, CEA and even less formal assessments of the overall merits of proposed social interventions are more commonly relied upon. Unless improvements are made in estimates of the value of life and other "intangibles," to the point where such estimates are consistent and credible, it is likely that CBA will remain a potentially powerful but underused technique.[18]

Summary

1. Unlike private decisions made in the marketplace, (social) cost–benefit analysis (CBA) involves evaluation of social benefits and social costs in public project analysis. Often markets do not exist to evaluate the benefits and costs entailed in such projects.

---

[17]See Brown and Burrows (1990) and Gastonis (1990).

[18]A 1993 issue of *Medical Care* did list over 3,000 studies using CBA and CEA analysis, however. See Elixhauser (1993).

2. CBA rests on the principle that society's welfare will be improved whenever the benefits of a project exceed its costs.

3. CBA represents an example of marginal analysis. The social optimum is achieved where marginal social benefit is equal to marginal social cost.

4. Though in principle CBA appears simple, it can be difficult to apply. The difficulties include identifying all the relevant costs and benefits, including third-party effects, assigning monetary values, and making projections over many years for projects with long lives.

5. The monetary values of future net benefits must be discounted. The choice of the appropriate discount rate remains controversial.

6. Health care projects often involve the need to value human life. The human capital approach and the willingness to pay approach have been the most widely applied methods.

7. Quality-adjusted life years (QALYs) are calculated by weighting each remaining year of an individual's life by the expected quality of life in the year in question. The expected quality is a probability-weighted average of quality-of-life scores associated with each of the possible health states that might occur for an individual.

8. Cost-effectiveness analysis (CEA), a truncated form of CBA, can be used when it is difficult to value the benefits of a project. CEA is used to compare the costs of alternative projects that achieve some desired objective.

9. The objective in CEA must nevertheless be quantifiable. Thus, costs are expressed, for example, as the cost of detecting a case of cancer or the cost of a year of life saved.

Discussion Questions

1. In what ways is social cost–benefit analysis similar to a consumer's decision on allocating his or her resources, or to a firm's investment decision? In what ways is it different?

2. Why do third-party effects have to be considered in the social decision?

3. Why are jobs created as a result of a social project not normally considered as a benefit?

4. Some suggest that a dollar value cannot be placed on life; that is, life is priceless. Explain the dilemma to social decision making that would be created by this view.

5. Why is the discount rate controversial? That is, so long as one discounts all projects that are considered at the same discount rate, is there a need to worry whether the rate is too high or too low?

6. What are some possible reasons to explain the kinds of EPA decisions described in footnote 12, under which a $35 million value is being placed on the life of applicators of a pesticide but only $60,000 on consumers?

7. How are QALYs similar to economic benefits? How do they differ?

8. Distinguish between cost–benefit analysis and cost-effectiveness analysis.

9. Cost–benefit analysis often is presented in terms of willingness to pay for a project. How is willingness to pay related to consumer demand?

Exercises

1. Using Figure 24.1, explain why a pollution abatement program that reduces discharge beyond Q_1 is inefficient.

2. Consider the following two projects. Both have costs of $5,000 in Year 1. Project 1 provides benefits of $2,000 in each of the first 4 years only. The second provides benefits of $2,000 for each of Years 6 to 10 only. Compute the net benefits using a discount rate of 6 percent. Repeat using a discount rate of 12 percent. What can you conclude from this exercise?

3. Consider the following table of costs and benefits from a governmental policy to clean the water in a local area.

Level of Abatement	Total Costs	Total Benefits
0%	$ 0	$ 0
10	10	80
20	22	150
30	40	200
40	70	240
50	105	280
60	150	320
70	210	350
80	280	375
90	350	385
100	420	390

   a. What level of abatement is most efficient by general economic criteria?
   b. Would a 70 percent level of abatement pass a benefit–cost test? Is it efficient?
   c. How would you respond to those who argue for 100 percent abatement?

4. Consider a project that costs $10,000 today. It will provide benefits of $4,000 at the end of Year 1, $3,500 at the end of Year 2, and $3,500 at the end of Year 3. If the discount rate is 6 percent, will this project be approved using cost–benefit analysis? Would your answer change if the discount rate is 5 percent? 4 percent?

5. Consider a hypothetical three-stage screening test for a cancer with the following rates of detection and costs:

	Number of Cases	
Stage	Detected	Total Costs
1	100	$200,000
2	105	$260,000
3	106	$300,000

   a. Calculate the average cost per cancer detected in the three stages.
   b. Calculate the marginal cost per cancer detected in the three stages.
   c. Suppose that the marginal benefit per treated case is $10,000 per person. What would be the optimal screening, given the costs?

CHAPTER 25

Economics of Mental Health and Substance Abuse

- ■ Incidence of Ailments

- ■ Nature of the Ailments and Treatments

- ■ Offset Effects

- ■ Treatment Supply

- ■ Treatment Demand

- ■ Financing

- ■ Conclusions

Over the past 25 years, there has been increased attention in the health care community to the treatment of mental health and substance abuse (either alcoholism or drug abuse). While formerly relegated to large state-run mental health hospitals, MH/SA, or alternatively ADM (alcoholism-drug-mental health) treatment and coverage have become major parts of the health budget and have assumed a major role in health care policy.

MH/SA illnesses and their treatments are different in many ways from most other types of health care. Most prominently, they are characterized by the stigma of the disease. People who need mental health therapy, or those with alcoholism or drug abuse problems, may be forced into treatment by involuntary commitment. They may also be shamed into seeking treatment, or in fact shamed into not seeking treatment.

Second, MH/SA illnesses, like many other chronic diseases, may represent long-term conditions without explicit indicators of cure. As a result, costs may be spread out over long periods of time; alternatively, outcomes of the treatment may be very difficult to measure. The frequent lack of conventional indicators makes it difficult to measure efficacy (does treatment work?) and costs of different treatment modalities (such as inpatient or outpatient care). Moreover, the difficulty in measuring treatment outcomes,

583

along with the stigmas attached to the diseases, may lead to particular skepticism in cost-effectiveness or cost–benefit evaluations regarding treatment.

In this chapter, we examine the special characteristics of MH/SA illnesses. We start with the difficulties in measuring the incidence of the various components (alcoholism, drug abuse, mental health). We follow with a discussion of types and locations of treatment, and we continue with an examination of aspects of demand and supply of care. We finish with a discussion of the importance of the mechanisms used to finance MH/SA care, and the implications of health care financing in a system of managed care.

INCIDENCE OF AILMENTS

Like other ailments, MH/SA ailments exact economic costs on patients who have them and those who must care for the patients. The costs to the individuals include reduced productivity, reduced quality of life regardless of productivity, and increased probability of death from conditions as various as suicide, cirrhosis of the liver, drunk driving, drug overdose, or AIDS. The costs to the society include a range of medical costs including inpatient and outpatient treatment as well as drug therapy. Criminal or violent behavior toward others may impose additional societal costs.

Where MH/SA conditions differ from many other conditions is in the stigma that adheres to those who present them.[1] Patients presumably have little embarrassment at presenting broken bones, infections, burns, or other traumas, but psychiatric disorder ailments such as psychoses or depression are often viewed as less acceptable by society. People prefer not to be viewed as "crazy" and may seek to hide the ailments.

Drug abuse and alcohol abuse present concerns that are similar to the analysis of mental health conditions. Although there are ample indications that various forms of substance abuse represent illness, there are numerous scholars and practitioners who believe that substance abuse is not a disease, and that substance abusers are responsible for their own ailments, and hence merit less attention than others with more conventional illnesses.

Medical ethicists Philip Boyle and Daniel Callahan (1995) discuss the unequal treatment between mental health and other health services:

> As is generally acknowledged by researchers but not the public, the causes of this unequal treatment arise in part from deep-seated convictions, if not biases. Service scandals and widely publicized crimes committed by homeless persons with mental illness fuel discrimination. In combination, these beliefs have conspired to minimize treatment and funding for mentally ill persons. Unlike those with a physical illness, persons with mental illness are often perceived to be the cause of their own problems and, for that reason, to be less entitled to generous benefits (pp. 9–10).

---

[1]Other conditions that often carry stigmas include sexually transmitted diseases, pregnancy out of wedlock, and epilepsy.

Moreover, mental health and substance abuse problems often occur together and are termed *comorbidities.* Figure 25.1 presents a Venn diagram that shows how alcoholism, mental health, and substance abuse conditions may overlap.

Goodman, Nishiura, and Hankin (1995) analyze a sample of employed workers and their dependents who worked for a group of large U.S. corporations from 1989 through 1991. All members of the sample had one or more "events" of either mental health, alcoholism, or substance abuse treatment in a three-year period. Figure 25.1 shows that of the 98,985 people with some inpatient MH/SA treatment, 76.8 percent had treatment for mental illness alone.

Although mental health was the most prevalent diagnosis, 55.3 percent of the 15,823 patients receiving inpatient treatment for alcoholism also had diagnoses for mental illness, substance abuse, or both. Of the 11,441 patients receiving drug abuse treatment, 56.6 percent also had diagnoses for mental illness, alcoholism, or both. Similar percentages are applicable to outpatient treatment as well.[2]

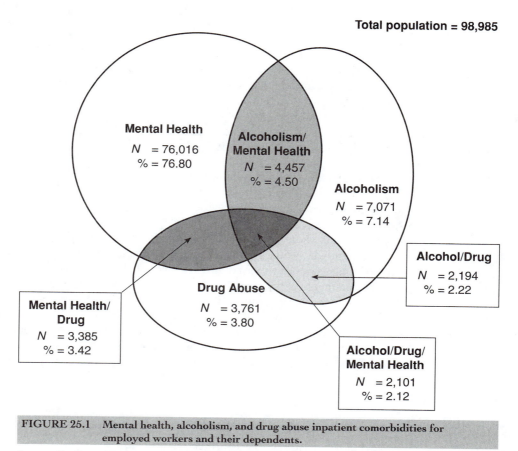

Total population = 98,985

Mental Health
N = 76,016
% = 76.80

Alcoholism/Mental Health
N = 4,457
% = 4.50

Alcoholism
N = 7,071
% = 7.14

Alcohol/Drug
N = 2,194
% = 2.22

Mental Health/Drug
N = 3,385
% = 3.42

Drug Abuse
N = 3,761
% = 3.80

Alcohol/Drug/Mental Health
N = 2,101
% = 2.12

FIGURE 25.1   Mental health, alcoholism, and drug abuse inpatient comorbidities for employed workers and their dependents.

Source: Goodman, Nishiura, and Hankin (1995).

Given these problems, the measurement of mental health incidence is a topic of considerable interest, if only to discover the extent of the problem. Kessler et al. (1994) present the most up-to-date estimates of lifetime and 12-month prevalence of 14 DSM-III-R psychiatric disorders from the National Comorbidity Survey (NCS).[3] The NCS was a national survey of noninstitutionalized persons between the ages of 15 and 54, conducted from September 1990 to February 1992. The NCS claimed to be the first survey to administer a structured psychiatric interview to a national probability sample in the United States.

Kessler and his colleagues estimated that nearly 50 percent of the respondents experienced at least one lifetime psychiatric disorder, and 40 percent of those sought professional help. This implies that 20 percent of the population saw a mental health provider in their lifetime.

It is appropriate to put such numbers in context. On the one hand, the fact that 60 percent of those with at least one lifetime psychiatric disorder did not seek professional help could be interpreted as a cause for alarm. On the other hand, there are numerous illnesses that come and go (the common cold probably has an annual incidence of at least 50 percent), without necessarily having permanent impacts on people's health. While incidence of mental health (as well as substance abuse) disorders is an important measure, particularly where underreporting is probable, any inferences about inadequate care must pass more rigorous analyses regarding marginal benefits and marginal costs. Phrased differently, treatment must be effective in order for its absence to be a problem.

NATURE OF THE AILMENTS AND TREATMENTS

Mental health and substance abuse ailments are chronic in nature. Following a clinical diagnosis, there are wide ranges of treatments, ranging from inpatient hospitalization to outpatient care (in clinics or providers' offices) to self-help groups, such as Alcoholics Anonymous.

Although there are numerous methods of measuring treatment outcomes, the chronic nature of the disease makes treatment evaluation difficult. If after treatment the patient halts his or her pattern of drug or alcohol abuse for a year, and then starts again, has the treatment been successful or not? If the patient has a relapse of mental illness due to a failure to take the prescribed drugs, does this constitute a failure in treatment? Critics of the evaluation of mental health or substance abuse regimens may gain insights from examining other chronic diseases such as asthma or diabetes.

Mental health and substance abuse treatment has evolved from the large-scale institutionalization that persisted into the 1950s, into a mixture of inpatient care, out-

---

[2]Of the 275,010 people with some outpatient MH/SA treatment, 90.1 percent had treatment for mental illness alone; 51.4 percent of the 18,138 patients receiving treatment for alcoholism also had diagnoses for mental illness, substance abuse, or both; and 56.6 percent of the 12,949 patients receiving drug abuse treatment also had diagnoses for mental illness, alcoholism, or both.

[3]While *incidence* refers to new cases, *prevalence* refers to the number of existing cases in a specified time period. The terms, while related, are not interchangeable.

patient care, and other less formal treatments. Table 25.1 shows how numbers of mental hospital inmates declined steadily.

In 1955, there were 3.4 times as many inpatient care episodes as outpatient care episodes; by 1983, there were 2.7 times as many outpatient as inpatient care episodes (Mechanic and Rochefort 1990), and the outpatient ratio has certainly been increasing since then. In the decade of the 1970s alone, the daily inpatient census was reduced by more than 50 percent. Reducing the inpatient component of MH/SA care has the potential to reduce costs considerably, if the quality of the care can be maintained. In the mental health field other possible substitutions involve shifts from mental health specialists to more general providers.

Goodman et al. (1994) examined the potential substitution of inpatient and outpatient alcoholism treatments using insurance claims data from a large Midwestern employer. The researchers looked at inpatient and outpatient alcoholism treatments, and inpatient and outpatient psychiatric treatments, and contrasted them to other non-MH/SA treatments in other settings.

The authors computed price indices for the various treatments, and they used those indices to calculate substitution elasticities among the various types and locations of treatment (readers may wish to review elasticity of substitution from Chapter 13). They found that the best substitute for inpatient alcoholism treatment was not outpatient alcoholism treatment (a relatively inexpensive treatment), but rather inpatient psychiatric treatment. Moreover, outpatient alcoholism treatment was not even as good a substitute for inpatient alcoholism treatment as outpatient psychiatric treatment was for inpatient psychiatric treatment. It should be emphasized that these results were specific to one company and one insurance plan, but they indicate that although outpatient treatment is considerably less expensive than inpatient treatment, given the way the care is actually provided, potential savings from substituting outpatient for inpatient care may be limited.

Wells and Sturm (1995) address substitution from mental health specialists to more general providers in the treatment of depression. Clinical depression is defined as a period of intense, often continuous feelings of sadness and hopelessness accompa-

TABLE 25.1   Average Daily Inpatient Census of Mental Patients, by Type of Organization, 1969–1988

Type	1969	1975	1979	1983	1986	1988
State and county mental hospitals	367,629	193,380	138,600	116,236	107,056	99,869
Veterans Administration medical centers	47,140	32,123	28,693	20,342	21,242	19,602
Private psychiatric hospitals	11,608	12,058	13,901	16,467	23,475	29,698
Nonfederal general hospitals with psychiatric services	17,808	22,874	23,110	34,328	34,437	35,902
Residential centers for children	12,406	16,164	18,054	15,826	22,650	23,092
All other (including community mental health centers)	6,240	10,989	11,026	20,970	19,670	19,673
Total	468,831	287,588	233,384	224,169	228,530	227,836

Source: Manderscheid and Sonnenschein (1992).

nied by cognitive and somatic symptoms that can require treatment. Prevailing diagnostic systems distinguish between two major categories of mood disorders: major depression, a severe episode of daily depressed mood accompanied by symptoms such as suicidal thoughts, weight loss, poor sleep, and poor concentration, lasting two weeks; and chronic depression, often called *dysthemia*.

Although a shift from mental health specialists to generalized medical providers can reduce treatment costs, Wells and Sturm find that it also produces poorer functional outcomes and does little to improve the value of care. Care for depression is much cheaper in general medical practice than in psychiatry, but health outcomes are worse in general practice because general medical patients are less likely to receive appropriate care during their visits. The authors caution, however, that psychiatric care is not more economically efficient because the higher rates of appropriate care are accompanied by greater use of ineffective minor tranquilizers and high visit costs.

OFFSET EFFECTS

Early studies of mental health and substance abuse treatment appeared to document an impressive finding that subsequent to treatment initiation, the costs and utilization of other types of non-MH/SA treatment also fell. It was thought that MH/SA treatment not only addressed the MH/SA conditions, but in addition it "offset" other sorts of treatment. It was argued, for example, that people with mental disorders presented vague and diffuse physical complaints to primary care physicians in an effort to receive treatment for underlying psychiatric symptoms. Once specialized mental health care was initiated, it was hypothesized that these visits to primary care providers would decline.

This type of analysis has been adapted to the broader policy framework by calculating substance abuse offsets with respect to reduced crime (i.e., treating people for substance abuse makes them less likely to rob others to pay for their habit). In this adaptation, MH/SA treatment not only improves people's health, but it also reduces utilization and costs of other societal resources.

Wells and Sturm, among others, note the weaknesses of many of the offset analyses. They point out that most studies of offset effects can neither distinguish between mental and physical health reasons for visits, nor can they classify visits according to provider type. As a result, researchers may see spurious "cost offsets" because patients of mental health or substance abuse specialists already have fewer visits to general medical providers than patients who receive their care in the general medical sector and whose visits are misclassified as medical visits. Furthermore, many of the analyses identify the impact of MH/SA treatment initiation as the "trigger" that reduces costs of episodes that are already declining in their intensity and need for treatment.

Many care providers, including clinicians who treat mental health and substance abuse, have viewed skepticism of offset effects as attacks on the effectiveness of MH/SA treatment. Yet, to evaluate MH/SA treatment on its ability to provide cost or utilization offsets or to reduce crime invokes stringent criteria that are not always applied to other sorts of morbidities. This would suggest that an economic evaluation of MH/SA treatment, particularly in the context of comparison with other treatments, should be conducted with the more narrow focus of cost-effectiveness, cost–utility, or cost–benefit analyses (see Chapter 24) with respect to the MH/SA ailment itself. This is particularly important in policy decisions regarding the inclusion of MH/SA benefits in broader health care reforms. Frank and McGuire (1995) argue that uncertainty of the cost estimates (and implicitly uncertainty of their benefits) led both the Congress and the Clinton administration to "shy away" from including broad coverage for MH/SA care in the 1993 health care reform proposals.

TREATMENT SUPPLY

Economic analysis of the supply of MH/SA treatment has focused almost entirely on mental health. Analysts term the mental health sector as a three-sector economy with publicly owned providers (including public hospitals and the Veterans Administration facilities) joining the for-profit and nonprofit sector. Although expenditures are jointly the results of supply-and-demand factors, economists address supply decisions in the context of responses to reimbursement or the substitution of resources. Demand decisions typically relate patient expenditures to visit prices or coinsurance.

Government has a major role in the mental health sector. In 1990, roughly 57 percent of all expenditures in the specialty mental health sector involved public dollars (Frank and Manning 1992). State governments are included through publicly owned hospitals and clinics; the government is also a major source of insurance coverage through the Medicare and Medicaid programs. Reimbursement is a key issue with the government as an insurer, with suppliers reacting in response to changing reimbursement policies.

Harrow and Ellis (1992) provide a useful discussion of mental health providers' responses to the reimbursement system. They note that most of the empirical literature has focused on inpatient length-of-stay supply response. A key feature of Medicaid is that provider reimbursement varies across the 50 states. Reimbursement policies may limit the number of covered days; various states also have length-of-stay review programs. Comparisons of inpatient lengths-of-stay across states under the Medicaid program reveal that inpatient psychiatric stays in states with limits on reimbursement can be over 30 percent shorter than stays in states without these limits.

The authors report that Medicare's Prospective Payment System (PPS) has induced 22 to 32 percent reductions in length of psychiatric stay. Providers appear to respond to reimbursement incentives on the outpatient side as well. Psychotherapists who are reimbursed on a fee-for-service basis provide 15 to 20 percent more visits than do their salaried colleagues.

In an application of analytical methods from the field of public finance, Frank and Salkever (1992) use models of charitable giving to investigate the impact of public mental hospitals on the supply of indigent psychiatric care by general hospitals. In particular, they seek to determine whether and how much public spending "crowds out" charitable care. They find little evidence of crowding out, indicating that the presence of public psychiatric hospitals tends to increase the total amount of care to mentally ill persons who are indigent.

TREATMENT DEMAND

Many of the elements of MH/SA treatment demand are similar to the impacts of coinsurance on health care demand and expenditures that were discussed in Chapters 6 and 11. A feature that is fundamental to MH/SA is the prevalence of both deductibles and coinsurance (as well as the possibility of either annual or lifetime limits). Given the chronic nature of some MH/SA treatment, and the possible selection of patients into insurance plans with generous coverage, this presents a considerable statistical problem.

Figure 25.2 shows what happens when researchers try to estimate health care demand in the presence of insurance. Consider (following Frank and Manning, 1992) a very simple policy with a $200 deductible, followed by a 50 percent coinsurance rate. Suppose that a consumer's demand for 12 monthly visits in a given year is totally price inelastic (i.e., unresponsive to price), and suppose that the out-of-pocket cost of a visit is $50. As shown in the diagram, the patient will purchase four visits at the full price of $50, plus an additional eight visits at the coinsured price of $25.

Recalling from Chapter 3 that regression analysis averages the deviations around a line, we see that even though the true elasticity is 0 (the patient would have purchased 12 visits regardless of the price), the estimated demand curve appears to be responsive to price (elastic). This analytical error occurs because increased use impacts the marginal price paid by the consumer. Analyses that do not account for this error will tend to give incorrect (or biased) estimates.[4]

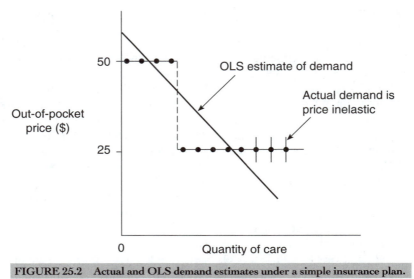

FIGURE 25.2   Actual and OLS demand estimates under a simple insurance plan.

Source: Adapted from Frank and Manning (1992).

---

[4]The corrections for these problems are beyond the scope of this text. See Frank and Manning (1992) for further discussion.

Using suitable corrections, Ellis and McGuire (1986a) calculated price elasticities of demand for outpatient mental health care based on an "expected" out-of-pocket price (that is, the price that a consumer, knowing his or her insurance rate, and expected utilization, expects to pay). Their point estimate at a 50 percent coinsurance rate was .

Keeler, Manning, and Wells (1988) use episode analysis to measure price elasticity of demand. Episode analysis seeks to characterize an illness from its beginning to its end, in principle a more natural grouping than monthly or annual expenditures.[5] The appropriate expenditures for a mental health episode beginning in September and lasting until March should be added for the entire six-month period, rather than split across two calendar years (unfortunately deductibles, coinsurance, and limits are often calculated by calendar year). The authors calculate a price elasticity of demand for outpatient mental health care of (compared to for ambulatory general medical care).

The estimation of MH/SA demand would appear to be a fertile opportunity to estimate the substitution of inpatient and outpatient care through price cross-elasticities. Goodman (1989) finds some substitution of mental health treatment on other medical treatment, and Goodman et al. (1994) examine the potential substitution of inpatient and outpatient care. Figure 25.1 implies considerable possibility of substitution but research on this topic has been limited.

FINANCING

Due to the difficulties in measuring outcomes, and the chronic nature of the ailments, policy analysts have feared that unlimited fee-for-service care would invite very high expenditures. As part of the Rand Health Insurance Experiment, for example, Newhouse and colleagues (1993) compared the cost and use of care by families assigned to a prepaid group practice (HMO) with that of families assigned to receive free care in the fee-for-service sector. Although fee-for-service and free care enrollees sought MH/SA care at the same rate, the fee-for-service population had mental health expenditures that were almost three times greater than those of the prepaid health plan enrollees ($69.70 versus $24.60 per enrollee in 1977 dollars). This may be attributed to a less hospital-intensive form of medicine practiced in the HMO sector than in the fee-for-service sector. In keeping with this result, most MH/SA coverage has been characterized by both substantial coinsurance rates and limits on numbers of visits in a given calendar period.

With the increasing market penetration of managed care plans, and with increasing coverage for MH/SA in managed care plans, employers, as agents for their employees, have looked more closely at *risk contracting*. In a risk contract, the care manager assumes some of the claims risk for a population and is responsible for providing and managing services. In the context of earlier chapters, HMOs and PPOs are prominent examples of risk contractors. A primary goal of risk contracting is to balance

---

[5]It is also a very labor-intensive analysis, which requires that treatments and outcomes be traced through clinic-based or insurance claims data.

the manager's incentives to reduce services against the decreased quality of care that may accompany the reduced services.

Carve-Outs

MH/SA treatment has a particular feature in many health insurance plans. Many insurers subcontract or *carve out* MH/SA treatment to vendors who manage and often pay for mental health (and usually substance abuse). Frank, McGuire, and Newhouse (1995) note two arguments in favor of the carve-out concept:

1. A specialty organization is helpful in managing costs and the quality and appropriateness of mental health (and presumably substance abuse) care.

2. A carve-out "protects" or "sets aside" a designated level of funding for MH/SA services. This addresses the familiar argument that care managers (again, such as HMOs or PPOs) have an incentive only to take on the "good risks" (i.e., those who won't cost much). A subbudget that identifies a specific level of funding for MH/SA care is analogous to a benefit mandate in the world of employer insurance. It would presumably reduce incentives for managed care providers to keep the more chronic users out of the system.

Capitation

One of the primary features of managed care is a capitation system under which vendors accept payment per person per year. If the patient costs less than the payment received, the vendor earns a profit, and vice versa. In a *pure capitation* contract all financial risk lies with the vendor. However, in a wide range of managed MH/SA contracts the more prevalent contract is a *soft capitation* contract, in which both the vendor and the payer share the risk.

Figure 25.3 compares the pure and the soft capitation models. In both, amount T represents an estimated or *target* claims cost per person in a given year. If all treatment costs are paid by the vendor, this can be represented as a 45-degree line from the origin. If all clients used exactly T dollars worth of services, it would indicate the breakeven point. (The intersection of the two lines is noted as point A.) In a pure capitation contract, any set of costs less than T (all points to the left of the breakeven point) accrues as profits to the vendor; conversely, all points to the right of the breakeven point indicate losses to the vendor.

In a soft capitation contract, the vendor and the payer share the risks. In a representative contract, if vendor costs fall below T, vendor profits are 50 percent of the cost shortfall as shown by the dotted line to the left of A, up to a limit of 5 percent of the target amount (indicated as point B). Any further shortfall in costs (moving farther to the left) accrues back to the payer.

Similarly, if vendor costs rise above T, the payer shares 50 percent of the risk, again up to a limit of 5 percent of the target amount (indicated as point C). Any further increase in costs (moving farther to the right) is the obligation of the payer. As Frank, McGuire, and Newhouse note, the range over which a vendor can increase profits or experience losses is quite limited, and in fact most of the risk goes to the payer.

Why do such contracts emerge in contrast to the pure capitation alternative, and what advantages do they present to the employer/payer? First, if vendors fear extra-

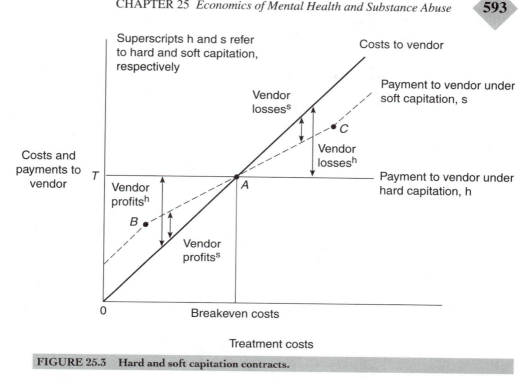

Superscripts h and s refer to hard and soft capitation, respectively

Costs to vendor

Vendor losses^s

Payment to vendor under soft capitation, s

Costs and payments to vendor

Vendor losses^h

Vendor losses^h

T

Vendor profits^h

A

Payment to vendor under hard capitation, h

B

Vendor profits^s

C

0

Breakeven costs

Treatment costs

FIGURE 25.3   Hard and soft capitation contracts.

ordinary expenses from insuring for MH/SA, the value of *T* may require a large risk premium. By offering to keep a large portion of the risk, the payer may elicit better bids from the vendors.

Second, limiting vendor profits means that a portion of the profits go back to the payer. This is particularly attractive to public employers who may find it embarrassing to disclose to voters that their vendors made considerable profits.

Third, contracting with vendors presents considerable information problems. Although in principle the employer's vendors are representing the employer's preferences, monitoring the vendors to make sure this is the case is difficult and time-consuming. Pure capitation, in the eyes of the employer, may lead to unacceptable reductions in quantity and quality of care. It follows that soft capitation may induce vendors to align their practices more toward the preferences of the insured workers and their families.

It is clear, then, that in the context of the cost-cutting attributes of managed care, soft capitation has less capacity for cost savings. This is because the reduced incentives to limit patient treatment may also reduce incentives to contain costs. Frank, McGuire, and Newhouse note that vendor contracts increasingly have performance indicators, such as phone answering and referral practices, but these fall far short of any sort of measurement that tries to relate the marginal benefits to the marginal costs of service. The authors note the necessity of developing a payment system that creates incentives to economize while limiting profits stemming from undertreatment.

CONCLUSIONS

This chapter has addressed some of the particular economic aspects of mental health and substance abuse. Unlike many other conditions, MH/SA may be undercounted and undertreated due to certain stigmas that are attached by individuals and by society. Yet attempts to include MH/SA treatment in more comprehensive health care coverages often meet with opposition because of fears of the high costs of treatment that have few easily measured outcomes.

MH/SA conditions and treatments raise many questions regarding level of care and the accompanying costs. These questions include the appropriate mixtures of inpatient versus outpatient care, general versus specialty provider, and the design of contracts with incentives neither to undertreat nor to overspend. They represent typical and troubling examples of the trade-offs between quantity and quality of care and patient outcomes that face all health care systems.

Summary

1. MH/SA illnesses and their treatments are different in many ways from most other types of health care. Most prominently, they are characterized by the stigma of the disease.

2. MH/SA illnesses may be chronic long-term conditions without explicit indicators of cure. As a result, costs may be spread out over long periods of time; alternatively, outcomes of the treatment may be very difficult to measure.

3. Mental health and substance abuse problems often occur together and are termed *comorbidities.*

4. Mental health and substance abuse treatment has evolved from the large-scale institutionalization that persisted into the 1950s into a mixture of inpatient care, outpatient care, and other less formal treatments.

5. Early studies of mental health and substance abuse treatment appeared to indicate that subsequent to treatment initiation, the costs and utilization of other types of non-MH/SA treatment also fell. Careful examination of such offset effects has indicated that much of the perceived impact is spurious.

6. Much of the literature on supply of care measures the response of length of inpatient stay to specific reimbursement schemes. Comparisons across states under the Medicaid program reveal that inpatient psychiatric stays in states with reimbursement limits can be over 30 percent shorter than stays in states without these limits.

7. The chronic nature of some MH/SA treatment and the possible selection of patients into insurance plans with generous coverage, along with the prevalence of both deductibles and coinsurance (as well as the possibility of either annual or lifetime limits) lead to considerable problems in measuring demand elasticities. In general mental health care is more price elastic than ambulatory general medical care.

8. With increasing coverage for MH/SA, there has been particular interest in risk con-tracting. In a risk contract, a manager assumes some of the claims risk for a popu-lation and is responsible for providing and managing services.

9. In a capitation system vendors accept a fixed payment per person per year. If the patient costs less than the payment received, the vendor earns a profit, and vice versa. In a pure capitation contract all financial risk lies with the vendor, but a wide range of managed MH/SA care features soft capitation contracts, in which both the vendor and the payer share the risk.

10. Soft capitation has less capacity for cost savings because the reduced incentives to undertreat patients also reduce incentives to contain costs.

Discussion Questions

1. Provide a detailed comparison between the analysis of treatment and treatment outcome for a broken leg, and the analysis of treatment and treatment outcome for an episode of alcohol abuse.

2. What are comorbidities? What is the importance of comorbidities in the treatment of MH/SA disorders?

3. Provide examples of treatment substitution for MH/SA disorders. How would you guess that these compare with other more traditional ailments?

4. How do vendors determine target rates for capitation plans?

5. How are offsets defined in the health services literature? What arguments are made in support of the offset hypothesis? What arguments are made in opposition?

6. In estimating demand for MH/SA care, how does the chronic nature of the ailment affect the estimates of price elasticity?

Exercises

1. Suppose that one is estimating the costs of alcoholism treatment, and one has the following regression:

$C = 40 + 25 \cdot$ (number of alcoholism visits) $+ 10 \cdot$ (number of psychiatric visits)

a. What is the alcoholism treatment cost if the patient has three alcoholism visits and one psychiatric visit?

b. How much do estimated alcoholism treatment costs rise for patients with three alcoholism visits and two psychiatric visits? Why?

2. Suppose that a patient has ten visits per year for mental therapy, at a price of $30 per visit, that is paid out of pocket. If, as the literature suggests, the price elasticity of demand is about -0.6, what would happen to the number of visits if the out-of-pocket price were to rise to $40? What would happen to total expenditures?

3. In Question 2, what would happen to the number of visits at the original price of $30 if a 50 percent coinsurance policy were provided? What would happen to patient expenditures and to total expenditures?

4. In Table 25.1 calculate the percentage change in inpatient census for mental patients from 1969 to 1979 across the numerous categories. Then calculate the percentage changes from 1979 to 1988. What does this tell you about the trends in inpatient hospitalization? How might you explain these trends?

5. Figure 25.3 shows a contract with both hard capitation and 50 percent soft capitation. Suppose that a contract was drawn in which the vendor received 75 percent of the difference between target T and expenses, if expenses were less than T, and 75 percent of the difference if expenses were greater than T. How would you draw this on Figure 25.3? Discuss the incentives that would accrue to the vendor.

Glossary

Items in italics are defined elsewhere in the glossary.

Actuarially Fair   Insurance under which expected payouts equal the premiums paid by beneficiaries.

Adverse Selection   A situation often resulting from *asymmetric information* in which individuals are able to purchase insurance at rates which are below actuarially fair rates plus *loading costs.*

Agency Relationship   A situation in which one person (agent) makes decisions on behalf of another person (principal).

Aggregate Demand (for cigarettes)   (*See* Market Demand)

Allocative Efficiency   (*See* Efficiency)

Alternative Delivery System (ADS)   Insurance and organizational arrangements for health care delivery which are alternatives to traditional *fee-for-service* (FFS) arrangements.

Assignment   (*See* Participation/Assignment)

Asymmetric Information   Situations in which the parties on the opposite sides of a transaction have differing amounts of relevant information.

Average Cost   Total cost represents the sum of all fixed costs and variable costs in the *short run.* Average cost equals total cost divided by the quantity of output and also equals the sum of average variable cost (AVC) and average fixed cost (AFC). In the *long run,* average total cost represents the minimum possible cost per unit of producing any given level of output when there are no fixed costs.

Balance Billing   The practice of collecting from the patient the difference between the charge and the insurance reimbursement.

Barrier-to-Entry   Impediments to the unrestricted flow of factors into or out of an industry or occupation (e.g., control over natural resources, licensure, patents).

Budget Constraint   The line that is the collection of points representing combinations of goods that the consumer is just able to afford.

Capitation   A method of reimbursement under which a provider is paid a fixed amount per person regardless of the amount of services rendered.

Cardinal Utility   A quantitative measure of the value of a good in terms of metrically measurable utility. It is used in the study of risk and insurance.

Case-Mix Index   A numerical measure of the assortment of patient cases treated by a given hospital, so that a higher value indicates a greater average degree of complexity of the cases.

Certificate-of-Need (CON)   Regulations which require health care providers to obtain approval from state planning agencies for capital expenditures which exceed various threshold levels (e.g., $500,000).

Ceteris Paribus   Other things being held constant.

Coefficient of Variation   A measure of dispersion equal to the standard deviation divided by the mean (and sometimes multiplied by 100).

Coinsurance (Rate)   The share of costs which are paid by the beneficiary of a health policy (often after some *deductible*).

Comparative Statics   The analysis which calculates the level of a new equilibrium, given changed values of one or more economic parameters, such as prices or income.

Competition   (*See* Perfect Competition)

Concentration Ratio   The share of the market sales or production accounted for by a certain number of the largest firms. Often the four-firm ratio is used.

Copayment   Amounts paid by the insurance beneficiary as a result of *coinsurance* and *deductibles*.

Cost–Benefit Analysis (CBA)   A method of comparing the monetary value of all benefits of a social project with all costs of that project.

Cost-Effectiveness Analysis (CEA)   A method which tries to find the least cost method of achieving a desired objective(s) associated with a social project.

Cost Sharing   (*See also* Copayment) Methods of financing health care which require some direct payments for services by patients.

Cost Shifting   Increasing revenues from some payers to offset uncompensated care costs and lower net payments from other payers.

Cross (Price) Elasticity of Demand   (*See also* Elasticity) The percentage change in the quantity demanded of one good resulting from a one percent change in the price of another good.

Deductible   The amount of health care charges for which a beneficiary is responsible before the insurer begins payment.

Demand Function   The relationship between quantity demanded and price (and other independent variables such as income and tastes). One could study individual demand as well as market demand.

Depreciation   The change in the value of a good over time, due to deteriorating physical characteristics or technical obsolescence.

Diagnosis-Related Groups (DRGs)   A set of case types established under the Prospective Payment System (PPS) identifying patients with similar conditions and processes of care. There are currently 495 DRGs in Medicare's Prospective Payment System, each of which is assigned a relative weight that compares its costliness to the average for all DRGs.

Discounting—Discount Rate   The process of converting sums to be received at a future date to a present value. The interest rate which is used is called the discount rate.

Discrete Choice Analysis   Statistical analysis in which the variable to be explained is limited among alternatives, typically to values of 0 or 1.

Economic Profit (*See also* Monopoly Profit) The return over and above which is necessary to keep the firm from exiting the market over the *long run*. These profits are also called above normal profits, excess profits and supra normal profits.

Economies of Scale Situations in which the *long-run* average costs of a firm decline as output increases.

Economies of Scope Situations in which a firm can jointly produce two or more goods more cheaply than under separate production of the goods.

Edgeworth Box (in Consumption) A diagram that shows all possible allocations of fixed amounts of goods and services between two people.

Efficiency (*See also* Pareto Efficiency) *Technical efficiency* occurs when the firm produces the maximum possible sustained output from a given set of inputs. This idea is distinguished from *allocative efficiency*—situations in which either inputs or outputs are put to their best possible uses in the economy so that no further gains in output or welfare are possible. Both allocative and technical efficiency are prerequisites for *Pareto Efficiency*.

Elasticity Percentage change in some dependent variable (e.g., quantity demanded) resulting from a one percent change in some independent variable (e.g., price). Elasticities which exceed one in absolute value are considered elastic; elasticities less than one are inelastic.

Elasticity of Substitution (*See also* Elasticity) The percentage change in the capital–labor ratio resulting from a one percent change in relative factor prices.

Equilibrium Price (Quantity) The price (quantity) at which the quantity demanded and the quantity supplied are equal.

Expected Value A measure used with a probability distribution of returns. The expected value is the sum of each probability multiplied by its corresponding return.

Experience Good A good for which evaluation is difficult prior to experience or purchase.

Externality A case in which a consumer (producer) affects the utility (costs) of another consumer (producer) through actions which lie outside the price system.

Fee-for-Service (FFS) A method of payment under which the provider is paid for each procedure or service that is provided to a patient.

Firm Any entity that transforms inputs to some product or service that is sold in the marketplace.

First Fundamental Theorem of Welfare Economics Under specified conditions, competitive markets are *Pareto efficient*.

Fixed Costs (TFC and AFC) Costs which do not vary with output. They are expressed either as total fixed cost (TFC) or average fixed cost (AFC).

Frontier Analysis A statistical analysis of firm efficiency that attempts to identify the best possible production practice and interprets firm inefficiency as a departure from the best possible production practice, or frontier.

Galbraith Effect The effect of advertising on market demand for the product.

Game Theory A model that analyzes economic behavior as a series of strategic moves and countermoves by rival agents.

Gross National Product (GNP)—Gross Domestic Product (GDP) GNP is the current value of all final goods and services produced by a country in a given period of time such as one year. GDP is a closely related measure which includes the value associated only with domestic factors of production.

Group Model HMO   An HMO organization in which the insurer contracts with group practices to provide care.

Health and Health Status   (*See also* Morbidity Rate *and* Mortality Rate) Measures of the physical and emotional well-being of an individual or a defined population. *Mortality* and *morbidity rates* are often used to measure health status.

Health Care   Goods and services used as inputs to produce health. In some analyses, one's own time and knowledge used to maintain and promote health are considered in addition to conventional health care inputs.

Health Care Financing Administration (HCFA)   Agency of the United States Department of Health and Human Services (DHHS). HCFA is responsible for administering the financing and quality assurance programs for *Medicare* and the Federal participation in *Medicaid.*

Health Maintenance Organization (HMO)   A managed care plan that integrates financing and delivery of a comprehensive set of health care services to an enrolled population. HMOs may contract with or directly employ health care providers.

Human Capital   A form of intangible capital that includes the skills and other knowledge that workers have or acquire through education, training, and health care that yields valuable productive services over time.

Identification Problem   In econometric analysis, the inability to distinguish between two relationships (such as demand and supply) which contain the same variables (such as price and quantity).

Income Effect   (*See also* Substitution Effect) The effect on quantity demanded that results from the change in real income associated with a relative change in the price of the good or service under study.

Income Elasticity of Demand   (*See also* Elasticity) Percentage change in quantity demanded resulting from a one percent change in income.

Indemnity   Health insurance under which the insurer's liability is determined by a fixed predetermined amount for a covered event.

Indifference Curve   Shows all combination of goods which provide a constant level of satisfaction (*utility*) to the individual under study.

Inefficiency   (*See* Efficiency *and* Pareto Efficiency)

Infant Mortality Rate   The ratio of the number of deaths in infants one year or less during a year divided by the number of live births during the year.

Inferior Good   (*See also* Normal Good) A good or service for which demand decreases as income increases.

Internal Rate of Return   That discount rate that will equate the time streams of costs and returns of an investment. It is a measure of the profitability of an investment.

Isoquant (Isoproduct Curve)   All combinations of factors of production yielding a constant level of output.

Labor–Leisure Trade-off   The line that is the collection of points representing the combinations of leisure time and earnings from work that are possible for a person.

Law of Demand   There is an inverse relationship between price and quantity demanded, *ceteris paribus.*

Law of Diminishing Returns   After some point, the marginal product of a variable input must diminish.

Loading Costs   Administrative and other costs associated with underwriting an insurance policy.

Long Run   (*See also* Short Run) A period of time sufficient to permit a firm to vary all factors of production.

Long-Term Care   Ongoing health and social services provided for individuals who need assistance on a continuing basis because of physical or mental disability. Services can be provided in an institution, the home, or the community, and include informal services provided by family or friends as well as formal services provided by professionals or agencies.

Luxury good   A good that richer people tend to buy in greater proportions, so that its *income elasticity* is greater than one.

Managed Care   Any payment or delivery arrangement used by a health plan or provider to control or to coordinate use of health services to contain health expenditures, improve quality, or both.

Managed Care Plan   A health plan that uses managed care arrangements and has a defined system of selected providers that contract with the plan. Enrollees have financial incentives to use participating providers that agree to furnish a broad range of services to them.

Mandated Benefits   Coverage in health insurance policies for certain services which are mandated by state insurance statutes.

Marginal   Incremental; a one unit increase.

Marginal Cost   The increase in total cost resulting from a one unit increase in output.

Marginal Labor (Factor) Cost   The addition to total labor (factor) costs associated with an additional unit of labor (factor of production).

Marginal Product   The addition to total output resulting from an additional unit of the variable input.

Marginal Rate of Substitution   The amount of one commodity given up per unit increase in another commodity while maintaining the same level of satisfaction.

Marginal Rate of Technical Substitution   The amount of one factor of production given up per unit increase in another factor of production while maintaining the same level of output.

Marginal Rate of Transformation   The slope of the production possibilities curve, and the rate at which society can transform one good into another.

Marginal Revenue   The addition to total revenue associated with a one unit increase in output.

Marginal Revenue Product   The addition to a firm's total revenue associated with employing one more unit of a variable input.

Marginal Utility   The extra utility gained from consuming one more unit of a good holding others constant. Utility is a measure of the satisfaction from consuming goods.

Market Demand   The total demand for a good by all consumers in the market.

Market Structure   How an industry is organized in terms of the number and distribution of firms and how firms compete among themselves.

Medicaid   Health insurance programs administered by the states for qualifying low income beneficiaries. The Federal government establishes minimum standards and provides matching grants. The program became law in 1965.

Medicare   The federal health insurance program established in 1965 for the elderly and other selected groups.

Medicare—Part A   Medicare Hospital Insurance which covers beneficiaries for inpatient hospital, home health, hospice, and limited skilled nursing facility services. Beneficiaries are responsible for deductibles and copayments.

Medicare—Part B   Medicare Supplementary Medical Insurance which covers Medicare beneficiaries for physician services, medical supplies, and other outpatient treatment. Beneficiaries are responsible for monthly premiums, copayments, deductibles, and balance billing.

Medigap Policy   A privately purchased insurance policy that supplements Medicare coverage and meets specified requirements set by federal statute and the National Association of Insurance Commissioners.

Monopoly (Power)   Situations in which a firm faces a negatively sloped demand curve. In a *pure monopoly,* there is no other firm which produces a close substitute for the firm's product. Thus the demand curve facing the monopolist is the market demand curve.

Monopoly Profit (Rent)   The return over and above a *normal profit* resulting from *monopoly power.*

Monopsony   Situations in which a firm faces a positively sloped supply curve in the product or factor market because it is the only buyer.

Moral Hazard   An insurance term which represents the disincentives created by insurance for individuals to take measures which would reduce the amount of care demanded. In the health services literature, it is more commonly used to express the additional quantity of health care demanded, resulting from a decrease in the net price of care attributable to insurance.

Morbidity Rate   The rate of incidence of disease in a particular population.

Mortality Rate   The death rate for a particular population. The crude death rate is the ratio of deaths during a year divided by midyear population. Because age is so important, the age-adjusted mortality rate is a measure which takes into account a population's age distribution.

Necessity   A good whose consumption does not vary greatly with changes in peoples' incomes. More generally, a good with an *income elasticity* less than one.

Network Model HMO   An HMO made up by a network of group practices.

Nominal Value   (*See also* Real Value) The money value measured in current dollars.

Nonprofit Firm   A firm that is constrained by law from distributing any residual of income over costs to any party.

Normal Good   (*See also* Inferior Good) A good or service for which demand increases as income increases.

Normal Return (Normal Profit)   The return just sufficient to retain factors of production in an industry or an occupation in the long run. The return equal to the *opportunity cost* of a factor of production.

Nursing Facility   An institution that provides skilled nursing care and rehabilitation services to injured, functionally disabled, or sick persons.

Offer Curve   A set of points summarizing the amount of a good that an individual will offer for trade, given his or her preferences, endowment, and the prices of other goods.

Opportunity Cost   The value of the best alternative which is forgone in order to get or produce more of the commodity under consideration.

Ordinal Utility   Utility as evaluated through relative levels of satisfaction, when the particular unit of utility is not essential. Examples of ordinal numbers are 1st, 2nd, and 3rd.

Pareto Efficiency (Optimum)   (*See also* Efficiency) Situation in which it is impossible to improve the level of welfare of one party without hurting the welfare level of another party. Situation in which the level of welfare of one or more parties can be improved without hurting any other party are Pareto improvements.

Participation/Assignment   Situation in which a provider agrees to accept the third-party payer's payment in full thereby relieving the patient of any balance (except for applicable patient copayments).

Peer Review Organization (PRO)   An organization that contracts with HCFA to investigate the quality of health care furnished to Medicare beneficiaries and to educate beneficiaries and providers. PROs also conduct limited review of medical records and claims to evaluate the appropriateness of care provided.

Perfect Competition   A market structure in which there are (1) numerous buyers and sellers, (2) perfect information, (3) free entry and exit, and (4) a homogeneous product.

Play or Pay   Insurance proposal that would require employers to either provide minimal levels of health insurance to their employees or pay into a fund which would be used to provide coverage.

Preferred Provider Organization (PPO)   An arrangement under which an enrollee is given financial incentives (e.g., no *copayments*) to seek care from selected physicians and hospitals with which the payer has contracted.

Prepaid Group Practice (PGP)   A *prepayment* arrangement under which participating providers agree to provide services to eligible enrollees in return for a fixed capitated payment.

Prepayment—Prepaid Plans   Health insurance proposal which provides unlimited amounts of covered services in return for a fixed predetermined premium.

Present (Discounted) Value (PV or PDV)   (*See also* Discounting) The value of a stream of returns to be received at future dates, discounted to the equivalent of present dollars.

Price Discrimination   The sale of goods or services to different individuals at different prices.

Price Elasticity of Demand   (*See also* Elasticity) The percentage change in quantity demanded resulting from a 1 percent change in price.

Price Elasticity of Supply   (*See also* Elasticity) The percentage change in quantity supplied resulting from a 1 percent change in price.

Price Index   Expresses the current prices of a group of goods relative to the prices of these goods in a base year. A price index, often used to convert *nominal values* to *real values,* shows how much prices of those goods have changed since the base year.

Production Function   The relationship between the maximum output that can be produced corresponding to any combination of factor inputs.

Production Possibilities Curve (Transformation Curve)   A relationship showing all combination of goods that an economy can produce with given amounts of input factors and the existing technology. The slope of the curve is the *marginal rate of transformation* showing the amount of one good which must be given up for a one unit increase in the other good.

Prospective Payment System (PPS)   The method of hospital reimbursement phased in by *Medicare* beginning in 1983 under which hospitals were reimbursed a fixed amount determined by the *Diagnosis-Related Groups* (DRGs) of their admissions.

Public Good (Pure)   A good (e.g., national defense) that no one can be prevented from consuming, nonexcludable, and that can be consumed by one person without depleting it for another, i.e., nonrival. The marginal cost of providing the good to another consumer is zero.

Rate Regulation (RR)   Regulations administered largely at the state level that define the terms under which hospitals are reimbursed.

Real Value   (*See also* Nominal Value) Monetary values that are adjusted for changes in the general level of prices relative to some arbitrarily selected base year.

Regression Analysis   Statistical analysis that posits a linear relationship between a variable to be explained, and one or more (in multiple regression) explanatory variables, in the form $y = a + bx$.

Relative Value Scale   A system that assigns relative weights to health care procedures or services. These are sometimes used as guides by providers to price their services and by third-party payers to determine reimbursement levels.

Rent (Economic Rent)   The remuneration to a factor of production, over and above that amount that is necessary to induce its supply in the market.

Reputation Good   A good for which consumers rely on information provided by friends, neighbors, and others.

Resource-Based Relative Value Scale (RBRVS)   A relative value scale used in *Medicare* reimbursement that is based on the resources involved in providing a service.

Risk Aversion   The degree to which a certain income is preferred to a risky alternative with the same expected income.

Risk Selection   Enrollment choices made by health plans or enrollees on the basis of perceived risk relative to the premium to be paid.

Roemer's Law   The proposed positive relationship between the availability of hospital beds and a population's utilization of those beds. It is also referred to as Say's Law for hospital beds.

Search Good   A good whose characteristics can be fully evaluated upon inspection.

Second Fundamental Theorem of Welfare Economics   Any *Pareto efficient* outcome can, in principle, be achieved by competitive markets, given an appropriate initial endowment.

Short Run   (*See also* Long Run) Situations in which the firm is not able to vary all its inputs. There is at least one factor of production that is fixed.

Small Area Variations   The large variations in the per capita rates of utilization across small, homogeneous areas for many medical and surgical procedures.

Social Insurance   Government insurance programs in which eligibility and premiums are not determined by the practices common to private insurance contracts.

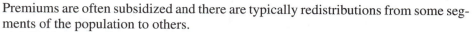

Premiums are often subsidized and there are typically redistributions from some segments of the population to others.

Social Welfare Function   A decision rule under which society ranks all possible distributions of goods and services.

Staff Model HMO   An HMO in which physicians are directly employed by the HMO.

Substitutes   Substitutes in consumption are goods that satisfy the same wants (e.g., beef and chicken) so that an increase in the price of one will increase the demand for the other. Substitutes in production are alternative goods which a firm can produce (e.g., corn and soybeans for a farmer) so that an increase in the price of one will lead to a decrease in the supply of another.

Substitution Effect   (*See also* Income Effect) The change in quantity demanded resulting from a relative change in commodity prices, holding real income constant.

Supplier-Induced Demand (SID)   The change in demand associated with the discretionary influence of providers, especially physicians, over their patients. Demand that is provided for the self-interests of providers rather than solely for patient interests.

Target Income Hypothesis   A model under which providers are thought to select a specified income level, and to adjust their amount of services provided or fees in order to reach this level.

Technical Efficiency   (*See* Efficiency)

Technological Change   A change in the process by which factors of production combine to produce outputs.

Theorem of the Second Best   The economic theorem stating that the correction of some but not all market imperfections, in cases where there are more than one imperfection, will not necessarily improve society's welfare.

Third-Party Effect   (*See* Externality)

Time Costs   The money value of the time lost through travel or waiting when consuming a product or service.

Uncompensated Care   Care rendered by hospitals or other providers without payment from the patient or a government-sponsored private insurance program. It includes both charity care, which is provided without expectation of payment, and bad debts, for which the provider has made an unsuccessful effort to collect payment due from the patient.

Usual, Customary, and Reasonable (UCR) Reimbursement   A system of insurance reimbursement under which the third-party payer restricts payment to the maximum of several limits (screens) which are established.

Utility and Utility Function   Utility represents satisfaction or the level of welfare of an individual, measured in *cardinal* or *ordinal* terms. The utility function expresses the person's utility as a function of all possible combinations of goods and services.

Utilization Review (UR)   Programs that attempt to determine whether specific services are medically necessary and delivered at an appropriate level and cost.

Variable Costs (TVC and AVC)   Costs associated with variable factor(s) of production often expressed as total variable cost (TVC) or average variable cost (AVC).

Welfare   A measure of an individual's or a society's level of well-being.

Welfare Loss or Deadweight Loss   A measure of the net loss of society's welfare resulting from a misallocation of resources, usually situations in which the marginal benefits of a good are not equal to marginal costs.

Yardstick Competition   A regulatory pricing policy in which an average of the marginal costs of all competing firms is used as a standard of payment to induce the firm to engage in cost-cutting innovations.

References

Abel-Smith, Brian, *Cost Containment in Health Care.* London: Bedford Square, 1984.

Acton, Jan P., "Demand for Health Care Among the Urban Poor with Special Emphasis on the Role of Time," in Richard Rosett, ed., *The Role of Health Insurance in the Health Services Sector.* New York: Neal Watson, 1976.

Acton, Jan P., "Nonmonetary Factors in the Demand for Medical Services: Some Empirical Evidence," *Journal of Political Economy,* 83 (1975): 595–614.

Adamache, Killard W., and Louis F. Rossiter, "The Entry of HMOs into the Medicare Market: Implications for TEFRA's Mandate," *Inquiry,* 23 (1986): 349–364.

Adamache, Killard W., and Frank Sloan, "Unions and Hospitals: Some Unresolved Issues," *Journal of Health Economics,* 1 (1982): 81–108.

Aday, Lu Ann, Ronald Andersen, and Gretchen Fleming, *Health Care in the United States: Equitable for Whom?,* Beverly Hills, CA: Sage, 1980.

Aigner, Dennis J., C. A. Knox Lovell, and Peter Schmidt, "Formulation and Estimation of Stochastic Frontier Production Function Models," *Journal of Econometrics,* 6 (1977): 21–37.

Akerlof, George A., "The Market for 'Lemons': Qualitative Uncertainty and the Market Mechanism," *Quarterly Journal of Economics,* 84 (1970): 488–500.

Albion, Mark S., and Paul W. Farris, *The Advertising Controversy: Evidence on the Economic Effects of Advertising.* Boston: Auburn House, 1981.

Alchian, Armen A., and Harold Demsetz, "Production, Information Costs, and Economic Organization," *American Economic Review,* 62 (1972): 777–795.

Altman, Stuart H., and Marc A. Rodwin, "Halfway Competitive Markets and Ineffective Regulation: The American Health Care System," *Journal of Health Politics, Policy and Law,* 13 (1988): 323–339.

Andersen, Ronald, and Lee Benham, "Factors Affecting the Relationship Between Family Income and Medical Care Consumption," in H. Klarman, ed., *Empirical Studies in Health Economics.* Baltimore: Johns Hopkins, 1970.

Anderson, Gerard F., "Universal Health Care Coverage in Korea," *Health Affairs,* 8 (1989): 24–33.

Anderson, Geoffrey M., et al., "Use of Coronary Bypass Surgery in the United States and Canada," *Journal of the American Medical Association,* 269 (1993): 1661–1666.

Anderson, Keith B., "Regulation, Market Structure, and Hospital Costs: Comment," *Southern Economic Journal,* 58 (1991): 528–534.

Anderson, Odin W., *Health Services as a Growth Enterprise in the United States Since 1875,* 2nd ed. Ann Arbor, MI: Health Administration Press, 1990.

Anderson, Odin W., and Ellen M. Morrison, "The Worth of Medical Care: A Critical Review," *Medical Care Review,* 46 (1989): 121–155.

Archibald, Robert, Clyde Haulman, and Carlisle Moody, "Quality, Price, Advertising, and Published Quality Ratings," *Journal of Consumer Research,* 9 (1983): 347–356.

Arnould, Richard J., Lawrence W. Debrock, and John W. Pollard, "Do HMOs Produce Specific Services More Efficiently?," *Inquiry,* 21 (1984): 243–253.

Arrow, Kenneth J., "Uncertainty and the Welfare Economics of Medical Care," *American Economic Review,* 53 (1963): 941–973.

Arrow, Kenneth J., "Some Ordinalist-Utilitarian Notes on Rawls's Theory of Justice," *Journal of Philosophy,* 70 (1973): 245–262.

Arrow, Kenneth J., *Social Choice and Individual Values.* New York: Wiley, 1975.

Auster, Richard D., Irving Leveson, and Deborah Sarachek, "The Production of Health, an Exploratory Study," *Journal of Human Resources,* 4 (1969): 411–436.

Auster, Richard D., and Ronald L. Oaxaca, "Identification of Supplier Induced Demand in the Health Care Sector," *Journal of Human Resources,* 16 (1978): 327–342.

Bain, Joe S., *Barriers to New Competition.* Cambridge, MA: Harvard, 1956.

Baltagi, Badi H., and Dan Levin, "Estimating Dynamic Demand for Cigarettes Using Panel Data: The Effects of Bootlegging, Taxation and Advertising Reconsidered," *Review of Economics and Statistics,* 68 (1986): 148–155.

Bator, Francis M., "The Simple Analytics of Welfare Maximization," *American Economic Review,* 47 (1957): 22–59.

Baumol, William J., *Business Behavior, Value and Growth,* rev. ed. New York: Harcourt, Brace & World, 1967.

Baumol, William J., "On the Social Rate of Discount," *American Economic Review,* 58 (1968): 788–802.

Bays, Carson W., "Cost Comparisons of For Profit and Nonprofit Hospitals," *Social Science and Medicine,* 13C (1979): 219–225.

Bays, Carson W., "Specification Error in the Estimation of Hospital Cost Functions," *Review of Economics and Statistics,* 62 (1980): 302–305.

Bays, Carson W., "Why Most Private Hospitals Are Nonprofit," *Journal of Policy Analysis and Management,* 2 (1983): 366–385.

Bays, Carson W., "The Determinants of Hospital Size: A Survivor Analysis," *Applied Economics,* 18 (1986): 359–377.

Becker, Edmund R., and Frank A. Sloan, "Hospital Ownership and Performance," *Economic Inquiry,* 23 (1985): 21–36.

Becker, Gary S., and Kevin J. Murphy, "A Theory of Rational Addiction," *Journal of Political Economy,* 96 (1988): 675–700.

Behrman, Jere R., and Barbara L. Wolfe, "Does More Schooling Make Women Better Nourished and Healthier?: Adult Sibling Random and Fixed Effects Estimates for Nicaragua," *Journal of Human Resources,* 24 (1989): 644–663.

Benham, Lee, "The Effects of Advertising on the Price of Eyeglasses," *Journal of Law and Economics,* 15 (1972): 421–477.

Berger, Mark C., et al., "Valuing Changes in Health Risks: A Comparison of Alternative Measures," *Southern Economic Journal,* 53 (1987): 967–984.

Berger, Mark C., and J. Paul Leigh, "Schooling, Self-Selection and Health," *Journal of Human Resources,* 24 (1989): 433–455.

Berle, Adolphe A., and Gardner C. Means, *The Modern Corporation and Private Property.* New York: Macmillan, 1932.

Birnbaum, Howard, Christine Bishop, A. James Lee, and Gail Jensen, "Why Do Nursing Home Costs Vary?," *Medical Care,* 19 (1981): 1095–1107.

Bishop, Christine E., "Nursing Home Cost Studies and Reimbursement Issues," *Health Care Financing Review,* 1 (1980): 47–64.

Blanchard, Garth A., Chee W. Chow, and Eric Noreen, "Information Asymmetry, Incentive Schemes, and Information Biasing: The Case of Hospital Budgeting Under Rate Regulation," *Accounting Review,* 61 (1986): 1–15.

Blank, David M., and George J. Stigler, *The Demand and Supply of Scientific Personnel.* New York: National Bureau of Economic Research, 1957.

Blendon, Robert J., et al., "Satisfaction with Health Systems in Ten Nations," *Health Affairs,* 9 (1990): 185–192.

Blendon, Robert J., et al., "Who Has the Best Health Care System? A Second Look," *Health Affairs,* 14 (1995): 220–230.

Blomquist, Glenn C., "The Value of Human Life: An Empirical Perspective," *Economic Inquiry,* 19 (1981): 157–164.

Bond, Ronald, et al., *Staff Report on Effects of Restrictions on Advertising and Commercial Practice in the Professions: The Case of Optometry,* Federal Trade Commission. Washington, D.C.: Government Printing Office, 1980.

Bopp, Kenneth D., "How Patients Evaluate the Quality of Ambulatory Medical Encounters: A Marketing Perspective," *Journal of Health Care Marketing,* 10 (1990): 6–15.

Borjas, George J., H. E. Frech III, and Paul B. Ginsburg, "Property Rights and Wages: The Case of Nursing Homes," *Journal of Human Resources,* 17 (1983): 232–246.

Bosworth, Barry, and Gary Burtless, "Effects of Tax Reform on Labor Supply, Investment, and Saving," *Journal of Economic Perspectives,* 6 (1992): 3–25.

Boyle, Philip J., and Daniel Callahan, "Managed Care in Mental Health: The Ethical Issues," *Health Affairs,* 14 (1995): 7–22.

Brennan, Troyen A., et al., "Incidence of Adverse Events and Negligence in Hospitalized Patients," *New England Journal of Medicine,* 324 (1991): 370–376.

Bromberg, Michael D., and Thomas C. Goodwin, "Grassroots Politics and Health Care: Effects of Medicare Budget Cuts," *Healthcare Financial Management,* 42 (1988): 20, 22, 100.

Brook, Robert H., et al., "Does Free Care Improve Adults' Health?: Results from a Randomized Controlled Trial," *The New England Journal of Medicine,* 309 (1983): 1426–1434.

Brook, Robert H., et al., "Appropriateness of Acute Medical Care for the Elderly: An Analysis of the Literature," *Health Policy,* 14 (1990): 225–242.

Brown, Douglas M., "Do Physicians Underutilize Aides?", *Journal of Human Resources,* 23 (1988): 342–355.

Brown, Kaye, and Colin Burrows, "The Sixth Stool Guaiac Test: $47 Million that Never Was," *Journal of Health Economics,* 9 (1990): 429–445.

Brown, Lawrence D., "Afterward," *Journal of Health Politics, Policy and Law,* 13 (1988): 361–363.

Browning, Edgar K., and William R. Johnson, "Taxation and the Cost of National Health Insurance," in Mark V. Pauly, ed., *National Health Insurance: What Now, What Later, What Never?* Washington, D.C.: American Enterprise Institute, 1980.

Buchanan, James, *The Limits of Liberty.* Chicago: University of Chicago Press, 1975.

Burstein, Philip L., and Jerry Cromwell, "Relative Incomes and Rates of Return for U.S. Physicians," *Journal of Health Economics,* 4 (1985): 63–78.

Cady, John F., *Drugs on the Market.* Lexington, MA: Lexington, 1975.

Carlson, Rick, *The End of Medicine.* New York: Wiley Interscience, 1975.

Carr, W. John, and Paul J. Feldstein, "The Relationship of Cost to Hospital Size," *Inquiry,* 4 (1967): 45–65.

Carroll, Norman V., and W. Gary Erwin, "Patient Shifting as a Response to Medicare Prospective Payment," *Medical Care,* 25 (1987): 1161–1167.

Chaloupka, Frank J., "Rational Addictive Behavior and Cigarette Smoking," *Journal of Political Economy,* 99 (1991): 722–742.

Chaloupka, Frank J., and Henry Saffer, "Clean Indoor Air Laws and the Demand for Cigarettes," *Contemporary Policy Issues,* 10 (1992): 72–83.

Chiswick, Barry R., "The Demand for Nursing Home Care: An Analysis of the Substitution Between Institutional and Noninstitutional Care," *Journal of Human Resources,* 11 (1976): 295–316.

Christianson, Jon B., et al., "The HMO Industry: Evolution in Population Demographics and Market Structures," *Medical Care Review,* 48 (1991): 3–46.

Clark, Derek, and Jan Abel Olsen, "Agency in Health Care with an Endogenous Budget Constraint," *Journal of Health Economics,* 13 (1994): 231–251.

Clark, Jane Deane, "Variation in Michigan Hospital Use Rates: Do Physician and Hospital Characteristics Provide the Explanation?," *Social Science and Medicine,* 30 (1990): 67–82.

Clark, Robert Charles, "Does the Nonprofit Form Fit the Hospital Industry?," *Harvard Law Review,* 93 (1980): 1417–1489.

Coffey, Rosanna M., "The Effect of Time Price on the Demand for Medical Care Services," *Journal of Human Resources,* 18 (1983): 407–424.

Cohen, Harold A., "Variations in Cost Among Hospitals of Different Sizes," *Southern Economic Journal,* 33 (1967): 355–366.

Comanor, William S., and Thomas A. Wilson, *Advertising and Market Power.* Cambridge, MA: Harvard, 1974.

Comanor, William S., and Thomas A. Wilson, "The Effect of Advertising on Competition: A Survey," *Journal of Economic Literature,* 17 (1979): 453–476.

Commerce Clearing House, *Physicians' Medicare Fee Schedules.* Chicago, IL: 1990, 1992.

Conrad, Robert F., and Robert P. Strauss, "A Multiple-Output Multiple-Input Model of the Hospital Industry in North Carolina," *Applied Economics,* 15 (1983): 341–352.

Cooper, Philip F., and Alan C. Monheit, "Does Employment-Related Health Insurance Inhibit Job Mobility," *Inquiry,* 30 (Winter 1993): 400–416.

Corman, Hope, and Michael Grossman, "Determinants of Neonatal Mortality Rate in the U.S.: A Reduced Form Model," *Journal of Health Economics,* 4 (1985): 213–236.

Corman, Hope, Theodore J. Joyce, and Michael Grossman, "Birth Outcome Production Function in the United States," *Journal of Human Resources,* 22 (1987): 339–360.

Cowing, Thomas G., and Alphonse G. Holtmann, "Multiproduct Short-Run Hospital Cost Functions: Empirical Evidence and Policy Implications from Cross-Section Data," *Southern Economic Journal,* 49 (1983): 637–653.

Cowing, Thomas G., Alphonse G. Holtmann, and Susan Powers, "Hospital Cost Analysis: A Survey and Evaluation of Recent Studies," *Advances in Health Economics and Health Services Research,* 4 (1983).

Coyte, Peter C., "Canada," in Jean-Jacques Rosa, ed., *Advances in Health Economics and Health Services Research, Supplement 1: Comparative Health Systems.* Greenwich, CT: JAI Press, 1990.

Coyte, Peter C., et al., "Waiting Times for Knee-Replacement Surgery in the United States and Ontario," *New England Journal of Medicine,* 331 (1994): 1068–1071.

Cromwell, Jerry, and Janet B. Mitchell, "Physician-Induced Demand for Surgery," *Journal of Health Economics,* 5 (1986): 293–313.

Cropper, Maureen L., et al., "The Determinants of Pesticide Regulation: A Statistical Analysis of EPA Decision Making," *Journal of Political Economy,* 100 (1992): 175–197.

Culyer, A. J., "The Normative Economics of Health Care Finance and Provision," *Oxford Review of Economic Policy,* 5 (1989): 34–58.

Culyer, A. J., and Andrew Meads, "The United Kingdom: Effective, Efficient, Equitable?," *Journal of Health Politics, Policy and Law,* 17 (1992): 667–688.

Culyer, A. J., Eddy van Doorslaer, and Adam Wagstaff, "Utilization as a Measure of Equity by Mooney, Hall, Donaldson and Gerard: Comment," *Journal of Health Economics,* 11 (1992): 93–98.

Daniels, Norman, "Health Care Needs and Distributive Justice," *Philosophy and Public Affairs,* 10 (1981): 146–179.

Daniels, Norman, "Equity of Access to Health Care: Some Conceptual and Ethical Issues," *Milbank Memorial Fund Quarterly/Health and Society,* 60 (1982): 51–81.

Daniels, Norman, *Just Health Care.* Cambridge: Cambridge University Press, 1985.

Davis, Karen, and Roger Reynolds, "The Impact of Medicare and Medicaid on Access to Medical Care," in Richard Rosett, ed., *The Role of Health Insurance in the United States Health Services Sector.* New York: Neal Watson, 1976.

Davis, Mark A., "On Nursing Home Quality: A Review and Analysis," *Medical Care Review,* 48 (1991): 129–166.

de Lissovoy, Gregory, et al., "Preferred Provider Organizations One Year Later," *Inquiry,* 24 (1987): 127–135.

DesHarnais, Susan, James Chesney, and Steven Fleming, "Trends in Regional Variations in Hospital Utilization and Quality During the First Two Years of the Prospective Payment System," *Inquiry,* 25 (1988): 374–382.

DesHarnais, Susan, et al., "The Early Effects of the Prospective Payment System on Inpatient Utilization and the Quality of Care," *Inquiry,* 24 (1987): 7–16.

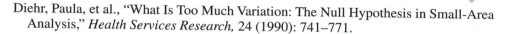

Diehr, Paula, et al., "What Is Too Much Variation: The Null Hypothesis in Small-Area Analysis," *Health Services Research,* 24 (1990): 741–771.

DiFranza, Joseph R., et al., "RJR Nabisco's Cartoon Camel Promotes Camel Cigarettes to Children," *Journal of the American Medical Association,* 266 (December 11, 1991): 3149–3153.

DiMasi, Joseph A., et al., "Cost of Innovation in the Pharmaceutical Industry," *Journal of Health Economics,* 10 (1991): 107–142.

Dobson, Allen, and Elizabeth W. Hoy, "Hospital PPS Profits: Past and Prospective," *Health Affairs,* 7 (1988): 126–129.

Donabedian, Avedis, "Evaluating the Quality of Medical Care," *Milbank Memorial Fund Quarterly/Health and Society,* 44 (1966): 166–203.

Donabedian, Avedis, *The Definition of Quality and Approaches to Its Assessment.* Ann Arbor: Health Administration Press, 1980.

Dor, Avi, "Non-minimum Cost Functions and the Stochastic Frontier: On Applications to Health Care Providers," *Journal of Health Economics,* 13 (1994): 329–334.

Dorfman, Robert, and Peter O. Steiner, "Optimal Advertising and Optimal Quality," *American Economic Review,* 44 (1954): 826–836.

Douglas, Stratford, and Govind Hariharan, "The Hazard of Starting Smoking: Estimates from a Split Population Duration Model," *Journal of Health Economics,* 13 (1994): 213–230.

Dranove, David, "Demand Inducement and the Physician/Patient Relationship," *Economic Inquiry,* 26 (1988): 281–298.

Dranove, David, "The Five Ws of Utilization Review," American Enterprise Institute Conference on Health Policy Reform, October 1991.

Dranove, David, "A Problem with Consumer Surplus Measures of the Cost of Practice Variations," *Journal of Health Economics,* 14 (1995): 243–251.

Dranove, David, and Kenneth Cone, "Do State Rate Setting Regulations Really Lower Hospital Expenses?" *Journal of Health Economics,* 4 (1985): 159–165.

Dranove, David, Mark Stanley, and Carol Simon, "Is Hospital Competition Wasteful?," *RAND Journal of Economics,* 23 (1992): 247–262.

Dranove, David, and Paul Wehner, "Physician-Induced Demand for Childbirths," *Journal of Health Economics,* 13 (1994): 61–73.

Dranove, David, and William D. White, "Agency and the Organization of Health Care Delivery," *Inquiry,* 24 (1987): 405–415.

Duncan, R. Paul, "Uncompensated Hospital Care," *Medical Care Review,* 49 (1992): 265–330.

Dunn, Daniel L., et al., "Economies of Scope in Physicians' Work: The Performance of Multiple Surgery," *Inquiry,* 32 (1995): 87–101.

Dyck, Frank J., et al., "Effect of Surveillance on the Number of Hysterectomies in the Province of Saskatchewan," *New England Journal of Medicine,* 296 (1977): 1326–1328.

Easley, David, and Maureen O'Hara, "The Economic Role of the Nonprofit Firm," *Bell Journal of Economics,* 14 (1983): 531–538.

Economic Report of the President, Transmitted to the Congress. February 1985. Washington, D.C.: United States Government Printing Office, 1985.

Eddy, David M., "Clinical Decision Making; From Theory to Practice," *Journal of the American Medical Association,* 263 (January 19, 1990): 441–443.

Eisenberg, J. M., *Doctors' Decisions and the Cost of Medical Care.* Ann Arbor, MI: Health Administration Press, 1986.

Elixhauser, Anne, ed., "Health Care Cost-Benefit and Cost Effectiveness Analysis (CBA/CEA)," *Medical Care,* 31 (1993): JS1–JS150.

Ellis, Randall P., and Thomas G. McGuire, "Cost Sharing and Patterns of Mental Health Care Utilization," *Journal of Human Resources,* 21 (1986a): 359–380.

Ellis, Randall P., and Thomas G. McGuire, "Provider Behavior Under Prospective Reimbursement," *Journal of Health Economics,* 5 (1986): 129–151.

Enthoven, Alain C., "National Health Service: Some Reforms that Might be Politically Feasible," *The Economist,* 22 (1985): 61–64.

Enthoven, Alain C., "Why Managed Care Has Failed to Contain Health Costs," *Health Affairs,* 12 (1993): 27–43.

Ermann, Danny, "Hospital Utilization Review: Past Experience, Future Directions," *Journal of Health Politics, Policy and Law,* 13 (1988): 683–704.

Ernst, Richard L., and Donald E. Yett, *Physician Location and Specialty Choice.* Ann Arbor, MI: Health Administration Press, 1985.

Escarce, José J., "Explaining the Association Between Surgeon Supply and Utilization," *Inquiry,* 29 (1992): 403–415.

Escarce, José J., "Would Eliminating Differences in Physician Practice Style Reduce Geographic Variations in Cataract Surgery Rates?" *Medical Care,* 12 (1993): 1106–1118.

Escarce, José J., et al., "Diffusion of Laparoscopic Cholecystectomy Among General Surgeons in the United States," *Medical Care,* 33 (1995): 256–271.

Eskin, Gerald J., "A Case for Test Marketing Experiments," *Journal of Advertising Research,* 15 (1975): 27–33.

Eskin, Gerald J., and Penny H. Barron, "Effect of Price and Advertising in Test-Market Experiments," *Journal of Marketing Research,* 14 (1977): 499–508.

Evans, Robert G., " 'Behavioral' Cost Functions for Hospitals," *Canadian Journal of Economics,* 4 (1971): 198–215.

Evans, Robert G., "Supplier-Induced Demand; Some Empirical Evidence and Implications," in Mark Perlman, ed., *The Economics of Health and Medical Care.* London: Macmillan, 1974.

Fein, Rashi, *Medical Care, Medical Costs.* Cambridge, MA: Harvard, 1986.

Feinglass, Joe, and James J. Holloway, "The Initial Impact of the Medicare Prospective Payment System on U.S. Health Care: A Review of the Literature," *Medical Care Review,* 48 (1991): 91–115.

Feldman, Roger, and J. Begun, "Effects of Advertising: Lessons from Optometry," *Journal of Human Resources,* 13 (Supplement 1978): 247–262.

Feldman, Roger, and Bryan Dowd, "Is There a Competitive Market for Hospital Services?" *Journal of Health Economics,* 5 (1986): 277–292.

Feldman, Roger, and Bryan Dowd, "A New Estimate of the Welfare Loss of Excess Health Insurance," *American Economic Review,* 81 (1991): 297–301.

Feldman, Roger, and Michael A. Morrisey, "Health Economics: A Report on the Field," *Journal of Health Politics, Policy and Law,* 15 (1990): 627–646.

Feldman, Roger, and Richard M. Scheffler, "The Union Impact on Hospital Wages and Fringe Benefits," *Industrial Labor Relations Review,* 35 (1982): 196–206.

Feldman, Roger, et al., "Effects of HMOs on the Creation of Competitive Markets for Hospital Services," *Journal of Health Economics,* 9 (1990): 207–222.

Feldstein, Martin S., *Economic Analysis for Health Service Efficiency.* Amsterdam: North-Holland, 1967.

Feldstein, Martin S., "Hospital Cost Inflation: A Study of Nonprofit Price Dynamics," *American Economic Review,* 61 (1971): 853–872.

Feldstein, Martin S., "The Welfare Loss of Excess Health Insurance," *Journal of Political Economy,* 81 (1973): 251–280.

Feldstein, Martin S., "The High Cost of Hospitals—And What to Do About It," *The Public Interest,* 48 (1977): 40–54.

Feldstein, Paul J., "Forecasts of Costs in the Hospital Sector," in *Proceedings: Health Care in the American Economy: Issues and Forecasts.* Chicago: Health Services Foundation, 1977.

Feldstein, Paul J., "The Emergence of Market Competition in the U.S. Health Care System. Its Causes, Likely Structure, and Implications," *Health Policy,* 6 (1986): 1–20.

Feldstein, Paul J., *Health Care Economics,* 3rd ed. New York: Wiley, 1988.

Finkler, Merton D., and David D. Wirtschafter, "Cost-Effectiveness and Data Envelopment Analysis," *Health Care Management Review,* 18 (1993): 81–88.

Fisher, Elliott S., et al., "Hospital Readmission Rates for Cohorts of Medicare Beneficiaries in Boston and New Haven," *New England Journal of Medicine,* 331 (1994): 989–995.

Flexner, Abraham, *Medical Education in the United States and Canada, Bulletin No. 4.* New York: Carnegie Foundation for the Advancement of Teaching, 1910.

Flynn, Marilyn L., and Yong-Soon Chung, "Health Care Financing in Korea: Private Market Dilemmas for a Developing Nation," *Journal of Public Health Policy,* 2 (1990): 238–253.

Folland, Sherman T., "Health Care Need, Economics and Social Justice," *International Journal of Social Economics,* 13 (1986): 98–116.

Folland, Sherman T., "Advertising by Physicians: Behavior and Attitudes," *Medical Care,* 25 (1987): 311–326.

Folland, Sherman T., "A Critique of Pure Need: An Analysis of Norman Daniels's Concept of Health Care Need," *International Journal of Social Economics,* 17 (1990): 36–45.

Folland, Sherman T., and Robert Kleiman, "The Effect of Prospective Payment under DRGs on the Market Value of Hospitals," *Quarterly Review of Economics and Business,* 30 (1990): 50–68.

Folland, Sherman T., and Miron Stano, "Sources of Small Area Variations in the Use of Medical Care," *Journal of Health Economics,* 8 (1989): 85–107.

Folland, Sherman T., and Miron Stano, "Small Area Variations: A Critical Review of Propositions, Methods, and Evidence," *Medical Care Review,* 47 (1990): 419–465.

Fontana, John P., "Hospital Marketing Is Here to Stay," *Hospital Topics,* 62 (1984): 12–13.

Foster, Stuart A., and Wilpen L. Gorr, "Federal Health Policy and the Geographic Diffusion of Physicians: A Macro-Scale Analysis," *Policy Sciences,* 25 (1992): 117–134.

Fournier, Gary M., and Jean M. Mitchell, "Hospital Costs and Competition for Services: A Multiproduct Analysis," *Review of Economics and Statistics,* 74 (1992): 627–634.

Frank, Richard G., and Willard G. Manning, Jr., eds., *Economics and Mental Health.* Baltimore: The Johns Hopkins University Press, 1992.

Frank, Richard G., and Thomas G. McGuire, "Estimating Costs of Mental Health and Substance Abuse Coverage," *Health Affairs,* 14 (1995): 102–115.

Frank, Richard G., Thomas G. McGuire, and Joseph P. Newhouse, "Risk Contracts in Managed Mental Health Care," *Health Affairs,* 14 (1995): 50–64.

Frank, Richard G., and David S. Salkever, "Do Public Mental Health Hospitals Crowd Out Care for Indigent Psychiatric Patients in Nonprofit General Hospitals?" in Richard G. Frank and Willard G. Manning, Jr., eds., *Economics and Mental Health.* Baltimore: The Johns Hopkins University Press, 1992.

Frank, Richard G., and David S. Salkever, "Nonprofit Organizations in the Health Sector," *Journal of Economic Perspectives,* 8 (1994): 129–144.

Frank, Richard G., and W. Pete Welch, "The Competitive Effects of HMOs: A Review of the Evidence," *Inquiry,* 22 (1985): 148–161.

Frech, H. E. III, "The Property Rights Theory of the Firm: Empirical Results from a Natural Experiment," *Journal of Political Economy,* 84 (1976): 143–152.

Frech, H. E. III, "The Property Rights Theory of the Firm: Some Evidence from the U.S. Nursing Home Industry," *Zeitschrift Fur Staatswissenschaft,* 141 (1985): 146–166.

Frech, H. E. III, "The United States," *Advances in Health Economics and Health Services Research Supplement 1: Comparative Health Systems.* Greenwich, CT: JAI Press, 1990: 43–75.

Frech, H. E. III, and Paul B. Ginsburg, "Optimal Scale in Medical Practice: A Survivor Analysis," *Journal of Business,* 47 (1974): 23–36.

Frech, H. E. III, and Paul B. Ginsburg, "The Cost of Nursing Home Care in the United States: Government Financing, Ownership, and Efficiency," in J. van der Gaag and Marc Perlman, eds., *Health, Economics, and Health Economics.* Amsterdam: North-Holland, 1981.

Frech, H. E. III, and Paul B. Ginsburg, "Competition Among Health Insurers, Revisited," *Journal of Health Politics, Policy and Law,* 13 (1988): 279–291.

Frech, H. E. III, and Lee R. Mobley, "Resolving the Impasse on Hospital Scale Economies: A New Approach," *Applied Economics,* 27 (1995): 286–296.

Freshnock, Larry, *Physicians and Public Attitudes on Health Care Issues.* Chicago: American Medical Association, 1984.

Friedman, Milton, and Simon Kuznets, *Income from Independent Professional Practice.* New York: National Bureau of Economic Research, 1945.

Fuchs, Victor R., "The Contribution of Health Services to the American Economy," in Victor R. Fuchs, ed., *Essays in the Economics of Health and Medical Care.* New York: National Bureau of Economic Research, 1972.

Fuchs, Victor R., *Who Shall Live?* New York: Basic Books, Inc., 1974.

Fuchs, Victor R., "The Supply of Surgeons and the Demand for Operations," *Journal of Human Resources,* 13 (Supplement 1978): 35–56.

Fuchs, Victor R., "Economics, Health, and Post-Industrial Society," *Milbank Memorial Fund Quarterly/Health and Society,* 57 (1979): 153–182.

Fuchs, Victor R., "Time Preference and Health: An Exploratory Study," in Victor R. Fuchs, ed., *Economic Aspects of Health.* Chicago: The University of Chicago Press, 1982: 93–120.

Fuchs, Victor R., "The Clinton Plan: A Researcher Examines Reform," *Health Affairs,* 13 (1994): 102–114.

Fuchs, Victor R., "Economics, Values, and Health Care Reform," Presidential Address to the American Economic Association, *American Economic Review,* 86 (1996): 1–24.

Fuchs, Victor R., and James S. Hahn, "How Does Canada Do It? A Comparison of Expenditures for Physicians' Services in the United States and Canada," *New England Journal of Medicine,* 323 (1990): 884–890.

Fuchs, Victor R., and Marcia J. Kramer, "Determinants of Expenditures for Physicians' Services in the United States 1948–68," National Bureau of Economic Research, National Center for Health Services Research and Development, DHEW Publication No. (HSM) 73–3013, December 1972.

Gabel, Jon, and Dan Ermann, "Preferred Provider Organizations: Performance, Problems, and Promise," *Health Affairs,* 4 (1985): 24–40.

Gabel, Jon, and Gail A. Jensen, "The Price of State Mandated Benefits," *Inquiry,* 26 (1989): 419–432.

Galbraith, John K., *The Affluent Society.* Boston: Houghton Mifflin, 1958.

Gastonis, Constantine, "The Long Debate on the Sixth Guaiac Test: Time to Move on to New Grounds," *Journal of Health Economics,* 9 (1990): 495–497.

Gaumer, Gary L., "Regulating Health Professionals: A Review of the Empirical Literature," *Milbank Memorial Fund Quarterly/Health and Society,* 62 (1984): 380–416.

Gaumer, Gary L., et al., "Effects of State Prospective Reimbursement Programs on Hospital Mortality," *Medical Care,* 27 (1989): 724–736.

Gauthier, Anne K., et al., "Administrative Costs in the U.S. Health Care System: The Problem or the Solution?," *Inquiry,* 29 (1992): 308–320.

Gaynor, Martin, and Mark V. Pauly, "Compensation and Productive Efficiency in Partnerships: Evidence from Medical Group Practice," *Journal of Political Economy,* 98 (1990): 544–573.

Gaynor, Martin, and Solomon Polachek, "Measuring Information in the Market: An Application to Physician Services," *Southern Economic Journal,* 60 (1994): 815–831.

Gerdtham, Ulf-G, et al., "An Econometric Analysis of Health Care Expenditure: A Cross-Section Study of the OECD Countries," *Journal of Health Economics,* 11 (1992): 63–84.

Gertler, Paul J., "Subsidies, Quality, and the Regulation of Nursing Homes," *Journal of Public Economics,* 38 (1989): 33–52.

Gertler, Paul J., and Donald M. Waldman, "Quality-Adjusted Cost Functions and Policy Evaluation in the Nursing Home Industry," *Journal of Political Economy,* 100 (1992): 1232–1256.

Gibson, Robert M., and Marjorie Smith Mueller, "National Health Expenditures, Fiscal Year 1976," *Social Security Bulletin,* 40 (1977): 3–32.

Ginsburg, Paul B., "Public Insurance Programs: Medicare and Medicaid," in H. E. Frech III, ed., *Health Care in America.* San Francisco: Pacific Research Institute for Public Policy, 1988.

Goddeeris, John H., "Insurance and Incentives for Innovation in Medical Care," *Southern Economic Journal,* 51 (1984a): 530–539.

Goddeeris, John H., "Medical Insurance, Technological Change, and Welfare," *Economic Inquiry,* 22 (1984b): 56–67.

Goddeeris, John H., "Economic Forces and Hospital Technology: Lessons from the United States Experience," *International Journal of Technology Assessment in Health Care,* 3 (1987): 223–240.

Goddeeris, John H., and Thomas P. Bronken, "Benefit-Cost Analysis of Screening," *Medical Care,* 23 (1985): 1242–1255.

Goldberg, Lawrence G., and Warren Greenberg, "The Effect of Physician-Controlled Health Insurance," *Journal of Health Politics, Policy and Law,* 2 (1977): 48–78.

Goodman, Allen C., "Estimation of Offset and Income Effects on the Demand for Mental Health," *Inquiry,* 26 (1989): 235–248.

Goodman, Allen C., and Janet R. Hankin, "Baltimore's Elderly Jews," Johns Hopkins University, Center for Metropolitan Planning and Research, 1981.

Goodman, Allen C., Eleanor Nishiura, and Janet R. Hankin, "Mental Health, Drug Abuse, and Alcoholism Comorbidities," Detroit, MI: Wayne State University, 1995.

Goodman, Allen C., Miron Stano, and John M. Tilford, "Applications and Extensions of the Grossman Health Care Model," Detroit, MI: Wayne State University, 1995.

Goodman, Allen C., and John M. Tilford, "Estimation of Health Care Substitution Effects with a Mixed Multinomial Logit Model," Detroit, MI: Wayne State University, manuscript, 1992.

Goodman, Allen C., et al., "Short Term Alcoholism Treatment: Prices and Substitution Effects," Detroit, MI: Wayne State University, 1994.

Goodman, John C., "Health Insurance: States Can Help," *The Wall Street Journal,* October 17, 1991: A14.

Gordon, Margaret S., *Social Security Policies in Industrial Countries.* Cambridge: Cambridge University Press, 1988.

Gornick, Marian, et al., "Twenty Years of Medicare and Medicaid: Covered Populations, Use of Benefits, and Program Expenditures," *Health Care Financing Review, Annual Supplement,* 6 (1985): 13–59.

Graddy, Elizabeth, "Interest Groups or the Public Interest—Why Do We Regulate Health Occupations?," *Journal of Health Politics, Policy and Law,* 16 (1991): 25–49.

Grannemann, Thomas W., Randall S. Brown, and Mark V. Pauly, "Estimating Hospital Costs: A Multiple-Output Analysis," *Journal of Health Economics,* 5 (1986): 107–127.

Green, Lee A., and Mark P. Becker, "Physician Decision Making and Variation in Hospital Admission Rates for Suspected Acute Cardiac Ischemia," *Medical Care,* 32 (1994): 1086–1097.

Grossman, Michael, *The Demand for Health: A Theoretical and Empirical Investigation.* New York: Columbia (for the National Bureau of Economic Research), 1972a.

Grossman, Michael, "On the Concept of Health Capital and the Demand for Health," *Journal of Political Economy,* 80 (1972b): 223–255.

Grossman, Michael, and Theodore J. Joyce, "Unobservables, Pregnancy Resolutions, and Birth Weight Production Functions in New York City," *Journal of Political Economy,* 98 (1990): 983–1007.

Grossman, Sanford, and Joseph E. Stiglitz, "Information and Competitive Price Systems," *American Economic Review,* 66 (1976): 246–253.

Grytten, Jostein, Fredrik Carlsen, and Rune Sorensen, "Supplier Inducement in a Public Health Care System," *Journal of Health Economics,* 14 (1995): 207–229.

Guterman, Stuart, and Allen Dobson, "Impact of Medicare Perspective Payment System for Hospitals," *Health Care Financing Review,* 7 (1986): 97–114.

Haas-Wilson, Deborah, "Consumer Information and Providers' Reputations: An Empirical Test in the Market for Psychotherapy," *Journal of Health Economics,* 9 (1990): 321–333.

Hadley, Jack, *More Medical Care, Better Health?* Washington, D.C.: Urban Institute, 1982.

Hadley, Jack, "Medicare Spending and Mortality Rates of the Elderly," *Inquiry,* 25 (1988): 485–493.

Hadley, Jack, and Stephen Zuckerman, "The Role of Efficiency in Hospital Rate Setting," *Journal of Health Economics,* 13 (1994): 335–340.

Hadley, Jack, Stephen Zuckerman, and Judith Feder, "Profits and Fiscal Pressure in the Prospective Payment System," *Inquiry,* 26 (1989): 354–365.

Hall, Thomas D., and Cotton M. Lindsay, "Medical Schools: Producers of What? Sellers to Whom?," *Journal of Law and Economics,* 23 (1980): 55–80.

Ham, Chris, and Mats Brommels, "Health Care Reform in the Netherlands, Sweden, and the United Kingdom," *Health Affairs,* 13 (1994): 106–119.

Hamilton, James L., "The Demand for Cigarettes: Advertising, the Health Scare, and the Cigarette Advertising Ban," *Review of Economics and Statistics,* 54 (1972): 401–411.

Hamilton, James L., "The Effect of Cigarette Advertising Bans on Cigarette Consumption," *Proceedings of the Third World Conference on Smoking and Health.* Washington, D.C.: U.S. DHEW, 1975.

Hanke, Steve H., and Richard A. Walker, "Benefit-Cost Analysis Reconsidered: An Evaluation of the Mid-States Project," *Water Resources Research,* 10 (1974): 898–908.

Reprinted in Robert H. Haveman and Julius Margolis, eds., *Public Expenditure and Policy Analysis,* 2nd ed. Chicago: Rand-McNally, 1977.

Hansen, W. Lee, "Shortages and Investment in Health Manpower," in *The Economics of Health and Medical Care: Proceedings of the Conference on the Economics of Health and Medical Care May 10–12, 1962.* Ann Arbor, MI: University of Michigan, 1964.

Hansmann, Henry B., "The Role of Nonprofit Enterprise," *Yale Law Journal,* 89 (1980): 835–901.

Harris, Jeffrey E., "The Internal Organization of Hospitals: Some Economic Implications," *Bell Journal of Economics,* 8 (1977): 467–482.

Harrow, Brooke S., and Randall P. Ellis, "Mental Health Providers' Response to the Reimbursement System," in Richard G. Frank, and Willard G. Manning, Jr., eds., *Economics and Mental Health.* Baltimore: The Johns Hopkins University Press, 1992.

Havighurst, Clark C., "The Questionable Cost-Containment Record of Commercial Health Insurers," in H. E. Frech III, ed., *Health Care in America.* San Francisco: Pacific Research Institute for Public Policy, 1988.

Hay, Joel W., "Is Too Much Being Spent on AIDS?," *The Wall Street Journal,* October 3, 1989.

Hay, Joel W., and Gerard Anderson, "The Hospital Services Market: A Disequilibrium Analysis," *Southern Economic Journal,* 54 (1988): 656–665.

Hay, Joel W., and Michael J. Leahy, "Physician-Induced Demand: An Empirical Analysis of the Consumer Information Gap," *Journal of Health Economics,* 1 (1982): 231–244.

Headen, Alvin E., Jr., "Wages, Returns to Ownership, and Fee Responses to Physician Supply," *Review of Economics and Statistics,* 72 (1990): 30–37.

Health Insurance Association of America, *Source Book of Health Insurance Data,* various years.

Hemenway, David, et al., "Physicians' Responses to Financial Incentives: Evidence from a For-Profit Ambulatory Center," *New England Journal of Medicine,* 322 (1990): 1059–1063.

Henke, Klaus-Dirk, "The Federal Republic of Germany," in Jean-Jacques Rosa, ed., *Advances in Health Economics and Health Services Research, Supplement 1: Comparative Health Systems.* Greenwich, CT: JAI Press, 1990.

Henke, Klaus-Dirk, Margaret A. Murray, and Claudia Ade, "Global Budgeting in Germany: Lessons for the United States," *Health Affairs,* 13 (1994): 7–21.

Hershey, John C., et al., "Health Insurance Under Competition: Would People Choose What Is Expected?," *Inquiry,* 21 (1984): 349–360.

Hibbard, Judith H., and Edward C. Weeks, "Does the Dissemination of Comparative Data on Physician Fees Affect Consumer Use of Services?," *Medical Care,* 27 (1989): 1167–1174.

Hillman, Alan L., Mark V. Pauly, and Joseph J. Kerstein, "How Do Financial Incentives Affect Physicians' Clinical Decisions and the Financial Performance of Health Maintenance Organizations?" *New England Journal of Medicine,* 321 (1989): 86–92.

Hinrichs, Karl, "The Impact of German Health Insurance Reforms on Redistribution and the Culture of Solidarity," *Journal of Health Politics, Policy and Law,* 20 (1995): 653–687.

Hirshleifer, Jack, and Amihai Glazer, *Price Theory and Applications,* 5th ed., Englewood Cliffs, NJ: Prentice Hall, 1992.

Hitiris, Theo, and John Posnett, "The Determinants and Effects of Health Expenditure in Developed Countries," *Journal of Health Economics,* 11 (1992): 173–181.

Hochban, Jacquelyn, et al., "The Hill-Burton Program and Changes in Health Services Delivery," *Inquiry,* 18 (1981): 61–69.

Hodgkin, Dominic, and Thomas G. McGuire, "Payment Levels and Hospital Response to Prospective Payment," *Journal of Health Economics,* 13 (1994): 1–29.

Hodgson, Thomas A., "Cigarette Smoking and Lifetime Medical Expenditures," *Milbank Quarterly,* 70 (1992): 81–125.

Holtmann, Alphonse G., and Todd L. Idson, "Wage Determination of Registered Nurses in Proprietary and Nonprofit Nursing Homes," *Journal of Human Resources,* 28 (1993): 55–79.

Hornbrook, Mark C., and Alan C. Monheit, "The Contribution of Case-Mix Severity to the Hospital Cost-Output Relation," *Inquiry,* 22 (1985): 259–271.

Hsiao, William C., "Resource-Based Relative Value Scale: An Option for Physician Payment," *Inquiry,* 24 (1987): 360–361.

Hsiao, William C., "Medical Savings Accounts: Lessons from Singapore," *Health Affairs,* 14 (1995): 260–266.

Hsiao, William C., Daniel L. Dunn, and Diana K. Verrilli, "Assessing the Implementation of Physician-Payment Reform," *New England Journal of Medicine,* 328 (1993): 928–933.

Hurd, Richard W., "Equilibrium Vacancies in a Labor Market Dominated by Nonprofit Firms: The 'Shortage of Nurses,' " *Review of Economics and Statistics,* 55 (1973): 234–240.

Hurst, Jeremy W., "Reform of Health Care in Germany," *Health Care Financing Review,* 12 (1991): 73–86.

Hurwitz, Mark A., and Richard E. Caves, "Persuasion or Information? Promotion and the Shares of Brand Name and Generic Pharmaceuticals," *Journal of Law and Economics,* 31 (1988): 299–320.

Hyman, David N., *Public Finance,* 3rd ed. Chicago: Dryden Press, 1990.

Illich, Ivan, *Medical Nemesis.* New York: Bantam Books, 1976.

Ingbar, Mary Lee, and Lester D. Taylor, *Hospital Costs in Massachusetts.* Cambridge, MA: Harvard, 1968.

James, John H., "Reforming the British National Health Service: Implementation Problems in London," *Journal of Health Politics, Policy and Law,* 20 (1995): 653–687.

Jeffers, James, Michael Bognanno, and J. Bartlett, "On the Demand Versus Need for Medical Services and the Concept of Shortage," *American Journal of Public Health,* 61 (1971): 46–63.

Jensen, Gail A., and Kevin D. Cotter, "Choice of Purchasing Arrangements in Insurance Markets," Detroit, MI: Department of Economics, Wayne State University, manuscript, November 1987.

Jensen, Gail A., and Michael A. Morrisey, "The Role of Physicians in Hospital Production," *Review of Economics and Statistics,* 68 (1986): 432–442.

Jensen, Gail A., and Michael A. Morrisey, "Group Health Insurance: A Hedonic Price Approach," *Review of Economics and Statistics,* 72 (1990): 38–44.

Johnston, Jack, "Advertising and the Aggregate Demand for Cigarettes: A Comment," *European Economic Review,* 14 (1980): 117–125.

Jolin, Leanne D., et al., "US Medical School Finances," *Journal of the American Medical Association,* 266 (August 21, 1991): 985–990.

Jonas, Steven, *An Introduction to the U.S. Health Care System,* 3rd ed. (1st and 2nd editions by Milton Roemer). New York: Springer Publishing Co., 1992.

Journal of the American Medical Association, 265 (May 15, 1991).

Joyce, Theodore, Andrew D. Racine, and Naci Mocan, "The Consequences and Costs of Maternal Substance Abuse in New York City: A Pooled Time-Series, Cross-section Analysis," *Journal of Health Economics,* 11 (1992): 297–314.

Juba, David A., *Price Setting in the Market for Physicians' Services: A Review of the Literature,* U.S. Department of Health, Education and Welfare, Health Care Financing Administration, HEW Publication No. (HCFA) 03012 9–79, GPO 1979.

Kamien, Morton I., and Nancy L. Schwartz, *Market Structure and Innovation.* Cambridge: Cambridge University Press, 1982.

Katz, Steven J., Lawrence F. McMahon, and Willard G. Manning, "Comparing the Use of Diagnostic Tests in Canadian and U.S. Hospitals," *Medical Care,* 34 (1996): 117–125.

Keeler, Emmett B., and John E. Rolph, "The Demand for Episodes of Treatment in the Health Insurance Experiment," *Journal of Health Economics,* 7 (1988): 337–367.

Keeler, Emmett B., Willard G. Manning, Jr., and Kenneth B. Wells, "The Demand for Episodes of Mental Health Services," *Journal of Health Economics,* 7 (1988): 369–392.

Kenkel, Donald S., "The Demand for Preventive Medical Care," *Applied Economics,* 26 (1994): 313–325.

Kessel, Reuben, "Price Discrimination in Medicine," *Journal of Law and Economics,* 1 (1958): 20–53.

Kessides, Ioannis N., "Advertising, Sunk Costs, and Barriers to Entry," *Review of Economics and Statistics,* 68 (1986): 84–95.

Kessler, Ronald C., et al., "Lifetime and 12-month Prevalence of DSM-III-R Psychiatric Disorders in the United States," *Archives of General Psychiatry,* 51 (1994): 8–19.

Klarman, Herbert E., "The Road to Cost-Effectiveness Analysis," *Milbank Memorial Fund Quarterly/Health and Society,* 6 (1982): 585–603.

Klausen, Liv Marit, Trand E. Olsen, and Alf Erling Risa, "Technological Diffusion in Primary Health Care," *Journal of Health Economics,* 13 (1992): 439–452.

Kleinman, Joel C., Marsha Gold, and Diane McKue, "Use of Ambulatory Care by the Poor: Another Look at Equity," *Medical Care,* 19 (1981): 1011–1029.

Kooreman, Peter, "Data Envelopment Analysis and Parametric Frontier Estimation: Complementary Tools," *Journal of Health Economics,* 13 (1994): 345–346.

Krahn, Murray D., et al., "Screening for Prostate Cancer: A Decision-Analytic View," *Journal of the American Medical Association,* 272 (September 14, 1994): 773–780.

Krasny, Jacques, and Ian R. Ferrier, "A Closer Look at Health Care in Canada," *Health Affairs,* 10 (1991): 152–158.

Krizay, John, and Andrew Wilson, *The Patient as Consumer.* Lexington, MA: Lexington, 1974.

Krueger, Alan B., and Uwe E. Reinhardt, "The Economics of Employer Versus Individual Mandates," *Health Affairs,* 13 (1994): 34–53.

Kwoka, John E., Jr., "Advertising and the Price and Quality of Optometric Services," *American Economic Review,* 74 (1984): 211–216.

Labelle, Roberta, Gregg Stoddard, and Thomas Rice, "A Re-Examination of the Meaning and Importance of Supplier-Induced Demand," *Journal of Health Economics,* 13 (1994): 347–368.

Lalonde, Marc, *A New Perspective on the Health of Canadians.* Office of the Canadian Minister of National Health and Welfare, Ottawa, 1974.

Lamberton, C. E., W. D. Ellington, and K. R. Spear, "Factors Determining the Demand for Nursing Home Services," *Quarterly Review of Economics and Business,* 26 (1986): 74–90.

Lambin, J. J., *Advertising, Competition and Market Conduct in Oligopoly Over Time.* Amsterdam: North-Holland, 1976.

Langwell, Kathryn M., and Lyle M. Nelson, "Physician Payment Systems: A Review of History, Alternatives and Evidence," *Medical Care Review,* 43 (1986): 5–58.

Laugesen, Murray, and Chris Meads, "Tobacco Advertising Restrictions, Price, Income, and Tobacco Consumption in OECD Countries, 1960–1986," *British Journal of Addiction,* 86 (1991): 1343–1354.

Lave, Judith R., and Lester B. Lave, "Hospital Cost Functions," *American Economic Review,* 60 (1970): 379–395.

Lee, Maw L., "A Conspicuous Production Theory of Hospital Behavior," *Southern Economic Journal,* 38 (1971): 48–58.

Lee, Roger I., and Lewis W. Jones, *The Fundamentals of Good Medical Care.* Publication of the Committee on the Costs of Medical Care. Chicago: University of Chicago, 1933.

Lee, Robert H., and Jack Hadley, "Physicians' Fees and Public Medical Care Programs," *Health Services Research,* 16 (1981): 185–203.

Leffler, Keith B., "Physician Licensure: Competition and Monopoly in American Medicine," *Journal of Law and Economics,* 21 (1978): 165–186.

Leffler, Keith B., "Persuasion or Information? The Economics of Prescription Drug Advertising," *Journal of Law and Economics,* 24 (1981): 45–74.

Leffler, Keith B., and Cotton M. Lindsay, "Student Discount Rates, Consumption Loans, and Subsidies to Professional Training," *Journal of Human Resources,* 16 (1981): 468–476.

Legnini, Mark W., et al., "Changes in Connecticut Hospital Use Rates: Have Small-Area Variations Been Affected?," *Inquiry,* 27 (1990): 51–60.

Lerner, Arthur N., "Federal Trade Commission Antitrust Activities in the Health Care Services Field," *Antitrust Bulletin* (1984): 205–224.

Levit, Katherine R., et al., "National Health Expenditures, 1993," *Health Care Financing Review,* 16 (1994): 247–294.

Lewin, Lawrence, Robert Derzon, and Rhea Margulies, "Investor-Owneds and Nonprofits Differ in Economic Performance," *Hospitals,* 55 (July 1, 1981): 52–58.

Lewin, Lawrence, Timothy J. Eckels, and Linda B. Miller, "Setting the Record Straight: The Provision of Uncompensated Care by Not-for-Profit Hospitals," *New England Journal of Medicine,* 318 (1988): 1212–1215.

Lewis, Karen, "Comparison of Use by Enrolled and Recently Disenrolled Populations in a Health Maintenance Organization," *Health Services Research,* 19 (1984): 1–22.

Lewit, Eugene M., and Douglas Coate, "The Potential for Using Excise Taxes to Reduce Smoking," *Journal of Health Economics,* 1 (August 1982): 121–145.

Lewit, Eugene M., Douglas Coate, and Michael Grossman, "The Effects of Government Regulation on Teenage Smoking," *Journal of Law and Economics,* 24 (1981): 545–569.

Link, Charles, and John Landon, "Monopsony and Union Power in the Market for Nurses," *Southern Economic Journal,* 41 (1975): 649–659.

Linn, Margaret W., Lee Gurel, and Bernard S. Linn, "Patient Outcome as a Measure of Quality of Nursing Home Care," *American Journal of Public Health,* 4 (1977): 337–344.

Linnerooth, Joanne, "The Value of Human Life: A Review of the Models," *Economic Inquiry,* 17 (1979): 52–74.

Littrup, Peter J., Allen C. Goodman, and Curtis J. Mettlin, "The Benefit and Cost of Prostate Cancer Early Detection," *CA—A Cancer Journal for Clinicians,* 43 (May/June 1993): 134–149.

LoGerfo, James P., et al., "Rates of Surgical Care in Prepaid Group Practices and the Independent Setting: What Are the Reasons for the Differences?" *Medical Care,* 17 (1979): 1–10.

Long, Millard F., "Efficient Use of Hospitals," in Selma J. Mushkin, ed., *The Economics of Health and Medical Care.* Ann Arbor, MI: University of Michigan, 1964.

Luft, Harold S., "How Do Health-Maintenance Organizations Achieve Their "Savings?" *New England Journal of Medicine,* 298 (1978): 1336–1343.

Luft, Harold S., *Health Maintenance Organizations: Dimensions of Performance.* New York: John Wiley & Sons, 1981.

Luft, Harold S., "Health Maintenance Organizations and the Rationing of Medical Care," *Milbank Memorial Fund Quarterly/Health and Society,* 60 (1982): 268–306.

Luft, Harold S., "Translating the U.S. HMO Experience to Other Health Systems," *Health Affairs,* 10 (1991): 172–186.

Luft, Harold S., et al., "Does Quality Influence Choice of Hospital?" *Journal of the American Medical Association,* 263 (June 6, 1990): 2899–2906.

Lynch, James, and Drue Schuler, "Consumer Evaluation of the Quality of Hospital Services from an Economics of Information Perspective," *Journal of Health Care Marketing,* 10 (1990): 16–22.

Maddala, G. S., *Limited Dependent and Qualitative Variables in Econometrics.* Cambridge: Cambridge University Press, 1983.

Madrian, Brigitte C., "Employment-Based Health Insurance and Job Mobility: Is There Evidence of Job-Lock?" *Quarterly Journal of Economics,* 109 (May 1994): 27–54.

Maioni, Antonia, "Nothing Succeeds Like the Right Kind of Failure: Postwar National Health Insurance Initiatives in Canada and the United States," *Journal of Health Politics, Policy and Law,* 20 (1995): 5–30.

Manderscheid, Ronald W., and M. A. Sonnenschein, eds., *Mental Health, United States, 1992*. Washington, DC: U.S. Government Printing Office, 1992.

Manning, Willard G., Jr., and Richard G. Frank, "Econometric Issues in the Demand for Mental Health Care Under Insurance," in Richard G. Frank and Willard G. Manning, Jr., eds., *Economics and Mental Health*. Baltimore: The Johns Hopkins University Press, 1992.

Manning, Willard G., et al., "A Controlled Trial of the Effect of a Prepaid Group Practice on Use of Services," *New England Journal of Medicine,* 310 (1984): 1505–1510.

Manning, Willard G., et al., "Health Insurance and the Demand for Medical Care: Evidence from a Randomized Experiment," *American Economic Review,* 77 (1987): 251–277.

Marder, William D., and Stephen Zuckerman, "Competition and Medical Groups: A Survivor Analysis," *Journal of Health Economics,* 4 (1985): 167–176.

Marks, Daniel B., et al., "Use of Medical Resources and Quality of Life After Acute Myocardial Infarction in Canada and the United States," *New England Journal of Medicine,* 331 (1994): 1130–1135.

Massaro, Thomas A., and Yu-Ning Wong, "Positive Experience with Medical Savings Accounts in Singapore," *Health Affairs,* 14 (1995): 267–271.

Mauldon, Jane, "The Effect of Marital Disruption on Children's Health," *Demography,* 27 (1990): 431–446.

Maynard, Alan, "The United Kingdom," in Jean-Jacques Rosa, ed., *Advances in Health Economics and Health Services Research, Supplement 1: Comparative Health Systems*. Greenwich, CT: JAI Press, 1990: 1–26.

Mayo, John W., and Deborah A. McFarland, "Regulation, Market Structure, and Hospital Costs," *Southern Economic Journal,* 55 (1989): 559–569.

Mayo, John W., and Deborah A. McFarland, "Regulation, Market Structure, and Hospital Costs: Reply," *Southern Economic Journal* (1991): 535–538.

McCarthy, Thomas R., "The Competitive Nature of the Primary-Care Physician Services Market," *Journal of Health Economics,* 4 (1985): 93–117.

McGuinness, Tony, and Keith Cowling, "Advertising and the Aggregate Demand for Cigarettes," *European Economic Review,* 6 (1975): 311–328.

McKay, Niccie L., "The Prisoner's Dilemma: An Obstacle to Cooperation in Health Care Markets," *Medical Care Review,* 51 (1994): 179–204.

McKeown, Thomas, *The Modern Rise of Population*. New York: Academic Press, 1976.

McKinlay, John B., and Sonja M. McKinlay, "The Questionable Contribution of Medical Measures to the Decline of Mortality in the United States in the Twentieth Century," *Milbank Memorial Fund Quarterly/Health and Society,* 55 (1977): 405–428.

McLaughlin, Catherine G., "Market Responses to HMOs: Price Competition or Rivalry?," *Inquiry,* 25 (1988): 207–218.

McLaughlin, Catherine G., "The Dilemma of Affordability: Health Insurance for Small Business," in *American Health Policy: Critical Issues for Reform,* Robert B. Helms, ed. Washington, DC: AEI Press, 1993: 152–166.

McLaughlin, Catherine G., and Wendy K. Zellers, "Small Business and Health Care Reform," The University of Michigan School of Public Health, 1994.

McLaughlin, Catherine G., et al., "Small-Area Variation in Hospital Discharge Rates: Do Socio-economic Variables Matter?," *Medical Care,* 27 (1989): 507–521.

McPherson, Klim, et al., "Small-Area Variations in the Use of Common Surgical Procedures: An International Comparison of New England, England, and Norway," *New England Journal of Medicine,* 307 (1982): 1310–1313.

Mechanic, David, and David A. Rochefort, "Deinstitutionalization: An Appraisal of Reform," *Annual Review of Sociology,* 16 (1990): 301–327.

Medicare and Medicaid, Prospective Payment Assessment Commission: Medicare and the Health System. Report to Congress. Chicago: Commerce Clearing House, Inc., 1991.

Miller, Robert H., and Harold S. Luft, "Managed Care Plan Performance Since 1980: A Literature Analysis," *Journal of the American Medical Association,* 271 (May 18, 1994): 1512–1519.

Mills, Edwin S., *Studies in the Structure of the Urban Economy.* Baltimore: Johns Hopkins, 1972.

Mills, Edwin S., and Bruce W. Hamilton, *Urban Economics,* 5th ed. New York: Harper Collins, 1994.

Mitchell, Janet B., and Jerry Cromwell, "Physician Behavior Under the Medicare Assignment Option," *Journal of Health Economics,* 1 (1982): 245–264.

Mitchell, Janet B., and Jerry Cromwell, "Impact of All-or-Nothing Assignment Requirement Under Medicare," *Health Care Financing Review,* 4 (1983): 59–78.

Mobley, Lee R., and H. E. Frech III, "Firm Growth and Failure in Increasingly Competitive Markets: Theory and Application to Hospital Markets," *Journal of the Economics of Business,* 1 (1994): 77–93.

Moffit, Robert E., "Surprise, A Government Health Plan that Works," *The Wall Street Journal* (April 2, 1992): A14.

Monroe, Kent B., "Buyers' Subjective Perceptions of Price," *Journal of Marketing Research,* 10 (1973): 70–80.

Montgomery-Karp, Beverly, "Market Demands Call for New Treatment," *Advertising Age,* 54 (September 26, 1983): M9–11.

Moon, Ok-Ryun, "The National Health Insurance Policy Issues in Korea," *Korean Journal of Public Health,* 42 (1989): 98–114.

Mooney, Gavin, et al., "Utilization as a Measure of Equity: Weighing Heat?" *Journal of Health Economics,* 10 (1991): 475–480.

Mooney, Gavin, et al., "Reweighing Heat: Response to Culyer, van Doorslaer and Wagstaff," *Journal of Health Economics,* 11 (1992): 199–205.

Moore, Gordon T., "Will the Power of the Marketplace Produce the Workforce We Need?," *Inquiry,* 31 (1994): 276–282.

Moore, Michael J., "Death and Tobacco Taxes," Working Paper No. 5153, National Bureau of Economic Research, Inc., Cambridge, MA, June 1995.

Morrisey, Michael A., "Movies and Myths: Hospital Cost Shifting," *Business Economics,* 30 (1995): 22–25.

Mott, Peter D., "Hospital Utilization by Health Maintenance Organizations: Separating Apples from Oranges," *Medical Care,* 24 (1986): 398–406.

Mueller, Curt D., and Alan C. Monheit, "Insurance Coverage and the Demand for Dental Care," *Journal of Health Economics,* 7 (1988): 59–72.

Mullahy, John, and Jody L. Sindelar, "Alcoholism, Work, and Income," *Journal of Labor Economics,* 11 (1993): 494–520.

Mushkin, Selma J., *Biomedical Research: Costs and Benefits.* Cambridge, MA: Ballinger, 1979.

Mwabu, Germano, Martha Ainsworth, and Andrew Nyamete, "Quality of Medical Care and Choice of Medical Treatment in Kenya: An Empirical Analysis," *Journal of Human Resources,* 28 (1993): 838–862.

Nelson, Phillip, "Information and Consumer Behavior," *Journal of Political Economy,* 78 (1970): 311–329.

Nelson, Phillip, "Advertising as Information," *Journal of Political Economy,* 82 (1974): 729–754.

Newbold, Paul, *Statistics for Business and Economics,* 4th ed. Englewood Cliffs, NJ: Prentice-Hall, 1995.

Newhauser, Duncan, and Ann M. Lewicki, "What Do We Gain from the Sixth Stool Guaiac?," *New England Journal of Medicine,* 293 (1975): 226–228.

Newhouse, Joseph P., "Toward a Theory of Nonprofit Institutions: An Economic Model of a Hospital," *American Economic Review,* 60 (1970): 64–74.

Newhouse, Joseph P., "Medical-Care Expenditures: A Cross-National Survey," *Journal of Human Resources,* 12 (1977): 115–125.

Newhouse, Joseph P., *The Economics of Medical Care.* Reading, MA: Addison-Wesley, 1978a.

Newhouse, Joseph P., "The Structure of Health Insurance and the Erosion of Competition in the Medical Marketplace," in W. Greenberg, ed., *Competition in the Health Care Sector: Past, Present and Future.* Germantown, MD: Aspen Systems, 1978b.

Newhouse, Joseph P., "The Demand for Medical Care Services: A Retrospect and Prospect," in J. van der Gaag and M. Perlman, eds., *Health, Economics, and Health Economics*. Amsterdam: North-Holland, 1981: 85–102.

Newhouse, Joseph P., "Has the Erosion of the Medical Marketplace Ended?" *Journal of Health Politics, Policy and Law*, 13 (1988): 263–277.

Newhouse, Joseph P., "Medical Care Costs: How Much Welfare Loss?" *Journal of Economic Perspectives*, 6 (1992): 3–21.

Newhouse, Joseph P., "Frontier Estimation: How Useful a Tool in Health Economics?" *Journal of Health Economics*, 13 (1994): 317–322.

Newhouse, Joseph P., Geoffrey Anderson, and Leslie L. Roos, "Hospital Spending in the United States and Canada: A Comparison," *Health Affairs*, 7 (1988): 6–16.

Newhouse, Joseph P., and Daniel J. Byrne, "Did Medicare's Perspective Payment System Cause Length of Stay to Fall?," *Journal of Health Economics*, 7 (1988): 413–416.

Newhouse, Joseph P., and Lindy J. Friedlander, "The Relationship Between Medical Resources and Measures of Health: Some Additional Evidence," *Journal of Human Resources*, 15 (1980): 200–218.

Newhouse, Joseph P., and Charles E. Phelps, "New Estimates of Price and Income Elasticities of Medical Care Services," in Richard Rosett, ed., *The Role of Health Insurance in the Health Services Sector*. New York: Neal Watson, 1976.

Newhouse, Joseph P., John E. Ware, and Cathy A. Donald, "How Sophisticated Are Consumers About the Medical Care Delivery System?" *Medical Care*, 19 (1981): 316–328.

Newhouse, Joseph P., et al., *How Have Location Patterns Affected the Availability of Medical Services?* Publication R-2872-HJK/HHS/RWJ, Rand, Santa Monica, CA, May 1982.

Newhouse, Joseph P., et al., "Are Fee-for-Service Costs Increasing Faster than HMO Costs?," *Medical Care*, 23 (1985): 960–966.

Newhouse, Joseph P., et al., *Free for All? Lessons from the RAND Health Insurance Experiment*. Cambridge, MA: Harvard University Press, 1993.

Nozick, Robert, *Anarchy, State, and Utopia*. New York: Basic Books, 1974.

Nyman, John A., "Testing for Excess Demand in Nursing Home Markets," *Medical Care*, 31 (1993): 680–693.

Nyman, John A., et al., "Changing Physician Behavior: Does Medical Review of Part B Medicare Claims Make a Difference?," *Inquiry*, 27 (1990): 127–137.

O'Brien, Jack, Borje O. Saxberg, and Howard L. Smith, "For-Profit or Not-for-Profit Nursing Homes: Does It Matter?," *The Gerontologist*, 23 (1983): 341–348.

Oberg, Charles N., and Cynthia Longseth Polich, "Medicaid: Entering the Third Decade," *Health Affairs*, 7 (1988): 83–96.

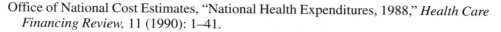

Office of National Cost Estimates, "National Health Expenditures, 1988," *Health Care Financing Review,* 11 (1990): 1–41.

Office of National Cost Estimates, "National Health Expenditures, 1990," *Health Care Financing Review,* 13 (1991): 29–54.

Office of the President, *The President's Comprehensive Health Reform Program,* February 6, 1992.

Okun, Arthur, *Efficiency and Equity: The Big Tradeoff.* Washington, DC: Brookings, 1975.

Olkin, Ingram, and Jerome Sacks, "Cross-Disciplinary Research in the Statistical Sciences," Hayward, CA: Institute of Mathematical Statistics, September 1988.

Parker-Pope, Tara, "Antismoking Sentiment Flares in Europe's Smoke-Filled Cafes," *The Wall Street Journal* (August 28, 1995): B1.

Parkin, David, Alistair McGuire, and Brian Yule, "Aggregate Health Care Expenditures and National Income: Is Health Care a Luxury Good?" *Journal of Health Economics,* 6 (1987): 109–128.

Pattison, Robert, and Hallie Katz, "Investor-Owned and Not-for-Profit Hospitals: A Comparison Based on California Data," *The New England Journal of Medicine,* 309 (1982): 347–353.

Paul, Chris, "Physician Licensure and the Quality of Medical Care," *Atlantic Economic Journal,* 12 (1984): 18–30.

Pauly, Mark V., "The Economics of Moral Hazard: Comment," *American Economic Review,* 58 (1968): 531–537.

Pauly, Mark V., *Medical Care at Public Expense: A Study in Applied Welfare Economics.* New York: Praeger, 1971.

Pauly, Mark V., "Is Medical Care Really Different?," in Warren Greenberg, ed., *Competition in the Health Care Sector.* Germantown, MD: Aspen Systems, 1978.

Pauly, Mark V., "A Primer on Competition in Medical Markets," in H. E. Frech III, ed., *Health Care in America.* San Francisco: Pacific Research Institute for Public Policy, 1988a.

Pauly, Mark V., "Is Medical Care Different? Old Questions, New Answers," *Journal of Health Politics, Policy and Law,* 13 (1988b): 227–237.

Pauly, Mark V., "Editorial: A Re-Examination of the Meaning and Importance of Supplier-Induced Demand," *Journal of Health Economics,* 13 (1994a): 369–372.

Pauly, Mark V., "Making a Case for Employer-Enforced Individual Mandates," *Health Affairs,* 13 (1994b): 21–33.

Pauly, Mark V., and John C. Goodman, "Tax Credits for Health Insurance and Medical Savings Accounts," *Health Affairs,* 14 (1995): 126–139.

Pauly, Mark V., and Michael Redisch, "The Not-for-Profit Hospital as a Physician's Cooperative," *American Economic Review,* 63 (1973): 87–100.

Pauly, Mark V., and Mark A. Satterthwaite, "The Pricing of Primary Care Physicians' Services: A Test of the Role of Consumer Information," *Bell Journal of Economics,* 12 (1981): 488–506.

Pauly, Mark V., et al., "A Plan for 'Responsible National Health Insurance,' " *Health Affairs,* 10 (1991): 5–25.

Peabody, John W., Sung-Woo Lee, and Stephen R. Bickel, "Health Care for All in the Republic of Korea: One Country's Experience with Implementing Universal Health Care," *Health Policy,* 31 (1995): 29–42.

Peltzman, Sam, "Toward a More General Theory of Regulation," *Journal of Law and Economics,* 19 (1976): 211–248.

Pernick, Martin S., "The Cultural Ecology of Health: Science, Values, and Society in the History of American Medicine," manuscript of book in progress, 1991.

Petroshius, Susan M., and Kent B. Monroe, "Effect of Product Line Pricing Characteristics on Product Evaluations," *Journal of Consumer Research,* 13 (1987): 511–519.

Pfaff, Martin, "Differences in Health Care Spending Across Countries: Statistical Evidence," *Journal of Health Politics, Policy and Law,* 15 (1990): 1–67.

Pharmaceutical Manufacturers Association, "Facts at a Glance," Washington, DC, May 1987.

Phelps, Charles E., *Health Economics.* New York: Harper Collins, 1992.

Phelps, Charles E., "Welfare Loss from Variations: Further Considerations," *Journal of Health Economics,* 14 (1995): 253–260.

Phelps, Charles E., and Cathleen Mooney, "Correction and Update on 'Priority Setting in Medical Technology Assessment,' " *Medical Care,* 30 (1992): 744–751.

Phelps, Charles E., and Stephen T. Parente, "Priority Setting in Medical Technology and Medical Practice Assessment," *Medical Care,* 28 (1990): 703–723.

Phlips, Louis, *The Economics of Imperfect Information.* Cambridge: Cambridge University Press, 1988.

Physician Payment Review Commission, *Annual Report to Congress,* April 5, 1995.

Pindyck, Robert S., and Daniel L. Rubinfeld, *Microeconomics,* 2nd ed. New York: Macmillan, 1992.

Pitt, Laura, *1988 January Update of Medicare Enrollments in HMOs.* Excelsior, MN: InterStudy, 1988.

Politzer, Robert M., Charles A. Yesalis, and Jerald M. Katzoff, "The Hidden Supply of Foreign Medical Graduates," *Medical Care,* 27 (1989): 1046–1057.

Pollard, Michael R., and Robert F. Leibenluft, *Antitrust and the Health Professions,* Office of Policy and Planning, Federal Trade Commission, 1981.

Prospective Payment Review Commission, *Medicare Prospective Payment and the American Health Care System,* Report to Congress, June 24, 1991, Commerce Clearing House, Inc., Chicago, IL, 1991.

Prospective Payment Assessment Commission, *Medicare and the American Health Care System,* Report to Congress, June 1995.

Quick, Jonathan D., M. R. Greenlick, and K. L. Roghmann, "Prenatal Care and Pregnancy Outcome in an HMO and General Population: A Multivariate Cohort Analysis," *American Journal of Public Health,* 71 (1981): 381–390.

Raffel, Marshall W., and Norna K. Raffel, *The U.S. Health System: Origins and Functions,* 4th ed. Albany, NY: Delmar, 1994.

Rakich, Jonathon S., "The Canadian and U.S. Health Care Systems: Profiles and Policies," *Hospital & Health Services Administration,* 36 (1991): 25–42.

Rathwell, Tom, "Health Care in Canada: A System in Turmoil," *Health Policy,* 24 (1994): 5–17.

Rawls, John, *A Theory of Justice.* Cambridge, MA: Belnap Press of the Harvard University Press, 1971.

Rayack, Elton, "The Physician Service Industry," in *The Structure of American Industry,* 6th ed., Walter Adams, ed. New York: Macmillan, 1982.

Register, Charles A., and Edward R. Bruning, "Profit Incentives and Technical Efficiency in the Production of Hospital Care," *Southern Economic Journal,* 53 (1987): 899–914.

Reinhardt, Uwe E., "A Production Function for Physician Services," *Review of Economics and Statistics* (1972): 55–65.

Reinhardt, Uwe E., "Economists in Health Care: Saviors, or Elephants in a Porcelain Shop?," *American Economic Review,* 79 (1989): 337–342.

Reinhardt, Uwe E., "Germany's Health Care System: It's Not the American Way," *Health Affairs,* 13 (1994a): 22–24.

Reinhardt, Uwe E., "Planning the Nation's Health Workforce: Let the Market In," *Inquiry,* 31 (1994b): 250–263.

Renn, Steven C., et al., "The Effects of Ownership and System Affiliation on the Economic Performance of Hospitals," *Inquiry,* 22 (1985): 219–236.

Rhee, Sang-O, et al., "USMGs Versus FMGs: Are There Performance Differences in the Ambulatory Setting?" *Medical Care,* 24 (1986): 248–258.

Rice, Dorothy, *Estimating the Cost of Illness.* U.S. Public Health Service Publication No. 947–6, Washington, D.C.: GPO, May 1966.

Rice, Thomas H., "The Impact of Changing Medicare Reimbursement Rates on Physician-Induced Demand," *Medical Care,* 21 (1983): 803–815.

Rice, Thomas H., and Roberta J. Labelle, "Do Physicians Induce Demand for Medical Service?" *Journal of Health Politics, Policy and Law,* 14 (1989): 587–600.

Rifkind, Basil M., et al., "Distribution of High Density and Other Lipoproteins in Selected LRC Prevalence Study Populations: A Brief Survey," *Lipids,* 14 (1979): 105–112.

Rizzo, John A., "Physician Advertising Revisited," *Medical Care,* 26 (1988): 1238–1244.

Rizzo, John A., and Richard J. Zeckhauser, "Advertising and Entry: The Case of Physician Services," *Journal of Political Economy,* 98 (1990): 476–500.

Rizzo, John A., and Richard J. Zeckhauser, "Advertising and the Price, Quantity, and Quality of Primary Care Physician Services," *Journal of Human Resources,* 27 (1992): 381–421.

Roberts, Mark J., and Larry Samuelson, "An Empirical Analysis of Dynamic, Nonprice Competition in an Oligopolistic Industry," *Rand Journal of Economics,* 19 (1988): 200–220.

Rochaix, Lise, "Information Asymmetry and Search in the Market for Physicians' Services," *Journal of Health Economics,* 8 (1989): 53–84.

Roemer, Milton I., "Bed Supply and Hospital Utilization: A National Experiment," *Hospitals, J.A.H.A.* 35 (1961): 988–993.

Roemer, Milton I., and William Shonick, "HMO Performance: The Recent Evidence," *Milbank Memorial Fund Quarterly/Health and Society,* 51 (Summer 1973): 271–317.

Rolph, Elizabeth S., Paul B. Ginsburg, and Susan D. Hosek, "The Regulation of Preferred Provider Arrangements," *Health Affairs,* 6 (1987): 32–45.

Romeo, Anthony A., Judith L. Wagner, and Robert H. Lee, "Prospective Reimbursement and the Diffusion of New Technologies in Hospitals," *Journal of Health Economics,* 3 (1984): 1–24.

Rosett, Richard N., and Lien-fu Huang, "The Effect of Health Insurance on the Demand for Medical Care," *Journal of Political Economy,* 81 (1973): 281–305.

Rosko, Michael D., and Robert W. Broyles, *The Economics of Health Care.* New York: Greenwood, 1988.

Rossiter, Louis F., and Gail R. Wilensky, "A Reexamination of the Use of Physician Services: The Role of Physician-Initiated Demand," *Inquiry,* 20 (1983): 162–172.

Rossiter, Louis F., and Gail R. Wilensky, "Identification of Physician-Induced Demand," *Journal of Human Resources,* 19 (1984): 231–244.

Rotfeld, Herbert J., and Kim B. Rotzoll, "Advertising and Product Quality: Are Heavily Advertised Products Better?," *Journal of Consumer Affairs,* 10 (1976): 37–47.

Rouleau, Jean L., et al., "A Comparison of Management Patterns after Acute Myocardial Infarction in Canada and the United States," *New England Journal of Medicine,* 328 (1993): 779–784.

Rublee, Dale A., "Medical Technology in Canada, Germany and the United States: An Update," *Health Affairs,* 13 (1994): 113–117.

Ruffin, Roy J., and Duane E. Leigh, "Charity, Competition, and the Pricing of Doctors' Services," *Journal of Human Resources,* 8 (1973): 212–222.

Russell, Louise B., "The Diffusion of Hospital Technologies: Some Econometric Evidence," *Journal of Human Resources,* 12 (1977): 482–502.

Russell, Louise B., *Educated Guesses: Making Policy About Medical Screening Tests.* Berkeley: University of California Press, 1994.

Saffer, Henry, "Alcohol Advertising Bans and Alcohol Abuse: An International Perspective," *Journal of Health Economics,* 10 (1991): 65–79.

Safriet, Barbara J., "Impediments to Progress in Health Care Workforce Policy: License and Practice Laws," *Inquiry,* 31 (1994): 310–317.

Salkever, David S., and Thomas W. Bice, *Hospital Certificate-of-Need Controls: Impact on Investment, Costs, and Use.* Washington, DC: American Enterprise Institute, 1979.

Salop, Stephen C., "Information and Monopolistic Competition," *American Economic Review,* 66 (1976): 240–245.

Salvatore, Dominick, *Schaum's Outline Series: Microeconomic Theory,* 2nd ed. New York: McGraw-Hill, 1983.

Sassone, Peter G., and William A. Schaffer, *Cost-Benefit Analysis: A Handbook.* New York: Academic Press, 1978.

Satterthwaite, Mark A., "Consumer Information, Equilibrium Industry Price, and the Number of Sellers," *Bell Journal of Economics,* 10 (1979): 483–502.

Scanlon, William J., "A Theory of the Nursing Home Market," *Inquiry,* 17 (1980): 25–41.

Schaefer, Mark E., "Demand Versus Need for Medical Services in a General Cost Benefit Setting," *American Journal of Public Health,* 65 (1975): 293–295.

Scheffler, Richard M., "The United Mine Workers' Health Plan: An Analysis of the Cost-Sharing Program," *Medical Care,* 22 (1984): 247–254.

Scherer, F. Michael, *Innovation and Growth: Schumpeterian Perspectives.* Cambridge, MA: MIT, 1984.

Schieber, George J., and Jean-Pierre Poullier, "Overview of International Comparisons of Health Care Expenditures," *Health Care Financing Review,* 10 (Annual Supplement 1989): 1–7.

Schieber, George J., and Jean-Pierre Poullier, "International Health Spending: Issues and Trends," *Health Affairs,* 10 (1991): 106–116.

Schmalensee, Richard, *The Economics of Advertising.* Amsterdam: North-Holland, 1972.

Schmalensee, Richard, "A Model of Advertising and Product Quality," *Journal of Political Economy,* 86 (1978): 485–503.

Schneider, Lynne, Benjamin Klein, and Kevin M. Murphy, "Governmental Regulation of Cigarette Health Information," *Journal of Law and Economics,* 24 (1981): 575–612.

Schneider, Markus, "Health Care Cost Containment in the Federal Republic of Germany," *Health Care Financing Review,* 12 (1991): 87–101.

Schneyer, Solomon, J. Steven Landefeld, and Frank H. Sandifer, "Biomedical Research and Illness: 1900–1979," *Milbank Memorial Fund Quarterly/Health and Society,* 59 (1981): 44–58.

v. D. Schulenburg, J. -Matthias, "Germany: Solidarity at a Price," *Journal of Health Politics, Policy and Law,* 17 (1992): 715–738.

Schultz, T. Paul, "Introduction: Symposium on Investments in Women's Human Capital and Development," *Journal of Human Resources,* 28 (1993): 689–693.

Schwartz, Michael, et al., "Small Area Variations in Hospitalization Rates: How Much You See Depends on How You Look," *Medical Care,* 32 (1994): 189–201.

Schwartz, William B., "In the Pipeline: A Wave of Valuable Medical Technology," *Health Affairs,* 13 (1994): 70–79.

Scitovsky, Anne A., "Changes in the Costs of Treatment of Selected Illnesses, 1971–1981," *Medical Care,* 23 (1985): 1345–1357.

Scitovsky, Anne A., and Nelda McCall, "Changes in the Costs of Treatment of Selected Illnesses, 1951–1964–1971," National Center for Health Services Research, DHEW Publication No. (HRA) 77-3161, 1977.

Scitovsky, Tibor, "The Benefits of Asymmetric Markets," *Journal of Economic Perspectives,* 4 (1990): 135–148.

Seldon, Barry J., and Khowsrow Doroodian, "A Simultaneous Model of Cigarette Advertising: Effects on Demand and Industry Response to Public Policy," *Review of Economics and Statistics,* 71 (1989): 673–677.

Sexton, Thomas R., et al., "Evaluating Managerial Efficiency of Veterans Administration Medical Centers Using Data Envelopment Analysis," *Medical Care,* 27 (1989): 1175–1185.

Shain, Max, and Milton I. Roemer, "Hospital Costs Relate to the Supply of Beds," *Modern Hospital,* 92 (1959): 71–73.

Shalit, Sol S., "A Doctor-Hospital Cartel Theory," *Journal of Business,* 50 (1977): 1–20.

Shleifer, Andrei, "A Theory of Yardstick Competition," *Rand Journal of Economics,* 16 (1985): 319–327.

Short, Pamela F., and Peter Kemper, "Nursing Home Financing Reform: How Would It Affect Expenditures for Nursing Home Care," *Inquiry,* 31 (1994): 141–152.

Shortell, Stephen M., *A Model of Physician Referral Behavior: A Test of Exchange Theory in Medical Practice.* Chicago: Center for Health Administration Studies, 1973.

Shortell, Stephen M., Robin R. Gillies, and David A. Anderson, "The New World of Managed Care: Creating Organized Delivery Systems," *Health Affairs,* 13 (Winter 1994): 46–64.

Showstack, Jonathon A., et al., "Fee-for-Service Physician Payment: Analysis of Current Methods and Evidence," *Inquiry,* 16 (1979): 230–246.

Silver, Morris, "An Economic Analysis of Variations in Medical Expenses and Work-Loss Rates," in H. Klarman, ed., *Empirical Studies in Health Economics.* Baltimore: Johns Hopkins, 1970.

Sindelar, Jody, "The Declining Price of Health Insurance," in H. E. Frech III, ed., *Health Care in America.* San Francisco: Pacific Research Institute for Public Policy, 1988.

Skinner, Jonathon, "What Do Stochastic Cost Functions Tell Us About Inefficiency?," *Journal of Health Economics,* 13 (1994): 323–328.

Skocpol, Theda, "The Rise and Resounding Demise of the Clinton Plan," *Health Affairs,* 14 (1995): 66–87.

Sloan, Frank A., "Rate Regulation as a Strategy for Hospital Cost Control: Evidence from the Last Decade," *Milbank Memorial Fund Quarterly/Health and Society,* 61 (1983): 195–221.

Sloan, Frank A., "Property Rights in the Hospital Industry," in H. E. Frech III, ed., *Health Care in America.* San Francisco: Pacific Research Institute for Public Policy, 1988.

Sloan, Frank A., and Edmund R. Becker, "Internal Organization of Hospitals and Hospital Costs," *Inquiry,* 28 (1981): 224–239.

Sloan, Frank A., Roger D. Feldman, and A. Bruce Steinwald, "Effects of Teaching on Hospital Costs," *Journal of Health Economics,* 3 (1983): 1–28.

Sloan, Frank A., Michael A. Morrisey, and Joseph Valvona, "Effects of the Medicare Prospective Payment System on Hospital Cost Containment: An Early Appraisal," *Milbank Quarterly,* 66 (1988a): 191–219.

Sloan, Frank A., Michael A. Morrisey, and Joseph Valvona, "Medicare Prospective Payment and the Use of Medical Technologies in Hospitals," *Medical Care,* 26 (1988b): 837–853.

Sloan, Frank A., and A. Bruce Steinwald, "Effects of Regulation on Hospital Costs and Input Use," *Journal of Law and Economics,* 23 (1980): 81–109.

Sloan, Frank A., et al., "Diffusion of Surgical Technology: An Exploratory Study," *Journal of Health Economics,* 5 (1986): 31–61.

Sloan, Frank A., et al., "The Demise of Hospital Philanthropy," *Economic Inquiry,* 28 (1990): 725–743.

Smith, Francis B., *The Retreat of Tuberculosis 1850–1950.* London: Croom Helm, 1988.

Sonnenfeld, Sally T., et al., "Projections of National Health Expenditures Through the Year 2000," *Health Care Financing Review,* 13 (1991): 1–27.

Spence, A. Michael, "Monopoly, Quality, and Regulation," *Bell Journal of Economics,* 6 (1975): 417–429.

Stano, Miron, "Individual Health Accounts: An Alternative Health Care Financing Approach," *Health Care Financing Review,* 3 (1981): 117–125.

Stano, Miron, "An Analysis of the Evidence on Competition in the Physician Services Markets," *Journal of Health Economics,* 4 (1985): 197–211.

Stano, Miron, "A Further Analysis of the Physician Inducement Controversy," *Journal of Health Economics,* 6 (1987): 227–238.

Stano, Miron, et al., "The Effects of Physician Availability on Fees and the Demand for Doctors' Services," *Atlantic Economic Journal,* 13 (1985): 51–60.

Starr, Paul, *The Social Transformation of American Medicine.* New York: Basic Books, 1982.

Starr, Paul, "Health Care for the Poor: The Past Twenty Years," in Sheldon Danziger and Daniel Weinberg, eds., *Fighting Poverty: What Works and What Doesn't.* Cambridge, MA: Harvard, 1986.

Steinwald, A. Bruce, and Laura A. Dummit, "Hospital Case-Mix Change: Sicker Patients or DRG Creep?," *Health Affairs,* 8 (1989): 35–47.

Stigler, George J., "The Economics of Information," *Journal of Political Economy,* 69 (1961): 213–225.

Stigler, George J., "The Theory of Economic Regulation," *Bell Journal of Economics,* 2 (1971): 3–21.

Stiglitz, Joseph E., *Economics of the Public Sector,* 2nd ed. New York: Norton, 1988.

Strauss, John, et al., "Gender and Life-Cycle Differentials in the Patterns and Determinants of Adult Health," *Journal of Human Resources,* 28 (1993): 791–837.

Strumwasser, Ira, et al., "The Triple Option Choice: Self-Selection Bias in Traditional Coverage, HMOs and PPOs," *Inquiry,* 26 (1989): 432–441.

Sullivan, Daniel, "Monopsony Power in the Market for Nurses," *Journal of Law and Economics,* 32 (1989): S135-S179.

Surgeon General of the United States, *Reducing the Health Consequences of Smoking: 25 Years of Progress, Executive Summary.* U.S. Department of Health and Human Services, Public Health Service, Office on Smoking and Health, Rockville, Maryland, 1989.

Svorny, Shirley, "Should We Reconsider Licensing Physicians," *Contemporary Policy Issues,* 10 (1992): 31–38.

Telser, Lester G., "Advertising and Competition," *Journal of Political Economy,* 72 (1964): 537–562.

Temin, Peter, "An Economic History of American Hospitals," in H. E. Frech III, ed., *Health Care in America: The Political Economy of Hospitals and Health Insurance.* San Francisco: Pacific Research Institute for Public Policy, 1988.

Teplensky, Jill D., et al., "Hospital Adoption of Medical Technology: An Empirical Test of Alternative Models," *Health Services Research,* 30 (1995): 437–466.

Thomas, Lewis, *The Lives of a Cell.* New York: Viking, 1974.

Toxic Substances Board, *Health or Tobacco: An End to Tobacco Advertising and Promotion.* Department of Health, Wellington, New Zealand, May 1989.

Tremblay, Carol Horton, and Victor J. Tremblay, "The Impact of Cigarette Advertising on Consumer Surplus, Profit, and Social Welfare," *Contemporary Economic Policy,* 13 (1995): 133–124.

Trigg, Andrew B., and Nick Bosanquet, "Tax Harmonization and the Reduction of European Smoking Rates," *Journal of Health Economics,* 11 (1992): 329–346.

Tye, Joe B., Kenneth E. Warner, and Stanton A. Glantz, "Tobacco Advertising and Consumption: Evidence of a Causal Relationship," *Journal of Public Health Policy,* 8 (1987): 492–508.

U.S. Department of Commerce, *Statistical Abstract of the United States,* Washington, DC (various years).

U.S. Department of Health and Human Services, Public Health Service, *Health United States 1994,* May 1995.

U.S. Department of Health and Human Services, Public Health Service, *Seventh Report to the President and Congress on the Status of Health Personnel in the United States,* DHHS Publication No. HRS-P-OD-90–1, March 1990.

U.S. Department of Health and Human Services, *Report of the Expert Panel on Population Strategies for Blood Cholesterol Reduction,* NIH Publication No. 90–3046, November 1990.

U.S. Department of Justice and Federal Trade Commission, *Statements of Enforcement Policy and Analytical Principles Relating to Health Care and Antitrust,* September 27, 1994.

U.S. Department of Labor, Bureau of Labor Statistics, *Occupational Outlook Handbook,* 1990–91 Edition, April 1990.

Valdez, R. Burciaga, Robert H. Brook, William H. Rogers, et al., "Consequences of Cost-Sharing for Children's Health," *Pediatrics,* 75 (1985): 952–961.

Valdmanis, Vivian G., "Ownership and Technical Efficiency of Hospitals," *Medical Care,* 28 (1990): 552–561.

van Doorslaer, Eddy, and Adam Wagstaff, "Equity in the Delivery of Health Care: Some International Comparisons," *Journal of Health Economics,* 11 (1992): 389–411.

van de Ven, Wynand P. M. M., and Rene C. J. A. van Vliet, "Consumer Information Surplus and Adverse Selection in Competitive Health Insurance Markets: An Empirical Study," *Journal of Health Economics,* 14 (1995): 149–169.

Viscusi, W. Kip, "Promoting Smokers' Welfare with Responsible Taxation," *National Tax Journal,* 57 (1994): 547–558.

Vita, Michael G., "Exploring Hospital Production Relationships With Flexible Functional Forms," *Journal of Health Economics,* 9 (1990): 1–21.

Vitaliano, Donald F., and Mark Toren, "Cost and Efficiency in Nursing Homes: A Stochastic Frontier Approach," *Journal of Health Economics,* 13 (1994): 281–300.

Volinn, Ernest, Kathleen M. Turczyn, and John D. Loeser, "Patterns in Low Back Pain Hospitalization: Implications for the Treatment of Low Back Pain in an Era of Health Care Reform," *Clinical Journal of Pain,* 10 (1994): 64–70.

Wagstaff, Adam, "Estimating Efficiency in the Hospital Sector: A Comparison of Three Statistical Cost Frontier Models," *Applied Economics,* 21 (1989): 659–672.

Wagstaff, Adam, "QALYs and the Equity-Efficiency Trade-Off," *Journal of Health Economics,* 10 (1991): 21–41.

Warner, Kenneth E., and Linda M. Goldenhar, "The Cigarette Advertising Broadcast Ban and Magazine Coverage of Smoking and Health," *Journal of Public Health Policy,* 10 (1989): 32–42.

Warner, Kenneth E., et al., "Promotion of Tobacco Products: Issues and Policy Options," *Journal of Health Politics, Policy and Law,* 11 (1986): 367–392.

Wasserman, Jeffrey, et al., "The Effects of Excise Taxes and Regulations on Cigarette Smoking," *Journal of Health Economics,* 10 (1991): 43–64.

Wedig, Gerard J., "Health Status and the Demand for Health: Results on Price Elasticities," *Journal of Health Economics,* 7 (1988): 151–163.

Weeks, William B., et al., "A Comparison of the Educational Costs and Incomes of Physicians and Other Professionals," *New England Journal of Medicine,* 330 (1994): 1280–1286.

Weisbrod, Burton A., "Costs and Benefits of Medical Research: A Case Study of Poliomyelitis," *Journal of Political Economy,* 79 (1971): 527–544.

Weisbrod, Burton A., "Toward a Theory of the Voluntary Non-Profit Sector in a Three-Sector Economy," in Edmund S. Phelps, ed., *Altruism, Morality, and Economic Theory.* New York: Russell Sage Foundation, 1975.

Weisbrod, Burton A., *The Nonprofit Economy.* Cambridge, MA: Harvard, 1988.

Weisbrod, Burton A., "The Health Care Quadrilemma: An Essay on Technological Change, Insurance, Quality of Care, and Cost Containment," *Journal of Economic Literature,* 29 (1991): 523–552.

Wells, Kenneth B., and Roland Sturm, "Care for Depression in a Changing Environment," *Health Affairs,* 14 (1995): 78–89.

Wells, William, John Burnett, and Sandra Moriarity, *Advertising: Principles and Practice.* Englewood Cliffs, NJ: Prentice Hall, 1989.

Wennberg, John E., "Dealing with Medical Practice Variations: A Proposal for Action," *Health Affairs,* 3 (1984): 6–32.

Wennberg, John E., and F. J. Fowler, "A Test of Consumer Contribution to Small Area Variations in Health Care Delivery," *Journal of the Maine Medical Association,* 68 (1977): 275–279.

Wennberg, John E., Jean L. Freeman, and William J. Culp, "Are Hospital Services Rationed in New Haven or Overutilized in Boston?" *The Lancet,* I:(1987): 1185–1189.

Wennberg, John E., et al., "Changes in Tonsillectomy Rates Associated with Feedback and Review," *Pediatrics,* 59 (1977): 821–826.

Wennberg, John E., et al., "Hospital Use and Mortality Among Medicare Beneficiaries in Boston and New Haven," *New England Journal of Medicine,* 321 (1989): 1168–1173.

Wickizer, Thomas M., John R. C. Wheeler, and Paul J. Feldstein, "Does Utilization Review Reduce Unnecessary Hospital Care and Contain Costs?" *Medical Care,* 27 (1989): 632–647.

Wickizer, Thomas M., John R. C. Wheeler, and Paul J. Feldstein, "Have Hospital Inpatient Cost Containment Programs Contributed to the Growth in Outpatient Expenditures?" *Medical Care,* 29 (1991): 442–451.

Wilensky, Gail R., and Louis F. Rossiter, "Economic Advantages of Board Certification," *Journal of Health Economics,* 2 (1983): 87–94.

Wilson, George W., and Joseph M. Jadlow, "Competition, Profit Incentives, and Technical Efficiency in the Provision of Nuclear Medicine Services," *Bell Journal of Economics,* 13 (1982): 472–482.

Wittink, Dick R., "Advertising Increases Sensitivity to Price," *Journal of Advertising Research,* 17 (1977): 27–33.

Wittman, Donald, "Efficient Rules in Highway Safety and Sports Activity," *American Economic Review,* 72 (1982): 78–90.

Wolfe, Barbara L., "Health Status and Medical Expenditures: Is There a Link?," *Social Science and Medicine,* 22 (1986): 993–999.

Wolfe, Barbara L., and Jere R. Behrman, "Women's Schooling and Children's Health: Are the Effects Robust with Adult Sibling Control for the Women's Childhood Background?," *Journal of Health Economics,* 6 (1987): 239–254.

Wolinsky, Frederick, *The Sociology of Health: Principles, Practitioners, and Issues.* Belmont, CA: Wadsworth, 1988.

Woods, Robert, and P. R. Andrew Hinde, "Mortality in Victorian England: Models and Patterns," *Journal of Interdisciplinary History,* 18 (1987): 27–54.

Woolhandler, Steffie, and David U. Himmelstein, "The Deteriorating Administrative Efficiency of the U.S. Health Care System," *New England Journal of Medicine,* 324 (1991): 1253–1258.

Wyszewianski, Leon, John R. C. Wheeler, and Avedis Donabedian, "Market-Oriented Cost-Containment Strategies and Quality of Care," *Milbank Memorial Fund Quarterly/Health and Society,* 60 (1982): 518–550.

Yett, Donald E., *An Economic Analysis of the Nurse Shortage.* Lexington, MA: Lexington Books, 1975.

Zeckhauser, Richard J., and D. Marks, "Sign-Posting: Selected Product Information and Market Function," John F. Kennedy School of Government, manuscript, 1989.

Zimmerman, David R., et al., "Development and Testing of Nursing Home Quality Indicators," *Health Care Financing Review,* 16 (1995): 107–127.

Zuckermann, Stephen, Jack Hadley, and Lisa Iezzoni, "Measuring Hospital Efficiency with Frontier Cost Functions," *Journal of Health Economics,* 13 (1994): 255–280.

Zwanziger, Jack, and Glen A. Melnick, "The Effects of Hospital Competition and the Medicare PPS Program on Hospital Cost Behavior in California," *Journal of Health Economics,* 7 (1988): 301–320.

Name Index

Subject Index

I